MAKING CHOICES IN SEXUALITY

MAKING CHOICES IN SEXUALITY
RESEARCH AND APPLICATIONS

Susan McCammon
David Knox
Caroline Schacht

East Carolina University

Brooks/Cole Publishing Company

I⊤P® An International Thomson Publishing Company

Pacific Grove • Albany • Belmont • Bonn • Boston • Cincinnati • Detroit • Johannesburg • London • Madrid
Melbourne • Mexico City • New York • Paris • Singapore • Tokyo • Toronto • Washington

Sponsoring Editor: *Marianne Taflinger*
Project Development Editor: *Penelope Sky*
Marketing Team: *Michael Campbell, Alicia Barelli,
    and Christine Davis*
Editorial Assistant: *Scott Brearton*
Production Coordinator: *Laurel Jackson*
Production Service: *PC&F, Inc.*
Permissions Editor: *Linda Rill*

Indexer: *James Minkin*
Interior Design: *PC&F, Inc.*
Cover Design: *Vernon T. Boes*
Cover Photo: *Jason Hawkes, Tony Stone Images*
Photo Researcher: *PC&F, Inc.*
Typesetting: *PC&F, Inc.*
Cover Printing: *Phoenix Color Corporation*
Printing and Binding: *World Color*

For more information, contact:

BROOKS/COLE PUBLISHING COMPANY
511 Forest Lodge Road
Pacific Grove, CA 93950
USA

International Thomson Publishing Europe
Berkshire House 168-173
High Holborn
London WC1V 7AA
England

Thomas Nelson Australia
102 Dodds Street
South Melbourne, 3205
Victoria, Australia

Nelson Canada
1120 Birchmont Road
Scarborough, Ontario
Canada M1K 5G4

International Thomson Editores
Seneca 53
Col. Polanco
11560 México, D. F., México

International Thomson Publishing GmbH
Königswinterer Strasse 418
53227 Bonn
Germany

International Thomson Publishing Asia
221 Henderson Road
#05-10 Henderson Building
Singapore 0315

International Thomson Publishing Japan
Hirakawacho Kyowa Building, 3F
2-2-1 Hirakawacho
Chiyoda-ku, Tokyo 102
Japan

Printed in the United States of America

10 9 8 7 6 5 4 3 2 1

Library of Congress Cataloging-in-Publication Data

McCammon, Susan.
    Making choices in sexuality : research and applications / by Susan
McCammon, David Knox, and Caroline Schacht.
        p. cm.
    ISBN 0-534-35595-1 (softcover)
    1. Sex. 2. Hygiene, Sexual. 3. Sex (Biology) 4. Sex
(Psychology) 5. Computer sex. I. Knox, David, [date]–   .
II. Schacht, Caroline. III. Title.
HQ21.M113 1997
306.7—dc21   97-41780
                                                 CIP

To our children,

Andrew and Reagin,

Lisa and Dave,

and Isabelle,

as they wrestle with making sexual choices for themselves.

ABOUT THE AUTHORS

Susan L. McCammon, Ph.D., is an Associate Professor of Psychology at East Carolina University. She teaches in the M.A. program in Clinical Psychology, as well as undergraduate and graduate sections of the sexual behavior course. She directed the Women's Studies Program from 1992–1995 and currently serves on the executive committee of the program. Her most recent publications include co-authored articles with graduate students and other faculty examining behavioral aspects of homonegativity, as well as a book chapter on teaching about trauma. She is a member of the editorial board of the *Journal of Traumatic Stress* and the *National Women's Studies Association Journal.* Her community activities include chairing the local county coalition on adolescent pregnancy prevention and attending the Little League baseball games in which her 10- and 12-year old sons play.

David Knox, Ph.D., is Professor of Sociology at East Carolina University, where he teaches courses in human sexuality, marriage, and the family. He is a marriage and family therapist with a clinical focus in sexual problems. He is the author or co-author of 10 books and 30 professional articles. He and Caroline Schacht are married.

Caroline Schacht received her master's degrees in sociology and family relations from East Carolina University, where she teaches in the Sociology Department. Her clinical work includes marriage, family, and sex therapy. She is also a divorce mediator and the co-author of several books, including *Choices in Relationships* and *Understanding Social Problems.*

BRIEF CONTENTS

Contents

PREFACE

Sexuality is a personal topic that affects both your individual and your community life in your society. The theme of *Making Choices in Sexuality* is to encourage you to take charge of your life by making deliberate, informed sexual choices and to provide an understanding of how society and culture influence your sexual choices. You'll be introduced both to fundamental information on human sexuality and to the tools you'll need to make informed sexual decisions. Human sexuality is not just an academic aspect of psychology, sociology, anthropology, and biology; it is also a study of how you live your life and with what level of satisfaction, depth, and meaning. We hope this text will be helpful as you explore the components of sexual functioning and consider what sexual expression matches the seriousness or permanence of your relationships, the role of sensual desire, and your capacity for intimacy. We hope you will take this study seriously but will have fun and enjoy it, too.

After our 900-page text was published in 1993, students complained that it was "too heavy"—referring not to the level of difficulty, but to the weight of their backpacks. They also complained that the price was too high. We hope this book will be less physically heavy, but we also hope that its scholarly level, depth of coverage, and intellectual appeal are evident and that we continue to hear our favorite compliment: "This is one textbook I've read from cover to cover!"

We have designed the text to emphasize the theme of choice because students often do not realize the possibilities of alternatives to their choices. Nor do students often realize the consequences of their sexual choices to their long-term psychological and physical health, their relationships, and the quality of their lives. Because information is valuable only to the extent that you *make choices* with it, in this text you will discover several features to make

you aware and more conscious of the choices you make. The "Choices" features in this book include the following:

PERSONAL CHOICES discusses specific choices you might face regarding an issue we are discussing in the text. For example, in the discussion of sexual fantasy, a Personal Choices box addresses the issue "Should You Share Your Sexual Fantasies with Your Partner?" Other examples of the Personal Choices feature include "Which Method of Contraception Should You Use?" "Should You Be Tested for HIV or Other STDs?" and "How Do You Choose Whether to Have an Abortion?"

SELF-ASSESSMENTS provides a scale for you to complete in order to measure a particular aspect of your sexuality and to compare your score with those of other adults who have taken the self-assessment. Examples include the Student Sexual Risks Scale, the Homophobia Scale, and the Reiss Premarital Sexual Permissiveness Scale. Other self-assessments allow you to measure locus of control (Chapter 1); attitudes toward feminism (Chapter 2); menstruation (Chapter 3); condom use (Chapter 5); and abortion (Chapter 8); motive for having children (Chapter 6); expectations of the effects of alcohol (Chapter 9); empathy regarding rape (Chapter 11); level of erotophilia or erotophobia (Chapter 13); and the sexual double standard (Chapter 15).

SOCIAL CHOICES identifies social issues with which our society is confronted. Examples include "Should a Couple Be Able to Select the Sex of Their Unborn Child?" "Should Homosexual Marriage Be Legal?" and "Should Condoms Be Available in High Schools?"

THINK ABOUT IT asks you to reflect on the content just presented and to use critical thinking skills in evaluating sexual issues. For example, in Chapter 5, on sexually transmitted diseases, a "Think About It" feature asks: "Why are many individuals who are in high-risk categories for acquiring HIV and other STDs also the least likely to be tested for STDs?" In Chapter 8, on abortion and adoption, a "Think About It" feature asks: "Which of the strategies for reducing the need for abortion could be embraced by both pro-life and pro-choice advocates? How can opposition between advocacy groups be transformed into cooperative efforts to reduce the need for abortion?"

NATIONAL AND INTERNATIONAL DATA features are presented to address students' interest in "what is normal" and "what is common." To replace speculation with facts, we have provided data from national and international samples. For example, the exposure of extramarital affairs in celebrities' private lives has led to the speculation that such affairs are rampant everywhere. But a 1997 study by M. W. Wiederman (see Chapter 14) on a national sample of U.S. adults reveals that only 22.7% of the men and 11.6% of the women reported ever having extramarital sex. Only 4.1% of the currently married men and 1.7% of the currently married women reported having had extramarital sex in the 12 months preceding the study. A global perspective is added by reports of international data, such as the United Nations Population Fund statistic that 2,000,000 girls (ages 5 to 15) are introduced into the commercial sex market each year (see Chapter 12).

DIVERSITY IN SEXUALITY features present evidence that sexual values, attitudes, and behaviors differ not only among individuals, but in the same individual across time. Symbols are used throughout the text to draw attention to diversity content. For example, in Chapter 11, the incidence of acquaintance rape in gay relationships is noted, as well as the incidence of unwanted sexual aggression in a study at the Chinese University of Hong Kong. Part III of the text is devoted to such diversity as expressed by women and men, diversity in various cultures, diversity of sexual orientation, and paraphilias.

CUTTING-EDGE CONTENT is crucial because of ongoing changes in values, behaviors, and social policies related to sexuality. For example, as we go to press, the U.S. Supreme Court is meeting to rule on yet

another facet of the abortion issue. The following lists some of the current controversial topics discussed in each chapter:

Chapter 1   CHOICES IN SEXUALITY
The 1997 *Psychology Today* Body Image Survey
Sexuality on the Internet
Body piercing

Chapter 2   SEX RESEARCH AND THEORY
Collecting sexuality data through "talking computers"
Public funding for sex research

Chapter 3   ANATOMY AND PHYSIOLOGY
New mammogram guidelines
Legislation concerning women's right to breast-feed in public

Chapter 4   COMMUNICATION AND SEXUALITY
Honesty and dishonesty in communication
Issues concerning disclosure to one's partner of an STD infection

Chapter 5   SEXUALLY TRANSMITTED DISEASES
1997 data from the Centers for Disease Control and Prevention
Global statistics on STDs
How STDs facilitate transmission of HIV
Use of computers in STD prevention
Postexposure HIV treatment
Condom availability in high schools
Needle-exchange programs

Chapter 6   PLANNING CHILDREN AND BIRTH CONTROL
How old is too old to become a parent?
Ethnicity or nationality and preferred family size
Having a child without a partner

Chapter 7   PREGNANCY AND PARENTHOOD
Cloning
Should criminal prosecution be instituted for fetal abuse?

Chapter 8   ABORTION AND ADOPTION
Reducing the need for abortion
Abortion rates and policies outside the United States

ANCILLARIES FOR THE INSTRUCTOR

Instructor's Resource Guide (ISBN: 0-534-35622-2) Includes supplementary lecture notes, ideas for classroom activities, and teaching tips.

Test Bank (ISBN: 0-534-35623-0) Includes multiple-choice, true/false, and discussion questions, all keyed to the text.

Computerized Test Bank (Macintosh ISBN: 0-534-35624-9; Windows ISBN: 0-534-35626-5; DOS ISBN: 0-534-35625-7) An electronic version of the printed test bank.

Practice Tests (ISBN: 0-534-35627-3)

Web Resource (http://psychstudy.brookscole.com) This web site allows students and faculty to easily explore the most current information about all aspects of sexuality.

Acknowledgments

We would like to thank the following reviewers for their valuable comments and suggestions: Charles R. Baffi, Virginia Polytechnic Institute; Kenneth C. Becker, University of Wisconsin–LaCrosse; Thomas E. Billimek, San Antonio College; Roy O. Darby, University of South Carolina–Beaufort; Kathleen Dolan, Georgia State University; Martha M. Ellis, Collin County Community College; Randy D. Fisher, University of Central Florida; Timothy L. Hulsey, Southwest Texas State University; Chrystyna Kosarchyn, Longwood College; Jerald J. Marshall, University of Central Florida; Barbara Miller, Pasadena City College; Carol Plugge, Lamar University; Peggy Skinner, South Plains College; Margaret M. Smith, Oregon State University; Sherman K. Sowby, California State University, Fresno; Mary Ann Watson, Metropolitan State College of Denver; Deborah R. Winters, New Mexico State University; and Michael Young, University of Arkansas.

Marianne Taflinger provided the vision for this book. Her direction, faith, and support for the project have brought it to fruition. The authors would also like to thank Karen Crowell of the Health Affairs Library at the East Carolina University School of Medicine, who served as research consultant for the project; Anna Dougherty of Circulation, Joyner Library at East Carolina University; Pat Guyette and Jessica Hilliard of Inter-Library Services, Joyner Library at East Carolina University; Tracy Everette, Stacie Hatfield, Jennipher Huckle, Wandy Nieves, and Johanna Gartz for tracking down sources and references; M.S. Dar for information about Islamic sexuality; Linda Rill, who kept up with permissions; Karen Sampson, production editor, for her patience and professionalism; Laurie Jackson, production coordinator, who kept the project on track; and Vernon Boes for ensuring a cover that reflects the "choices" theme of the text.

Susan McCammon would like to thank Mike for his love and patience and Maxine for spoiling her grandchildren while Susan worked on the manuscript. She is also grateful to Clem Handron and Beverly Harju for their encouragement and suggestions.

We are always interested in ways to improve the text, and we invite your feedback and suggestions for new ideas and material to include in subsequent editions. We are also interested in dialogue with professors and students and invite you to write us at East Carolina University, Greenville, NC 27858; or send us e-mail at one of the following addresses:

MCCAMMONS@MAIL.ECU.EDU
DAVIDKNOX@prodigy.net
UHXP97B@prodigy.com

Susan McCammon
David Knox
Caroline Schacht

BACKGROUND FOR
SEXUAL CHOICES

PART 1

CHOICES IN SEXUALITY

Chapter 1

Elements of Human Sexuality

Sexual Self-Concept
Behaviors
Cognitions
Values
Emotions
Anatomy and Physiology
Interpersonal Relationships
Diversity
PERSONAL CHOICES: Why Take a Course in Human Sexuality?

Q UESTION If most college students already know about sex, why might it be helpful to take a course in human sexuality?

Do You Make Your Own Sexual Choices?

Emotional Influences
Cultural Constraints
Previous Decisions
Alcohol and Drug Use
Peer and Partner Pressure
Family Factors
Locus of Control
SELF-ASSESSMENT: Internality, Powerful Others, and Chance Scales
PERSONAL CHOICES: Do You or Other Factors Control Your Sexual Choices?

Q UESTION To what degree are your sexual choices products of your free will or products of previous experiences and current social influences?

Nature of Sexual Choices

Not to Decide Is to Decide
Choices Involve Trade-Offs
Choices Include Selecting a Positive or Negative View
Choices Produce Ambivalence and Uncertainty
Some Choices Are Revocable; Some Are Not

Q UESTION When you are confronted with a sexual choice and are not sure what to decide, is it best to avoid making a choice until you are sure about what to do?

Making Sexual Choices

Basic Decision-Making Steps
Important Skills for Decision Making

Q UESTION What are examples of individual, couple, and group sexual choices?

Social Changes and Sexual Choices

Sex in the Media
Sexuality on the Internet
SOCIAL CHOICES: Government Control of Sexual Content on the Internet
Birth Control Availability and Technology
Increased Rates of Divorce and Cohabitation
Women in the Workplace
Social Movements
HIV Infection and AIDS
Reproductive and Medical Technology

Q UESTION How are the sexual choices with which you are confronted today different from those your parents and grandparents may have faced?

*R*emember that sex is not out there, but in here, in the deepest layer of your own being. There is not only a morning after—there are lots of days and years afterwards.

Jacob Neusner in *Words of Wisdom*

What do the following questions have in common?

- Is abstinence the best choice for me at this point in my life?
- Is sex with a new person worth the risk of contracting HIV or other STDs?
- How and when do I bring up the issue of using a condom with a new partner?
- How much do I tell my new partner about my previous sexual experiences (masturbation, number of sexual partners, homosexual encounters)?
- Do I disclose to my partner that I have fantasies about sex with other people?
- What type of birth control should I and my partner use?
- Should posting of "indecent" material be banned on the Internet?

Each of these questions involves making a sexual choice. One of the main goals of this text is to emphasize the importance of making deliberate and informed choices about your sexuality. The alternative is to let circumstances and others decide for you. Informed decision making involves knowledge of the psychological, physiological, and psychosocial components of sexual functioning, personal values, and the interaction between cultural values and sexual behaviors. We begin by identifying the various elements of human sexuality.

ELEMENTS OF HUMAN SEXUALITY

Human sexuality is a complex and multifaceted concept. The various elements of human sexuality include sexual self-concept, behaviors, thoughts, values, emotions, anatomy and physiology, interpersonal relationships, and diversity.

Sexual Self-Concept

Your *sexual self-concept* includes your body image and sense of identity as a sexual individual and partner. *Body image* refers to the perception of one's own physical appearance and is influenced by cultural definitions of attractiveness. Various industries perpetuate Americans' obsessions with their appearance, including the fashion, weight loss, and cosmetic industries. Forty thousand breast implants, 50,000 eyelid procedures, and 51,000 liposuction surgeries are performed every year (Spiegler, 1996). Fifty-six percent of the women and 43% of the men in *Psychology Today's* 1997 Body Image Survey reported that they were dissatisfied with their overall appearance (see Figure 1.1). Twenty-five percent of the women and 17% of the men said that they would sacrifice 3 years of their life if they could be the weight they wanted.

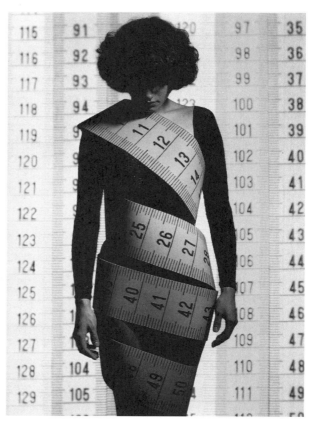

Our society encourages us to have bodies that conform to certain culturally defined measurements.

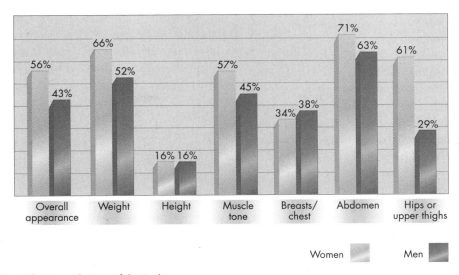

FIGURE 1.1 Dissatisfaction with Parts of the Body
This chart shows the percentages of 4000 respondents to a 1997 *Psychology Today* survey who reported feeling dissatisfied with specific parts of their bodies. **Source:** Garner, 1997.

Body image and sexual experiences are linked. "The less attractive I feel, the less I desire sex," reported one of the respondents in the survey (Garner, 1997). In another study of 212 university students, the researchers found that men, persons who exercised, those who perceived themselves to be physically attractive/sexually desirable and good sexual partners had higher body image scores than women, nonexercisers, etc. (Holmes, Chamberline, & Young, 1994). The following boxed insert on body piercing reflects how some people change their body image by piercing.

Body Piercing

Body piercing, as well as tattooing, are ways of enhancing one's self-identity and body image. No longer a highly stigmatized practice carried out in the back rooms of adult bookstores or a practice specific to primitive societies, body piercing is making its way into heavily patronized studios. Myers (1992) and Sanders (1988) conducted participant observation studies about the who and why of body piercing. Myers (1992) reported that his subjects were "sane, successful people." By doing so, he made it clear that he wanted to counter the emphasis in the psychological literature on aberrant behavior, self-mutilation, and the repugnance that mainstream society tends to feel toward body piercing. While some may regard body piercing as a biological perversion, the latter actually involves such acts as physically maiming or burning one's body.

Although body mutilation in primitive societies is ritualistic and is considered a sign of social position, body piercing in the United States seems to function by giving individuals a strong sense of self and a connection with others, by marking relationship events in commitment ceremonies, by enhancing people's feeling about their bodies, by providing the rush of the piercing experience, and by giving people a way to rebel against mainstream society. While the most common places of body piercing are the face or ears, some pierce their tongues, nipples, abdomen, buttocks, and genitals. Body piercing is not without risk in that it sometimes results in infection.

Sources: Myers, J. (1992). Nonmainstream body modification: Genital piercing, branding, burning and cutting. *Journal of Contemporary Ethnography, 21,* 267–306.

Sanders, C. (1988). Marks of mischief: Becoming and being tattooed. *Journal of Contemporary Ethnography, 16,* 395–432.

Behaviors

Human sexuality encompasses a variety of behaviors. Although people commonly associate the word *sex* with *intercourse*, vaginal intercourse is only one of many sexual behaviors. Masturbation, oral sex, breast stimulation, manual genital stimulation, and anal intercourse are also sexual behaviors. We discuss the range of sexual behaviors in Chapter 13, "Individual and Interpersonal Sexual Behaviors."

Some behaviors may or may not be experienced as sexual, depending on the context and the definitions used by the respective partners. For example, kissing, touching, and caressing may be considered sexual behaviors with a lover, but not with a friend.

Cognitions

What determines whether a kiss is a sexual behavior or an expression of affection? The meaning or cognition an individual attaches to a particular kiss, as well as to anatomy, plays an important role in sexuality. These meanings are largely influenced by cultural definitions. Americans, for example, are taught to view the naked breasts of adult women as erotic and inappropriate to display in public. In other societies, such as the Chavantez Indian tribe in Brazil, women's breasts are not viewed as erotic.

Cognitions in sexuality also include sexual fantasies. Indeed, engaging in sexual fantasies is one of the most common types of sexual behavior (Meston, Trapnell, & Gorzalka, 1996). Given the central role that cognitions play in human sexuality, what is the most important sexual organ of the body? Answer: the brain!

Values

Sexual values are definitions of what is right and wrong, or what is good and bad, regarding sexuality. In a national study of college students, 54% of the men and 42% of the women agreed with the statement, "If two people really like each other, it's all right for them to have sex even if they've known each other for only a very short time" (American Council on Education & University of California, 1996). Although values serve as moral guidelines for sexual behavior, what a person values is sometimes different from what a person does. More than half of a national sample of adults who said that premarital sex is always wrong also said that they themselves had sex before they were married (Michael, Gagnon, Laumann, & Kolata, 1994).

Sexual values not only guide individual sexual behavior, but they also guide social policies related to sexual issues. Policies concerning sex with a minor, prostitution, sex in the media, sex education, same-sex marriage, abortion, and other sexuality-related issues are largely shaped by public values concerning sexuality. We discuss sexual values in Chapter 12.

Emotions

Emotions are an important element of human sexuality. We may be happy or unhappy with our sexual self-concept. Emotional feelings of love, trust, and intimacy may lead to the development of a sexual relationship. Within sexual relationships, emotions affect sexual involvement. For example, anger often decreases one's interest in sexual interactions (Beck & Bozman, 1995). Various aspects of our sexuality also elicit emotions. Fantasizing about someone other than our partner may produce feelings of guilt, as well as feelings of excitement. Viewing erotic material may elicit feelings of disgust or feelings of enjoyment. Sexual interactions may elicit feelings of intimacy or feelings of guilt, shame, anger, frustration, fear, or disappointment.

Anatomy and Physiology

Human sexual anatomy refers to the external genitalia, secondary sex characteristics (such as a deepened voice in males) and internal reproductive organs of women and men; physiology refers to the functioning of the genitals and reproductive system. Anatomy also refers to other aspects of our physical body such as height, weight, appearance, and shape. We discuss sexual anatomy and physiology in Chapter 3.

Interpersonal Relationships

While masturbation and sexual fantasies can occur outside the context of a relationship, much of sexuality occurs in the context of an interpersonal relationship. Such relationships may be heterosexual or homosexual, nonmarital, marital, or extramarital, casual or intimate, personal or business-related (as in phone sex and prostitution), and brief or long-term. The type of emotional and social relationship a couple has affects the definition and quality of their sexual relationship.

Based on a random sample of 3432 U.S. adults, regarding physical pleasure and emotional satisfaction with their partners

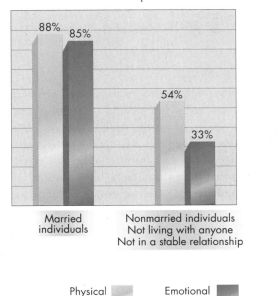

Source: Michael et al., 1994, p. 125.

The distribution of power in a relationship also influences sexual choices, especially for women who traditionally have been assigned to submissive, powerless roles. A woman who perceives herself as having little power in the relationship may feel less able to make sexual choices that contradict the wishes of her more domineering partner.

Diversity

Sexual behaviors, cognitions, emotions, values, and relationships vary within the same person, between people, and between cultures. For example, the same person may have multiple sex partners at one age, but may be monogamous or celibate at another age. The more diverse the population of a society, the more the members of that society vary in the types of sexual behaviors they engage in and in their sexual thoughts, feelings, values, and relationships. Given the ethnic, racial, and religious diversity of the population in the United States, the sexual diversity and variability among members of the U.S. population is not surprising.

When a cross-cultural perspective is considered, variations in sexuality become even more extensive. For example, although homosexual behavior is viewed as a variant sexual lifestyle in the United States, in the New Guinea Highlands, it is regarded as a pathway to heterosexuality (Herdt, 1981, 1989). Among the Sambia (New Guinea Highlands), preadolescent boys are taught to perform fellatio (oral sex) on older unmarried males and ingest their sperm. They do this believing it enables them to produce their own sperm in adulthood, thereby ensuring their ability to impregnate their wives.

Evidence of cultural diversity is also illustrated when comparing 356 Asian American and 346 non-Asian undergraduate students attending college in the United States. Thirty-six percent of the Asian American women, compared to 69% of non-Asian U.S. women, reported having engaged in sexual intercourse. Thirty-five percent of Asian American men, compared to 63% of non-Asian U.S. men, reported having engaged in intercourse (Meston et al., 1996). These differences reflect the fact that Asian parents have traditionally been more successful in restricting access to the opposite sex by emphasizing academic pursuits rather than dating and love relationships.

THINK ABOUT IT

Suppose you were a parent of an adolescent child who was going to take a sex education class in school, and you discovered that the topics covered in this class were limited to sexual anatomy and reproductive physiology. If you could influence the school board to broaden the content of the sex education curriculum, would you? What elements of human sexuality, other than anatomy and physiology, would you suggest be included in the curriculum?

PERSONAL CHOICES

Why Take a Course in Human Sexuality?

College students take courses in human sexuality for a variety of academic, personal, and career-related reasons. Some students sign up for human sexuality courses because they fulfill social science or elective requirements for graduation. Others take such courses to examine their own sexuality and gain knowledge that may help them make informed sexual choices. Still other students study human sexuality in preparation for careers as sex educators or therapists. Knowledge about sexuality is also very important for persons in a variety of occupational fields, including psychology, nursing, health education, and medicine.

DO YOU MAKE YOUR OWN SEXUAL CHOICES?

Most people would answer "yes" to this question, believing they consciously make decisions about sexual matters and act accordingly. For example, when confronted with whether to insist on using a condom before having intercourse, a person may elect to require a condom, tell the partner, and either get a condom or decide not to have intercourse. But more than half (52%) of respondents in an adult sample who had two sex partners in the previous 12 months reported that they "never" used a condom (Michael et al., 1994). If we are in control of our decisions, yet still make some very dangerous decisions, what makes us override our rational thinking, causing us to make questionable choices? There are various influences affecting the sexual choices we make; we review some of them in the following pages.

Emotional Influences

Arthur Schopenhauer, the German philosopher, noted that rather than wanting something because we have reasons for it, we tend to find reasons for something because we want it. In effect, Schopenhauer believed that we are driven by emotions and that we construct explanations for what we do as an afterthought. Love is a powerful emotion that influences sexual choices. ℮ Data from 280 homosexual men who participated in a longitudinal study in upstate New York revealed that in spite of their knowledge about how HIV is transmitted, many homosexual men continue to take chances and risk HIV infection through sexual transmission. Love is a central reason.

In all the years of the study, we have noted that men in committed relationships and men just falling in love take chances for HIV infection that they did not take with more casual partners. Men were more willing to have unprotected anal sex even if they did not know the loved man's sero-status. (Ames, Atchinson, & Rose, 1995, p. 68) ℮

Cultural Constraints

Sexual choices are also influenced by social and cultural values, roles, norms, and laws. For example, the current emphasis on the social value of safe sex has increased the number of individuals who are choosing to use condoms. Traditional gender roles taught women that they should not initiate sexual intimacy and taught men to be the initiator in relationships. The changing roles of women and men have led to more women choosing to initiate sex in their relationships. Although infidelity is not uncommon, most spouses remain sexually faithful because of the strong social norm that says married people should not have sexual relations outside of marriage. Finally, governmental laws and policies may affect sexual choices by restricting or allowing, for example, access to abortion, prostitution, and certain methods of birth control. Additionally, sexual harassment laws and policies influence individuals' choices about how to interact with their employees, co-workers, and students.

Previous Decisions

Sexual choices are often affected by previous sexual choices. A partner who has chosen not to use pregnancy prevention may be faced with a choice about whether to continue or terminate an unwanted pregnancy. An individual in a committed relationship who has chosen to have an affair must also decide whether or not to disclose the affair to the partner. A person who has chosen to engage in unprotected, high-risk sexual behavior may then be faced with the choice of whether or not to be tested for HIV and other STDs, and whether or not to disclose this infection to his or her partner.

Alcohol and Drug Use

Alcohol and drug use affect one's mood, judgment, and sexual choices. Researchers Sigmon and Gainey (1995) found that condom use decreases with alcohol use. Almost half (48%) of the men and 43% of the women in one study of college students reported not using protection during sex after they had been drinking (Sigmon & Gainey, 1995). The researchers concluded that alcohol consumption not only impairs judgment, but also lowers inhibitions and often results in individuals making sexual choices that they would not have made if they were sober.

Alcohol and other drugs affect not only what choices we make, but whether we make a choice at all. How can a person choose to have sex or not, or to use a condom or not, if that person has passed out from alcohol or other drug use? The answer is, one cannot.

Peer and Partner Pressure

Finally, sexual choices are influenced by our peers. In a study of undergraduate women and men who were college virgins, the respondents reported that being a virgin was not easy because they were under pressure from peers and partners to have intercourse (Sprecher & Regan, 1996). Muehlenhard and Cook (1988) reported that almost two-thirds of the college men in their sample had experienced unwanted intercourse largely due to peer pressure and fear of appearing inexperienced or shy. In another study, an inner-city adolescent girl described her experience with peer pressure:

> There was only one of us besides myself that didn't have sex. The rest of them all had sex and I was the oldest one and they was all like, "when you gonna do it?" and I was known as the girl that, you know, was never gonna do it. (Rosenthal, Lewis, & Cohen, 1996, p. 734)

Family Factors

Various family factors, including family composition and relationships, values, and economic resources, influence sexual choices. For example, your family's economic resources may influence your choices about what type of birth control to use, whether to seek sexual health care (such as Pap tests and mammograms), and whether to continue an unplanned pregnancy. If your parents are an interracial couple or have values that are accepting of interracial couples, you may be more likely to choose to date individuals of various races. Conversely, if your parents have racist views and disapprove of interracial couples, you may be less likely to choose to date individuals of a different race. If you already have two children of the same sex, you may be more likely to choose to have a third child than you would if you already had one child of each sex.

Family members can also influence your choices by giving directives such as, "If you are going to have sex, use a condom every time" or "Before you decide to have sex, tell me and I'll take you to a doctor and get you birth control pills." A student in the authors' class talked about how her parents influenced her choice to have an abortion when she was 17: "My parents made me have an abortion. . . . They wouldn't allow me to have a baby."

Locus of Control

Psychologists use the term *locus of control* to refer to an individual's beliefs about the source or cause of his or her successes and failures. A person with an *internal locus of control* believes that successes and failures in life are attributable to his or her own abilities and efforts. A person with an *external locus of control* believes that successes and failures are determined by fate, chance, or some powerful external source (such as other individuals). This chapter's Self-Assessment on internality, powerful others, and chance allows you to assess the degree to which you believe your life is controlled by you or by external factors.

PERSONAL CHOICES

Do You or Other Factors Control Your Sexual Choices?

One basic assumption of this text is that humans have free will or the capacity to make their own choices. The belief in free will implies that although heredity and environment may influence our choices, individuals are ultimately in charge of their own destinies. Even when our lives are affected by circumstances or events that we do not choose, we can still choose how to view and respond to those circumstances and events.

An alternative and competing assumption of this text is *determinism*—the idea that our choices are largely determined by heredity and environment. Being born with a particular sexual orientation reflects determinism; how one views and acts upon one's sexual orientation reflects free will.

INTERNALITY, POWERFUL OTHERS, AND CHANCE SCALES

To assess the degree to which you believe you have control over your own life (I = Internality), the degree to which you believe other people control events in your life (P = Powerful Others), and the degree to which you believe chance affects your experiences or outcomes (C = Chance), read each of the following statements and select a number from minus three to plus three.

−3	−2	−1	+1	+2	+3
Strongly Disagree	Disagree	Slightly Disagree	Slightly Agree	Agree	Strongly Agree

Subscale

I 1. Whether or not I get to be a leader depends mostly on my ability.

C 2. To a great extent my life is controlled by accidental happenings.

P 3. I feel like what happens in my life is mostly determined by powerful people.

I 4. Whether or not I get into a car accident depends mostly on how good a driver I am.

I 5. When I make plans, I am almost certain to make them work.

C 6. Often there is no chance of protecting my personal interests from bad luck happenings.

C 7. When I get what I want, it's usually because I'm lucky.

P 8. Although I might have good ability, I will not be given leadership responsibility without appealing to those in positions of power.

I 9. How many friends I have depends on how nice a person I am.

C 10. I have often found that what is going to happen will happen.

P 11. My life is chiefly controlled by powerful others.

C 12. Whether or not I get into a car accident is mostly a matter of luck.

P 13. People like myself have very little chance of protecting our personal interests when they conflict with those of strong pressure groups.

C 14. It's not always wise for me to plan too far ahead because many things turn out to be a matter of good or bad fortune.

P 15. Getting what I want requires pleasing those people above me

C 16. Whether or not I get to be a leader depends on whether I'm lucky enough to be in the right place at the right time.

P 17. If important people were to decide they didn't like me, I probably wouldn't make many friends.

I 18. I can pretty much determine what will happen in my life.

I 19. I am usually able to protect my personal interests.

P 20. Whether or not I get into a car accident depends mostly on the other driver.

I 21. When I get what I want, it's usually because I worked hard for it.

P 22. In order to have my plans work, I make sure that they fit in with the desires of other people who have power over me.

I 23. My life is determined by my own actions.

C 24. It's chiefly a matter of fate whether or not I have a few friends or many friends.

Scoring: Each of the subscales of Internality, Powerful Others, and Chance are scored on a six-point Likert format from minus three to plus three. For example, the eight Internality items are 1, 4, 5, 9, 18, 19, 21, 23. A person who has strong agreement with all eight items would score a plus 24; strong disagreement, a minus 24. After adding and subtracting the item scores, add 24 to the total score to eliminate negative scores. Scores for Powerful Others and Chance are similarly derived.

Continued on following page.

From "Differentiating Among Internality, Powerful Others and Chance," by H. Levenson, 1981. In H. M. Lefcourt (Ed.), *Research with the Locus of Control Construct, Vol. 1*, pp. 57–59. Copyright © 1981 by Academic Press, Inc. Reprinted by permission.

Rather than view sexual choices as something we control or as something that is controlled by other factors, we might consider how each view contributes to our understanding of sexual choices. In Table 1.1, we present some of the advantages and disadvantages of these two views.

A team of researchers (Mirowsky, Ross, & Van Willigen, 1996) analyzed survey data of 2031 Americans and found that the overwhelming majority believe they are in control of their own choices and destinies. Ninety-three percent agreed with "I am responsible for my own success."

THINK ABOUT IT

Identify the last sexual choice you made. To what degree was your choice influenced by social and cultural values, roles, norms, and laws? Was your choice influenced by alcohol or drugs, peer pressure, family factors, previous decisions, emotions, or a combination of these factors?

NATURE OF SEXUAL CHOICES

Understanding the nature of sexual choices may provide insight into your own sexual choices.

Not to Decide Is to Decide

Not making a decision is a decision by default. For example, if you are having oral, vaginal, or anal intercourse and do not decide to use a latex condom with nonoxynol-9, you have made a decision to increase your risk for contracting HIV or another STD. If you are having vaginal intercourse and do not decide to use birth control, you have decided to risk pregnancy. If you do not decide to confront a sexual harassment situation, you have decided to allow the harassment to continue.

Choices Involve Trade-Offs

All choices involve trade-offs or disadvantages, as well as advantages. The choice to cheat on your partner may provide excitement, but it may also produce

TABLE 1.1 Who Controls Our Choices? Advantages and Disadvantages of Different Views

ADVANTAGES	DISADVANTAGES
View 1: We Control Our Choices	
Gives individuals a sense of control over their lives. Encourages individuals to take responsibility for their choices.	Blames individuals for their unwise sexual choices. Fails to acknowledge the influence of social and cultural factors on sexual choices.
View 2: Other Factors Influence Our Choices	
Recognizes how emotions, peers, and cultural factors influence our lives and choices. Implies that making changes in our social and cultural environment may be necessary to help us make better choices.	Blames social and cultural factors for our own sexual choices. Discourages individuals from taking responsibility for their behaviors and choices.

feelings of guilt and may lead to the breakup of your relationship. The choice to tell your partner of an indiscretion may deepen your feelings of intimacy, but by doing so, you may risk your partner's leaving you. The choice to have an abortion may enable you to avoid the hardship of continuing an unwanted pregnancy, but it may also involve feelings of guilt, anxiety, or regret. Likewise, the choice to continue an unwanted pregnancy may enable you to experience the joy of having a child and allow you to avoid the guilt associated with having an abortion, but it may also involve the hardships of parenting or placing the baby for adoption.

Choices Include Selecting a Positive or Negative View

Regardless of your circumstances, you can choose to view a situation in positive terms. The skill of developing a positive view can be used in unlimited situations. The discovery of your partner having an affair can be viewed as an opportunity to open channels of communication with your partner and strengthen your relationship. One woman reported that dealing with her diagnosis of genital herpes helped her avoid potential partners that were not willing to work through the complications in the relationship. @ Being rejected by one's parents because of sexual orientation may be viewed positively as an opportunity to develop closer relationships with those family members who accept homosexuality. @

Conflicting messages about abortion may increase ambivalence among women who face the choice of whether to continue an unwanted pregnancy or have an abortion.

Choices Produce Ambivalence and Uncertainty

Choosing among options often creates *ambivalence*— conflicting feelings that produce uncertainty or indecisiveness about the next course of action. Many sexual choices involve ambivalence. For example, consider the conflicting feelings and uncertainty that would accompany the following decisions:

- When and with whom should I become sexually active?
- Should I report a family member who has sexually abused me?
- Should I have an abortion or continue an unwanted pregnancy?
- Should I keep an unplanned child that was conceived in a casual relationship or place the baby for adoption?
- Should I come out of the closet and tell my family that I am gay?
- Should I accept my co-worker's invitation to spend the night together at a conference (which means cheating on my partner)?
- Should I forgive my partner for having an affair or should I terminate the relationship?

Ambivalence is much more common in societies that allow and encourage its members to choose from a variety of options. In the United States, for example, individuals have the option of choosing to have an abortion, to engage in nonmarital sex, to file sexual harassment charges, and to use a variety of birth control methods. In other societies, legal abortion may not be available, nonmarital sex may be severely punished, sexual harassment may not be against the law, and birth control methods may not be available or affordable.

Ambivalence is also more prevalent in societies where there are conflicting norms and values. In the United States, individuals may be ambivalent about abortion because there are conflicting values regarding abortion, as evidenced by the pro-choice and antiabortion movements. Similarly, the decision of whether to engage in nonmarital sex may produce ambivalence because of the conflicting norms and values regarding nonmarital sex. One's parents and religion may convey that nonmarital sex is wrong, whereas one's peers and the media may indicate that it is acceptable and desirable.

Some Choices Are Revocable; Some Are Not

Some sexual choices are revocable; that is, they can be changed. For example, a person who has chosen to have sex with multiple partners can subsequently decide to be faithful to one partner or to abstain from sexual relations. An individual who, in the past, has chosen to accept being sexually unsatisfied in a pair-bonded relationship can decide to address the issue or seek sex therapy.

Although many sexual choices can be modified or changed, some cannot. You cannot eliminate the effects of some sexually transmissible diseases, undo an abortion, or be a virgin once you have had intercourse.

What has been your most difficult sexual decision? What were the trade-offs involved in your options? To what degree were you ambivalent about making your choice?

MAKING SEXUAL CHOICES

Chopra (1994) emphasizes the importance of making conscious decisions in our lives. Making wise sexual decisions is a complex art that requires a great deal of thought and effort. Following basic decision-making steps may help you think through your sexual decisions to make the best choices. Willingness to learn from previous decisions is also important for making wise sexual choices.

Basic Decision-Making Steps

The basic steps in decision making include the following:

1. Identifying and exploring alternative courses of action
2. Seeking information that makes the short-term and long-term consequences clear for each choice
3. Weighing the positive and negative consequences for each alternative
4. Selecting an alternative that has maximum positive consequences and minimal negative consequences
5. Implementing one's decision

Deepak Chopra (1994, p. 42) offers the following suggestion for making choices:

> When you make any choice—any choice at all—you can ask yourself two things: First of all, "What are the consequences of this choice that I am making?" . . . Secondly, "Will this choice that I'm making now bring happiness to me and to those around me?"

Important Skills for Decision Making

A variety of skills are helpful when making decisions. Information gathering skills, such as reading and library or computer research, may be helpful in identifying alternative courses of action and projecting negative and positive consequences of various alternatives. Implementing one's decision may require skills in assertiveness and the ability to resist social pressure from peers or parents.

Sometimes sexual choices are made by couples or groups, rather than by individuals. For example, a couple may be faced with the choice of whether to have a vasectomy, whether to seek sex therapy, or whether to take fertility drugs to get pregnant. A group, such as a state legislature, may be faced with the decision of whether to provide sex education in the public schools, and if so, at what grade levels and with what curriculum. When decisions are made by couples or groups, additional decision-making skills are needed including communication and listening skills that enable individuals to effectively convey and listen to each other's ideas and concerns. Negotiation and collaboration skills are also important for couple and group decision making.

Another decision-making skill is the ability to learn from past experience. We have all made decisions we regret. Making poor decisions is inevitable to some degree; it is part of growing up and part of life. To learn from our experiences, we might ask ourselves, "What could we have done differently?" and "What will we do differently in the future to avoid making a similar mistake?" Many students report that making sexual decisions when they have drunk too much alcohol increases the risk of unintended pregnancy and HIV or other STD infection. Moderating or reducing the level of drinking results in reducing the risks of such consequences.

We also can learn from the experiences of others, such as friends and family members. The positive

TABLE 1.2 Best and Worst Choices—Student Experiences

BEST CHOICE	WORST CHOICE
Ending my relationship with someone I loved who was unfaithful to me.	Cheating on my partner; it wasn't worth it. The guilt has been almost unbearable.
Insisting on using a condom with a person I had just met. I later found out the person had an STD.	Cheating on my partner.
Forgiving my partner for cheating on me.	Cheating on my partner.
Getting out of a relationship with someone who was married.	Getting into a relationship with someone who was married.
Waiting for more than a year to have sex in a relationship.	Getting drunk and having sex with people I didn't know.
Getting out of a sex- and drug-focused relationship.	Having unprotected sex on a one-night stand.
Getting out of a relationship with a partner who was jealous.	Trying to make my partner jealous.

experiences that come with making good choices and the negative experiences that come with making poor choices are yet another way we can learn. Table 1.2 describes some of the best and worst choices reported by students in the authors' classes. As you read the table above, think about what each student may have learned from his or her best and worst choices.

——————— **THINK ABOUT IT** ———————

What decision-making steps did you use when making the most difficult sexual choice you have faced? Which steps did you omit? What did you learn from your best and worst sexual choice?

SOCIAL CHANGES AND SEXUAL CHOICES

The new generation of young adults known as *Generation X* is difficult to characterize. Members of Generation X, who are younger than the baby boomers from the prosperous years following World War II, have not experienced the Vietnam War and have grown up in a time of economic uncertainty. Traditional family forms, virginity until marriage, and "till death do us part" marriages have been replaced to some extent by alternative lifestyles, early sexual activity, and relatively high divorce rates. The cultural and social climate for choices are different for this generation. Some of the recent social changes that have affected human sexuality are discussed in detail in the following pages.

Sex in the Media

Media, particularly television, are major factors in the social changes surrounding sexuality. Dennis Rodman dressing up like a woman, Elaine and Jerry talking about faking an orgasm on an episode of *Seinfeld*, and

Women continue to be displayed as sex objects in the media.

Hugh Grant confessing to Jay Leno on *The Tonight Show* that he "did a bad thing" by hiring a prostitute are examples of how sex pervades the media. Television talk shows such as *Oprah, Geraldo,* and *Rolanda* often feature sexual issues such as date rape, infidelity, and transsexualism. Music videos are often erotic; lyrics, too, may contain sexual messages. Movies and television shows display explicit sexuality, and magazine, television, and billboard advertisements often display sexual images. Even T-shirts and bumper stickers contain sexual implications (such as "Scuba divers do it deep").

Media portrayals and discussions of sexuality have had both positive and negative influences on sexual choices. On the positive side, reports on sexual abuse, date rape and the "date rape drug" Rohypnol have helped to bring these abuses into public awareness. Media attention on HIV infection and other sexually transmitted diseases provides a valuable public educational service. Colleges and universities, billboards, subways, buses, and other public places often display educational posters with such messages as "Use condom sense," and "Against her will is against the law."

On the negative side, the media have been criticized for portraying women as sexual objects, depicting sexuality in violent contexts, and contributing to women's negative body images and self-concepts by portraying desirable women as only those who are young and beautiful. The media also may be criticized for exposing youth to sexually explicit images before they are old enough to make responsible sexual choices. Researcher Robert Lichter, codirector of the Center for Media and Public Affairs, noted that there are about 10,000 scenes of suggested intercourse, sexual comment, or innuendo during one year of average television viewing and that over 80% of intercourse acts are extramarital (cited in Hinds, 1996). Edwards (1996a) reported that prime-time television has 25 instances of sexual behavior for every 1 instance of preventative behavior or comment. *SIECUS,* the Sexuality Information and Education Council of the United States, emphasizes the major responsibility the media must assume for presenting the "complexities of human sexuality at all stages of the life cycle in a manner that is accurate, sensitive to diversity, and free of exploitation, gratuitous sexual violence, and dehumanizing sexual portrayals" (SIECUS, 1996, p. 21).

Sexuality on the Internet

In 1994, for the first time ever, personal computers outsold televisions in the United States (Shannon & Dwyer, 1996). Access to the Internet and the World Wide Web has opened up all sorts of new communication channels. For some, erotic photos and movies of all descriptions are accessed by a few keystrokes. Individuals can exchange nude photos, have explicit sexual dialogue, and arrange to have "phone sex" or meet in person.

Sex on the Internet has both positive and negative consequences and poses many ethical dilemmas. The advantages are educational, social, emotional, cognitive, and improved sexual health.

As a sex education tool, the various search engines allow individuals to surf the Net for recent, accurate sex information. New information on the treatment of STDs and sexual dysfunctions are available instantly and anonymously. Go Ask Alice (which can be found on the Web at www.columbia.edu/cu/healthwise/) is an interactive question and answer sex information resource sponsored by Columbia University. Alice fields questions on sex, relationships, drugs, and other topics. No question is taboo.

Socially, the Internet serves as a mechanism to connect individuals who want to meet others with similar interests. Various mate matching or dating services provide an unlimited pool of individuals from which to choose and participants may connect on-line immediately. This alternative for meeting others is particularly valuable for persons with limited time or mobility. Matt Fischer of *Netguide* magazine identified over 27 sites on the Internet where people can meet (Miller, 1995). One such site in cyberspace is match.com (http://match.com). The following reflects the experience of a divorced woman who met a new partner on-line.

"Never thought I'd be alone, this far down the line" is a lyric from the Eagles' classic hit, "Wasted Time." It described my plight. I was 28, recently divorced from an eight-year marriage, and alone. I didn't want to complicate my life by getting involved with anyone at work and I didn't like the loud smoky bar routine. Alone one night, I turned on my computer, logged onto one of the commercial services, and went to one of the bulletin boards where a lot of people "hang out." I posted a note entitled, "Make me laugh." I thought this was innocuous enough as I did not want to appear desperate.

To my surprise, I received over 50 responses. Most (85%) were from guys seeking cybersex, a few shared jokes, and still fewer just wanted to talk. Soon I was regularly sending notes to men in five different states. After several weeks I fell in love with one of them, arranged to meet him, and fell deeper in love. But he was recently divorced and didn't want to tie himself to one partner. I was heartbroken and alone again . . . but turned my computer back on.

A man from Arizona began to pique my interest. Suddenly we began to E-mail each other nightly and share our histories, interests, values, and goals. Within a short time, I knew I had discovered my soulmate and fell even more deeply in love with this man than the previous cyberman. After a photo exchange, hours of phone conversations, and enormous phone bills (I mean $400 monthly phone bills), we met and discovered that we had found the love of our lives.

Quickly we planned to meet each others' family and were married in six weeks. Although this sounds very impulsive, we discussed every imaginable issue and just felt that this was "right." Although we met six states away from each other via computer, we now live in our home and are rearing our twins born last month. Meeting "on-line" certainly worked for us.

(Doebbler, 1997)

Emotionally, the Internet may connect separated lovers. An end-of-the-day E-mail is one way some pair-bonded partners maintain their long-distance relationships. Others may be unhappy in their personal and interpersonal lives and may derive immense satisfaction from on-line love relationships.

Cognitively, the Internet may meet sexual fantasy needs. Individuals with similar sexual interests and fetishes may exchange photos and play out their sexual fantasies on-line. Sexual health is enhanced on-line by the safe sex quality of Internet sex. Individuals can share sexual fantasies on-line with no risk of contracting STDs.

But sexuality on the Internet has its disadvantages, including dependence on Net relationships and infidelity. Because social, emotional, and sexual connections with others can be made through the computer, such connections may encourage quick relationship fixes and may discourage face-to-face

relationship reality. Might people become so socially isolated with their computer relationships that they neglect the development of their live interpersonal skills and relationships?

Infidelity is also a concern. Does developing an on-line emotional relationship involving the exchange of sexual fantasies constitute being unfaithful to one's partner? Does such interaction degrade the value of faithfulness an individual has toward one's partner and relationship?

Just as individuals make personal choices about what they choose to access on the Internet, governments debate what should be on the menu (see Social Choices).

Birth Control Availability and Technology

The Comstock Act passed by Congress in 1873 prohibited the mailing of obscene matter; this included advertisements for methods of contraception. Anthony Comstock, the author of the bill, also influenced the passage of legislation in New York that made it illegal to provide verbal contraceptive information. Today, methods of birth control are widely available. You can place an order for condoms via the phone, through the mail, or over the Internet. Condoms and spermicides may be purchased at a number of stores in your community. In 1997, a major drug company began direct advertising to consumers featuring its injectible contraceptive (Depo-Provera) in national magazine ads and a television ad.

More recent changes in birth control availability and technology include the development of a female condom, and the availability of postcoital contraception, specifically RU-486 and the use of birth control pills for emergency contraception. Although published data confirm the effectiveness of emergency contraception, it is infrequently prescribed and public awareness is low (Trussell, Ellerston, & Stewart, 1996). However, this method may be important to young women, due to their patterns of sexual behavior and contraceptive use (Gold, Schein, & Coupey, 1997).

Increased Rates of Divorce and Cohabitation

Since the 1960s, both the number of divorces and the divorce rate have more than doubled (National

Center on Health Statistics, 1997). This increased divorce rate has affected sexual behavior. For example, divorced individuals are more likely to report having a higher number of sexual partners than individuals who are married.

Although not all U.S. adults approve of cohabitation, for many, living together has become an acceptable stage of progression toward marriage, or even an alternative to marriage. Almost half of the U.S. adult population in their thirties report that they have lived with a partner (Nock, 1995). The number of cohabiting couples has grown from half a million in 1970 to more than 3.6 million today (Saluter, 1996).

Did increased social acceptance of sex outside of marriage lead to increased rates of cohabitation? Or

NATIONAL DATA

Individuals reporting having had between two and four sexual partners

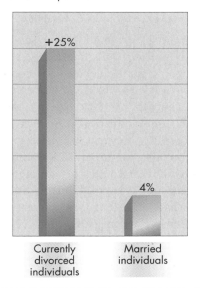

+25% — Currently divorced individuals

4% — Married individuals

Source: Michael et al., 1994.

did increased rates of living together lead to increased social acceptance of sex outside of marriage? The answer is both. However, the result is the same: Without the stigma and social disapproval previously associated with sex outside of marriage and cohabitation, individuals are more likely to choose these options today than they were in previous generations.

Women in the Workplace

With more than 90% of women earning an income at some time in their lives and more than 60% of wives working outside the home, women are becoming increasingly financially independent from men. This has resulted in delayed marriages, increased singlehood, and higher divorce rates. Increased female workforce participation also has increased the potential for sexual relationships with co-workers and incidents of sexual harassment at work. Finally, women's increased career commitment has affected childbearing choices—U.S. women are having fewer children and they are conceiving at later ages.

Birth control is widely available in the United States today and is even being advertised in national magazines.

GOVERNMENT CONTROL OF SEXUAL CONTENT ON THE INTERNET

Should the government censor sexual content on the Internet? This question is the focus of an ongoing public debate that concerns protecting children from sexually explicit content on the Internet. In February 1995, President Clinton signed into law the Communications Decency Act (CDA), making it illegal not only to send "indecent material" to a minor, but also "to display in a manner available to a person under 18 years of age any comment, request, suggestion, proposal, image, or other communication that . . . depicts or describes, in terms patently offensive as measured by contemporary community standards, sexual or excretory activities or organs." Moments after President Clinton signed the law, the American Civil Liberties Union and 19 other groups and individuals filed suit to overturn the CDA. These opponents argued that the law's definitions of "indecency" and "patently offensive" were vague.

Some sexual content on the Internet clearly violates public mores and laws. For example, in the summer of 1996, police in the United States captured 13 pedophiles (adults who have a predominant or exclusive sexual interest in prepubescent children) who were videotaping the sexual abuse of young girls and broadcasting it on the Internet (Cusack, 1996). However, much sexual content on the Internet is not uniformly viewed as harmful or inappropriate, and may even be helpful and educational (Edwards, 1996b). Critics of the CDA argued that it would restrict access to legitimate information on the Internet such as literature, art, research data, counseling and self-help discussion groups, and sexual health information. John Troyer, a graduate student at the University of California at San Francisco, joined the lawsuit against the CDA to protect the "Safer Sex Page" that he operates (DeLoughry, 1996). This page features videotaped instructions for putting on a condom correctly and other information intended to protect people from contracting the HIV virus.

In June 1996, after hearing arguments, a panel of three federal judges declared the decency law

unconstitutional on the grounds that it violated the First Amendment rights of computer users. The U.S. Justice Department asked the court to reinstate the law, and in December 1996, the U.S. Supreme Court decided to review the Communications Decency Act. Deputy Solicitor General Seth P. Waxman warned that the Internet "threatens to give every child a free pass into the equivalent of every adult bookstore and every adult video store in the country" (Savage, 1997, p. 18A). However, a unanimous Supreme Court said the Act's broad restriction on posting "indecent" material was inconsistent with free speech.

Other governments have adopted restrictive Internet policies. In Singapore, the government requires Internet service providers to block access to certain web sites that contain pornography or inflame political, religious, or racial sensitivities (Fluendy, 1997). China's largest service provider blocks at least 100 sites, including *Playboy*. Vietnam allows electronic mail, but does not allow access to the Net's other resources.

But in the United States, it will be up to parents, not the government, to regulate children's use of the Internet. Software products, such as Net Nanny, Surfwatch, CYBERsitter, CyberPatrol, and Time's Up, are being marketed to help parents control what their children view on the Internet. These software programs allow parents to block unapproved web sites and categories (such as pornography), block transmission of personal data (such as address and telephone numbers), scan pages for sexual material before they are viewed, and track Internet usage. A more cumbersome solution is to require Internet users to provide passwords or identification numbers that would verify their ages before allowing access to certain web sites.

Another alternative is for parents to use the Internet with their children both to monitor what their children are viewing, and to teach their children values about what they believe is right and wrong on the Internet. Some parents believe that children must learn how to safely surf the Internet. One parent reported that the Internet is like a busy street, and

Continued on following page.

just as you must teach your children how to safely cross in traffic, you must teach them how to avoid giving information to strangers on the Internet.

Sources: Cusack, J. (1996, November). The murky world of Internet porn. *World Press Review*, 8–9.

DeLoughry, T. J. (1996, February 16). Upset with internet law: Students join ACLU in lawsuit challenging limit on "indecent" content. *The Chronicle of Higher Education*, A21, A26.

Edwards, M. (1996a). The Net and the Web: Unlimited potential to communicate sexuality issues. *SIECUS Report, 25,* 2.

Edwards, M. (1996b). We have a responsibility to dialogue with the media. *SIECUS Report, 24,* 5.

Fluendy, S. (1997, January). Can the Net be censored? *World Press Review,* 46.

Savage, D. (1997, March 20). Justices try to salvage online porn restrictions. *News and Observer,* Raleigh, NC, p. 18A.

Social Movements

At least three social movements have influenced sexual choices—the sexual revolution, the women's movement, and the gay liberation movement. The *sexual revolution* created a cultural openness about sexuality, which, in turn, caused the frequency of intercourse and the number of sexual partners before marriage to increase. Statistically, 90% of women born between 1933 and 1942 were either virgins or had had premarital intercourse only with the men they married. In contrast, women born between 1963 and 1974 were much more likely to have had intercourse before marriage with a greater number of partners (Michael et al., 1994, p. 97). Hence, the sequence had changed from dating, love, maybe intercourse with a spouse-to-be, then marriage and parenthood . . . to affection or love and sex with a number of partners, maybe living together, then marriage and children. Those who broke up before or during the living together stage would re-enter the cycle. "Given the current late age at marriage, young people are sexually active between seven and ten years prior to marriage" (Jones, Tepperman & Wilson, 1995, p. 66).

The *women's movement* has also influenced sexual choices. In the 19th century and earlier, few voices protested the subordinate status of women in our society. The women's movement emerged to fight for equal rights and opportunities and against sexual exploitation. This movement supports the belief that women should have the right to make choices regarding their bodies and reproduction, thus advocating access to sex education, contraception, and abortion. The women's movement has sensitized women to their rights to equality in sexual interaction such as initiating and terminating relationships, requiring respect from their partners, and expecting their partners to be attentive to their sexual needs.

The *gay liberation movement* increased the visibility of gay people. In 1996, there were over 138 gay-oriented newspapers, magazines, and arts and entertainment guides in the United States (Carey & Visgaitis, 1997). Such exposure has increased the viability of the gay lifestyle as a sexual choice. In effect, more gays will come "out of the closet" as Ellen DeGeneres did on nationwide television in 1997.

HIV Infection and AIDS

One of the most significant social changes affecting sexuality has been the spread of the human immunodeficiency virus (HIV) and acquired immune deficiency syndrome (AIDS). The threat of contracting HIV has put a new fear in sexual relationships—the fear that sexual activity may result in a potentially fatal disease. Concern over HIV and AIDS may affect numerous sexual choices, including the following:

- Should I have oral, vaginal, or anal intercourse?
- Should I have sex with a new partner?
- Should I engage in extrapartner sex?
- Should I have multiple sex partners?
- Should I require HIV testing before having sex with a new partner?
- Should I require the use of a condom during each act of sex?
- Should I continue a sexual relationship with a partner who has had sex outside the relationship?

Concern over HIV and AIDS does not, however, always result in cautious sexual behavior. For example, only 63% of 4000 university students said that they always used protection during penile/vaginal intercourse, and only 3% said that they used protection when participating in oral sex (Latman & Latman, 1995).

Recent technological advances, such as the successful cloning of a rhesus monkey, may offer the possibility of new reproductive alternatives.

Reproductive and Medical Technology

Advances in reproductive technology include artificial insemination and test tube fertilizations. These technologies allow infertile couples, single women, and lesbians to conceive. Cloning may someday provide another alternative in reproductive technology; however, recent advances in this field have come under heavy scrutiny. Following the announcement by researchers at the Oregon Regional Primate Research Center that they had cloned a pair of rhesus monkeys, President Clinton banned the use of federal funds for human cloning. Anticloning measures were then introduced in the House of Representatives. Public opinion may, however, be reversed by an infertile couple arguing that cloning may offer their only chance to bear a child. @ Gay rights advocates may also emphasize the value of cloning for same-sex couples. @

New medical technology has also created other choices. Due to the development of prenatal testing such as ultrasound and amniocentesis, pregnant women face new choices: "Should I undergo prenatal testing?" and "If the tests reveal fetal abnormalities, should I continue the pregnancy?" Medical technology now allows men with erection difficulties to choose to have penile implants or to use medication that induces erection. An individual experiencing gender dysphoria (a condition in which one's gender identity does not match one's biological sex), may choose to undergo transsexual surgery to change his or her gender.

Many of the sexual choices that individuals face today are not the same as those our parents, grandparents, and great-grandparents confronted. For example, as discussed earlier, individuals in previous generations could not choose to use certain methods of birth control because they were either prohibited by law or had not yet been developed. Sexual choices of earlier generations were not influenced by HIV and AIDS because these diseases were unknown until the 1980s. Likewise, the sexual choices faced by our children and the generations to come will reflect future social changes.

—————— **THINK ABOUT IT** ——————

Explain how each of the social changes mentioned earlier influenced your own sexuality and sexual choices. For example, how has the media's openness about sexuality influenced your sexual choices?

KEY TERMS

ambivalence 12	internal locus of control 9
body image 4	
determinism 9	locus of control 9
external locus of control 9	sexual revolution 19
	sexual self-concept 4
free will 9	SIECUS 15
gay liberation movement 19	women's movement 19
HIV/AIDS 19	

SUMMARY POINTS

This chapter emphasized the broad concept of sexuality, the theme of sexual choices, the many influences on our sexual choices, and recent social changes affecting sexuality in our society.

Elements of Human Sexuality

Although most college students are informed about the basics of sexual anatomy and reproduction, human sexuality involves several other elements, including sexual self-concept, behaviors, cognitions, values, emotions, anatomy and physiology, interpersonal relationships, and diversity.

Do You Make Your Own Sexual Choices?

Although people have free will to make their own sexual choices, such choices are influenced by their emotions, cultural constraints, previous decisions, alcohol and drugs, peers and intimate partners, and family factors.

Nature of Sexual Choices

We are continually making choices, many of which are difficult because they involve trade-offs, or disadvantages as well as advantages. Choices that result in irrevocable outcomes, such as becoming a parent or having an abortion, are among the most difficult choices individuals may face. However, we cannot avoid making choices because not to choose is, itself, a choice. For example, if we have oral, vaginal, or anal intercourse and have not decided to use a condom, we have made a decision to risk contracting and transmitting HIV and other sexually transmissible diseases.

Making Sexual Choices

Individuals, couples, and groups may profit from following basic decision-making steps including identifying and exploring alternative courses of action, seeking information that helps project short-term and long-term consequences, weighing the positive and negative consequences for each alternative, and implementing the decision. Being willing to learn from past decisions is also an important factor in effective decision making.

Social Changes and Sexuality

Each new generation faces new sexual choices due to social changes. Some changes that influence today's decisions include sex in the media, sex on the Internet, birth control availability and technology, increased rates of divorce and cohabitation, women in the workplace, social movements, HIV infection and AIDS, and reproductive and medical technology.

REFERENCES

American Council on Education & University of California. (1996). *The American freshman: National norms for Fall, 1996.* Los Angeles: Los Angeles Higher Education Research Institute.

Ames, L. J., Atchinson, A. B., & Rose, D. T. (1995). Love, lust, and fear: Safer sex decision making among gay men. *Journal of Homosexuality, 30,* 53–73.

Beck, J. G., & Bozman, A. W. (1995). Gender differences in sexual desire: The effects of anger and anxiety. *Archives of Sexual Behavior, 24,* 595–612.

Carey, A. R., & Visgaitis, G. (1997, March 14). Ad spending in gay press. *USA Today,* p. D1.

Chopra, D. (1994). *The seven spiritual laws of success.* San Rafael, CA: Ambr-Allen.

Doebbler, S. (1997). Mate selection on line. Used by permission.

Edwards, M. (1996a). The Net and the Web: Unlimited potential to communicate sexuality issues. *SIECUS Report, 25,* 2.

Edwards, M. (1996b). We have a responsibility to dialogue with the media. *SIECUS Report, 24,* 5.

Garner, D. M. (1997). The 1997 body image survey results. *Psychology Today, 30,* 30–44.

Gold, M. A., Schein, A., & Coupey, S. M. (1997). Emergency contraception: A national survey of adolescent health experts. *Family Planning Perspectives, 29,* 15–19, 24.

Herdt, G. (1981). *Guardians of the flutes: Idioms of masculinity.* New York: McGraw-Hill.

Herdt, G. (1989, June). *Sexuality and masculine development up to middle adolescence among Sambia (Papua New Guinea).* Paper presented at the annual meeting of the International Academy of Sex Research, Princeton, NJ.

Hinds, M. (1996). *The troubled American family: Which way out of the storm?* Washington, DC: National Issues Forums Institute.

Holmes, T., Chamberlin, P., & Young, M. (1994). Relations of exercise to body image and sexual desirability among a sample of university students. *Psychological Reports, 74,* 920–922.

Jones, C. L., Tepperman, L., & Wilson, S. J. (1995). *The futures of the family.* Englewood Cliffs, NJ: Prentice Hall.

Latman, N. S., & Latman, A. I. (1995). Behavioral risk of human immunodeficiency virus/acquired immunodeficiency syndrome in the university student community. *Sexually Transmitted Diseases, 22,* 104–109.

Meston, C. M., Trapnell, P. D., & Gorzalka, B. B. (1996). Ethnic and gender differences in sexuality: Variations in sexual behavior between Asian and non-Asian university students. *Archives of Sexual Behavior,* 25, 33–72.

Michael, R. T., Gagnon, J. H., Laumann, E. O., & Kolata, G. (1994). *Sex in America: A definitive survey.* Boston: Little, Brown.

Miller, L. (1995, February 9). Looking for love in cyberspace. *USA Today,* p. 6d.

Mirowsky, J., Ross, C.E., & Van Willigen, M. (1996). Instrumentalism in the land of opportunity: Socioeconomic causes and emotional consequences. *Social Psychology Quarterly* 59, 322–337.

Muehlenhard, C. L., & Cook, S. W. (1988). Men's self-reports of unwanted sexual activity. *Journal of Sex Research, 24,* 58–72.

National Center for Health Statistics. (1997). *Births, marriages, divorces, and deaths for August 1996.* Monthly Vital Statistics Report (Vol. 45, No. 8.), Hyattsville, MD: Public Health Service.

Nock, S. L. (1995). A comparison of marriages and cohabiting relationships. *Journal of Family Issues, 16,* 53–76.

Reinisch, J. J., Hill, C. A., Sanders, S. A., & Ziemba-Davis, M. (1995). High-risk sexual behavior at a Midwestern university: A confirmatory survey. *Family Planning Perspectives, 27,* 79–82.

Rosenthal, S. L., Lewis, L. M., & Cohen, S. S. (1996). Issues related to the sexual decision-making of inner-city adolescent girls. *Adolescence, 31*(123), 731–739.

Saluter, A. F. (1996). *Marital Status and Living Arrangements: March 1994* (U.S. Bureau of the Census, Current Population Reports, Series P20-484). Washington, DC: U.S. Government Printing Office.

Shannon, D., & Dwyer, C. (1996). Sexuality education and the Internet: The next frontier. *SIECUS Report 25,* 3–6.

SIECUS. (1996). *SIECUS Position Statements on Human Sexuality, Sexual Health and Sexuality Education and Information 1995–1996.* 24, 21–23.

Sigmon, S. B., & Gainey, R. (1995). High-risk sexual activity and alcohol consumption among college students. *College Student Journal, 29,* 128.

Spiegler, M. (1996). Breast implants: Once is not enough. *American Demographics, 18,* 13.

Sprecher, S., & Regan, P. C. (1996). College virgins: How men and women perceive their sexual status. *The Journal of Sex Research, 33,* 3–15.

Trussell, J., Ellerston, C., & Stewart, F. (1996). The effectiveness of the Yuzpe regimen of emergency contraception. *Family Planning Perspectives, 28,* 58–64, 87.

Sex Research and Theory

Chapter 2

The Interdisciplinary Nature of Sex Research

QUESTION What three disciplines approach sex research questions from different perspectives?

Conducting Sex Research: A Step-by-Step Process

Identifying a Research Question
Reviewing the Literature
Formulating a Hypothesis and Operationalizing
   Variables

QUESTION How does scientific sex research differ from casual observations of sexual attitudes and behaviors?

Methods of Data Collection

Experimental Research
PERSONAL CHOICES: Should People Who Are
   Infected with HIV or Have AIDS Participate in
   Experimental Research?
Survey Research
PERSONAL CHOICES: Should You Participate in
   Sex Research as a Subject?
Field Research
Direct Laboratory Observations
Case Studies
Historical Research
SOCIAL CHOICES: Should Taxpayers Support
   Funding for Sex Research?

QUESTION Which method of data collection would you use if you wanted to assess attitudes toward abortion? Which method would you select to assess a person's abortion experience?

Levels of Data Analysis

Description
Correlation
Causation
Reliability
Validity

QUESTION What conditions must be met before you can say that X causes Y (for example, drinking alcohol [X] causes sexual aggression [Y])?

Theories of Sexuality

Biological Theories
Psychological Theories
Sociological Theories
SELF-ASSESSMENT: Attitudes Toward Feminism
   Scale

QUESTION Which provides the best explanation for human sexual behavior: biological theory, psychological theory, or sociological theory?

Eclectic View of Human Sexuality

QUESTION What is an eclectic view of an older diabetic man's difficulty with achieving erection?

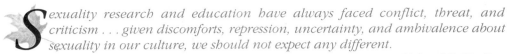

exuality research and education have always faced conflict, threat, and criticism . . . given discomforts, repression, uncertainty, and ambivalence about sexuality in our culture, we should not expect any different.

Richard P. Keeling
President of Society for the
Scientific Study of Sex, 1996

Students taking courses in human sexuality are often kidded about being in such classes. Their peers may tease and joke with them saying things like, "Does the class have a lab?" or "What do you have to do to get an A?" People who study human sexuality in their occupational fields are also subjected to ridicule. Nevertheless, professional sex researchers are engaged in serious and important work.

This chapter focuses on the science of sexuality. The scientific study of sexuality—also called *sexology*—involves identifying important questions related to sexuality issues and finding answers based on scientific methods of investigation. Knowledge can be based on a variety of sources, including common sense, intuition, tradition, and authority. But the problem with these sources is that they often provide false or misleading information. Scientific knowledge is based on empirical evidence or systematic observation that enables researchers to test ideas. Compared to common sense, intuition, tradition, and authority, scientific knowledge is a more reliable source of knowledge because it is both objective and verifiable. The principle of *objectivity* dissuades researchers from letting their personal values and biases affect their research results. *Verifiability* means that scientists must report in detail how they did their research so the research study can be scrutinized and duplicated by other researchers. In this way, research is subject to critical examination by other researchers.

THE INTERDISCIPLINARY NATURE OF SEX RESEARCH

The study of sexuality is an interdisciplinary field that incorporates a number of different professions, including psychology, medicine, sociology, family studies, public health, social work, counseling and therapy, history, and education. Basically, the study of

sexuality can be divided into three broad approaches: biosexology, psychosexology, and sociosexology.

Biosexology is the study of the biological aspects of sexuality. Studies in this field focus on such topics as the physiological and endocrinological aspects of sexual development and sexual response, the role of evolution and genetics in our sexual development, the physiology of reproduction, and the development of new contraceptives. Biosexology is also concerned with the effects of drugs, medications, disease, and exercise on sexuality.

Psychosexology involves the study of how psychological processes influence and are influenced by sexual development and behavior. For example, how do emotions and motivations affect sexual performance, the use of contraception, and safe-sex practices? What psychological processes are involved in the development of sexual aggression and other forms of sexual deviance? How do various sexual and reproductive experiences (such as pregnancy, rape, infertility, or sexual dysfunction) affect the emotional state of the individual?

Sociosexology is concerned with how social and cultural forces influence and are influenced by sexual attitudes, beliefs, and behaviors. For example, how do culture, age, race, socioeconomic status, and gender influence a person's attitudes toward masturbation, homosexuality, abortion, and pregnancy before marriage? Sociosexology is also concerned with how social policy and social institutions (marriage, religion, economics, law and politics, and the health care system) influence and are influenced by human sexuality. Finally, this approach studies how sexual processes affect and are affected by intimate relationships.

_____ **THINK ABOUT IT** _____

In the sexuality education you received from parents, peers, and school programs, which category of sex information received the most emphasis: biosexology, psychosexology, or sociosexology?

Conducting Sex Research: A Step-by-Step Process

Conducting sex research, like all scientific research, involves following basic steps in the scientific process. These steps include identifying a research question, reviewing the literature, formulating a hypothesis, operationalizing variables, and collecting data.

Identifying a Research Question

A researcher's interest in a particular research question may be based on a personal life experience or it may involve concern about certain human or social problems. Some researchers are hired by the government, by industry, or by some other organization to conduct research and investigate questions that are of interest to the organization.

Alfred C. Kinsey and his colleagues conducted the first large study of human sexuality, the results of which they published in *Sexual Behavior in the Human Male* (1948) and *Sexual Behavior in the Human Female* (1953). The project began with various questions about the frequency of and the motivations for certain beliefs and behaviors. Issues studied included such things as nonmarital and marital intercourse, attitudes toward sexuality, and how social factors such as education and income affect sexual behavior.

Not all questions that concern us can be answered through scientific research. Questions involving values, religion, morality, and philosophical issues often fall outside the domain of science. For example, scientific research cannot answer the question of whether abortion is right or wrong. Scientific research can, however, reveal information that may help us make or evaluate our own moral or value choices. For example, researchers can investigate the psychological, social, physical, and economic consequences of various sexual decisions. Regarding abortion, researchers can identify the consequences of aborting a child, rearing a child as a single parent, placing a child with an adoptive family, or rearing a child with the father.

Reviewing the Literature

Numerous journals publish research on human sexuality, including *Journal of Sex Research, Archives of Sexual Behavior, Journal of Sex Education and Therapy, Journal of Homosexuality, Family Planning Perspectives,* and many others. Reviewing the literature enables researchers to discover what other researchers have already learned about a topic, provides researchers with ideas about new research questions, and suggests ways to conduct research.

Formulating a Hypothesis and Operationalizing Variables

In order to answer their research questions, researchers must transform their questions into testable hypotheses. A *hypothesis* is a tentative and testable proposal or an educated guess about the outcome of a research study. Hypotheses often involve predictions about the relationships between particular variables. A *variable* is any measurable event or characteristic that varies or is subject to change. The *dependent variable* is the variable that is measured to assess what, if any, effect the independent variable has on it. The *independent variable* is the variable that is presumed to cause or influence the dependent variable. Here are two examples of sex research hypotheses and the variables involved.

1. Hypothesis: Teenage birth rates are higher among nonwhites than among whites.
   Independent Variable: race
   Dependent Variable: teenage birth rates
2. Hypothesis: High alcohol consumption is associated with lower condom use.
   Independent Variable: alcohol consumption
   Dependent Variable: condom use

Kinsey and his colleagues are credited with conducting the first large-scale study of sex research, in which more than 11,000 respondents were interviewed.

Because human sexual behavior and attitudes are complex and influenced by many factors, researchers often assess the effects of several independent variables on one or more dependent variables. ℮ For example, Waldner-Haugrud and Magruder (1996) conducted research to assess how several independent variables (including religion, parents' political ideology, parents' socioeconomic status, the importance of school, and the importance of heterosexual friends) affected adolescent homosexuals' expressions of a gay or lesbian identity. The researchers found that among gay males, the conservative political ideology of parents, higher socioeconomic status, and the importance of heterosexual friends inhibited sexual identity expression. Among lesbians, religion and the importance of school inhibited sexual identity expression. ℮

You might wonder how the researchers defined and measured homosexual identity expression. Another way of asking this question is: "How did the researchers operationalize the variable 'homosexual identity expression'?" When researchers operationalize a variable (or develop an *operational definition* of a variable), they specify how a variable is to be measured. For example, in order to get a driving while intoxicated (DWI) conviction, the courts have operationally defined intoxication by measuring the level of alcohol in a person's blood. In North Carolina, for example, a blood alcohol level of .08 is the legal definition of "driving while impaired" resulting in the automatic loss of that person's license.

Some variables, such as age, gender, and educational attainment are easy to measure—the researcher simply asks the respondents to indicate their age, gender, and highest level of education achieved. However, researchers must carefully consider how they will operationalize variables such as sexual satisfaction, rape, sexual desire, pornography, sexual orientation, and many others because there are many possible ways to measure these variables. In the study referred to previously on homosexual adolescents' sexual identity expression, the researchers operationalized homosexual identity expression by asking respondents to answer five questions on a 5-point scale (1 = not important; 5 = extremely important) in order to assess behaviors indicating gay or lesbian identity expression. These questions included: "How important are lesbian/gay organizations, groups, and meetings to you?" and "How important are gay or lesbian friends to you?" Responses on the five-item scale were added to yield a composite score assessing homosexual identity expression.

Considering your personal, academic, or professional interests, what research question about sexuality would you be interested in investigating? Based on your research question, what hypothesis could you formulate and how might you operationalize your independent and dependent variables?

METHODS OF DATA COLLECTION

After identifying a research question, reviewing the literature, formulating a hypothesis, and operationalizing variables, researchers collect data. Methods of data collection include experimental research, survey research, field research, direct laboratory observations, case studies, and historical research.

Experimental Research

Experimental research involves manipulating the independent variable in order to determine how it affects the dependent variable. In conducting an experiment, the researcher recruits participants and randomly assigns them either to an experimental group or a control group. After measuring the dependent variable in both groups, the researcher exposes participants in the experimental group to the independent variable (also known as the experimental treatment). Then the researcher measures the dependent variable in both groups again and compares the experimental group with the control group. Any differences between the groups may be due to the experimental treatment.

For example, a team of researchers wanted to assess the effects of aerobic exercise (independent variable or experimental treatment) on the frequency of sexual behavior (dependent variable) in elderly men (White et al., 1990). After randomly assigning the men (alike in age, weight, etc.) to either the experimental group (the group that was to begin exercising) or the control group (the group that did not exercise), the researchers measured the current frequency of sexual behavior of men in each group. After a period of time during which the men in the experimental group engaged in regular exercise, the researchers once again measured the dependent variable (frequency of sexual behavior). The researchers compared the sexual frequency of men in both groups and concluded that the men who exercised reported more frequent sexual behavior than the men who did not exercise.

The major strength of the experimental method is that it provides information on causal relationships; that is, it shows how one variable affects another. A primary weakness is that experiments are often conducted on small samples, usually in artificial laboratory settings. For this reason, the findings may not be generalizable to other people in natural settings.

PERSONAL CHOICES

Should People Who Are Infected with HIV or Have AIDS Participate in Experimental Research?

Individuals who are infected with HIV and/or have AIDS may face the choice of whether or not to participate in a form of experimental research called *clinical trials.* AIDS and HIV clinical trials are experimental research studies that test new drug treatments for AIDS and HIV infection in volunteers who are HIV positive or have AIDS. Currently, clinical trials are underway to develop treatments that may stop HIV's destruction of the immune system, help rebuild a damaged immune system, and prevent or cure the various opportunistic infections that result from a damaged immune system.

In considering whether or not to participate in clinical trials, people who are HIV infected or who have AIDS might consider the risks and benefits of doing so. These risks and benefits can be summarized as:

Risks:

– Experimental drugs may not have any beneficial effects or may even be harmful.

– New drugs may have unanticipated and unpleasant side effects.

– Clinical trials may require a lot of the participant's time and frequent trips to the study site.

Benefits:

+ Patients gain access to new treatments that are not available to the public.

+ Experimental drugs are often provided free of charge to participants.

+ Participants receive expert medical care at leading health care facilities.

+ Participants have a chance to help others by contributing to medical research.

Survey Research

Survey research involves eliciting information from respondents using questions. An important part of survey research is selecting a *sample,* or a portion of the population in which the researcher is interested. Ideally, samples are representative of the population being studied. A *representative sample* allows the researcher to assume that responses obtained from the sample are similar to those that would be obtained from the larger population. Thus, the information obtained from a representative sample can be generalized to the larger population. For example, Michael et al. (1994) conducted a national sex survey based on a representative sample of U.S. adults. The results of their survey, published in the book *Sex in America,* are generalized to the rest of the U.S. adult population that did not participate in the survey.

One of the flaws of the original Kinsey sex research (see page 25) was that rather than selecting a representative sample of U.S. adults, he studied mostly white people in Indiana. Thus, Kinsey's findings are not generalizable to the larger population of U.S. adults. Most sex research studies are not based on representative samples. For example, only two of 152 professional articles published in professional journals on homosexuality were based on representative samples (Sell & Petrulio, 1996). Let the reader beware!

Popular books on sexuality and "sex studies" published in popular magazines are often based on nonrepresentative samples. *Sex on Campus* by Elliott and Brantly (1997) was hyped in the media as "the naked truth about the real sex lives of college students." But only one in ten of the 20,000 college students who were mailed a 151-item questionnaire for this study returned the questionnaire. Thus, we know nothing about the sexual attitudes and behaviors of the 90% who did not return the questionnaire.

One of the disadvantages of face-to-face interviews is that the respondent may be embarrassed, which can cause distorted answers.

Details magazine published the survey as "the current state of student unions" (Sohn, 1997).

After selecting a sample, survey researchers either interview people or ask them to complete written questionnaires.

INTERVIEWS In *interview survey research,* trained interviewers ask respondents a series of questions and either take written notes or tape-record the respondents' answers. Interviews may be conducted over the telephone or face-to-face. Data for *Sex in America* (Michael et al., 1994) were collected by 220 trained interviewers who conducted face-to-face interviews with 3432 U.S. adults.

One advantage of interview survey research is that it enables the researcher to clarify questions for the respondent and follow up on answers to particular questions. Face-to-face interviews provide a method of surveying individuals who do not have a telephone or mailing address. For example, some AIDS-related research attempts to assess high-risk behaviors among street youth and intravenous drug users, both high-risk groups for HIV infection. These groups may not have a telephone or address due to their transient lifestyle. However, these groups may be accessible if the researcher locates their hangouts and conducts face-to-face interviews.

A major disadvantage of interview research is the lack of privacy and anonymity. Respondents may feel embarrassed or threatened when asked to answer questions about sexual attitudes and behaviors. As a result, some respondents may choose not to participate and those who do may conceal or alter information to give socially desirable answers to interviewers' questions (such as "No, I have never had intercourse with someone other than my spouse during my marriage" or "Yes, I use condoms each time I have sex"). Another disadvantage of interview survey research is the expense. The average cost of each interview in the Michael et al. (1994) study was $450 (which included the interviewer training, transportation to the respondents' homes, and computer data entry). Telephone interviews cost less money, but they usually yield less information.

Although face-to-face interviews are often conducted one on one, sometimes they are held in a small group, called a *focus group*. Advantages of focus group research include the minimal expense of time and money and the fact that it allows participants to interact and raise new issues for the researcher to investigate. A disadvantage is the limited sample size, which means that the data from focus groups may not be representative of the larger research population.

QUESTIONNAIRES Instead of conducting face-to-face or phone interviews, researchers may develop questionnaires that they either mail or give to a sample of respondents. One researcher (Taylor, 1997) placed an ad in the newspaper asking persons who had had an extramarital affair to send their names and addresses to the researcher who would send out the questionnaires. He received 70 responses. Because researchers do not ask respondents to write their names on questionnaires, questionnaire research provides privacy and anonymity to the research participants. This reduces the likelihood that respondents will provide answers that are intentionally inaccurate or distorted. Questionnaire surveys also quickly provide large quantities of data that can be analyzed relatively inexpensively as compared to face-to-face or telephone surveys, which typically yield less data yet take a great deal of time to complete.

The major disadvantage of mail questionnaires is that it is difficult to obtain an adequate response rate. Many people do not want to take the time or make the effort to complete a questionnaire, and others may not be able to read or understand the questions. Typically, only 20 to 40% of individuals in a sample complete and return a mail questionnaire. In contrast, the response rate for a face-to-face interview is usually about 95% (Nachmias & Nachmias, 1987). A low response rate is problematic because nonrespondents (those people who do not respond to the survey) are usually different from those people who do respond. For example, nonrespondents are more likely than respondents to be poorly educated (Nachmias & Nachmias, 1987). Also, because respondents do not constitute a representative sample, the researcher may not be able to generalize the research findings to the larger population.

As noted, studies on sexuality and relationships are commonly found in popular magazines such as *Cosmopolitan, Playboy,* and *Details.* Sometimes these magazines conduct their own research or ask readers to complete questionnaires and mail them to magazine editors. The survey results are published in subsequent issues of such magazines. The results of magazine surveys should be viewed with caution because the data are not based on representative samples.

"TALKING" COMPUTERS The newest method for conducting survey research is asking respondents to provide answers to a computer that "talks." Romer et al. (1997) found that respondents rated computer interviews about sexual issues more favorably than face-to-face interviews and that the former were reliable. Respondents reported the privacy of computers as a major advantage.

PERSONAL CHOICES

Should You Participate in Sex Research as a Subject?

As a student at a college or university, you may be asked to complete a questionnaire or participate in an interview as part of a sex research project being conducted by a professor or graduate student. Before deciding whether to participate in the study, you may want to be sure that the research follows established ethical guidelines for research with human participants. These include being informed by the researcher(s) about the nature and purpose of the study, being protected from physical or psychological harm, being guaranteed anonymity and confidentiality, and having the option to choose not to participate (or to discontinue participation) without penalty.

Individuals who participate in sexuality research benefit the larger society. The sexual information they share with researchers, which are later disseminated in professional journals, may enable all of us to make more informed sexual and relationship choices.

Field Research

Field research involves observing and studying social behaviors in settings in which they occur naturally. Two types of field research are participant observation and nonparticipant observation. In *participant observation* research, the researcher participates in the phenomenon being studied in order to obtain an insider's perspective of the people and/or behavior being observed. Mason-Schrock (1996) studied transsexuals by attending support groups over a 15-month period and going to the group's annual party. Other sex researchers have studied "body piercing parties" (Myers, 1992), swinging (Bartell, 1970), nude beaches (Douglas, Rasmussen & Flanagan, 1977), strip clubs (Petersen & Dressel, 1982), and homosexuality in public restrooms (Humphreys, 1970) as participants. In the latter study, the researcher acted in the role of "lookout."

In *nonparticipant observation* research, the investigators observe the phenomenon being studied but do not actively participate in the group or the activity. For example, a researcher could study nude beaches and strip clubs as an observer without being a nudist or a stripper.

The primary advantage of field research is that it yields detailed descriptive information about the behaviors, values, emotions, and norms of those being studied. A disadvantage of field research is that the individuals being studied may alter their behaviors if they know they are being observed. If researchers do not let the individuals know they are being studied, the researchers may be violating ethical codes of research conduct. Another potential problem with field research is that the researcher's observations are subjective and may be biased. In addition, because field research is usually based on small samples, the findings may not be generalizable.

Direct Laboratory Observation

William Masters and Virginia Johnson, of the Masters and Johnson Institute in Saint Louis, conducted *direct laboratory observation* of 694 individuals who engaged in sexual behavior over a 12-year period. The findings were published in *Human Sexual Response* (1966). We will review many of their observations about human sexual response in the next chapter.

One problem with laboratory observation research is the use of volunteers. Are those who volunteer to participate in such research similar to those who do not? Some research suggests they are not. Research volunteers have been found to be more sexually experienced, more interested in sexual variety, and less guilty about sex than nonvolunteers (Bogaert, 1996; Strassberg & Lowe, 1995).

Case Studies

A *case study* is a research approach that involves conducting an in-depth, detailed analysis of an individual, group, relationship, or event. Data obtained in a case study may come from interviews, observations, or analysis of records (medical, educational, and legal). Skeen (1991) conducted ten case studies of individuals reflecting different aspects of sexuality including a woman's discovery that she was a lesbian, a prostitute and her adjustment to leaving that profession, a rock and roll band leader and his sexual encounters, an incest survivor, and a person with AIDS.

Like field research, case studies yield detailed descriptive information about the experiences of individuals. The case study method also allows rare cases of sexual phenomena to be investigated. For example, three researchers conducted a case study of a 31-year-old man who had his penis, scrotum, and testicles cut off in a fight (Szasz, McLoughlin, & Warren, 1990). Their report described the "return to erection, orgasmic, and ejaculation capabilities after penile replantation" (p. 344). The main disadvantage of the case study method is that findings based on a single case are not generalizable.

Historical Research

Historical research involves investigating sexuality and sexual issues through the study of historical documents. Data sources used in conducting historical research include newspapers, magazines, letters, literature (such as novels and poetry), diaries, medical texts and popular health manuals, court records, hospital records, prison records, and official (government) statistics on such topics as birth rates, arrest and conviction rates, sexually transmittable diseases (STDs), and nonmarital pregnancies.

Historical sexuality research provides information about the changing nature of sexual behavior, norms, social control, and socially constructed meanings of sexuality. Historical sexuality research has also linked sexuality to issues of power and social conflict in U.S. history (Duggan, 1990). In an analysis of sexuality in U.S. life from colonial times to the present, D'Emilio and Freedman (1988) traced changes in sexual themes from a reproductive emphasis in the 18th century, to a focus on gender relations in the 19th century, to a concern for eroticism in the 20th century. Historical research led Freedman and D'Emilio (1990) to conclude that "the very term 'sexuality' is a modern construct which originated in the 19th century" (p. 483).

Although the cost of a research study varies with the nature of the research question, the method of research used, and the number of participants, research is usually expensive. Who pays for sex research? Funding may come from private organizations and corporations, universities, or government agencies. This chapter's Social Choices section discusses whether taxpayers should pay for sex research.

SHOULD TAXPAYERS SUPPORT FUNDING FOR SEX RESEARCH?

While many taxpayers and politicians value sex research and support public funding of sex research studies, others object to sexuality research and oppose funding it with tax dollars. Researchers who conducted The National Health and Social Life Survey (Michael et al., 1994), a national survey on American sexual behavior, sought government funding for the project on the premise that the data would be helpful in understanding and solving social problems such as transmission of HIV and other STDs and teenage pregnancy. But the Senate refused funding because it feared public opposition to funding sex research with tax dollars. Senator Jesse Helms introduced an amendment to a National Institute of Health bill that specifically prohibited the government from paying for such a study. The amendment passed by a vote of 66 to 34. To conduct The National Health and Social Life Survey study, researchers solicited funds from the private sector.

Abramson (1990, p. 150) suggested that public resistance to funding sexuality research may stem from negative feelings surrounding sexuality. "Sexual science invokes a variety of emotional responses (e.g., disgust, shame, guilt, etc.) which directly undermine both the legitimacy and progress of sex research." However, in order to answer important questions about such issues as the spread of HIV and other STDs, teenage pregnancy, child sexual abuse, pornography, sexual dysfunctions, and the role of sexuality in intimate relationships, we need to support sexuality research. If we fail to do so, "future generations will find it incomprehensible—perhaps unconscionably negligent—that so little effort was marshaled to obtain data on and establish a science of human sexual behavior" (Abramson, 1990, p. 162).

However, some sexuality-related research may not deserve public funding on the grounds that it harms human participants and, therefore, violates ethical research standards. For example, the Public Citizens' Health Research Group revealed that "the U.S. Government is funding studies in some developing countries which will allow over 1,000 infants to die unnecessarily from HIV infections" (Kaye, 1997, p. 3). In experiments with pregnant HIV-infected women in Asia, Africa, and the Caribbean, researchers have been investigating whether the antiviral drug AZT or other drugs will reduce the transmission of HIV from mother to child. Many women in these studies are not receiving AZT, even though research has already established that AZT can reduce HIV transmission from mother to child by about two-thirds. Instead of receiving a proven therapy (AZT), many women in these studies are receiving a placebo or an unproven treatment. Dr. Sidney Wolfe, director of the Health Research Group calls these studies "Tuskegee, Part Two, and this time many more people will die" (Kaye, 1997, p. 3). Wolfe's reference was to the study that began in 1932 in Tuskegee, Alabama, in which African American men with syphilis were not offered effective treatment so that researchers could study the long-term effects of syphilis.

Another questionable research project funded by the National Institute of Health would randomize individuals who are injection drug users to receive or not receive sterile syringes from a needle exchange program (Alaskan Needle Exchange Study, 1997). Half of the participants in this study would be prevented from using the needle exchange program, even though other research suggests that needle exchange programs can reduce the transmission of HIV and do not lead to an increase in drug use. Critics of this research have made efforts to stop the funding for this project.

Sources: Abramson, P. R. (1990). Sexual science: Emerging discipline or oxymoron? *Journal of Sex Research, 27,* 147–165.

Alaskan Needle Exchange Study, (1997, spring). *Public Citizen News,* p. 8.

Kaye, M. W. (1997, spring). Tuskegee, Part Two. *Public Citizen News,* p. 3.

Michael, R. T., Gagnon, J. H., Laumann, E. O., & Kolata, G. (1994). *Sex in America: A definitive survey.* Boston: Little, Brown.

Earlier in this chapter, you were asked to formulate a sex research question and hypothesis based on your personal, academic, or professional interests. Which method of research would you select to answer your research question? What are the advantages and disadvantages of using the method you selected?

LEVELS OF DATA ANALYSIS

After collecting data on a research question, researchers analyze the data to test their hypotheses. There are three levels of data analysis: description, correlation, and causation.

Description

The goal of many sexuality research studies is to describe sexual processes, behaviors, and attitudes, as well as the people who experience them. Descriptive research may be qualitative or quantitative. Qualitative descriptions are verbal narratives that describe details and nuances of sexual phenomena. Quantitative descriptions of sexuality are numerical representations of sexual phenomena. Quantitative descriptive data analysis may involve computing the following: means (averages), frequencies, mode (the most frequently occurring observation in the data), median (the middle data point; half of the data points are above and half are below the median), and range (a measure of dispersion, comprising the highest and lowest values of a variable in a set of observations).

Descriptive quantitative research findings should be interpreted with caution. For example, research suggests that in regard to motivations for sexual intercourse, men emphasize the desire for sexual pleasure, conquest, and relief of sexual tension more often than women, who emphasize emotional closeness and affection (Townsend & Levy, 1990). Does this mean that women never emphasize sexual pleasure and men never emphasize emotional closeness? Of course not! What these findings mean is that men generally tend to emphasize sexual pleasure and women tend to emphasize emotional closeness.

While these generalizations are based on averages, they do not account for the range of variability among women and men. Indeed, some men are more concerned about intimacy than some women, and some women are more interested in sexual pleasure than some men. As you read the research findings in this text, remember that they are generalizations, not absolute truths.

Correlation

Researchers are often interested in the relationships among variables. Remember that a variable is simply a measurable item or characteristic that is subject to change. *Correlation* refers to a relationship among two or more variables. Correlational research may answer such questions as "What is the relationship between sex and attitudes toward masturbation?", "What factors are associated with engaging in high-risk sexual behavior (such as the failure to use condoms)?", and "What is the relationship between homophobia and religion?"

If there is a correlation or relationship between two variables, then a change in one variable is associated with a change in the other variable. A *positive correlation* exists when both variables change in the same direction. For example, in general, the greater the number of sexual partners a person has, the greater the chances are of contracting a sexually transmissible disease. As variable A (number of sexual partners) increases, variable B (chances of contracting an STD) also increases. Therefore, we may say that there is a positive correlation between the number of sexual partners and contracting STDs. Similarly, we might say that as the number of sexual partners decreases, the chance of contracting STDs decreases. Notice that in both cases, the variables change in the same direction.

A *negative correlation* exists when two variables change in opposite directions. For example, there is a negative correlation between condom use and contracting STDs. This means that as condom use increases, the chance of contracting STDs decreases.

Students often make the mistake of thinking that if two variables decrease, the correlation is negative. To avoid making this error, remember that in a positive correlation, it does not matter whether the variables increase or decrease, as long as they change in the same direction.

Sometimes the relationship between variables is curvilinear. A *curvilinear correlation* exists when two variables vary in both the same and opposite directions. For example, suppose that if you have one alcoholic beverage, your desire for sex increases. With two drinks, your sexual desire increases more, and three drinks raise your interest even higher. So far, there is a positive correlation between alcohol consumption (variable A) and sexual desire (variable B); as one variable increases, the other also increases. But suppose after four drinks, you start feeling sleepy, dizzy, or nauseous, and your interest in sex decreases. After five drinks, you are either vomiting or semiconscious, and sex is of no interest to you. There is now a negative correlation between alcohol consumption and sexual desire; as alcohol consumption increases, sexual interest decreases. Figure 2.1 illustrates how positive, negative, and curvilinear correlations look when they are plotted on a graph.

A fourth type of correlation is called a spurious correlation. A *spurious correlation* exists when two variables appear to be related but only because they are both related to a third variable. When the third variable is controlled through a statistical method in which a variable is held constant, the apparent relationship between the dependent and independent variables disappears.

For example, some research suggests that the more religiously devout you are, the more likely you are to contract a sexually transmissible disease (Smith & Walters, 1988). How can that be? Is there something about being religiously devout that, in and of itself, leads to STDs? The explanation is that religiously devout unmarried individuals are less likely to plan intercourse, and therefore, when they do have intercourse, they often are not prepared in terms of having a condom with them. Therefore, the correlation between religious devoutness and STDs is spurious. These variables appear to be related only because they are both related to a third variable (in this case, condom use).

Causation

If data analysis reveals that two variables are correlated, we know only that a change in one variable is associated with a change in the other variable. We cannot assume, however, that a change in one variable causes a change in the other variable unless our data collection and analysis are specifically designed to assess causation. The research method that best allows us to assess causal relationships is the experimental method.

In order to demonstrate causality, three conditions must be met. First, the research must demonstrate that variable *A* is correlated with variable *B*. In other words, a change in variable *A* must be associated with a change in variable *B*. Second, the researcher must demonstrate that the observed correlation is nonspurious. A nonspurious correlation is a relationship

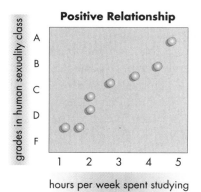
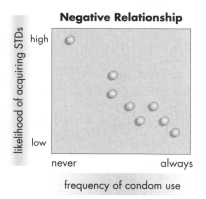
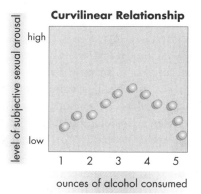

FIGURE 2.1 Graphs Depicting Positive, Negative, and Curvilinear Relationships

between two variables that cannot be explained by a third variable. A nonspurious correlation suggests that there is an inherent causal link between the two variables. As we saw earlier, the correlation between religious devoutness and sexually transmissible diseases is spurious because a third variable—condom use—explains the correlation. Third, the researcher must demonstrate that the presumed cause (variable *A*) occurs or changes prior to the presumed effect (variable *B*). In other words, the cause must precede the effect.

For example, suppose a researcher finds that there is a negative correlation between marital conflict and frequency of marital intercourse (as marital conflict increases, frequency of marital intercourse decreases). In order to demonstrate that marital conflict causes the frequency of marital intercourse to decrease, the researcher must show that the marital conflict preceded the decrease in marital intercourse. Otherwise, the researcher cannot be sure whether marital conflict causes a decrease in marital intercourse or a decrease in marital intercourse causes marital conflict.

Reliability

An important aspect of data analysis involves assessing reliability. *Reliability* refers to the consistency of a measuring instrument or technique; that is, the degree to which we can depend on the measure to give the same results from one administration to the next. Measures of reliability are made on scales and indexes (such as those in the Self-Assessment sections of this text), on instruments that measure physiological processes, and on specific information-gathering techniques, such as the survey methods described earlier.

Various statistical methods exist for determining reliability; however, the most frequently used method in sex research is called the "test-retest method" (Lief, Fullard, & Delvin, 1990). The test-retest method involves gathering data on the same group of people twice (usually 1 or 2 weeks apart) using a particular instrument or method and then correlating the results. If the results are the same (or highly correlated), the instrument or method is considered reliable.

Test-retest correlations also provide a measure of the stability of self-reported estimates of sexual activities. For example, Kinsey et al. (1948, 1953) reported test-retest data for the adult, heterosexual, college-educated portion of their sample. In general, incidence questions ("Have you ever performed . . .") on intercourse, same-sex contact, masturbation, petting, and animal contact elicited answers that were highly reliable (0.90–0.95), whereas questions about the frequency of these behaviors produced answers that were much less reliable (0.58–0.67).

Validity

Measures that are perfectly reliable may be absolutely useless unless they also have a degree of validity. *Validity* refers to the extent to which a research instrument measures what it intends to measure. Validity measures are important in research that uses scales or indexes, such as those included in the various Self-Assessments in this text. Scales and indexes are tools designed to measure complex or abstract attitudes, traits, or behaviors. Rather than measure an attitude, trait, or behavior by asking respondents a single question, scales and indexes provide a more valid measure by including multiple questions about the attitude, trait, or behavior of interest. A score on a scale or index is more likely to reflect the property being measured than is a measure based on a response to one question or item.

Validity is also an important concern for sex research that is based on self-report data. Much of the data obtained through sex research are self-report data, or information that individuals provide through interviews or questionnaires. While we may assume that self-report data are accurate, they may not be. Individuals often report inaccurate information about their sexual lives due to embarrassment or fear of disapproval from the interviewer, or to project a desired image of themselves. Individuals may also provide inaccurate data due to recall difficulty. They may not accurately remember, for example, how many sex partners they have had in their lifetime.

THINK ABOUT IT

Why might questionnaire survey research yield more valid data than interview survey research?

THEORIES OF SEXUALITY

A *theory* is a set of ideas designed to answer a question or explain a particular phenomenon. In this section, we review various theoretical perspectives and their applications to human sexuality.

Biological Theories

Biological theories of sexuality include both physiological theories and evolutionary theories. *Physiological theories* of sexuality describe and explain how physiological processes affect and are affected by sexual behavior. Cardiovascular, respiratory, neurological, and endocrinological functioning, as well as genetic factors, are all involved in sexual processes and behaviors. For example, what physiological processes are involved in sexual desire, arousal, lubrication, erection, and orgasm? How do various drugs and medications affect sexual functioning? How do various hormones affect sexuality? To what degree are behavioral differences between women and men attributable to their different hormonal makeups?

Evolutionary or *sociobiological theories* of sexuality explain human sexual behavior and sexual anatomy on the basis of human evolution. According to evolutionary theories of sexuality, sexual behaviors and traits evolve through the process of natural selection. Through *natural selection,* individuals who have genetic traits that are adaptive for survival are more likely to survive and pass on their genetic traits to their offspring. For example, the evolutionary theory of rape suggests that use of forceful tactics to inseminate females may have been naturally selected to favor "males who can inseminate large numbers of females using whatever methods necessary (including force)" (Ellis, 1989, p. 15). On the other hand, females enhance their reproductive potential by mating with males who will help care for the offspring they produce, so females have evolved tendencies to avoid and resist forced copulation (Ellis, 1989).

Psychological Theories

Biological theories do not account for the influence of personality, learning, thoughts, and emotions on human sexuality. These aspects of sexuality are explained by psychological theories, including psychoanalytic theories, learning theories, and cognitive/affective theories.

PSYCHOANALYTIC THEORIES *Psychoanalytic theory,* originally developed by Sigmund Freud (1856–1939), emphasizes the role of unconscious processes in our lives. This theory dominated the early views on the nature of human sexuality. A basic knowledge of Freud's ideas about personality structure are important for understanding his theories of sexuality.

Freud believed that each person's personality consists of the id, ego, and superego. The *id* refers to instinctive biological drives, such as the need for sex, food, and water. Freud saw human sexuality as a biological force that drove individuals toward the satisfaction of sexual needs and desires. Indeed, one of Freud's most important contributions was his belief that infants and children are sexual beings who possess a positive sexual drive that is biologically wired into their systems.

Another part of the personality, the *ego,* deals with objective reality as the individual figures out how to obtain the desires of the id. The ego also must be realistic about social expectations. Whereas the id is self-centered and uninhibited, the ego is that part of the person's personality that inhibits the id in order to conform to social expectations. While the id operates on the "pleasure principle," the ego operates on the "reality principle." The ego ensures that individuals do not attempt to fulfill every need and desire whenever they occur. Freud would see rape as a failure of the ego to function properly.

The *superego* is the conscience, which functions by guiding the individual to do what is morally right and good. It is the superego that creates feelings of guilt when the ego fails to inhibit the id, and the person engages in socially unacceptable behavior.

Freud emphasized that personality develops in stages. When we successfully complete one stage, we are able to develop to the next stage. If we fail to successfully complete any given stage, we become fixated or stuck in that stage. Psychoanalysis untangles the repressed feelings created by a fixation at an earlier stage so that mature sexuality may emerge. The four basic psychosocial stages Freud identified are the oral, anal, phallic, and genital stages (see

Table 2.1). Latency is not a stage, but a period of time when psychosexual development is dormant or on hold.

Freud developed his theories during a time of sexual repression. "Freud, up against the Victorian era, was impressed by the importance of sex in human life" (Wisdom, 1992, p. 17). He proposed that *libido* (the sex drive) was the most important of human instincts. However, even though his libido theory has been described as "a great piece of thinking" (p. 20) and "ingenious" (p. 36), it has been criticized as overemphasizing sexual motivation for behavior.

Some clinicians and theorists initially attracted to psychoanalytic interpretations of human behavior later extended Freud's work (Anna Freud, Erikson, and other ego-analysts). They, along with more culturally oriented writers such as Karen Horney, recognized the importance of childhood personality development, but they believed that social, rather than sexual, factors were dominant in personality for-

mation (Ford & Urban, 1963). They felt that the need to emerge from the helpless controlled state of an infant to that of an independent, autonomous individual was the driving force of the individual. Sex played a minor role in the drive for independence.

Even Freud acknowledged that what he had to say about women was "certainly incomplete and fragmentary and does not always sound friendly" (Freud, 1989, p. 670). For example, he described the "momentous discovery" made by little girls that initiates the phallic phase. "They notice the penis of a brother or playmate, strikingly visible and of large proportions, at once recognize it as the superior counterpart of their own small and inconspicuous organ, and from that time forward fall victim to envy for the penis" (p. 673). Modern feminists were not the first to criticize his ideas; in the 1920s and early 1930s, some psychoanalysts, such as Ernest Jones and Karen Horney "did not accept Freud's verdict that women are virtually failed men, and said so in private and in print" (p. 670).

TABLE 2.1   Freud's Four Stages of Psychosocial Development

Stage	Age	Characteristics
Oral	Womb to 18 months	Pleasures are derived primarily from meeting oral needs of sucking, licking, and chewing. Pleasure principle dominates, and id focuses on meeting pleasure needs.
Anal	1½ to 3 years	Pleasures shift to anal needs and are derived from retention and elimination of urine and feces. Pleasure principle and id are still dominant mechanisms.
Phallic	3 to 6 years	Pleasures shift to stimulation of genitals. Girls discover they have no penis. Masturbation may be practiced, and ego negotiates with id and superego for social control of sexual impulses. Oedipus and Electra complexes develop during this period.
(Latency) Genital	6 years to puberty	Repression of sexual urges.
	Adolescence	Shift away from immature masturbation to appropriate peer-sex interaction.

Erikson (1950) also acknowledged that individuals progress through a series of stages as they develop, but unlike Freud, he felt that the states were psychosocial, not psychosexual. Erikson believed that central developmental tasks did not involve seeking oral, anal, and genital pleasures but rather establishing basic trust with people. Also, Erikson felt that personality formation did not end in adolescence, but was a lifelong process (most contemporary psychologists agree).

Some of Freud's concepts are also difficult to verify using the standards of scientific objectivity required today. The presence of unconscious processes operative in the Oedipus and Electra complexes are very difficult to assess empirically. Freud's ideas, according to Wisdom (1992, p. 13) "should all be regarded, not as hypotheses, still less as established, but as great seminal ideas like those all the known sciences have sprung from." It should also be noted that Freud was a psychiatrist whose observations were based on people with problems. Hence, his sample of human behavior may have been biased toward psychopathology.

In her critique of Freud's writings, Millett (1970) characterized Freudian psychology as tragic in that fallacious interpretations of feminine character were made upon valid clinical observations. The patients who provided his clinical data were the basis of his generalizations about all women.

In spite of the many criticisms of Freudian theory, Freud is credited with discovering the sexuality of children. He demonstrated that "infantile sexual development had profound consequences for the adult's erotic life and character structure . . ." (Person, 1987, p. 385). Although generally identified as promoting a loosening of traditional puritanical sexual inhibitions, Freud actually rationalized antagonistic relations between the sexes and ratified traditional roles (Millett, 1970).

In contrast to Freud's psychoanalytic view of sexuality, other psychological theories explain human sexual attitudes and behaviors as learned. Learning theories include operant learning theory, classical conditioning theory, and social learning theory.

OPERANT LEARNING THEORY *Operant learning theory,* largely developed by B. F. Skinner, emphasizes that behavior is a function of the consequences that follow the occurrence of a behavior. Operant learning

theory states that the consequences of a behavior influence whether or not that behavior will occur in the future. Consequences that follow a behavior may maintain or increase the behavior, or may decrease or terminate it. A consequence that maintains or increases a behavior is known as *reinforcement.* A consequence that decreases or terminates a behavior is known as *punishment.* A partner who has been reinforced for initiating sexual behavior is likely to do so again. A partner who has been punished for initiating sexual behavior is less likely to do so in the future.

CLASSICAL CONDITIONING THEORY *Classical conditioning* is a process whereby a stimulus and a response that are not originally linked become linked. Pavlov, a Russian physician of the early 1900s, observed that the presence of food caused dogs to salivate. As salivation is a natural reflex to the presence of food, we call food an *unconditioned stimulus.* However, if Pavlov rang a bell and then gave the dogs food, the dogs soon learned that the bell meant that food was forthcoming, and they would salivate at the sound of the bell. Hence, the bell became a *conditioned stimulus* because it had become associated with the food and was now capable of producing the same response as the food (an unconditioned stimulus).

Sexual fetishes can be explained on the basis of classical conditioning. A fetish is a previously neutral stimulus that becomes a conditioned stimulus for erotic feelings. For example, some people have a feather, foot, or leather fetish and they respond to these stimuli in erotic ways. But there is nothing about a feather that would serve to elicit erotic feelings unless the feather has been associated with erotic feelings in the past.

How might a person become conditioned to respond to a feather as an erotic stimulus? Perhaps the person may have masturbated and picked up a feather and rubbed it on his or her genitals. Or the person may have observed a stripper in person or on a video who used a feather as part of the erotic dance. In either case, the feather would become a conditioned stimulus and would elicit erotic feelings in the same way the masturbation and stripper did as an unconditioned stimulus.

SOCIAL LEARNING THEORY Another learning-based approach to understanding human sexuality is the social learning theory, which is largely based on the work of Albert Bandura. The *social learning theory* emphasizes the process of learning through observation and imitation. Observational learning occurs through observing a model who demonstrates attitudes and behavior. For example, we may imitate the sexual attitudes and behaviors that we observe in our parents, peers, and in the media. The television industry's adoption of a program ratings system stems from concern about the sexual behaviors and values children learn through observing sexuality on television. Social scientists have studied the effects of exposure to sexually explicit material that contains aggression toward women. In a review of this research, Davis and Bauserman (1993) concluded that most men exposed to this material do not report an increased likelihood of sexual aggression after exposure. Men who were already prone to aggression toward women or psychoticism were the exception.

COGNITIVE/AFFECTIVE THEORIES *Cognitive/affective theories* of sexuality emphasize the role of thought processes and emotions in sexual behavior. The importance of cognitions in human life was recognized nearly 2000 years ago by Epictetus, a philosopher who said, "Man is disturbed not by things but by the view that he takes of them." Aaron Beck and Albert Ellis are modern-day therapists who emphasize that irrational cognitions often result in sexual problems. For example, one wife said that her husband ejaculated as quickly as he could because he did not like her and he wanted to frustrate her by making sure that she did not have an orgasm. Her thinking or cognition created resentment and unhappiness. Through cognitive therapy (which is based on cognitive theory), she examined her beliefs and how they contributed to her sexual problems with her husband. With the help of her sex therapist, she changed how she viewed her husband's early ejaculation, focusing on it as a learned behavior rather than as an expression of his presumed negative feelings for her. Together they used the "squeeze technique" (discussed in Chapter 10 under "Resolving Sexual Dysfunctions") to help the husband learn how to delay his ejaculation. Once he was able to do this, the wife's cognitions changed to "my husband loves me and cares about my being sexually satisfied."

Emotions are connected to cognitions. As the above example illustrates, changing the wife's cogni-

tions resulted in her having different emotional feelings about her husband and herself. Affective theories of sexuality emphasize the fact that emotions (such as love, fear, anxiety, embarrassment, and frustration) may precede sexual expression, may be a component of sexual expression, and/or may be a consequence of sexual activity.

Sociological Theories

Sociological theories of human sexuality explain how society and social groups affect and are affected by sexual attitudes and behaviors. The various sociological theoretical perspectives on human sexuality include symbolic interaction, structural-functional, conflict, feminist, and systems theory.

SYMBOLIC INTERACTION THEORY *Symbolic interaction theory* (developed by Max Weber, George Simmel, and Charles Horton Cooley) suggests that human attitudes and behavior are influenced by social definitions and meanings, and that these definitions and meanings are learned through interaction with others. For example, our definitions of what are appropriate and inappropriate sexual behaviors are learned through our relationships with others. Sexual self-concepts, including body image and perception of one's self as an emotional and sexual partner, are also influenced by interactions with others.

According to the symbolic interaction view of sexuality, humans respond to their definitions of situations rather than to objective situations themselves. For example, your response to seeing a woman breast-feeding her infant in public is influenced by

Symbolic interactionists emphasize that your reaction to this photo is affected by your definition of what you see.

your definition of the event: Do you see a mother engaging in a natural, nurturing behavior? Or do you define the event as an inappropriate or even offensive display of public nudity? When you encounter a male college student who has not experienced sexual intercourse, do you view him as a person with high moral standards or as a "weirdo" or "nerd"?

Our definitions of situations and behaviors are largely influenced by the societies in which we live. In the United States, female breasts are defined as an erotic, sexual part of the female body; women can be arrested for exposing their naked breasts in public. Other societies attach no sexual significance to female breasts. In these societies, female breasts are exposed in public and the sight or touch of a woman's breast (to a heterosexual man) will not produce an erection or physiological response, since no sexual meaning is attached to them. Also, while men who wear women's clothes are defined in the United States as cross-dressers or transvestites, in Myanmar (formerly Burma), men dress like women for religious reasons. By doing so, they confirm that they are married to the spirit god of Mangudon and can function as an intermediary for those seeking good fortune and success (Coleman, 1990).

An important component of symbolic interaction theory is the concept of *social scripts* (developed by John Gagnon), which are shared interpretations and expected behaviors of a social situation. Women and men have different patterns of sexual attitudes and behaviors, partly because women and men learn different social scripts for sexual behavior. Men often learn, for example, to seek sexual activity early in a relationship whereas women learn to postpone sexual involvement until they are in a loving, committed relationship. College fraternities have been criticized because some teach social scripts to their members that encourage sexual coercion of women. For example, some fraternities teach social scripts emphasizing the importance of masculinity and maintaining a macho image, and encourage excessive alcohol consumption and taking advantage sexually of women who are under the influence of alcohol or drugs (Martin & Hummer, 1989).

STRUCTURAL-FUNCTIONAL THEORY *Structural-functional theory* (developed by Talcott Parsons and Robert Merton) views society as a system of interrelated parts that influence each other and work together to achieve social stability. The various parts

TODAY'S GREEKS CALL IT DATE RAPE.
Just a reminder from Pi Kappa Phi. Against her will is against the law

In recent years, many fraternities have actively campaigned against sexual exploitation of women and have made attempts to change the social scripts that some fraternity men learn.

of society include family, religion, government, economics, and education. Structural-functional theory suggests that social behavior may be either functional or dysfunctional. Functional behavior is behavior that contributes to social stability; dysfunctional behavior disrupts social stability. The institution of marriage, which is based on the emotional and sexual bonding of individuals, may be viewed as functional for society because it provides a structure in which children are born and socialized to be productive members of society. Hence, there is great social approval for sex within marriage; children created by a married couple are cared for by the parents and not by welfare, as is more common of children born to single parents. Similarly, extramarital sex is viewed as dysfunctional because it is associated with divorce, which can disrupt the care and socialization of children. In a nationally representative telephone survey, 90% of respondents said that unplanned pregnancy is "somewhat of a big problem" in the United States, and 89% cited a decline in moral standards as contributing to the problem. Never-married women with children, women in general, low-income respondents, Hispanics, and people aged 65 or older were especially likely to believe that barriers to accessible contraceptives (such as cost or the inability to obtain contraceptives) contribute largely to many unplanned pregnancies (Mauldon & Delbanco, 1997).

Structural-functional theory also focuses on how parts of society influence each other, and how changes in one area of society produce or necessitate changes in another. For example, some religious leaders denounce education programs that offer condoms to students. Similarly, the educational system in a society affects the birth rate in that society—low educational attainment is associated with high birth rates. Hence, reducing population growth in developing countries requires increasing the educational attainment of women in these countries. The economic institution in the United States, which includes more women in the workforce today than in previous generations, has influenced the government to establish laws concerning sexual harassment and family leave.

CONFLICT THEORY While structural-functional theory views society as comprised of different parts working together, *conflict theory* views society as comprised of different parts competing for power and resources. Conflict theory (as developed by Karl Marx and Ralf Dahrendorf) explains social patterns by looking at which groups control and benefit from a particular social pattern. Conflict theory also explains why some aspects of sexuality and sexual behavior are (or are not) defined as deviant. For example, from a conflict perspective, prostitution and homosexuality are threats to our capitalistic system— prostitution offers women an alternative source of income, and homosexuality fails to produce new members of society for the workforce. Thus, prostitution and homosexuality are defined as deviant in order to dissuade individuals from adopting these lifestyles.

FEMINIST THEORY Feminist theory overlaps with conflict theory; both explain social patterns by examining which groups have the power and resources to meet their needs. *Feminist theory* specifically focuses on the imbalance of power and resources between women and men, and how these imbalances affect sexuality. For example, why are prostitutes (most of whom are women) more socially stigmatized and more likely to be arrested than "johns" (customers of prostitutes, most of whom are men)? "Efforts to punish pimps and clients have been only moderately effective because neither enforcement customs nor public outcries support prosecuting men" (Davis, 1993, p. xii). Feminist theory suggests that these social patterns are due to the power imbalance between men and women, and the fact that men primarily make and enforce the laws. Feminist theory also suggests that rape and sexual assault may be viewed as an abuse of power that some men engage in as an attempt to intimidate women. (Up until the mid-90s, husbands could legally rape their wives in some states.) Liberal feminists emphasize educational and legal remedies for discrimination and unequal treatment of women. Radical feminists believe that it will take more revolutionary changes in institutions and social organizations before political, economic, and social conditions become more equitable.

Socialist feminist theory is critical of *patriarchy*— a system of social organization in which the father is the head of the family and family descent is traced through the male line (meaning that wives and children take the last name of the husband and father). Patriarchy involves the connotation that women and children are the property of their fathers and/or husbands. Cultural attitudes toward women and children as property may contribute to some cases of abuse (including sexual abuse) of women and children.

Finally, multicultural feminists emphasize the diversity among women of different classes and races. For example, women with low incomes, African-American women, and Latino women may experience different forms of oppression that must be addressed.

The following Self-Assessment allows you to assess your attitudes toward feminism.

ATTITUDES TOWARD FEMINISM SCALE

Following are statements on a variety of issues. Left of each statement is a place for indicating how much you agree or disagree. Please respond as you *personally* feel and use the following letter code for your answers:

A—Strongly Agree   B—Agree   C—Disagree   D—Strongly Disagree

_____ 1. It is naturally proper for parents to keep a daughter under closer control than a son.

_____ 2. A man has the right to insist that his wife accept his view as to what can or cannot be afforded.

_____ 3. There should be no distinction made between woman's work and man's work.

_____ 4. Women should not be expected to subordinate their careers to home duties to any greater extent than men.

_____ 5. There are no natural differences between men and women in sensitivity and emotionality.

_____ 6. A wife should make every effort to minimize irritation and inconvenience to her husband.

_____ 7. A woman should gracefully accept chivalrous attentions from men.

_____ 8. A woman generally needs male protection and guidance.

_____ 9. Married women should resist enslavement by domestic obligations.

_____ 10. The unmarried mother is more immoral and irresponsible than the unmarried father.

_____ 11. Married women should not work if their husbands are able to support them.

_____ 12. A husband has the right to expect that his wife will want to bear children.

_____ 13. Women should freely compete with men in every sphere of economic activity.

_____ 14. There should be a single standard in matters relating to sexual behavior for both men and women.

_____ 15. The father and mother should have equal authority and responsibility for discipline and guidance of the children.

_____ 16. Regardless of sex, there should be equal pay for equal work.

_____ 17. Only the very exceptional woman is qualified to enter politics.

_____ 18. Women should be given equal opportunities with men for all vocational and professional training.

_____ 19. The husband should be regarded as the legal representative of the family group in all matters of law.

_____ 20. Husbands and wives should share in all household tasks if both are employed an equal number of hours outside the home.

_____ 21. There is no particular reason why a girl standing in a crowded bus should expect a man to offer her his seat.

_____ 22. Wifely submission is an outmoded virtue.

_____ 23. The leadership of a community should be largely in the hands of men.

_____ 24. Women who seek a career are ignoring a more enriching life of devotion to husband and children.

_____ 25. It is ridiculous for a woman to run a locomotive and for a man to darn socks.

_____ 26. Greater leniency should be adopted towards women convicted of crime than towards male offenders.

Continued on following page.

_____ 27. Women should take a less active role in courtship than men.

_____ 28. Contemporary social problems are crying out for increased participation in their solution by women.

_____ 29. There is no good reason why women should take the name of their husbands upon marriage.

_____ 30. Men are naturally more aggressive and achievement-oriented than women.

_____ 31. The modern wife has no more obligation to keep her figure than her husband to keep down his waist line.

_____ 32. It is humiliating for a woman to have to ask her husband for money.

_____ 33. There are many words and phrases which are unfit for a woman's lips.

_____ 34. Legal restrictions in industry should be the same for both sexes.

_____ 35. Women are more likely than men to be devious in obtaining their needs.

_____ 36. A woman should not expect to go to the same places or to have quite the same freedom of action as a man.

_____ 37. Women are generally too nervous and high-strung to make good surgeons.

_____ 38. It is insulting to women to have the "obey" clause in the marriage vows.

_____ 39. It is foolish to regard scrubbing floors as more proper for women than mowing the lawn.

_____ 40. Women should not submit to sexual slavery in marriage.

_____ 41. A woman earning as much as her male date should share equally in the cost of their common recreation.

_____ 42. Women should recognize their intellectual limitations as compared with men.

Reproduced by permission of Bernice Lott, Department of Psychology, University of Rhode Island.

Scoring: Score your answers as follows: A = +2, B = +1, C = -1, D = -2. Because half the items were phrased in a pro-feminist and half in an antifeminist direction, you will need to reverse the scores (+2 becomes -2, etc.) for the following items: 1, 2, 6, 7, 8, 10, 11, 12, 17, 19, 21, 23, 25, 26, 27, 30, 33, 35, 36, 37, and 42. Now sum your scores for all the items. Scores may range from +84 to -84.

Interpreting your score: The higher your score, the higher your agreement with feminist (Lott used the term "women's liberation") statements. You may be interested in comparing your score, or that of your classmates, with those obtained by Lott (1973) from undergraduate students at the University of Rhode Island. The sample was composed of 109 men and 133 women in an introductory psychology class, and 47 additional older women who were participating in a special Continuing Education for Women (CEW) program. Based on information presented by Lott (1973), the following mean scores were calculated: Men = 13.07, Women = 24.30, and Continuing Education Women = 30.67.

More recently, Biaggio, Mohan, and Baldwin (1985) administered Lott's questionnaire to 76 students from a University of Idaho introductory psychology class and 63 community members randomly selected from the local phone directory. Although they did not present the scores of their respondents, they reported they did not find differences between men and women. Unlike Lott's students, in Biaggio et al.'s sample, women were not more pro-liberation than men. Biaggio et al. (1985, p. 61) stated, "It seems that some of the tenets of feminism have taken hold and earned broader acceptance. These data also point to an intersex convergence of attitudes, with men's and women's attitudes toward liberation and child rearing being less disparate now than during the period of Lott's study." It would be interesting to determine if there are differences in scores between members of each sex in your class.

Biaggio, M. K., Mohan, P. J., & Baldwin, C. (1985). Relationships among attitudes toward children, women's liberation, and personality characteristics. *Sex Roles, 12,* 47–62.

Lott, B. E. (1973). Who wants the children? Some relationships among attitudes toward children, parents, and the liberation of women. *American Psychologist, 28,* 573–582.

SYSTEMS THEORY **Systems theory** (developed by Murray Bowen) emphasizes the interpersonal and relationship aspects of sexuality. One application of systems theory is in the area of sexual dysfunctions. For example, while a biological view of low sexual desire emphasizes the role of hormones or medications and a psychological view might emphasize negative cognitions and emotions regarding sexual arousal, a systems perspective views low sexual desire as a product of the interaction between two partners. Negative and conflictual interaction between partners can affect their interests in having sex with one another.

Table 2.2 presents different theoretical explanations for various sexuality observations.

TABLE 2.2 Sexuality Observations and Theoretical Explanations

OBSERVATIONS	THEORY
1. Men are more sexually aggressive than women.	*Operant Learning* Men have been reinforced for being sexually aggressive. Women have been punished for being sexually aggressive. *Social Script* Our society scripts men to be more aggressive and women to be more passive sexually. Each sex learns through interactions with parents, peers, and partners that this is normative behavior. *Physiological* Men have large amounts of androgen and women have larger amounts of progesterone, which accounts for male aggressiveness and female passivity.
2. Pornography is consumed primarily by men.	*Operant Learning* Men derive erotic pleasure (reinforcement) from pornography. *Social Script* Men script each other to regard pornography as desired entertainment. Men swap pornography, which reflects a norm regarding pornography among males. Women rarely discuss pornography with each other. *Evolutionary* Men are biologically wired to become erect in response to visual sexual stimuli.
3. Men in most societies are allowed to have a number of sexual partners.	*Structural-Functional* In many societies, women outnumber men. Polygyny potentially provides a mate for every woman. *Conflict Theory* Social, political, and economic power of men provides the context for men to exploit women sexually by making rules in favor of polygyny. *Evolutionary* Men are biologically wired for variety; women for monogamy. These respective wirings produce reproductive success for the respective sexes.

Continued on following page.

TABLE 2.2 Sexuality Observations and Theoretical Explanations *(continued)*

Observations	Theory
4. Women and men tend to report lower levels of sexual desire in their elderly years.	*Social Script* Aging women and men learn social scripts that teach them that elderly persons are not expected to be sexual. *Systems* Elderly persons are often not in a relationship that elicits sexual desire. *Biological* Hormonal changes in the elderly account for decreased or absent sexual desire (physiological). There is no reproductive advantage for elderly women to be sexually active; there is minimal reproductive advantage for elderly men to be sexually active (evolutionary).
5. Extradyadic relationships, including marital infidelity, are common.	*Operant Learning* Immediate interpersonal reinforcement for extradyadic sex is stronger than delayed punishment for infidelity. *Biological* Humans (especially men) are biologically wired to be sexually receptive to numerous partners. *Structural-Functional* Infidelity reflects the weakening of the family institution. *Systems* Emotional and sexual interactions between couples are failing to meet the needs of one or both partners.

THINK ABOUT IT

Do you think that the different theoretical explanations for human sexuality are necessarily incompatible? Or can biological, psychological, and sociological theories each contribute unique insights to our understanding of various aspects of sexuality?

ECLECTIC VIEW OF HUMAN SEXUALITY

While some scholars who study human sexuality focus on one theoretical approach, others recognize that each theoretical approach may contribute in combination with others. We prefer the latter, *eclectic view,* whereby we use multiple perspectives to understand a phenomenon. For example, in her synthesis of biological, psychological, and social aspects of sexuality in aging women, psychologist Barbara Sherwin (1991) concluded that "human sexual behavior is multidetermined" (p. 194). Sherwin suggested that sexual desire or libido in aging women is influenced by biological, psychological, and sociocultural factors. Estrogen deficiency is a biological factor that plays an important role in determining sexual response (such as pelvic vasocongestion and vaginal lubrication) in aging women. Changes in sexual response patterns of older women may, in turn, influence psychological variables, such as subjective arousal, desire, and self-concept.

Other influences on sexuality in aging women include the following psychosocial and cultural variables:

1. Availability of a sexual partner who is interested in and capable of engaging in sexual activity. Older women are frequently widowed or divorced, and if they do have a partner, the partner may not be interested in sex or may have erection difficulties.

2. Socioeconomic status and level of education. Sherwin cited three studies of Swedish, United States, and Belgian pre- and postmenopausal women that found decreased sexual interest among lower socioeconomic status groups. This finding was attributed to the notion that education leads to greater freedom from cultural inhibitions and sexual stereotypes.

3. Cultural views and stereotypes of aging women. In some societies, older women are accorded higher status, and postmenopausal sexuality is characterized by openness and playfulness. The United States, on the other hand, has traditionally devalued older women and stereotyped them as being asexual.
(Sherwin, 1991)

Table 2.3 illustrates the value of integrating various theoretical approaches in the assessment and treatment of a hypothetical case of a diabetic man (Fred) seeking medical treatment for erection difficulties. This illustration was presented by Schover and Jensen (1988) in their book *Sexuality and Chronic Illness*.

TABLE 2.3 An Integrative Model Applied to the Case of Fred

Psychological Factors	Physiological Factors	Relationship Factors	Social Factors
Assessment			
• Poor compliance with diabetic diet • Anxiety about long-term diabetic complications	• Mild pelvic vascular deficit • Heavy smoker • Wife's post-menopausal vaginal atrophy	• Poor communication of affect and sexual preferences • Decrease in expressing affection since sexual problem began • Sexual routine is performance-oriented; focus on erections and intercourse • Wife overprotective of husband's health, encouraging him to take passive role	• Primary care physician disapproves of sexuality for older adults • Insurance does not cover couple therapy
Treatment			
• Encourage more active role for Fred in controlling his diet and quitting smoking • Use cognitive behavioral techniques, such as self-monitoring, positive thinking, and self-reinforcement	• Quit smoking • Educate couple on water-based vaginal lubricants; use vaginal estrogen cream if conservative treatment fails	• Communication training • Negotiation on expressing caring more effectively in nonsexual contexts • Sensate focus and enrichment of sexual routine • Give wife insight into husband's need to actively control his health; enlist her support for his efforts in that direction	• With Fred's permission, send assessment report to his physician; follow with phone call to increase physician's knowledge of clinic services • Sliding fee scale; reduce planned sessions from 15 to 10

Source: Schover and Jensen, 1988.

Why is it important to look at a sexual phenomenon or problem from different theoretical perspectives? Choose an aspect of your own sexuality or sexual experience and think about how you might view it from an eclectic theoretical perspective.

KEY TERMS

SUMMARY POINTS

Research and theory provide ways of discovering and explaining new information about human sexuality. They are the bedrock of sexology as a discipline.

The Interdisciplinary Nature of Sex Research

Sexology, the scientific study of sexuality, is an interdisciplinary field that incorporates various fields including psychology, medicine, sociology, family studies, public health, social work, therapy, history, and education. Sexology can be divided into three broad disciplinary approaches: biosexology, psychosexology, and sociosexology. Biosexology is the study of the biological aspects of sexuality, such as: the physiological and endocrinological aspects of sexual development and sexual response; the role of evolution and genetics in sexual development; the physiology of reproduction; the development of new contraceptives; and the effects of drugs, medications, disease, and exercise on sexuality.

Psychosexology involves the study of how psychological processes, such as emotions, cognitions, and personality, influence and are influenced by sexual development and behavior. Sociosexology is concerned with how social and cultural forces influence and are influenced by sexual attitudes, beliefs, and behaviors.

Conducting Sex Research: A Step-By-Step Process

Unlike casual observations of sexuality, scientific sex research is conducted according to a systematic process. After identifying a research question, a researcher reviews the literature on the subject, formulates a hypothesis, operationalizes the research variables, and collects data using one of several scientific methods of data collection.

Methods of Data Collection

Experimental research, survey research, field research, direct laboratory observation, case studies, and historical research each have advantages and disadvantages. The major strength of the experimental method is that it provides information on causal relationships; that is, it shows how one variable affects another. A primary weakness of this method is that experiments are often conducted on small samples in artificial laboratory settings, so the findings may not be generalizable to other people in natural settings.

An advantage of interview survey research is that it enables the researcher to clarify questions for the respondent and pursue answers to particular questions. Face-to face-interviews can be conducted with individuals who do not have a telephone or mailing address. A major disadvantage of interview research is lack of privacy and anonymity, which often causes some respondents to choose not to participate, to conceal, or to alter information. Questionnaire survey research provides privacy and anonymity to the research participants, which reduces the likelihood that they will provide answers that are intentionally inaccurate or distorted. Questionnaire surveys are also less expensive and time-consuming than face-to-face or telephone surveys. The major disadvantage of mail questionnaires is that it is difficult to obtain adequate response rates.

An advantage of field research is that it yields detailed descriptive information about the behaviors, values, emotions, and norms of those being studied. A disadvantage of field research is that the individuals being studied may alter their behaviors if they know they are being observed. Also, the researcher's observations and interpretations may be biased, and the findings may not be generalizable.

Masters and Johnson conducted direct laboratory observation of sexual response patterns in women and men. One disadvantage of direct laboratory observation research is that volunteers who participate in such research are not representative of the larger population.

Like field research, case studies yield detailed descriptive information about the experiences of individuals. The case study method also allows rare cases of sexual phenomena to be investigated. The main disadvantage of the case study method is that findings based on a single case are not generalizable.

Historical research involves investigating sexuality and sexual issues through the study of historical documents. Historical research provides information on how sexual behavior, attitudes, and norms have changed with time.

Levels of Data Analysis

Levels of data analysis include description (qualitative or quantitative), correlation (positive, negative, curvilinear, or spurious), and causation. Determining causation is difficult because human experiences are influenced by so many factors, that it is almost impossible to isolate one factor to assess it's effects.

Reliability means that there is consistency in measurement, or that the same results occur with repeated measurements. Validity refers to the extent to which a research instrument measures what it is intended to measure.

Theories of Sexuality

Biological, psychological, and sociological theories each contribute unique insights to our understanding of various aspects of sexuality. Biological theories include physiological and evolutionary theories. Psychological theories include psychoanalytic, operant learning, classical conditioning, social learning, and cognitive/affective theories. Sociological theories include symbolic interaction, structural-functional, conflict, feminist, and systems theories.

Eclectic View of Human Sexuality

Many aspects of human sexuality are best explained by using an eclectic theoretical approach that considers biological, psychological, and sociological explanations. For example, for a diabetic man with erection difficulties, physiological explanations would involve pelvic vascular changes attributable to diabetes; psychological explanations would focus on the anxiety that might trigger such difficulty; and sociological explanations would focus on the relationship with his partner and the fact that his family physician may disapprove of his interest in sex "at his age." Biological treatments might involve the diabetic man quitting smoking (in order to improve vascular circulation); psychological treatment may involve changing cognitions so that erection is not viewed as essential to sexual pleasure; and sociological treatment may involve changing cultural views regarding sexuality among aging persons and incorporating sex therapy into health care insurance plans.

REFERENCES

Bartell, D. (1970). Group sex among the mid-Americans. *Journal of Sex Research, 6,* 113–130.

Bogaert, A. F. (1996). Volunteer bias in human sexuality research: Evidence for both sexuality and personality differences in males. *Archives of Sexual Behavior, 25,* 125–140.

Coleman, E. (1990). Expanding the boundaries of sex research. *Journal of Sex Research, 27,* 473–480.

Davis, C. M., & Bauserman, R. (1993). Exposure to sexually explicit materials: An attitude change perspective. *Annual Review of Sex Research, IV*, 121-209.

Davis, N. J. (Ed.). (1993) *Prostitution: An international handbook on trends, problems, and policies.* Westport, CT: Greenwood.

D'Emilio, J., & Freedman, E. B. (1988). *Intimate matters: A social history of sexuality in America.* New York: Harper and Row.

Douglas, J. D., Rasmussen, P. H., & Flanagan, C. A. (1977). *The nude beach.* Beverly Hills, CA: Sage.

Duggan, L. (1990). From instincts to politics: Writing the history of sexuality in the U.S. [Review essay]. *Journal of Sex Research, 27,* 95-109.

Elliott, L., & Brantley, C. (1997). *Sex on campus: The naked truth about the real sex lives of college students.* New York: Random House.

Ellis, L. (1989). *Theories of rape: Inquiries into the causes of sexual aggression.* New York: Hemisphere.

Erikson, E. H. (1950). *Childhood and society.* New York: W. W. Norton.

Ford, D. H., & Urban, H. B. (1963). *Systems of psychotherapy: A comparative study.* New York: Wiley.

Freedman, E. B., & D'Emilio, J. (1990). Problems encountered in writing the history of sexuality: Sources, theory and interpretation. *The Journal of Sex Research, 27,* 482-495.

Freud, S. (1989). Some physical consequences of the anatomical distinction between the sexes. In P. Gay (Ed.), *The Freud reader.* New York: W. W. Norton. (Original work published in 1925).

Humphreys, L. (1970). *Tearoom trade: Impersonal sex in public places.* Chicago: Aldine.

Kinsey, A. C., Pomeroy, W. B., & Martin, C. E. (1948). *Sexual behavior in the human male.* Philadelphia: Saunders.

Kinsey, A. C., Pomeroy, W. B., Martin, C. E., & Gebhard, P. H. (1953). *Sexual behavior in the human female.* Philadelphia: Saunders.

Lief, H. I., Fullard, W., & Delvin, S. J. (1990). A new measure of adolescent sexuality: SKAT-A. *Journal of Sex Education and Therapy, 16,* 79-91.

Martin, P. Y., & Hummer, R. A. (1989). Fraternities and rape on campus. *Gender and Society, 3,* 457-473.

Mason-Schrock, D. (1996). Transsexuals' narrative construction of the 'True Self.' *Social Psychology Quarterly, 59,* 176-192.

Masters, W. H., & Johnson, V. E. (1966). *Human sexual response.* Boston: Little, Brown.

Mauldon, J., & Delbanco, S. (1997). Public perceptions about unplanned pregnancy. *Family Planning Perspectives, 29,* 25-34, 40.

Michael, R. T., Gagnon, J. H., Laumann, E. O., & Kolata, G. (1994). *Sex in America: A definitive survey.* Boston: Little, Brown.

Millett, K. (1970). *Sexual politics.* New York: Avon.

Myers, J. (1992). Nonmainstream body modification: Genital piercing, branding, burning and cutting. *Journal of Contemporary Ethnography, 21,* 267-306.

Nachmias, D., & Nachmias, C. (1987). *Research methods in the social sciences* (3rd ed.). New York: St. Martin's Press.

Petersen, D. M., & Dressel, P. L. (1982). Equal time for women: Social notes on the male strip show. *Urban Life, 11,* 185-208.

Person, E. S. (1987). A psychoanalytic approach. In J. H. Greer & W. T. O'Donohue (Eds.), *Theories of human sexuality* (pp. 385-410). New York: Plenum Press.

Romer, D., Hornik, R., Stanton, B., Black, M., Li, X., Ricardo, I., & Feigelman, S. (1997). "Talking" computers: A reliable and private method to conduct interviews on sensitive topics with children. *The Journal of Sex Research, 34,* 3-9

Schover, L. R., & Jensen, S. B. (1988). *Sexuality and chronic illness: A comprehensive view.* New York: Guilford Press.

Sell, R. L., & Petrulio, C. (1996). Sampling homosexuals, bisexuals, gays, and lesbians for public health research: A review of the literature from 1990 to 1992. *Journal of Homosexuality, 30,* 31-48.

Sherwin, B. B. (1991). The psychoendocrinology of aging and female sexuality. In J. Bancroft, C. M. Davis, & H. J. Ruppel (Eds.), *Annual review of sex research* (Vol. 2, pp. 181-198). Lake Mills, Iowa: The Society for the Scientific Study of Sex.

Skeen, D. (1991). *Different sexual worlds: Contemporary case studies of sexuality.* Lexington, MA: Lexington Books.

Smith, R., & Walters, J. (1988). *Sexual guilt.* Unpublished paper, University of Georgia, Department of Child and Family Development, Athens. Used by permission.

Sohn, A. (1997, May). 1997 College sex survey. *Details,* 159-163.

Strassberg, D. S., & Lowe, K. (1995). Volunteer bias in sexuality research. *Archives of Sexual Behavior 24,* 369-382.

Szasz, G., McLoughlin, M. G., & Warren, R. J. (1990). Return of sexual functioning following penile replant surgery. *Archives of Sexual Behavior, 19,* 343-348.

Taylor, R. (1997). *Love affairs: Marriage and infidelity.* Amherst, NY: Prometheus Books.

Townsend, J. M., & Levy, G. D. (1990). Effects of potential partner's physical attractiveness and socioeconomic status on sexuality and partner selection. *Archives of Sexual Behavior, 19,* 149-164.

Waldner-Haugrud, L. K., & Magruder, B. (1996). Homosexual identity expression among lesbian and gay adolescents: An analysis of perceived structural associations. *Youth & Society, 27*(3), 313-333.

White, J. R., Case, D. A., McWhirter, D., & Mattison, A. M. (1990). Enhanced sexual behavior in exercising men. *Archives of Sexual Behavior, 19,* 193-210.

Wisdom, J. O. (1992). *Freud, women and society.* New Brunswick: Transaction.

ANATOMY AND PHYSIOLOGY

Female External Anatomy and Physiology

Female Internal Anatomy and Physiology

Male External Anatomy and Physiology

Male Internal Anatomy and Physiology

Models of Human Sexual Response

Hormones and Sexual Response

Private Parts is the title of a 1997 film featuring television and radio personality Howard Stern. Its title was no doubt selected to commercially capitalize on the connotation with human sexual anatomy. Although we have emphasized that human sexuality is a broader concept than anatomy, knowledge of sexual anatomy and physiology is important in making choices in sexuality. If we think of the human body as a special type of machine, anatomy refers to the machine's parts, and physiology refers to how the parts work. Technically, anatomy is the study of body structure, and physiology is the study of bodily functions. *Sexual anatomy* refers to internal and external genitals, which are also called sex organs. *Sexual physiology* refers to the vascular, hormonal, and central nervous system processes involved in genital functioning. Sexual sensations involve the whole body—not just the sex organs. Furthermore, what happens above the neck—in the brain—largely influences sexual functioning.

FEMALE EXTERNAL ANATOMY AND PHYSIOLOGY

Despite living in a culture that seems sexually obsessed, many women do not know the correct scientific names for their genitalia (Tavris, 1992). Little girls are usually taught only that they have a vagina, which becomes the word for everything "down there." Actually, the vagina is an internal sexual organ that is not visible externally. External sex organs of the female include the mons veneris, labia, clitoris, urethral opening, and vaginal opening (see Figure 3.1).

The external female genitalia are collectively known as the *vulva* (VUHL-vuh), which is a Latin term meaning "covering." Female genitalia differ in size, shape, and color, resulting in considerable variability in appearance (see Figure 3.2).

Mons Veneris

The soft cushion of fatty tissue that lies over the pubic bone is called the *mons veneris* (mahns vuh-NAIR-ihs), which is Latin for "mound of Venus" (Venus being the goddess of love).

The mons acts as a cushion to protect the pubic region during intercourse. Since this area is filled with many nerve endings, women often find gentle stimulation of this area to be highly pleasurable. Also know as the mons pubis, this area becomes covered with hair during puberty.

Labia

The *labia majora* (LAY-bee-uh muh-JOR-uh), or "major lips," are two elongated folds of fatty tissue that extend from the mons veneris to the *perineum* (pair-uh-NEE-uhm)—the area of skin between the opening of the vagina and the anus. Located between the labia majora lie two hairless, flat folds of skin called the *labia minora* (muh-NOR-uh), or "minor lips," that cover the urethral and vaginal openings. The labia minora join at the top to form the prepuce, or hood, of the clitoris. It is not uncommon for the labia minora to protrude beyond the labia majora. In fact, in some societies, such as the Hottentot tribe in South Africa, this is considered desirable. For this reason, the women purposely attempt to elongate their minor lips by pulling on them.

The labia minora have numerous nerve endings, making them very sensitive to tactile stimulation. They also have a rich supply of blood vessels; during sexual stimulation, the labia minora become engorged with blood, causing them to swell and change color. With prolonged stimulation, the inner surfaces of the labia minora receive a small amount of mucous secretion from the small *Bartholin's* (BAR-toh-linz) *glands,* which are located at the base of the minor lips. This does not significantly contribute to vaginal lubrication, however, and the main function of these glands remains unknown.

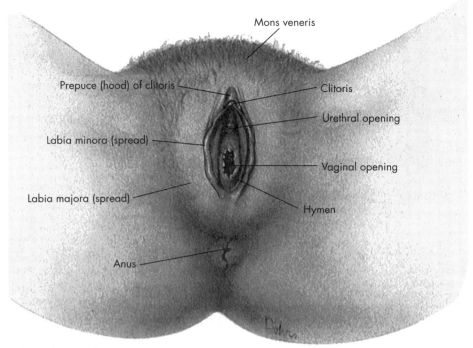

FIGURE 3.1   External Female Genitalia

Clitoris

The most sensitive organ of the female genitalia is the *clitoris* (KLIHT-uh-ruhs)—a sensory organ located at the top of the labia minora (see Figure 3.3). The word "clitoris" is derived from the Greek word meaning "to hide." The clitoris is extremely sensitive to touch, pressure, and temperature and is unique in that it is an organ whose only known function is to provide sexual sensations and erotic pleasure. In a sexually unaroused woman, the only visible part of the clitoris is the glans—a small external knob of tissue located just below the clitoral hood. The size of the clitoral glans, about one-quarter inch in diameter and one-quarter to one inch in length, is not related to the subjective experience of pleasure. The shaft of the clitoris, which is hidden from view by the clitoral hood, divides into two much larger structures called *crura* (CROO-ruh), which are attached to the pubic bone.

The clitoris develops embryologically from the same tissue as the penis and has as many or more

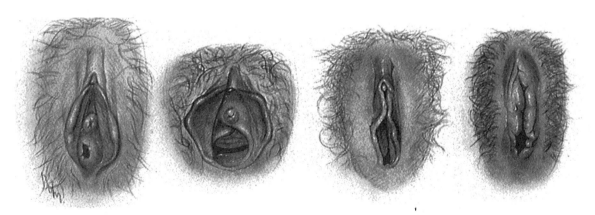

FIGURE 3.2   Variations in the Vulva

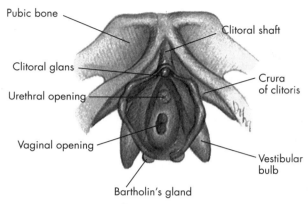

Pubic bone
Clitoral shaft
Clitoral glans
Crura of clitoris
Urethral opening
Vaginal opening
Vestibular bulb
Bartholin's gland

FIGURE 3.3 Anatomy of the Clitoris

nerve endings. The body of the clitoris consists of a spongy tissue that fills with blood during sexual arousal. This results in a doubling or tripling of its original size. Like the penis, stimulation of any part of the female body may result in engorgement or swelling of the clitoris. However, it is incorrect to describe the clitoris as a "miniature penis" because the clitoris does not have a reproductive or urinary function. With sufficient sexual arousal, the glans of the clitoris disappears beneath the clitoral hood.

Vaginal Opening

The area between the labia minora, called the *vestibule,* includes the urethral opening and the vaginal opening, or *introitus* (ihn-TROH-ih-tuhs). The vaginal opening, like the anus, is surrounded by a ring of sphincter muscles. Although the vaginal opening can expand to accommodate the passage of a baby at childbirth, these muscles can involuntarily contract under conditions of tension, making it difficult to insert an object (such as a tampon) into the vagina.

The vaginal opening is sometimes partially covered by a thin mucous membrane called the *hymen.* Throughout history, the hymen has been regarded as proof of virginity. A newly wed woman who was found to be without a hymen was often returned to her parents, disgraced by exile, or even tortured or killed. 🖋 It has been a common practice in many societies to display a bloody bedsheet after the wedding night as proof of the bride's virginity. In Japan and other countries, sexually experienced women sometimes have plastic surgeons reconstruct their hymens before marriage. 🖋 The hymen is, however,

a poor indicator of virginity. Some women are born without hymens or with incomplete hymens. For other women, hymens are accidentally ruptured by vigorous physical activity or by insertion of a tampon. In some women, the hymen stretches during sexual intercourse without tearing. Most doctors cannot determine whether a woman is a virgin by simply examining her vaginal opening.

Urethral Opening

Above the vaginal opening but below the clitoris is the urethral opening, which allows urine to pass from the body. A short tube called the *urethra* connects the bladder (where urine collects) with the urethral opening. Small glands called Skene's glands—developed from the same embryonic tissue as the male prostate gland—are located just inside the urethral opening.

Because of the shorter length of the female urethra and its close proximity to the anus, women are more susceptible than men to *cystitis,* or bladder inflammation. The most common symptom is frequent urination accompanied by burning sensations. Women (and men) with these symptoms should see a health care practitioner. A common cause of cystitis is the transmission of bacteria that live in the intestines to the urethral opening. Women can avoid cystitis by cleansing themselves from the vulva toward the anus after a bowel movement and by avoiding vaginal intercourse after anal intercourse.

However, if one participates in anal intercourse, a condom should be considered for health reasons (AIDS, herpes, HPV, syphilis, gonorrhea, and so on). If one chooses to proceed from anal intercourse to vaginal intercourse, a new condom should be used. If a condom is not used, it would be advisable to very carefully wash the penis as well as urinate to possibly "flush out" unwanted microorganisms. It is not a good idea to have vaginal intercourse after anal intercourse, but if this occurs, precautions are imperative.

The Female Breasts

The female breasts are designed to provide milk for infants and young children (see Social Choices for a discussion of public breastfeeding). However, they are not considered part of the reproductive system, and their development is considered to be a secondary sex characteristic like pubic hair. (*Secondary sex characteristics* are those that differentiate males and females that are not linked to reproduction.)

Female breasts begin to develop during puberty in response to increasing levels of estrogen. This hormone has a similar effect if injected in males.

Each adult female breast consists of 15 to 20 mammary, or milk-producing, glands, that are connected to the nipple by separate ducts (see Figure 3.4). The soft consistency and the size of the breasts are due to fatty tissues that loosely pack between the glands. Breasts vary in size and shape; it is common for a woman to have one breast that is slightly larger than the other. The nipples are made up of smooth muscle fibers with numerous nerve endings, making them sensitive to touch. The nipples are kept lubricated during breastfeeding by secretions of oil from the *areola* (uh-ree-OH-lah), the darkened area around the nipple. This area becomes permanently darker after pregnancy. There is no relation between the size or shape of breasts and their sensitivity. Many women enjoy having their breasts stimulated; however, others derive no particular pleasure from such stimulation.

_____ **THINK ABOUT IT** _____

During your childhood and adolescence, what, when, and how did you learn about external female sexual anatomy? Does your experience differ from the way you want your children to learn?

PERSONAL CHOICES

When Should a Woman Conduct Breast Self-Examinations and Have a Mammogram?

Breast cancer is the most common cancer in women; an estimated 180,200 new cases of invasive breast cancer are diagnosed annually (American Cancer Society, 1997). A woman with breast cancer is much more likely to survive if the cancer is detected and treated early, before it develops to an advanced stage and spreads to other parts of the body.

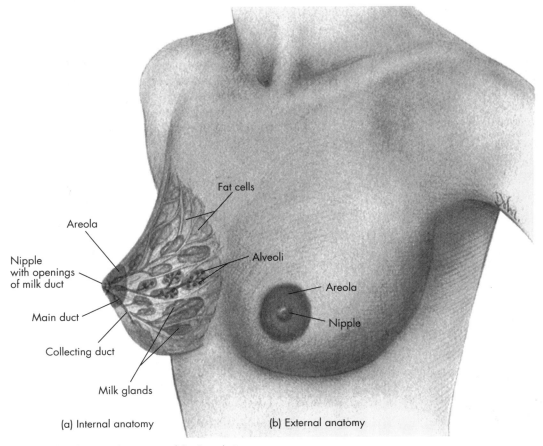

Fat cells

Areola

Nipple with openings of milk duct

Main duct

Collecting duct

Milk glands

Alveoli

Areola

Nipple

(a) Internal anatomy

(b) External anatomy

FIGURE 3.4 Internal and External Anatomy of the Female Breast

Most breast lumps are discovered by women themselves. Although the majority of breast lumps are not cancerous, the American Cancer Society (1997) recommends that all women ages 20 and older examine their breasts each month (preferably after menstruation) to feel for unusual lumps and look for any changes in the contour of each breast, such as swelling, dimpling of skin, or changes in the nipple. Any of these observations, as well as discharge that results from gently squeezing each nipple, should be reported to a doctor immediately.

Some breast tumors are too small to feel during a physical breast examination. A *mammogram* is a low-dose x-ray technique used by a radiologist to detect small tumors inside the breast. If a lump or nodule is found, a breast biopsy is taken, which involves removing breast tissue for examination under the microscope. The American Cancer Society issued new guidelines in the spring of 1997 that include the recommendation that all women should have a mammogram every year beginning at age 40. Although mammograms are safe, it is important to ensure that one is receiving a low-dose mammogram and that the facility performing the mammogram is certified by the American College of Radiology.

FEMALE INTERNAL ANATOMY AND PHYSIOLOGY

The internal sex organs of the female include the vagina, uterus, and paired Fallopian tubes and ovaries (see Figure 3.5).

Vagina

The word "vagina" is derived from a Latin word meaning "sheath." The *vagina* is a 3- to 5-inch long muscular tube that extends from the vulva to the cervix of the uterus. The vagina is located behind the bladder and in front of the rectum and points at a 45° angle toward the small of the back. The walls of the vagina are normally collapsed; thus, the vagina is really a potential space rather than an actual one. The walls of the vagina have a soft, pliable, mucosal surface similar to that of the mouth. During sexual arousal, the vaginal walls become engorged with blood, and the consequent pressure causes the mucous lining to secrete drops of fluid. The vagina functions as a passageway for menstrual flow and as the birth canal, as well as an organ for sexual intercourse. The vagina can expand by as much as two inches in length and diameter during intercourse.

Some people erroneously believe that the vagina is a dirty part of the body. In fact, the vagina is a self-cleansing organ. The bacteria that are found naturally in the vagina help to destroy other potentially harmful bacteria. In addition, secretions from the vaginal walls help maintain the vagina's normally acidic environment. The use of feminine hygiene sprays, as well as excessive douching, can cause irritation, allergic reactions, and vaginal infection by altering the natural, normal chemical balance of the vagina.

The lower third of the vagina is surrounded by the muscles of the pelvic floor, including the *pubococcygeus* (pyoo-boh-kahk-SIH-jee-us, or PC) and the levator ani. These muscles can influence sexual functioning, in that if they are too tense, vaginal entry may be difficult or impossible. On the other hand, some degree of muscle tone is probably desirable. Some sex therapists have advocated performing *Kegel exercises* (voluntarily contracting the PC muscle, as though stopping the flow of urine after beginning to urinate, several times at several sessions per day). However, there is no clear evidence that deficient tone interferes with intercourse satisfaction or that such exercises improve it (Bancroft, 1989).

The "G Spot"

In 1950, German gynecologist Edward Grafenberg reported that he found a highly sensitive area on the anterior wall of the vagina one to two inches into the vaginal canal. This area, named the "Grafenberg spot" or *G spot*, swells during stimulation. Although a woman's initial response may be a perceived need to urinate, continued stimulation may lead to orgasm. Some researchers have reported finding the G spot in every one of more than 400 women (Ladas, Whipple, & Perry, 1982). However, data obtained by other researchers (Darling, Davidson, & Conway-Welch, 1990), indicate that only 66% of 1230 professional women who completed a questionnaire reported "an especially sensitive area in their vagina which, if stimulated, produced pleasurable feelings." Of these women, 73% reported that stimulating this sensitive area during sexual arousal produced an orgasm. Research conducted at the Masters and Johnson Institute found that less than 10% of a sample of over 100 women who were carefully examined had an area of heightened sensitivity in the front wall of the vagina (Masters, Johnson, & Kolodny, 1989). Other researchers dispute the existence of the G spot altogether.

> The "G spot" does not exist as such, and the potential professional use of this term would be not only incorrect but also misleading. . . . The entire extent of the anterior wall of the vagina (rather than one specific spot), as well as the more deeply situated tissues, including the urinary bladder and urethral region, are extremely sensitive, being richly endowed with nerve endings. (Hock, 1983, p. 166)

According to Tavris (1992, p. 230), the story of the G spot illustrates the tendency of sexologists to "reduce sexuality to its component muscles, tissues, arteries, nerve endings, and 'magic spots.'" Although the notion of finding and pushing the right button for physical bliss may be appealing, sexual response is more complex, as Tavris points out: "The reason, as Grafenberg, himself, acknowledged so long ago, is that sex occurs in many places, beginning in the brain and including, but not limited to, various interesting anatomical parts" (p. 241).

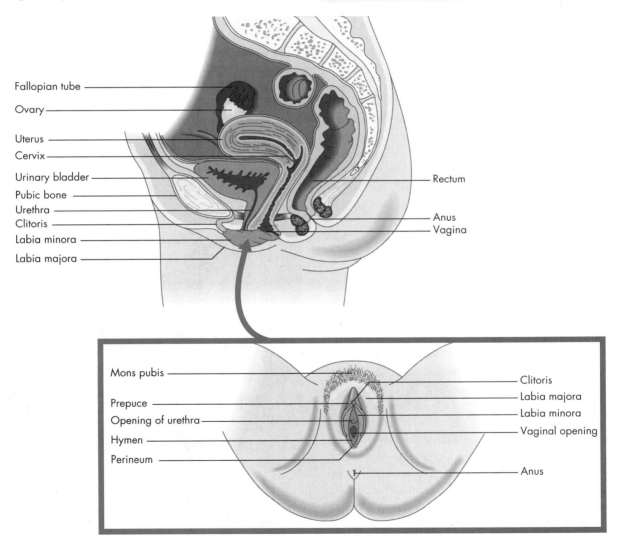

FIGURE 3.5 Female Reproductive Anatomy

SHOULD WE PROTECT A WOMAN'S RIGHT TO BREAST-FEED IN PUBLIC?

In the United States, a woman's breasts are considered erotic and sexual; women can be arrested under obscenity, lewdness, or public nudity laws for exposing their breasts in public. This taboo on women publicly exposing their breasts has resulted in a heated debate over women's right to breast-feed in public.

Although it is not against the law to breast-feed in public in any state, nursing mothers often experience harassment, intimidation, and discrimination for breast-feeding in public. Nursing mothers have been asked either to stop breast-feeding or to leave public places, including restaurants, malls, libraries, parks, bus stations, pools, movie theaters, hotel lobbies, department stores, and even doctors' offices. In Connecticut, a woman was breast-feeding her infant in her car in the back parking lot of a restaurant when a police officer tapped on the window and told her to either stop nursing or go somewhere else (Nieves, 1996). One mother explained, "Breasts are seen as sex objects, so when we nurse, some people just can't handle it" (Warren 1995, p. A3).

In 1993, Florida became the first state to pass legislation guaranteeing women the right to breast-feed in public. At least 14 states have passed breast-feeding legislation. Various cities and counties have also amended ordinances or enacted laws that protect breastfeeding. Such legislation is not being enacted because it is currently illegal to breast-feed in public, but because of the public perception that breastfeeding is indecent exposure. The legislation typically states that breastfeeding is not indecent exposure, and thus not criminal behavior. New York was the first state to create a civil rights law guaranteeing a woman's right to breast-feed in public. Violation of this law is a violation of a mother's civil rights. The New York law provides women with legal recourse if they are prevented from breastfeeding.

Several states have enacted legislation dealing with other breast-feeding issues (Baldwin & Friedman, 1997). For example, Idaho and Iowa enacted legislation allowing breast-feeding mothers to be exempted from jury duty. Florida and Texas have created worksite breast-feeding support policies for all state employees. These policies address such issues as work schedule flexibility and accessible locations and privacy for pumping breast milk or nursing. Texas encourages businesses to create supportive worksite breast-feeding policies by allowing businesses that develop such policies to use the designation "mother-friendly" in their promotional materials.

In other states, the controversy continues over granting women the right to breast-feed in public. In spring 1995, a California Assembly committee killed a bill that would have permitted mothers to breast-feed in any public place and would have protected breast-feeding women from harassment by those who find nursing offensive. Some committee members who opposed the bill claimed that the bill was unnecessary because breast-feeding is already legal. Others feared that such a bill would lead to frivolous lawsuits and public nudity. Assemblyman George House, who opposed the bill, explained: "I'm

Continued on following page.

Some people are offended by the sight of a woman breast-feeding in public, even though most breast-feeding women do so discreetly.

certainly not against motherhood and childbearing and healthy babies, [but] there are other body functions that are natural but not necessarily . . . decent at a particular time" (Warren, 1995, p. A30).

Studies show that breastfeeding has significant benefits for both mother and infant. Breastfed children have lower rates of death, meningitis, childhood leukemia and other cancers, diabetes, respiratory illness, bacterial and viral infections, ear infections, allergies, obesity, and developmental delays. Women who breastfeed have a lower risk for breast and ovarian cancers. Yet only about half of all new mothers try to breast-feed, and many quit after a short time. One reason they quit is because they feel discomfort from people who give disapproving looks, no matter how discreet they try to be in public. A nutritionist who supports legislation guaranteeing the right to breast-feed in public commented that "after impressing on women the importance of breastfeeding, we send them out to the cruel world where all our efforts are undermined by someone who says, 'You're gross.'" . . . The bottom line is, we are mammals and breasts were made for making milk. People forget that" (Smith, 1995, p. E3).

There are also economic arguments for supporting breastfeeding. One study found that the national WIC (Women and Infant Care) program could save $93 million a month in lower food costs if all mothers breast-fed their infants. Each breast-fed baby saves $478 in WIC and other health care costs for the first six months (reported in Baldwin & Friedman, 1997). In addition, because breast-fed infants have lower rates of illnesses, employed mothers who breast-feed their babies take fewer sick days from work (Hordern, 1994). Fewer sick days means higher productivity and profits for the corporate sector.

Baldwin and Friedman (1997), two national experts on breastfeeding and the law, suggest that legislation supporting breastfeeding may help increase public awareness and acceptance of this practice.

> As the legal system continues to recognize and encourage breastfeeding, a message is sent to the public at large that breastfeeding is an important issue; one that has an impact on our lives and the futures of our children. But society's views and taboos are not easily changed. Legislation that recognizes the importance of breastfeeding is just one step toward helping our society become more supportive of breastfeeding. (p. 2)

Sources: Baldwin, E.N., & Friedman, K.A. (1997). A current summary of breastfeeding legislation in the U.S. La Leche League [Website]. Available: http://www.lalechleague.org/lawBills.html. June 17, 1997.

Hordern, B. B. (1994, April). Breast-feeding and the bottom line. *Working Woman*, 18.

Nieves, E. (1996, September 15). Public furor over nursing baby in a car. *The New York Times*, p. 45(L).

Rohter, L. (1993, March 4). Florida approves measure on right to breast-feed in public. *The New York Times*, p. A18.

Smith, L. (1995, April 12). Bill protects nursing moms from harassment. *Los Angeles Times*, p. E3.

Warren, J. (1995, May 11). Panel kills bill on breast-feeding. *Los Angeles Times*, A3, A30.

Uterus

The *uterus* (YOOT-uh-ruhs), or womb, resembles a small, inverted pear. In women who have not given birth, it measures about three inches long and three inches wide at the top. It is here in the uterus that a fertilized ovum implants and develops into a fetus. No other organ is capable of expanding as much as the uterus does during pregnancy. Held in the pelvic cavity by ligaments, the uterus is generally perpendicular to the vagina. However, 1 in every 10 women has a uterus that tilts backward. Although this poses no serious problems, it may cause discomfort with some positions during intercourse.

The broad, rounded part of the uterus is the *fundus,* and the narrower portion, which projects into the vagina, is the *cervix.* The cervix feels like a small, slippery bump (like the end of one's nose) at the top of the vagina. The opening of the cervix (through which semen and menstrual flow both pass) is normally the diameter of a pencil, but at childbirth, it dilates to about 4 inches to allow the passage of the baby. Secretory glands located in the cervical canal produce mucus that differs in consistency at different stages of the menstrual cycle.

Fallopian Tubes

The *Fallopian* (fuh-LOH-pee-uhn) *tubes,* or oviducts, extend about 4 inches laterally from either side of the uterus to the ovaries. It is in the Fallopian tubes that fertilization normally occurs. The tubes transport the ovum, or egg, from an ovary to the uterus, but the tubes do not make direct contact with the ovaries.

The funnel-shaped ovarian end of the tubes, or infundibulums (in-fun-DIB-u-lumz), are close to the ovaries and have fingerlike projections called fimbria (FIM-bree-ah), which are thought to aid in picking up eggs from the abdominal cavity.

Passage of an egg through one of the tubes each month, which takes about 3 days, is aided by the sweeping motion of hairlike structures, or cilia, on the inside of the tube. Occasionally, a fertilized egg becomes implanted in a site other than the uterus, resulting in an *ectopic pregnancy.* The most common type of ectopic pregnancy occurs within a Fallopian tube and poses a serious health threat to the woman unless surgically removed.

Tying off the Fallopian tubes so that egg and sperm cannot meet is a common type of female sterilization. The tubes can also be blocked by inflammation; serious infections can result in permanent scarring and even sterility.

Ovaries

The *ovaries* (OH-vuh-reez), which are attached by ligaments on both sides of the uterus, are the female gonads—comparable to the testes in the male. These two almond-shaped structures have two functions: producing ova and producing the female hormones estrogen and progesterone. At birth, the ovaries combined have about 2 million immature ova, each contained within a thin capsule to form a follicle. Some of the follicles begin to mature at puberty, but only about 400–500 mature ova will be released in a woman's lifetime.

PERSONAL CHOICES

When Should a Woman Have a Pap Test and Pelvic Exam?

In 1997, an estimated 14,500 cases of invasive cervical cancer were diagnosed (American Cancer Society, 1997). Death rates from cervical cancer declined 48% between 1971–1973 and 1991–1993, primarily due to the increased prevalence of Pap screening. For a *Pap test* (named after Dr. Papanicolaou, who originated the technique), a small sample of cells is swabbed from the cervix, transferred to a slide, and examined under a microscope. This test is very valuable in the detection of cervical cancer and should be performed annually in women who are (or have been) sexually active or who have reached the age of 18. Women who smoke, have first intercourse at an early age, have human papillomavirus (the virus that causes genital warts), have multiple sex partners, or have partners who have had multiple sex partners are at an increased risk for cervical cancer. Cervical cancer is almost 100% curable when detected and treated early.

Cancer of the uterine corpus (or body) and ovary are more common than cancer of the cervix; an estimated 34,900 cases of uterine cancer and 26,800 cases of ovarian cancer were diagnosed in 1997 (American Cancer Society, 1997). However, the Pap test is not effective in detecting these types of cancers. A thorough annual pelvic examination performed by a health care practitioner is recommended for early detection of these cancers.

Menstruation

When girls reach the ages of 12 or 13 years, a part of the brain called the hypothalamus signals the pituitary gland at the base of the brain to begin releasing *follicle-stimulating hormone* (FSH) into the bloodstream. It is not known what causes the pituitary gland to release FSH at this time, but the hormone stimulates a follicle to develop and release a mature egg from the ovary. If the egg is fertilized, it will implant itself in the endometrium of the uterus, which has become thick and engorged with blood vessels in preparation for implantation. If the egg is not fertilized, the thickened tissue of the uterus is sloughed off. This flow of blood, mucus, and dead tissue (about 2–3 ounces worth) is called *menstruation,* or *menses,* from the Latin mensis or "month." The time of first menstruation is called *menarche.* Except during pregnancy, this process will repeat itself at monthly intervals until menopause. The average menstrual cycle is 28 days, but this varies from cycle to cycle and woman to woman. Some cycles range anywhere from 22 to 35 days (Singer & Haning, 1995).

PHASES OF THE MENSTRUAL CYCLE The menstrual cycle can be divided into four phases: preovulatory (follicular), ovulatory, postovulatory (luteal), and menstrual. The preovulatory phase begins with the release of FSH from the pituitary gland, stimulating the growth of a follicle in one ovary. As the follicle grows, it secretes increasing amounts of estrogen. This causes growth of the endometrium in the uterus along with an increase in the cervical mucus, providing a hospitable environment for sperm. Estrogen also signals the pituitary gland to stop any further release of FSH and to begin secreting luteinizing hormone (LH). When the levels of estrogen reach a critical point, there is a surge in blood levels of LH, followed by ovulation within 36 hours. During *ovulation,* the follicle moves to the periphery of the ovary and expels the ovum into the abdominal cavity. Ovulation occurs about 14 days before the start of menstruation, regardless of cycle length.

In the postovulatory phase, the empty follicular sac (now called the corpus luteum) secretes estradiol-17B and progesterone. These hormones cause the endometrium to thicken further, building up nutrients. If the egg is fertilized and implants in the uterine wall, the lining of the uterus is maintained during pregnancy by continuous secretions of estradiol-17B and progesterone from the ovary. If fertilization does not occur, the corpus luteum disintegrates, the levels of the two hormones maintaining the endometrium decrease, and menstruation begins. During menstruation, which lasts from 2 to 8 days, the endometrial matter is sloughed off (see Figure 3.6).

ATTITUDES TOWARD MENSTRUATION In many societies throughout history, menstruating women were thought to have special powers or to be unclean. They have been blamed for such phenomena as crop failure and dogs going mad. They also have been feared as sources of contamination for their sexual partners. 🍃 Indeed, Chinese men believe that having sex with a menstruating woman causes illness, because it disrupts the balance of Yang (male) and Yin (female) energy (Tang Siu, Lai, & Chung, 1996). In India, some believe that men who touch menstruating women must be decontaminated and purified by a priest (Ullrich, 1977). 🍃

You can explore your own attitudes about menstruation by completing the Menstrual Attitude Self-Assessment Questionnaire.

PROBLEMS OF THE MENSTRUAL CYCLE Various problems have been associated with the menstrual cycle. Although most adolescent girls have regular monthly periods, irregularity, or *oligomenorrhea,* is not unusual. The interval between periods may be highly variable. A missed period may or may not indicate pregnancy. Issues such as anxiety, overwork,

relationship problems with her partner, or fear of being pregnant can cause a woman to miss her period, as can intense training for competitive athletics. Some women have periods only once a year. If the menstrual cycle has not stabilized by age 17, a gynecologist should be consulted. Spotting or bleeding between periods also indicates the need for a checkup.

Amenorrhea is the absence of menstruation for 3 or more months when a woman is not pregnant, menopausal, or breast-feeding. A pituitary or ovarian tumor or a metabolic disease are possible causes of amenorrhea; hence, a physician should be consulted. Excessive or prolonged menstruation, or *menorrhagia,* may suggest other problems. These include uterine infection and tumors.

Some women experience painful menstruation, or *dysmenorrhea,* symptoms of which can include spasmodic pelvic cramping and bloating, headaches, and backaches. In addition, they may feel tense, irritable, nauseated, and depressed. As the result of the hormone changes, some women retain excess body fluids and experience painful swelling of the breasts (mastalgia) during menstruation. Dysmenorrhea is caused by prostaglandins, chemicals in the menstrual flow that cause spasms of the uterus, and can be relieved by prostaglandin inhibitors. Masters and Johnson (1966) reported that orgasms provided relief from painful menstruation by speeding up the menstrual flow, thus eliminating the prostaglandins. Some women who experience dysmenorrhea report less intense symptoms after taking birth control pills, which contain estrogen and progesterone and disrupt the normal hormonal changes of the menstrual cycle. During ovulation, some women complain of lower abdominal pains, referred to as "mittelschmerz" (or middle pain).

Painful menstruation can also be caused by endometrial tissue growing outside the uterus (in the Fallopian tubes or abdominal cavity, for example). This condition is known as *endometriosis.* These tissues deteriorate during menstruation, just as the lining of the uterus normally does, and a painful infection can result when the tissue cannot be expelled. Treatment ranges from aspirin to surgery.

Finally, some women experience *premenstrual syndrome* (PMS)—physical and psychological symptoms caused by hormonal changes from the time of ovulation to the beginning of, and sometimes during, menstruation. There are over 150 symptoms

Events occurring between day 1 of menstrual cycle (first day of flow) and day 14 (ovulation):

Pituitary gland releases FSH, LH.

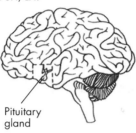

Pituitary gland

Pituitary gland monitors estrogen levels and reduces FSH and LH production when estrogen level is high enough.

Ovary produces estrogen.

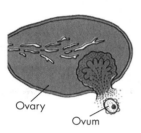

Ovary

Ovum

Ovum matures and leaves follicle (ovulation).

Follicle becomes corpus luteum.

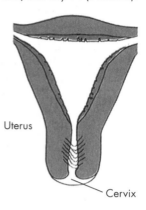

Uterus

Cervix

After shedding, endometrium begins to build up.

(a) In the first part of the monthly cycle, an ovarian follicle (an ovum with its surrounding sac of cells) begins to mature. The follicle grows. Ovulation is the bursting of this follicle, which frees the now ready ovum.

Events occurring between ovulation and day 1 of next menstrual cycle:

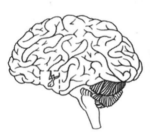

Lower FSH and LH levels.

Corpus luteum produces progesterone.

Lower estrogen production.

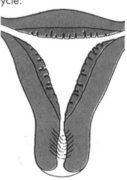

Thickened endometrium is maintained by progesterone.

(b) If fertilized, the ovum settles in the uterus. Simultaneously, the uterus prepares for the ovum by building up its lining (the **endometrium**), storing extra blood and glycogen in it to provide nourishment for the growth of an embryo. Meanwhile, the empty follicular sac develops into the **corpus luteum** ("yellow body"), a sort of remote control device that releases the hormone progesterone that will maintain pregnancy-favoring conditions in the uterus. (It is the corpus luteum for which the pituitary hormone, luteinizing hormone, is named.)

Events occurring on day 1 of next menstrual cycle:

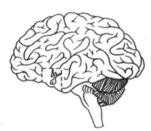

FSH and LH levels begin to rise.

Corpus luteum begins degenerating; progesterone level begins to decline; estrogen level begins to rise.

Uterine lining is shed.

(c) If fertilized and implanted, the ovum produces a factor to maintain these conditions and support pregnancy. If the ovum is shed the conditions for pregnancy cannot be maintained. The corpus luteum withers away, the hormonal climate changes, and the cycle begins again.

FIGURE 3.6 Physiology of the Female Reproductive System

MENSTRUAL ATTITUDE QUESTIONNAIRE (MAQ)

The following scale measures attitudes and expectations toward menstruation. To complete the MAQ, rate each statement on a 7-point scale (disagree strongly = 1, agree strongly = 7). Men can also complete the questionnaire by substituting the word *women* in items using the first person. For example, instead of "Menstruation is something I just have to put up with," revise the item to read "Menstruation is something women just have to put up with."

Subscale 1

1. A woman's performance in sports is not affected negatively by menstruation.* _5_
2. Women are more tired than usual when they are menstruating. _7_
3. I expect extra consideration from my friends when I am menstruating. _1_
4. The physiological effects of menstruation are normally no greater than other usual fluctuations in physical state.* _3_
5. Menstruation can adversely affect my performance in sports. _____
6. I feel as fit during menstruation as I do any other time of the month.* _____
7. I don't allow the fact that I'm menstruating to interfere with my usual activities.* _____
8. Avoiding certain activities during menstruation is often very wise. _____
9. I am more easily upset during my premenstrual or menstrual periods than at other times of the month. _____
10. I don't believe my menstrual period affects how well I do on intellectual tasks.* _____
11. I realize that I cannot expect as much of myself during menstruation, compared to the rest of the month. _____
12. Women just have to accept the fact that they may not perform as well when they are menstruating. _____

Subscale 2

1. Menstruation is something I just have to put up with. _____
2. In some ways, I enjoy my menstrual periods.* _____
3. Men have a real advantage in not having the monthly interruption of a menstrual period. _____
4. I hope it will be possible someday to get a menstrual period over within a few minutes. _____
5. The only thing menstruation is good for is to let me know I'm not pregnant. _____
6. Menstruation provides a way for me to keep in touch with my body.* _____

Subscale 3

1. Menstruation is a recurring affirmation of womanhood. _____
2. Menstruation allows women to be more aware of their bodies. _____
3. Menstruation provides a way for me to keep in touch with my body. _____
4. Menstruation is an obvious example of the rhythmicity that pervades all of life. _____
5. The recurrent monthly flow of menstruation is an external indication of a woman's general good health. _____

Subscale 4

1. I can tell my period is approaching because of breast tenderness, backache, cramps, or other physical signs. _____
2. I have learned to anticipate my menstrual period by the mood changes that precede it. _____

Continued on following page.

3. My own moods are not influenced in any major way by the phase of my menstrual cycle.* _____
4. I am more easily upset during my premenstrual or menstrual periods than at other times of the month. _____
5. Most women show a weight gain just before or during menstruation. _____

Subscale 5

1. Others should not be critical of a woman who is easily upset before or during her menstrual period.* _____
2. Cramps are bothersome only if one pays attention to them. _____
3. A woman who attributes her irritability to her approaching menstrual period is neurotic. _____
4. I barely notice the minor physiological effects of my menstrual periods. _____
5. Women who complain of menstrual distress are just using that as an excuse. _____

6. Premenstrual tension/irritability is all in a woman's head. _____
7. Most women make too much of the minor physiological effects of menstruation. _____

Scoring   A mean is computed for each subscale by dividing the sum of items by the number of items in each factor (reversing the scoring of items where necessary). An * indicates items for reverse scoring. (For example, a rating of 1 is changed to 7, 2 is changed to 6, 3 is changed to 5.)

Interpretation   A higher score indicates stronger endorsement of the concept measured by each subscale. Following is a summary of data obtained from four different samples. You may want to compare your scores with these groups.

Psychometric Information   Brooks-Gunn and Ruble (1980) investigated the replicability and internal consistency of the factors. They reported high Cronbach's alpha coefficients ranging from 0.90 to 0.97 for each factor (presented here as subscales) across two samples. There was high congruence between the same factors across the two samples.

Summary Statistics for the Menstrual Attitude Questionnaire

	SAMPLE			
	COLLEGE WOMEN	COLLEGE WOMEN	COLLEGE MEN	ADOLESCENT GIRLS
Factor Scores	(N = 191)	(N = 154)	(N = 82)	(N = 72)
1. Menstruation as a debilitating event	(mean) 3.39 (SD) 1.09	3.61 0.98	4.45 0.73	3.75 1.28
2. Menstruation as a bothersome event	4.18 1.26	4.65 1.09	4.13 0.93	3.99 1.54
3. Menstruation as a natural event	4.64 1.09	4.51 1.04	4.55 0.93	4.62 0.84
4. Anticipation and prediction of the onset of menstruation	3.79 1.16	4.98 1.11	5.04 0.74	3.85 1.34
5. Denial of any effect of menstruation	2.73 0.96	3.17 1.05	2.83 0.79	3.12 1.08

associated with PMS, including tension, irritability, mood swings, lethargy, migraines, acne, backaches, joint pain, weight gain (due to increased appetite and water retention), and breast tenderness. Dietary treatment for PMS involves eliminating caffeine, salt, and alcohol from the diet and eating several small meals or snacks every 2 to 4 hours. Some women find various methods of stress reduction helpful, such as meditation, yoga, aerobic exercise, and afternoon naps. Physicians may prescribe diuretics to relieve the increased water retention, and antidepressant medication, such as Prozac or Zoloft, to relieve emotional PMS symptoms. Some antidepressants, however, have negative side effects, including reduced orgasmic capacity.

At the same time, it is also possible that some women are particularly susceptible to behavioral influence by hormonal fluctuation. Sexuality researcher John Bancroft (1989, 1991) reviewed evidence that women are quite variable in their immunity or susceptibility to hormonal influence. He suggested that as we learn more about different hormonal sensitivities, this will inform our understanding of women's wide range of experiences of premenstrual syndrome, postnatal depression, menopause, and sexual desire or receptivity.

--------- **THINK ABOUT IT** ---------

Carol Tavris, a social psychologist and writer on women's issues, noted that "biomedical researchers have taken a set of bodily changes that are normal to women over the menstrual cycle, packaged them into a 'Premenstrual Syndrome,' and sold them back to women as a disorder, a problem that needs treatment. . . . " (1992, p. 133). How might drug companies, physicians, and men benefit from defining women's normal menstrual changes as a "disorder"?

MALE EXTERNAL ANATOMY AND PHYSIOLOGY

Male external sexual and reproductive anatomy includes the penis and the scrotum. Like the vulva, male genitalia differ in appearance, and no single example can be labeled "normal" (see Figure 3.7).

Penis

The *penis* (PEE-nihs) is the primary male sex organ, which, in the unaroused state, is soft and hangs between the legs. When sexually stimulated, the penis enlarges, hardens, and becomes erect, enabling penetration of the vagina. The penis not only functions reproductively (depositing sperm in the female's vagina), but also contains the passageway from the bladder to eliminate urine.

The visible, free-hanging portion of the penis consists of the body, or shaft, and the smooth, rounded *glans* at the tip. Like the glans of the female clitoris, the glans of the penis has numerous nerve endings. The penis is especially sensitive to touch on the raised rim, or *corona,* and on the *frenulum,* the thin strip of skin on the underside, which connects the glans with the body. The body of the penis is not nearly as sensitive as the glans. The urethral opening, or meatus, through which urine is expelled from the

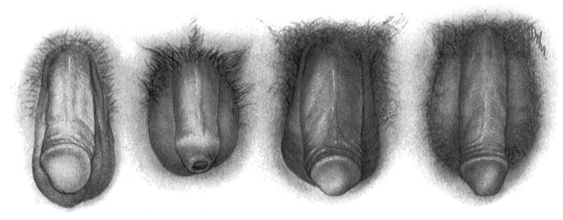

FIGURE 3.7 Variations in External Male Genitalia

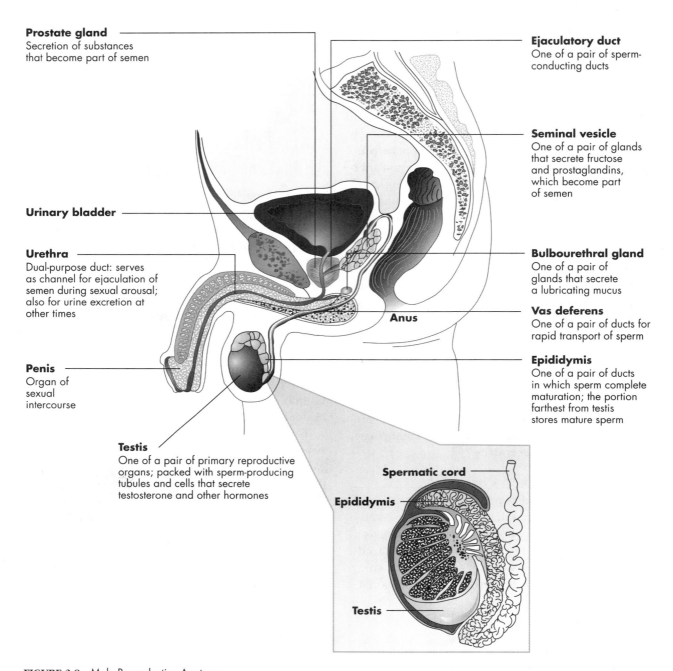

Prostate gland
Secretion of substances
that become part of semen

Urinary bladder

Urethra
Dual-purpose duct: serves
as channel for ejaculation of
semen during sexual arousal;
also for urine excretion at
other times

Penis
Organ of
sexual
intercourse

Testis
One of a pair of primary reproductive
organs; packed with sperm-producing
tubules and cells that secrete
testosterone and other hormones

Ejaculatory duct
One of a pair of sperm-
conducting ducts

Seminal vesicle
One of a pair of glands
that secrete fructose
and prostaglandins,
which become part
of semen

Bulbourethral gland
One of a pair of
glands that secrete
a lubricating mucus

Vas deferens
One of a pair of ducts for
rapid transport of sperm

Epididymis
One of a pair of ducts
in which sperm complete
maturation; the portion
farthest from testis
stores mature sperm

Anus

Spermatic cord

Epididymis

Testis

FIGURE 3.8   Male Reproductive Anatomy

body, is normally located at the tip of the glans. Occasionally, the urethral opening is located at the side of
the glans, a minor anatomical defect that may prevent depositing the sperm at the cervical opening;
this can be surgically corrected.

Unlike the penises of some other mammalian
species, the human penis has no bone. Nor is the
penis a muscle that the man can contract to cause

erections. In cross-section, the penis can be seen to
consist of three parallel cylinders of tissue containing
many cavities, two corpora cavernosa (cavernous
bodies) and a corpus spongiosum (spongy body)
through which the urethra passes (see Figure 3.8).
Each is bound in its own fibrous sheath. The spongy
body can be felt on the underside when the penis is
erect. The penis has numerous blood vessels, and

when it is stimulated, the arteries dilate and blood enters faster than it can leave, as venous outflow is reduced. The cavities of the cavernous and spongy bodies fill with blood, and pressure against the fibrous membranes causes the penis to become erect. Like the clitoris, the penis is attached to the pubic bone by the inner tips of the cavernous bodies, called *crura*.

The root of the penis consists of the crura and the inner end of the spongy body, which is expanded to form the bulb. Two muscles surround the root of the penis and aid in ejaculation and urination. Voluntary and involuntary contractions of these muscles result in a slight jerking of the erect penis.

The glans of the penis is actually the expanded front end of the spongy body. The skin of the penis, which is extremely loose to enable expansion during erection, folds over most of the glans. This foreskin, or prepuce, is fixed at the border between the glans and body of the penis. Small glands beneath the foreskin secrete small amounts of oils that have no known physiological function. These oily secretions can become mixed with sweat and bacteria to form *smegma*, a cheesy substance similar to that which can build up under the clitoral hood in women.

Circumcision, the surgical procedure in which the foreskin of the penis is pulled forward and cut off, has been practiced for at least 6000 years. Circumcision is a religious rite for members of the Jewish and Moslem faiths. In some societies, circumcision is often performed very crudely and without anesthesia as a puberty rite to symbolize the passage into manhood. In the United States, when the procedure is done it is generally performed within the first few days after birth. The primary reason for performing circumcision today is to ensure proper hygiene and to maintain tradition. The smegma that can build up under the foreskin can potentially be a breeding ground for infection. However, proper hygiene can be accomplished in the uncircumcised male by pulling back the foreskin and cleaning the glans during normal bathing.

NATIONAL DATA

The percentage of circumcisions performed on male babies varies from 80.1% in the Midwest to 34.2% in the West, with an average of 62.7% for the United States.

Source: National Center for Health Statistics, 1994.

Scrotum

The *scrotum* (SCROH-tuhm) is the sac located below the penis that contains the testicles. Beneath the skin is a thin layer of muscle fibers that contract when it is cold, helping to draw the testicles closer to the body, In hot environments, the muscle fibers relax, and the testicles are suspended further away from the body. Sweat is produced by the numerous glands in the skin of the scrotum. These responses help regulate the temperature of the testicles. Sperm can only be produced at a temperature several degrees lower than normal body temperature, and any variation can result in sterility.

THINK ABOUT IT

Unlike female genitals, which are somewhat hidden from view and untouched during urination, male external genitalia are easily visible and are touched and held during urination. How might these differences between female and male genitalia affect the sexual knowledge, attitudes, and behaviors of women and men?

MALE INTERNAL ANATOMY AND PHYSIOLOGY

The male internal organs include the testicles (where sperm is produced), a duct system to transport the sperm out of the body, the seminal vesicles, and the prostate gland (see Figure 3.9).

Testes

The paired *testes,* or *testicles,* are the male gonads that develop from the same embryonic tissue as the female gonads (the ovaries). The translation of the Latin "testes" is "witness." In biblical times, it was the custom when giving witness to hold the testicles of the person to whom one was making an oath (hence, "testifying"). The Romans adopted this custom, except that they held their own testes while testifying. In essence, a man's word was literally as good as his testes (Rosen & Beck, 1988).

The two oval-shaped testicles are suspended in the scrotum by the spermatic cord and enclosed within a fibrous sheath. It is normal for the left testicle to hang lower than the right one in right-handed men, and the reverse is true in left-handed men. However, the two testicles should be about the same size, and if one is noticeably larger, a physician should be consulted. The testes are very sensitive to pressure; some men find gentle touching of the scrotum to be sexually arousing, while others find this type of stimulation unpleasant.

The function of the testes is to produce spermatozoa and male hormones. Billions of sperm are produced each month in the seminiferous tubules, and the male hormone testosterone is produced in the interstitial or Leydig's cells, that are located between the seminiferous tubules (see Figure 3.10).

Duct System

The several hundred seminiferous (sehm-uh-NIHF-er-uhs) tubules come together to form a tube in each testicle called the *epididymis* (ehp-uh-DIHD-uh-miss), the first part of the duct system that transports sperm. The epididymis, which can be felt on the top of each testicle, is a C-shaped, highly convoluted tube, which if uncoiled would measure 20 feet in length. The sperm spend from 2 to 6 weeks traveling through the epididymis as they mature; they are reabsorbed by the body if ejaculation does not occur.

The sperm leave the scrotum through the second part of the duct system, the *vas deferens* (vas DEF-uh-renz), or ductus deferens. These 14- to 16-inch-long paired ducts transport the sperm from the epididymis up and over the bladder to the prostate gland, where the sperm mix with seminal fluid to form semen (see Figure 3.9). As we will discuss in Chapter 6, one form of male sterilization involves cutting and tying off each vas deferens.

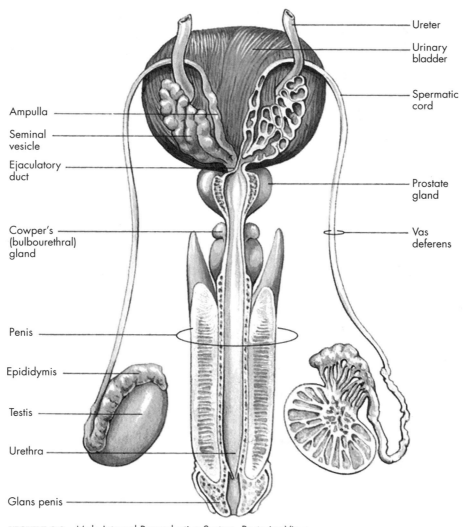

FIGURE 3.9 Male Internal Reproductive System, Posterior View

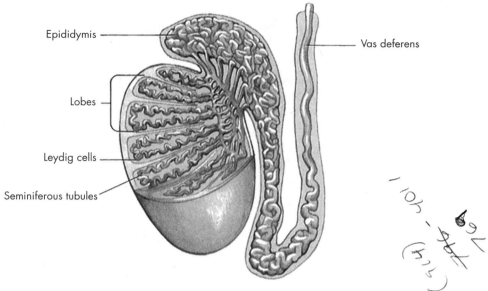

FIGURE 3.10 Cross-Section of Testicle

The final portion of the duct system is about 8 inches long and is divided into prostatic, membranous, and penile portions. In the prostatic portion, the previously paired duct system joins together to form the final common pathway. The male urethra transports urine from the bladder, as well as semen. The urethral sphincter muscles surround the membranous portion of the urethra, enabling voluntary control of urination. The penile portion of the urethra runs through the corpus spongiosum, and the urethral opening is at the top of the glans. As in women, transmission of bacteria to the urethral opening can result in inflammation of the urethra (urethritis) and bladder. The most common symptoms are frequent urination accompanied by a burning sensation and discharge. Men should consult a health care practitioner if these symptoms appear.

Seminal Vesicles and Prostate Gland

The *seminal vesicles* resemble two small sacs about 2 inches in length located behind the bladder. They are mistakenly called vesicles because it was once believed that they were storage areas for semen. The seminal vesicles, however, secrete their own fluids that mix with sperm and fluids from the prostate gland. Substances secreted from the seminal vesicles include fructose and prostaglandins. Sperm that reach the ejaculatory duct as a result of both muscular contractions of the epididymis and vas and the sweeping motion of hairlike cilia on their inner walls are made active by fructose. Prostaglandins induce contractions of the uterus, possibly aiding movement of the sperm within the female.

Much of the seminal fluid comes from the *prostate gland* (see Figure 3.8), a chestnut-sized structure located below the bladder and in front of the rectum. In the prostate, the ejaculatory ducts join the initial portion of the urethra from the bladder to form a single common passageway for urine and semen. The prostate enlarges at puberty as the result of increasing hormone levels. It normally shrinks as men get older, but in some cases, it becomes larger and constricts the urethra, interfering with urination. Surgical removal of the prostate may be required. The prostate is also a common site of infection, resulting in an inflamed condition called prostatitis. Major symptoms are painful ejaculation or defecation. The condition can be treated with antibiotics. Some men develop prostate cancer. Among men, prostate cancer is the most common type of all new causes of cancer, and the risk increases with age. All men should have their prostate checked annually, a procedure in which the physician inserts a finger into the rectum and palpates the prostate to check for any abnormalities. (See the Personal Choices section for further information.)

Anatomy and Physiology   67

When Should a Man Have a Prostate Rectal Exam?

The most common type of cancer in U.S. men is prostate cancer. In 1997, an estimated 334,500 new cases of prostate cancer were diagnosed, and an estimated 41,800 deaths from prostate cancer were reported (American Cancer Society, 1997). Prostate cancer incidence rates are 66% higher for African American men than they are for white men. More than 80% of all prostate cancers are diagnosed in men over the age of 65.

The most common procedure for detecting prostate cancer is a digital rectal exam. The health care professional inserts a gloved, lubricated finger into the rectal canal and then rotates the finger to see if the size of the prostate is normal and to check for any unusual lumps in the rectum. The American Cancer Society recommends that every man aged 40 and more should have a digital rectal exam as part of

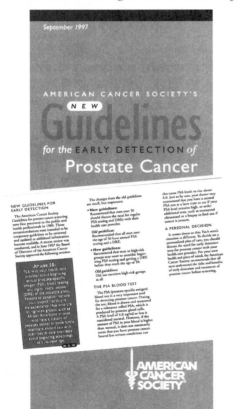

This American Cancer Society public education pamphlet encourages men to get prostate rectal exams.

his regular annual physical checkup. In addition, men who are over 50 should also have an annual protein specific antigen (PSA) test, which can provide additional information about the early presence of a cancerous growth. Because of the frequency of "false positives," however, a prostate biopsy is normally advised by the physician if the patient has a positive PSA result along with a family history of prostate cancer.

THINK ABOUT IT

Do you think that most young adults know more about the internal reproductive systems of women or of men? Why?

MODELS OF HUMAN SEXUAL RESPONSE

Various sexologists have described patterns or stages of human sexual response. In 1906, Havelock Ellis offered a two-stage model of human sexual response. This consisted of tumescence and detumescence, or the buildup and release of sexual energy. Beach, in 1956, also proposed a two-stage model while studying the act of copulation in rats. In the following decade, Masters and Johnson made a quantum knowledge leap with their laboratory studies of human sexual response.

Masters and Johnson's Four-Stage Model of Sexual Response

William Masters and Virginia Johnson (1966) were the first sexologists to propose a four-stage model describing sexual response. Their model assumes that people are sexually programmed to respond to "adequate sexual stimulation" (Janssen & Everaerd, 1993) and focuses on genital response. This model includes the following stages: excitement, plateau, orgasm, and resolution.

EXCITEMENT PHASE During the excitement phase, individuals become sexually aroused in response to hormonal, tactile, auditory, visual, olfactory, cognitive, and relationship stimuli. For both women and men, the excitement phase of sexual response is characterized by peripheral arousal (increases in heart rate, blood pressure, respiration, and overall muscle tension) and genital arousal (*vasocongestion,* or increased blood flow to the genital region). In men, increased blood flow to the penis causes erection, or *tumescence;* in women, vasocongestion results in vaginal lubrication and engorgement of external genitals (labia majora, labia minora, and clitoris). During sexual excitement, the labia turn a darker color, and the upper two-thirds of the vagina expands in width and depth.

Physiological signs of sexual excitement are not always linked to feeling sexually aroused (Tavris, 1992). Men can feel aroused without becoming erect, and women can feel aroused without becoming lubricated. Conversely, men can have erections without feeling sexually aroused, and women can become lubricated without feeling aroused. For example, a man can have an erection as a response to fear, anger, exercise, or waking up. Women can become lubricated as a response to nervousness, excitement, or fear. Nevertheless, erection on the part of the man and lubrication on the part of the woman are usually indicative of sexual arousal. The source of the vaginal lubrication in women is the moisture from the small blood vessels that lie in the vaginal walls. This moisture is forced through the walls as the vaginal tissues engorge and produce a "sweating" of the vaginal barrel.

PLATEAU PHASE   After reaching a high level of sexual arousal, women and men enter the plateau phase of the sexual response cycle. In women, the lower third of the vagina constricts and the upper two-thirds expands, presumably to form a pool to catch the semen. At the same time, the clitoris withdraws behind the clitoral hood, providing insulation for the extremely sensitive glans of the clitoris. Direct clitoral stimulation at this time may be painful or unpleasant because the glans has a tremendous number of nerve endings concentrated in a small area. Even though the clitoris is under the hood, it continues to respond to stimulation of the area surrounding it.

During the plateau phase, the penis increases slightly in diameter, and the size of the testes increases considerably—from 50 to 100%. In some men, the head (glans) of the penis turns a deep red-purple color.

Other changes occur in both women and men: *myotonia* (muscle contractions), *hyperventilation* (heavy breathing), *tachycardia* (heart rate increase),

and blood pressure elevation. Also, some women and men experience a "sex flush" that looks like a measles rash on parts of the chest, neck, face, and forehead. This flush sometimes suggests a high level of sexual excitement or tension.

Cognitive factors are also important in the maintenance of the plateau phase. Individuals in this stage must continue to define what is happening to them in erotic terms. Without such labeling, there will be a return to prearousal levels of physiological indicators.

ORGASM PHASE   *Orgasm* is the climax of sexual excitement and is experienced as a release of tension involving intense pleasure. Physiologically, in both women and men, orgasm involves an increase in respiration, heart rate, and blood pressure. Although everyone is different, as is each person's experience of orgasm, researchers have provided some information on the various experiences of women and men.

1. *Female orgasm.*   Physiologically, the orgasmic experience for women involves simultaneous rhythmic contractions of the uterus, the outer third of the vagina, and the rectal sphincter. These contractions begin at 0.8-second intervals and then diminish in intensity, duration, and regularity (Masters and Johnson, 1966). A mild orgasm may have only 3 to 5 contractions, while an intense orgasm may have 10 to 15 contractions.

   Bancroft (1989) characterized the controversy regarding the nature of the woman's orgasm as one of the most intriguing debates in the field of human sexuality. Freud is credited with starting this debate. He differentiated between sexual pleasure resulting from stimulation of the clitoris and the pleasure resulting from coitus. He stated the "the elimination of clitoridal sexuality is a necessary precondition for the development of femininity" (Freud, 1925/1989, p. 675). According to Freud, sexual satisfaction and release from "the tension of the libido" that come from intercourse result in the highest intensity of pleasure and are achieved through a different mechanism from other types of sexual pleasure. Making the "clitoral-vaginal transfer" was seen as an indicator of sexual maturity.

   Based on their study of physiology of sexual response, Masters and Johnson (1966) stated that clitoral stimulation (either direct or indirect) is

masters + Johnson

necessary for orgasm. They identified only one type of orgasm, refuting the categories of clitoral and vaginal orgasm.

Subsequently, Singer (1973) hypothesized that orgasms resulting from clitoral stimulation occur more easily and therefore are more likely to be observed in laboratory settings. Singer concluded that there are two basic variations in female orgasmic experiences, vulval orgasms and uterine orgasms. *Vulval orgasms* result primarily from manual stimulation of the clitoris and are characterized by spastic contractions of the outer third of the vagina. In contrast, *uterine orgasms* are caused by deep intravaginal stimulation and involve contractions in the uterus as well as vagina. *Blended orgasms* are those in which women experience both vulval contractions and deep uterine enjoyment. While women report varying degrees of emotional fulfillment with different types of orgasm, no type is viewed as more mature or proper.

Some women define orgasm in yet another way: forty percent of 1171 women reported that they experienced an "ejaculation" at the moment of orgasm (Darling et al., 1990).

2. *Male orgasm.* Male orgasm and ejaculation are not one and the same process, although in most men the two occur simultaneously. Orgasm refers specifically to the pleasurable, rhythmic muscular contractions in the pelvic region and the release of sexual tension. Ejaculation refers to the release of semen that usually accompanies orgasm. Orgasm without ejaculation is not uncommon in boys before puberty. It also can occur if the prostate is diseased or as a side effect of some medications. Ejaculation without orgasm is less common but can occur in some cases of neurological illness (Brackett, Bloch, & Abae, 1994).

Unlike female orgasm, orgasm in men occurs in two stages. In the first stage, there is a buildup of fluid from the prostate, seminal vesicles, and vas deferens in the prostatic urethra (the area behind the base of the penis and above the testes). Once this pool of semen collects, the man enters a stage of ejaculatory inevitability; he knows he is going to ejaculate and cannot control or stop the process. The external appearance of semen does not occur until several seconds after the man experiences ejaculatory inevitability due to the distance the semen must travel through the urethra.

In the second stage of orgasm, the penile muscles contract two to three times at 0.8-second intervals, propelling the semen from the penis. The contractions may then continue at longer intervals. The more time that has passed since the last ejaculation, the greater number of contractions, and the greater the volume of ejaculate and sperm count.

The subjective experience of orgasm in men begins with the sensation of deep warmth or pressure that accompanies ejaculatory inevitability, followed by intensely pleasurable contractions involving the genitals, perineum (the area between the anus and the scrotum), rectum, and anal sphincter. The process of semen traveling through the urethra may be experienced as a warm rush of fluid or a shooting sensation.

RESOLUTION PHASE   After orgasm, the *resolution phase* of the sexual response cycle begins, which involves the body's return to its preexcitement condition. In women, the vagina begins to shorten in both width and length, and the clitoris returns to its normal anatomic position. In men, there is usually (though not always) a loss of erection, and the testes decrease in size and descend into the scrotum. In both women and men, breathing, heart rate, and blood pressure return to normal. A thin layer of perspiration may appear over the entire body.

In the resolution phase, individuals may prefer to avoid additional genital stimulation. "My clitoris feels very sensitive—almost burns—and I don't want it touched after I orgasm." This statement characterizes the feelings of some women. Other women say their clitoris tickles when touched after orgasm. A man often wants to lie still and avoid stimulation of the head of the penis. When sexual arousal does not result in orgasm, resolution still takes place, but more gradually. Some women and men experience an unpleasant sensation of sexual tension or fullness in the genital area due to prolonged vasocongestion in the absence of orgasm.

DIFFERENT SEXUAL RESPONSE CYCLES OF WOMEN AND MEN   Although the subjective experience of orgasm may be similar for women and men (Vance & Wagner, 1976), there are distinct differences in the patterns of sexual response.

1. *Alternative cycles in women.* Masters and Johnson (1966) stated that a woman may experience the sexual response cycle in one of three ways. When there is sufficient and continuous stimulation, the most usual pattern is a progression from excitement through plateau to orgasm to resolution, passing through all phases and returning to none of these stages for a second time. Experientially, the woman gets excited, enjoys a climax, and cuddles in her partner's arms after one orgasm. If she is masturbating, she relaxes and savors the experience.

   In another pattern (again, assuming sufficient and continuous stimulation), the woman goes from excitement to plateau to orgasm to another or several orgasms and then to resolution. The interval between orgasms varies; in some cases, it is only a few seconds. In effect, the woman gets excited, climbs through the plateau phase, and bounces from orgasm to orgasm while briefly reaching the plateau phase between orgasms. In a study (Darling, Davidson, & Jennings, 1991) of 805 professional nurses, 48% of the respondents reported that they had experienced "multiple orgasm" at least once (43% usually did so). The number of orgasms reported during a multiorgasmic experience ranged from two to 20. Forty percent reported that each successive orgasm was stronger, 16% said they were weaker, and 9% reported no difference.

   Still another pattern of female sexual response is to move through the sequence of phases of the sexual response cycle but skip the orgasm phase. The woman gets excited and climbs to the plateau phase but does not have an orgasm. Insufficient stimulation, distraction, or lack of interest in the partner (if one is involved) are some of the reasons for not reaching orgasm (other reasons are discussed in Chapter 10, Sexual Dysfunctions and Sex Therapy). The woman moves from the plateau phase directly to the resolution phase.

2. *Alternative cycles in men.* Men typically progress through the sexual response cycle in a somewhat different pattern. Once sexual excitement begins, there is usually only one pattern—excitement through plateau to orgasm. (It is recognized that, for a variety of physiological and psychological reasons, the male may plateau but not have an orgasm.) Following orgasm, most men experience a longer *refractory period* than women, during which the person cannot be sexually aroused. During the refractory period, the penis usually becomes flaccid, and further stimulation (particularly on the glans of the penis) is not immediately desired. However, some men remain erect after orgasm and desire continued stimulation.

   The desire and ability to have another erection and begin stimulation depends on the man's age, fatigue, and the amount of alcohol or other drugs in his system. In general, the older, exhausted, alcohol-intoxicated individual will be less interested in renewed sexual stimulation than the younger, rested, sober man. The time of the refractory period varies. As noted previously, some men maintain an erection after orgasm and skip the refractory period to have another orgasm (see Figure 3.11).

When the sexual response cycles of women and men are compared, three differences are noticeable:

1. Whereas men usually climax once (some men report multiple orgasms whereby they have an orgasm but do not ejaculate), women's responses are more variable. They may have an orgasm once, more than once, or not at all.
2. When the woman does experience more than one climax, she may be capable of doing so throughout her life span, although this may vary, depending on the type of orgasm. In contrast, the man usually needs a longer refractory period before he is capable of additional orgasms, especially as he ages (Bancroft, 1989).
3. Orgasm in men is never accompanied by urination, whereas this may occur in women. In a sample of 281 women, 32% reported that they expelled urine during orgasm "occasionally" (Darling et al., 1990, p. 41).

Although the Masters and Johnson model is the most widely presented model of human sexual response, it has been criticized on several counts. First, the idea of a four-stage process is arbitrary and imprecise. Psychologist Carole Wade noted that the "stages" of sexual response "are not like the stages of

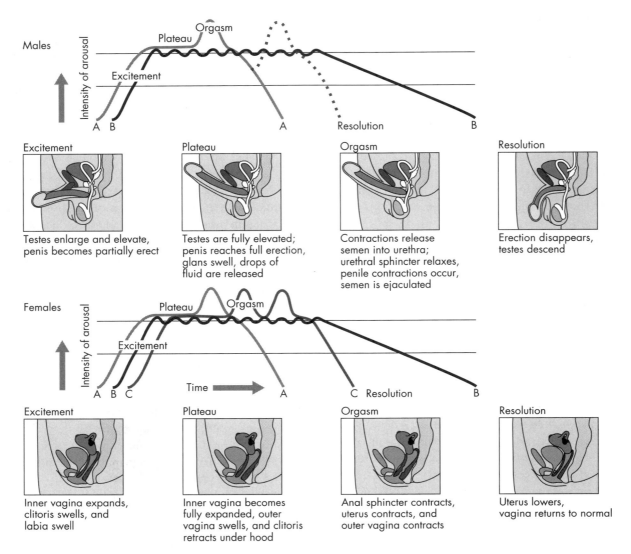

Males

Intensity of arousal

Orgasm

Plateau

Excitement

A B   A   Resolution   B

Excitement

Testes enlarge and elevate, penis becomes partially erect

Plateau

Testes are fully elevated; penis reaches full erection, glans swell, drops of fluid are released

Orgasm

Contractions release semen into urethra; urethral sphincter relaxes, penile contractions occur, semen is ejaculated

Resolution

Erection disappears, testes descend

Females

Intensity of arousal

Plateau   Orgasm

Excitement

Time

A B C   A   C   Resolution   B

Excitement

Inner vagina expands, clitoris swells, and labia swell

Plateau

Inner vagina becomes fully expanded, outer vagina swells, and clitoris retracts under hood

Orgasm

Anal sphincter contracts, uterus contracts, and outer vagina contracts

Resolution

Uterus lowers, vagina returns to normal

FIGURE 3.11 Human Sexual Response
The four phases as described by sex researchers Masters and Johnson. The letters indicate different basic patterns of sexual response.
Source: From *Healthy for Life,* by Brian K. Williams and Sharon N. Knight, 1994, p. 827. Brooks/Cole Publishing Company. Reprinted by permission.

a washing machine. You don't hear a 'click click' when it shifts to a new phase of the cycle" (quoted in Tavris, 1992, p. 226).

Second, the Masters and Johnson model virtually ignores cognitive and emotional states and focuses almost exclusively on objective physiological measures (Tiefer, 1991). The measurement of these physiological changes (primarily changes in the genitals) may be taken to represent sexuality, rather than being seen as one component of it. Their model of sexual response deemphasizes the emotional, spiritual, and intimacy aspects of sexuality and sexual interaction. Nevertheless, the research of Masters and Johnson

paved the way for the more recently developed field of psychophysiology (Laan & Everaerd, 1995).

Helen Kaplan's Three-Stage Model of Sexual Response

In an effort to emphasize the motivational and psychological aspects of human sexual response, Helen Kaplan (1979) proposed a three-stage model consisting of desire, excitement, and orgasm. The desire phase involves "the experience of specific sensations that motivate the individual to initiate or become responsive to sexual stimulation" (Rosen & Beck, 1988, p. 42). Sexual desire involves feeling "horny," sexy, or interested in sex; this stage may be accompanied by genital sensations.

Kaplan's excitement and orgasm phases are very similar to those of Masters and Johnson; both models focus on vasocongestion and genital contractions in these two phases. The primary criticism of Kaplan's model is that she suggests that desire is a necessary prerequisite for excitement. However, desire is not necessary for arousal or orgasm to occur. ✍ Garde and Lunde (1980) noted that about one-third of a representative sample of Danish women did not report experiencing desire despite "adequate arousal" and orgasm. ✍

PERSONAL CHOICES

Should You Engage in Sexual Behavior When Desire Is Low?

It is not unusual when one partner wants to engage in sex and the other does not. Should the partner who has low sex interest or desire agree to participate anyway, or should the partner who wants sex masturbate or wait until another time?

But there are also times when the partner with low sex desire wants to feel desire and wants to engage in sexual behavior. Should he or she? Moser noted:

> People may engage in sex, even frequently, but for reasons other than their own desires (e.g., marital duty, to prove that they can, as a form of self-treatment, to become pregnant, to promote intimacy, to please the partner, for self-esteem. (1992, p. 66)

Beck, Bozman, and Qualtrough (1991) found that 82% of 86 college women and 60% of 58 college men reported engaging in sexual behavior when they had low sex desire. Their primary reasons for doing so were to please their partners.

Aside from pleasing the partner, another potential positive outcome from choosing to engage in sexual behavior independent of desire is that the individual may experience desire following involvement in sexual behavior. Cognitive behavior therapists conceptualize this phenomenon as "acting oneself into a new way of feeling rather than feeling oneself into a new way of acting." Rather than wait for the feelings of sexual desire to occur before engaging in sexual behavior, the person acts as though there is feeling, only to discover that the

feeling sometimes follows. An old French saying reflects this phenomenon: *"L'appétit vient avec mangent,"* which translates into "The appetite comes with eating."

We are not suggesting that an individual who lacks sexual desire should routinely initiate sexual behavior with his or her partner or comply with the partner's wishes. Individuals should respect their own feelings and preferences and should not feel coerced into engaging in sexual behavior when they do not want to do so. Often more is involved than just the frequency of lovemaking. Masters, Johnson, and Levin (1974) presented the scenario of a husband who would welcome intercourse four times a week, while his wife thinks twice a week would be adequate. Rather than recommending a numerical compromise of three times a week, which might leave the husband frustrated and the wife feeling imposed on, the couple was encouraged to explore the situation they were in to determine what factors were affecting each partner. Was he feeling a need for more care and warmth, or feeling especially loving and energetic? Was she worried about financial pressures, or preoccupied with her new job? In this way, even if their sexual needs were disparate, they could approach each other to find out how best to show their care and concern for each other and respond to the partner's emotional strain. Virginia Johnson observed that for two individuals with different needs, moods, and senses of timing, their desires don't always dovetail perfectly. "But," she asked, "how can the two of you reconcile those differences in a spirit of love?" (p. 40).

Bancroft's Four Features of Sexual Response

More recently, researchers have offered perspectives and schema for studying sexual response. Four essential features were identified by Bancroft (1989): sexual appetite, peripheral arousal (increased heart rate, blood pressure, breath rate), genital responses, and central arousal. The first three of these have been discussed already.

Central arousal refers to the brain, the central nervous system, and the cognitions and emotions involved in transmitting and processing sexual stimuli. The way in which events are cognitively labeled and subjectively experienced is essential to defining sexual arousal (Janssen & Everaerd, 1993) and may involve both automatic and controlled processing of sexual meaning and context. Laan and Everaerd

(1995) hypothesized that genital arousal occurs because of automatic processing of erotic cues, although conscious cognitive processing may interfere with one's feeling sexual. For example, most women responded within seconds with increased vaginal vasocongestion to an erotic film depicting sexual activity (Laan, Everaerd, van Bellen, & Hanewald, 1994). Genital response occurred even when the women evaluated the stimuli negatively. The researchers speculate that genital response to sexual stimuli is adaptive from an evolutionary perspective, helping our species to survive. However, this "involuntary" response is not the only vehicle for sexual arousal; sexual imagery and fantasy, as well as appraisal of sex or the sex partner, can also increase or decrease arousal.

What we know about the brain localization of sexual functions is almost entirely dependent on studies of animals. The limbic system, which influences emotions and motivation, includes a number of sites where stimulation brings about erection or ejaculation in rats and monkeys. Studies of lesions in the preoptic and hypothalamic areas reveal an effect on copulatory behavior that may be important in humans as well (Bancroft, 1989).

LeVay (1994) described a study by a research group at Kyushu University in Japan, in which the natural electrical activity of hypothalamic neurons was recorded during sexual activity. The researchers placed a male monkey in a chairlike restraint and painlessly immobilized his head so stable recordings could be obtained. The monkey could press a button, which brought another chair toward him, in which an estrous female monkey sat. When they copulated (despite the restraints), the neuronal activity in the medial preoptic area was closely related to the monkey's state of sexual arousal. When the monkey saw the female and pressed the button to move her toward him, the cells discharged at a high rate; the rate dropped during copulation and almost stopped completely after ejaculation. The same pattern was not observed in control experiments with a banana available in the other chair. Although the monkey ate the banana with enthusiasm, the neuronal activity was not affected. This finding leads to speculation that such neuronal activity in the medial preoptic area may mediate how aroused one becomes by certain faces.

Inputs from the olfactory system and cerebral cortex may also trigger sexual activity. Without question, sexual thoughts and complicated sexual behaviors, such as mate selection, require the involvement of large regions of the cerebral cortex. LeVay (1994) suggested a cortex-hypothalamus-cortex circuit in which regions of the central cortex signal the hypothalamus and combine with olfactory inputs, sensory inputs from the genitals, and sex hormones circulating in the bloodstream, to set the level of neuronal activity in the preoptic area. "These neurons in turn send signals down to the brain stem and spinal cord to influence the mechanics of sex, but they also send signals back to wide areas of the cerebral cortex that very likely influence sexual ideation and complex sexual behavior" (p. 81).

_____ **THINK ABOUT IT** _____

What feature added by Bancroft is essential to the understanding of human sexual response?

HORMONES AND SEXUAL RESPONSE

Hormones are chemical messengers that typically travel from cell to cell via the bloodstream. The hypothalamus and pituitary gland near the center of the brain regulate the endocrine system's secretion of hormones into the bloodstream (see Figure 3.12). The reproductive hormones (estrogens, progesterone, and androgens) are mainly produced in the gonads. They influence reproductive development through *organizing* and *activating* effects (Bancroft, 1991). Organizing effects include anatomical differentiation (the development of male or female genitals) and some differentiation of brain structure. At puberty, they lead to the development of secondary sex characteristics. Activating effects include influences on behavior and affective states. For example, researchers have studied the role of reproductive hormones and their possible influence on adolescent aggression and behavior problems, adolescent sexuality, and the menstrual cycle and related mood changes.

Manley (1990) summarized how little is known about the hormonal influences on human sexual

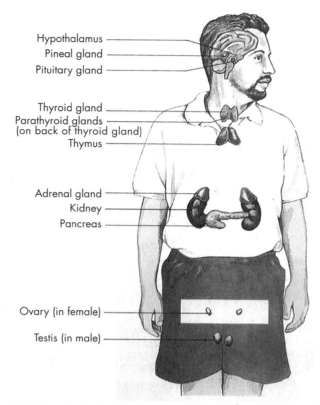

Hypothalamus
Pineal gland
Pituitary gland

Thyroid gland
Parathyroid glands
(on back of thyroid gland)
Thymus

Adrenal gland
Kidney
Pancreas

Ovary (in female)

Testis (in male)

FIGURE 3.12 Endocrine System
Endocrine glands produce and release chemical regulators
called hormones that affect sexual functioning.

response: "The role of hormones in human sexual
behavior is not well understood because not enough
is known and what is known is not clear" (p. 338). In
regard to what is known, androgen increases sexual
desire in both men and women. Indeed, when both
men and women are deprived of testosterone (a primary type of androgen), they lose all sexual desire
(Kaplan, 1974). Estrogen and progesterone have less
specific effects and "may have no specific effect on
sexual behavior" (p. 53).

Researchers have attempted to correlate the
amount of specific hormones in the bloodstream
with sexual behavior in humans. In a study (Heiman,
Rowland, Hatch, & Gladue, 1991) of premenopausal
women between the ages of 21 and 45, hormone levels of cortisol, prolactin, luteinizing hormone, and
testosterone were assessed as the participants viewed
both erotic and neutral videotapes. Few consistent

changes in hormone levels and few correlations with
behavioral arousal signs were observed. The authors
commented on the "complexity and subtlety of endocrine interactions with sexual response" (p. 171).
They suggested that compared to that of women, the
sexual behavior of men may be more affected by hormonal factors.

Researchers have attempted to study the relative
importance of psychosocial factors and hormone levels on sexual behavior. Udry, Talbert, and Morris
(1986) noted that in female adolescents, peer group
sexual activity (whether their close friends were sexually active), rather than hormonal levels, was the
most reliable predictor of sexual behavior. Male adolescents, on the other hand, were more likely to be
influenced by testosterone levels than by their peer
group (Udry, Billy, Morris, Groff, & Raj, 1985).

THINK ABOUT IT

What are the implications of viewing sexual interest as a product of hormones versus social and
psychological influences? How would the respective views affect the way individuals feel about
their own sexuality and that of their partners?

KEY TERMS

amenorrhea 59
areola 53
Bartholin's glands 50
blended orgasm 70
cervix 57
circumcision 65
clitoral orgasm 70
clitoris 51
corona 63
cystitis 52
dysmenorrhea 59
ectopic pregnancy 58
endometriosis 59
epididymis 66
excitement phase 68
fallopian tubes 57
follicle-stimulating
    hormone 58
frenulum 63
fundus 57
glans 63

"G spot" 54
hormone 74
hymen 52
hyperventilation 69
introitus 52
Kegel exercises 54
labia majora 50
labia minora 50
mammogram 54
menarche 58
menorrhagia 59
menstruation/
    menses 58
mons veneris 50
myotonia 69
oligomenorrhea 59
orgasm 69
ovaries 58
Pap test 58
penis 63
perineum 50

SUMMARY POINTS

This chapter has examined the basics of female and male internal and external sexual anatomy. We have also reviewed some models for human sexual response, as well as the effect that hormones have on human sexuality.

Female External Anatomy and Physiology

Female external sexual anatomy includes the mons veneris, labia, clitoris, vaginal opening, and urethral opening. The clitoris is the most sensitive part of a woman's sexual anatomy. Even though the female breasts provide the important function of nourishing offspring, they are secondary sex characteristics and are not considered part of the female reproductive anatomy.

Female Internal Anatomy and Physiology

The vagina, pubococcygeus muscle, uterus, Fallopian tubes, and ovaries comprise the internal sexual anatomy of the female. Fertilization of the female egg, or ovum, usually occurs in the Fallopian tubes.

Around the ages of 12 or 13 years, the hypothalamus in females signals the pituitary gland to begin releasing follicle-stimulating hormone (FSH) into the bloodstream. This hormone stimulates a follicle to develop and release a mature egg from the ovary. If the egg is fertilized, it will normally implant itself in the endometrium of the uterus, which will be thick and engorged with blood vessels in preparation for implantation. If the egg is not fertilized, the thickened tissue of the uterus is shed. This flow of blood, mucus, and tissue is called menstruation.

Male External Anatomy and Physiology

The penis and scrotum make up the external anatomy of the male. Penile erection is caused by dilation of the numerous blood vessels within the penis, which results in blood entering the penis faster than it can leave. The trapped blood within the penis creates pressure and results in penile erection.

Male Internal Anatomy and Physiology

The testes, duct system, seminal vesicles, and prostate gland make up the internal sexual anatomy of the male. Sperm (long cells with a thin, motile tail) are produced in the testes. Semen is the mixture of sperm and seminal fluid. Most seminal fluid comes from the prostate gland, but a small amount is also secreted by two Cowper's, or bulbourethral, glands that are located below the prostate gland.

Models of Human Sexual Response

The Masters and Johnson's model of sexual response involves four phases: excitement, plateau, orgasm, and resolution. These elements are genitally focused. Bancroft's four features of sexual response include sexual appetite, peripheral arousal, genital responses, and central arousal. The latter involves the brain, central nervous system, and the cognitions and emotions involved in transmitting and processing sexual stimuli. The way in which events are cognitively labeled and subjectively experienced is essential to one's sexual experience.

Hormones and Sexual Response

The role of hormones in human sexual response is not well understood. However, research has shown that androgen increases sexual desire in both women and men. When women and men are deprived of testosterone (a type of androgen), they lose sexual desire. Compared to that of women, the sexual behavior of men may be more affected by hormonal factors.

REFERENCES

American Cancer Society. (1997). *Cancer facts & figures—1997.* (Available from the American Cancer Society, 1599 Clifton Road NE, Atlanta, GA 30329-4251, (404) 320-3333).

Bancroft, J. H. (1989). *Human sexuality and its problems* (2nd ed.). New York: Churchill Livingston.

Bancroft, J. (1991). Reproductive hormones. In M. Rutter & P. Casaer (Eds.), *Biological risk factors for psychosocial disorders* (pp. 260-310). Cambridge: Cambridge University Press.

Beck, J. G., Bozman, A. W., & Qualtrough, T. (1991). The experience of sexual desire: Psychological correlates in a college sample. *Journal of Sex Research, 28,* 443-456.

Brackett, N. L., Bloch, W. E., & Abae, M. (1994). Neurological anatomy and physiology of sexual function. In C. Singer & W. J. Weiner (Eds.), *Sexual dysfunction: A neuro-medical approach* (pp. 1-42). Armonk, NY: Furura.

Darling, C. A., Davidson, J. K., & Conway-Welch, C. (1990). Female ejaculation: Perceived origins, the Grafenberg spot/area, and sexual responsiveness. *Archives of Sexual Behavior, 19,* 29-47.

Darling, C. A., Davidson, J. K., Sr., & Jennings, D. A. (1991). The female sexual response revisited: Understanding the multiorgasmic experience in women. *Archives of Sexual Behavior, 20,* 527-540.

Freud, S. (1989). Some psychical consequences of anatomical distinction between the sexes. In P. Gay (Ed.), *The Freud reader.* New York: Norton. (Original work published in 1925).

Garde, K., & Lunde, I. (1980). Female sexual behavior: A study in a random sample of 40-year-old women. *Maturitas, 2,* 225-240.

Heiman, J. R., Rowland, D. L., Hatch, J. P., & Gladue, B. A. (1991). Psychophysiological and endocrine responses to sexual arousal in women. *Archives of Sexual Behavior, 20,* 171-186.

Hock, Z. (1983). The G spot. *Journal of Sex and Marital Therapy, 9,* 166-167.

Janssen, E., & Everaerd, W. (1993). Determinants of male sexual arousal. *Annual Review of Sex Research, 4,* 211-245.

Kaplan, H. (1974). *The new sex therapy.* New York: Brunner/Mazel.

Kaplan, H. (1979). *Disorders of sexual desire.* New York: Brunner/Mazel.

Laan, E., & Everaerd, W. (1995). Determinants of female sexual arousal: Psychophysiological theory and data. *Annual Review of Sex Research, 6,* 32-76.

Laan, E., Everaerd, W., van Bellen, G., & Hanewald, G. (1994). Women's sexual and emotional responses to male and female produced erotica. *Archives of Sexual Behavior, 23,* 153-170.

Ladas, A. K., Whipple, B., & Perry, J. D. (1982). *The G spot and other recent discoveries about human sexuality.* New York: Holt, Rinehart and Winston.

LeVay, S. (1994). *The sexual brain.* Cambridge, MA: MIT Press.

Manley, G. (1990). Endocrine disturbances and sexuality, In C. I. Fogel & D. Lauvr (Eds.), *Sexual health promotion* (pp. 337-359). Philadelphia: W. B. Saunders.

Masters, W. H., & Johnson, V. E. (1966). *Human sexual response.* Boston: Little, Brown.

Masters, W. H., Johnson, V. E., & Kolodny, R. C. (1989). *Human sexuality* (4th ed.). New York: HarperCollins.

Moser, C. (1992). Lust, lack of desire, and paraphilias: Some thoughts and possible connections. *Journal of Sex and Marital Therapy, 18,* 65-69.

National Center for Health Statistics. (1994). Circumcisions performed [Website]. Available: http://www.cirp.org/CIRP/library/statistics/USA/ 1991-1994.

Rosen, R. C., & Beck, J. G. (1988). *Patterns of sexual arousal: Psychophysiological processes.* New York: Guilford Press.

Singer, D. B., & Haning, Jr., R. V. (1995). The menstrual cycle. In D. R. Coustan, R. V. Haning, & D. B. Singer (Eds.), *Human reproduction: Growth and development* (pp. 1-14). Boston: Little, Brown.

Singer, I. (1973). *The goals of human sexuality.* New York: Norton.

Tang, C. S., Siu, B. N., Lai, F. D., & Chung, T. K. H. (1996). Heterosexual Chinese women's sexual adjustment after gynecologic cancer. *The Journal of Sex Research, 33,* 189-195.

Tavris, C. (1992). *The mismeasure of woman.* New York: Simon & Schuster.

Tiefer, L. (1991). Historical, scientific, clinical, and feminist criticisms of "The Human Sexual Response Cycle" model. *Annual Review of Sex Research, 2,* 1-23.

Udry, J. R., Billy, J. O. G., Morris, N. M., Groff, T. R., & Raj, M. H. (1985). Serum androgenic hormones motivate sexual behavior in adolescent boys. *Fertility and Sterility, 43,* 90-94.

Udry, J. R., Talbert, L. M., & Morris, N. M. (1986). Biosocial foundations for adolescent female sexuality. *Demography, 23,* 217-229.

Ullrich, H. E. (1977). Caste differences between Brahmin and non-Brahmin women in a South Indian village. In A. Schlegel (Ed.), *Sexual stratification: A cross-cultural view* (pp. 94-108). New York: Columbia University Press.

Vance, E. B., & Wagner, N. N. (1976). Written descriptions of orgasm: A study of sex differences. *Archives of Sexual Behavior, 5,* 87-98.

Whipple, B., Cerdes, C. A., & Komisaruk, B. R. (1996). Sexual response to self-stimulation in women with complete spinal cord injury. *The Journal of Sex Research, 33,* 231-240.

COMMUNICATION AND SEXUALITY

y wife said I don't listen to her—at least I think that's what she said.

Laurence J. Peter
Humorist

Mary is involved in an emotional and sexual relationship with Tom. Cunnilingus is the only way she can experience an orgasm, but she is reluctant to talk to Tom about her need. She has a dilemma: If she chooses to tell Tom, she risks his disapproval and his rejection of doing what she asks. If she does not tell Tom about her need, she risks growing resentful and feeling dissatisfied in the relationship.

Bob has drifted into a flirtatious relationship with a woman in his office. He is emotionally and sexually attracted to her. He knows she feels the same. Bob is also in love with Karen and is committed to her emotionally and sexually. Should he tell Karen about his attraction to the woman at work? Should he disclose that he has dreamed about her? How open should he be?

Carol and her husband, Dean, get into frequent arguments. Their pattern is that after arguing, they "cool off" by not talking to each other for a few hours. Then, Dean usually approaches Carol for sex as a way to "make up." Carol always wants to talk about their conflict and resolve it before having sex, but she is afraid that if she rejects Dean's sexual advances, he will become angry again. What should she do?

The individuals in these scenarios would probably ask themselves two questions: "What should I say?" and "How should I say it?" These two questions reflect the awareness that *communication* involves both information and the process of exchanging information between individuals. The information, or messages exchanged between individuals, is referred to as the content of the communication. The way in which the information is delivered, received, and responded to is referred to as the process of communication.

In this chapter, we will discuss the importance of communication in achieving intimacy, relationship, and sexual satisfaction; we will review some principles of effective communication; we will discuss honesty in relationships; and we will examine how conflicts in relationships can be resolved. Our premise is that good communication patterns are associated with relationship and sexual satisfaction.

INTIMACY, RELATIONSHIP, AND SEXUAL SATISFACTION

Most U.S. adults value being in an intimate love relationship. Although we commonly use and hear the term "sexual intimacy," not all sexual encounters are intimate. Likewise, not all intimate relationships are sexual. *Intimacy* refers to the emotional closeness and bond between two individuals. Although two newly acquainted individuals may experience strong feelings of passion toward one another, intimacy develops over time as they disclose their views, values, histories, goals, fears, dislikes, and preferences to each other. This process of *self-disclosure,* or communicating personal information to another person, is "the single factor which most influences a couple's level of intimacy" (Waring, 1988, p. 38). Disclosing personal information is not only essential for the development of an intimate love relationship, it is also important for maintaining intimacy with one's partner over time.

In addition to helping to achieve and maintain intimacy, communication is also important for relationship satisfaction. Individuals who are happy with their intimate partners often make such statements as "I feel like I can tell my partner anything"; "We don't keep anything from each other"; and "We are open and honest with each other about our feelings." In interviews with 30 couples who reported that they had been happily married for an average of 32 years, researchers (Billingsley, Lim, & Jennings, 1995) noted that openness about likes and dislikes, feelings, and preferences was a common theme with these couples. The couples also discussed problems with each other and listened to each other's point of view. In another study of 402 married individuals, satisfaction with sexual communication was significantly associated with marital satisfaction, marital cohesion, and sexual satisfaction (Cupach & Comstock, 1990).

Just as good communication is associated with satisfaction in intimate relationships, poor communication is associated with unhappy relationships. Individuals in unhappy relationships make statements

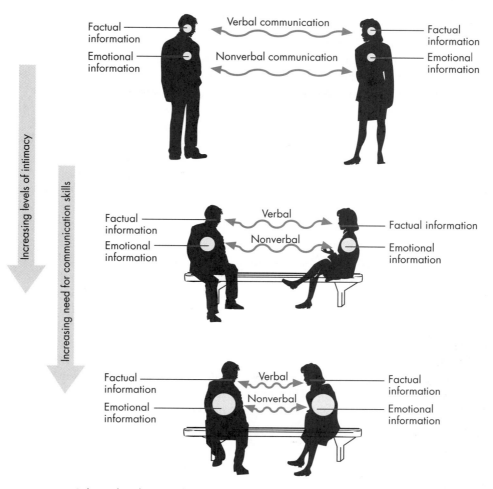

Increasing levels of intimacy

Increasing need for communication skills

Verbal communication

Nonverbal communication

Factual information

Emotional information

Factual information

Emotional information

Verbal

Nonverbal

Factual information

Emotional information

Factual information

Emotional information

Verbal

Nonverbal

Factual information

Emotional information

Factual information

Emotional information

FIGURE 4.1 Relationships begin with signals. The more effective our signals—verbal as well as nonverbal—the more likely we are to build good relationships.

like "He never talks about his feelings"; "We are constantly arguing about something"; "She doesn't listen to me"; "He often criticizes me"; and "I can't trust her; she has lied too many times." In some cases, poor communication creates dissatisfaction in the relationship; in others, dissatisfaction in the relationship leads to poor communication. "In either case, sexual satisfaction and relationship satisfaction are clearly interconnected . . . and both are affected by the ability and willingness of partners to interact effectively with one another" (Cupach & Metts, 1991, p. 93). The ability to interact effectively requires the understanding and use of basic principles of effective communication.

THINK ABOUT IT

Can individuals who are not sexually involved with one another have an intimate relationship?

Can individuals who are sexually involved with one another have a relationship that is not intimate? How can individuals avoid confusing "relationship intimacy" with "sexual intimacy"?

PRINCIPLES OF EFFECTIVE COMMUNICATION IN INTIMATE RELATIONSHIPS

As important as communication is for developing and sustaining fulfilling and enduring relationships, few U.S. adults have received training or education in the art of communication. In this section, we provide a "crash course" in some of the principles of effective communication that are used in intimate and sexual relationships.

Initiate Discussion of Important Issues

Effective communication means addressing important issues. If you wait until your partner brings up an issue, it may never happen. In a study of 203 undergraduates, women were significantly more likely than men to initiate discussions of a problem in their relationships (Knox, Hatfield, & Zusman, in press).

With the potential risk for HIV and STD infection, talking about safer-sex issues with a new sexual partner should be a requirement. Two researchers asked 252 university women and 207 university men whether it was "very likely" they would bring up a variety of issues with new potential sexual partners. The issues and percentages are presented in the table below (Gray & Saracino, 1991, p. 261). The percentages reflect the reluctance college students have to bringing up safer-sex issues.

Sometimes partners do not address issues because they fear their partners will view the issues as trivial. A general guideline for this dilemma is: "If the issue is important to you, then the issue is important enough to discuss with your partner." Another obstacle to discussing important issues is fear of rejection. This chapter's Social Choices feature examines issues related to disclosing one's sexual health history to one's partner.

Choose Good Timing

The phrase "timing is everything" can be applied to interpersonal communication. In general, it is best to discuss important or difficult issues when partners are alone together in private with no distractions, both partners have ample time to talk, and both partners are rested and sober. Avoid discussing important issues when you or your partner are tired or under unusual stress. If one partner (or both) is very upset, it may be best to wait a while until things have "cooled off" before discussing an issue. If you are not sure whether the timing is right, you can always ask your partner by saying something like "I would like for us to discuss how we are going to deal with this unplanned pregnancy. Is this a good time for us to talk about it?" Likewise, if your partner brings up an issue and it is not a good time for you to discuss the matter, suggest a specific alternative time and place to have the discussion. Good timing in communication also means that information should be communicated at a time that allows the receiver to make an informed response. For example, discussions about sexual issues, such as pregnancy prevention, STD protection, and monogamy, should occur *before* partners engage in sexual activity.

Issue	Percentage of College Students
Discuss condom use before having intercourse	54%
Ask to have a monogamous relationship	49%
Insist on using a condom before intercourse	40%
Ask how many sexual partners he or she has had	27%

Some discussions may be difficult to initiate, but intimate communication is important in creating and maintaining a good relationship.

ONE'S SEXUAL HEALTH STATUS: TO TELL OR NOT TO TELL?

Individuals often struggle over whether, or how, to tell a partner about their sexual health condition or history. If a person in a committed relationship becomes infected with an STD, that individual, or his or her partner, may have been unfaithful and had sex with someone outside of the relationship. Thus, disclosure about an STD may also mean confessing one's own infidelity or confronting one's partner about his or her possible infidelity. (However, the infection may have occurred prior to the current relationship but was undetected.) For women in abusive relationships, telling their partner that they have an STD involves fear that their partner will react violently (Rothenberg & Paskey, 1995). Individuals who are infected with an STD and who are beginning a new relationship face a different set of concerns. Will their new partner view them negatively? Will they want to continue the relationship? Individuals with herpes disclosed the following feelings about and reactions to telling their partners about it.

> I have done several experiments to see how women react to herpes. Experiment 1 was to tell the individual in an upfront manner on the first date. Over dinner . . . I would whisper, "I guess I should tell you something." I would try and make it a little funny by stating, "Before you fall madly in love with me and we run away to Las Vegas and get married . . . " In every case, five out of five, the first date was the last!
>
> Experiment 2 was to tell the lady that I had herpes after I felt the time was right for intimacy . . . Second verse almost the same as the first. Four out of five never saw me again. ("Treatment Update," 1997, pp. 3–4)
>
> I decided to use herpes as a yardstick by which to measure whether a man's affections were real or not for me and as a yardstick as to his strength and maturity in helping me to manage and live with the disease. (Silver, Auerbach, Vishniavsky, & Kaplowitz, 1986, p. 170)
>
> If someone rejects me because of herpes, I genuinely feel I've weeded that person out. (Hill, 1987, p. 5)
>
> One night over Irish coffee, I suddenly fell in love with a man whom I'd been dating casually for several

months. We began kissing madly, and eventually I felt I must tell him I have herpes. After I got the words out, he looked at me with delight and said, "Does that mean you're planning to sleep with me? That's marvelous!" ("Treatment Update," 1997, pp. 3–4)

Although telling a partner about having an STD may be difficult and embarrassing, avoiding disclosure or lying about having an STD represents a serious ethical violation. The responsibility to inform a partner that one has an STD—*before* having sex with that partner—is a moral one. But there are also legal reasons for disclosing one's sexual health condition to a partner. If you have an STD and you do not tell your partner, you may be liable for damages if you transmit the disease to your partner. In over half the states, transmission of a communicable disease, including many STDs, is considered a crime. Penalties

Couples considering sexual contact should discuss the potential for contracting or transmitting STDs and agree on what steps they will take to reduce the risk.

Continued on following page.

depend on whether the crime is regarded as a felony (which may involve a five-year prison term) or a misdemeanor (which may involve a fine of $100) (Davis & Scott, 1988). If you have an STD and do not tell your sex partner, you may also be sued if your partner contracts a disease from contact with you. According to one attorney, the number of personal-injury lawsuits arising from STDs is on the rise ("Litigation of the 90s," 1996).

Some states and cities have partner notification laws that require health care providers to advise all persons with serious sexually transmitted diseases about the importance of informing their sex or needle-sharing partner (or partners). Partner notification laws may also require health care providers to either notify any partners the infected person names or forward the information about partners to the Department of Health, where public health officers notify the partner (or partners) that he or she has been exposed to an STD and schedule an STD testing appointment. The privacy of the infected individual is protected by not revealing his or her name to the partner being notified of potential infection. In cases where the infected person refuses to identify partners, standard partner notification laws require doctors to undertake notification without cooperation, if they know who the partner or spouse is (Norwood, 1995).

Sources: Davis, M., & Scott, R. S. 1988. *Lovers, doctors and the law.* New York: Harper & Row.

Hill, T. (1987, Summer). Herpes and relationships. *The Helper, 9*(2), 1, 3–5.

Litigation of the 90s: Personal injury suits from STDs. (1996, February 16). *American Medical News, 39*(7), 23.

Norwood, C. (1995). Mandated life versus mandatory death: New York's disgraceful partner notification record. *Journal of Community Health, 20*(2), 161–170.

Rothenberg, K. H., & Paskey, S. J. (1995). The risk of domestic violence and women with HIV infection: Implications for partner notification, public policy, and the law. *American Journal of Public Health, 85*(11), 1569–1576.

Silver, P. S., Auerbach, S. M., Vishniavsky, N., & Kaplowitz, L. G. (1986). Psychological factors in recurrent genital herpes infection: Stress, coping style, social support, emotional dysfunction, and symptom recurrence. *Journal of Psychosomatic Research, 30,* 163–171.

Treatment Update. (1997, Summer). *The Helper, 19*(2), 3–4.

Give Congruent Messages

The process of communication involves both verbal and nonverbal messages. *Verbal messages* are the words individuals say to each other. *Nonverbal messages* include facial expressions, gestures, bodily contact, and tone of voice. What happens when verbal and nonverbal messages do not match? For example, suppose Lashanda and Brian are giving feedback about the last time they had sex. Lashanda says to Brian, "It was good"; yet she has a sullen facial expression and tone of voice and does not make eye contact. Lashanda's verbal and nonverbal messages are not congruent—they do not match. When this happens, the other partner typically gives more weight to the nonverbal message (L'Abate & Baga-rozzi, 1993). In this scenario, Brian would probably give more weight to the nonverbal message, thus believing that Lashanda did not enjoy their most recent sexual experience. He might also feel that she was not being honest with him.

This chapter's Self-Assessment feature assesses the verbal and nonverbal ways in which partners communicate interest in sexual interactions.

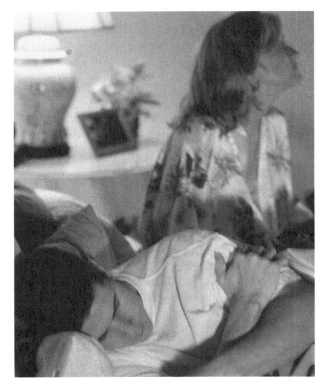

This man's nonverbal behavior is communicating his feelings toward his wife.

THE SEXUAL SIGNALING BEHAVIORS INVENTORY

When you think your partner can be persuaded to have sex though he or she has not yet become aware of your desire, what do you usually do? Check all items that apply.

_____ **A.** ask directly

_____ **B.** use some code words with which (s)he is familiar

_____ **C.** use more eye contact

_____ **D.** use touching (snuggling, kissing, etc.)

_____ **E.** change appearance or clothing

_____ **F.** remove clothing

_____ **G.** change tone of voice

_____ **H.** make indirect talk of sex

_____ **I.** do more favors for the other

_____ **J.** set mood atmosphere (music, lighting, etc.)

_____ **K.** share a drink

_____ **L.** tease

_____ **M.** look at sexual material

_____ **N.** play games such as chase or light "roughhousing"

_____ **O.** make compliments ("I love you," "You're nice")

_____ **P.** use some force

_____ **Q.** use "suggestive" body movements or postures

_____ **R.** allow hands to wander

_____ **S.** lie down

_____ **T.** other (describe _____)

This scale was developed by Dr. Clinton Jesser (1978), a sociology professor who was interested in determining how college students communicate to their heterosexual partners when they want coitus (sexual intercourse). He wondered whether women would use more indirect signals than men and whether men would evaluate women's indirect communication as more desirable. He surveyed 153 students at a large midwestern university and examined the responses of the 50 men (90%) and 75 women (71%) in the sample who were coitally experienced. The most frequently reported signals were "use touching (snuggling, kissing, etc.)" and "allow hands to wander," which were both endorsed by more than 70% of the men and the women. The next most frequent item was "ask directly," which was reported by 58% of the women and 56% of the men. Although there was essentially no difference in the reports of men and women who said they ask directly, women were more likely to report using eye contact, changing their appearance or clothing, and changing their tone of voice. The women who used the direct approach (42 of the 75) were no more likely to be rebuffed than those using an indirect approach. No formal checks of the reliability or validity of this measure have been made, although Dr. Jesser noted that more women report being direct than are perceived by men as being direct. Dr. Jesser (1988) suggested that the Sexual Signaling Behaviors Inventory could be used with gay and lesbian participants.

Minimize Criticism; Maximize Compliments

Research on marital interaction has consistently shown that one brutal "zinger" can erase 20 acts of kindness (Notarius & Markman, 1994). Because intimate partners are capable of hurting each other so deeply, it is important not to criticize your partner. Calling a partner "fat," "stupid," or a "lousy lover" can devastate a partner.

Conversely, complimenting your partner and making positive remarks can enhance the relationship. Not only are sincere compliments and positive remarks good to hear, they can create a self-fulfilling prophecy effect. A partner who is often told that he or she is an attentive and affectionate lover is more likely to behave accordingly to make these expectations come true than a partner who receives no feedback or negative feedback.

Making positive statements is particularly important during the beginning and end of a discussion. In psychology, the term "primacy/recency effect" refers to the tendency of individuals to remember best what occurs first and last in a sequence. After discussing a difficult issue, partners may be more likely to come away with a positive feeling about the interaction if it begins and ends with positive comments. For example, suppose your partner tries a new sexual intercourse position with you that you find unpleasant. You might tell your partner, "I didn't enjoy that, please don't do it again." Or, you could say, "I am glad that you feel comfortable enough with me to try new things, but that position was a bit uncomfortable and painful for me. I'd rather be on top. Being able to tell you what I like and don't like is one of the things I like most about our relationship."

Suppose you are so upset with your partner about an issue that you begin a discussion by blurting out a negative comment. You can still end the conversation on a positive note by saying something positive like "Thank you for listening to my anger and allowing me to vent." Or, if your partner begins a discussion with a negative remark, such as "Our sex life is so boring, you never want to try anything new," you can respond with a positive comment, such as "Thank you for telling me about your frustration with our sex life. It is important for me to know how you feel."

Communicate Feelings

In intimate relationships, it is important to communicate feelings as well as thoughts. It sounds simple, but many people are not in touch with their feelings, or they confuse feelings with thoughts. If you listen to yourself and to others, you will hear people communicating thoughts, but these thoughts are often labeled as feelings. For example, the statement "I feel that we should be tested for STDs" is communicating an idea, not an emotion. Feelings include sadness, fear, anger, joy, excitement, guilt, boredom, anxiety, frustration, and depression. "We should be tested for STDs" is not an emotion. The statement "I am afraid to have sex with you because we have not been tested for STDs" is expressing a feeling—fear.

In order to communicate emotions, a person must first recognize and label, or describe, the emotions.

Unfortunately, many people learn to hide and repress unpleasant feelings. Before you can communicate your emotions to a partner, you must first get in touch with your feelings and give yourself permission to feel them. You must also let "those around you experience their feelings . . ." (Hendricks & Hendricks, 1990, p. 101). When your partner is sad and begins to cry, instead of saying "Please don't cry," consider saying, "It's OK to cry; let yourself feel as sad as you are." When your partner is afraid, instead of saying, "There's nothing to be afraid of; everything will be all right," consider saying, "Listen to your fear; it is trying to tell you something." Attempts to cover up or minimize unpleasant feelings may be made with the best intentions; however, repressing your emotions or interrupting the emotions of your partner often serves to prolong the emotional state rather than to resolve it.

Tell Your Partner What You Want

In a relationship, it is important for partners to tell each other what they want and to do so in a positive, rather than negative, way. Rather than complain about what you don't want, it is helpful to make requests for, or statements about, what you do want. Table 4.1 provides examples of how complaints can be reframed into requests.

One common error people make when communicating is not being specific enough about what they want. When you tell your partner what you want, make sure you communicate clearly and precisely. Table 4.2 presents examples of vague and specific communication.

Of course, before you can say what you want in a relationship, you must first know what you want. In some relationships, one partner (or both) has a pattern of saying, "I don't know" to common questions, such as "What movie do you want to see tonight?" or "Where do you want to go to eat?" Hendricks and Hendricks (1990, p. 145) suggest that "knowing and saying what you want is one of the most powerful skills you can learn." They state that barriers to knowing and saying what we want can be overcome by phrasing what we want in our mind and out loud. Assertiveness training, which is available at many college counseling centers and public mental health facilities, is also useful in helping individuals learn how to express what they want. If you want to use a condom with a new sexual partner, your ability to

TABLE 4.1 Reframing Complaints into Requests

COMPLAINTS	REQUESTS
I don't like to make love when you are sweaty and dirty.	I would like you to take a shower before we make love.
Don't rub so hard.	Please rub more softly.
I don't want you to stay up so late at night.	I would like you to come to bed earlier.
Leave me alone, I'm trying to get ready for work!	I prefer to have sex in the evening when we can relax and take our time.
Whenever I ask you to massage me you end up wanting to have sex with me.	Sometimes, I would like for you to give me a massage without expecting sex to follow.

assertively tell your partner what you want may mean the difference between health and disease or life and death. Assertiveness and communication training has been successfully used to promote condom use in HIV high-risk groups ("Sexual Assertiveness Training Promotes Condom Use," 1995).

Make Statements Instead of Asking Questions

When partners are uncomfortable or unwilling to express their feelings and wants, they may put their statements in the form of questions. For example, partners who have difficulty expressing what they want may ask the question "Do you think we should see a sex therapist?" instead of making the statement "I would like for us to see a sex therapist."

Transforming statements into questions allows partners to mask or hide their true feelings, thoughts, and desires and thus interferes with the development and maintenance of relationship intimacy. Begin listening to your questions and those of your partner

and try to discern which questions are really statements that are masking feelings, wants, or both. When you catch yourself or your partner doing this, rephrase the question into a statement. And remember the rule: Only ask a question when you don't know something that you need to know.

Ask Open-Ended Questions

When you want information from your partner, it is helpful to ask open-ended questions. An *open-ended question* is a broad question designed to elicit a lot of information. In contrast, a *closed-ended question* can be answered in one word. Open-ended questions are useful in finding out your partner's feelings, thoughts, and desires. Table 4.3 provides examples of open- and closed-ended questions.

One way to use open-ended questions in a sexual relationship is to follow the *touch-and-ask-rule*, whereby each touch and caress is accompanied by the question "How does that feel?" The partner then

TABLE 4.2 Examples of Vague and Specific Communication

VAGUE	SPECIFIC
I want more foreplay.	I want us to kiss and stroke each other more than we do now. I mean, maybe for 15 minutes or so.
I'd like us to try something new.	I'd like us to use a vibrator.
I heard about a new erotic video.	I'd like for us to watch an X-rated video together.

TABLE 4.3 Open-Ended and Closed-Ended Questions

OPEN-ENDED QUESTIONS	CLOSED-ENDED QUESTIONS
What are your views on condom use?	Do you want to use a condom?
What can I do to please you sexually?	Do you like to receive oral sex?
Tell me your thoughts about having children.	Do you want to have children?
How can I be a better sex partner?	Are you happy with our sex life?
What are your views on abortion?	Do you believe in abortion?

gives feedback. By using this rule, a couple can learn a lot about how to please each other. Guiding and moving the partner's hand or body are also ways of giving feedback.

Use Reflective Listening

One of the most important communication skills is the art of *reflective listening*, or restating the meaning of what your partner has said to you in a conversation. When you use reflective listening, your partner is more likely to feel that you are truly listening and that you understand his or her feelings, thoughts, and desires. In practicing reflective listening, it is important to repeat both the ideas or thoughts expressed by your partner, as well as the emotions that your partner has conveyed. For example, suppose that after you have made love your partner says, "Next time, can we spend a little more time on foreplay?" You might respond by reflecting back your partner's message: "It sounds like you are feeling frustrated because you didn't get enough foreplay, and in the future, you would like us to have more foreplay before we have intercourse." Another example of a reflective statement you could use is this example: "You feel frustrated that we didn't take more time to be loving and affectionate before having sex. It sounds like having more foreplay is important to you."

Using the technique of reflective listening is particularly difficult when one partner blames or criticizes the other. When people are blamed or criticized, they typically respond by withdrawing from the interaction, attacking back (through blaming or criticizing the other person), or defending or explaining themselves. Each of these responses may produce further conflict and frustration. Alternatively, instead of withdrawing, attacking back, or defending and explaining, the listener can simply reflect back what the partner has said. At some point in the discussion, the criticized partner may and should express his or her thoughts, feelings, and views on the situation. But it is best to first acknowledge the other person's feelings and thoughts through reflective listening. In Table 4.4, we present an example of a critical or accusatory remark, followed by four types of possible responses. Compare the reflective listening response with the other three responses.

Use "I" Statements

"I" statements focus on the feelings and thoughts of the communicator without making a judgment on others. Because "I" statements are a clear and nonthreatening way of expressing what you want and how you feel, they are likely to result in a positive change in the listener's behavior.

In contrast, "you" statements blame or criticize the listener and often result in increasing negative feelings and behavior in the relationship. For example, suppose you are angry at your partner for being late. Rather than say, "You are always late and irresponsible" (which is a "you" statement), you might respond with, "I get upset when you are late and would feel better if you called me when you will be delayed." The latter focuses on your feelings and a desirable future behavior rather than blaming the partner for being late.

Applying the communication principles presented in this chapter to everyday interactions can enhance both individual and relationship well-being and increase your sexual satisfaction with your partner. The principles and techniques are fairly simple, but

TABLE 4.4 Four Responses to A Critical or Accusatory Remark

CRITICAL OR ACCUSATORY REMARK
"You told me you had never slept with anyone before. You lied to me."

FOUR POSSIBLE RESPONSES
1. Withdraw from the interaction: "I can't handle this; I'm leaving."
2. Attack back: "Well, you didn't tell me you had herpes. That's lying too, you know!"
3. Defend or explain: "Being a virgin seemed so important to you; I didn't want to disappoint you. I didn't mean to hurt you."
4. Reflective listening: "You are angry at me for telling you I hadn't slept with anyone when I really had. You wish that I had been truthful with you."

just because it is simple doesn't mean it is easy. To apply effective communication techniques, you must first abandon old patterns of communication. Replacing old communication patterns with new ones is not an easy task, but most couples report that it is worth the effort.

_____ THINK ABOUT IT _____

Which of the principles of effective communication would you most want your partner, or future partner, to understand and practice? Which of the principles would your partner most want you to use?

PERSONAL CHOICES

What Should You Do When Your Partner Will Not Communicate?

One of the most frustrating experiences in relationships is when one partner wants and tries to communicate, but the other partner will not. If your partner will not communicate with you, you might try the following (Duncan & Rock, 1993).

1. Change your strategy. Rather than trying to coax your partner into communicating, become less available for conversation and stop trying to initiate or maintain discussion. Keep it short if a discussion does start. This strategy removes the pressure on the partner to communicate, and shifts the power in the relationship.

2. Interpret silence in a positive way, such as "We are so close we don't always have to be talking," or "I feel good when you're quiet because I know that it means everything is all right between us." This negates any power your partner might be expressing through silence.

3. Focus less on the relationship and more on satisfying yourself. When you do things for yourself, you need less from others in the way of attention and assurance.

HONESTY AND DISHONESTY IN INTERPERSONAL COMMUNICATION

Although the movie *Liar Liar,* starring Jim Carrey, was a parody of honesty, most individuals value honesty in their relationships. "Truthtelling is . . . the foundation of authenticity, self-regard, intimacy, integrity, and joy. We know that closeness requires honesty, that lying erodes trust, that the cruelest lies are often 'told' in silence" (Lerner, 1993, p. 15). Despite the importance of honesty or, to use Lerner's term, truth-telling, "deception is part of everyday existence" (p. 9). Mothersill (1996, p. 913) observed, ". . . and as for lying, we all lie all the time."

Forms of Dishonesty and Deception

Dishonesty and deception take various forms. In addition to telling an outright lie, people may exaggerate the truth, pretend, or conceal the truth. They may put up a good front, be two-faced, or tell a partial truth. People also engage in self-deception when they deny or fail to acknowledge their own thoughts, feelings, values, beliefs, priorities, goals, and desires. When individuals are not honest with themselves, they also are not honest with others. As Lerner (1993) notes, "We can be no more honest with others than we are with the self" (p. 13).

Another form of dishonesty occurs when people withhold information or are silent about particular issues. Lerner (1993) comments on the difference between lying and withholding information:

> In contrast to how we react to stated lies, we are slower to pass negative judgment on what is *withheld*. After all, no one can tell "the whole truth" all the time. . . . Deception through silence or withholding may be excused, and even praised: "My daughter is lucky I never told her about her father," "The doctor was kind enough to spare her the truth about her illness." (pp. 12–13)

Privacy Versus Secrecy and Deception

In virtually every relationship, there are things that partners have not shared with each other about themselves or their past. There are times when partners do not share their feelings and concerns with each other. But when is withholding information about yourself an act of privacy, and when is it an act of secrecy or deception? Privacy involves information that is nobody else's business. When we withhold private information, we are creating or responding to boundaries between ourselves and other people. There may be no harm done in maintaining aspects of ourselves as "private" and not to be disclosed to others. Indeed, it is healthy to have and maintain boundaries between the self and others. However, the more intimate the relationship, the greater our desire is to share our most personal and private selves with our partner. And the greater the emotional consequences of not sharing.

We often withhold information or keep secrets in our intimate relationships for what we believe are good reasons; we believe we are protecting our partner from anxiety or hurt feelings, protecting ourselves from criticism and rejection, and protecting our relationship from conflict and disintegration (Zagorin, 1996). In intimate relationships, however, keeping secrets can block opportunities for healing, resolution, self-acceptance, and deeper intimacy between partners. Taylor (1997) suggested that deception in intimate relationships is a form of infidelity.

> Any betrayal is an infidelity, even the slightest and most commonplace deception. Someone who withholds from a spouse knowledge of personal finances, of associates, of how time away from home is spent, or anything whatever that would be of interest to the other, is being faithless. Equally to the point, such infidelity can be far worse than sexual inconstancy. (p. 10)

Extent of Lie-Telling Among College Students

According to research, lying is rampant among relationships involving college students. More than 85% of 50 undergraduates reported that they had lied to their partners (Saxe, 1991). Most of these lies (41%) were about involvement with other partners. In another study, 77 college students kept diaries of their daily social interactions and reported telling two lies a day (DePaulo, Kirkendol, Kashy, Wyer, & Epstein, 1996). Participants said they did not regard their lies as serious and did not plan them or worry about being caught.

Table 4.5 presents the lies that a sample of the authors' students reported having told to a current or past partner.

PERSONAL CHOICES

Is Honesty Always the Best Policy?

Good communication often implies open communication, but how much honesty is good for a relationship? Duncan and Rock (1993, p. 49) emphasized that it is a myth that always being honest is critical for a relationship to work.

> Being open with someone who will use the information to manipulate you or gain power over you is like playing poker and showing your cards before you bet. An open and honest expression must be interpreted as such by the receiver of the message for it to be truly open and honest. Openness is not the only way, and in some situations, not the best way.

TABLE 4.5 Lies University Students Reported Having Told a Current or Past Partner (Number in Sample = 137)

Lie	Male	Female	Total Number of Students Reporting Lie	Percentage of Sample Reporting Lie
Number of previous partners	11%	20%	42	30.6
Had an orgasm	1	23	33	24.1
You're the best	8	8	22	16.1
It was good	2	15	23	16.8
I love you	7	8	21	15.3
I'm a virgin	3	5	11	8.0
You're the biggest	0	7	10	7.3
I like oral sex	4	1	8	5.8
I'm on my period	0	4	6	4.4
I've never cheated	1	3	5	3.6
Yes, I want to	0	1	2	1.5
Age	1	2	3	2.2
I'll call	2	0.01	3	2.2
I've got a headache	1	2	3	2.2
No, I don't have AIDS or an STD	1	0.01	2	1.5
I'll pull out	2	0	2	1.5
I'm too tired	1	0.01	2	1.5
I'm on the Pill	0	0.01	1	0.75
I don't have protection	1	0	1	0.75
You're beautiful	1	0	1	0.75
Reported having told no lies	1	6	9	6.6

Source: Knox et al., 1993.

When the issue is an extramarital affair, spouses might consider the consequences before disclosing. Pepper Schwartz cautions women especially to think twice before confessing. "According to my research, only confess if you want to end your marriage, or if the relationship is so bad that you are willing to risk ending it in order to help it" (quoted by Van Matre, 1992, p. d-8).

Some couples, however, may find that the disclosure of an affair by one partner forces them to examine problems in their relationship, seek marriage therapy, or both. In such cases, disclosure may ultimately result in bringing the couple closer together in an emotional sense.

Although complete dishonesty in the form of withholding may or may not be an advisable option

Individuals differ in terms of how honest they are with one another.

in the case of an extradyadic indiscretion, other situations might call for tempered honesty. A particular situation in which tempered honesty may be the best policy is when you are extremely upset. In this situation, you may honestly feel and think horrible things about your partner. If you express such thoughts and feelings, they may be difficult to retract later when you are calm. At such times, it may be best to not be totally honest about your thoughts and feelings. Instead, admit you are upset and either wait until you are calm to talk about the problem or refrain from expressing thoughts that are hurtful to your partner.

Though honesty may be tempered with kindness in some situations, in others it is probably best to be completely honest. Specific information that should not be withheld from the partner includes previous marriages and children, a sexual orientation different from what the partner expects, alcohol or other drug addiction, having a sexually transmitted disease (such as HIV or genital herpes), and any known physical disabilities (such as sterility). Disclosures of this nature include anything that would have a significant impact on the relationship.

PERSONAL CHOICES

Should You Tell Your Partner You Are Attracted to Other People?

Partners who stay together for a long time will likely, at some time and at some level, be attracted to someone outside the relationship. Whether such attrac-

tions or interests are to be disclosed to the partner may depend on the nature of the personalities of the individuals, the nature of the relationship with the partner, and the nature and extent of the attraction. Some couples decide to share such feelings and have relationships in which the partners are not insecure or defensive about such disclosures. Other couples decide it is much too painful to disclose or to hear of such interests. Still other couples ignore the issue. No one strategy might be considered best, because different strategies may have both positive and negative outcomes for different couples. However, it is important for couples to acknowledge that such attractions are likely to occur and to agree on the nature and extent of the desired disclosure.

THINK ABOUT IT

To what degree are individuals honest with others? Make the case for and against being completely open with one's partner.

RESOLVING CONFLICT IN RELATIONSHIPS

Beyond effective and honest communication, both women and men value conflict management skills (Burleson, Kunkel, Samter, & Werking, 1996). Skills in conflict resolution are important for maintaining relationship satisfaction. Of 343 university students surveyed, 56% reported having a very troublesome relationship within the past 5 years. Of those who had a troubled relationship, most (69%) reported talking to the partner in an attempt to resolve the problem (19% avoided discussing the problem, and 18% avoided the partner) (Levitt, Silver, & Franco, 1996). The most troublesome behaviors of partners were being selfish, manipulative, demanding, and possessive. In another study of 203 undergraduates, the most to least difficult relationship problems to discuss were (in that order) the future of the relationship, ex-partners, sex, and jealousy (Knox, Hatfield, & Zusman, in press).

Howard Markman is head of the Center for Marital and Family Studies at the University of Denver. He and his colleagues have been studying 150 couples at yearly intervals (beginning before marriage) to determine those factors most responsible for marital success. They have found that communication skills that reflect the ability to handle conflict, which they call "constructive arguing," is the single biggest predictor of marital success over time (Marano, 1992). According to Markman:

> Many people believe that the causes of marital problems are the differences between people and problem areas such as money, sex, children. However, our findings indicate it is not the differences that are important, but how these differences and problems are handled, particularly early in marriage. (Marano, 1992, p. 53)

There is also merit in developing and using conflict negotiation skills before problems develop. Not only are individuals more willing to work on issues when things are going well, but they have not developed negative patterns of response that are difficult to change.

This section describes principles and techniques that are helpful in resolving interpersonal conflict. Such principles and techniques permit a couple to manage present and future conflict by emphasizing the "process" of their interaction and negotiation and not focusing on "fixing" a specific problem (Kolevzon & Jenkins, 1992).

Address Any Recurring Issues

Some couples are uncomfortable talking about issues that plague them. They fear that a confrontation will further weaken their relationship. Pam is jealous that Mark spends more time with other people at parties than with her. "When we go someplace together," she blurts out, "he drops me to disappear with someone else for two hours." Her jealousy is spreading to other areas of their relationship. "When we are walking down the street and he turns his head to look at another woman, I get furious." If Pam and Mark don't discuss her feelings about Mark's behavior, their relationship may deteriorate as a result of a negative response cycle: He looks at another woman, she gets angry, he gets angry at her getting angry and finds that he is even more attracted to other women, she gets angrier because he escalates his looking at other women, and so on.

To bring the matter up, Pam might say, "I feel jealous when you spend more time with other women at parties than with me. I need some help in dealing with these feelings." By expressing her concern in this way, she has identified the problem from her perspective and asked for her partner's cooperation in handling it.

When discussing difficult relationship issues, it is important to avoid attacking, blaming, or being negative. Such reactions reduce the motivation of the partner to talk about an issue and thus reduce the probability of a positive outcome (Forgatch, 1989).

Focus on What You Want (Rather Than What You Don't Want)

Dealing with conflict is more likely to result in resolution if the partners focus on what they want rather than what they don't want. For example, rather than tell Mark she doesn't want him to spend so much time with other women at parties, Pam might tell him that she wants him to spend more time with her at parties.

Find Out Your Partner's Point of View

We often assume that we know what our partner thinks and why our partner does things. Sometimes we are wrong. Rather than assume how our partner thinks and feels about a particular issue, we might ask our partner open-ended questions in an effort to get him or her to tell us thoughts and feeling about a particular situation. Pam's words to Mark might be "What is it like for you when we go to parties?" "How do you feel about my jealousy?"

Once your partner has shared his or her thoughts about an issue with you, it is important for you to summarize your partner's perspective in a nonjudgmental way. After Mark has told Pam how he feels about their being at parties together, she can summarize his perspective by saying, "You feel that I cling to you more than I should, and you would like me to let you wander around without feeling like you're making me angry." (She may not agree with his view, but she knows exactly what it is—and Mark knows that she knows.)

Generate Win-Win Solutions to the Conflict

A *win-win solution* is one in which both people involved in a conflict feel satisfied with the agreement or resolution to the conflict. It is imperative to look for win-win solutions to conflicts. Solutions in which one person wins and the other person loses involve one person not getting his or her needs met. As a result, the person who "loses" may develop feelings of resentment, anger, hurt, and hostility toward the winner and may even look for ways to get even.

Win-win solutions increase the intimacy between partners.

In this way, the winner is also a loser. In intimate relationships, one winner really means two losers.

Generating win-win solutions to interpersonal conflicts often requires brainstorming. The technique of *brainstorming* involves suggesting as many alternatives as possible without evaluating them. Brainstorming is crucial to conflict resolution because it shifts the partners' focus from criticizing each other's perspective to working together to develop alternative solutions. Any solution may be an acceptable one as long as the solution is one of mutual agreement.

Evaluate and Select a Solution

After generating a number of solutions, each solution should be evaluated and the best one selected. In evaluating solutions to conflicts, it may be helpful to ask the following questions.

1. Does the solution satisfy both individuals? (Is it a win-win solution?)
2. Is the solution specific? Does the solution specify exactly who is to do what, how, and when?
3. Is the solution realistic? Can both parties realistically follow through with what they have agreed to do?
4. Does the solution prevent the problem from recurring?
5. Does the solution specify what is to happen if the problem recurs?

Kurdek (1995) emphasized that conflict resolution styles that stress agreement, compromise, and humor are associated with marital satisfaction, whereas conflict engagement, withdrawal, and defensiveness styles are associated with lower marital satisfaction. In his own study of 155 married couples, the style in which the wife engaged the husband in conflict and the husband withdrew was particularly associated with low marital satisfaction for both spouses.

THINK ABOUT IT

Think about the last conflict you had in a relationship. Which of the conflict resolution steps, if any, did you and your partner follow?

KEY TERMS

brainstorming 94	open-ended question 87
closed-ended question 87	reflective listening 88
communication 80	self-disclosure 80
intimacy 80	touch-and-ask rule 87
"I" statements 80	verbal message 84
nonverbal message 84	win-win solution 93

SUMMARY POINTS

This chapter focused on the value of good communication to relationship and sexual satisfaction, the principles of effective communication, the issue of honesty in relationships, and conflict resolution in relationships through generating win-win solutions.

Intimacy, Relationship, and Sexual Satisfaction

Good communication and self-disclosure are important factors in creating and maintaining intimacy, relationship, and sexual satisfaction. Poor communication is associated with unhappy relationships. In some cases, poor communication creates dissatisfaction in the relationship; in other cases, dissatisfaction in the relationship leads to poor communication.

Principles of Effective Communication in Intimate Relationships

Effective communication in intimate relationships is based on understanding and using various communication principles. These include initiating discussions about important issues, giving congruent messages, minimizing negative remarks and maximizing positive remarks, expressing feelings, and practicing reflective listening. Applying these communication principles to everyday interactions can enhance both individual and relationship well-being and increase sexual satisfaction between partners. Although these principles and techniques are fairly simple, abandoning old patterns of communication and replacing these old patterns with new ones is not easy.

Honesty and Dishonesty in Interpersonal Communication

Most individuals value honesty in their relationships. Honest communication is associated with trust and intimacy. Despite the importance of honesty in relationships, deception occurs frequently in interpersonal relationships.

Lying is rampant among college student relationships. Partners sometimes lie to each other about previous sexual relationships, how they feel about each other, and how they experience each other sexually. In one study, more than 85% of 50 undergraduates reported that they had lied to their partners; in another study, 77 college students kept diaries of their daily social interactions and reported telling two lies a day.

Telling lies is not the only form of dishonesty. People exaggerate, minimize, tell partial truths, pretend, and engage in self-deception. A partner may withhold information or keep secrets in order to protect the other partner, preserve the relationship, or both. However, the more intimate the relationship, the greater our desire to share our most personal and private selves with our partner, and the greater the emotional consequences of not sharing. In intimate relationships, keeping secrets can block opportunities for healing, resolution, self-acceptance, and deeper intimacy between partners.

Resolving Conflict in Relationships

Having a plan to communicate about conflicts is essential. Such a plan includes deciding to address recurring issues rather than suppress them, asking the partner for help in resolving the issue, finding out the partner's point of view, summarizing the partner's perspective in a nonjudgmental way, brainstorming for alternative win-win solutions, and selecting a plan of action.

REFERENCES

Billingsley, S., Lim, M., & Jennings, G. (1995). Themes of long-term, satisfied marriages consummated between 1952-1967. *Family Perspectives, 29,* 283-295.

Burleson, B. R., Kunkel, A. W., Samter, W., & Werking, K. J. (1996). Men's and women's evaluations of communication skills in personal relationships: When sex differences make a difference—and when they don't. *Journal of Social and Personal Relationships, 13,* 201-224.

Cupach, W. R., & Comstock, J. (1990). Satisfaction with sexual communication in marriage: Links to sexual satisfaction and dyadic adjustment. *Journal of Social and Personal Relationships, 7,* 179-186.

Cupach, W. R., & Metts, S. (1991). Sexuality and communication in close relationships. In K. McKinney & S. Sprecher (Eds.), *Sexuality in close relationships* (pp. 93-110). Hillsdale, NJ: Lawrence Erlbaum Associates.

DePaulo, B. M., Kirkendol, S. E., Kashy, D. A., Wyer, M. M., & Epstein, J. A. (1996). Lying in everyday life. *Journal of Personality and Social Psychology, 70*(5), 979-997.

Duncan, B. L., & Rock, J. W. (1993). Saving relationships: The power of the unpredictable. *Psychology Today, 26,* 46-51, 86, 95.

Forgatch, M. S. (1989). Patterns and outcome in family problem solving: The disrupting effect of negative emotion. *Journal of Marriage and the Family, 51,* 115-124.

Gray, L. A., & Saracino, M. (1991). College students' attitudes, beliefs and behaviors about AIDS: Implications for family life educators. *Family Relations, 40,* 258-263.

Hendricks, G., & Hendricks, K. (1990). *Conscious loving: The journey to co-commitment.* New York: Bantam Books.

Knox, D., Hatfield, S., & Zusman, M. (in press). College student discussion of relationship problems. *College Student Journal.*

Kolevzon, M. S., & Jenkins, L. A. (1992). *The relationship self-assessment inventory (RSAI): A guide to resolving conflict in couples therapy.* Paper presented at the 54th Annual Conference, National Council on Family Relations, Orlando, FL.

Kurdek, L. A. (1995). Predicting change in marital satisfaction from husbands' and wives' conflict resolution styles. *Journal of Marriage and the Family, 57,* 153-164.

L'Abate, L., & Bagarozzi, D. A. (1993). *Sourcebook of marriage and family interaction.* New York: Brunner/Mazel.

Lerner, H. G. (1993). *The dance of deception: Pretending and truth-telling in women's lives.* New York: HarperCollins.

Levitt, M. J., Silver, M. E., & Franco, N. (1996). Troublesome relationships: A part of human experience. *Journal of Social and Personal Relationships, 13,* 523-536.

Marano, H. E. (1992, January/February). The reinvention of marriage. *Psychology Today, 49,* 48-53, 85.

Mothersill, M. (1996). Some questions about truthfulness and lying. *Social Research, 63,* 913-929.

Notarius, C., & Markman, H. (1994). *We can work it out: Making sense of marital conflict.* New York: Putnam.

Saxe, L. (1991). Lying: Thoughts of an applied social psychologist. *American Psychologist, 46*(4), 409-415.

Sexual assertiveness training promotes condom use. (1995, November 6). *American Medical News, 38*(41), 42.

Taylor, R. (1997). *Love affairs: Marriage and infidelity.* Amherst, NY: Prometheus Books.

Van Matre, L. (1992, August 28). Honesty can be worst policy in affair. *The Daily Reflector,* d-8.

Waring, E. M. (1988). *Enhancing marital intimacy through facilitating cognitive self-disclosure.* New York: Brunner/Mazel.

Zagorin, P. (1996). The historical significance of lying and dissimulation. *Social Research, 63,* 863-912.

HEALTH AND
REPRODUCTIVE SEXUAL CHOICES

SEXUALLY TRANSMITTED DISEASES

Sexually Transmitted Diseases: A Pandemic

The Scope of the Problem: U.S. and Global
    Statistics on STDs
Sexually Transmitted Diseases in the United
    States: Who Is at Risk?
PERSONAL CHOICES: Should You Be Tested for
    HIV and Other STDs?

QUESTION What is the most common sexually
transmitted disease in the United States and
throughout the world?

Consequences of Sexually Transmitted Diseases

Health Consequences
Economic Consequences
Psychological Consequences

QUESTION Is HIV/AIDS the only STD with serious
health consequences?

Modes of Transmission, Symptoms, and Treatment for Sexually Transmitted Diseases

Chlamydia
Gonorrhea
Human Papilloma Virus (HPV) or Genital Warts
Genital Herpes
Syphilis

Human Immunodeficiency Virus and Acquired
    Immunodeficiency Syndrome
Hepatitis B
Nongonococcal Urethritis
Chancroid
Vaginitis
Pubic Lice
Scabies

QUESTION Which sexually transmitted diseases
remain in the body and have no cure?

Prevention and Control of Sexually Transmissible Diseases

Modification of High-Risk Sexual Behavior
SELF-ASSESSMENT: The UCLA Multidimensional
    Condom Attitudes Scale
SOCIAL CHOICES: Should Condoms Be Available
    in High Schools?
Public and Private Sexual Health Services
Syringe-Exchange Programs
Computer Technology: A Revolution in STD
    Intervention

QUESTION How does the prevention and control
of STDs, such as chlamydia, herpes, gonorrhea,
chancroid, syphilis, and trichomoniasis, help in
the prevention of HIV infection?

*S*ome students have a hard time understanding that the consequence of one
unprotected sexual encounter may not be reversible.

American College Health Association

In the last two decades, there has been great knowledge expansion of sexually transmitted diseases (STDs). Researchers have identified new diseases, gained a better understanding about how some STDs are transmitted and progress, and developed new treatments for many STDs. The explosion of STD research has been paralleled by the unprecedented cultural visibility of STDs. Once considered a "hidden epidemic," sexually transmitted diseases have come into the public's view through school sex and health education, public service announcements, and mass media coverage. Yet, despite the fact that much information has been shed on STDs, many Americans—even educated adults—remain largely ignorant of these diseases. In a 1995 government study, approximately one-third of a sample of U.S. women and men could not name any STD other than AIDS (Sternberg, 1996).

In addition, most young adults have not been tested for HIV and other STDs. Many people are infected and do not even know it. When it comes to using condoms and other safer sex practices, studies reveal some serious gaps between what individuals know they should do and what they actually do. Despite public education campaigns that encourage sexually active people to "use condom sense," many people do not use condoms consistently or correctly. Those individuals who *do* use condoms do not realize that condoms *reduce* the risk of STD transmission, but do not eliminate entirely the possibility of STD infection.

This chapter presents information about sexually transmitted diseases. How widespread are the problems? Who is at risk? What behaviors are associated with contracting STDs? What are the health, economic, and psychological consequences of STDs? What choices can you make to reduce your risk of acquiring an STD? What can society do to control and prevent the spread of STDs?

NATIONAL DATA

A national survey of women from ages 18 to 60

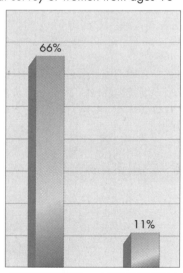

66%

11%

Little knowledge about STDs (other than HIV/AIDS)

Aware that STDs can be more harmful to women than to men

Source: Committee on Prevention and Control of STDs, 1997.

SEXUALLY TRANSMITTED DISEASES: A PANDEMIC

Sexually transmitted diseases represent a major individual and public health concern. Of the top ten most frequently reported diseases in the United States in 1995, five were sexually transmitted diseases (SIECUS Fact Sheet, 1997). In 1995, STDs accounted for 87% of all cases reported that year among the ten most frequently reported diseases in the United States.

An overview of U.S. and global statistics on STDs reveals how widespread sexually transmitted diseases are. The consequences of STDs—their impact on physical health, economics, and psychological well-being—convey the seriousness of the STD pandemic.

TABLE 5.1 Incidence Rates of the Most Common STDs in the United States

STD	ANNUAL ESTIMATED INCIDENCE
Chlamydia	4 million
Trichomoniasis	3 million
PID (pelvic inflammatory disease)*	1 million
Gonorrhea	800,000
HPV (human papilloma virus) or genital warts	500,000 to 1 million
Genital Herpes	200,000 to 500,000
Syphilis	101,000
HIV/AIDS	80,000

*Although PID is generally not considered an STD, it results from some untreated STDs, including chlamydia and gonorrhea.

Source: *SIECUS,* 1997 (25).

The Scope of the Problem: U.S. and Global Statistics on STDs

Sexually transmitted diseases are widespread in the United States and many other countries throughout the world.

U.S. STATISTICS ON STDS   In the United States, at least one person in four will contract an STD at some point in his or her lifetime (SIECUS Fact Sheet, 1997). Table 5.1 presents the annual estimated incidence of the eight most common STDs in the United States.

GLOBAL STATISTICS ON STDS   Sexually transmitted diseases and their consequences represent major public health problems, especially for developing countries that lack resources for preventing and treating STDs. Six out of ten women in many countries have an STD (1997 UNFPA Report, 1997). Chlamydia is the most common STD in the world, affecting about 50 million individuals annually (Aitken & Reichenbach, 1994).

INTERNATIONAL DATA

More than 300 million cases of STDs reported in 1997 were caused by gonorrhea, chlamydia, syphilis, or chancroid. Most of these cases occurred in developing countries.

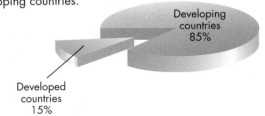

Developing countries 85%

Developed countries 15%

Source: Chernesky, 1997.

One of the most urgent public health concerns around the globe is the spread of HIV and AIDS.

Current projections of the AIDS pandemic suggest that by the year 2000, between 40 and 110 million of the world's people will be infected with the virus, and there will have been 20 million AIDS-related deaths (Pinkerton & Abramson, 1997). As Figure 5.1 illustrates, Africa has suffered the highest incidence of AIDS cases.

Sexually Transmitted Diseases in the United States: Who Is at Risk?

Various factors are associated with an increased risk of acquiring an STD.

INDIVIDUALS WITH MULTIPLE SEX PARTNERS   The more sexual partners an individual has, the higher the risk of being exposed to a sexually transmissible disease.

NATIONAL DATA

Based on a national representative sample of United States adults, number of sexual partners reported since the age of 18

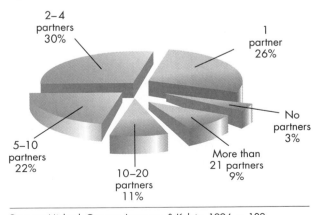

2–4 partners 30%

1 partner 26%

No partners 3%

More than 21 partners 9%

10–20 partners 11%

5–10 partners 22%

Source: Michael, Gagnon, Laumann, & Kolata, 1994, p. 102.

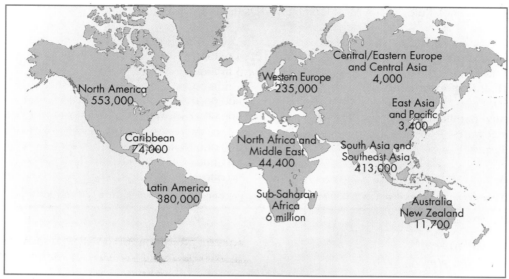

FIGURE 5.1 Global Distribution of AIDS Cases Over the Past Two Decades   **Source:** Data from *Weekly Epidemiological Record* of the World Health Organization.

RELATIONSHIP STATUS   In a national study comparing people who were not married (never married, divorced, separated, or widowed) to those who were married or living together, the people who were not married reported having more sexual partners (Michael et al., 1994). Thus, being single is associated with a higher STD risk than being married or living with a partner.

NATIONAL DATA

Wives and husbands having had extramarital sex, as reported in a national sample

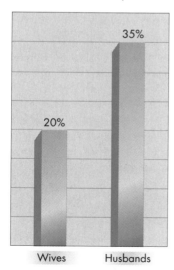

Source: Michael et al., 1994.

Catania et al. (1995, p. 1497) noted, however, that "although the process of partnering through legal marriage or cohabitation imparts some degree of risk reduction, this reduction may at times be illusory." This is because heterosexuals with histories of risk factors for HIV seldom obtain testing prior to cohabitation or marriage and do not regularly use condoms with their primary partners. In addition, married couples and partners living together may still have sexual partners outside of their primary relationships.

Married and cohabiting individuals are more likely to use condoms with secondary partners than with primary partners, thus placing their primary partners at risk for STDs.

ADOLESCENTS AND YOUNG ADULTS   In the United States, adolescents and young adults are the age group with the greatest risk of acquiring an STD. For example, rates of chlamydia and gonorrhea in women are highest among 15- to 19-year-olds (Centers for Disease Control, 1995).

STD rates are high among adolescents and young adults because they are more likely to have multiple sexual partners, their partners may be at higher risks of being infected, and they may be more likely to engage in intercourse without using condoms. Young adolescent girls have an increased risk of HIV infection due, in part, to their minimal vaginal mucus production, which provides less of a barrier to HIV. Young girls also have an increased presence

Every year, many young adults account for the major percentage of sexually transmitted diseases in the United States.

Young adults 70%

Other 30%

Source: Binson, Dolcini, Pollack, & Catania, 1993.

About 1 in 4 sexually experienced teenagers acquire a sexually transmitted disease.

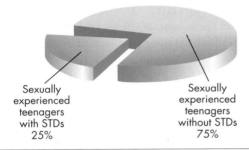

Sexually experienced teenagers with STDs 25%

Sexually experienced teenagers without STDs 75%

Source: SIECUS Fact Sheet, 1997.

of cervical ectopy, which increases their risk of acquiring HIV and chlamydia. *Cervical ectopy* refers to an outgrowth of membranous tissue from the cervix toward the vagina. This outgrowth of cervical tissue, common in adolescent girls, is more susceptible to some STDs than the more protective membranous tissue of the vagina (Hankins, 1996).

WOMEN   Women are biologically more susceptible than men to becoming infected if exposed to STDs. A woman who has one act of unprotected intercourse with a man infected with gonorrhea has up to a 90% chance of contracting the disease. In contrast, a man who has one act of unprotected intercourse with a woman infected with gonorrhea has about a 30% chance of becoming infected (SIECUS Fact Sheet, 1997). Likewise, male-to-female transmission of HIV is 2 to 4 times more efficient than female-to-male transmission (Hankins, 1996). This is due to the larger mucosal surface area exposed to the virus in women, the greater amount of virus present in semen as compared with vaginal secretions, and the shortness and location of the female urethra.

Also, women who engage in anal intercourse have an increased risk of acquiring HIV due to the potential for anal tears or rectal abrasions during anal intercourse, which can facilitate entry of HIV and the poor protection of the membranous tissue of the rectal lining. In a survey of U.S. adults, nine percent of women reported having engaged in anal intercourse in the past year (Michael et al., 1994). Although lesbians are not immune from HIV and other STD infections, women who have sexual relations only with women (and whose partners do likewise) have a substantially lower risk of acquiring STDs than heterosexual women.

HOMOSEXUAL MALES AND BISEXUAL MALES AND THEIR FEMALE PARTNERS   In the United States, HIV rates are highest among gay and bisexual men. This is due to the high rate of anal intercourse—a high-risk sexual behavior—among gay and bisexual men. However, worldwide, most cases of HIV and AIDS are found among the heterosexual population.

SUBSTANCE USE   Current media campaigns warn of the dangers of combining alcohol and drugs with sex ("Get drunk, get high, get AIDS"). Drinking alcohol or using drugs is associated with an increased risk of acquiring HIV and other STDs. One study of more than 1200 sexually active adolescents revealed that adolescents engaged in riskier sexual behaviors when they used alcohol or drugs (Cooper, Pierce, & Huselid, 1994). In a laboratory experiment involving 20 men, participants were randomly assigned to an experimental group who drank vodka and tonic to achieve a blood alcohol level of .08%, or to a control group who drank only tonic (Gordon & Carey, 1996). All participants then completed a battery of tests related to condom use. Compared to the men who did not consume alcohol, those who consumed alcohol tended to report more negative attitudes toward condoms (they believed, for example, that condoms decrease pleasure or that discussing condom use with a partner is embarrassing) and lower self-efficacy regarding the initiation of condom use in sexual encounters. Using alcohol and other recreational drugs not only affects judgment and attitudes about sexual behavior, but it may also damage immune systems, making individuals more susceptible to infectious diseases in general.

USERS OF ILLEGAL INJECTION DRUGS AND THEIR PARTNERS AND OFFSPRING   In the United States, injection of illegal drugs is the risk behavior most frequently associated with heterosexual and perinatal transmission of HIV. According to a recent estimate, the majority of new HIV infections in the United States each year occur among intravenous drug users, their sexual partners, and their offspring (Holmberg, 1996).

NATIONAL DATA

As of June 1997, about one-third of the cases of adolescent and adult AIDS reported to the Centers for Disease Control (CDC) were associated with intravenous drug use.

Source: Centers for Disease Control, 1997.

INDIVIDUALS WHO HAVE BEEN SEXUALLY ABUSED Women who have been sexually abused during childhood are twice as likely to become infected with STDs as women who do not have such histories. Individuals who have been raped or sexually assaulted are also at risk for acquiring an STD, as rapists rarely use condoms. Forced sexual activity is also more likely to result in vaginal or anal abrasions, thereby increasing susceptibility to HIV.

LOWER SOCIOECONOMIC STATUS   Rates of STDs are higher among populations that are economically disadvantaged. This is because individuals in lower socioeconomic conditions tend to lack health insurance, have inadequate access to health care, and receive inadequate education (including education related to STDs). Because racial and ethnic minorities are disproportionately represented among the poor, rates of STDs are higher among minority populations. For example, according to a U.S. Department of Health and Human Services report, gonorrhea rates among African American adolescents (15 to 19 years of age) are more than 26 times greater than the rate among white adolescents. The rate of syphilis among African Americans is nearly 60 times that of whites; among Hispanics, the syphilis rate is 4 times that of whites. In 1995, 91% of all reported cases of congenital syphilis occurred in babies born to African American or Hispanic mothers (Centers for Disease Control, 1995).

In addition, minority racial and ethnic groups are, on the average, younger, and (as noted earlier) youths

have higher STD risks. Finally, minorities tend to live in concentrated areas of poverty; this "creates potential sex partner pools of high risk and high STD prevalence and perhaps reinforces risky behaviors" (Aral, 1996, p. 14).

URBAN DWELLERS   Rates of HIV and other STDs are higher in urban areas than in rural areas. This is primarily because individuals with high risk factors tend to be concentrated in urban areas.

ENGAGING IN HIGH-RISK SEXUAL BEHAVIOR   The term "high-risk" implies that certain traits determine who will become infected with an STD. Kerr (1990, p. 431) noted that "the concept of high-risk groups has led many persons to falsely believe that they are not susceptible to HIV infection since they do not fall into one of these groups." Many rural Americans deny the possibility that their friends and neighbors might be infected with HIV. Even though inner cities have higher rates of HIV, AIDS cases in rural U.S. areas rose by 80% between 1991 and 1995, outpacing the increases of 47% for large urban areas and 64% for smaller urban areas (McMillan, 1996).

It is not the group one belongs to, but rather the behaviors one practices, that puts one at risk for STD infection. Anyone who engages in risky sexual behavior is susceptible to acquiring STDs. With some exceptions (such as sexual victimization and mother-child transmission), STDs result from people choosing to engage in behaviors that place them at risk. It is these choices, rather than people's group affiliation, that most influences STD transmission. Table 5.2 presents various behaviors and their level of STD risk.

PERSONAL CHOICES

Should You Be Tested for HIV and Other STDs?

Many people do not get tested for HIV and other STDs because they believe they are not infected. Several STDs are asymptomatic; that is, they often do not produce symptoms. Thus, individuals may have an STD and not know it. Other individuals believe that if they are not in a high-risk category (if they are not gay men, do not have multiple partners, or do not use needles to inject drugs), then they are not at

TABLE 5.2 Which Sexual Behaviors Are Most Risky?

Extremely High Risk	Moderate Risk
Unprotected anal and vaginal intercourse Sharing needles (for drug use and body piercing)	Unprotected oral sex on a man or woman Unprotected oral-anal contact (rimming) Unprotected fisting or intercourse using one or more fingers Sharing devices that draw blood (such as whips) Sharing unprotected sex toys (such as dildos) Allowing body fluids to come in contact with broken skin and mucous membranes

Low Risk	No Risk
Deep (French) kissing Anal and vaginal intercourse with a condom used correctly Fisting or intercourse using one or more fingers protected by a finger cot* or latex glove Oral-anal contact (rimming) with a dental dam** Oral sex on a man or woman using a condom or dental dam	Dry kissing Hugging and nongenital touching Massage Using vibrators or sex toys (not shared) Masturbation (alone or with partner)

 * A *finger cot* is a mini-condom worn on the finger(s) for finger intercourse.

** A *dental dam* is a latex square used to cover the anus or vagina during oral sex. Household plastic wrap or a condom cut lengthwise can be used as a substitute for a dental dam.

---

risk for HIV and other STDs. Yet, anyone who has engaged in unprotected intercourse (vaginal or anal) or oral-genital contact, or anyone who has shared drug needles, may possibly have HIV or another STD. Some individuals do not get tested for HIV and other STDs because they fear the results may indicate they are infected. For this same reason, some individuals get tested, but never follow up to get the results.

With HIV and other STDs, what you don't know *can* hurt you. The longer an STD goes undiagnosed and untreated, the more likely it is that it will produce serious health consequences including sterility, cancer, and death. The sooner an infected individual is tested and diagnosed, the sooner that individual can begin treatment for the disease and begin to alter sexual or needle-sharing behavior, thereby reducing the risk of transmitting the disease to others. Early detection of HIV enables the infected individual to begin interventions that slow the growth of HIV and prevent opportunistic diseases. An HIV-infected individual whose disease is detected and treated in the early stages has a better prognosis for living longer with a higher quality of life than an individual whose HIV

infection is detected during later stages. Early detection of other STDs can prevent or minimize the negative health effects they might otherwise produce. Because of the ulcerations caused by genital herpes, syphilis, and chancroid, and the inflammation caused by gonorrhea, chlamydia, and trichomoniasis, these infections facilitate transmission of HIV. Therefore, rapid diagnosis and treatment of these STDs may help prevent sexual transmission of HIV (Chernesky, 1997).

Getting tested for HIV and other STDs requires an investment of time, effort and potentially, money. Getting tested also requires individuals to overcome any embarrassment and fear associated with discussing their sexual behaviors with health care providers, having their genitals examined, and coping with the possibility of being told they have an STD.

Where do individuals go to get tested for HIV and other STDs, and what do the tests involve? STD testing is available at most local public health centers, STD clinics, family planning clinics, private health care providers, hospitals, and university health centers. One can also get tested for HIV in the privacy of the home. One type of HIV test can be bought at pharmacies, college health centers, and public health clinics, or it can be ordered through the mail for a cost of around $50. The test involves pricking a finger, putting three drops of blood on a special card, and mailing the card to a laboratory. To obtain the results, one calls the company's toll-free number after 7 days and gives them the personal identification number that was included with the test kit. HIV counselors are available to discuss your test results and give advice and information.

Some STD testing involves getting a sample of the person's blood or urine and testing it for the presence of a particular STD. Testing for chlamydia in women involves a health care provider inserting a cotton swab inside the vagina to obtain a specimen that is then cultured. This swab procedure is done during a pelvic exam. For men, chlamydia testing involves a health care provider inserting a cotton swab into the penis. Although a urine test has been developed to detect chlamydia, it is not commonly used because data on its credibility are lacking. A recently developed oral HIV test involves placing a specially treated pad between the lower cheek and gum for 2 minutes. The pad soaks up fluid that is then tested for HIV antibodies.

THINK ABOUT IT

Why are many individuals who are in high-risk categories for acquiring HIV and other STDs also the least likely to be tested for STDs?

CONSEQUENCES OF SEXUALLY TRANSMITTED DISEASES

Most teenagers and adults today are aware that HIV and AIDS can cause serious health consequences. However, the emphasis on HIV/AIDS may be inadvertently overshadowing the seriousness of other STDs. In addition to health consequences, HIV and other STDs can cause psychological distress and can also place an economic burden on individuals and society.

Health Consequences

Untreated STDs can result in severe health consequences. Women are more likely than men to suffer serious health consequences from contracting STDs. Women are less likely to produce symptoms, and are, therefore, less likely to be diagnosed until severe problems develop.

INTERNATIONAL DATA

The World Bank estimates that STDs, excluding AIDS, are the second leading cause of death among women, ages 15 to 44, in the developing world.

Source: Committee on Prevention and Control of STDs, 1997.

Untreated sexually transmitted diseases may cause *pelvic inflammatory disease (PID)*—a major health problem in women of reproductive age, often requiring hospitalization and surgery. PID is associated with complications such as infertility, ectopic pregnancy, and chronic abdominal pain. In the United States, chlamydia—the most common STD—causes the majority of PID in women.

NATIONAL DATA

In the United States, an estimated 1 million women experience an episode of PID each year.

Source: Committee on Prevention and Control of STDs, 1997.

Some American women are infertile because of tubule damage caused by PID resulting from an STD.

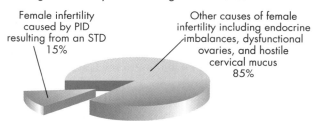

Female infertility caused by PID resulting from an STD 15%

Other causes of female infertility including endocrine imbalances, dysfunctional ovaries, and hostile cervical mucus 85%

Source: SIECUS Fact Sheet, 1997.

STDs are also associated with health problems for pregnant women and infants. Various STDs may be transmitted to the fetus, newborn, or infant through the placenta (congenital infection), during passage through the birth canal (perinatal infection), or after birth through breastfeeding or close contact. Health consequences include spontaneous abortion, stillbirth, and premature delivery.

For both women and men, STDs increase the level of susceptibility to HIV. Individuals with active genital herpes, syphilis, chancroid infection, chlamydia, gonorrhea, or trichomoniasis are three to five times more likely to contract HIV than noninfected individuals (SIECUS Fact Sheet, 1997). This is partly because tissue inflammation, ulcerations, and open sores associated with STDs provide the HIV virus with entries into partners' bloodstreams.

The health consequences of HIV and AIDS have caused great alarm; AIDS causes more deaths than any other STD. The largest number of deaths related to STDs other than AIDS is caused by cervical and other cancers associated with the human papilloma virus, and liver disease cancer caused by the hepatitis B virus (Committee on Prevention and Control of STDs, 1997). Untreated syphilis can cause serious damage to the cardiovascular system and nervous system, and may also cause blindness and death.

In Asia and Africa, 2 million individuals each year are permanently blinded by chlamydial infections (Aral & Holmes, 1991). The rate of blindness due to chlamydia is much lower in the United States, due to the climate and the fact that medication is readily available to control the infection.

Economic Consequences

The economic costs of STDs place a burden on individuals and their families and drain the tax dollars that support public health insurance (such as Medicaid) and public health care facilities.

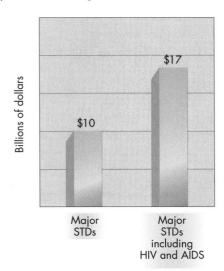

Source: Donovan, 1997.

Individuals with AIDS (and their families) are particularly hard hit by the financial costs associated with this disease. Medicines alone can cost over a thousand dollars per month. A volunteer at a community AIDS support organization commented, "There are days when our clients must make a decision about whether they will eat that day or take their medicine" (B. Baker, personal communication, 1997).

Annual medication costs of $10,000 to $20,000 are prohibitive to many U.S. families. Needless to say, the drug therapies "are out of reach of the 90 percent of the world's HIV-infected people, who live in developing countries" (Pinkerton & Abramson, 1997, p. 373).

Psychological Consequences

Individuals who learn they are infected with a sexually transmissible disease often experience psychological consequences similar to those experienced with other life crises. These psychological reactions include shock, withdrawal from social interaction, anger (especially at the person who gave them the infection), fear, shame, and depression.

Telling one's partner (or a potential partner) that one has an STD can be very stressful. Individuals infected with an STD often encounter rejection. One woman with herpes stayed in an unhappy relationship for seven years because "she felt that no one but the man who gave her herpes would ever want her" (Winning the War in Your Mind, 1997, p. 1). (See Chapter 4, "Social Choices" for a discussion about telling your partner about your sexual health status.)

Individuals with HIV and AIDS are prone to high levels of psychological distress. In a sample of 736 people with AIDS, more than 40% scored above a cutoff for significant depressive symptoms on a scale measuring depression (Fleishman & Fogel, 1994). The levels of psychological distress among individuals in this sample were lower in those who had high levels of social support from friends and family members.

The psychological effects of having an STD partly depend on the coping strategies used by the infected individual. In one study of individuals with AIDS, researchers identified three coping strategies individuals used after finding out they were infected with HIV (Fleishman & Fogel, 1994). These strategies include "avoidance coping," "positive coping," and "seeking social support" (see Table 5.3). Researchers found that individuals who used positive coping strategies experienced fewer depressive symptoms, whereas individuals who used avoidance coping or sought social support experienced greater depressive

TABLE 5.3 Coping Strategies Used by Individuals After Learning They Are HIV-Positive

POSITIVE COPING STRATEGY

1. Try to learn more about AIDS.
2. Tell yourself to accept it.
3. Think about people who were less fortunate than you.
4. Look on the bright side.
5. Make plans for the future.

AVOIDANCE COPING STRATEGY

1. Try to push it out of your mind.
2. Think about better times in the past.
3. Make yourself feel better by drinking or taking drugs.
4. Avoid being with people.
5. Go on as if nothing happened.
6. Keep your feelings to yourself.
7. Keep others from knowing how bad things are.
8. Let yourself feel so angry that you want to hit or smash something.

SEEKING SOCIAL SUPPORT COPING STRATEGY

1. Ask friends or relatives for advice.
2. Seek sympathy and understanding from friends.

Source: Fleishman & Fogel, 1994.

symptoms. Regarding the latter finding, researchers suggested that support seeking may be a response to, rather than a cause of, distress.

——————— THINK ABOUT IT ———————

If the health consequences for common STDs (such as chlamydia, gonorrhea, and human papilloma virus) were as serious for men as they are for women, do you think more men would insist on using condoms?

MODES OF TRANSMISSION, SYMPTOMS, AND TREATMENT FOR STDS

There are more than 25 sexually transmissible infectious diseases. In this section, we provide an overview of the more common and serious STDs.

Chlamydia

Chlamydia trachomatis (CT), also referred to simply as *chlamydia* (clah-MID-ee-uh), is a bacterium that can infect the genitals, eyes, and lungs. Chlamydia is the most frequently occurring STD on college campuses, and many health officials believe it is the most common sexually transmitted disease.

MODES OF TRANSMISSION CT is easily transmitted directly from person to person through sexual contact. The microorganisms are found most often in the urethra of men; the cervix, uterus, and Fallopian tubes of women; and in the rectum of both women and men. CT infections can also occur indirectly (through contact with a towel containing bacteria, for example).

Genital-to-eye transmission of the bacteria can also occur. If a person with a genital CT infection rubs his or her eye (or touches the eye of a partner) after touching his or her infected genitals, the bacteria can be transferred to the eye (and vice versa). In addition, an infant can get CT while passing through the cervix of its infected mother during delivery.

SYMPTOMS Chlamydia rarely shows obvious symptoms, which accounts for it being known as "the silent disease." About one in four infected men, and between 50 and 70% of infected women, experience no initial symptoms. Because women and men infected with CT usually do not know they have the disease, they infect new partners unknowingly, who then infect others unknowingly.

Although CT often has no symptoms, symptoms sometimes do occur. In men, symptoms include pus from the penis, sores on the penis, sore testes, or a bloody stool. In women, symptoms include low-back pain, pelvic pain, boils on the vaginal lips, or a bloody discharge. Symptoms in either sex may include sores on the tongue, sores on the fingers, low-grade fever, pain during urination, or frequent urge to urinate.

TREATMENTS Chlamydia can be effectively treated with antibiotics, such as tetracycline. Left untreated, chlamydia can lead to pelvic inflammatory disease, sterility, arthritis, blindness, miscarriage, and premature birth.

Gonorrhea

Also known as "the clap," "the whites," "morning drop," and "the drip," *gonorrhea* is a bacterial infection.

MODES OF TRANSMISSION   Individuals most often contract gonorrhea through sexual contact with someone who is carrying the gonococcus bacteria. Gonococci cannot live long outside the human body. Even though these bacteria can be cultured from a toilet seat, there are no documented cases of gonorrhea being transmitted in any way other than intimate physical contact. These bacteria thrive in warm, moist cavities, including the urinary tract, cervix, rectum, mouth, and throat. A pregnant woman can transmit gonorrhea during childbirth by causing an eye infection in the newborn.

SYMPTOMS   Although some infected men show no signs, 80% exhibit symptoms between 3 and 8 days after exposure. They begin to discharge a thick, white pus from the penis and start to feel pain or discomfort during urination. They may also have swollen lymph glands in the groin. Women are more likely to show no signs of the infection (70 to 80% have no symptoms), but when they do, the symptoms may include a discharge from the vagina, along with a burning sensation. More often, a woman becomes aware of gonorrhea only after she feels extreme discomfort, which is usually a result of the untreated infection traveling up into her uterus and Fallopian tubes.

TREATMENTS   Gonorrhea is treated with antibiotics. A major problem with new cases of gonorrhea is that the emergence of new strains of the bacteria are resistant to penicillin and tetracycline. The current recommended treatment for gonorrhea is Ceftriaxone (Noris, 1995).

Undetected and untreated gonorrhea is dangerous. Inflammation of the Fallopian tubes resulting from gonorrhea may cause infertility or ectopic pregnancies in women. Pregnant women could also have a miscarriage or a premature or stillborn infant. Both men and women could develop meningitis (inflammation of the tissues surrounding the brain and spinal column), arthritis, and sterility. In men, the urethra can become blocked, necessitating frequent visits to a physician to clear the passage for urination.

Human Papilloma Virus (HPV) or Genital Warts

There are more than 60 types of *human papilloma virus (HPV)*. More than a dozen of these can cause warts (called *genital warts* or *condyloma*) or more subtle signs of infection in the genital tract.

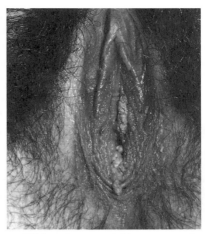

In some cases, HPV produces no visible symptoms. In other cases, HPV produces visible warts on the genital region.

MODES OF TRANSMISSION   HPV can be transmitted through vaginal or rectal intercourse and through fellatio and cunnilingus. It is also possible for HPV to be transmitted from an infected pregnant woman to her infant.

SYMPTOMS   Human papilloma virus infects the skin's top layers. It can remain inactive for months or years before any obvious signs of infection appear. Often, small to large warts or bumplike growths appear within 3 to 6 months after exposure. Warts may be pink or red and may appear in clusters or alone. In women, genital warts most commonly develop on the vulva, in the vagina, or on the cervix. They can also appear on or near the anus. In men, the warts appear most often on the penis, but can appear on the scrotum, the anus, or within the rectum. Although rare, HPV also can produce warts in areas of the mouths of both sexes.

Only one in three cases of HPV infection is symptomatic by the presence of warts; thus many infected individuals remain undiagnosed and may unknowingly transmit the infection to others (Tobin, 1997). The seriousness of HPV is that some strains seem to lead to cervical cancer.

TREATMENTS   Health care providers disagree about the efficacy of treating HPV when there are no detectable warts. When the warts can be seen by visual inspection or by colposcope, however, various treatments may be recommended depending on the number of warts and their location, the availability of equipment, the training of health care providers, and the preferences of the patient. Treatment options for removing warts include cryotherapy (freezing), surgical removal, laser surgery, cauterization (burning), and topical application of chemicals such as podophyllin.

Treatment of warts destroys some infected cells, but not all of them. HPV is present in a wider area of skin other than just the precise wart location; therefore, recurrence of genital warts is not uncommon, even after treatment. Patients are advised to schedule follow-up visits with their health care practitioners, check themselves regularly for visible warts, and talk with their sexual partners about using condoms to reduce the risk of transmitting the infection.

Genital Herpes

The term "herpes" refers to more than 50 related viruses. One type of herpes virus is *herpes simplex virus type 2 (HSV-2)*, also known as *genital herpes*. Another type of herpes, known as *herpes simplex virus type 1 (HSV-1)*, or *lip herpes*, originates in the mouth.

Because of the increase in fellatio and cunnilingus, HSV-1 herpes can be found in the genitals, and HSV-2 can be found on the lips.

One in five Americans age 12 or older carries the genital herpes virus—a 30% increase since the late 1970s. About 90% of these individuals do not know they are infected (Fleming et al., 1997).

MODES OF TRANSMISSION The herpes virus is spread by direct skin-to-skin contact, such as kissing and oral, vaginal, or anal sex with an infected individual. Pregnant women can transmit the herpes virus to their newborn infants, causing brain damage or death. Herpes may also be spread from one part of the body to another by touching the infected area and then touching another area of the body. For example, touching a herpes infection and then rubbing one's eye can result in a herpes infection of the eye (ocular herpes), which could potentially lead to blindness.

Some people believe that herpes can only be spread when there are obvious signs or symptoms of the infection. However, herpes may be active without causing signs or symptoms. Herpes is often transmitted by people who are unaware that they are infected and by people who do not realize that their herpes infection is in its active phase. One woman described her experience contracting herpes:

I had contracted herpes from a partner who had a case of "unrecognized" herpes—never a severe or noticeable outbreak, never any past problems with this condition. Being a sexually cautious person—I was a virgin at the time—I was floored when my symptoms showed up, much to the surprise of my partner as well. ("Personal Perspectives," 1997, p. 4)

SYMPTOMS When a person is first infected with herpes, symptoms usually appear within two weeks after exposure. The initial symptoms of oral herpes infection often include small pimples or blisters ("cold sores" or "fever blisters") on the mouth or face. Genital herpes produces sores in the genital areas of women and men, and skin lesions may appear on the thigh or buttocks. These sores, resembling blisters or pimples, eventually crust over and scab. In the two to four weeks it takes for herpes sores to heal, some people experience a second outbreak of lesions, and some will have flulike symptoms including fever, aches, and swollen glands.

After the symptoms of genital herpes subside (the sores dry up, scab over, and disappear, and the infected person feels well again), the virus settles in the nerve cells in the spinal column. HSV-2 causes repeated outbreaks in about one-third of those who are infected.

Stress, menstruation, sunburn, fatigue, and the presence of other infections seem to be related to the reappearance of herpes symptoms. Although such recurrences are usually milder and of shorter duration than the initial outbreak, the resurfacing of the symptoms can occur throughout a person's life.

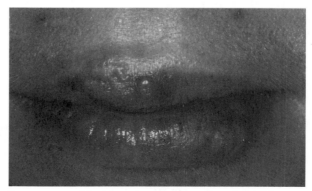

One symptom of lip herpes is an eruption of small painful blisters or sores in the mouth area.

Symptomatic recurrences of genital herpes average one per year. Symptomatic recurrences of oral herpes typically occur four or five times per year.

The herpes virus is most contagious when a person has visible herpes sores. However, infected people may have a mild recurrence, yet be unaware that they are contagious. Aside from visible sores, symptoms such as itching, burning, or tingling sensations at the sore site, also indicate that a person is contagious. Some infected individuals may not experience any symptoms of herpes recurrence, yet may still be at risk for transmitting the virus to their partners.

TREATMENTS   Although there is no cure for the herpes virus, the symptoms may be treated with prescription ointments such as Zovirax™ (acyclovir) or Immu-Vir™. These ointments, applied directly on the sores, help to relieve pain, speed healing, and reduce the amount of time that live viruses are present in the sores. Prescription medication taken in capsule form (acyclovir, valacyclovir, and famciclovir) is also used to speed healing and reduce the rate of recurring episodes of genital herpes. In 1997 the Food and Drug Administration (FDA) approved the marketing of generic versions of Glaxo Wellcome's pioneering drug for herpes treatment, Zovirax brand acyclovir. Generic acyclovir, now available at retail pharmacies, costs about half of the price of Zovirax. A year's supply of generic acyclovir costs about $700; the same supply of Zovirax costs about $1500 ("Treatment Update," 1997). It is also helpful to keep the sores clean and dry, take hot sitz baths three times a day, and wear loose-fitting cotton underwear to enhance air circulation. Proper nutrition, adequate sleep and exercise, and avoidance of physical or mental stress help people better cope with recurrences.

Researchers are making progress toward developing a vaccine to prevent herpes infection. A new type of herpes vaccine is now being tested in human clinical trials ("Treatment Update," 1997). Pregnant women with herpes can have cesarean deliveries to prevent exposure of newborns to the herpes virus.

Herpes cold sores may be treated with topical applications of penciclovir cream. Sold under the name Denavir,® this prescription medication is the first antiviral cream approved in the United States for cold sores ("New Treatment for Cold Sores," 1997).

Syphilis

Syphilis is a sexually transmissible disease caused by bacteria. In the late 1980s and early 1990s, syphilis rates in the United States increased dramatically, causing an increase in concern about this disease.

MODES OF TRANSMISSION   Syphilis is transmitted through kissing or having genital contact with an infected individual. The spirochete bacteria enter the body through mucous membranes that line various body openings, such as the inside of the cheek, the vagina, and the urethra of the penis. Syphilis can also be transmitted from an infected pregnant woman to her unborn baby.

SYMPTOMS   Syphilis progresses through identifiable stages. Each of these stages—primary, secondary, latent, and tertiary—involves different symptoms.

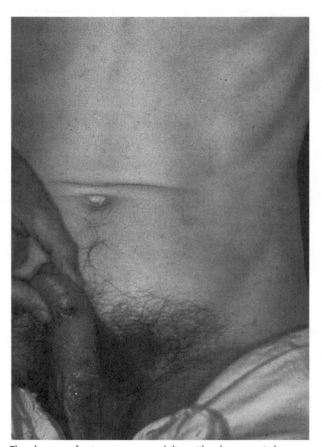

The chancre of primary-stage syphilis neither hurts nor itches and, if left untreated, will disappear in 3 to 5 weeks. However, the syphilis bacteria are still present and doing great harm.

In stage one (primary-stage syphilis), a small sore or chancre will appear at the site of infection between 10 and 90 days after exposure. The chancre, which appears on the tip of the man's penis, in the labia or cervix of the woman, or in either partner's mouth or rectum, neither hurts nor itches and, if left untreated, will disappear in 3 to 5 weeks. The disappearance leads infected people to believe that they are cured (this is one of the tricky aspects of syphilis). In reality, the disease is still present and doing great harm, even though there are no visible symptoms.

During the second stage (secondary-stage syphilis), beginning from 2 to 12 weeks after the chancre has disappeared, other signs of syphilis may become evident including a rash all over the body or on the hands or feet. Syphilis has been called "the great imitator" because it mimics so many other diseases (mononucleosis, cancer, and psoriasis, for example). Welts and swelling of the lymph nodes can also occur, as well as fever, headaches, sore throat, and hair loss. Whatever the symptoms, they too will disappear without treatment, perhaps causing the person to again believe that nothing is wrong.

Following the secondary stage is the latency stage, during which there are no symptoms and the person is not infectious. However, the spirochetes are still in the body and can attack any organ at any time.

Tertiary syphilis—the third stage—can cause serious disability or even death. Heart disease, blindness, brain damage, loss of bowel and bladder control, difficulty in walking, and erectile dysfunction can result.

TREATMENTS Treatment for syphilis is similar to that for gonorrhea. Penicillin or other antibiotics are effective. Infected persons treated in the early stages can be completely cured with no ill effects. If the syphilis has progressed into the tertiary stage, however, damage that has been done cannot be repaired.

Human Immunodeficiency Virus and Acquired Immunodeficiency Syndrome

Human immunodeficiency virus (HIV) attacks the white blood cells (T-lymphocytes) in human blood, and causes AIDS. *AIDS (acquired immunodeficiency syndrome)* is characterized by a breakdown of the body's immune system that makes individuals vulnerable to a variety of opportunistic diseases. Before 1993, a diagnosis of AIDS was made only when an HIV-infected individual developed one of more than twenty serious illnesses delineated by the Centers for

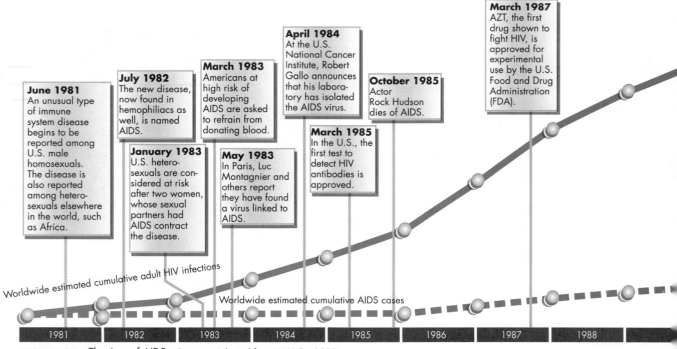

June 1981
An unusual type of immune system disease begins to be reported among U.S. male homosexuals. The disease is also reported among heterosexuals elsewhere in the world, such as Africa.

July 1982
The new disease, now found in hemophiliacs as well, is named AIDS.

January 1983
U.S. heterosexuals are considered at risk after two women, whose sexual partners had AIDS contract the disease.

March 1983
Americans at high risk of developing AIDS are asked to refrain from donating blood.

May 1983
In Paris, Luc Montagnier and others report they have found a virus linked to AIDS.

April 1984
At the U.S. National Cancer Institute, Robert Gallo announces that his laboratory has isolated the AIDS virus.

March 1985
In the U.S., the first test to detect HIV antibodies is approved.

October 1985
Actor Rock Hudson dies of AIDS.

March 1987
AZT, the first drug shown to fight HIV, is approved for experimental use by the U.S. Food and Drug Administration (FDA).

Worldwide estimated cumulative adult HIV infections

Worldwide estimated cumulative AIDS cases

1981 1982 1983 1984 1985 1986 1987 1988

FIGURE 5.2 The Age of AIDS **Source:** Adapted from W.H.O., 1992.

Disease Control and Prevention (CDC), such as *Pneumocystis carinii* pneumonia, pulmonary tuberculosis, cervical cancer, or Kaposi's sarcoma (a form of cancer). Since 1993, the definition of AIDS has been expanded to include anyone with HIV whose immune system is severely impaired, as indicated by a T-cell (or CD4 cell) count of less than 200 cells per cubic millimeter of blood. T-cell counts in healthy people not infected with HIV range from 800 to 1200 per cubic millimeter of blood.

Not all people who are HIV-infected progress to AIDS. About 3% are what is referred to as long-term nonprogressors—people who have been infected but have not suffered any apparent damage to their immune systems in 20 years (Gorman, 1996).

MODES OF TRANSMISSION Transmission of HIV infection is influenced by the stage of the disease in the infected partner. HIV is more infectious in the early stages and again in the later stages, after AIDS symptoms have started to appear (Pinkerton & Abramson, 1997). The human immunodeficiency virus can be transmitted in various ways.

HIV-attacks white blood cells. T-cells

mid-1996
25.5 million cumulative HIV infections

1992
12 million to 14 million worldwide

October 1997
Researchers announced they have identified a molecule (called a chemokine) that prevents HIV from infecting all cell types. The discovery offers hope for developing new HIV treatments.

September 1997
New HIV drug "cocktails" shown to be less effective against HIV infection than previously thought because HIV is developing a resistance to the drugs.

July 1995
The CDC published recommendations that all pregnant women receive HIV counseling and undergo voluntary HIV testing.

December 1995
The FDA approved use of saquinavir—the first of a new class of drugs called "protease inhibitors" used to slow the growth of HIV.

February 1994
A landmark study demonstrated that HIV-infected pregnant women can reduce the risk of transmitting HIV to their fetus by taking AZT during pregnancy. Shortly after, the National Institute of Allergies and Infectious Diseases recommended that all HIV-infected pregnant women receive AZT treatment.

October 1991
Basketball player Magic Johnson announces that he is infected with HIV.

May 1992
Montagnier and Gallo agree that the viruses they found were the same.

October 1994
The National Institute of Allergies and Infectious Diseases announced a new test that measures HIV viral load, allowing doctors to better assess the effectiveness of various drugs in treating HIV patients.

October 1991
FDA approves anti-AIDS drug, ddI.

June 1992
FDA approves a third drug, ddc.

June 1996
The FDA approved nevirapine—the first of a new class of drugs called "non-nucleosides" that, like protease inhibitors, slows the growth of HIV (each class of HIV drugs attacks the virus in a different stage in its replication cycle).

April 1990
Hemophiliac Ryan White, 18, dies of AIDS.

Millions — 7, 6, 5, 4, 3, 2, 1, 0

989   1990   1991   1992   1993   1994   1995   1996   1997

1. *Sexual contact.* HIV is found in several body fluids of infected individuals, including blood, semen, and possibly vaginal secretions. During sexual contact with an infected individual, the virus enters a person's bloodstream through the rectum, vagina, penis (the uncircumcised penis is at greater risk because of the greater retention of the partner's fluids), and possibly the mouth during oral sex. Saliva, sweat, and tears are not body fluids through which HIV is transmitted. Although the proportion of U.S. adult and adolescent AIDS cases involving men who have sex with men has declined from 53% in 1995 to 47% in 1997, men who have sex with men still account for the largest proportion of reported AIDS cases (Centers for Disease Control, 1997).

2. *Intravenous drug use.* Drug users who are infected with HIV can transmit the virus to other drug users with whom they share needles, syringes, and other drug-related implements.

3. *Blood transfusion.* HIV can be transmitted by receiving HIV-infected blood or blood products. Currently, all blood donors are screened, and blood is not accepted from high-risk individuals. Blood that is accepted from donors is tested for the presence of HIV. However, prior to 1985, donor blood was not tested for HIV. Individuals who received blood or blood products prior to 1985 may have been infected with HIV.

4. *Mother-child transmission of HIV.* A pregnant woman infected with HIV can infect her unborn child. Studies suggest that between 13 and 30 percent of infants born to HIV-infected women become infected during pregnancy or delivery (Bauman, 1997). However, azidothymidine (AZT) taken by the mother twelve weeks before birth seems to reduce by two-thirds the transmission of HIV by the mother (Laurence, 1994). Although rare, HIV can be transmitted through breastfeeding (Phair & Chadwick, 1992). It is not the breast milk, but the blood that can result from the baby's chewing on the mother's nipple, that can transmit HIV.

5. *Organ or tissue transplants and donor semen.* Receiving transplant organs and tissues, as well as receiving semen for artificial insemination, could involve risk of contracting HIV if the donors have not been tested for HIV. Such testing is essential, and recipients should insist on knowing the HIV status of the organ, tissue, or semen donor.

6. *Occupational transmission of HIV.* Certain occupational workers regularly come into contact with human blood, and are therefore susceptible to occupational transmission of HIV. Health care workers (such as nurses and physicians), laboratory technicians, morgue technicians, rescue workers, dentists, police officers, prison guards, and other individuals who are likely to come into contact with bleeding individuals should use protection such as latex gloves before making physical contact with an injured or bleeding individual. Latex gloves also should be used by lay persons when coming in contact with another person's blood, and should be part of every first-aid kit.

NATIONAL DATA

As of June 1997, the following data were documented.

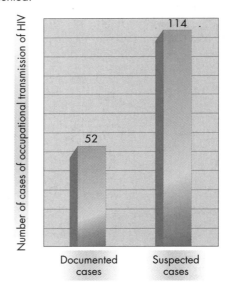

Source: Centers for Disease Control and Prevention, 1997.

SYMPTOMS   HIV/AIDS is known as a spectrum illness—although everyone infected with HIV has the same disease, they may have different symptoms at different stages. Some HIV-infected individuals display no symptoms at all for many years after exposure. Unless they are tested for HIV, many HIV-infected individuals don't know they are infected. When symptoms do appear, they may include swollen lymph glands, oral thrush (a white coating or spotting in the mouth), and memory problems. If full-blown AIDS develops, severe immune system breakdown can lead to the onset of illnesses such as *Pneumocystis carinii* pneumonia, pulmonary tuberculosis, cervical cancer, and Kaposi's sarcoma (a form of cancer).

TREATMENTS   Presently, there is no cure for HIV/AIDS and no vaccine to prevent infection. Treatments are available to inhibit HIV growth and to fight or prevent opportunistic diseases. Drugs used to slow HIV growth include azidothymidine (AZT), dideoxyinosine (DDI), protease inhibitors, and non-nucleosides. These drugs do not cure HIV, but they do slow the progression of the disease and increase survival rates in patients. About 25 other drugs are used to treat and prevent opportunistic diseases (such as pneumonia) associated with AIDS. Some drugs are used to treat HIV-infected mothers to reduce the risk of transmitting HIV to their infants.

A new "morning after" treatment has also been developed to prevent HIV infection after exposure to the virus. A study of health care workers who were exposed to HIV found that treatment with antiretroviral drugs (such as zidovudine) after exposure decreases the odds of HIV infection by 79% (Katz & Gerberding, 1997). The drug treatment must begin within 72 hours after exposure to HIV and continues for 4 weeks. Drugs, laboratory monitoring, and office visits for this postexposure treatment can cost between $400 and $800. The availability of HIV postexposure treatment raises some serious concerns. It may increase resistance to antiretroviral drugs and "may lead people to have unsafe sexual relations in the belief that they will be protected from infection if they begin treatment after the exposure" (Katz & Gerberding, 1997, p. 1098). An increase in high-risk behavior may lead to an increase in HIV infection rates, as postexposure treatment reduces, rather than eliminates the risk of becoming HIV-infected. Nevertheless, some clinicians are prescribing postexposure HIV treatment to individuals who are exposed through sexual contact. The *AIDS/HIV Treatment Directory,* published quarterly by the American Foundation for AIDS Research, summarizes recent drug treatment developments.

Treatment for HIV and AIDS also includes adopting lifestyle habits that promote well-being: a balanced diet, ample rest, regular exercise, and relaxation. According to the U.S. Centers for Disease Control,

people with AIDS are 20 times more likely to contract salmonella, a contaminant of undercooked poultry and eggs, and 200 to 300 times more likely to develop listeria infections from poultry, meat, and raw fish. Therefore, AIDS patients should eat only well-done meats, fish, and eggs. It is also important for persons with HIV/AIDS to avoid stressors on the immune system, such as tobacco, recreational drugs, and other STDs. Establishing a supportive network of family and friends is also essential in managing the stress of having HIV/AIDS.

Hepatitis B

Hepatitis B is an inflammatory disease of the liver caused by a virus. Other forms of hepatitis viruses include types A, C, D, and E.

MODES OF TRANSMISSION   Hepatitis B (HBV) is most often transmitted through vaginal, oral, or anal sexual contact with an infected individual. Infection may also occur from transfusions of contaminated blood or from sharing contaminated personal items, such as razors or needles (used for steroid injections, drug use, body piercing, or tattoos). Pregnant women may also transmit hepatitis B to their newborns.

SYMPTOMS   The symptoms of hepatitis B infection, which take 2 to 6 months to appear, include skin rash, muscle and joint pain, fatigue, loss of appetite, nausea and vomiting, headache, fever, dark urine, jaundice, and liver enlargement and tenderness.

TREATMENTS   There is no treatment for curing hepatitis B; people usually recover naturally and develop immunity to future infection. While the disease is running its course, health care professionals recommend rest, a high-protein diet with lots of fluids, and the avoidance of alcohol and drugs that may stress the liver. As many as 10% of those infected with hepatitis B become carriers of the virus for several years or even their lifetime. Some hepatitis B infections lead to cirrhosis of the liver or liver cancer.

Currently, the only effective vaccine for prevention of an STD is the hepatitis B vaccine. The Centers for Disease Control and Prevention recommend that all adolescents and young adults receive a hepatitis B vaccination. The vaccine is given in the arm in three separate doses.

Nongonococcal Urethritis (NGU)

Nongonococcal urethritis (NGU) is an infection of the urethra—the tube that carries urine from the bladder. NGU is caused by several different sexually transmitted organisms. The most common and most serious organism that causes NGU is chlamydia.

MODES OF TRANSMISSION   Organisms that cause nongonococcal urethritis are transmitted through sexual contact and from mother to newborn. Because individuals with NGU are often asymptomatic, they unknowingly transmit infection to their partners.

SYMPTOMS   In men, symptoms of NGU include penile discharge, burning during urination, and burning or itching around the opening of the penis. Some men will experience no symptoms, or have symptoms so mild they go unnoticed. In women, symptoms of NGU may include vaginal discharge, burning during urination, abdominal pain, bleeding between periods, and fever. Many infected women show no symptoms.

TREATMENTS   Once identified, NGU is treated with tetracycline or other antibiotics. Even when symptoms are mild or nonexistent, untreated NGU can cause damage to the reproductive organs and lead to infertility, result in miscarriages, and cause eye, ear, and lung infections in newborns.

Chancroid

Also known as "soft chancre," *chancroid* is most common in tropical countries. In the United States, chancroid is predominantly seen among immigrants or U.S. citizens who travel to developing countries.

MODES OF TRANSMISSION   Chancroid is transmitted through either sexual contact with the chancroid ulcer or discharge from infected local lymph glands.

SYMPTOMS   Two to five days after exposure, a small papule forms at the site of contact. This lesion develops into an ulcer that exudes pus, bleeds easily, and is very painful. Local lymph glands enlarge, become inflamed, and may drip pus. The difference between a chancroid and a chancre is that the former is soft and painful.

TREATMENTS   Chancroid is treated with antibiotics such as erythromycin or Ceftriaxone.

Vaginitis

Two types of *vaginitis,* or vaginal infection, include trichomoniasis and candidiasis. Most women get vaginitis at some time in their lives, and many do not develop it from sexual contact.

Vaginal infection may be caused by bacteria from the rectum being transferred to the vagina. This can result from improper hygiene, or from anal intercourse or manipulation combined with vaginal intercourse or manipulation. Vaginal infection may also result from foreign objects, such as tampons and diaphragms, being left in the vagina too long. ☮Lesbians can transmit vaginal infections between partners through direct vulva-to-vulva contact or hand-to-vulva contact.☮

TRICHOMONIASIS   Although some infected women show no symptoms, *trichomoniasis* is usually characterized by a foul-smelling, thin, frothy discharge that may be green, yellow, gray, or white and causes an irritating rash in the vulva. The inner thighs may also become irritated if the discharge is allowed to come in contact with the skin. Left untreated, the irritation continues and causes pain during intercourse. The woman may also infect her male partner, who may experience irritation and pain during intercourse.

Diagnosis is made by examining mucus from the vagina or penis under a microscope. Since trichomoniasis may occur with syphilis or gonorrhea, a specific diagnosis is essential. Antibiotics, such as metronidazole (Flagyl), are usually effective in treating trichomoniasis. Because the partner may harbor trichomoniasis organisms without symptoms, both the woman and her sexual partner should be treated.

CANDIDIASIS   *Candidiasis,* also known as monilia and fungus, is a yeast infection caused by *Candida albicans.* Candidiasis tends to occur in women during pregnancy, when they are on oral contraceptives, or when they have poor resistance to disease. Symptoms of candidiasis include vaginal irritation, itching, thick cottage cheeselike discharge, and pain during intercourse. Treatment involves antifungal suppositories or creams to be inserted into the vagina. Antibiotics are not effective because candida are not bacteria.

Pubic Lice

Pubic lice, also called "crabs," attach themselves to the base of coarse pubic hair and suck blood from the victim. Their biting the skin to release the blood causes severe itching. Pubic lice are caught from an infected person, often through sexual contact, and also may be transmitted by contact with toilet seats, clothing, and bedding that harbor the creatures. Applications of gamma benzene hexachloride, sold under the brand name of Kwell, will usually kill the lice within 24 hours.

Scabies

Scabies results from a parasite, *Sarcoptes scabiei,* that penetrates the skin and lays eggs. The larvae of these eggs burrow tunnels under the skin and cause intense itching. Although genitals are a prime target for the mites, the groin, buttocks, breasts, and knees may also be infested with them. Since the itching is intense, scabies sufferers tend to scratch the affected area, which may result in bleeding and spreading the scabies. Treatment includes applying gamma benzene hexachloride (Kwell) or crotamiton (Eurax) and a thorough cleaning of self, clothing, and bedding.

--- **THINK ABOUT IT** ---

Although it is important to recognize STD symptoms, keep in mind that many individuals infected with an STD experience no symptoms. According to the United Nations Population Fund, about half of all infected women worldwide may experience no symptoms (*1997 UNFPA Report,* 1997).

PREVENTION AND CONTROL OF SEXUALLY TRANSMISSIBLE DISEASES

Due to the serious health consequences of AIDS, STD prevention and control efforts in recent years have largely focused on preventing transmission of HIV. However, given the potentially serious health consequences of other STDs—including the increased susceptibility to HIV infection—prevention and control of all STDs is warranted. Researchers have found that HIV-infected men who have another STD have a higher concentration of HIV in their semen compared to HIV-infected men who do not have a concurrent STD. In one study, the concentration of HIV in the semen of HIV-infected men was eight times higher in men who had another STD than in those who did not have a concurrent STD (Cohen, et al., 1997). Thus, the risk of HIV transmission via semen is increased by

concurrent infection with a sexually transmitted disease. Ulcerations, lesions, or sores caused by many sexually transmitted diseases provide a site for HIV to enter the bloodstream. Because STDs facilitate transmission of HIV, efforts to prevent, detect, and treat STDs may help reduce HIV transmission. It is estimated, for example, that treating or preventing 100 cases of syphilis among high-risk groups would prevent 1200 HIV infections during a 10-year period (Committee on Prevention and Control of STDs, 1997). Efforts to prevent and control STDs involve modification of high-risk behaviors, public and private sexual health care delivery, syringe-exchange programs, and the use of computer technology.

Modification of High-Risk Sexual Behavior

The most reliable ways to avoid getting a sexually transmitted disease is to avoid injecting drugs and avoid sexual contact. In a nationwide study of sex education teachers, abstinence was one of the most commonly cited goals of sex education (Forrest & Silverman, 1989). Yet, the majority of the U.S. population begins engaging in sexual intercourse during their teenage years.

Abstinence from sexual intercourse does not mean that a person is immune from acquiring an STD. Even virgins are at risk for STDs. A study of over 2000 students in grades 9 through 12 found that 47% reported they were virgins (Schuster, Bell, & Kanouse, 1996). However, of those who were virgins, 9%, 10% and 1% reported they had engaged in fellatio with ejaculation, cunnilingus, and anal sex, respectively. Most (86%) of those who engaged in fellatio reported that they never used a condom. The researchers noted that "although remaining a virgin all but eliminates the possibility of becoming pregnant, activities such as fellatio, cunnilingus, and anal intercourse can spread sexually transmitted diseases" (Schuster et al., 1996, p. 1570).

Individuals (including virgins) who are sexually active may reduce their risks of acquiring an STD by having sexual contact only with one partner who is not infected, who is monogamous, and who does not inject drugs. Rather than rush into sexual relationships, allow time to build trusting, caring, and honest relationships in which you can share your sexual histories. Physical intimacy and pleasure may be achieved by practicing *outercourse*—activities that do

THE UCLA MULTIDIMENSIONAL CONDOM ATTITUDES SCALE

Indicate your level of agreement with each of the following items by writing a number from 1 to 7 next to each item, based on the following answer key.

1	2	3	4	5	6	7
Very Strongly Disagree	Strongly Disagree	Disagree Slightly	Neither Agree Nor Disagree	Agree Slightly	Agree Strongly	Agree Very Strongly

Reliability and Effectiveness

1. Condoms are an effective method of birth control. _____

2. Condoms are an effective method of preventing the spread of AIDS and other sexually transmitted diseases. _____

3. I think condoms are an excellent means of contraception. _____

4. Condoms are unreliable. _____

5. Condoms do not offer reliable protection. _____

Pleasure

6. The use of condoms can make sex more stimulating. _____

7. Condoms ruin the sex act. _____

8. Condoms are uncomfortable for both partners. _____

9. Condoms are a lot of fun. _____

10. Use of a condom is an interruption of foreplay. _____

Identity Stigma

11. Men who suggest using a condom are really boring. _____

12. If a couple is about to have sex and the man suggests using a condom, it is less likely that they will have sex. _____

13. Women think men who use condoms are jerks. _____

14. A woman who suggests using a condom does not trust her partner. _____

Embarrassment About Negotiation and Use

15. When I suggest using a condom, I am almost always embarrassed. _____

16. It is really hard to bring up the issue of using condoms to my partner. _____

17. It is easy to suggest to my partner that we use a condom. _____

18. I'm comfortable talking about condoms with my partner. _____

19. I never know what to say when my partner and I need to talk about condoms or other protection. _____

Embarrassment About Purchase

20. It is very embarrassing to buy condoms. _____

21. When I need condoms I often dread having to get them. _____

22. I don't think that buying condoms is awkward. _____

23. It would be embarrassing to be seen buying condoms in a store. _____

24. I always feel really uncomfortable when I buy condoms. _____

Scoring: Reverse-score the following items: 4, 7, 8, 10, 11, 12, 13, 14, 15, 16, 19, 20, 21, 23, 24. To reverse-score, make the following changes in your answers: 1 = 7; 2 = 6; 3 = 5; 4 = 4 (no change); 5 = 3; 6 = 2; 7 = 1.

After reversing the scores of the items indicated, compute a mean (average) score for each of the scale's subsections. The higher the score, the more positive your attitudes toward condoms. You might pencil your mean scores in the spaces provided and compare them with those obtained in a study of 239 students ages 15 to 35 (mean age = 19) (Helweg-Larsen & Collins, 1994).

Continued on following page.

Subsection	Mean Score ·	Men	Women
1. Reliability and Effctiveness (measures attitudes toward the reliability and effectiveness of condoms)	_____	5.4	5.3
2. Pleasure (measures the pleasure associated with condom use)	_____	4.1	4.3
3. Identity Stigma (measures the stigma attached to being a condom user)	_____	5.6	6.2
4. Embarrassment About Negotiation and Use (measures the embarrassment associated with the negotiation and use of condoms)	_____	4.8	4.8
5. Embarrassment About Purchase (measures the embarrassment associated with the purchase of condoms)	_____	4.3	3.5*

Discussion: After analyzing the scores of 239 students on the Multidimensional Condom Attitudes Scale, researchers found that overall, men were less embarrassed about purchasing condoms than women, whereas women were more positive about issues related to identity stigma. (Helweg-Larsen & Collins, 1994).

From "The UCLA Multidimensional Condom Attitudes Scale: Documenting the Complex Determinants of Condom Use in College Students," by M. Helweg-Larsen & B.E. Collins, 1994, *Health Psychology*, *13*(3), 224–237. Copyright © 1994 by the American Psychological Association. Reprinted by permission of the author.

not involve exposing a partner to blood, semen, or vaginal secretions. Outercourse includes hugging, cuddling, masturbating, fantasizing, massage, and body-to-body rubbing with clothes on. Also, carefully inspect your partner's genitals before sexual contact, as well as your own. Although some STDs produce no visible signs, it is possible to see herpes blisters, chancres, genital warts, and rashes. If you notice anything unusual about your partner's genitals (or your own), abstain from sexual contact and seek a medical examination. Showering or washing the genital area with soap and water both before and after sexual activity is also helpful in preventing infections. And finally, use of condoms and dental dams during vaginal and anal intercourse, fellatio, and cunnilingus are also important. Before reading further, you may want to assess your attitudes toward condoms (see Self-Assessment).

Studies have shown that consistent, correct condom use reduces the overall risk of acquiring and transmitting HIV and other STDs. However, condoms do not offer a 100% guarantee against the transmission of STDs for a variety of reasons. First, condoms are not always used consistently and correctly. Using a condom "most of the time" or "almost always" is not the same as using one every time a person engages in vaginal or anal intercourse or fellatio. It is also important to use a condom correctly (see Table 5.4 on correct condom use). Even when used correctly, condom breakage and slippage may still occur.

NATIONAL DATA

Data from the 1991 follow-up survey of the National Survey of Adolescent Males (NSAM) were collected from 1676 young men aged 17–22. Of those men using condoms in the previous 12 months, 23% experienced at least one condom break. Of all condoms used, 2.5% broke.

Source: Lindberg, Sonenstein, Ku, & Levine, 1997.

The NSAM survey found that experience with condoms and knowledge about them seemed to reduce the risk of condom breakage. Unfortunately, only about half of the men who had used condoms reported having recent sex education. Since condom failure

TABLE 5.4 Correct Condom Use

1. Use only condoms that are made in the United States or Japan. Condoms that are made in other countries may not have been tested for effectiveness.

2. Check the expiration date of the condom. Do not use condoms that have passed the expiration date.

3. Store condoms in a cool, dry place. Do not keep condoms in wallet or car, where they can become hot, and do not keep them in the refrigerator.

4. Use only latex or polyurethane condoms for fellatio and vaginal or anal intercourse. Natural lamb-skin condoms are an ineffective barrier against HIV.

5. Use condoms with a reservoir tip, or pinch $\frac{1}{2}$" at the tip of the condom to collect the semen.

6. Unroll the condom slowly and carefully onto the erect penis before the first contact of penis to vagina, anus, or mouth.

7. Make sure there is no air trapped inside the condom. (If there is, it could cause breakage.) Have a spare condom available in case you find a tear or a hole in the one you are using.

8. Use only water-based lubricants, such as K-Y™ or other personal lubricants. Products containing oil, such as vaseline, baby oil, and lotions, can destroy latex products.

9. Unless you are allergic to spermicides, use condoms that contain the spermicide Nonoxynol-9, or put a drop of spermicide inside the tip of the condom. For added protection, use an application of spermicide in the vagina or anus before intercourse in addition to the use of condoms. Some studies have found Nonoxynol-9 to be effective in killing HIV and other STDs.

10. Remove the penis from the partner immediately after ejaculation, before the penis loses its erection. Hold the condom securely on the base of the penis while withdrawing it from the partner, and be careful not to spill the contents.

11. Never reuse a condom.

reduces confidence in the method, education about how to respond to breakage (insert spermicide into the vagina or wash the penis and vulva with soap and water, and seek postcoital contraception), and how to prevent it, may encourage condom use (Lindberg, et al., 1997).

Condoms may be less effective when used during anal intercourse than vaginal intercourse because condom breakage and slippage rates may be higher. In a review of the literature on condom slippage and breakage during anal intercourse, Silverman and Gross (1997) reported that in retrospective surveys, in which participants are asked to recall the number of condoms used during a particular period and the number that had failed during anal intercourse, rates of condom breakage ranged from 0.5% to 6% and slippage rates ranged from 3.8% to 5%. In prospective studies, in which participants were followed over a period of time to elicit condom use, slippage, and breakage experience, slippage rates ranged from 0% to 33% and breakage rates ranged from 0% to 32%. Finally, condoms do not protect against all STDs because some STD infections, such as HPV and herpes, can occur on the testicles, around the anus, and in other areas that are not protected by the condom.

Research on condom use has identified a number of factors that influence whether or not an individual uses condoms. These factors include the following:

- Perceived susceptibility (the degree to which an individual feels he or she is at risk for contracting an STD)
- Perceived seriousness of STDs (the degree to which an individual views STDs as having severe or serious consequences)
- Belief that using condoms will reduce the risk of STDs
- Belief that the benefits of using condoms will outweigh any of the costs (inconvenience, decreased pleasure, expense, and so on)
- Sense of *self-efficacy* regarding condom use; that is, the person's belief that he or she has the skills and abilities necessary to use condoms in a variety of circumstances in the face of various obstacles, such as a reluctant or unwilling partner
- A person's intention to use condoms
- A person's perception of the degree to which social norms expect condom use

SHOULD CONDOMS BE AVAILABLE IN HIGH SCHOOLS?

By the time they reach the 12th grade, the majority of U.S. students have engaged in sexual intercourse. Unprotected teenage sexual activity contributes to teenage pregnancy and the high rate of STDs among adolescents, who constitute one-quarter of the 12 million new STD cases each year. School programs that provide condoms are designed to reduce teenage pregnancy and the spread of STDs by increasing condom use by reducing teenagers' embarrassment when buying condoms, eliminating the cost, and improving access. An evaluation of a small sample of students from Philadelphia high schools, nine of which implemented health resource drop-in centers (offering reproductive health information, condoms, and general health referrals), showed encouraging trends toward a decline in unprotected intercourse in schools making high use of the clinics (Furstenberg, Geitz, Teitler, & Weiss, 1997).

In a survey of 431 U.S. schools that have condom availability programs in place, nearly all offered condoms as part of a more comprehensive program involving other components such as counseling, sex education, or HIV education (Kirby & Brown, 1996). In 81% of the schools in this survey, either active or passive parental consent was required before a student could obtain a condom. Ten percent of schools required active consent, in which students obtained written parental consent in order to receive condoms. In the 71% of schools that required passive consent, the school sent notices home to parents indicating that they must sign the form or contact someone at the school only if they wished to withhold consent. After parental consent, the second most common requirement was counseling, which was mandatory in about half (49%) of the schools with condom availability programs. "During counseling, students are commonly informed that abstinence is the safest method of protection against STDs; they are also instructed about the proper methods of storing and using condoms" (Kirby & Brown, 1996, p. 199).

In most schools with condom availability programs, condoms are free of charge. Only 3% of schools with such programs make condoms available to students through vending machines, at a cost of about 25¢ per condom. In most condom availability programs, students must ask an adult (principal, teacher, counselor, nurse, or other) for condoms. Only 5% of the schools in the Kirby and Brown survey provided condoms in bowls or baskets.

Chances are, the high school you attended did not make condoms available to students. Only 2.2% of all public high schools and 0.3% of all high school districts in the United States make condoms available to students (Kirby & Brown, 1996). Why are these programs not widely implemented? Some parents are afraid that increased condom availability will encourage students to be more sexually active. However, evaluation of the Philadelphia school health resource centers found that condom availability did not increase the level of sexual activity among the students (Furstenberg et al., 1997). In some states, there are legal restrictions against such programs. Although many states require high schools to provide instruction in HIV or STD prevention, 19 states prohibit or restrict availability of (or in some cases, information about) contraceptives to students through school health and education programs (Committee on Prevention and Control of STDs, 1997). Segments of the population, as well as powerful conservative groups such as the Family Research Council and Focus on the Family strongly oppose school condom availability on the premise that giving young people condoms might seem to condone their sexual activities or encourage promiscuity. Parents opposed to condom availability programs have filed suits against school districts, claiming that such programs usurped their parental rights. In 1993, a New York state appellate court ruled in favor of those opposed to New York City's school condom availability program, which was the first program in the nation to make condoms available without parental consent. The result was that the public schools implemented the program, but allowed parents an "opt-out" option whereby they could send notification to the school if they did not want their children to have

Continued on following page.

access to condoms. Less than 1% of parents of high school students in the New York City school system have chosen that option (Mahler, 1996). More recently, the Massachusetts supreme judicial court upheld a lower court ruling rejecting parents' claim that school condom availability programs violate their rights. The parents challenged the court's ruling, but the U.S. Supreme Court declined to review the case. In refusing to hear this case, "the Supreme Court has, for now, left resolution of these issues in the hands of the states" (Mahler, 1996, p. 77).

Parental opposition to school condom availability programs is in contrast to the recommendation of such organizations as The American School Health Association, the American College of Obstetricians and Gynecologists, the National Medical Association, and the National Institute of Medicine that condoms be made available to adolescents as part of comprehensive school health and STD prevention programs.

At present, it is uncertain whether or not the public will demand, or even allow, public schools to implement this recommendation throughout the United States. Giving teenagers condoms contradicts moral values that are against nonmarital sexual relations. However, as one school official responded, "This is not a matter of morality, it is a matter of life and death (Seligmann et al., 1991, p. 61).

Sources: Committee on Prevention and Control of STDs. (1997). The hidden epidemic: Confronting sexually transmitted diseases. *SIECUS Report, 25*(3), 4–14.

Furstenberg, F. F., Getiz, L. M., Teitler, J. O., & Weiss, C. C. (1997). Does condom availability make a difference? An evaluation of Philadelphia's health resource centers. *Family Planning Perspectives, 29*, 123–127.

Kirby, D. B., & Brown, N. L. (1996). Condom availability programs in U.S. schools. *Family Planning Perspectives, 28*, 196–202.

Mahler, K. (1996). Condom availability in the schools: Lessons from the courtroom. *Family Planning Perspectives, 28*(2), 75–77.

Seligmann, J., Beachy, L., Gordon, J., McCormick, J., & Starr, M. (1991, December 9). Condoms in the classroom. *Newsweek, 61.*

Attitudes toward pregnancy prevention and use of other birth control methods also influence condom use. A study of nearly 2,900 high school students in Miami revealed that the more the students knew about HIV and AIDS, the less emphasis they placed on pregnancy prevention, and as the importance of pregnancy prevention decreased, so did the frequency of using condoms (Langer, Zimmerman, & Katz, 1997). Young men who were dating someone steadily and who felt pregnancy prevention was more important than AIDS prevention were the most likely to report they used condoms often. Female, Hispanic, and African American students were the most likely to put equal emphasis on pregnancy and AIDS prevention. A study of women served in 17 clinics in southeastern Texas found that most women who selected an injectable contraceptive did not use condoms to protect themselves from STD exposure (Sangi-Haghpeykar, Poindexter, & Bateman, 1997).

Numerous school, clinic, and community programs have been designed and implemented to prevent STDs by modifying high-risk sexual behaviors. HIV and STD prevention programs utilize a variety of instructional techniques, including group discussions, role-plays, lectures, videos, and peer counseling. Such programs typically provide education about sex, STDs, and contraception; encourage abstinence and

responsible sexual decision making; teach behavioral skills in sexual communication and condom use; and provide condoms (Card et al., 1996).

One of the more controversial STD prevention strategies involves making condoms available to high school students. This chapter's Social Choices section looks at this controversy.

Public and Private Sexual Health Services

Sexual health services, including STD screening, diagnostic testing, and treatment for STDs, are provided by public clinics, agencies, health centers and private health care providers. A screening test, or a test used for screening purposes, is one that is applied to someone with no symptoms or signs of the disease being assessed. If the person has either symptoms or signs of a particular STD, the test is not a screening test but a diagnostic test. In addition to screening, diagnostic testing, and STD treatment, sexual health services may perform the following functions:

- Identify persons who are unaware, misinformed, or in denial of their risks for HIV and other STDs and facilitate an accurate self-perception of risks
- Teach clients how to reduce their risks of acquiring or transmitting an STD
- Refer clients to resources providing psychosocial support to facilitate desired behavior changes

- Provide referrals to drug treatment services for clients whose substance abuse problems increase their STD risks
- Provide family planning information and referrals for women of childbearing ages who are infected or at high risk for contracting HIV or other STDs
- Provide referrals for any necessary medical and psychosocial services
- Communicate to clients the responsibility to notify sex and needle-sharing partners

Most public health departments, community health centers, and other agencies (such as Planned Parenthood) also provide condoms free of charge (Frost & Bolzan, 1997).

Primary health care providers, in both public and private settings, can play an important role in preventing STD transmission. However, many primary providers neglect to assess their clients' risk behaviors, screen for STDs, or provide counseling concerning safer sex. One study found that in a sample of over 2000 teenage females, only 57% of those who were sexually experienced had ever had a pelvic exam (Paperny, 1997). Despite the prevalence of chlamydia among adolescents, one study done in San Diego, California, revealed that less than half of primary health care clinicians who provided adolescent health care routinely screened sexually active adolescent girls for chlamydia; less than 20% routinely screened sexually active boys (Gunn, Veinbergs, & Friedman, 1997). The researchers recommended that primary care providers expand routine chlamydia screening to all sexually active adolescents.

Many groups at high risk for STDs have infrequent contact with health care services for a variety of reasons. For example, many high-risk individuals either do not have health insurance, or their health insurance plan may not cover screening and other preventive health services related to STDs, or they may require copayments and deductibles that they cannot afford to pay. Health care reform might include provisions for full coverage of STD testing and treatment for insured individuals and their partners.

Cost is not the only barrier to STD services; many individuals do not have easy access to sexual health services. To improve accessibility, more STD prevention and control programs need to be delivered through alternative approaches, such as school health programs, peer teen outreach, and mobile clinics.

Syringe-Exchange Programs

Syringe-exchange programs are designed to reduce the transmission of HIV that is associated with drug injection by providing sterile syringes in exchange for used, potentially HIV-contaminated, syringes. (Another method is to sterilize a shared needle with bleach after each use.) Other services that are sometimes provided by such programs include latex condom distribution, HIV testing and counseling, primary health care services, and outreach efforts to reach subpopulations of intravenous drug users (such as youth, homeless, or those who inject steroids).

Syringe-exchange programs are a major component of HIV-prevention strategies in most developed countries. In the United States, these programs are controversial. Advocates point to the importance of providing sterile needles for drug users to prevent HIV transmission. Critics, on the other hand, argue that syringe-exchange programs condone and promote drug use and have successfully lobbied for a federal ban that prohibits federal spending on syringe-exchange programs.

Despite the controversy over, and lack of federal support for, syringe-exchange programs, there has been a rapid growth of such programs.

NATIONAL DATA

The number of U. S. syringe exchange programs from 1993 to 1995 and the number of syringes exchanged from 1992 to 1994

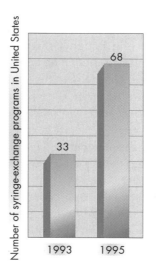

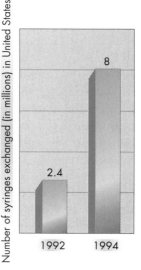

Source: Paone, Des Jarlais, Clark, & Shi, 1996.

The majority of syringe-exchange programs (70%) operate in five states: California, New York, Washington, Connecticut, and Hawaii. In a 1995 survey of 60 syringe-exchange programs, 33 reported that they operated in a state in which such programs were legal (55%); the remaining 27 programs (45%) operated in a state in which they were illegal (Paone et al., 1996). The legal status of a program affected the services it delivered. Programs that had legal status tended to have adequate supplies, funding for adequate disposal for biohazardous wastes, more operating hours, and formal arrangements with drug-treatment programs. The researchers strongly suggest expansion of syringe-exchange programs by lifting the ban on federal funding and repealing state laws that make them illegal.

Computer Technology: A Revolution in STD Intervention

Federal, state, and local governments each provide funding of public sexual health services at STD clinics and health departments. However, government downsizing, the economic crises faced by some large jurisdictions (including Los Angeles and the District of Columbia), and the increased need for sexual health services that accompanied the HIV/AIDS epidemic, has left many public sexual health facilities short on staff and funds. In response to these cutbacks, clinics of the future are expected to implement computer technology that will perform a range of functions, including eliciting personal and confidential behavioral risk data from clients, gathering medical and social data, generating personalized scripts (including educational messages), referring patients to other providers, and providing specific risk-reducing behavioral information and material. "Implementing modern computer technology into the clinic setting can decrease the number of support staff, essentially do away with paper functions such as record keeping and laboratory surveillance, supplement behavioral risk assessments of clients, and deliver interventions such as counseling" (Conlon, 1997, p. 13).

Computer technology in sexual health care facilities may not only reduce the cost of providing such services (fewer staff are needed), but also may provide more reliable information about clients' symptoms, high-risk behaviors, and sexual histories. Traditionally, sexual health care providers have obtained such sensitive information through face-to-face interviews. But individuals, especially adolescents, are reluctant to divulge sexual and drug use information due to guilt, embarrassment, mistrust, and fear of disapproval. The development of an interactive multimedia computer program "Youth Health Provider" was designed to obtain a thorough behavioral and health history, identify problem areas and health needs, provide problem-specific health advice and local referrals, administer health education videos, and dispense specific printed take-home materials. Examples of questions asked by the Youth Health Provider computer program include "Does it burn or hurt when you urinate or pee lately?" and "Would you like to learn more about how not to get STDs?" The program also asks participants if they have any lumps or sores in, on, or around their genitals or have experienced any pus, drip, or discharge from their penises or vaginas. Of more than 4000 teens ages 13 to 19 who used the Youth Health Provider program, 85% indicated they were totally honest in responding to the computer's questions, and 89% said they preferred the computer interview over a face-to-face interview or written questionnaire (Paperny, 1997).

Evaluation research on computer technology designed to reduce HIV/STD risk has shown promising results. One such series of interactive video programs, "The Choice Is Yours—Preventing HIV/STDs," was designed to provide the decision-making skills and information necessary to make competent decisions, and to teach the social skills needed to deal safely with sexual situations (Noell, Ary, & Duncan, 1997). Separate programs were developed for each of three races (Hispanic, African American, and white) at each of two age levels (middle school and high school). In a randomized experiment involving 827 students, those who participated in the video program showed significant changes in their believing that sex occurs as a result of decisions (versus "it just happens"), their believing that even a single incident of unprotected sex can result in an STD or pregnancy, their intentions and attitudes toward the use of condoms, and their self-efficacy in remaining abstinent. Figure 5.2 presents an example of a scenario flowchart from the video program.

In addition to "The Choice Is Yours" program, a wide range of interactive computer programs have

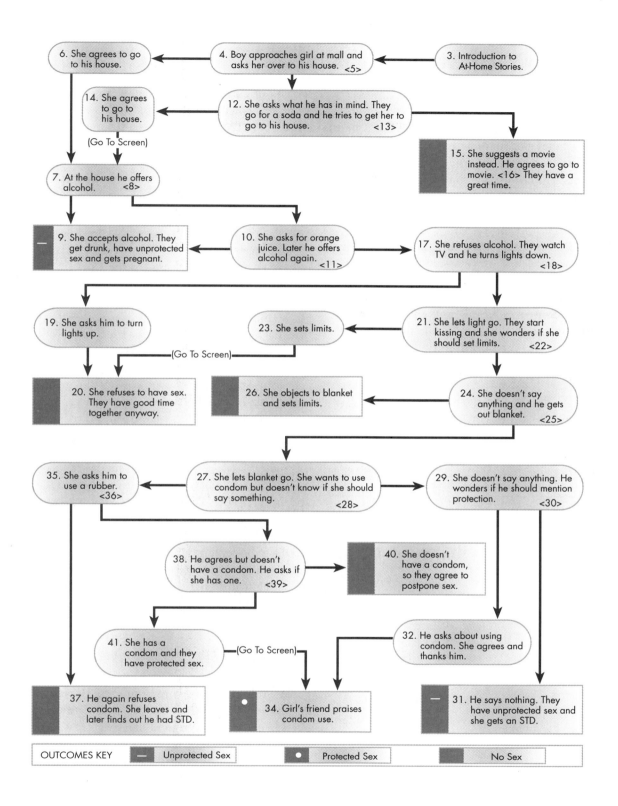

FIGURE 5.3 Scenario Flowchart from "The Choice Is Yours": A Computer Video Program Designed to Prevent STDs
Source: Noell et al., 1997.

been developed to help prevent transmission of HIV/STDs. "Life Challenge," developed by the New York State Department of Health, uses a time travel/adventure game format to provide information on STDs and allow participants to practice negotiating safe sex with a partner. Users record and play back their responses as they negotiate with their selected computerized partner about whether or not to have sex and whether or not to use a condom. An evaluation of the program found that users had significant gains in STD knowledge and self-efficacy scores (Thomas, Cahill, & Santilli, 1997).

The various programs, services, and technology designed to control and prevent sexually transmitted diseases require public support and funding. In an era of spending cutbacks, securing funds for STD prevention and control is an ongoing challenge. With this challenge comes the opportunity to reduce disease and death and the opportunity to improve the health and well-being of the U.S. population.

THINK ABOUT IT

Suppose you are responsible for deciding whether condoms should be available in the public school system your children are attending. What would you recommmend and why? How would you respond to disagreements with your recommendation?

KEY TERMS

acquired immunodefi-
    ciency syndrome
    (AIDS) 112
candidiasis 116
cervical ectopy 103
chancroid 116
chlamydia 108
condyloma 109
dental dam 105
finger cot 105
genital herpes 110
genital warts 109
gonorrhea 108
hepatitis B 115
herpes simplex virus
    type 1 (HSV-1) 110
herpes simplex virus
    type 2 (HSV-2) 110

human immunodeficiency
    virus (HIV) 112
human papilloma virus
    (HPV) 109
lip herpes 110
nongonococcal
    urethritis 116
outercourse 117
pelvic inflammatory
    disease (PID) 106
protease inhibitors 115
pubic lice 116
scabies 117
self-efficacy 120
syphilis 111
syringe-exchange
    program 123
trichomoniasis 116
vaginitis 116

SUMMARY POINTS

As more individuals have more sex with more partners, the risk of contracting a sexually transmitted disease increases. The physical, psychological, and economic effects of STDs can be dramatic; thus, individual and social efforts to prevent and treat STDs are warranted.

Sexually Transmitted Diseases: A Pandemic

In the United States, at least one person in four will contract an STD at some point in his or her lifetime. The most common STD in the United States and around the world is chlamydia. Of the top ten most frequently reported diseases in the United States in 1995, more than half (87%) of all cases were sexually transmitted diseases. Certain categories of individuals, including adolescents and young adults, gay and bisexual men and their partners, users of illegal injection drugs and their partners, women, singles, minorities, and urban dwellers are at higher risk for acquiring an STD. However, it is not the group one belongs to, but the behaviors one practices, that puts one at risk for STD infection. Anyone who engages in high-risk behaviors is susceptible to acquiring STDs. It is therefore important for individuals who have engaged in high-risk behaviors (such as intercourse or oral sex without a condom) to get tested for HIV and other STDs. The longer an STD goes undiagnosed and untreated, the more likely it is that it will produce serious health consequences including sterility, cancer, and death. The sooner an infected individual is tested and diagnosed, the sooner that individual can begin treatment for the disease and begin altering high-risk behaviors, thereby reducing the risk of transmitting the disease to others.

Consequences of Sexually Transmitted Diseases

Most individuals today are aware that HIV/AIDS cause serious health consequences. However, the emphasis on HIV/AIDS may be inadvertently overshadowing the seriousness of other STDs. Women are more likely than men to suffer serious health consequences from contracting STDs because they are less likely to produce symptoms, and are therefore less likely to be diagnosed until severe problems develop. Untreated sexually transmitted diseases may cause pelvic inflammatory disease (PID)—a major health problem in women of reproductive age, often requiring hospitalization and surgery. PID is associated with such complications as infertility, ectopic pregnancy, and chronic abdominal pain. STDs are also associated with health problems for pregnant women and infants. Various STDs may be transmitted to the fetus, newborn, or infant through the placenta (congenital infection), during passage through the birth canal (perinatal infection), or after birth through breastfeeding or close contact. Health consequences include spontaneous abortion, stillbirth, and premature delivery.

AIDS causes more deaths than any other STD. The largest number of deaths related to STDs other than AIDS is caused by cervical and other cancers associated with human papilloma virus, and liver disease/cancer caused by hepatitis B virus. Untreated syphilis can also cause serious damage to the cardiovascular system and nervous system, as well as blindness and death. In addition to health consequences, HIV and other STDs may cause psychological distress and can also place an economic burden on individuals and society.

Modes of Transmission, Symptoms, and Treatment for STDs

There are more than 25 infectious diseases that are transmissible through sexual contact. Other modes of transmission for various STDs include needle sharing, mother-child transmission (from infected pregnant woman to fetus or newborn), blood transfusions, and occupational transmission.

Although some STDs may produce symptoms such as blisters and bumps (herpes) or painless chancres or sores (first-stage syphilis), many STDs often produce no symptoms, especially in women. For example, most women infected with gonorrhea or chlamydia experience no symptoms and many HIV infected individuals show no symptoms until their condition progresses to AIDS.

Bacterial STDs, including chlamydia, gonorrhea, syphilis, chancroid, and nongonococcal urethritis, are treated with antibiotics. There are no cures for viral STDs, such as herpes, human papilloma virus (HPV), and HIV, although symptoms may be treated and disease progression slowed with various medications, procedures, and lifestyle alterations.

Prevention and Control of Sexually Transmissible Diseases

Currently, the only effective method for prevention of an STD is the hepatitis B vaccine. Although this vaccine is available, it has not been implemented on a wide scale. For both women and men, STDs increase susceptibility to HIV. Individuals with genital herpes, syphilis, chancroid infection, chlamydia, gonorrhea, or trichomoniasis are three to five times more likely to contract HIV than noninfected individuals. Therefore, the prevention of STDs helps to prevent HIV infection.

STD prevention and control programs and strategies include modifying high risk behaviors by increasing the use of condoms and delaying initiation of sexual activity (encouraging abstinence). Various public and private sexual health care services provide STD screening and testing, treatment, and counseling. Some high schools are providing condoms to students, along with a comprehensive program in sex/STD education and health care. Syringe-exchange programs attempt to reduce HIV transmission among users of illegal injection drugs by providing clean, sterile needles in exchange for used ones. Finally, computer technology offers a wide range of applications for STD prevention.

REFERENCES

Aitken, I., & Reichenbach, L. (1994). Reproductive and sexual health services: Expanding access and enhancing quality. In G. Sen, A. Germain, & L. C. Chen (Eds.), *Population policies reconsidered: Health, empowerment, and rights,* (pp. 177-192). Boston: Harvard School of Public Health.

Aral, S. O. (1996). The social context of syphilis persistence in the southeastern United States. *Sexually Transmitted Diseases, 23*(1), 9-15.

Aral, S. O., & Holmes, K. K. (1991). Sexually transmitted diseases in the AIDS era. *Scientific American, 264,* 62-69.

Bauman, K. A. (1997). Women and AIDS. In J. Rosenfeld (Ed.), *Women's health in primary care* (pp. 399-419). Baltimore, MD: Williams & Wilkins.

Binson, D., Dolcini, M. M., Pollack, L. M., & Catania, J. A. (1993). Multiple sex partners among young adults: the National AIDS Behavioral Surveys (NABS). *Family Planning Perspectives, 25*(268).

Card, J. J., Niego, S., Mallari, A., & Farrell, W. S. (1996). The Program Archive on Sexuality Health & Adolescence: Promising "prevention programs in a box." *Family Planning Perspectives, 28,* 210-220.

Catania, J. A., Binson, D., Dolcini, M., Stall, R, Choi, K. H., Pollack, L. M., Hudes, E., Canchola, J., Phillips, K., Moskowitz, J. T., & Coates, T. J. (1995). Risk factors for HIV and other sexually transmitted diseases and prevention practices among U.S. heterosexual adults: Changes from 1990 to 1992. *American Journal of Public Health, 85*(11), 1492-1499.

Centers for Disease Control. (1995). *Summary of Notifiable Diseases, United States, 1995.* Washington, DC: U.S. Department of Health and Human Services.

Centers for Disease Control. (1997). *HIV/AIDS Surveillance Report 9,* (No. 1). Washington, DC: U.S. Department of Health and Human Services.

Chernesky, M. A. (1997). How can industry, academia, public health authorities, and the sexually transmitted diseases diagnostics initiative work together to help control sexually transmitted diseases in developing countries? *Sexually Transmitted Diseases, 24*(2), 61-63.

Cohen, M. S., Hoffman, I. F., Royce, R. A., Kazembe, P., Dyer, J. R., Daly, C. C., Zimba, D., Vernazza, P. L., Maida, M., Fiscus, S. A. Eron Jr., J. J., & the AIDSCAP Malawi Research Group. (1997). Reduction of concentration of HIV-1 in semen after treatment of urethritis: Implications for prevention of sexual transmission of HIV-1. *Lancet, 349* (9069), 1868-1873.

Committee on Prevention and Control of STDs. (1997). The hidden epidemic: Confronting sexually transmitted diseases. *SIECUS Report, 25*(3), 4-14.

Conlon, R. T. (1997). Introducing technology into the public STD clinic. *Health Education & Behavior, 24*(1), 12-19.

Cooper, M., Pierce, R. S. , & Farmer Huselid, R. (1994). Substance use and sexual risk taking among black adolescents and white adolescents. *Health Psychology, 13*(3), 251-262.

Davis, M., & Scott, R. S. (1988). *Lovers, doctors and the law.* New York: Harper & Row.

Donovan, P. (1997). Confronting a hidden epidemic: The Institute of Medicine's report on sexually transmitted diseases. *Family Planning Perspectives, 29*(2), 87-89.

Fleishman, J. A., & Fogel, B. (1994). Coping and depressive symptoms among people with AIDS. *Health Psychology, 13*(2), 156-169.

Fleming, D. T., McQuillan, G. M., Johnson, R. E., Nahmias, A. J., Aral, S. O., Lee, F. K., & St. Louis, M. E. (1997). Herpes simplex virus type 2 in the United States: 1976-1994. *New England Journal of Medicine, 333*(16), 1105-1111.

Forrest, J. D., & Silverman, J. (1989). What public school teachers teach about preventing pregnancy, AIDS and sexually transmitted diseases. *Family Planning Perspectives, 21,* 65-72.

Frost, J. J., & Bolzan, M. 1997. The provision of public-sector services by family planning agencies in 1995. *Family Planning Perspectives, 29*(1), 6-14.

Gordon, C. M., & Carey, M. P. (1996). Alcohol's effects on requisites for sexual risk reduction in men: An initial experimental investigation. *Health Psychology, 15*(1), 56-60.

Gorman, C. (1996, February 12). Battling the AIDS virus. *Time,* 62-65.

Gunn, R. A., Veinbergs, E., & Friedman, L. S. (1997). Notes from the field: Adolescent Health Care Providers: Establishing a dialogue and assessing sexually transmitted disease prevention practices. *Sexually Transmitted Diseases, 24*(2), 90-93.

Hankins, C. (1996). Sexual transmission of HIV to women in industrialized countries. *World Health Statistics Quarterly, 49,* 106-112.

Hill, T. (1987, summer). Herpes and relationships. *The Helper, 9*(2), 1, 3-5.

Holmberg, S. D. (1996). The estimated prevalence and incidence of HIV in 96 large metropolitan areas. *American Journal of Public Health, 86,*642-651.

Katz, M. H., & and Gerberding, J. L. (1997). Postexposure treatment of people exposed to the human immuno-deficiency virus through sexual contact or injection-drug use. *New England Journal of Medicine, 336*(15), 1097-1099.

Kerr, D. L. (1990). AIDS SPEAK: Sensitive and accurate communication and the HIV epidemic. *Journal of School Health, 60,* 431-432.

Kirby, D. B., & Brown, N. L. (1996). Condom availability programs in U.S. schools. *Family Planning Perspectives, 28,*196-202.

Langer, L. M., Zimmerman, R. S., & Katz, J. (1997). Which is more important to high school students: Preventing pregnancy or preventing AIDS? *Family Planning Perspectives, 29,* 67-69, 75.

Laurence, J. (1994, spring). Keeping infants safe from HIV. *The AmFar Report,* 1-3.

Lindberg, A. D., Sonenstein, F. L., Ku, L., & Levine, G. (1997). Young men's experience with condom breakage. *Family Planning Perspectives, 29,* 128-131, 140.

Litigation of the 90s: Personal injury suits from STDs. (1996 February 16). *American Medical News, 39*(7), 23.

McMillan, J. (1996, November, 15). Preventing AIDS in rural America. *The Chronicle of Higher Education,* A10.

Michael, R. T., Gagnon, J. H., Laumann, E. O., & Kolata, G. (1994). *Sex in America: A definitive survey.* Boston: Little, Brown. (1994).

New treatment for cold sores. (1997, Spring). *The Helper, XIX*(1), 10.

1997 UNFPA Report—The Right to Choose: Reproductive Rights and Health. (1997). *Popline* (World Population News Service), *19,* 4-5.

Noell, J., Ary, D., & Duncan, T. (1997). Development and evaluation of a sexual decision-making and social skills program: "The Choice Is Yours—Preventing HIV/STDs." *Health Education & Behavior, 24*(1), 87-101.

Noris, J. (1995). *Professional guide to diseases* (5th ed). Springhouse, PA: Springhouse.

Paone, D., Des Jarlais, D., Clark, J., & Shi, Q. (1996). Syringe-exchange programs in the United States: Where are we now? *AIDS & Public Policy Journal, 11*(3), 144-147.

Paperny, D. M. N. (1997). Computerized health assessment and education for adolescent HIV and STD prevention in health care settings and schools. *Health Education & Behavior, 24*(1), 54-70.

Personal perspectives. (1997, Summer). *The Helper, XIX*(2), 3-4, 11.

Phair, J. P., & Chadwick, E. G. (1992). Human immunodeficiency virus infection and AIDS. In S. T. Shulman, J. P. Phair, & H. M. Sommers (Eds), *The biological and clinical basis of infectious diseases* (4th ed., pp. 380-393). Philadelphia: W. B. Saunders.

Pinkerton, S. D., & Abramson, P. R. (1997). Condoms and the prevention of AIDS. *American Scientist, 85,* 364-373.

Sangi-Haghpeykar, H., Poindexter III, A. N., & Bateman, L. (1997). Consistency of condom use among users of injectable contraceptives. *Family Planning Perspectives, 29,* 67-69, 75.

Schuster, M. A., Bell, R. M., & Kanouse, D. E. (1996). The sexual practices of adolescent virgins: Genital sexual activities of high school students who have never had vaginal intercourse. *American Journal of Public Health, 86*(11), 1570-1576.

SIECUS Fact Sheet. (1997). Sexually transmitted diseases in the United States. *SIECUS Report, 25*(3), 22-24.

Silverman, B. G., & Gross, T. P. (1997). Use and effectiveness of condoms during anal intercourse. *Sexually Transmitted Diseases, 24*(1), 11-17.

Sternberg, S. (1996). Risky sex breeds neglected epidemic. *Science News,* (150), 343.

Thomas, R., Cahill, J., & Santilli, L. (1997). Using an interactive computer game to increase skill and self-efficacy regarding safer sex negotiation: Field results. *Health Education and Behavior 24,* 71-86.

Tobin, M. (1997). Sexually transmitted diseases. In J. Rosenfeld (Ed.), *Women's Health in Primary Care* (pp. 383-397). Baltimore, MD: Williams & Wilkins.

Treatment update. (1997, Summer). *The Helper, XIX*(2), 1, 5-8.

Winning the war in your mind. (1997, Spring). *The Helper, XIX*(1), 1, 5-7.

Planning Children and Birth Control

Chapter 6

Do You Want to Have Children?

Social Influences Motivating Individuals to Have Children
Individual Motivations for Having Children
Lifestyle Changes and Economic Costs
SELF-ASSESSMENT: An Instrument to Assess Motivation for Parenthood
SOCIAL CHOICES: How Old Is Too Old to Become a Parent?
PERSONAL CHOICES: Choices Resulting from New Reproductive Technologies

QUESTION If personal freedom is such an important value in American society, why do over 90% of both women and men opt to radically alter their child-free lifestyle and divert their economic resources to have children?

How Many Children Do You Want?

None—The Child-Free Alternative
One Child?
Two Children?
Three Children?
Four or More Children?
PERSONAL CHOICES: Should You Choose to Have a Child Without a Partner?

QUESTION What are the unique challenges faced by individuals who decide to have a child without a partner?

Birth Control

Hormonal Contraceptives
Condom
Intrauterine Device (IUD)
Diaphragm
Cervical Cap
Vaginal Spermicides
Periodic Abstinence
Nonmethods: Withdrawal and Douching
Emergency Contraception
Effectiveness of Various Contraceptive Choices
SELF-ASSESSMENT: Contraceptive Comfort and Confidence Scale

QUESTION What options are available for an individual who had unprotected intercourse and wants to avoid a pregnancy? How soon after the event must the person take the prescribed medication?

Sterilization

Female Sterilization
Male Sterilization

QUESTION If the goals are efficiency and cost-effectiveness, should the man or the woman be sterilized?

In a 1996 survey conducted by the American Council on Education and the University of California, a national sample of 251,232 first-year college students ranked raising a family as their second most important goal in life (being financially secure was number one). Although becoming a parent is considered by many to be one of the most rewarding experiences in life, it also brings lifestyle changes, economic concerns, and other challenges. In their 1995 study of 50 successful marriages, Wallerstein and Blakeslee (1995) found that for couples who have children, learning how to expand their "circle" to include children and learning how to balance raising the children with their own relationships were major developmental tasks. Parenthood, therefore, should begin with planning.

NATIONAL DATA

The percentage of births that were unwanted, based on the National Maternal and Infant Health Survey

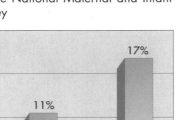

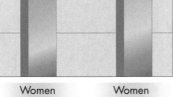

Source: Kost & Forrest, 1995.

Family planning has benefits for both the mother and the child. Having several children at short intervals increases the chances of premature birth, infectious disease, and death of the mother or the baby.

Parents can minimize such risks by planning fewer children with longer intervals in between. Women who plan their pregnancies can also modify their behaviors and seek preconception care from a health care practitioner to maximize their chances of having healthy pregnancies and babies. For example, women planning pregnancies can make sure they eat properly and avoid alcohol and other substances that could harm developing fetuses or embryos. (Preconception care is discussed in Chapter 7.)

Couples may also benefit from family planning by pacing the financial demands of parenthood. Having children 4 years apart helps to avoid having more than one child in day care or college at the same time.

Conscientious family planning may also reduce the number of unwanted births. This may benefit society by enabling people to avoid having children they cannot feed and clothe adequately—children whose rearing may have to be subsidized by taxpayers. Finally, family planning is essential to halting the continuing expansion of the world population.

INTERNATIONAL DATA

By the year 2000, the world's population is projected to be 6.1 billion.

Source: *Statistical Abstract of the United States: 1997,* Table 1334.

Without population control—particularly in countries such as China (which will have over a billion people by the year 2000)—increased food shortages, unchecked urban growth, environmental damage (including water, soil, and air pollution), depletion of our planet's natural resources, and destruction of the ozone layer will result. Although most population growth will occur in Africa and South Asia, four industrialized countries (the United States, Canada, Australia, and New Zealand) are also projected to continue their growth (Independent Commission on Population and Quality of Life, 1996). Sadik (1992, p. 134) suggested that "population may be the key to all the issues that will shape the future:

economic growth; environmental security; and the health and well-being of countries, communities, and families."

In this chapter, we encourage you to consider three basic questions:

- Do you want to have children?
- How many?
- What form of birth control will you use to ensure the family size you want?

DO YOU WANT TO HAVE CHILDREN?

In the United States, children are an expected part of one's adult life. In this section, we examine the social influences that motivate individuals to want children. We also discuss the difficulties associated with parenthood.

NATIONAL DATA

The percentage of women between the ages of 18 and 34 in the United States who expect to have children

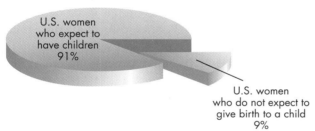

U.S. women who expect to have children 91%

U.S. women who do not expect to give birth to a child 9%

Source: *Statistical Abstract of the United States: 1997,* Table 107.

Social Influences Motivating Individuals to Have Children

Our society tends to encourage childbearing, an attitude known as *pronatalism*. Our family, friends, religions, government, and schools help us develop positive attitudes toward parenthood. Cultural observances also function to reinforce these attitudes.

FAMILY   Our experience of being reared in families encourages us to have families of our own. Our parents are our models. If they married, we marry. If they had children, we have children. Some parents exert a much more active influence. "I'm 73 and don't have much time. Will I ever see a grandchild?" asked the

mother of an only child. Other remarks parents have made include "If you don't hurry up, your younger sister is going to have a baby before you do," "We're setting up a trust fund for your brother's child, and we'll do the same for yours," "Did you know that Nash and Marilyn (the adult child's contemporaries) just had a daughter?" "I think you'll regret not having children when you're old," and "Don't you want a son to carry on your name?"

FRIENDS   Our friends who have children influence us to do likewise. After sharing an enjoyable weekend with friends who had a little girl, one husband wrote to the host and hostess, "Lucy and I are always affected by Karen—she is such a good child to have around. We haven't made up our minds yet, but our desire to have a child of our own always increases after we leave your home." This couple became parents 16 months later.

RELIGION   Religion may be a powerful influence on the decision to have children. Roman Catholics are taught that having children is the basic purpose of marriage and gives meaning to the union. Although many Catholics use contraception and reject their church's emphasis on procreation, some internalize the church's message. One Catholic woman said, "My body was made by God, and I should use it to produce children for Him. Other people may not understand it, but that's how I feel." Judaism also has a strong family orientation. Couples who choose to be child-free are less likely than couples with children to adhere to any set of religious beliefs.

GOVERNMENT   The tax structures imposed by our federal and state governments support parenthood. Married couples without children pay higher taxes than couples with children, although the reduction in taxes is not sufficient to offset the cost of rearing a child and is not large enough to be a primary inducement to have children.

Governments in other countries have encouraged or discouraged childbearing in different ways. In the 1930s, as a mark of status for women contributing to the so-called Aryan race, Adolf Hitler bestowed the German Mother's Cross—a gold cross for eight or more children, a silver cross for six or seven, and a bronze cross for four or five—on Nazi Germany's most fertile mothers.

China, on the other hand, has a set of incentives to encourage families to have only one child. Couples who have only one child are given a "one-child glory certificate," which entitles them to special priority housing, better salaries, a 5% supplementary pension, free medical care for the child, and an assured place for the child in school. If the couple has more than one child, they may lose their jobs, be assigned to less desirable housing, and be required to pay the government back for any benefits they have received. India once had a policy similar to China's, but it was repealed after its passage led the people to force Indira Gandhi out of office. 🍃

CULTURAL OBSERVANCES   Our society reaffirms its approval of parents every year by identifying special days for Mom and Dad. Each year on Mother's Day and Father's Day (and now Grandparents' Day), parenthood is celebrated across the nation with cards, gifts, and embraces. There is no cultural counterpart (such as Child-Free Day) for people who choose not to have children.

Despite general pronatalism in our society, it is important to point out that our society is also antinatalistic and relegates children, particularly poor children, to a rather low priority in terms of importance (Kozol, 1995). Witness the recent budget cuts in governmental programs that benefit children—education at all levels, school breakfast/lunch programs, Temporary Assistance to Needy Families (TANF), food stamps, Head Start, child care, welfare, and so on. In addition, there is a continuous fight to get corporations to implement or enforce any family policies (from family leaves to flextime to on-site day care). Profit and money—not children—are priorities.

Finally, although people are generally tolerant of their own children, they often exhibit antinatalistic behavior in reference to the children of others. Notice the unwillingness of some individuals to sit next to a child on an airplane or the existence of some apartments—indeed, entire communities—that cater to the elderly and prohibit children.

Individual Motivations for Having Children

Individual motivations, as well as social influences, play important roles in making the decision to have children. Some of these motivations are conscious, such as the desire for love and companionship with one's own offspring and the desire to be personally fulfilled by having a child. Other motivations are more difficult to perceive—having a child as an attempt to recapture childhood and youth, for example. The motivations for having children are similar for homosexual and heterosexual individuals (Benkov, 1994).

🍃 In premodern societies (before industrialization and urbanization) and in some parts of China and Korea today, spouses try to have as many children as possible because children are an economic asset (Jones, Tepperman, & Wilson, 1995). At an early age, children work as farm hands or in other jobs for wages that they give to their parents. Children are also expected to take care of their parents when the parents are elderly. In China and Korea, the eldest son is expected to take care of his aging parents by earning money for them and by marrying and bringing his wife into their home to physically care for them. Her parents need their own son and daughter-in-law for old-age insurance. Beyond their economic value and old-age insurance, children are regarded as a symbol of virility for the man, a source of prestige for the woman, and as a sign of good fortune for the couple. In modern societies, large numbers of children are economic liabilities rather than assets. 🍃

Unconscious motivations may also be operative. Two examples include wanting a child in order to compete with a sibling and having a child in order to gain acceptance and approval from one's parents and peers (Michaels, 1988). It is sometimes thought that teenagers have children because they want someone who will love them (Parnell, Swicegood, & Stevens, 1994).

Lifestyle Changes and Economic Costs of Parenthood

Although there are numerous potential positive outcomes for becoming a parent, there are also drawbacks. Every parent knows that parenthood involves difficulties as well as joys. Some of the difficulties associated with parenthood are discussed next.

LIFESTYLE CHANGES   Becoming a parent often involves changes in lifestyle. Daily living routines become focused around the needs of the children. Living arrangements change to provide space for another person in the household. Some parents change their work schedule to allow them to be home more. Food shopping and menus change to accommodate the appetites of children. A major lifestyle change is the loss of freedom of activity and flexibility in one's personal schedule.

Lifestyle changes are particularly dramatic for women. The time and effort it takes to be pregnant and rear children often competes with the time and energy needed to build a career. "The assumption underlying all highly paid careers is that work will take priority over everything else" (Jones et al., 1995, p. 110). Because few women can count on their husbands to take over—let alone share—the work of child-rearing, many women face a dilemma of children versus career. As we have noted elsewhere in this text, most sacrifice their career.

FINANCIAL COSTS   Meeting the financial obligations of parenthood is difficult for many parents. Demographers note that high-income families spend more money on rearing their children than low- or middle-income families.

NATIONAL DATA

According to the U.S. Department of Agriculture, the estimated cost of rearing a child by family income group from birth through age 17 (does not include college*)

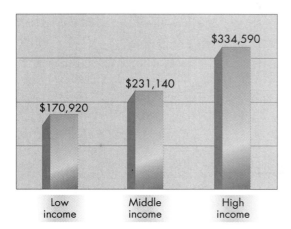

$170,920 — Low income
$231,140 — Middle income
$334,590 — High income

*College expenses significantly increase the cost of rearing a child.

Source: Schwiesow & Staimer, 1994, p. a1.

NATIONAL DATA

The expenses incurred for four years of college, including tuition and fees, books and supplies, room and board, transportation, and miscellaneous expenses

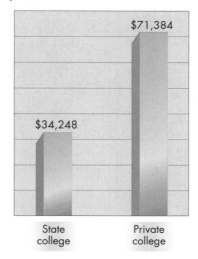

$34,248 — State college
$71,384 — Private college

Source: *Statistical Abstract of the United States: 1995,* Table 288.

Regardless of the lifestyle changes and economic costs, most people are motivated to have children. This chapter's Self-Assessment allows you to assess your own motivations for having a child.

Because of lifestyle and economic considerations, some women put off having a child until they are older. How old is too old? Should the government intervene? We address these concerns in this chapter's Social Choices section.

PERSONAL CHOICES

Choices Resulting from New Reproductive Technologies

The development of various reproductive technologies (discussed further in chapter 6) has created a new range of choices with regard to family planning. Examples of such choices are presented in the following paragraphs.

Example One   A young woman who wants to delay pregnancy and child-rearing until after she has established herself professionally in a career may, in her

AN INSTRUMENT TO ASSESS MOTIVATION FOR PARENTHOOD

Indicate the answer you feel is the best by placing a one (1) in front of it. Rank the remaining answers (2, 3, and 4) to show your order of preference.

1. Parents expect their children
   F ( ) to fulfill the purpose of life.
   I ( ) to strengthen the family.
   A ( ) to be healthy and happy.
   N ( ) to follow in their footsteps.

2. Men want children because
   N ( ) they would like to prove their sexual adequacy.
   F ( ) it is a natural instinct.
   I ( ) they need them to enhance their social status.
   A ( ) they like children.

3. A mother expects her daughter
   I ( ) to give her companionship and affection.
   F ( ) to take the place in the world for which she is destined.
   N ( ) to be like herself.
   A ( ) to be happy and well.

4. Men want children because
   I ( ) children hold the marriage together.
   A ( ) they like to care and provide for children.
   F ( ) it is a function of the mature adult.
   N ( ) they want to perpetuate themselves.

5. A father expects his son
   A ( ) to be happy and well.
   F ( ) to take the place in the world for which he is destined.
   I ( ) to give him companionship and affection.
   N ( ) to be like himself.

6. Women want children because
   A ( ) they like children.
   I ( ) they need them to enhance their social status.
   N ( ) they would like to prove their sexual adequacy.
   F ( ) it is a natural instinct.

7. Generally, people want children because
   F ( ) they are destined to reproduce.
   A ( ) they desire to help someone grow and develop.
   N ( ) they can create someone in their own image.
   A ( ) they provide companionship.

8. A father expects his daughter
   N ( ) to believe in him.
   A ( ) to be happy and well.
   F ( ) to take her place in the world.
   I ( ) to give him companionship and affection.

9. Women want children because
   I ( ) children hold the marriage together.
   F ( ) it is a function of the mature adult.
   A ( ) they like to care and provide for children.
   N ( ) they want to perpetuate themselves.

10. Women want children because
    F ( ) they are destined to reproduce.
    A ( ) they desire to help someone grow and develop.
    I ( ) they provide companionship.
    A ( ) they create someone in their own image.

11. Generally, people want children because
    A ( ) they like to care and provide for children.
    N ( ) they want to perpetuate themselves.
    I ( ) children hold the marriage together.
    F ( ) it is a function of the mature adult.

Continued on following page

12. A mother expects her son
  F ( ) to take his place in the world.
  I ( ) to give her companionship and affection.
  A ( ) to be happy and well.
  N ( ) to believe in her.

13. Men want children because
  I ( ) they provide companionship.
  N ( ) they create someone in their own image.
  F ( ) they are destined to reproduce.
  A ( ) they desire to help someone grow and develop.

14. Generally, people want children because
  F ( ) it is a natural instinct.
  A ( ) they like children.
  I ( ) they need them to enhance their social status.
  N ( ) they would like to prove their sexual adequacy.

Scoring   The Child Study Inventory is composed of sentences related to motivations for parenthood. Each sentence is followed by four completion choices. Each choice following the relevant sentence can be categorized into one of the basic CSI motivational categories: Altruistic (A), Narcissistic (N), Fatalistic (F), Instrumental (I).

Scoring is accomplished for each of the four categories by summing the rankings of all completion choices in that category (e.g., all rankings of altruistic choices to obtain an altruistic motivation score). A low score indicates high preference for a given category.

For a more detailed subdivision of scores, the user may score "motivational" items (#2, 4, 6, 7, 9, 10, 11, 13, 14) and "expectancy" items (#1, 3, 5, 8) separately.

youth, have her healthy eggs extracted, frozen, and artificially inseminated later when she is in her 40s or 50s. Doing so would reduce some of the risks associated with birth defects in women who elect to have children during middle age. Alternatively, a middle-aged woman may want to use an egg from a younger woman and have it fertilized with her partner's sperm and artificially inseminated.

What are the disadvantages of delaying pregnancy through the use of reproductive technologies? Risk to the fetus and risk to the mother are the predominant problems. While some of the risks to the fetus can be avoided by using a "young" egg ("old" eggs are much more likely to be defective), the middle-aged pregnant woman is much more likely to be diabetic, be overweight, and have high blood pressure, which may also affect the fetus negatively.

In addition, what are the implications for the child who will have two elderly parents who may die before her or his graduation from high school? Joni Mitchell decided to have a baby at age 52 and was

implanted with a fertilized egg from a young woman. (Her husband was the sperm donor.) She said of the implications for her age and its effect on her child, "If I can raise him or her until age 30, then he should be able to make it on his own" (quoted in Gorman, 1991, p. 62).

Example Two   Couples who have genetic histories that include sickle-cell anemia or cystic fibrosis may have such defects tested for in several embryos and implant only those without the defects. But if embryos can be destroyed because of a genetic defect, can sex of the child also be used as a basis for discarding the embryo?

─────── **THINK ABOUT IT** ───────

How much of the decision to have children do you feel is biologically driven, socially induced, or personally motivated? How much of the desire for children is conscious and deliberate, and how much is a result of people's tendency to drift from one stage of life to the next?

HOW OLD IS TOO OLD TO BECOME A PARENT?

Arceli Keh of Highland, California, became a mother at the age of 63 (Hellmich, 1997); Tony Randall had a child at the age of 77; and Strom Thurmond was in his eighties when he became a father. Situations like these are becoming more common, and questions are now being asked about the appropriateness of elderly individuals becoming parents. Should social policies on this issue be developed?

When Tony Randall's daughter, Julia, begins college, her father will be 95. Arceli Keh will be 81 when her daughter, Cynthia, begins college. "So what?" Arceli says, "My mother is in *her* eighties and she's helping me with Cynthia" (Peterson & Hellmich, 1997).

There are advantages and disadvantages of having a child as an elderly parent. The primary developmental advantage for the child of retirement-aged parents is the attention the parents can devote to their offspring. Not distracted by their career, these parents have more time to nurture, play with, and teach their children. There is abundant evidence that children benefit cognitively, emotionally, and socially from concentrated attention during their early developmental years (Ramsburg, 1997; *Starting Points for Young Children,* 1994).

Elderly parents are also less likely to divorce. The median age of women who divorce is 33; for men, it is 36 (*Statistical Abstract of the United States: 1997,* Table 149). Two researchers (Amato & Keith, 1991, p. 54) analyzed data in 37 studies from 81,000 people and concluded that "divorce (or permanent separation) has broad negative consequences for quality of life in adulthood." Children who experience divorce are more likely to experience depression and lower life satisfaction and are more likely to have a divorce in their own marriages.

The primary disadvantage of having a child in the later years is that the parents are likely to die before, or early in, the child's adult life. The daughter of James Dickey, the Southern writer, lamented the fact that her late father (to whom she was born when he was in his fifties) would not be present at her graduation or wedding.

There are also medical concerns for both the mother and the baby during pregnancy in later life. Although maternal and fetal outcomes for women delivering babies after the age of 45 are "generally good" (Dildy et al., 1996), there is an increased risk of morbidity and mortality for the mother. These risks are typically a function of chronic disorders that go along with aging, such as diabetes, hypertension, and cardiac disease (Cunningham et al., 1997). Stillbirths, congenital malformations, and infant mortality are also higher in women in their late thirties and forties (Fretts et al., 1995; Cunningham et al., 1997). However, prenatal testing can identify the risk of Down syndrome and any chromosome abnormality (Bahado-Singh et al., 1996), and negative neonatal outcomes are not inevitable (Bianco et al., 1996). Based on a review of the studies on pregnancy and childbirth in women over 35, Cunningham et al. (1997, p. 577) noted:

> Women should realistically appraise the risks of pregnancy later in life, but should not necessarily fear delaying childbirth. Pregnancy after 35 is increasingly common in our society, and improved obstetrical care has made advanced maternal age compatible with successful pregnancy for the great majority of such women.

Given that medical outcomes are usually manageable, government regulations in regard to how young a woman must be at pregnancy are not likely. In addition, control would be difficult. Fearing that she would not be accepted into the University of Southern California's Program for Assisted Reproduction, Arceli Keh did not tell them her real age. Instead, she told them she was 50.

Sources: Amato, P. R., & Keith, B. (1991). Parental divorce and adult well-being. *Journal of Marriage and the Family, 53,* 43–58.

Bahado-Singh, R. O., Deren, O., Tan, A., D'AnCona, R. L., Hunter, D., Copel, J. A., & Mahoney, M. J. (1996). Ultrasonographically adjusted

Continued on following page.

mid trimester risk of trisomy 21 and significant chromosomal defects in advanced maternal age. *American Journal of Obstetrics and Gynecology, 175,* 1563–1568.

Bianco, A., Stone, J., Lynch, L., Lapinski R., Berkowitz, B., & Berkowitz, R. L. (1996). Pregnancy outcome at age 40 and older. *Obstetrics and Gynecology, 87,* 917–922.

Cunningham, F. G., MacDonald, P. C., Gant, N. F., Leveno, K. J., Gilstrap, L. C., Harkins, G. D. V., & Clark, S. L. (Eds.). (1997). *Williams Obstetrics* (20th ed.). Stamford, CT: Appleton and Lange.

Dildy, G. A., Jackson, G. M., Flowers, G. K., Oshiro, B. T., Varner, N.W., & Clark S. L. (1996). Very advanced maternal age: Pregnancy after age 45. *American Journal of Obstetrics and Gynecology, 175,* 668–674.

Fretts, R. C., Schmittdiel, J., McLean, F.H., Usher, R. H., & Goldman, M. B. (1995). Increased maternal age and the risk of fetal death. *New England Journal of Medicine, 333,* 953–957.

Hellmich, N. (1997, April 24). Oldest new mom is 63. *USA Today,* p. 1A.

Peterson, K. S., & Hellmich, N. (1997, April 25). No shortage of opinion on 63-year-old mom. *USA Today,* p. 1A.

Ramsburg, D. (1997, April). Brain development in young children: The early years ARE learning years. *Parent News, 3,* 1–3.

Sparta, C. (1997, April 24). Tony Randall a daddy at 77. *USA Today,* p. 1A.

Starting points for young children. (1994). New York: Carnegie Corporation of New York.

Statistical Abstract of the United States: 1997, (117th ed.). (1997). Washington, DC: U.S. Bureau of the Census.

HOW MANY CHILDREN DO YOU WANT?

The national data chart that follows shows the percent of families in the United States who have children. Although more than half of the families do not have children at any given time, most either will have children someday or already have children who have left home.

NATIONAL DATA

The percentage of families in the United States who have children

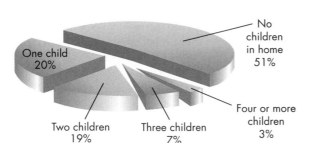

Source: *Statistical Abstract of the United Sates: 1997,* Table 77.

More than 90% of couples want children, but some do not. Jay Leno and his wife are an example of a child-free couple.

None—the Child-Free Alternative

NATIONAL DATA

Women in the United States between the ages of 18 and 34 who do not expect to have children

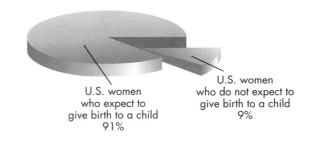

Source: *Statistical Abstract of the United States: 1997,* Table 107.

With two exceptions, the percentage of couples electing to remain child-free has remained relatively stable in the past 50 years. The two periods of exception occurred during the 1930s depression (when there were more child-free women) and during the 1950–1965 baby boom (when there were fewer child-free women) (Jones et al., 1995).

Women today who want to remain child-free tend to evidence greater interest in a career, to have an egalitarian relationship with their spouse, and to value freedom from the constraints of having children. Generally, wives in child-free marriages are more committed to remaining child-free than are their husbands (Jones et al., 1995, p. 113). Couples who put off having children are similar to couples who make it clear they do not ever want children. Both groups tend to be white, highly educated, career-oriented city dwellers (Jones et al., 1995).

Whites are most likely to consider marriage without children. African Americans, Native Americans, Mexican Americans and Asian Americans are more likely to be family-oriented and consider children an important part of family life (O'Hare, Pollard, Mann, & Kent, 1991; O'Hare & Felt, 1991; Ahlburg & De Vita, 1992). However, being upwardly mobile may sometimes override ethnic influence. African Americans who are striving to achieve social mobility are more likely to be voluntarily child-free (Boyd, 1989).

How happy are the marriages of couples who elect to remain child-free compared to the marriages of couples who opt for having children? While marital satisfaction declines across time for all couples whether or not they have children (MacDermid, Huston, & McHale, 1990), children tend to lessen marital satisfaction by decreasing spousal time together, spousal interaction, and agreement over finances. In addition, couples who have children report greater satisfaction before their children are born and after the children leave home. The greatest drop in marital satisfaction is during the time the children are teenagers. Child-free couples do not experience this roller-coaster ride (Glenn, 1991).

THINK ABOUT IT

Is the child-free lifestyle for you? If you get your primary satisfactions from interacting with adults and from your career, and if you require an atmosphere of freedom and privacy, perhaps the answer is yes. But if your desire for a child is at least equal to your desire for a satisfying adult relationship, career, and freedom, the answer may be no. The child-free alternative is particularly valuable to people who would find the demands of parenthood an unneccessary burden and strain.

One Child?

Bill and Hillary Clinton and their daughter, Chelsea, have drawn national attention to the one-child family. The number of children a couple chooses to have is influenced by the society in which the couple lives. In the United States, the two-child norm exerts enor-

The Clinton family has drawn national attention to the one-child family.

mous social pressure on parents of one child to have a second child. In China, the one-child family is actively encouraged and has resulted in a drop in the country's birthrate. Although most only children are stereotyped as being spoiled, selfish, and lonely, data suggest that they are happy, bright, and socially skilled. Toman said of only children:

> More than other children their age, only children look and act like little adults themselves. This is not only because they have usually spent more time with their parents than other children who have siblings, but also because they can learn how to behave toward a parent as the other parent would and not as another child does. There are no other children to identify with. An only child behaves toward his father the way his mother does, and vice versa. He can also make his parents help and protect him and do things for him more readily than other children can make their parents. Only children are the focus of their [parents'] attention anyway. They don't have to share their parents with other children. Cousins and other children may come to their house, to be sure, but they don't stay for long, and the only child clearly recognizes that he does not have to compete with these other children for his parents' favor. (1993, p. 26)

One consequence of China's overpopulation and subsequent development of a one-child policy is the pressure on parents to have sons rather than daughters as their children. As noted earlier, sons are valued to take care of parents in their old age. They do this by marrying women who become responsible for taking care of their husband's elderly parents. Daughters are of little value to their parents because they are expected to marry and to take care of their husband's parents. Even in the face of very stringent governmental regulations and policies, "the majority of Chinese women continued childbearing in pursuit of their traditional, culturally and economically determined goal of producing a male offspring to carry on the family line and to provide for old-age insurance" (Li, 1995, p. 582).

One way some Chinese parents ensure that their only child is a son is infanticide—the killing of infant daughters soon after they are born. A 1990 census in China revealed that 5% of infant girls were "missing"; it is suspected that these infants were killed by midwives on the orders of parents who were intent on having sons (Kristof, 1991).

Two Children?

The most preferred family size in the United States is the two-child family. Couples choose to have two children for several reasons. Some couples feel that a family is not complete without two children, and they want their firstborn to have a sibling and companion. Parents might have two children with the hope of having a child of each sex. Many mothers want a second child because they enjoyed their first child and want to repeat the experience. Others want to avoid having an only child because of the negative stereotypes associated with only children. Or parents may not want to "put all their eggs in one basket." For example, some parents fear that if they only have one child and that child dies or turns out to be disappointing, they will not have another opportunity to enjoy parenting.

Three Children?

Couples are more likely to have a third child, and to do so quickly, if they already have two girls rather than two boys. They are least likely to bear a third child if they already have a boy and a girl (Jones et al., 1995).

Some individuals may want three children because they enjoy children and feel that "three is better than two." In some instances, a couple that has two children of the same sex may want to try one more time to have a child of the other sex.

Having a third child creates a "middle child." This child is sometimes neglected, because parents of three children may focus more on the "baby" and the firstborn than on the child in between (Toman, 1993). However, an advantage to being a middle child is the chance to experience both a younger and an older sibling.

Four or More Children?

Men are more likely to want four or more children than women. Hispanics are more likely to want larger families than whites or African Americans (Rochell, 1995). Larger families have complex interactional patterns and different values. The addition of each subsequent child dramatically increases the possible relationships in the family. For example, in the one-child family, 4 interpersonal relationships are possible: mother-father, mother-child, father-child, and father-mother-child. In a family of four, 11 relationships are possible; in a family of five, 26; and in a family of six, 57.

In addition to relationships, values change as families get larger. Whereas members of a small family tend to value independence and personal development, large-family members necessarily value cooperation, harmony, and sharing. A parent of nine children said, "Meals around our house are a cooperative endeavor. One child prepares the drinks, another the bread, and still another sets the table. You have to develop cooperation, or nobody gets fed."

Each additional child also has a negative effect on the existing children by reducing the amount of parental time available. This finding is based on a national sample of 1403 mothers who noted they had less time for existing children when new children arrived (Menaghan & Parcel, 1995). Furthermore, each additional child dilutes the financial resources available so that things such as educational materials, money for college, and a computer are less easily attained as the number of children in a family increases. This latter effect translates into less education and lower grades for children in larger families (Downey, 1995).

PERSONAL CHOICES

Should You Choose to Have a Child Without a Partner?

Although women have traditionally taken on parenthood after marriage, an increasing number have begun to consider having children even though they do not have steady partners. Many of these women are in their thirties and feel that they may never get married. One single mother over the age of 30 said:

I could imagine going through life without a man, but I couldn't imagine going through life without a child. My biological clock started sounding like a time bomb. (quoted in Smolowe, 1990, p. 76)

Another single mother by choice explained:

My relationships were not developing along the course I had hoped. . . . I really love kids and feel I have a lot to offer. (quoted in Smolowe, 1990, p. 76)

Jean Renvoize (1985) interviewed 30 unmarried women who had made a conscious choice to have a baby with the intent of rearing their child alone. Of these women, the researcher said:

I expected to find a group of tough-minded, militant women somewhat on the defensive; instead I found mostly happy, fulfilled, strong, but gentle individuals who gave out warmth and a readiness to share with others. These were women who had made their choice after much deliberation, mostly at a mature age, and who knew in advance that nothing in life comes free. (p. 5)

The typical profile of the single mother by choice follows:

. . . a white, educated, financially stable, professional woman who may have a prior history of marriage and/or pregnancy. She usually comes from an intact traditional family, although the parental marriage may have been conflictual. (Miller, 1993, p. 22)

. . . They are personable and have been able to develop strong and lasting friendships. They are sensitive and thoughtful and all too aware of the potential pitfalls that confront them and their children. They are also highly committed to their role as parents. (p. 49)

An organization for women who want children and who may or may not marry is Single Mothers by Choice. The organization has more than 2000 members and provides support for unmarried women who are contemplating having a child. The organization also has "thinkers' groups" for women who are uncertain about whether or not to have a child. Most women attending these groups decide not to have children after they have considered the various issues. *Single Mothers by Choice* (Mattes, 1994) is a handbook detailing the various issues to consider when making such a decision.

Some of the problems faced by women who elect to rear children alone include the following:

1. *Satisfaction of the emotional and disciplinary needs of the child.* Perhaps the greatest challenge for single parents is satisfying the emotional needs of their children—alone. Children need love, which a parent may express in numerous ways—from hugs to helping with homework. But the single parent who is tired from working all day and who has no one else with whom to share parenting at night may be less able to meet the emotional needs of a child.

Single mothers also have more limited help in monitoring their children and disciplining them (Simons, Whitbeck, Beaman, & Conger, 1994). (It is recognized, however, that there are also many mothers who work outside the home and receive limited or no parenting help from their partner.) A single mother of three teenagers stated:

In this day and age of child-rearing it sure would be nice to be sharing the responsibility with someone else. I get tired of being a full-time policeman and everything else. (Richards & Schmiege, 1993, p. 280)

When compared with mothers living with partners, single mothers report more stress and more behavior problems with children. These single mothers also report more conflict with their daughters than with their sons (Webster-Stratton, 1989).

2. *Satisfaction of adult emotional needs.* Single parents have emotional needs of their own that children are often incapable of satisfying. The unmet need to share an emotional relationship with an adult can weigh heavily on the single parent. Shaw interviewed 25 single-parent women and noted that loneliness was one of their concerns.

Loneliness means lack of an adult companion to talk to, to hold, to be with, who loves them, who understands them, and puts them first, before anything else. . . . However, the fact that these women feel a need for "someone special" does not mean that they are more unhappy than other individuals in society who experience the same feelings. . . . On the contrary, they are for the most part extremely positive about themselves, and optimistic about their futures. (1991, p. 145)

3. *Satisfaction of adult sexual needs.* Some single parents regard their parental role as interfering with their sexual relationships. They may be concerned that their children will find out if they have a sexual encounter at home or be frustrated if they have to go away from home to enjoy a sexual relationship. Some choices with which they are confronted include "Do I wait until my children are asleep and then ask my lover to leave before morning?" "Do I openly acknowledge my lover's presence in my life to my children and ask them not to tell anybody?" "Suppose my kids get attached to my lover, who may not be a permanent part of our lives?"

4. *Lack of money.* Single-parent families, particularly those headed by women, report that money is always lacking.

NATIONAL DATA

The median income for female-headed, single-parent households versus two-parent households. Male-headed, single-parent households are generally less economically stressed because men typically make more money than women.

Source: *Statistical Abstract of United States: 1996,* Table 711.

Single-parent, never-married mothers are also more economically disadvantaged than single-parent mothers who are divorced or separated. Lino (1994) compared never-married mothers with those who had been divorced and found that their before-tax family income averaged $9820 compared to $18,580. Two other researchers (Gringlas & Weinraub, 1995) compared 21 solo mothers (mothers who reared their child alone since birth with no help from father) with 21 married mothers and found more stress and less support among the solo mothers.

5. *Guardianship.* If the other parent is completely out of the child's life, the single parent needs to appoint a guardian to take care of her or his child in the event of her or his own death or disability.

6. *Prenatal care.* Single women who decide to have a child have poorer pregnancy outcomes than married women. In a Finnish study of 56,596 infants, those who were born to single mothers were more likely to be born prematurely, to have low birth weights, and to die shortly after birth than those born to married mothers (Manderbacka, Merilainen, Hemminki, Rahkonen, & Teperi, 1992). The researchers hypothesized that the reason for such findings may have been the lack of social support for the pregnancy or the working conditions of the mother. Alternatively, the researchers considered that it is possible that healthier people are more likely to be selected as marriage partners (p. 514).

THINK ABOUT IT

When couples think about and plan for the family size they want, they rarely take into consideration the possibility of divorce. In deciding how many children you want (if you want any at all), it is not unrealistic to ask yourself how you would care for the child (or children) if you became divorced and either had primary custody of the children or had to make child support payments. Also, when divorced parents remarry, they often find themselves in families that are larger than what they originally planned. For example, a woman with two children who marries a man with three children suddenly has five children in her family unit. Given the high rates of divorce and remarriage, you may want to consider these issues when thinking about the number of children you intend to have.

BIRTH CONTROL

Before 1870 (when condoms were first mass marketed), abstinence was the only way a couple could ensure that the woman would not get pregnant.

Today, couples can separate their lovemaking from their babymaking with a variety of birth control procedures. But despite the development of various contraceptive methods, many women experience unintended pregnancies.

According to a report by the Alan Guttmacher Institute, in almost half of unintended pregnancies in the United States, the contraceptive method used simply did not work as it should have, or it was used inconsistently or incorrectly. However, slightly more than half of all unintended pregnancies occur among the 10% of U.S. women who report that they do not use any method of birth control ("Sixty Percent of U.S. Pregnancies Unintended," 1997). Some women may not be able to afford birth control methods or may live far from medical contraceptive service providers. "Others may be embarrassed to buy contraceptives or seek services, or reluctant to admit that they are having sex, or may be afraid of parental or community disapproval" (p. 1).

In the remainder of this chapter, we review methods of contraception. All contraceptive practices have one of two common purposes: to prevent the male sperm from fertilizing the female egg or to keep the fertilized egg from implanting itself in the uterus.

Hormonal Contraceptives

Hormonal contraceptives currently available to women include the "pill," Norplant, and Depo-Provera.

BIRTH CONTROL PILL   The birth control pill is the most commonly used method of all the nonsurgical forms of contraception. Although a small percentage of women who take the pill still get pregnant, it remains a very desirable birth control option.

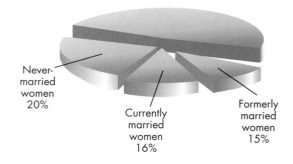
Although there are more than 40 brands available in North America, there are basically two types of birth control pills—the combination pill and the minipill. The combination pill contains the hormones estrogen and progesterone (also known as progestin), which act to prevent ovulation and implantation. The estrogen inhibits the release of the follicle-stimulating hormone (FSH) from the pituitary gland. Normally, follicles mature to become eggs, but without the release of FSH, follicles will not develop into eggs. Thus, estrogen blocks the release of FSH, which prevents the follicle from maturing into an egg.

The progesterone inhibits the release of luteinizing hormone (LH) from the pituitary gland, which during a normal cycle would cause the mature ovum to move to the periphery of the follicle and the follicle to rupture (ovulation). Hence, because of progesterone, there is no ovulation. In this case, the progestin blocks the LH, which would have caused ovulation.

Progesterone also causes the cervical mucus to become thick and acidic, thereby creating a hostile environment for the sperm. So, even if an egg were to mature and ovulation were to occur, the progesterone would ward off or destroy the sperm. Another function of progesterone is to make the lining of the uterus unsuitable for implantation.

The combination pill is taken for 21 days, during the first three weeks of the menstrual cycle. During the fourth week, the woman stops taking the pill, resulting in a lower hormone level. Three or four days after the last pill is taken, menstruation occurs, and the 28-day cycle begins again.

The second type of oral contraceptive, the minipill, contains the same progesterone found in the combination pill, but in much lower doses. The minipill contains no estrogen. Like the progesterone in the combination pill, the progesterone in the minipill provides a hostile environment for sperm and inhibits implantation of a fertilized egg in the uterus. In general, the minipill is somewhat less effective than other types of birth control pills and has been associated with a higher incidence of irregular bleeding.

Either the combination pill or the minipill should be taken only when prescribed by a physician who has detailed information about the woman's previous medical history. Contraindications—reasons for not prescribing birth control pills—include hypertension, impaired liver function, known or suspected tumors that are estrogen dependent, undiagnosed abnormal genital bleeding, pregnancy at the time of the examination, and a history of poor blood circulation. The major complications associated with taking oral contraceptives are blood clots and high blood pressure. Also, the risk of heart attack is increased in women over age 30, particularly for those who smoke or have other risk factors. Women over 40 should generally use other forms of contraception because the side effects of contraceptive pills increase with the age of the user. Infertility problems have also been noted in women who have used the combination pill for several years without the breaks in pill use recommended by most physicians.

Although the long-term negative consequences of taking birth control pills are still the subject of research, short-term negative effects are experienced by 25% of all women who use them. These side effects include increased susceptibility to vaginal infections, nausea, slight weight gain, vaginal bleeding between periods, breast tenderness, headaches, and mood changes (some women become depressed and experience a loss of sexual desire).

Finally, women should be aware that pill use is associated with an increased incidence of chlamydia and gonorrhea. One reason for this higher incidence of STDs is that sexually active women who use the pill sometimes erroneously feel that because they are protected from getting pregnant, they are also protected from contracting STDs. The pill provides no protection against STDs; a condom must be worn.

In spite of the negative consequences associated with birth control pill use, numerous studies involving hundreds of thousands of women show that the overall risk of pill use is lower than the risk of full-term pregnancy and giving birth.

Immediate health benefits are also derived from taking birth control pills. Oral contraceptives tend to protect the woman against breast tumors, ovarian cysts, rheumatoid arthritis, and inflammatory disease of the pelvis. They also regularize the woman's menstrual cycle, reduce premenstrual tension, and may reduce menstrual cramps and blood loss during menstruation. Finally, oral contraceptives are convenient, do not interfere with intercourse, and, most important, provide highly effective protection against pregnancy.

Whether to use birth control pills remains a controversial issue. Some women feel it harms their body to take birth control pills; others feel it harms their body not to take them. Whatever a woman's choice, it should be made in conjunction with the physician who knows her medical history. The physician should also alert the woman to the fact that any use of antibiotics while taking the pill may cancel the contraceptive effects of the pill.

NORPLANT   In the early 1990s, the FDA approved the use of *Norplant* (levonorgesterol), a long-acting reversible hormonal contraceptive consisting of six thin flexible silicone capsules about the size of matchsticks implanted under the skin of the upper arm. The major advantage of Norplant is that it provides continuous protection against pregnancy for up to 5 years. As a result of its association with silicone and reported side effects (migraine headaches, shortness of breath, menstrual irregularities, and weight gain), recent use has declined dramatically. Daily sales of Norplant have plummeted from 800 to 60. And out of one million women who have tried Norplant, 50,000 have retained lawyers to sue the company that manufactures it because they were not adequately warned of its potential problems (Cohen, 1995).

DEPO-PROVERA   A new FDA-approved alternative to Norplant is *Depo-Provera,* a synthetic compound similar to progesterone that is injected into the woman's arm or buttock. Depo-Provera protects a woman

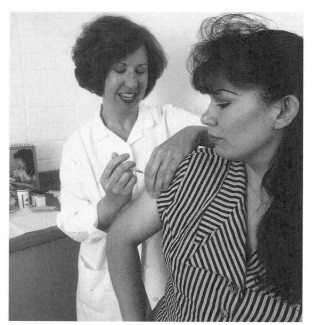

One shot of Depo-Provera protects a woman against pregnancy for three months.

against pregnancy for 3 months by preventing ovulation. It has been used by 30 million women worldwide since it was introduced in the late 1960s. For women who get their shot every 3 months, the failure rate is less than 1%.

Side effects of Depo-Provera include menstrual spotting, irregular bleeding, and some heavy bleeding the first few months of use. Mood changes, headaches, dizziness, and fatigue have also been observed. Some women report a weight gain of 3 to 5 pounds. Also, after stopping the injections, it takes an average of 18 months before the woman will become pregnant at the same rate as women who have not used Depo-Provera. The cost of injections is about $140 per year.

Oral contraceptives and Depo-Provera were designed for use by women. In recent years, researchers have tried to develop hormonal contraceptives for use by men. Dr. Ronald Swerdloff (1995) of the Harbor-UCLA Medical Center noted, "We have been able to show that reversible, safe, male hormonal contraception is a possibility." He and his colleagues injected 370 males once a day initially and, subsequently, once a week with synthetic testosterone. The desired effect was to lower sperm production so that men could have regular intercourse with only a 1.4% failure rate of pregnancy. Men who share the responsi-

bility for contraception are most likely to use a male injectable contraceptive (Ringheim, 1995). However, further testing and refinement will take several years before a male hormonal contraceptive is commercially available (Alexander, 1995). In this regard, it is noteworthy that hormonal pills for women were commercially available long before many of the problems related to them had been solved.

Condom

The condom is currently the only form of male contraception commercially available. The condom is a thin sheath made of latex or polyurethane. Unlike condoms made of latex, the polyurethane condom can be used with petroleum jelly; it avoids the latex allergy some people experience, blocks the HIV virus and other sexually transmitted diseases, and allows for greater sensitivity during intercourse.

NATIONAL DATA

In the United States, 14% of women ages 15 to 24, 15% of women ages 25 to 34, and 11% of women ages 35 to 44 use condoms as their method of contraception.

Source: *Statistical Abstract of the United States: 1997*, Table 110.

The condom works by rolling it over and down the shaft of the erect penis before intercourse (see Figure 6.1). When the man ejaculates, the sperm are caught inside the condom. When used in combination with a spermicidal lubricant that is placed on the inside of the reservoir tip of the condom, as well as a spermicidal or sperm-killing agent that the woman inserts inside her vagina, the condom is a highly effective contraceptive.

A latex or polyurethane condom with nonoxynol-9 (spermicide effective in killing the AIDS virus) is the contraceptive that best protects against HIV and other sexually transmitted diseases. Yet, 40% of sexually active college students reported not practicing "safe" sex (Morris & Schneider, 1992). Although denial ("I won't get an STD") is a major factor in not using a condom, some men say that condom use decreases sensation. However, others say having the partner put the condom on their penis during foreplay is an erotic experience, and the condom actually enhances pleasurable feelings during intercourse.

Pinch or twist the tip of the condom, leaving one-half inch at the tip to catch the semen.

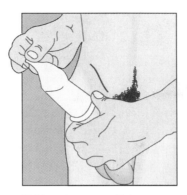

Holding the tip, unroll the condom.

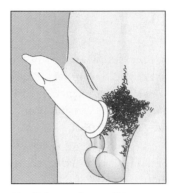

Unroll the condom until it reaches the pubic hair.

FIGURE 6.1   How to Put on a Condom

Like any contraceptive, the condom is effective only when used properly. It should be placed on the penis early enough to avoid any seminal leakage into the vagina. In addition, polyurethane or latex condoms with a reservoir tip are preferable, as they are less likely to break. Finally, the penis should be withdrawn from the vagina immediately after ejaculation, before the man's penis returns to its flaccid state. If the penis is not withdrawn and the erection subsides, semen may leak from the base of the condom into the vaginal lips. Alternatively, when the erection subsides, the condom will come off when the man withdraws his penis if he does not hold on to the condom. Either way, the sperm will begin to travel up the vagina to the uterus to fertilize the egg.

In addition to furnishing extra protection, spermicides also provide lubrication, which permits easy entrance of the condom-covered penis into the vagina. If no spermicide is used and the condom is not of the prelubricated variety, a personal lubricant, such as K-Y jelly, may be needed. (For more information about buying and using condoms, see Figure 6.2.)

THE FEMALE CONDOM   The female condom resembles a man's condom except that it fits in the woman's vagina to protect her from pregnancy, as well as HIV infection and other STDs. The vaginal condom is a large, lubricated, polyurethane adaptation of the male version. It is about 7 inches long and has flexible rings at both ends. It is inserted like a diaphragm, with the inner ring fitting behind the pubic bone against the   cervix; the outer ring remains outside the body and encircles the labial area (see Figure 6.3). Like the male version, the female condom is not reusable. Female condoms have been approved by the FDA and are being marketed under the brand names Femidom and Reality. The one-size-fits-all device is available without a prescription and sells for about $2.25 (per condom).

The female condom allows a woman to control her exposure to some STD infections.

How to Buy and Use Condoms

Materials: Buy latex or polyurethane, not natural membrane or lambskin. Latex and polyurethane are less apt to leak and better able to protect against HIV transmission. Inexpensive foreign brands are suspect.

Sizes: The Food and Drug Administration says condoms must be between 6 and 8 inches in length when unrolled. (The average erect penis is 6½ inches long.) Condoms labeled *Regular* are 7½ inches. Instead of "Small" for condoms under 7½ inches, manufacturers use labels such as *Snug Fit*. Instead of "Large" for condoms over 7½ inches, manufacturers use labels such as *Max* or *Magnum*.

Shapes: Most condoms are *straight-walled*. Some, however, are labeled *contoured*, which means they are anatomically shaped to fit the penis and thus are more comfortable.

Tips: Some condoms have a *reservoir* at the end to catch semen upon ejaculation. Others do not have a reservoir, in which case they should be twisted at the tip after being put on.

Plain or lubricated: Condoms can be purchased *plain* (unlubricated) or *lubricated,* which means they feel more slippery to the touch. There are four options:

1. Buy a plain condom and don't use a lubricant.
2. Buy a plain condom and use your own water-based personal lubricant product (such as K-Y Jelly or Astroglide).
3. Buy a lubricated condom pregreased with silicone-, jelly-, or water-based lubricants.
4. Buy a *spermicidally lubricated* condom that contains *nonoxynol-9,* a chemical that kills sperm and HIV. This is probably the best option.

Strength: A standard condom will do for vaginal and oral sex. Some people believe an *"extra strength"* condom is less apt to break during anal sex, although this is debatable.

Gimmicks: In addition, condoms come with all kinds of other features:

1. *Colors:* Red, blue, green, and yellow are safe. Avoid black and "glow in the dark," says the FDA, because the dyes may rub off.
2. *Smell and taste:* Latex smells and tastes rubbery, but some scented condoms mask this odor.
3. *Adhesive:* Condoms are available with adhesive to hold them in place so they won't slip off during withdrawal.
4. *Marketing gimmicks:* Some condoms are sold with ribs, nubs, bumps, and so on. It is questionable how much increased stimulation these features provide.

How to Use

Storage: Condoms should be stored in a cool, dry place. Keeping them in a hot glove compartment or wallet in the back pocket for weeks can cause the latex to fail.

Opening package: Look to see whether the foil or plastic packaging is not broken; if it is, don't use the condom. Open the package carefully. Fingernails can easily damage a condom.

Inspection: Make sure the condom is soft and pliable. Don't use it if it's brittle, sticky, or discolored. Don't try to test it for leaks by unrolling, stretching, or blowing it up; this will only weaken it.

Putting it on: Put the condom on before any genital contact to prevent exposure to fluids. Hold the tip of the condom, and unroll it directly onto the erect penis. (If the man is not circumcised, pull back the foreskin before rolling on the condom.) Gently pinch the tip to remove air bubbles, which can cause the condom to break. Condoms without a reservoir tip need a half-inch free at the tip.

Lubricants: *Important!* If you're using a lubricant of your own, *don't use an oil-based lubricant.* Oil-based lubricants—such as hand lotion, baby oil, mineral oil, and Vaseline—can reduce a latex condom's strength by 90% in as little as 60 seconds. Saliva is not recommended either.

Use a water-based or silicone-based product designed for such use, such as K-Y Jelly or spermicidal compounds containing nonoxynol-9.

Add lubricant to the outside of the condom before entry. If not enough lubricant is used, the condom can tear or pull off.

FIGURE 6.2 Condoms

Continued on next page.

The vaginal condom is durable and does not tear like latex male condoms, but it is trickier to use. The actual effectiveness rate (against STDs) of the vaginal condom has not been sufficiently studied. A major advantage of the female condom is that like the male counterpart, it protects against transmission of the HIV virus and other STDs. Placement may occur up to 8 hours before use, allowing greater spontaneity (Stifel & Anderson, 1997). Women and men who have used the vaginal condom are generally satisfied with the device (Gregersen & Gregersen, 1990).

In one study of 52 women ages 18–57, 79% reported that they had used the female condom at least once. Of those who reported use, 73% of the respondents and 44% of their partners preferred the female condom to the male condom (Gollub, Stein, & El-Sadr, 1995).

Intrauterine Device (IUD)

The *intrauterine device,* or IUD, is a small object that is inserted by a physician into the woman's uterus through the vagina and cervix (see Figure 6.4). The device is thought to prevent implantation of the fertilized egg in the uterine wall. As a result of infertility and miscarriage problems associated with IUDs and subsequent lawsuits against manufacturers by persons who were damaged by the device, use in the United States is now minimal. However, current studies suggest that the rates of pelvic inflammatory disease, ectopic pregnancy, or resultant infertility are lower for newer IUDs than previously suspected (Stifel & Anderson, 1997).

NATIONAL DATA

U.S. women ages 15–44 who use the IUD as their method of contraception

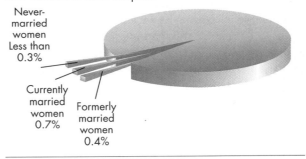

Never-married women Less than 0.3%

Currently married women 0.7%

Formerly married women 0.4%

Source: *Statistical Abstract of the United States: 1997,* Table 110.

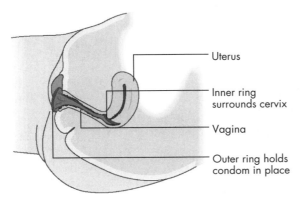

Uterus

Inner ring surrounds cervix

Vagina

Outer ring holds condom in place

FIGURE 6.3 The Female Condom
The 6 1/2-inch-long sheath lines the vagina and is held in place by two plastic rings.

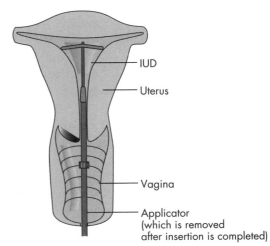

IUD

Uterus

Vagina

Applicator (which is removed after insertion is completed)

FIGURE 6.4 The IUD, as It Is Inserted by a Health Care Practitioner

Planning Children and Birth Control 149

Diaphragm

Use of the diaphragm in the United States is also minimal.

NATIONAL DATA

U.S. women ages 15–44 who use the diaphragm as their method of contraception

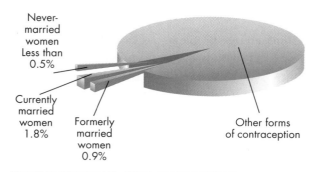

- Never-married women Less than 0.5%
- Currently married women 1.8%
- Formerly married women 0.9%
- Other forms of contraception

Source: *Statistical Abstract of the United States: 1997,* Table 110.

The *diaphragm* is a shallow rubber dome attached to a flexible, circular steel spring. Varying in diameter from 2 to 4 inches, the diaphragm covers the cervix and prevents sperm from moving beyond the vagina into the uterus. This device should always be used with a spermicidal jelly or cream.

To obtain a diaphragm, a woman must have an internal pelvic examination by a physician or nurse practitioner, who will select the appropriate size diaphragm and instruct the woman on how to insert it. The woman will be told to apply one teaspoonful of spermicidal cream or jelly on the inside of the diaphragm and around the rim before inserting it into the vagina (no more than 2 hours before intercourse). The diaphragm must also be left in place for 6 to 8 hours after intercourse to permit any lingering sperm to be killed by the spermicidal agent (see Figure 6.5).

After the birth of a child, a miscarriage, abdominal surgery, or the gain or loss of ten pounds, a woman who uses a diaphragm should consult her physician or health care practitioner to ensure a continued good fit. In any case, the diaphragm should be checked every 2 years for fit.

A major advantage of the diaphragm is that it does not interfere with the woman's hormonal system and has few, if any, side effects. Also, for couples who feel that menstruation diminishes their capacity to enjoy intercourse, the diaphragm is sometimes used to catch the menstrual flow for a brief time.

On the negative side, some women feel that use of the diaphragm with the spermicidal gel is messy and a nuisance. For some, the use of the gel may produce an allergic reaction. Furthermore, some partners feel that the gel makes oral-genital contact less enjoyable. Finally, if the diaphragm does not fit properly or is left in place too long (more than 24 hours), pregnancy or toxic shock syndrome (respectively) can result.

Cervical Cap

The *cervical cap* is a contraceptive device made of rubber or polyethylene that fits tightly over the cervix and is held in place by suction. Like the diaphragm, the cervical cap, which is used in conjunction with spermicidal cream or jelly, prevents sperm from entering the uterus. Cervical caps are fitted by health care practitioners. They have been widely available in

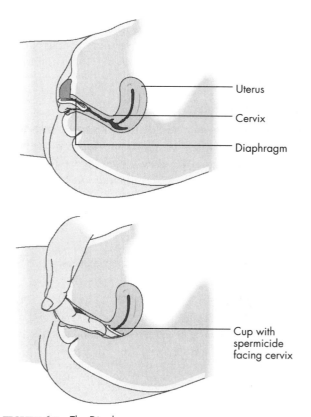

- Uterus
- Cervix
- Diaphragm
- Cup with spermicide facing cervix

FIGURE 6.5 The Diaphragm

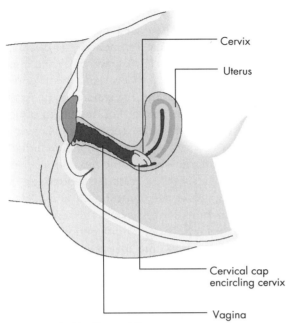

FIGURE 6.6   The Cervical Cap

Each time intercourse is repeated, more spermicide must be applied. Spermicide must be left in place for at least 6 to 8 hours after intercourse; douching or rinsing the vagina should not be done during this period. One advantage of using spermicides is that they are available without a prescription or medical examination. They also do not affect the woman's hormonal system and have few side effects. A major noncontraceptive benefit of some spermicides is that they offer some protection against the transmission of sexually transmitted diseases, including HIV. However, spermicides should never be depended upon alone to be effective in preventing STD transmission.

Periodic Abstinence

Also referred to as natural family planning, rhythm method, and fertility awareness, *periodic abstinence* involves refraining from sexual intercourse during the 1 to 2 weeks each month when the woman is thought to be fertile (see Figure 6.8).

Europe for some time and were approved for marketing in the United States in 1988. The cervical cap cannot be used during menstruation because the suction cannot be maintained. The effectiveness, problems, risks, and advantages are similar to those of the diaphragm (see Figure 6.6).

Vaginal Spermicides

A *spermicide* is a chemical that kills sperm. Vaginal spermicides come in several forms, including foam, cream, jelly, and suppository. In the United States, the active agent in most spermicides is nonoxynol-9, which has been shown to kill many organisms that cause sexually transmitted diseases (including HIV). Creams and gels are intended for use with a diaphragm. Suppositories are intended for use alone or with a condom. Foam is marketed for use alone but can also be used with a diaphragm or condom.

Spermicides must be applied before the penis comes near the vagina (appropriate applicators are included when the product is purchased), no more than 20 minutes before intercourse (see Figure 6.7). While foam is effective immediately, suppositories, creams, or jellies require a few minutes to allow the product to melt and spread inside the vagina. (Package instructions specify the exact time required.)

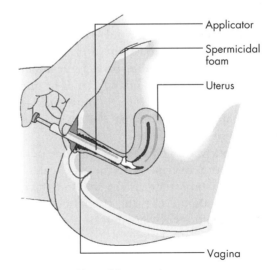

FIGURE 6.7   Vaginal Spermicides
Among the sperm-killing chemicals offered are foams, jellies, creams, suppositories, and films.

Days	Risk of conception
1	
2	
3	*Menstruation:* low-risk days for
4	unprotected intercourse
5	
6	Low-risk days for unprotected intercourse
7	
8	Possibly risky days,
9	if 28-day cycle varies by 8–9 days
10	
11	Risky days for unprotected intercourse
12	
13	
14	*Ovulation:* Risky days for unprotected intercourse
15	
16	
17	Risky: ovum may still be present
18	
19	Risky days for unprotected intercourse
20	
21	
22	
23	
24	
25	Low-risk days for unprotected intercourse
26	
27	
28	

FIGURE 6.8 The Calendar Method of Family Planning
Most women's cycles are not a consistent 28 days but may vary anywhere from 21 to 35 days.

Women who use periodic abstinence must know their time of ovulation and avoid intercourse just before, during, and immediately after that time. Calculating the fertile period involves three assumptions: (1) ovulation occurs on day 14 (plus or minus 2 days) *before the onset of the next menstrual period;* (2) sperm remain viable for 2–3 days; and (3) the ovum survives for 24 hours.

There are four ways of predicting the time period during which the woman is fertile: the calendar method, the basal body temperature method, the cervical mucus method, and the hormone-in-urine method. These methods may not only be used to avoid pregnancy, they may also be used to facilitate conception if the woman wants to become pregnant. We provide only basic instructions here for using periodic abstinence as a method of contraception. Individuals considering this method should consult with a trained health practitioner for more detailed instruction.

CALENDAR METHOD   The calendar method is the oldest and most widely practiced method of avoiding pregnancy through periodic abstinence. The calendar method allows women to calculate the onset and duration of their fertile period. When using the calendar method to predict when the egg is ready to be fertilized, the woman keeps a record of the length of her menstrual cycles for 8 months. The menstrual cycle is counted from day one of the menstrual period through the last day before the onset of the next period. She then calculates her fertile period by subtracting 18 days from the length of her shortest cycle and 11 days from the length of her longest cycle. The resulting figures indicate the range of her fertility period (Wheeler, 1995). It is during this time that the woman must abstain from intercourse if pregnancy is not desired.

For example, suppose that during an 8-month period, a woman had cycle lengths of 26, 32, 27, 30, 28, 27, 28 and 29 days. Subtracting 18 from her shortest cycle (26) and 11 from her longest cycle (32), she knows the days that the egg is likely to be in the fallopian tubes. To avoid getting pregnant, she must avoid intercourse on days 8 through 21 of her cycle.

THINK ABOUT IT

The calendar method of predicting the "safe" period may be unreliable for two reasons. First, the next month the woman may ovulate at a different time than any of the previous 8 months. Second, sperm life varies; they may live long enough to meet the next egg in the fallopian tubes.

BASAL BODY TEMPERATURE (BBT) METHOD   This method is based on determining the time of ovulation by measuring temperature changes that occur in the woman's body shortly after ovulation. The basal body temperature is the temperature of the body at rest on waking in the morning. To establish her BBT, the woman must take her temperature before she gets out of bed for 3 months. Shortly before, during, or right after ovulation, the woman's BBT usually rises about 0.4–0.8 degrees Fahrenheit. Some women notice a temperature drop about 12 to 24 hours before it begins to rise after ovulation. Intercourse must be avoided from the time the woman's temperature drops until her temperature has remained elevated for 3 consecutive days. Intercourse may be resumed on the night of the third day after the BBT has risen and remained elevated for 3 consecutive days.

CERVICAL MUCUS METHOD   The cervical mucus method, also known as the Billings method of natural family planning, is based on observations of changes in the cervical mucus during the woman's monthly cycle. The woman may observe her cervical mucus by wiping herself with toilet paper.

The woman should abstain from intercourse during her menstrual period because the mucus is obscured by menstrual blood and cannot be observed, and ovulation can occur during menstruation. After menstruation ceases, intercourse is permitted on days when no mucus is present or thick mucus is present in small amounts. Intercourse should be avoided just prior to, during, and immediately after ovulation if pregnancy is not desired. Before ovulation, mucus is cloudy, yellow or white, and sticky. During ovulation, cervical mucus is thin, clear, slippery, and stretchy and resembles raw egg white. This phase is known as the "peak symptom." During ovulation, some women experience ovulatory pain referred to as *mittelschmerz.* Such pain may include feelings of heaviness, abdominal swelling, rectal pain or discomfort, and lower abdominal pain or discomfort on either side. Mittelschmerz is useful for identifying ovulation but not for predicting it. Intercourse may resume 4 days after the disappearance of the peak symptom and continue until the next menses. During this time, cervical mucus may be either clear and watery, or cloudy and sticky, or there may be no mucus noticed at all.

Advantages of the cervical mucus method include that it requires the woman to become familiar with her reproductive system, and it can give early warning about some STDs (which can affect cervical mucus). However, the cervical mucus method requires the woman to distinguish between mucus and semen, spermicidal agents, lubrication, and infectious discharges. Also, the woman must not douche because she will wash away what she is trying to observe.

HORMONE-IN-URINE METHOD   A hormone is released into the bloodstream of the ovulating woman 12 to 24 hours prior to ovulation. Women can purchase over-the-counter tests, such as First Response and Ovutime, that are designed to ascertain if they have ovulated.

Nonmethods: Withdrawal and Douching

Because withdrawal and douching are not effective in preventing pregnancy, we call them "nonmethods" of birth control.

Also known as coitus interruptus, *withdrawal* is the practice whereby the man withdraws his penis from the vagina before he ejaculates. The advantages of coitus interruptus are that it requires no devices or chemicals, and it is always available. The disadvantages of withdrawal are that it does not provide protection from STDs, it may interrupt the sexual response cycle and diminish the pleasure for the couple, and it is very ineffective in preventing pregnancy.

Withdrawal is not a reliable form of contraception for two reasons. First, a man can unknowingly emit a small amount of preejaculatory fluid (stored in the prostate or penile urethra or in the Cowper's glands), which may contain sperm. This fluid contains more sperm after the man has recently ejaculated; one drop can contain millions of sperm. In addition, the man may lack the self-control to withdraw his penis before ejaculation, or he may delay his withdrawal too long and inadvertently ejaculate some semen near the vaginal opening of his partner. Sperm deposited there can live in the moist vaginal lips and make their way up the vagina.

Although some women believe that douching is an effective form of contraception, it is not. Douching refers to rinsing or cleansing the vaginal canal. After intercourse, the woman fills a syringe with water or a spermicidal agent and flushes (so she assumes) the sperm from her vagina. But in some cases, the fluid will actually force sperm up through the cervix. In other cases, a large number of sperm may already have passed through the cervix to the uterus, so the douche may do little good. Sperm may be found in the cervical mucus within 90 seconds after ejaculation.

In effect, douching does little to deter conception and may even encourage it. In addition, douching is associated with an increased risk for pelvic inflammatory disease and ectopic pregnancy.

Emergency Contraception

Also referred to as *postcoital contraception, emergency contraception* refers to various types of morning-after pills that are used primarily in three circumstances: when a woman has unprotected intercourse, when a contraceptive method fails (such as condom breakage or slippage), and when a woman is raped. Emergency contraception methods should be used only in emergencies—those times when unprotected intercourse has occurred and medication can be taken within 72 hours of exposure.

COMBINED ESTROGEN-PROGESTERONE The most common morning-after pills are the combined estrogen-progesterone oral contraceptives routinely taken to prevent pregnancy. In higher doses, they serve to prevent ovulation, fertilization of the egg, or transportation of the egg to the uterus. They may also make the uterine lining inhospitable to implantation. Known as the "Yuzpe method" after the physician who proposed it, four tablets of combined estrogen-progesterone are ingested. The first two tablets are taken within 72 hours of unprotected intercourse; two more tablets are taken 12 hours later. Side effects of combined estrogen-progesterone emergency contraception pills (sold under the trade name Ovral) include nausea, vomiting, and breast tenderness. The pregnancy rate is 1.2% if combined estrogen-progesterone is taken within 12 hours of unprotected intercourse, 2.3% if taken within 48 hours, and 4.9% if taken within 48 to 72 hours (Rosenfeld, 1997).

MIFEPRISTONE (RU-486) *Mifepristone,* also known as *RU-486,* is a synthetic steroid that effectively inhibits implantation of a fertilized egg. Given in a single 600-mg dose within 72 hours after unprotected intercourse, the endometrium is made unsuitable for implantation. Side effects of RU-486 may include nausea, vomiting, and breast tenderness. The pregnancy rate associated with RU-486 is 1.6%, which suggests that RU-486 is an effective means of emergency contraception (Rosenfeld, 1997).

Postcoital methods of contraception are controversial. Some people regard them as a form of abortion; others regard them as a means of reducing the need for abortion. Recent reviewers of research on new methods of emergency contraception (von Hertzen & Van Look, 1996) urged that as soon as researchers are able to establish the lowest effective dose of mifepristone, this method of emergency contraception should be more available in clinical practice and will be helpful in avoiding unwanted pregnancies and unnecessary abortions.

According to one expert, the wide availability and knowledge of emergency contraception in the Netherlands have contributed to the lower teenage pregnancy and abortion rates as compared to the United States and the United Kingdom (Haspels, 1994).

Effectiveness of Various Contraceptive Choices

In Table 6.1, we present data on the effectiveness of various contraceptive methods in preventing pregnancy and protecting against sexually transmitted

TABLE 6.1 Methods of Contraception and Sexually Transmitted Disease Protection from a Woman's Perspective

METHOD	ESTIMATED EFFECTIVENESS AGAINST STD	CONTRACEPTIVE EFFECTIVENESS HIGH[a]	AVERAGE[a]	BENEFITS	DISADVANTAGES	COST[b]
Condom	30–60%	98%	88%	Entails male responsibility; offers high level of protection; is inexpensive; available OTC[c]	Difficult to negotiate; entails lack of control for woman; may be seen as interrupting sex; may imply unfaithfulness	$0.50
Female condom	Insufficiently studied	Insufficiently studied	85%[d]	Offers high level of protection against sexually transmitted disease/HIV; available OTC[c]	Is visible; is expensive; requires negotiation	$2.25
Contraceptive film[d]	50%	99%	79%	Is easy to use; requires no negotiation; available OTC[c]	Requires 15 minutes' waiting time; must be applied within 1 hour of intercourse	$1.00
Spermicidal suppository	50%	99%	79%	Is easy to use; is inexpensive; requires no negotiation; available OTC[c]	Requires 15 minutes' waiting time; must be inserted within 1 hour of intercourse	$0.50

Continued on following page.

TABLE 6.1 (*continued*)

Method	Estimated Effectiveness Against STD	Contraceptive Effectiveness High[a]	Contraceptive Effectiveness Average[a]	Benefits	Disadvantages	Cost[b]
Contraceptive foam	50%	99%	79%	Is available OTC[e]; requires no waiting time after insertion; requires no negotiation	Requires applicator	$0.50
Jelly/cream	50%	99%	79%	Is available OTC; inexpensive; requires no negotiation	Requires applicator; must be applied within 1 hour of intercourse	$5.00 per tube
Cervical cap	50–70% for cervical pathogens, 0% for others	98%	82%	Is comfortable; can be used repeatedly over 2+ days; is cheaper over reproductive life; requires no waiting time after insertion; no UTIs[g], rarely requires refitting; may require no negotiation (if not felt by partner); offers excellent cervical protection with nonoxynol-9 use	Must be fitted; 20–40% of women not able to be fitted[f]; requires initial outlay of $100–$150; vaginal spermicide for best protection against sexually transmitted disease	$0.10 estimated per use over time
Diaphragm	50–75% for cervical pathogens	99%	82%	Requires no waiting time after insertion; fits nearly all women; may require no negotiation (if not felt by partner); is cheaper over reproductive life	Must be removed after 10–12 hours; may need to be refitted; carries increased risk of UTIs for some women; requires initial outlay of $50–$75	$0.10 estimated per use over time
Pill	None	96%	99%	Is convenient; is removed from sex act; affords high contraceptive efficacy	Offers no protection against sexually transmitted disease/HIV and may raise risk; is expensive	$12–$24/ month
Intrauterine device	None	99%	96%	Is not user dependent	Carries high initial cost; entails risk of PID associated with insertion	$150–$300 per insertion

[a]Highest observed effectiveness; "typical" user effectiveness.
[b]Per act of intercourse, based on average cost to consumer.
[c]Over the counter.
[d]Use-effectiveness rate presented at Food and Drug Administration hearings on Reality, January 31, 1992.
[e]Marketed as VCF (vaginal contraceptive film) in the United States and as C-film in the United Kingdom.
[f]Rate depends on criteria for a good fit, and practitioner criteria have varied widely.
[g]Urinary tract infection.

Source: Adapted from Rosenberg & Gollub, 1992.

diseases. Table 6.1 also describes the benefits, disadvantages, and costs of various methods of contraception. Not included in the chart is the obvious and most effective form of birth control, abstinence. Its cost is the lowest and it also eliminates the risk of HIV and STD infection from intercourse.

THINK ABOUT IT
Individuals rarely use one method of birth control throughout their fertile years. Which methods seem most suitable, and why, for each stage of a person's life?

STERILIZATION

Unlike the temporary and reversible methods of contraception just discussed, sterilization is a permanent surgical procedure that prevents reproduction. Sterilization may be a contraceptive method of choice when the woman should not have more children for health reasons or when individuals are certain about their desire to have no more children or to remain child-free. Many couples complete their intended childbearing in their late twenties or early thirties, leaving more than 15 years of continued risk of unwanted pregnancy. Because of the risk of pill use at older ages and the lower reliability of alternative birth control methods, sterilization has become the most popular method of contraception among married women who have completed their families.

Slightly more than half of all sterilizations are performed on women. Although male sterilization is easier and safer than female sterilization, women feel more certain they will not get pregnant if they are sterilized. "I'm the one that ends up being pregnant and having the baby," said one woman, "so I want to make sure that I never get pregnant again."

Female Sterilization

Although a woman may be sterilized by removal of her ovaries (*oophorectomy*) or uterus (*hysterectomy*), these operations are not normally undertaken for the sole purpose of sterilization, because the ovaries produce important hormones (as well as

eggs) and because both procedures carry the risks of major surgery. But sometimes there is another medical problem requiring hysterectomy.

The usual procedures of female sterilization are the salpingectomy and a variant of it, the laparoscopy. *Salpingectomy,* also known as tubal ligation or tying the tubes (see Figure 6.9), is often performed under a general anesthetic while the woman is in the hospital just after she has delivered a baby. An incision is made in the lower abdomen, just above the pubic line, and the fallopian tubes are brought into view one at a time. A part of each tube

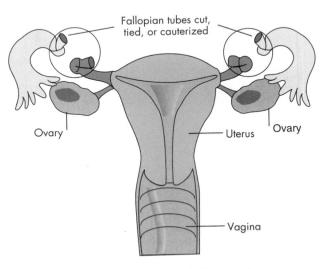

FIGURE 6.9 Female Sterilization: Tubal Sterilization
The fallopian tubes are interrupted surgically—cut and tied or blocked—to prevent passage of the eggs from the ovaries to the uterus.

CONTRACEPTIVE COMFORT AND CONFIDENCE SCALE

The following series of questions, which are adapted from the Contraceptive Comfort and Confidence Scale (Hatcher et al., 1990), is designed to help you assess whether the method of contraception that you are using or may be considering using in the future is or will be effective for you.

Most individuals will have a few "yes" answers. "Yes" answers predict potential problems. If you have more than a few "yes" responses, you may want to talk to your physician, counselor, partner, or friend. Talking it over can help you decide whether to use this method or how to use it so it will really be effective for you. In general, the more "yes" answers you have, the less likely you are to use this method consistently and correctly.

In choosing a method of contraception, you might want to keep in mind that if you want a highly effective method of contraception *and* a method that is highly effective in preventing transmission of STDs, you may have to use *two* methods (Cates & Stone, 1992). Hence, any method of contraception (except abstinence, of course) should be combined with condom use for maximum protection against STDs.

Method of birth control you are currently using or are considering using: Answer "yes" or "no" to the following questions.

_____ 1. Have you had problems using this method before?

_____ 2. Are you afraid of using this method?

_____ 3. Would you really rather not use this method?

_____ 4. Will you have trouble remembering to use this method?

_____ 5. Have you ever become pregnant using this method? (Or, has your partner ever become pregnant using this method?)

_____ 6. Will you have trouble using this method correctly?

_____ 7. Do you still have unanswered questions about this method?

_____ 8. Does this method make menstrual periods longer or more painful?

_____ 9. Does this method cost more than you can afford?

_____ 10. Could this method cause you or your partner to have serious complications?

_____ 11. Are you opposed to this method because of religious beliefs?

_____ 12. Is your partner opposed to this method?

_____ 13. Are you using this method without your partner's knowledge?

_____ 14. Will using this method embarrass your partner?

_____ 15. Will using this method embarrass you?

_____ 16. Will you enjoy intercourse less because of this method?

_____ 17. Will your partner enjoy intercourse less because of this method?

_____ 18. If this method interrupts lovemaking, will you avoid using it?

_____ 19. Has a nurse or doctor ever told you (or your partner) NOT to use this method?

_____ 20. Is there anything about your personality that could lead you to use this method incorrectly?

_____ 21. Does this method leave you at risk of being exposed to HIV or other sexually transmissible infections?

Total number of YES answers: _____

From *Contraceptive Technology 1990–1992*, by R. A. Hatchter, F. Stewart, J. Trussell, D. Kowal, F. Guest, G. K. Stewart, W. Cates, 1990, 15th ed. rev., p. 150. Reprinted by permission of Irvington Publishers, Inc.

is cut out, and the ends are tied, clamped, or cauterized (burned). The operation takes about 30 minutes. In the United States, about 700,000 such procedures are performed annually; the cost is around $2554.

Although the cost of female sterilization appears high, the cost of using the pill for 5 years is $1784. Over time, female sterilization is actually cheaper (Trussell et al., 1995).

A less expensive and quicker (about 15 minutes) form of *salpingectomy*, which is performed on an outpatient basis, is the *laparoscopy*. Often using local anesthesia, the surgeon inserts a small, lighted viewing instrument (laparoscope) through the woman's abdominal wall just below the navel through which the uterus and the fallopian tubes can be seen. The surgeon then makes another small incision in the lower abdomen and inserts a special pair of forceps that carry electricity to cauterize the tubes. The laparoscope and the forceps are then withdrawn, the small wounds are closed with a single stitch, and small bandages are placed over the closed incisions. (Laparoscopy is also known as "the band-aid operation.")

As an alternative to reaching the fallopian tubes through an opening below the navel, the surgeon may make a small incision in the back of the vaginal barrel (vaginal tubal ligation).

These procedures for female sterilization are over 95% effective, but sometimes they have complications. In rare cases, a blood vessel in the abdomen is torn open during the sterilization and bleeds into the abdominal cavity. When this happens, another operation is necessary to find the bleeding vessel.

Male Sterilization

NATIONAL DATA

Married men ages 20–39 who have had a vasectomy

Married men with vasectomy ages 20–39
12%

Source: Forste, Tanfer, & Tedrow, 1995.

Vasectomies are the most frequent form of male sterilization. They are usually performed in the physician's office under a local anesthetic. *Vasectomy* involves the physician's making two small incisions, one on either side of the scrotum, so that a small

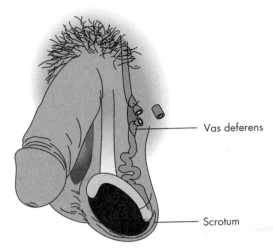

FIGURE 6.10 Male Sterilization: Vasectomy
A pair of incisions is made in the scrotum, and the vas deferens—the tubes connecting the testes and the urethra—are cut and tied off to prevent the passage of sperm to the urethra.

portion of each vas deferens (the sperm-carrying ducts) can be cut out and tied closed (see Figure 6.10). Sperm are still produced in the testicles, but since there is no tube to the penis, they remain in the epididymis and eventually dissolve. The procedure takes about 15 minutes and costs about $800. The man can leave the physician's office within a short time. Men most likely to seek a vasectomy are in their thirties or older, have been married more than 8 years, and already have three children (Forste et al., 1995).

Because sperm do not disappear from the ejaculate immediately after a vasectomy (some remain in the vas deferens above the severed portion), couples should use another method of contraception until the man has had about 20 ejaculations. The man is then asked to bring a sample of his ejaculate to the physician's office for examination under a microscope for a sperm count. In about 1% of the cases, the vas deferens grows back and the man becomes fertile again. In other cases, the man may have more than two tubes, which the physician was not aware of.

A vastectomy does not affect the man's desire for sex, ability to have an erection or an orgasm, amount of ejaculate (sperm comprise only a minute portion of the seminal fluid), or health. Although in some instances a vasectomy may be reversed, a man should get a vasectomy only if he does not want to have a biological child.

THINK ABOUT IT

Why has more research been conducted on female birth control and sterilization than on male birth control and sterilization?

KEY TERMS

cervical cap 150	Norplant · 145
diaphragm 150	oophorectomy 156
Depo-Provera 145	periodic abstinence 151
emergency contraception 153	postcoital contraception 153
female condom 147	RU-486 154
hysterectomy 156	salpingectomy 156
intrauterine device 149	spermicide 151
laparoscopy 158	vasectomy 158
mifepristone 154	withdrawal 153

SUMMARY POINTS

Having a family is a major goal for most individuals. Family planning is helpful in achieving one's family goals in terms of timing, number of children, and the interval between children. Over half (60%) of U.S. pregnancies are not planned.

Do You Want to Have Children?

Spouses, children, and society all benefit from family planning. The benefits include less health risk to mother and child, fewer unwanted children, decreased economic burden for the parents and society, and population control. The decision to become a parent is encouraged by family, friends, religions, government, and cultural observances. The reasons people give for having children include personal fulfillment and the desire for a close relationship with their offspring.

How Many Children Do You Want?

Some couples opt for a child-free lifestyle. Reasons women give for wanting to be child-free are more personal freedom, greater time and intimacy with their spouse, and career demands. Husbands are generally less committed than their wives to remaining child-free.

The most preferred family size in the United States is the two-child family. Some of the factors in a couple's decision to have more than one child are the desire to repeat a good experience, the feeling that two children provide companionship for each other, and the desire to have a child of each sex.

Birth Control

The primary methods of birth control discussed in this chapter are contraception and sterilization. With contraception, the risk of becoming pregnant can be reduced to practically zero, depending on the method selected and how systematically it is used. Contraception includes birth control pills, which prevent ovulation; the IUD, which prevents implantation of a fertilized egg; condoms and diaphragms, which are barrier methods, as well as vaginal spermicides and the rhythm method. Long-term methods include Norplant and Depo-Provera. These methods vary in effectiveness and safety.

Sterilization

Sterilization is a surgical procedure that prevents fertilization, usually by blocking the passage of eggs or sperm through the fallopian tubes or vas deferens, respectively. The procedure for female sterilization is called salpingectomy, or tubal ligation. Laparoscopy is a variation of tubal ligation. The most frequent form of male sterilization is vasectomy.

REFERENCES

Ahlburg, D. A., & De Vita, C. J. (1992). New realities of the American family. *Population Bulletin, 47,* 2–44.

Alexander, N. (1995, September). Future contraceptives. *Scientific American,* 136–141.

American Council on Education & University of California. (1996). *The American freshman: National norms for Fall, 1996.* Los Angeles: Los Angeles Higher Education Research Institute.

Benkov, L. (1994). *Reinventing the family: Lesbian and gay families.* New York: Crown Trade Paperbacks.

Boyd, R. L. (1989); Minority status and childlessness. *Sociological Inquiry, 59,* 331–342.

Cates, W., Jr., & Stone, K. M. (1992). Family planning, sexually transmitted diseases and contraceptive choice: A literature update—Part I. *Family Planning Perspectives, 24,* 75–82.

Cohen, S. (1995, October 1). Suits cite unexpected Norplant side effects. *The Charlotte Observer,* p. 19a.

Downey, D. (1995). Family size: Parental resources and children's education. *American Sociological Review, 60,* 746–761.

Forste, R., Tanfer, K., & Tedrow, L. (1995). Sterilization among currently married men in the United States, 1991. *Family Planning Perspectives, 27,* 100-107.

Glenn, N. D. (1991). Quantitative research on marital quality in the 1980s: A critical review. In A. Booth (Ed.), *Contemporary Families* (pp. 28-41). Minneapolis, MN: National Council on Family Relations.

Gollub, E. L., Stein, Z., & El-Sadr, W. (1995). Short-term acceptability of the female condom among staff and patients at a New York city hospital. *Family Planning Perspectives, 27,* 155-158.

Gorman, C. (1991, September 30). How old is too old? *Time,* 62.

Gregersen, E., & Gregersen, B. (1990). The female condom: A pilot study of the acceptability of a new female barrier method. *Acta Obstetricia et Gynecologica Scandinavica, 69,* 73.

Gringlas, M., & Weinraub, M. (1995). The more things change . . . single parenting revisited. *Journal of Family Issues 16,* 29-52.

Haspels, A. (1994). Emergency contraception: A review. *Contraception, 50,* 101-108.

Hatcher, R. A., Trussell, J., Stewart, F., Stewart, G. K., Kowal, D., Guest, F., Cates, W., Jr., & Policar, M. S. (1994). *Contraceptive technology: 1994-1996* (16th rev. ed). New York: Irvington.

Independent Commission of Population and Quality of Life. (1996). *Caring for the future: Making the next decades provide a life worth living.* New York: Oxford University Press.

Jones, C. L., Tepperman, L., & Wilson, S. J. (1995). *The futures of the family.* Englewood Cliffs, NJ: Prentice Hall.

Kost, K., & Forrest, J. D. (1995). Intention status of U.S. births in 1988: Differences by mothers' socioeconomic and demographic characteristics. *Family Planning Perspectives, 27,* 11-17.

Kozol, J. (1995). *Amazing grace: The lives of children and the conscience of a nation.* New York: Crown.

Kristof, N. D. (1991, June 17). A mystery from China's census: Where have young girls gone? *The New York Times,* pp. A1, A8.

Li, J. (1995). China's one-child policy: How well has it worked? A case study of Hebei Province, 1979-1988. *Population and Development Review, 21,* 563-585.

Lino, M. (1994). Economic status of families maintained by never-married mothers. *NCFR Annual Conference Proceedings: Families and Justice: From Neighborhoods to Nations* (Vol. 4, p. 32). Minneapolis: National Council on Family Relations.

MacDermind, S. M., Huston, T. L., & McHale, S. M. (1990). Changes in marriage associated with the transition to parenthood: Individual differences as a function of sex-role attitudes and changes in the division of household labor. *Journal of Marriage and the Family, 52,* 475-486.

Manderbacka, K. J., Merilainen, E., Hemminki, O., Rahkonen, O., & Teperi, J. (1992). Marital status as a predictor of perinatal outcome in Finland. *Journal of Marriage and the Family, 54,* 508-515.

Mattes, J. (1994). *Single mothers by choice.* New York: Times Books.

Menaghan, E. G., and Parcel, T. L. (1995). Social sources of change in children's home environments: The effects of parental occupational experiences and family conditions. *Journal of Marriage and the Family, 57,* 69-84.

Michaels, G. Y. (1988). Motivational factors in the decision and timing of pregnancy. In G. Y. Michaels & W. A. Goldberg (Eds.), *The transition to parenthood: Current theory and research* (pp. 23-61). New York: Cambridge University Press.

Miller, N. (1993). *Single parents by choice: A growing trend in family life.* New York: Insight Books.

Morris, J., & Schneider, D. (1992). Health risk behavior: A comparison of five campuses. *College Student Journal, 26,* 390-398.

O'Hare, W. P., & Felt, J. C. (1991, February). Asian Americans: America's fastest growing minority group. *Population Trends and Public Policy.* Washington DC: Population Reference Bureau.

O'Hare, W. P., Pollard, K. M., Mann, T. L., & Kent, M. M. (1991). African Americans in the 1900s. *Population Bulletin, 46,* 1-40.

Parnell, A. M., Swicegood, G., & Stevens, G. (1994). Nonmarital prepregnancies and marriage in the United States. *Social Forces, 73*(1), 263-287.

Renvoize, J. (1985). *Going solo: Single mothers by choice.* London: Routledge and Kegan Paul.

Richards, L. N., & Schmiege, C. (1993). Problems and strengths of single-parent families. *Family Relations, 42,* 277-285.

Ringheim, K. (1995). Evidence for the acceptability of an injectable hormonal method for men. *Family Planning Perspectives, 27,* 123-128.

Rochell, A. (1995, May 26). Who's having children: There's . . . real disparity in what people want. *The Atlanta Journal/The Atlanta Constitution,* p. ci.

Rosenfeld, J. (1997). Postcoital contraception and abortion. In J. Rosenfeld (Ed.), *Women's health in primary care.* (pp. 315-329). Baltimore: Williams & Wilkins.

Sadik, N. (1992). Public policy and private decisions: World population and world health in the 21st century. *Journal of Public Health Policy, 13,* 133-139.

Schwiesow, D. R., & Staimer, M. (1994, December 15). Charting the cost of kids. *USA Today,* p. A1.

Shaw, S. (1991). The conflicting experiences of lone parenthood. In M. Hardy & G. Grow (Eds.), *Lone parenthood* (pp. 143-145). Toronto, Ontario: University of Toronto Press.

Simons, R. L., Whitbeck, L. B., Beaman, J., & Conger, R. D. (1994). The impact of mothers' parenting, involvement by nonresidential fathers, and parental conflict on the adjustment of adolescent children. *Journal of Marriage and the Family, 56,* 356-374.

60% of U.S. Pregnancies Unintended. (1997). *POPLINE, 19,* 1. Washington, DC: Population Institute.

Smolowe, J. (1990, Fall). Last call for motherhood. *Time, 136,* No. 19, p. 76.

Stifel, E. N., & Anderson, J. (1997). Contraception. In J. Rosenfeld (Ed.), *Women's health in primary care* (pp. 289-313). Baltimore: Williams & Wilkins.

Swerdloff, R. (1995, August 7). Male contraception. In *Hard Copy.* New York, NY: National Broadcasting Company.

Toman, W. (1993). *Family constellation: Its effects on personality and social behavior.* New York: Springer.

Trussell, J., Leveque, J. A., Koenig, J. D., London, R., Borden, S., Henneberry, J., LaGuardia, K. D., Stewart, F., Wilson, T. G., Wysocki, S., & Strauss, M. (1995). The economic value of contraception: A comparison of 15 methods. *American Journal of Public Health, 85,* 949-503.

U.S. Bureau of the Census. (1995). *Statistical Abstract of the United States: 1995* (114th ed.). Washington, DC.

U.S. Bureau of the Census. (1996). *Statistical Abstract of the United States: 1996* (116th ed.). Washington, DC.

U.S. Bureau of the Census. (1997). *Statistical Abstract of the United States: 1997* (117 ed.). Washington, DC.

von Hertzen, H., & Van Look, P. F. A. (1996). Research on new methods of emergency contraception. *Family Planning Perspectives, 28,* 52-57, 88.

Wallerstein, J., & Blakeslee, S. (1995). *The good marriage.* Boston: Houghton Mifflin.

Webster-Stratton, C. (1989). The relationship of marital support, conflict, and divorce to parent perceptions, behaviors, and childhood conduct problems. *Journal of Marriage and the Family, 51,* 417-430.

Wheeler, C. A. (1995). Family planning. In D. R. Coustan, R. V. Haning, Jr., & D. B. Singer (Eds.), *Human reproduction: Growth and development* (pp. 359-377). Boston: Little, Brown.

PREGNANCY AND PARENTHOOD

I didn't know how babies were made until I was pregnant with my fourth child.

Loretta Lynn
Singer

In the spring of 1997, pregnancy and parenthood experienced a renewed cultural emphasis when news media disclosed that a 63-year-old woman had given birth to a healthy daughter at the University of Southern California Program for Assisted Reproduction. Arceli Keh (of Highland, California), whose husband was 60, had become pregnant through in vitro fertilization using a donated egg fertilized by her husband's sperm. While the event raised ethical issues about the ability of aging parents to care for their children, it also revealed the existence of two biological clocks. Dr. Richard Paulson noted that "the clock for the eggs and ovaries seems to run out much earlier than the one for the uterus" (Hellmich, 1997).

In this chapter, we address many of the choices and issues individuals and couples face in regard to getting pregnant and becoming parents. We begin with a discussion of fertilization and infertility and then take a look at the decisions individuals and couples confront in regard to these issues.

FERTILIZATION AND CONCEPTION

Fertilization takes place when a woman's egg, or ovum, unites with a man's sperm (see Figure 7.1). This may occur through sexual intercourse, artificial insemination, or in vitro fertilization.

At orgasm, the man ejaculates a thick white substance called semen, which contains about 300 million sperm. Once the semen is deposited in or near the vagina, the sperm begin to travel up the vagina, through the opening of the cervix, up the uterus, and into the fallopian tubes. If the woman has ovulated (released a mature egg from an ovary into a fallopian tube) within 8 hours, or if she ovulates during the 2 or 3 days the sperm typically remain alive, a sperm may penetrate and fertilize the egg. According to the World Health Organization, up to 50% of all fertilized ova do not progress beyond the first 3 weeks of development (Brent & Beckman, 1992).

Although popular usage does not differentiate between the terms "fertilization" and "conception,"

fertilization refers to the union of the egg and sperm, and *conception* refers to the fertilized egg that survives through implantation on the uterine wall. Hence, not all fertilizations result in conception. *Pregnancy* refers to the state of having conceived; this term emphasizes the developing fetus.

Since a woman is fertile for only a limited time each month, when is the best time to have intercourse to maximize the chance of pregnancy? In most healthy women, pregnancy results from having intercourse during a 6-day period ending on the day of ovulation (Wilcox, Weinberg, & Baird, 1995). There are several ways to predict ovulation. Many women have breast tenderness, and some experience a "pinging" sensation in their abdomen at the time of ovulation.

A woman may also detect ovulation by recording her basal body temperature and examining her cervical mucus. After menstruation, the vagina in most women is without noticeable discharge because the mucus is thick. As the time of ovulation nears, the mucus thins to the consistency of egg white, which may be experienced by the woman as increased vaginal discharge. If pregnancy is the goal, intercourse should occur during this time. In essence, the technology of the periodic abstinence method to avoid pregnancy (discussed in chapter 6) can be used to maximize the potential for pregnancy.

The position during intercourse may also be important for fertilization. In order to maximize the chance of fertilization, during intercourse, the woman should be on her back and a pillow should be placed under her buttocks after receiving the sperm so a pool of semen will collect near her cervix. She should remain in this position for about 30 minutes to allow the sperm to reach the fallopian tubes.

INFERTILITY

Infertility is defined as the inability to achieve a pregnancy after at least 1 year of regular sexual relations

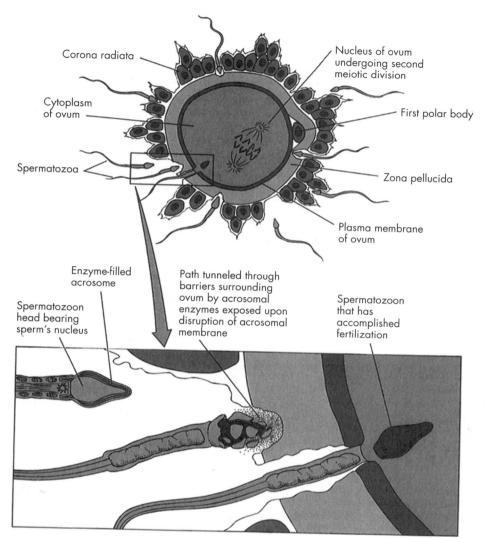

FIGURE 7.1 Process of Fertilization

without birth control, or the inability to carry a pregnancy to a live birth. Differentiations of infertility include the following:

1. Primary infertility—The woman has never conceived even though she wants to and has had regular sexual relations for the past 12 months.
2. Secondary infertility—The woman has previously conceived but is currently unable to do so even though she wants to and has had regular sexual relations for the past 12 months.
3. Pregnancy wastage—The woman has been able to conceive but has been unable to produce a live birth.

NATIONAL DATA

About 10 to 15% of U.S. couples of reproductive age are infertile.

Source: Rosenthal, 1997.

Causes of Infertility

Forty percent of infertility problems are attributed to the woman, 40% to the man, and 20% to both of them (Derwinski-Robinson, 1990). Some of the more common causes of infertility in men include low sperm production, poor semen motility, effects of sexually transmissible diseases (such as chlamydia, gonorrhea, and syphilis), and interference with the passage of sperm through the genital ducts due to an enlarged prostate. The causes of infertility in women include blocked fallopian tubes, endocrine imbalances that prevent ovulation, dysfunctional ovaries, chemically hostile cervical mucus that may kill sperm, and effects of sexually transmissible diseases.

Psychological Reactions to Infertility

Not being able to get pregnant may be a psychological crisis, a grief experience, and a situation that involves various choices. Regarding infertility as a crisis, one partner recalled:

> As I look back, I realize that neither of us was willing to apply the term "infertile" to us, even though several doctors had. We coped by changing doctors . . . and by keeping our desperation to ourselves. (Shapiro, 1988, p. 43)

Regarding the grief aspect of infertility, another infertile partner commented:

> Yet this is a different kind of grief. A death has finality to it, but infertility can go on indefinitely. It is like having a chronic illness; there is the continuing reminder of loss coupled with continued hope for a cure. Each month there is a new hope, the fantasy of being pregnant, and the conviction that this time it just has to work. (Lasker & Borg, 1987, p. 20)

Higgins (1990) reported changes couples experience when confronted with infertility. For example, their sexual relations may no longer be spontaneous but may become scheduled and regimented. Of this altered sex life, one respondent said:

> Making love requires such an effort. I just don't feel like it anymore. We have sex on schedule, and I'm relieved when my wife finishes ovulating so we don't have to subject ourselves to one more futile effort at making a baby. (Shapiro, 1988, p. 44)

The infertile couple may also avoid friends who have children, and they are often faced with a number of choices (Shapiro, 1988):

1. Whom should we tell? When employers question infertile individuals about missed days of work because they had to be away to take infertility tests, do these workers tell their employer the real reason for the absence? And do they tell friends and relatives about their plight? Shapiro (1988) noted that "countless infertile people who do decide to mention their infertility are surprised to learn that friends and relatives have had the same problem" (p. 115).

2. What do we tell? "Infertile people are afraid that their infertility may turn other people off, bore them, or cause them to feel pity" (p. 115). Some feel cautious about discussing the alternatives they are pursuing (such as engaging a surrogate or artificial insemination) for fear of disapproval or unwanted questions.

3. Should we pursue treatment? Once a diagnosis of infertility is made, some couples consider seeking assisted reproductive technology. A decision to pursue treatment should involve obtaining information about the potential side effects of any recommended medication, the risks of surgery, cost, the sequence of treatment, and how long treatment will go on.

4. Which alternatives should we pursue? Assuming that the couple is not able to have a child the traditional way (using their own egg and sperm united through sexual intercourse), they may choose from an array of alternatives to achieve the goal of having a child. One option is to adopt. Other alternatives are discussed in the following section.

THINK ABOUT IT

What operative cultural values make infertility a difficult adjustment for individuals and couples?

REPRODUCTIVE TECHNOLOGY

A number of technological innovations are available to assist women and couples in becoming pregnant. These include hormonal therapy, artificial insemination, ovum transfer, in vitro fertilization, gamete intrafallopian transfer, and zygote intrafallopian transfer.

Hormone Therapy

Drug therapies are often used to treat hormonal imbalances, induce ovulation, and correct problems in the luteal phase of the menstrual cycle. Frequently used drugs include Clomid, Pergonal, and human chorionic gonadotropin (HCG)—a hormone extracted from human placenta. These drugs stimulate the ovary to ripen and release an egg.

Although they are fairly effective in stimulating ovulation, hyperstimulation of the ovary can occur, which may result in permanent damage to the ovary.

Hormone therapy also increases the likelihood of ovulating multiple eggs, resulting in multiple births. The increase of triplets and higher-order multiple births over the last decade in the United States is largely attributed to the rise in use of ovulation-inducing drugs for treating infertility. In one U.S. study, 50% of triplet pregnancies were attributed to the use of ovulation-stimulating drugs, and 9% were attributed to in vitro fertilization and gamete intrafallopian transfer (Kiely, Kleinman, & Kiely, 1992). Infants of higher-order multiple births are at greater risk of having low birth weight, and experience higher infant mortality rates. Mortality rates have improved for these babies (the mortality rates in the mid-1980s were only half of those of the 1960s), but these low birth weight survivors may need extensive neonatal medical and social services (Kiely et al., 1992). Garel and Blondel (1992) interviewed 12 mothers one year following their deliveries of triplets in a public hospital in Paris. The mothers reported strained marriages, social isolation, and difficulty giving adequate attention to three children at the same time. Eight of the mothers reported psychological difficulties, and three had been treated for depression. The researchers recommended that families with triplets should receive increased attention, counseling, and support through specialized clinics, clubs, or home visits. The mothers stated that prior to a much-wanted pregnancy, parents can hardly anticipate the risks and hardships involved with having multiple children.

Artificial Insemination

When the sperm of the male partner are low in count or motility, sperm from several ejaculations may be pooled and placed directly into the cervix. This procedure is known as *artificial insemination* by the husband (AIH).

When sperm from someone other than a male partner is used to fertilize a woman, the technique is referred to as artificial insemination by donor (AID). Lesbians who want to become pregnant may use sperm from a friend or from a sperm bank. (Some sperm banks cater exclusively to lesbians.)

The American Fertility Society has issued a set of guidelines for donor insemination clinics and physicians. These include the following:

1. The donor's sperm should be screened for genetic abnormalities and sexually transmissible diseases.
2. All semen should be quarantined for 180 days and retested for HIV.
3. Fresh semen should never be used.
4. The donor should be under age 50 in order to diminish hazards related to aging (Foreman, 1990).

However, some physicians who regularly perform artificial inseminations do not test sperm donors for genetic defects or HIV status.

Sometimes the male partner's sperm is mixed with a donor's sperm, so that the couple has the psychological benefit of knowing that the male partner may be the biological father. One situation in which the male partner's sperm is not mixed with the donor's sperm is when the male partner is the carrier of a genetic disease, such as Tay-Sachs disease.

Artificial Insemination of a Surrogate Mother

In some instances, artificial insemination does not help a woman get pregnant. (Her fallopian tubes may be blocked, or her cervical mucus may be hostile to sperm.) The couple who still wants a child and has decided against adoption may consider parenthood through a *surrogate mother*. There are two types of surrogate mothers. One is the contracted surrogate mother who supplies the egg, is impregnated with the male partner's sperm, carries the child to term, and gives the baby to the man and his partner. A second type is the surrogate mother who carries a baby to whom she is not genetically related to term. As with AID, the motivation of the prospective parents is to have a child that is genetically related to at least one of them. For the surrogate mother, the primary motivation is to help childless couples achieve their aspirations of parenthood and to make money. (The surrogate mother is usually paid about $10,000.)

Legally, there are few guidelines for couples who engage a surrogate mother for procreative services. The surrogate can change her mind and decide to keep the child, as did a New Jersey surrogate mother in 1987. In what became known as the "Baby M Case," Mary Beth Whitehead decided she wanted to keep her baby, even though she had signed a contract to give up the baby to William Stern and his wife, Elizabeth, for $10,000. Whitehead turned down the fee and fled the state with the baby, who was found by private investigators and returned to the Sterns. Whitehead (1989) questioned the label applied to her of "surrogate mother," because she was the biological mother who provided the egg, carried the pregnancy to term, and gave birth. Initially, a judge upheld the surrogacy contract, severed Whitehead's parental rights, and presided over Elizabeth Stern's adoption of Baby M. A year later, the Supreme Court of New Jersey ruled surrogacy for hire was illegal because it resembled baby selling and reestablished Whitehead's parental rights. (It gave her liberal visitation rights.) However, the court ruled that Richard Stern was the primary custodial parent.

In another case in 1991, surrogate mother Elvie Jordon changed her mind when she discovered that the couple to whom she gave her baby were getting divorced. Jordon filed suit to get custody of her 17-month-old daughter, Marissa, who was living with Bob Moschetta (the biological father and ex-husband of Cindy Moschetta). A California superior court justice ruled that Elvie Jordon and Bob Moschetta (the biological mother and father) would share joint legal and physical custody of Marissa. (Cindy Moschetta was found to have no legal rights and was given no visitation privileges.)

Ovum Transfer

Another alternative for the infertile couple is *ovum transfer*. The sperm of the male partner is placed by a physician in a surrogate woman. After about 5 days, her uterus is flushed out (endometrial lavage), and the contents are analyzed under a microscope to identify the presence of a fertilized ovum. The fertilized ovum is then inserted into the uterus of the otherwise infertile partner. Although the embryo can also be frozen and implanted at a later time, fresh embryos are more likely to result in successful implantation (24% if fresh versus 8% if frozen) (Levran et al., 1990).

Infertile couples who opt for ovum transfer (also called embryo transfer) do so because the baby will be biologically related to at least one of them (the father) and the partner will have the experience of pregnancy and childbirth. As noted earlier, the surrogate woman participates out of her desire to help and infertile couple or to make money.

In Vitro Fertilization

About two million couples cannot have a baby because the woman's fallopian tubes are blocked or damaged, preventing the passage of eggs to the uterus. In some cases, blocked tubes can be opened via laser-beam surgery or by inflating a tiny balloon within the clogged passage. When these procedures are not successful (or when the woman decides to avoid invasive tests and exploratory surgery), *in vitro* (meaning "in glass") *fertilization,* also known as test-tube fertilization, is an alternative.

Using a *laparoscope* (a narrow, telescopelike instrument inserted through an incision just below the woman's navel to view the tubes and ovaries), the physician is able to see a mature egg as it is released from the woman's ovary. The time of release can be predicted accurately within 2 hours. When the egg emerges, the physician uses an aspirator to remove the egg, placing it in a small tube containing a stabilizing fluid. The egg is taken to the laboratory, put in a culture or petri dish, kept at a certain temperature-acidity level, and surrounded by sperm from the woman's partner (or donor). After one of these sperm fertilizes the egg, the egg divides and is implanted by the physician in the wall of the woman's uterus. Usually, several fertilized eggs are implanted in the hope that one will survive.

Occasionally, some fertilized eggs are frozen and implanted at a later time, if necessary. This procedure is known as *cryopreservation.* A separated or divorced couple may disagree over who owns the frozen embryos. Such was the case of Mary Sue Davis and Junior Davis, who took their disagreement to court. The court awarded the embryos to Mary Sue Davis (Fitzgerald, 1989).

Louise Brown of Oldham, England, was the first baby to be born by in vitro fertilization. Since her birth in 1978, over 300 clinics in the United States have emerged to duplicate this procedure, resulting in about 10,000 live births.

Other Reproductive Technologies

A major problem with in vitro fertilization is that only about 15 to 20% of the fertilized eggs will implant on the uterine wall. To improve this implant percentage (to between 40 and 50%), physicians place the egg and sperm directly into the fallopian tube, where they meet and fertilize. Then, the fertilized

SHOULD WE PURSUE HUMAN CLONING TECHNOLOGY?

In July, 1996, scientist Ian Wilmut of Scotland successfully cloned an adult sheep named Dolly. He did so by placing an udder cell from a 6-year-old sheep with an immature egg cell from another sheep and implanting the resulting embryo in a third sheep. This technological breakthrough has caused worldwide concern about the possibility of human cloning, which prompted quick European action that resulted in a ban on human cloning. President Clinton ordered a national commission to study the legal and ethical implications of cloning, which concluded that creating a child through cloning is morally unacceptable. However, Ruth Macklin, professor of bioethics at Albert Einstein College of Medicine, says that there is no evidence that human cloning is harmful. "In a democratic society, we don't usually pass laws outlawing something before there is actual or probable evidence of harm" (Macklin, 1997, p. 54).

One argument in favor of developing human cloning technology is that it has medical value; it may potentially allow everyone to have "their own reserve of therapeutic cells that would increase their chance of being cured of various diseases, such as cancer, degenerative disorders and viral or inflammatory diseases" (Kahn, 1997, p. 119). Human cloning technology could also provide an alternative reproductive route for couples who are infertile and for couples in which one partner is at risk for transmitting a genetic disorder to any offspring. Cloning technology may also provide a means of reproduction for single individuals and gay and lesbian couples. (Depending on one's personal values and beliefs, this could be viewed as a benefit or a drawback.)

Arguments against human cloning are largely based on moral and ethical considerations. In a national telephone poll of U.S. adults, 74% agreed that "it is against God's will to clone human beings" (Kluger, 1997). Critics of human cloning suggest that, whether used for medical therapeutic purposes or as a means of reproduction, human cloning is a threat to human dignity. Kahn (1997) explained that "creating human life for the sole purpose of preparing therapeutic material would clearly not be for the dignity of the life created" (p. 119). Kahn also suggests that "part of the individuality and dignity of a person probably lies in the uniqueness and unpredictability of his or her development" (p. 119). Cloned humans would be deprived of this individuality and dignity because they would be genetic carbon copies of other individuals. There is also concern that human cloning technology would be used by the "wrong people," such as oppressive dictators and fanatical terrorists, to reproduce and increase the members of their groups.

The current moratorium on human cloning research may not put a stop to it. Years ago, Scottish researchers studying in vitro fertilization were so intensely criticized for their work that they took their research "underground" until they perfected the technology (Kluger, 1997). Human cloning researchers could do the same. In the face of a moratorium on further research into human cloning, the future is uncertain. However, according to Arthur Caplan, director of the Center for Bioethics at the University of Pennsylvania, the first infant clone could possibly be created within the next 7 years (Kluger, 1997).

---

egg travels down into the uterus and implants. Since the term for sperm and egg together is "gamete," this procedure is called *gamete intrafallopian transfer,* or GIFT. This procedure, as well as in vitro fertilization, is not without psychological costs to the couple:

> The emotional response to the GIFT procedure is likely to be similar to that of patients undergoing in vitro fertilization, given the parallels in the proce-

dures. The experience of hormone therapy for the female, careful monitoring by laboratory tests, ultrasound scans, and pelvic exams, and the expectation that the male partner will produce a semen sample a few hours before the procedure—all contribute to the stress of the couple. (Shapiro, 1988, p. 18)

Zygote intrafallopian transfer (ZIFT) involves fertilizing the egg in a lab dish and placing the zygote or

DO YOU NEED PRECONCEPTION COUNSELING?

To determine whether you might benefit from preconception counseling, ask yourself the following questions:

- Do you have a major medical problem, such as diabetes, asthma, anemia, or high blood pressure?
- Do you know of any family members who have had a child with a birth defect or mental retardation?
- Have you had a child with a birth defect or mental retardation?
- Are you concerned about inherited diseases, such as Tay-Sachs disease, sickle-cell anemia, hemophilia, or thalassemia?
- Are you 35 years of age or older?
- Do you smoke, drink alcohol, or take illegal drugs?
- Do you take prescription or over-the-counter medications regularly?
- Do you use birth control pills?

- Do you have a cat?
- Are you a strict vegetarian?
- Are you dieting or fasting for any reason?
- Do you run long distances or exercise strenuously?
- Do you work with chemicals, toxic substances, radiation, or anesthesia?
- Do you suspect that you or your partner may have a sexually transmitted disease?
- Have you had German measles (rubella) or a German measles vaccination?
- Have you ever had a miscarriage, ectopic pregnancy, stillbirth, or complicated pregnancy?
- Have you recently traveled outside the United States?

If your answer to any of these questions is yes, you definitely should seek counseling from an obstetrician, nurse-midwife, or family practitioner 3 to 6 months before you hope to conceive a child.

From *An Invitation to Health*, 7th ed., by Diane Hales, 1997. Copyright © 1997 by Brooks/Cole Publishing Company. Reprinted by permission.

embryo directly into the fallopian tube. ZIFT has a success rate similar to gamete intrafallopian transfer.

Some infertility cases are the result of sperm that lack motility. In those cases, a physician may inject sperm directly into the egg by means of *microinjection*.

Eggs most likely to implant on the uterine wall are those whose shells have been poked open. To enhance implantation, physicians isolate an egg and drill a tiny hole in its protective shell. This procedure is known as *partial zona drilling* (PZD).

Infertile couples hoping to get pregnant through one of the 310 (as of 1997) in vitro fertilization (IVF) clinics should make informed choices by asking questions such as "What is the center's pregnancy rate for women with similar diagnoses? What percentage of these women have a live birth? How many cycles are attempted per patient?" The most successful reproductive technology programs report live birth rates of 20% (Rosenthal, 1997).

THINK ABOUT IT

There are no laws that prevent clinics or health care practitioners from providing single or lesbian women with assisted reproductive technology. Yet, some clinics refuse treatment to single or lesbian women, and many single and lesbian women who choose to become pregnant by donor insemination have trouble finding practitioners who will assist them (Rosenthal, 1997). Do you think that single or lesbian women should have the same access to reproductive technologies as married heterosexual women?

PRECONCEPTION CARE

Many women who plan their pregnancies want to enhance their health and well-being prior to conception to maximize their chance of having a healthy pregnancy and baby. In 1989, the U.S. Public Health

Service recommended that pregnancy-related health care services should begin *before* a woman becomes pregnant. *Preconception care* (also referred to as preconception counseling) includes risk assessment, interventions to reduce risk (such as treatment of infections and diseases and assistance with quitting smoking), and general health promotion (such as encouraging healthy eating, sleep, and exercise patterns). The risk assessment component of preconception care involves screening before pregnancy for medical, psychosocial, and genetic risk factors that might affect the health of the woman or her child (Acheson, 1997).

Preconception care often includes testing women from certain ethnic groups to assess if they are carriers of a genetic disease such as Tay-Sachs disease. Other examples of preconception care include immunizing nonpregnant women against rubella (live virus vaccines are contraindicated during pregnancy), diagnosing and controlling diabetes, advising the daily use of folate supplements to prevent neural tube (fetal brain and spine) defects, HIV testing and counseling, identifying and treating substance abuse, and advising women to avoid any substances (such as medications) that could harm a fetus.

Although all women can potentially benefit from preconception care, such care is particularly indicated for women who are at risk for pregnancy or child-birth complications. This chapter's Self-Assessment presents questions women can ask to determine whether they should seek preconception counseling.

THINK ABOUT IT

Medical ethicist Judith Boss (1994) observed that in the 1960s, there were two to three times more researchers working to seek a cure for Tay-Sachs disease than in the 1990s. Now, prenatal diagnosis for Tay-Sachs is emphasized, implying that abortion will follow a positive diagnosis. What do you think about Boss's charge that research on cures for genetic disorders (such as Tay-Sachs and sickle-cell anemia) has been put aside in favor of selective abortion?

PREGNANCY AND LABOR

Immediately after the egg and sperm unite, typically in the fallopian tube, the egg begins to divide and is pushed by hairlike cilia down the tube into the uterus, where it attaches itself to the inner wall. Furnished with a rich supply of blood and nutrients, the developing organism is called an *embryo* for the first 3 months and a *fetus* thereafter (see Figure 7.2).

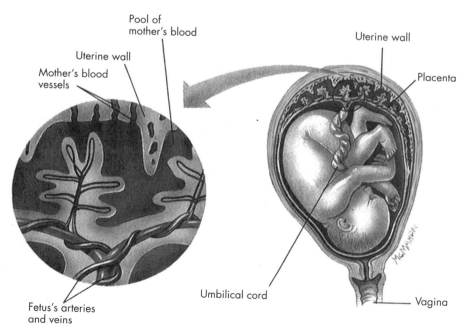

FIGURE 7.2 The Developing Embryo

Detecting pregnancy as early as possible is important. Not only does doing so enable the woman to begin prenatal precautions and medical care during the most vulnerable stage of fetal development, it also allows women with an unintended pregnancy time to consider if they want to have an abortion, which may then be performed when it is safest (early in pregnancy). Finally, early diagnosis may permit early detection of an *ectopic pregnancy*. Such a pregnancy involves the baby developing outside the uterus, such as in the cervix, abdominal area, or ovary (see Figure 7.3). Most ectopic pregnancies occur in the fallopian tube. An ectopic pregnancy is potentially dangerous, and signs of such a pregnancy should be taken seriously. These include sudden intense pain in the lower abdomen, irregular bleeding, or dizziness that persists for more than a few seconds.

New treatments for ectopic pregnancy include microsurgery incisions that allow the physician to remove the embryo while leaving the reproductive system intact. In some cases, methotrexate may be prescribed to destroy the pregnancy-related tissue.

NATIONAL DATA

Ectopic pregnancies account for 2% of all reported U.S. pregnancies. Ectopic pregnancy–related deaths account for 9% of all pregnancy-related deaths in the United States.

Source: Ectopic Pregnancy—United States, 1995.

Pregnancy Testing

Signs of pregnancy may include a missed period, morning sickness, enlarged and tender breasts, frequent urination, and excessive fatigue. However, pregnancy is best confirmed by laboratory tests and a physical examination.

Several laboratory tests of pregnancy have a high degree of accuracy. All of them depend upon the presence of a hormone produced by the developing embryo, human chorionic gonadotropin (HCG), which appears in the pregnant woman's urine. One procedure, formally known as the lutex agglutination inhibition immunologic slide test, detects HCG in

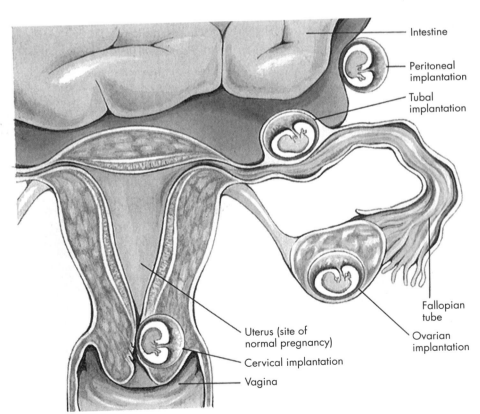

Intestine

Peritoneal implantation

Tubal implantation

Fallopian tube

Ovarian implantation

Uterus (site of normal pregnancy)

Cervical implantation

Vagina

FIGURE 7.3 Possible Sites of Ectopic Pregnancy

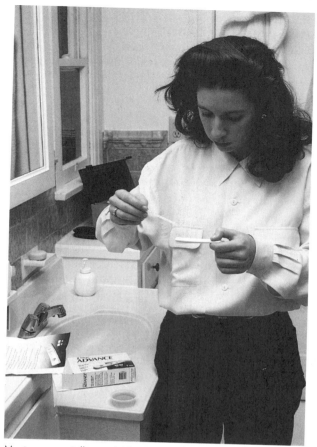

Most commercially available pregnancy tests are based on detecting the presence of a hormone called human chorionic gonadotropin in the woman's urine.

about 2 1/2 hours and can reveal if the woman is pregnant within 14 days after the first missed menstrual period. All commercially available pregnancy tests use the lutex agglutination principle and are reasonably reliable in providing information about the existence of a pregnancy. The most common error in the home pregnancy tests is that the woman takes the test too early in pregnancy and concludes that she is not pregnant when, in fact, she is (false negative).

HCG also appears in the bloodstream of the pregnant woman. A radioimmunoassay test, a laboratory examination of the blood, can suggest if the woman is pregnant within 8 days of conception. A new test, radioreceptorassay, also analyzes the blood and is 100% accurate on the first day after the first missed period. Pregnancy tests in which urine of the presumed pregnant woman is injected into a mouse, rabbit, or frog have been replaced by these tests.

If the laboratory test indicates pregnancy, the physician usually conducts a pelvic examination to find out if the woman's uterus has enlarged or changed color. These changes take place around the sixth week of pregnancy.

Physical Changes During Pregnancy

The usual course of a typical 266-day pregnancy is divided into trimesters, or 3-month periods, during which the woman may experience some discomfort due to physical changes (see Table 7.1). Women vary in the degree to which they experience these

TABLE 7.1   Side Effects of Pregnancy

	1st Trimester Week 0–14	2nd Trimester Week 15–26	3rd Trimester Week 27–40
Nausea	●		
Vomiting	●		
Frequent urination	●		
Leg cramps	●		●
Vaginal discharge	●		
Fatigue	●	●	●
Constipation	●	●	●
Swelling		●	●
Varicose veins		●	●
Backache		●	●
Heartburn		●	●
Shortness of breath		●	

changes. Some may experience few or none of the related symptoms, while others may experience many of them.

Prenatal Care and Prenatal Testing

As noted earlier in this chapter, some women seek preconception care to help ensure a healthy pregnancy and baby. Others do not receive pregnancy-related health care until after they become pregnant. Like preconception care, prenatal care involves receiving adequate nutrition, achieving adequate weight gain, and avoiding harmful substances such as alcohol, nicotine, illegal drugs, some medications, and toxic chemicals in the workplace. Vitamin and mineral supplements are commonly recommended, especially iron and folate (or folic acid) supplements.

Exercise is contraindicated for women who have certain risk factors (such as anemia, hypertension, pain of any kind, fetal distress, heart palpitations, or vaginal or uterine bleeding). In the absence of such risk factors, mild to moderate exercise is recommended and helps promote a sense of well-being and ease of labor/birth.

Pregnant women should eliminate their alcohol intake to avoid *fetal alcohol syndrome* (FAS), which refers to the possible negative consequences for the fetus and infant of the mother who drinks alcohol. Possible negative consequences for the developing infant include increased risk of low birth weight, growth retardation, facial malformations, and intellectual retardation. Avoiding alcohol intake during the early weeks of pregnancy is particularly critical; however, alcohol consumed in the later months may impede organ growth. "Professional advice to pregnant women is consistent: If you're pregnant, don't drink" (Travis, 1988, p. 121). And, since you usually do not know if you are pregnant for 1 to 2 months after fertilization, don't drink alcohol if you are not using a reliable method of contraception.

Smoking cigarettes during pregnancy is also associated with harm to the developing fetus. Negative consequences include lower birth weight babies, premature babies, and higher fetal or infant deaths (Acheson, 1997). Avoiding passive, secondary, or environmental smoke may also be in the best interest of the developing fetus.

Concerned about the health of their babies, some pregnant women avoid not only alcohol and nicotine, but also caffeine and such over-the-counter drugs as aspirin and antihistamines and prescription drugs such as amphetamines and tranquilizers. While there is no conclusive evidence that caffeine has a serious detrimental effect on the developing baby, a physician should be consulted in regard to continuing medications before and during pregnancy. "Ideally, consumption of nonprescription drugs should stop completely *prior* to conception" (Chez, 1991, p. 56).

Illegal drugs (also nonprescription drugs), such as marijuana and cocaine, should also be avoided. Cocaine has been associated with preterm labor and delivery, lower birth weight babies, limb defects, lower IQ, and oversensitivity to stimulation. These "crack" or "cocaine" babies may enter the world disadvantaged; however, since their mothers may have used various substances, it is difficult to isolate the specific effects of cocaine from malnutrition and lack of prenatal care (Brent & Beckman, 1992).

Despite the importance of prenatal care, more than 20% of U.S. women who delivered a live baby in 1993 did not receive prenatal care in the first trimester of pregnancy. Nearly 5% received prenatal care in the 3rd trimester or not at all (*Statistical Abstract of the United States: 1996,* Table 100). Disadvantaged populations are less likely to receive prenatal care due to lack of resources to pay for such care and lack of access to health care services.

Prenatal care may also involve prenatal (antenatal) testing. Such tests range from screening measures routinely used in prenatal care to invasive prenatal diagnostic tests. In the last decade, a test measuring maternal serum alpha-fetoprotein has become widely used as a screening measure for neural tube defects (Press & Browner, 1995). In the spring of 1997, the National Institutes of Health recommended routine prenatal genetic screening for cystic fibrosis, the most common inherited disease, which affects about 25,000 infants annually.

Ultrasound involves sound waves being intermittently beamed at the fetus, producing a detailed image on a video screen. It is a noninvasive test which immediately provides pictures of the maternal and fetal outlines and inner organs. Although its long-term effects are still being studied, it appears to be one of the safest procedures for the amount of information it provides. Ultrasound allows the physician to determine the length of gestation (the age of the fetus) and assess the presence of structural abnormalities. While ultrasound may reveal the fetus' genital area (depending on the position of the fetus), it is not considered a reliable test to determine the sex of the fetus.

Other prenatal tests are used to identify fetuses with chromosomal and biochemical defects. These procedures are usually offered to women who have a child with a birth defect, or some other risk factor (such as advanced maternal age, now defined at around 35 years of age). Their purpose is to detect defects early enough so that if the test is positive, the woman can either be prepared for the birth of a child with health problems or terminate the pregnancy. Their availability has provided to many people the confidence to initiate a pregnancy despite familial history of serious genetic disease or prior birth of affected children.

Amniocentesis (which is best performed in the 16th or 17th week of pregnancy) involves inserting a slender needle through the abdomen into the amniotic sac and taking about 1 ounce of fluid (see Figure 7.4). Fetal cells, which are present in this amniotic fluid, are sent to a laboratory, where they are cultured (permitted to multiply in a special medium) and then analyzed for defects.

Amniocentesis involves some risk. In rare cases (about 0.5% of the time, or 1 in 200 cases), the fetus may be damaged by the needle, even though an ultrasound scan has been used to identify its position. Congenital orthopedic defects, such as clubfoot, and premature birth have been associated with amniocentesis. Also, if no specific abnormality is detected (as is the case 97.5% of the time), this does not guarantee that the baby will be normal and healthy. Cleft palate, cleft lip, and most heart defects are not detected by amniocentesis.

Unfortunately, after the amniocentesis procedure at 16 to 17 weeks of gestation, an additional 3 or 4 weeks is required for cell tissue culture and karyotyping. By this time, the woman may be 20 to 22 weeks pregnant; the pregnancy is publicly visible, and she has probably felt fetal movement. Having

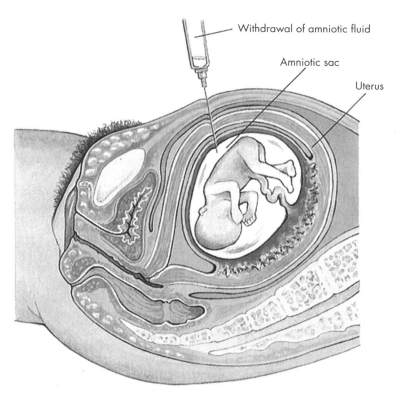

FIGURE 7.4 Amniocentesis

SHOULD CRIMINAL PROSECUTION BE INSTITUTED FOR FETAL ABUSE?

Should pregnant women who abuse alcohol, crack cocaine, and other drugs harmful to a fetus be prosecuted? Though over 100,000 infants have been exposed to such drugs while they were developing in their mothers, the courts have been reluctant to prosecute (Farr, 1995). Arguments against such prosecution are based on the difficulty of defining when the fetus becomes a person whose rights have been violated; the lack of warning to women that drug abuse during pregnancy may be a prosecutable offense; the vagueness of what exactly constitutes "the crime"; and the fact that fetal abuse is a lifestyle issue. Regarding the latter, many women who take drugs during their pregnancy live in poverty, which means they often lack prenatal care and have nutritional deficiencies. Indeed, prenatal care, drug treatment, and general health services are least accessible for poor and minority women. An additional problem is that sending pregnant women to jail or prison for drug abuse interferes with their ability to receive treatment during pregnancy.

The issue remains unresolved. Seven states continue to enact fetal abuse laws. For example, current legislation in Ohio is seeking to include fetal drug abuse in that state's definition of child abuse and neglect. Rhode Island is attempting to specify prenatal drug exposure that results in a baby's death as manslaughter (Shoop, 1992). "Yet there is no evidence that in the long run, such policies are either socially effective or economically sound. Instead, the research seems to call for a policy direction that emphasizes the provision of health and drug education" (Farr, 1995, p. 242).

Sources: Farr, K. A. (1995). Fetal abuse and the criminalization of behavior during pregnancy. *Crime and Delinquency, 41*, 235–245. Shoop, J. G. (1992). Fetal abuse conviction overturned in Florida. *Trial*, 16–17.

---

already made the emotional transition from the state of "being pregnant" to "going to have a baby," the woman and her partner would likely find it quite traumatic to face a diagnosis of a severe fetal abnormality this late in pregnancy (Evans & Johnson, 1992). To terminate a pregnancy that has progressed to 20 or 22 weeks, a saline or prostaglandin (induced miscarriage) abortion procedure is frequently used, which involves the delivery of the fetus. (Other procedures for terminating pregnancy are discussed in Chapter 18.)

In response to these problems, attempts have been made to move prenatal diagnosis into the first trimester of pregnancy. The major advantage of *chorionic villus sampling* (CVS) is that it can be done much earlier than amniocentesis, with the results available more quickly. Villi are the threadlike edges of the chorion, or membrane, surrounding the fetus. A small sample of the chorion can be obtained by passing a thin catheter, using ultrasound guidance, through the cervix and into the placenta (see Figure 7.5). Sometimes, due to the placement of the placenta, the villi must be extracted through the abdomen, as in amniocentesis. The villi can then be analyzed directly or cultured and the chromosomes studied (Johnson & Miller, 1992). In addition to diagnosis of Down syndrome and other chromosomal disorders, CVS has been shown to reliably diagnose Tay-Sachs disease, cystic fibrosis, sickle-cell anemia, and Duchenne muscular dystrophy (Evans & Johnson, 1992).

Considerable experience and coordination are needed to perform the procedure effectively and safely. The primary risk of the procedure is loss of the pregnancy, although there have been some reports of limb reduction deformities (Turner, 1992). Many clinics cite a slightly higher risk of pregnancy interruption for CVS than for amniocentesis.

When prenatal testing reveals a fetal abnormality, the choice to terminate the pregnancy may be extremely difficult. "The factor of choice is a tremendous emotional burden for women who choose to abort" (Rice, 1992, p. 279). Rice cautioned that men's feelings of shock, hurt, and disappointment may be overlooked. A partner may feel helpless, and yet responsible. He may feel he is not entitled to his grief, and try to discount his pain. Siblings may also feel a loss.

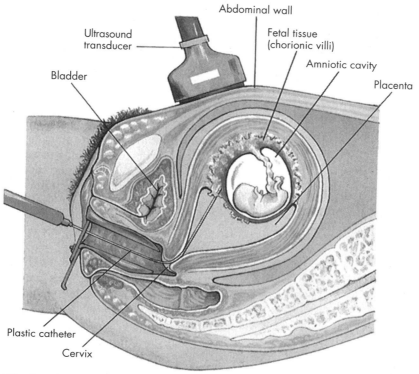

FIGURE 7.5 Chorionic Villus Sampling

Miscarriage

A *miscarriage,* also known as *spontaneous abortion,* is the unintended death of an embryo or fetus that occurs before the 20th week of pregnancy. Miscarriages are usually caused by chromosomal abnormalities in the developing zygote, embryo, or fetus (Acheson, 1997).

NATIONAL DATA

Miscarriage occurs in approximately 9% of medically confirmed pregnancies and in 31% of all pregnancies.

Source: Acheson, 1997.

Women who experience a miscarriage often feel intense grief. They may also feel guilt, anger, a sense of failure, and jealousy of other pregnant women or women with children. They may blame themselves for the miscarriage. Some feel that they are being punished for something they have done in the past—frequent, casual, anonymous premarital sex; an abortion; an extramarital affair. Others feel that they have failed not only as a woman or mother, but also in living up to the expectations of their partner, parents, and other children. (Women who have a miscarriage are often inappropriately urged to "try again" rather than focus on their grief.) Others are angry at the insensitivity of their friends who show little empathy for their feelings of sadness and emptiness at the loss of "their baby." Friends and family can be helpful by acknowledging the loss instead of attempting to minimize it.

Psychological Changes During Pregnancy

Affonso and Mayberry (1989) assessed the stresses of 221 women during and after pregnancy. Stress related to physical issues was the most frequently reported problem. "The total group identified fatigue, disturbed sleep, feeling physically restricted, and nausea or vomiting as the most common physical distresses" (p. 46). The second most frequently experienced stressor was associated "with 'weight gain' and feelings of being 'fat,' 'unattractive,' and 'distorted.'" (Affonso & Mayberry, 1989, p. 48)

The third most frequently reported concern during pregnancy was for the "baby's welfare and dealing with changes relative to household arrangements and restrictions in physical activities, especially as the woman nears childbirth" (Affonso & Mayberry, 1989, p. 49). Some of the women reported that they were plagued by such frequent thoughts as, "Something might happen to my baby," "Am I doing the right thing to protect my baby?", and "I shouldn't have done this because now I'm worried about how it affected my baby." (p. 49)

As women near the end of pregnancy, fears of pain, complications, and the threat of a cesarean are high-intensity stressors. At the beginning of pregnancy, some women feel trapped. They feel they have begun a course of action from which they cannot easily withdraw (Engel, 1990).

The man also experiences his own set of feelings during pregnancy. Shapiro (1987) interviewed 227 expectant and recent fathers and noted several concerns:

1. *Queasiness.* Respondents in Shapiro's study reported that their greatest fear before birth was coping with the actual birth process. They were queasy about being in the midst of blood and bodily fluids and felt they would faint or get sick. Most did neither.

2. *Worry over increased responsibility.* Over 80% reported feeling that they were now the sole support for three people. Many took second jobs or worked longer hours.

3. *Uncertain paternity.* Half of the men feared that the child their partner was carrying was not their own. "For most of them, such fears were based less on any real concern that the wife had been unfaithful than on a general insecurity brought on by being part of something as monumental as the creation of life" (p. 39).

4. *Fear of the loss of spouse, the child, or both.* Some men feared that both the wife and baby might die during childbirth and that they would be alone. They also feared that the baby would be brain-damaged or defective in some way.

5. *Fear of being replaced.* The words of one respondent reflect a common fear among expectant fathers—that of being replaced:

> The one thing that really scares me is that the best of our lives together will be gone as soon as the baby is born . . . in some ways, I'm feeling displaced. . . . (p. 42)

Some of the men had affairs late in their wife's pregnancy. These men perceived their wives to be more focused on and bonded with the impending baby than with them. Since they missed the attention they had received from their wife prior to pregnancy, they sought to replace that attention with that of other women.

Sex During Pregnancy

Sexual desire, behavior, and satisfaction may change during pregnancy. Eighty-one married couples provided information during the 13th and 14th weeks of pregnancy and again within 1 week after the birth of the baby. In regard to sexual desire, 40% of the women reported diminished sexual desire during the first and second trimesters. Seventy-four percent reported decreased sexual desire during the third trimester. Of their husbands, 9% and 17% reported decreased sexual desire the first and second trimesters, respectively, and 64% during the third trimester (Bogren, 1991).

Some pregnant women and their partners experience an increase in sexual desire during pregnancy. Changes in sexual desire may be related to the woman's changing physical appearance during pregnancy.

> Some women may perceive themselves as fat, ugly, and generally unattractive during their pregnancy. Others may find their enlarging breasts, rounding abdomens, and fuller shapes more womanly, appealing, and sexually desirable. Negative or positive feelings toward these changes in body image may influence a woman's sexual desire. (Wilkerson & Bing, 1988, p. 379)

In regard to sexual frequency, 41% of the women reported decreased sexual frequency during the first trimester, 40% during the second trimester, and 90% during the third trimester. The percentages of husbands reporting decreased frequencies for the first, second, and third trimester were 30%, 40%, and 83%, respectively (Bogren, 1991).

Are there conditions under which a pregnant woman should forego intercourse and orgasmic activity? Yes. Women who are experiencing vaginal bleeding or abdominal pain, those whose amniotic membrane has ruptured, and those whose cervix has begun to efface or dilate after 24 weeks should abstain from sexual intercourse (Engel, 1990). Also, those with a history of premature delivery or a history of miscarriage are encouraged to avoid intercourse during pregnancy (Gauna-Trujillo & Higgins, 1989).

Labor

The beginning of labor signals the end of pregnancy. Labor occurs in three stages, and although there are great variations, it lasts an average of 13 hours for the woman having her first baby (she is referred to as *primigravida*) and about 8 hours if the woman has given birth before (*multigravida*). Figure 7.6 illustrates the birth process.

It is not known what causes the onset of labor, which is marked by uterine contractions. But there

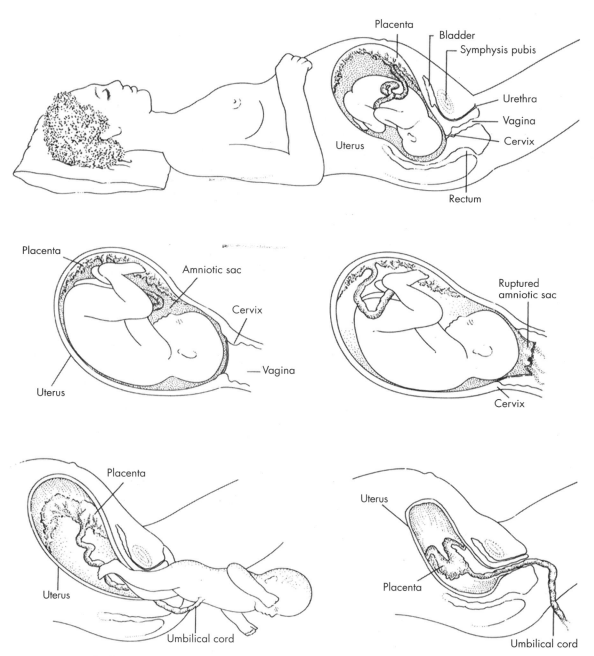

FIGURE 7.6 Stages of Labor

are distinctions between the contractions of true and preparatory (also known as Braxton-Hicks contractions) labor. Table 7.2 illustrates the respective differences.

FIRST STAGE OF LABOR   Labor begins with regular uterine contractions, at 15- to 20-minute intervals, that last from 10 to 30 seconds. The first stage lasts for about 9 hours if it is the first baby and about 5 hours in subsequent deliveries. During this first stage, the woman often has cramps and backache. The membranes of the amniotic sac may rupture, spilling the amniotic fluid.

Throughout the first stage, the uterine contractions become stronger, lasting for 30 to 45 seconds, and more frequent (every 3 to 5 minutes). These contractions result in effacement and dilation of the cervix. With *effacement,* the cervix flattens out and gets longer; with *dilation,* the cervical opening through which the baby will pass gets larger. At the end of the first stage, the cervix is dilated 3½ to 4 inches; contractions occur every 1 to 2 minutes and last up to a minute.

TABLE 7.2   Contractions Characteristic of True and Preparatory Labor

TRUE LABOR
Occur at regular intervals
Intervals gradually shorten
Intensity gradually increases
Discomfort in back and abdomen
Cervix dilates
Not affected by sedation

PREPARATORY LABOR
Occur at irregular intervals
Intervals remain long
Intensity remains the same
Discomfort chiefly in lower abdomen
Cervix does not dilate
Usually relieved by sedation

During the first stage, the baby is getting into position to be born. The fetal heart rate is monitored continually by stethoscope or ultrasound, and the woman's temperature and blood pressure are checked. She may experience leg cramps, nausea, or irritability during this first stage of labor.

SECOND STAGE OF LABOR   Also known as the expulsive stage of labor, the second stage begins when the cervix is completely dilated and ends when the baby is born. It lasts about 50 minutes if it is the woman's first baby, and 20 minutes for subsequent births. Uterine contractions may last 1½ minutes and be 1 to 2 minutes apart. These contractions move the baby further into the vaginal birth canal. The woman may help this process by pushing movements. The head of the baby emerges first, followed by the shoulders and trunk. While most babies are born head first, some are born breech. In a *breech birth,* the baby's feet or buttocks come out the vagina first. Breech deliveries are much more complicated.

To ease the birth, the physician may perform an episiotomy, which involves cutting the perineum (the area between the vagina and the anus) in one of two places to make a larger opening for the baby and to prevent uncontrolled tearing (see Figure 7.7).

Immediately after the baby is born, its nostrils are cleared of mucus using a small suction bulb. The umbilical cord is then clamped twice—about 1 and 2 inches from the infant's abdomen—and cut between the clamps. The baby is cleaned of placental matter and put in a temperature-controlled bassinet or held by the parents.

THIRD STAGE OF LABOR   After the baby is born, the placenta, or afterbirth, is delivered. Usually within 5 minutes after the birth of the baby, the placenta separates itself from the uterine wall and is expelled from the vagina. If it does not disengage easily and by itself, the birth attendant will manually remove it. If an episiotomy was done, the physician will repair it by stitching up the incision after the placenta is delivered.

The time from 1 to 4 hours after delivery is regarded by some physicians as a fourth stage of labor. During this time, the mother's uterus relaxes

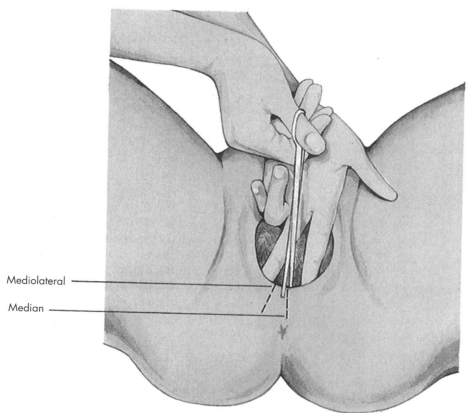

Mediolateral ——————

Median ——————

FIGURE 7.7 Alternative Episiotomy Sites

and returns to a more normal state. Bleeding of the cervix, which results from the detachment of the placenta from the uterine wall, stops.

Cesarean Childbirth

In the United States, a surprising number of babies are born by *cesarean section,* in which an incision is made in the woman's abdomen and the uterus and the baby is manually removed. During this procedure, the woman is put to sleep with general anesthesia or given a spinal injection, which enables her to remain awake and aware of the delivery.

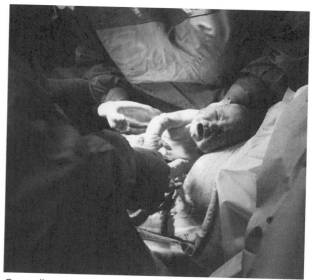

Generally, cesarean sections are performed only when medically necessary.

NATIONAL DATA

About 20% of U.S. births are cesarean births.

Source: Curtin, 1997.

Cesarean deliveries are most often performed when there would be risk to the mother or baby in a normal delivery. For example, cesarean sections are indicated when the fetus is positioned abnormally, the head is too large for the mother's pelvis, labor is not progressing properly, there is fetal distress, the woman has an active STD or diabetes, or develops toxemia during pregnancy. Travis (1988) identified additional reasons for cesarean sections, including convenience for the physicians, demand for perfect delivery outcomes and the threat of malpractice, decreased use of forceps, and increase in first pregnancy among older women.

Although cesareans are major surgery, the risk of death to the mother is low—about seven deaths per 10,000 births (Travis, 1988). When death occurs, it is usually the result of a preexisting condition, such as severe toxemia or heart disease—not a result of the surgery itself. The cesarean section, or C-section, is regarded as one of the safest of all abdominal surgeries and holds the record for the fewest postoperative problems.

There has been considerable criticism of physicians who routinely perform cesarean surgery when it is not medically indicated. C-sections, both primary and repeat, are more likely to occur on Fridays. The difference between Friday and Sunday births for C-sections was 50% in one study (National Center for Health Statistics, 1992). The implication is that C-sections are being performed in reference to the physician's social life, rather than the best interests of the mother and baby.

Some women who give birth through cesarean section experience negative psychological consequences. Travis (1988) noted that

> Mothers often feel a sense of failure because their role in delivery was peripheral rather than central. Additionally there may be feelings of anger or frustration directed toward the physician, husband, or infant. (p. 156)

Maternal and Infant Mortality

Maternal mortality refers to deaths that result from complications associated with pregnancy or childbirth. The major causes of maternal mortality include hemorrhage, unsafe induced abortion procedures, hypertension, obstructed labor, and infection (Freedman & Maine, 1993).

INTERNATIONAL DATA

Ninety-nine percent of the 585,000 women worldwide who die each year from pregnancy and childbirth-related causes are from less developed countries in Africa, Asia, and Latin America.

Source: Reproductive Health Priorities Identified, 1997.

High maternal death rates in developing countries stem from inadequate health care and family planning services.

In the United States, the maternal death rate has dropped considerably over the last few decades.

NATIONAL DATA

Between 1970 and 1990, the U.S. maternal death rate (number of deaths per 100,000 births and pregnancy complications) dropped from more than 20 to about 8.

Source: *Statistical Abstract of the United States: 1996,* Table 124.

Compared to less developed countries, the risk of dying from pregnancy or childbirth-related complications in the United States is relatively low.

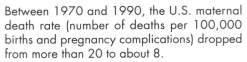

INTERNATIONAL DATA

In Bangladesh, Egypt, India, and Indonesia, more than 1 out of every 5 deaths among women in their childbearing years is related to pregnancy. By contrast, only 1 out of every 200 deaths among women of reproductive age in the United States is related to pregnancy.

Source: Freedman & Maine, 1993.

Infant mortality refers to deaths among infants under one year of age. In poorer countries, inadequate nutrition, impoverished living conditions, and lack of medical care contribute to high infant mortality rates (number of infant deaths per 1000 live births). For example, the infant mortality rate is 150 in Afghanistan, 121 in Somalia, and 97 in Pakistan (*Statistical Abstract of the United States: 1996,* Table 1327).

Like maternal mortality, the U.S. infant mortality rate has dropped over the last few decades—from about 20 in 1970 to about 8 in the 1990s (*Statistical Abstract of the United States: 1996,* Table 124). Although the U.S. infant mortality rate is low compared to developing countries, America lags behind other industrialized countries in infant health.

In the United States, both maternal and infant mortality rates vary by race, with minorities having significantly higher rates than whites. This is due to the disproportionate numbers of minorities who live in poverty and lack access to affordable health care. Hewlett (1992) reports that about half of all U.S. infant deaths are a direct result of their mothers receiving little or no prenatal care.

PERSONAL CHOICES

Should You Deliver in a Hospital or Have a Home Birth?

The American College of Obstetricians and Gynecologists views childbirth as a medical event that should take place in a hospital. Part of the reason why the medical profession does not advocate home births may be fear of being sued if something goes wrong during a home birth.

Although over 95% of all U.S. births do occur in the hospital, some expectant parents are concerned that traditional childbirth procedures are too impersonal, costly, and potentially dangerous. Those who opt for home births are primarily concerned about avoiding separation from the new infant, maintaining control over who can be present at the delivery, and avoiding what they view as unnecessary medical management (Sacks & Donnerfeld, 1984).

The nurse-midwife is most often asked to assist in home births. Some nurse-midwives are certified members of the American College of Nurse-Midwives and have successfully completed a master's degree in nurse-midwifery offered at various universities, including Georgetown, Emory, St. Louis, and Columbia. Two organizations—Association for Childbirth at Home (ACAH) and Home Oriented Maternity Experience (HOME)—help couples prepare for home births.

What is the relative safety of home versus hospital births? A study designed to answer this question revealed that except in special cases (such as when the mother has hypertension or diabetes), home births involve no extra risks compared to births in hospitals. However, the researchers warned that in cases of delayed labor, breech births, or fetal distress, a hospital is the safer environment (Holmes, 1988). European studies comparing planned home births to hospital deliveries confirmed that home birth can be a safe choice for women with low risk of obstetrical complications or poor perinatal outcomes (Remez, 1997). Factors associated with safe home births include low-risk pregnancies and quick access to adequate hospital services.

Rather than choose between having their baby in a hospital or at home, some prefer a birthing center, which is more likely to be available in larger metropolitan areas. Birthing centers provide special rooms for the woman to experience labor, and the staff is more likely to consist of certified nurse-midwives than obstetricians. National data from the United States suggest that low-risk mothers who choose to have their babies in birthing centers are no more likely to have poor birth outcomes or to require a cesarean section than are low-risk women who give birth in the hospital (Rooks et al., 1989).

THINK ABOUT IT

Travis (1988) suggested that the choice of whether to give birth at home or in a hospital is related to one's perspective on childbirth:

> Should childbirth be viewed as a natural process, usually resulting in spontaneous delivery of healthy alert infants to healthy attentive mothers? Or is it more appropriate to perceive the process as a medical event with relatively high risk of disease or death to both women and infants? (p. 150)

TRANSITION TO PARENTHOOD

Transition to parenthood refers to that period of time from the beginning of pregnancy through the first few months after the birth of the baby.

Goldberg and Michaels (1988) synthesized the research on the transition to parenthood and identified several factors and interventions that influence this transition (see Table 7.3). These factors and interventions help to explain "why some individuals and relationships adapt smoothly to the transition whereas others face numerous difficulties that may even reach crisis proportions" (Goldberg & Michaels, 1988, p. 351). More specific information on how the mother, father, and couple experience the transition to parenthood follows.

TABLE 7.3 Factors and Interventions Influencing the Transition to Parenthood

	PRECONCEPTION	PREGNANCY AND BIRTH	POSTNATAL
Factors associated with a smooth transition to parenthood	Well-functioning marriage Adequate social support network Good relationship with own parents Adequate socioeconomic status History of psychological health History of physical health Strong motivation to become a parent Social climate supportive of children and families	Supportive spousal relationship Adequate social support network (emotional, tangible, and cognitive support from family and friends) Adequate socioeconomic status Adequate prenatal care Good relationship with obstetrician Psychological health (low anxiety, low depression, high self-esteem, good self-concept, high autonomy, high affiliation) Medically and psychologically satisfactory birth experience	Well-functioning marriage; satisfaction with division of labor Psychological health Satisfaction with work and family roles Positive change and growth in self-concept Successful adaptation to parenthood (synchronous parent-infant interaction, development of secure attachment, sensitivity to child's developmental needs) Closer intergenerational ties Well-functioning social support network Adequate socioeconomic status Adequate well-baby care
Factors associated with a difficult transition to parenthood	History of psychiatric problems Low motivation to become a parent Psychological conflicts over femininity, masculinity History of physical health problems Economic hardship Marital distress Stress and deficits in support from family, friends, and community	Maternal anxiety and depression Psychological problems Economic problems Teenager; teenage head of household Advanced maternal or parental age Maternal or fetal medical complications during pregnancy Birth problems (maternal medical complications; birth of an ill, premature, or handicapped infant) Marital distress; lack of spousal support Stress and deficits in social support network	Poor adjustment to parenthood Reactivation of unresolved psychological needs Role conflict, strain, overload Extended postpartum depression Negative change in self-concept Guilt, ambivalence, grief, and mourning if infant is ill, premature, or handicapped Separation from infant due to maternal or infant health problems Financial problems Marital distress Stress and deficits in social support network

Continued on following page.

TABLE 7.3 Factors and Interventions Influencing the Transition to Parenthood *(Continued)*

	PRECONCEPTION	PREGNANCY AND BIRTH	POSTNATAL
Interventions (strategies to assist prospective and active parents at each phase of the transition to parenthood)	Learn decision-making skills to assist decisions about whether and when to have a baby Learn to use social support network effectively Couple (marital) therapy to resolve conflicts, work on communication skills	Childbirth preparation to impart educational information, promote spousal support, alleviate maternal experience of pain and need for medication during labor Preparation for parenthood—anticipatory guidance (what to expect from baby, changes to expect in lifestyle, marital and employment roles) Communication skills for couples Prenatal care Medical, educational, and social-psychological care for pregnant teenagers Government subsidies for economically disadvantaged women (the WIC program)	Informal support programs, such as drop-in center, peer support group, resource and referral Formal support programs, such as parent education, home visitors, counseling, group therapy Learn special caregiving for ill or handicapped infant Pediatric well-baby care Good-quality child care Emotional, tangible, and cognitive support from family and friends

Source: Michaels & Goldberg, 1988.

Transition to Motherhood

Although pregnancy and childbirth are sometimes thought of as a painful ordeal, some women describe the experience as fantastic, joyful, and unsurpassed. A strong emotional bond between a mother and her baby usually develops early, so that mother and infant resist separation. Sociobiologists suggest that there is a biological basis for the attachment between a mother and her offspring. The mother alone carries the fetus in her body for 9 months, lactates to provide milk, and produces oxytocin—a hormone from the pituitary gland (produced during the expulsive stage of labor) that has been associated with the onset of maternal behavior in lower animals.

POSTPARTUM BLUES Not all mothers feel joyous after childbirth. Emotional bonding may be temporarily impeded by a mild depression, characterized by irritability, crying, loss of appetite, and difficulty in sleeping. Between 50 to 70% of all new mothers experience "baby blues"—transitory symptoms of depression 24–48 hours after the baby is born. About 10% experience *postpartum depression*—a more severe reaction than "baby blues" (Kraus & Redman, 1986).

Postpartum depression is believed to be a result of the numerous physiological and psychological changes occurring during pregnancy, labor, and delivery. Although the woman may become depressed in the hospital, she more often experiences these feelings within the first month after returning home with her baby. Most women recover within a short time; some (about 5%) seek therapy to speed their recovery. To minimize "baby blues" and postpartum depression, one must recognize that having misgivings about the new infant is normal and appropriate. In addition, the woman who has negative feelings about her new role as mother should elicit help with the baby from her family so that she can continue to meet her personal and social needs.

CHOOSING PRIORITIES   For some women, motherhood is the ultimate fulfillment; for others, the ultimate frustration. Priorities must be established. When forced to choose between her job and family responsibilities (the babysitter does not show up, or the child is sick or hurt), the employed woman and mother (unlike the man and father) generally chooses the role of mother over the role of employee (Grant, Simpson, Rong, & Peters-Golden, 1990; LaRossa, 1988; Mischel & Fuhr, 1988). In spite of the stress associated with motherhood, it may be a profoundly happy time, particularly for mothers in their first marriage (Demo & Acock, 1996).

Transition to Fatherhood

Fatherhood is being given increased cultural visibility in our society. *U.S. News & World Report* devoted its lead article in one of its recent issues to "Why Fathers Count" and emphasized that among the greatest predictors of a positive outcome for children is the active presence of a father in the child's life (Minerbrook, 1995). Historically, the father's role in the United States has been to protect and provide for his family, but this role is expanding to include involvement in preparation for childbirth classes, presence in the birthing room, and child care. As to the latter, 93% of a random sample of 190 male college students reported that they intended to be the "new," involved father (Penland & Darling, 1992).

Sometimes, however, intentions fathers have to be involved with their children do not translate into specific behavior. Wayte (1994) observed that although fathers reported high rates of engagement (one-on-one interaction with their children) and accessibility (being available to the child), their level of responsibility did not change. Responsibility was defined in terms of ensuring that the child was appropriately cared for at *all* times. Job demands and making a living were the primary reasons for not increasing their responsibility in child care. Hence, the new image of the contemporary father taking responsibility for his children is more myth than reality.

The amount of time fathers spend with their children varies by society. Based on a comparison of over 1000 father-children pairs in both America and Japan, U.S. fathers spend about 1 hour on a weekday and 2 hours per day on the weekend with their sons.

Japanese fathers spend half that time with their sons. Both U.S. and Japanese fathers spend the same amount of time with their daughters—about a half hour per day during the week and about an hour and a third per day on the weekend. Having dinner and playing sports is the typical agenda of U.S. fathers and their children; having breakfast is the typical activity of Japanese fathers and their children. With regard to homework, 1 in 10 American fathers is involved every day, compared to 1 in 100 of Japanese fathers (Ishii-Kuntz, 1994).

Japanese fathers spend slightly more time with their daughters than with their sons. Japanese parents tend to be more protective of their daughters, and Japanese fathers are often saddened when their daughters marry, because they feel that they are "taken away." According to traditional partrilocal marriage residence custom among the Japanese (also practiced by Chinese and Korean families), when daughters marry, they leave their parents and go with their new husband to live in his parents' house. Hence, daughters leave their family of origin to become the daughter-in-law in the family of their husband. In contrast, adult sons form extended kin households and often stay close to the parents.

FATHERS WITH NEWBORNS AND OLDER CHILDREN
Fathers who participate in the delivery of their infants and have contact with them the first hour after birth experience an early context of communicating with and actively caring for their offspring (Briesemeister & Haines, 1988). However, the image of the father as an active and equal participant in child care is true of only a portion of middle-class professionals, such as educators, artists, physicians, and social workers. Mothers continue to perform over 90% of the active child care (LaRossa, 1988) and often feel overburdened (Biller, 1993).

In a study of 45 African American fathers of preschool children, two researchers observed that although the fathers spent less time taking care of their preschoolers than did the mothers (2.8 hours versus 6.7 hours per day), they "were accessible and involved with their children" (Ahmeduzzaman & Roopnarine, 1992, p. 705). Factors associated with greater involvement of the fathers included higher income, education, and stability of the marriage. In another study, 48% of African American fathers reported spending 3 or more hours a day feeding, dressing, bathing, and putting a preschooler to bed, in contrast to 32% of Hispanic fathers and 23% of non-Hispanic white fathers (Jacobsen & Edmondson, 1993).

INCREASED SENSE OF FINANCIAL RESPONSIBILITY

Given our society's expectation that fathers bear primary financial responsibility for their family, the birth of a baby sometimes "arouses anxieties in men about their capacity to provide" (Fedele, Golding, Grossman, & Pollack, 1988, p. 97). "Some fathers, fearing responsibility, run from it, leaving their families to fend for themselves without emotional or financial support" (Greenberg, 1986, p. 71). However, "many begin to put in more hours at work in order to bring home more money or to be a better father-provider" (Fedele et al., 1988, p. 97). Some wives regard this increased time away from home to earn more money as a "retreat from involvement with the baby and the whole family enterprise" (Cowan & Cowan, 1988, p. 136). Indeed, fathers are not likely to dramatically increase their involvement with children "as long as achievement in market work continues to grab a hunk of their attention" (LaRossa & Reitzes, 1993, p. 466). However, fathers who enjoy their work have higher self-esteem, which often translates into being less controlling and more accepting of their children (Grimm-Thomas & Perry-Jenkins, 1994).

JEALOUSY OF THE BABY

Some men are jealous of the baby and the attention that their wives divert from them to the baby. One new father said:

> My wife and I were really close. We would spend a lot of time together. We would walk together, hold each other, play cards, fish, or we would stay home and watch TV, lie on the couch together. Now whatever spare time we have together, the baby is there—and it's going to be that way for a long time. I couldn't accept that that's the way it has to be (quoted in Greenberg, 1986, p. 88).

Resolving this jealousy may require that the couple get help with child care so that they can spend more recreational and leisure time together. In addition, fathers may increase their involvement in child care so that child-centered activities become activities shared by the couple.

We have been discussing the adjustment of parents to babies who are healthy and normal. But about 1% or more of all births are babies with heart malformations, urogenital anomalies, cleft lip or palate, and various musculoskeletal anomalies (National Center for Health Statistics, 1992), which may make adjustment to parenthood more difficult. In addition, babies who cry a great deal and have irregular sleep patterns make adjustment on the part of the parents more difficult (Belsky & Rovine, 1990).

Transition to Couplehood

Researchers disagree on whether a baby increases or decreases marital happiness.

CHILDREN INCREASE MARITAL HAPPINESS

Some studies report that having a baby is associated with improving the marital relationship. Out of a total of 30,000 parents who responded to a magazine survey, 43% said they felt closer to their spouse after they had children (Greer, 1986). In another study of 75 fathers and 115 mothers, one researcher observed that couples who reported a high degree of marital satisfaction before the birth of their baby were more likely to experience positive changes as a result of the baby than were spouses who reported a low degree of marital satisfaction before the birth (Harriman, 1986).

CHILDREN DECREASE MARITAL HAPPINESS

Some research suggests that parenthood decreases marital happiness. A team of researchers (Lavee et al., 1996) studied 287 intact couples who had children living at

The birth of a baby changes a couple's relationship.

home and concluded that stress associated with rearing children negatively affected both their psychological well-being and perceived marital quality. The more economically stressed, the greater the effect. Cowan and Cowan (1992) followed 72 expectant couples and 24 child-free couples for 10 years. They noted a decrease in relationship satisfaction among parents as a result of unfulfilled expectations, different patterns of engagement into the role of parent, and different perceptions of their role as lover/partners. Both partners were surprised that the baby did not bring them closer together. The husbands viewed themselves less in the role of the parent than did the wives, and the wives viewed themselves less in the role of lover than did the husbands. The greater the discrepancies, the greater the unhappiness.

Cowan and Cowan (1992) have developed a program designed to assist couples in preparing for the changes that occur in the transition from spouse to parent. The following are some of their suggestions:

1. Share expectations. Discuss private notions about one's ideal family. Also share any anxieties about the new role and its impact on one's self, the relationship, and work.

2. Make time for talk, sex, and togetherness. Since the demands of the new baby will take time away from the couple, it is important to make time for communication, sex, and doing things together "even if the laundry or dinner dishes have to wait" (p. 78).

3. Don't be afraid of conflict. "Regard a fight as information that something is wrong in the relationship. The trick is not to worry that you are having a struggle, or to avoid a fight" (p. 78).

4. Talk with a friend or co-worker. Talking with others who have experienced the transition from spouse to parent helps alleviate one's feelings of aloneness and isolation. Be careful, however, not to divulge information that may result in the spouse's feeling betrayed. Some mental health centers offer parenting groups to discuss parenting concerns.

CHILDREN DO NOT AFFECT MARITAL HAPPINESS
Some research suggests that children neither increase nor decrease marital happiness. In a study comparing married couples who had children with those who did not have children, the researchers observed that, over time, the spouses in both groups reported declines in love feelings, marital satisfaction, doing things together, and positive interactions. The parents were no less happy in their marriages than the child-free couples. The researchers concluded that "the transition to parenthood is not an inescapable detriment to marital quality" (MacDermid, Huston, & McHale, 1990, p. 485).

THINK ABOUT IT

What might men and women do to prepare as individuals and as a couple for the transition to parenthood?

KEY TERMS

amniocentesis 175	infertility 164
artificial insemination 167	in vitro fertilization 168
breech birth 180	laparoscope 168
cesarean section 181	maternal mortality 182
chorionic villus sampling 176	microinjection 170
conception 164	miscarriage 177
cryopreservation 168	multigravida 179
dilation 180	ovum transfer 168
ectopic pregnancy 172	partial zona drilling 170
effacement 180	preconception care 171
embryo 171	postpartum depression 185
fertilization 164	pregnancy 164
fetal alcohol syndrome 174	primigravida 179
fetus 171	spontaneous abortion 177
gamete intrafallopian transfer 169	surrogate mother 167
infant mortality 182	ultrasound 174
	zygote intrafallopian transfer 169

SUMMARY POINTS

This chapter focuses on various medical, social, and psychological issues concerning pregnancy, infertility, and reproductive technologies. The transition to parenthood for women, men, and couples is also discussed.

Fertilization and Conception

Pregnancy begins with fertilization (a woman's egg unites with a man's sperm) and conception (the fertilized egg implants on the uterine wall).

Infertility

Infertility, the inability to achieve a pregnancy after at least 1 year of regular sexual relations without birth control, affects 15 to 20% of U.S. married couples. Common causes of male infertility include low sperm production and poor semen motility. Causes of female infertility include blocked fallopian tubes and impaired ovulation. The effects of some sexually transmissible diseases may result in infertility for both men and women.

Reproductive Technology

Reproductive technologies include hormone therapy, artificial insemination, artificial insemination of a surrogate mother, in vitro fertilization, and ovum transfer. Reproductive technology offers more choices regarding childbearing to infertile couples, single women, lesbians, and gay men.

Preconception Care

Preconception care includes risk assessment, interventions to reduce risk, and general health promotion prior to becoming pregnant. Women who want to maximize their chance of having a healthy pregnancy and baby may seek preconception care.

Pregnancy and Labor

Early signs of pregnancy include lack of menstruation, nausea and vomiting (morning sickness), enlarged and tender breasts, frequent urination, and fatigue. Pregnancy is best confirmed by laboratory tests and a physical examination. In the early stages of pregnancy, some women experience leg cramps, constipation, backache, varicose veins, swelling, heartburn, increased vaginal discharge, and shortness of breath. Prenatal care helps to ensure a healthy pregnancy and healthy baby. Miscarriages, which occur in about 9% of medically confirmed pregnancies, are usually caused by chromosomal abnormalities. Labor occurs in three stages. About 20% of U.S. births are cesarean births in which an incision is made in the woman's abdomen and uterus and the baby is manually removed.

Transition to Parenthood

The transition to parenthood involves that period of time from the beginning of pregnancy through the first few months after the birth of the baby. The transition is usually more profound for the mother, due to the fact that her hormonal system is altered. New mothers also may experience postpartum depression, and are confronted with reordering their priorities. Most women tend to place family considerations above career considerations.

The active participation of fathers in the lives of their children is one of the greatest predictors of positive outcomes for children. While over 90% of a sample of college students reported that they wanted to be actively involved in the lives of their children, only half reported that their fathers had been actively involved in their lives. In general, fathers tend to become more active as their children age. When U.S. fathers are involved with their children, it is more often with their sons. In most cases, wives and mothers are very influential in whether or not fathers have a close relationship with their children. Research findings regarding how children affect marital happiness are inconsistent. However, having children is associated with greater commitment and marital stability.

REFERENCES

Acheson, L. S. (1997). Caring for the pregnant woman and planning for the delivery. In J. Rosenfeld (Ed.), *Women's health in primary care* (pp. 331–350). Baltimore: Williams & Wilkins.

Affonso, D. D., & Mayberry, L. J. (1989). Common stressors reported by a group of childbearing American women. In P. N. Stern (Ed.), *Pregnancy and parenting* (pp. 41–55). New York: Hemisphere.

Ahmeduzzaman, M., & Roopnarine, J. L. (1992). Sociodemographic factors, functioning style, social support, and fathers' involvement with preschoolers in African American families. *Journal of Marriage and the Family, 54,* 699–707.

Belsky, J., & Rovine, M. (1990). Patterns of marital change across the transition to parenthood: Pregnancy to three years postpartum. *Journal of Marriage and the Family, 52,* 5–19.

Biller, H. B. (1993). *Fathers and families.* Westport, CT: Auburn House.

Bogren, L. Y. (1991). Changes in sexuality in women and men during pregnancy. *Archives of Sexual Behavior, 20,* 35–45.

Boss, J. A. (1994). First trimester prenatal diagnosis: Earlier is not necessarily better. *Journal of Medical Ethics, 20,* 146–151.

Brent, R. L., & Beckman, D. A. (1992). Principles of teratology. In M. I. Evans (Ed.), *Reproductive risks and prenatal diagnosis* (pp. 43–68). Norwalk, CT: Appleton & Lange.

Briesemeister, L. H., & Haines, B. A. (1988). The interactions of fathers and newborns. In K. L. Michaelson (Ed.), *Childbirth in America: Anthropological perspectives* (pp. 228–238). South Hadley, MA: Bergin & Garvey.

Chez, R. A. (1991). Identifying maternal/fetal risks before pregnancy *Medical Aspects of Human Sexuality, 25*, 54–58.

Cowan, P. A., & Cowan, C. P. (1988). Changes in marriage during the transition to parenthood: Must we blame the baby? In G. Y. Michaels & W. A. Goldberg (Eds.), *The transition to parenthood: Current theory and reasearch* (pp. 114–154). New York: Cambridge University Press.

Curtin, S. C. (1997, July 16). Rates of cesarean birth and vaginal birth after previous cesarean, 1991–1995. *Monthly Vital Statistics Report, 45*, (11).

Davis-Floyd, R. E. (1988). Birth as an American rite of passage. In K. L. Michaelson (Ed.), *Childbirth in America: Anthropological perspectives* (pp. 153–177). South Hadley, MA: Bergin & Carvey.

Demo, D. H., & Acock, A. C. (1996). Singlehood, marriage, and remarriage: The effects of family structure and family relationships on mother's well-being. *Journal of Family Issues, 17*, 388–407.

Derwinski-Robinson, B. (1990). Infertility and sexuality. In C. I. Fogel & D. Lauver (Eds.), *Sexual health promotion* (pp. 291–304). Philadelphia: W. B. Saunders.

Ectopic pregnancy—United States, 1990–1992. (1995). *Morbidity and Mortality Weekly Report, 44*, 46–67.

Engel, N. S. (1990). The maternity cycle and sexuality. In C. I. Fogel & D. Lauver (Eds.), *Sexual health promotion* (pp. 179–205). Philadelphia: W. B. Saunders.

Evans, M. I., & Johnson, M. P. (1992). Chorionic villus sampling. In M. I. Evans (Ed.), *Reproductive risks and prenatal diagnosis* (pp. 175–184). Norwalk, CT: Appleton & Lange.

Fedele, N. M., Golding, E. R., Grossman, F. K., & Pollack, W. S. (1988). Psychological issues in adjustment to first parenthood. In G. Y. Michaels & W. A. Goldberg (Eds.), *The transition to parenthood: Current theory and research* (pp. 85–113). New York: Cambridge University Press.

Fitzgerald, M. (1989, August 9). Couples fawn over frozen embryos, expert says. *USA Today*, p. 3A.

Foreman, S. (1990, March 26). Risk is small in hiding the identity of donor. *USA Today*, p. 7A.

Freedman, L. P., & Maine, D. (1993). Women's mortality: A legacy of neglect. In M. Koblinsky, J. Timyan, & J. Gay (Eds.), *The health of women: A global perspective* (pp. 147–170). Boulder, CO: Westview Press.

Garel, M., & Blondel, B. (1992). Assessment at 1 year of the psychological consequences of having triplets. *Human Reproduction, 7*, 729–732.

Gauna-Trujillo, B., & Higgins, P. G. (1989). Sexual intercourse and pregnancy. In P. N. Sern (Ed.), *Pregnancy and parenting* (pp. 31–40). New York: Hemisphere.

Goldberg, W. A., & Michaels, G. Y. (1988). Conclusion. The transition to parenthood: Synthesis and future directions. In G. Y. Michaels & W. A. Goldberg (Eds.), *The transition to parenthood: Current theory and research* (pp. 342–360). New York: Cambridge University Press.

Grant, L., Simpson, L. A., Rong, Z. L., & Peters-Golden, H. (1990). Gender, parenthood, and work hours of physicians. *Journal of Marriage and the Family, 52*, 39–49.

Greenberg, M. (1986). *The birth of a father*. New York: Continuum.

Greer, K. (1986, October). Today's parents: How well are they doing? *Better Homes and Gardens*, 36–46.

Grimm-Thomas, K., & Perry-Jenkins, M. (1994). All in a day's work: Job experiences, self-esteem, and fathering in working-class families. *Family Relations, 43*, 174–181.

Harriman, L. C. (1986). Marital adjustment as related to personal and marital changes accompanying parenthood. *Family Relations, 35*, 233–239.

Hellmich, N. (1997, April 24). Oldest new mom is 63. *USA Today*, p. e1.

Hewlett, S. (1992). *When the bough breaks: The cost of neglecting our children*. New York: HarperPerennial.

Higgins, B. S. (1990). Couple infertility: From the perspective of the close-relationship model. *Family Relations, 39*, 81–86.

Holmes, P. (1988). Squeeze on alternatives to hospital births. *New Statesman, 116*, 6.

Ishii-Kuntz, M. (1994). Parental involvement and perception toward fathers' roles: A comparison between Japan and the United States. *Journal of Family Issues, 15*, 30–48.

Jacobsen, L., & Edmondson, B. (1993, August). Father figures. *American Demographics*, 22.

Johnson, M. P., & Miller, O. J. (1992). Cytogenetics. In M. I. Evans (Ed.), *Reproductive risks and prenatal diagnosis* (pp. 237–249). Norwalk, CT: Appleton & Lange.

Kahn, A. (1997, March 13). Clone mammals . . . Clone man? *Nature, 383*, 119.

Kiely, J. L., Kleinman, J. C., & Kiely, M. (1992). Triplets and higher-order multiple births: Time trends and infant mortality. *American Journal of Diseases in Children, 146*, 862–868.

Kluger, J. (1997, March 10). Will we follow the sheep? *Time, 149*, 67, 70–72.

Kraus, M. A., & Redman, E. S. (1986). Postpartum depression: An interactional view. *Journal of Marital and Family Therapy, 12*, 63–74.

LaRossa, R. (1988). Fatherhood and social change. *Family Relations, 37*, 451–457.

LaRossa, R., & Reitzes, D. C. (1993). Continuity and change in middle class fatherhood, 1925–1939: The culture-conduct connection. *Journal of Marriage and the Family, 55,* 455–468.

Lasker, J. N., & Borg, S. (1987). *In search of parenthood.* Boston: Beacon Press.

Lavee, Y., Sharlin, S., & Katz, R. (1996). The effect of parenting stress on marital quality: An integrated mother-father model. *Journal of Family Issues, 17,* 114–135.

Lazarus, E. S. (1988). Poor women, poor outcomes: Social class and reproductive health. In K. L. Michaelson (Ed.), *Childbirth in America: Anthropological perspectives* (pp. 39–54). South Hadley, MA: Bergin & Garvey.

Levran, D., Dor, J., Rudak, E., Nebel, L., Ben-Shlomo, I., Ben-Rafael, Z., & Mashiach, S. (1990). Pregnancy potential of human oocytes—The effect of cryo-preservation. *New England Journal of Medicine, 323,* 1153–1156.

MacDermid, S. M., Huston, T. L., & McHale, S. M. (1990). Changes in marriage associated with the transition to parenthood: Individual differences as a function of sex-role attitudes and changes in the division of household labor. *Journal of Marriage and the Family, 52,* 475–486.

Macklin, R. (1997, March 10). Human cloning? Don't just say no. *U.S. News & World Report,* 64.

Michaelson, K. L. (1988). Childbirth in America: A brief history and contemporary issues. In K. L. Michaelson (Ed.), *Childbirth in America: Anthropological perspectives* (pp. 1–32). South Hadley, MA: Bergin & Garvey.

Minerbrook, S. (1995, October 30). Missing on the mall: Save the children. *U.S. News & World Report, 119*(17), 10–11.

Mischel, H. N., & Fuhr, R. (1988). Maternal employment: Its psychological effects on children and their families. In S. M. Dornbusch & M. H. Strober (Eds.), *Feminism, children and the new families* (pp. 194–195). New York: Guilford Press.

National Center for Health Statistics (1992). *Advance report of new data from the 1989 birth certificate.* (Monthly Vital Statistics Report, vol. 40, no. 12, suppl.). Hyattsville, MD: U.S. Public Health Service.

Office of Technology Assessment. (1988). *Artificial insemination: Practice in the United States, summary of a 1987 survey—Background paper.* Washington, DC: U.S. Government Printing Office.

Penland, M. R., & Darling, C. A. (1992). *Predicting fathering styles: Traditional vs. "new" fathers.* Paper, 54th Annual Conference, National Council on Family Relations, Orlando, FL.

Press, N., & Browner, C. H. (1995). Risk, autonomy, and responsibility: Informed consent for prenatal testing. *Hastings Center Report, 25*(3), S9–S12.

Remez, L. (1997). Planned home birth can be as safe as hospital delivery for women with low-risk pregnancies. *Family Planning Perspectives, 29,* 141–143.

Reproductive Health Priorities Indentified. (1997). *POPLINE, 19,* 1. Washington, DC: The Population Institute.

Rice, N. (1992). Psychological reaction to prenatal diagnosis and loss. In M. I. Evans (Ed.), *Reproductive risks and prenatal diagnosis* (pp. 277–282). Norwalk, CT: Appleton & Lange.

Rooks, J. P., Weatherby, N. L., Ernst, E. K., Stapleton, S., Rosen, D., & Rosenfield, A. (1989). Outcomes of care in birth centers. *New England Journal of Medicine, 321,* 1804–1811.

Rosenthal, M. B. (1997). Infertility. In J. Rosenfeld (Ed.), *Women's health in primary care* (pp. 351–362). Baltimore: Williams & Wilkins.

Sacks, S. R., & Donnerfeld, P. B. (1984). Parental choice of alternative birth environments and attitudes toward childrearing philosophy. *Journal of Marriage and the Family, 46,* 469–475.

Shapiro, J. L. (1987, January). The expectant father. *Psychology Today,* pp. 36–42.

Shapiro, C. H. (1988). *Infertility and pregnancy loss.* San Francisco: Jossey-Bass.

Statistical Abstract of the United States: 1996 (116th ed.). (1996). Washington, DC: U.S. Bureau of the Census.

Travis, C. B. (1988). *Women and health psychology: Biomedical issues.* Hillside, NJ: Lawrence Erlbaum Associates.

Turner, R. (1992). First-trimester chorionic villus sampling may raise risk of spontaneous abortion and limb abnormality. *Family Planning Perspectives, 24,* 45–46.

Wayte, D. (1994). Fatherhood and family roles: An examination of evidence of change. *Process: Family Systems Research and Therapy, 3,* 137–150.

Whitehead, M. (1989). *A mother's story: The truth about the Baby M case.* New York: St. Martin's Press.

Wilkerson, N. N., & Bing, E. (1988). Sexuality. In F. H. Nichols & S. S. Humenick (Eds.), *Childbirth education: Practice, research, and theory* (pp. 376–393). Philadelphia: W. B. Saunders Company.

Wilcox, A. J., Weinberg, C. R., & Baird, D. B. (1995). Timing of sexual intercourse in relation to ovulation. *The New England Journal of Medicine, 333,* 1517–1521.

ABORTION AND ADOPTION

Chapter 8

193

> *P*eople in crisis over a pregnancy must act. They may be just as ambivalent about abortion as most Americans or they may hold strong political views, but faced with the physical fact of an unplanned or risky pregnancy, they have no choice but to choose, finally and irreversibly, between birth and abortion.
>
> Kate Maloy
> Maggie Jones Patterson
> *Birth or Abortion?*

The following passage reflects the experience of millions of U.S. women each year who encounter a problem pregnancy and face the decision of whether to continue the pregnancy and parent the child, make an adoption plan for the child, or terminate the pregnancy through abortion.

> It was a big shock. I never thought it would happen to me. To other people, yes, but never in a million years would it happen to me. I looked at all my options and thought, how am I going to go to school, be a good mother, and work all at the same time? It seemed impossible. (Katelynn, age 19, quoted in Lindsay, 1997, p. 31)

Pregnancies that are terminated by induced abortion or are resolved by placing the infant for adoption are often referred to as "unintended" or "unwanted" pregnancies. However, neither of these terms reflect all pregnancies in which abortion or adoption is considered or carried out. Stotland (1996, p. 240) notes that:

> Some pregnancies are not consciously intended, but are tolerated or even welcomed when they are recognized or as they progress . . . Some pregnancies are wanted, but simultaneously experienced as unsupportable because of social or psychological circumstances . . . Therefore, the most accurate term may be . . . 'problem' pregnancy, which implies only that the pregnant woman considers the pregnancy a problem.

In this chapter, we discuss the two nonparenting options for resolving a 'problem pregnancy': abortion and adoption. We also emphasize an alternative to both abortion and adoption—the prevention of unwanted pregnancies and the provision of support for women who want to keep and parent their children.

ABORTION IN THE UNITED STATES

An abortion may be either an *induced abortion*, which is the deliberate termination of a pregnancy through chemical or surgical means, or a *spontaneous abortion* (miscarriage), which is the unintended termination of a pregnancy. In this text, however, we use the term "abortion" to refer to induced abortion.

Incidence of Abortion

Table 8.1 reflects the abortion rates and ratios in the United States for selected years. *Abortion rate* refers to the number of abortions per 1000 women aged 15 to 44; *abortion ratio* refers to the number of abortions per 1000 live births.

NATIONAL DATA

At current rates, an estimated 43% of U.S. women will have at least 1 abortion by the time they are 45 years old.

Source: *Facts in Brief*, 1996.

Since 1990, the number of abortions has dropped each year ("Abortion Surveillance," 1997). Reasons for the decreasing number of abortions include more single women keeping their babies, increased condom use, and more liberal attitudes toward single-parent families. In addition, lower abortion rates are associated with an increase in restrictive abortion policies,

TABLE 8.1 Abortion Rates and Ratios for Selected Years

	Number	Rate (No. of abortions per 1000 women aged 15–44)	Ratio (No. of abortions per 1000 live births)
1980	1,554,000	29	428
1985	1,589,000	28	422
1992	1,529,000	26	379
1993	1,330,414	22	334
1994	1,267,415	21	321

Sources: *Morbidity and Mortality Weekly Report, 1994* (1997), and *Statistical Abstract of the United States: 1995.*

such as those requiring parental consent and mandatory waiting periods (these policies are discussed later in the section on "Abortion Legislation in the United States") (Matthews, Ribar, & Wilhelm, 1997). Finally, the decreasing number of abortions is related to fewer abortion providers and limited access to health facilities offering the procedure, particularly in rural areas (Matthews, Ribar, & Wilhelm, 1997).

NATIONAL DATA

The number of abortion providers declined by 8% between 1988 and 1992. In 1992, 84% of all U.S. counties lacked an abortion provider.

Source: Henshaw & Van Vort, 1994.

Who Gets Abortions and Why?

Over half of U.S. women obtaining abortions are younger than 25. Although white women obtain more than half of all abortions, African American women are nearly three times as likely as white women to have an abortion, and Hispanic women are roughly two times as likely. Two-thirds of all abortions are obtained by never-married women, and a similar percentage of women who have abortions intend to have children in the future. Women who report no religious affiliation are more likely to have an abortion than women who belong to a religious organization (*Facts in Brief,* 1996; Henshaw & Kost, 1996; "Abortion Surveillance," 1997). Although these demographic characteristics are associated with a higher likelihood of having an abortion, women who choose abortion represent all backgrounds.

Women choose abortion for a variety of financial, emotional, interpersonal, and health reasons. The majority (about 60%) of women who have abortions became pregnant even though they used a method of contraception. In other words, they experienced contraceptive failure (*Facts in Brief,* 1996).

In North America, abortion is not typically relied on as a primary means of birth control. A Canadian study of women obtaining abortions between 1975 and 1993 revealed that 20% of the women had at least one previous abortion, and less than 2% had obtained three or more previous procedures (Millar, Wadhera, & Henshaw, 1997).

In a study of 92 pregnant women who sought an abortion (Barnett, Freudenberg, & Willie, 1992), the women reported seeking an abortion for the following reasons: fear that the children would cause difficulties with their training or work (46%); pressure from their partners to have an abortion (29%); or concern that their relationships with their partners were unstable (20%). Some women also chose abortions when their pregnancies resulted from rape or from infidelity.

NATIONAL DATA

Each year, an estimated 32,000 pregnancies result from rape.

Source: Holmes, 1996.

Abortion is also performed for health reasons concerning the woman or the fetus. Some women choose to abort after learning, through prenatal testing, that their fetus has a serious abnormality. Other women may choose to abort if their physician informs them that continuing the pregnancy would jeopardize their health or life. Abortions performed in order to protect the life or health of the woman are called *therapeutic abortions.* Women who have experienced severe postpartum psychiatric illness have a high risk of recurrence with subsequent deliveries. These woman may elect to have an abortion in order to avoid this recurrence, which can be "disabling, humiliating, and painful to the patient, [and] extremely stressful to her loved ones" (Stotland, 1996, p. 242). Some women with multifetal pregnancies (a common outcome of the use of fertility drugs) may have a procedure called *transabdominal first trimester selective termination.* In this procedure, the lives of some fetuses are terminated to increase the chance of survival for the others or to minimize the health risks associated with multifetal pregnancy for the woman.

Following are some questions that a woman considering abortion is likely to contemplate (Maloy & Patterson, 1992, p. 321):

> Did the woman love the man with whom she had become pregnant? Would he stay with her? Could she love the baby? Could she live with herself if she had a child and turned it over to strangers to raise? If she kept her child, could she care for it properly? Did she have marketable skills, an education, income? Would she ever acquire them if she went ahead with her pregnancy? Would the birth of another baby jeopardize the welfare of her existing children? Would the child be born with serious abnormalities? Would it suffer more than it would thrive?

Methods of Abortion

Prior to the availability of modern surgical techniques, abortion in the late 18th and early 19th centuries was performed by flushing the uterus with caustic substances (such as gunpowder, quinine, or oil of juniper) or by inserting sticks of silver nitrate into the cervix. In the following section, we look at modern-day methods of abortion. The procedure

NATIONAL DATA

Percentage of U.S. abortions that are performed in clinics or doctors' offices

U.S. abortions performed in clinics or doctors' offices 93%

Source: *Facts in Brief,* 1996.

used to perform an abortion depends largely on the stage of the pregnancy, as measured from the first day of the last menstrual period.

SUCTION CURETTAGE   Pregnancy may be terminated during the first 6 to 8 weeks through a procedure called *suction curettage,* also referred to as *vacuum aspiration.* After the administration of a local anesthetic (a general anesthetic may be used at the patient's request), a hollow plastic rod attached to a suction aspirator is inserted into the woman's uterus through the cervix (see Figure 8.2). The device suctions the fetal tissue out of the uterus into a container. Following the suction procedure, the physician may explore the uterine cavity with a small metal instrument (curette) to ensure that all the tissue has been removed. The procedure, which takes about 10 to 20 minutes, can be performed on an outpatient basis in a clinic or a physician's office. Following this procedure, the patient usually experiences some bleeding and cramping, which is normal.

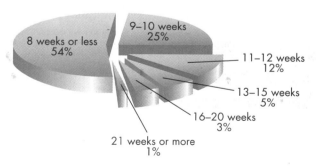

9–10 weeks 25%
8 weeks or less 54%
11–12 weeks 12%
13–15 weeks 5%
16–20 weeks 3%
21 weeks or more 1%

FIGURE 8.1   Percentage of U.S. Abortions Performed at Various Gestation Periods   **Source:** Abortion surveillance: Preliminary data—United States, 1994. (1997). *Morbidity and Mortality Weekly Report, 45,* 1123–1127.

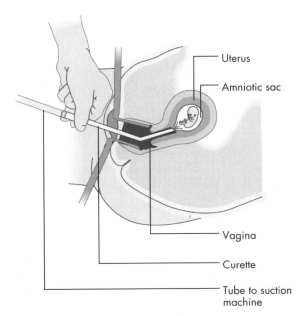

Uterus

Amniotic sac

Vagina

Curette

Tube to suction machine

FIGURE 8.2 Suction Curettage
The contents of the uterus are sucked out with a suction machine. This method is most often used during the first 3 months of pregnancy.

NATIONAL DATA

Percentage of all U.S. abortion facilities that provide services only through the 12th week of pregnancy

U.S. abortion facilities that provide services only through the 12th week of pregnancy 52%

Source: *Facts in Brief, 1996.*

DILATION AND SUCTION   *Dilation and suction (D & S),* a method of abortion used during the first 12 weeks of pregnancy, is essentially the same as suction curettage, except that the cervix is dilated before the suction procedure. Cervical dilation may be achieved by inserting laminaria into the cervix the day before the abortion is performed. Laminaria are dried, sterile rods of compressed seaweed stems that, when inserted into the cervix, absorb moisture and increase in diameter, thereby dilating the cervix. Cervical dilation may also be achieved by using a metal device designed to dilate the cervix just prior to the abortion. After suctioning the contents of the uterus, a metal surgical instrument is used to scrape any remaining fetal tissue and placenta from the uterine walls. (This method is also known as *dilation and curettage,* or *D & C.*) A local or general anesthetic may be used.

DILATION AND EVACUATION   *Dilation and evacuation (D & E),* an abortion procedure used in the second trimester of pregnancy (13 to 24 weeks' gestation), involves dilating the cervix and dismembering the fetus inside the uterus so that the body parts can be more easily suctioned out. Extraction instruments called ringed forceps are also used to remove the fetal tissue. A local or general anesthetic may be used.

INTACT DILATION AND EXTRACTION   An alternative to D & E is a procedure called *intact dilation and extraction (D & X),* which results in the whole fetus being aborted. After dilating the cervix, a physician pulls the fetus down into the birth canal, feet first. Then, with the rest of the body delivered and the head still lodged against the cervix, the physician inserts an instrument to make an opening in the base of the skull, inserts a suction catheter into this hole, evacuates the contents, and removes the fetus. An advantage of this procedure, if the fetus is malformed, is that certain types of testing can be more easily performed on an intact fetus to assess the woman's chances for a normal pregnancy in the future.

Abortion opponents have labeled dilation and extraction abortions *partial birth abortions* because the limbs and torso are typically delivered before the fetus has died. In many cases, D & X abortions are performed because the fetus has a serious defect, the woman's health is jeopardized by the pregnancy, or both. There are no reliable figures on how many D & Xs and other late-term abortions occur for nonmedical reasons.

NATIONAL DATA

Changes in Gallup poll results from April to July, 1996, indicated increased public support (57% to 71%) for banning late-term abortions by intact dilation and extraction.

Source: Moore, Newport, & Saad, 1996.

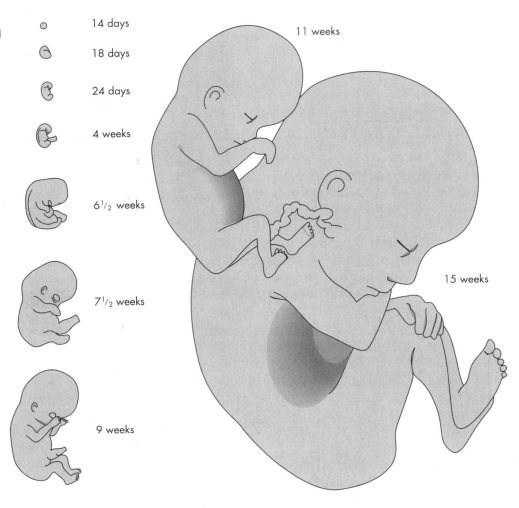

FIGURE 8.3 Actual Size Growth of the Embryo and Fetus from 2 to 15 Weeks after Conception

14 days

18 days

24 days

4 weeks

6½ weeks

7½ weeks

9 weeks

11 weeks

15 weeks

INDUCTION ABORTIONS Another abortion method used late in the second trimester involves inducing premature labor by injecting either saline or prostaglandins through the abdomen into the amniotic sac around the fetus. Prostaglandins may also be administered through vaginal suppositories. The injection or suppositories induce contractions that cause the cervix to dilate. An intravenous drip of oxytocin continues the labor contractions. The contractions are painful and can continue for several hours until the woman expels the fetus and placenta. Painkillers and local anesthesia are used to ease the woman's discomfort. This procedure must be performed in a hospital.

PHARMACEUTICAL ABORTION Also called *medical abortions*, *pharmaceutical abortions* involve the intentional termination of pregnancy through the use of pharmaceutical drugs. In 1997, the drug *RU-486* (mifepristone) became available in the United States after being approved by the U.S. Food and Drug Administration. The effects of mifepristone on the pregnant uterus include the onset of menstrual bleeding, sloughing off of the uterine lining, and stimulation of uterine contractions that help to dislodge the embryo. When within 6 weeks of the last menstrual period, mifepristone successfully aborts 90% of pregnancies (see Figure 8.4). Currently, mifepristone is used in conjunction with the injection or vaginal application of prostaglandins, resulting in a pregnancy termination rate of 95% (Lethbridge, 1995). After being examined by a physician to make sure the woman is less than 9 weeks pregnant, RU-486 is given, and 2 days later, a dose of prostaglandins is administered. A heavy menstrual flow follows. The woman makes a final visit to the physician to confirm that the abortion has been completed and to make sure the bleeding has stopped. Other drugs used to terminate pregnancies include methotrexate and misoprostol.

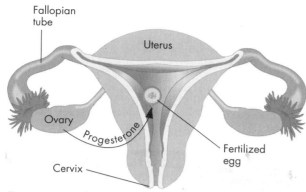

Progesterone, a hormone produced by the ovaries, is necessary for the implantation and development of a fertilized egg.

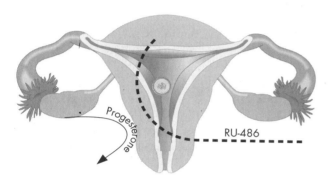

Taken early in pregnancy, RU-486 blocks the action of progesterone and makes the body act as if it isn't pregnant.

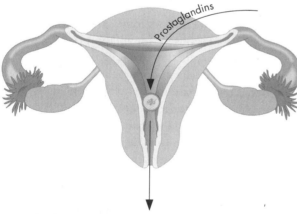

Prostaglandins, taken 2 days later, cause the uterus to contract and the cervix to soften and dilate. As a result, the fertilized egg is expelled in 97% of the cases.

FIGURE 8.4 How RU-486, Known as the Abortion Pill, Works

When women are offered a choice of surgical or medical abortion, most choose the medical method. The primary reasons for preferring medical

abortions include greater privacy and autonomy, less invasiveness, and greater naturalness (Winikoff, 1995). Another advantage of medical abortions is that drugs such as RU-486 can be dispensed by physicians in the privacy of their offices, which means women can avoid antiabortion forces that target abortion clinics.

Abortion Legislation in the United States

One of the most controversial political issues in U.S. society is abortion legislation. After a brief look at the historical background of abortion legislation, we will discuss the landmark *Roe v. Wade* case and more recent legislative action regarding abortion in the United States.

HISTORICAL BACKGROUND OF ABORTION LEGISLATION In the early postrevolution United States, abortion was neither prohibited nor uncommon. During this time, the states were governed by English common law, which permitted abortion until "quickening," the time when the woman could feel movement of the fetus inside her (usually in the fourth or fifth month of pregnancy) (Tribe, 1990). Even if an abortion was performed after quickening, the woman was immune from prosecution.

The legal control of abortion by statute began in 1821. Because thousands of women had died taking medically prescribed poisons to induce abortions, Connecticut passed a law prohibiting the use of poisons to induce postquickening abortions. This statute existed primarily to protect the lives of women. In 1828, New York enacted a law making abortion of an unquickened fetus a misdemeanor crime and abortion of a quickened fetus second-degree manslaughter, unless the abortion was necessary to preserve the woman's life (Sapiro, 1990).

In the mid-19th century, the American Medical Association led the campaign to criminalize abortion. Their concerns were both economic and moral (Petchesky, 1990). Formally trained physicians competed economically with midwives, who assisted not only in births, but also in abortions. Moral concerns in the medical community over abortion resulted, in part from advances in the scientific understanding of human development as a continuous process. This led physicians to question the relevance of the distinction between quickened and nonquickened fetuses (Tribe, 1990).

The movement to ban abortion was also spurred by concern over the increasing number of married, white, middle-class Protestant women who were having abortions in the mid-19th century. At the same time, immigrant and Catholic birthrates climbed. Medical professionals warned that "respectable women (white, middle-class Protestants) would be 'out-bred' by ignorant, lower-class aliens" (Petchesky, 1990, p. 82).

The medical profession opposed contraception, as well as abortion. Both contraception and abortion were associated with "obscenity, lewdness, sex, and worst of all, rebellious women" (Petchesky, 1990, p. 82) and were thus viewed as threats to traditional gender roles and conservative sexual values. Physicians condemned women who had abortions as "selfish" and criticized them for abandoning maternal and child care duties.

By 1900, abortion was illegal in all U.S. jurisdictions. In most states, the sole legal reason abortion could be performed was if continuation of the pregnancy threatened the life of the woman. Women who sought abortions for personal, social, or economic reasons were forced to seek more dangerous illegal abortions. In spite of the criminalization of abortion during this era, it is estimated that as many as one in three pregnancies was terminated by induced abortion (Rubin, 1987).

ROE V. WADE: A LANDMARK DECISION   The 20th-century movement to legalize abortion was led by advocates of women's rights and family planning. But the abortion rights movement did not gain ground until 1973, when the U.S. Supreme Court ruled in the famous *Roe v. Wade* case that any restriction on abortions during the first trimester of pregnancy was unconstitutional. This ruling declared that during the first 3 months of pregnancy, the decision to have an abortion would be between the pregnant woman and her physician. In the second trimester (the fourth through the sixth month of pregnancy), the state might regulate the abortion procedure (by requiring that the abortion take place in a hospital, for example) so as to protect the woman's health. During the last trimester, the state would have an interest in protecting the viable fetus, so the state might restrict or prohibit abortion. In effect, the Supreme Court ruled that the fetus is a potential life and not a "person" until the third trimester. The *Roe v. Wade* decision was based on the right to privacy; government intrusion in the doctor-patient relationship and a woman's reproductive decisions were seen as violations of that right.

ABORTION LEGISLATION SINCE *ROE V. WADE*   A number of abortion rulings and bills have been passed since the *Roe v. Wade* decision. Some of these are discussed below:

1. 1976—*Planned Parenthood of Central Missouri v. Danforth.* In the first post-Roe ruling, the Court overturned a law requiring a married woman to obtain her husband's consent for an abortion. This ruling stated that a woman's right to choose abortion is not subject to the veto of her partner in the pregnancy. The Court also stated that minors could not be blocked in obtaining an abortion by allowing their parents an absolute veto power.

2. 1976—The first of the Hyde amendments was passed, restricting Medicaid funding for abortions. Such restriction "turned out to be the most severe restriction that would pass constitutional muster in the Court until Webster" (Tribe, 1990, p. 151).

3. 1979—*Bellotti v. Baird.* The Court reconsidered the issue of requiring minors to obtain parental consent for abortion. It upheld a Massachusetts law requiring minors to notify both parents or obtain their consent for an abortion. The Court held that parental consent or notification does not infringe on a minor's rights if the minor can bypass the parents by obtaining a "judicial bypass." A minor may seek this judicial bypass from a judge, who will determine if the minor is "mature" enough to make the abortion decision herself and whether abortion is in the minor's best interest. Reasons why some minors choose to seek a court bypass include fear of parental disapproval, the father is absent from the home, and the desire to avoid contributing to stress in the family (Blum, Resnick, & Stark, 1990).

4. 1980—*Harris v. McRae* and *Williams v. Zbaraz.* The Court upheld the right of Congress and state legislatures to refuse to use public tax monies to pay for medically necessary abortions for poor women.

5. 1983—*Akron Center for Reproductive Health v. City of Akron.* The Court invalidated a variety

of restrictions on abortion, including state-imposed waiting periods and "informed consent" requiring that women seeking abortions be told that a fetus is a "human life," its precise gestational age, and that abortion is a major surgical procedure. The Supreme Court also declared unconstitutional regulations requiring that all abortions for women more than 3 months pregnant be performed in hospitals, rather than clinics; physicians tell women seeking abortions about possible alternatives, abortion risks, and that the fetus is a human life; there be at least a 24-hour waiting period between the time a woman signs a consent form and the abortion is performed; and all pregnant, unwed girls under 15 must obtain a parent's consent or have a judge's approval before having an abortion.

6. 1986—*Thornburgh v. American College of Obstetricians and Gynecologists.* The Court struck down requirements that women seeking abortions be provided with detailed descriptions of fetal development, be informed of particular risks, and be reminded of the possibility of assistance from the father or a social service agency. Imposition of a fixed waiting period was also ruled impermissible (Tribe, 1990).

7. 1989—*Webster v. Reproductive Health Services.* The court upheld various restrictions on abortion in Missouri. The Court declared that the state may prohibit "public facilities" and "public employees" from being used to perform or assist with abortions not necessary to save the life of the pregnant woman.

8. 1990—*Hodgson v. Minnesota* and *Ohio v. Akron Center for Reproductive Health.* In the Minnesota case, the Court declared that a state could require a pregnant minor to inform both her parents before having an abortion, so long as the law provides the option of a judicial bypass. In the Ohio case, the Court ruled that the state may require a minor to notify one parent, while allowing the judicial bypass alternative. The Court did not rule on whether judicial bypass must be offered as an alternative when notice to only one parent is required. The Court also upheld the constitutionality of requiring waiting periods before the abortion can be performed.

9. 1991—*Rust v. Sullivan.* The Supreme Court ruled that federally funded family planning clinics were prohibited from giving a woman any information about abortion. This prohibition (labeled by pro-choice advocates as the "gag rule") meant that when pregnant women attending these clinics asked for abortion information, they were told that the family planning clinic "does not consider abortion an appropriate method of family planning" (Marcus, 1991, p. 2).

10. 1992—*Planned Parenthood of Southeastern Pennsylvania v. Casey.* The Supreme Court upheld by a vote of 5 to 4 the right of a woman to obtain an abortion but affirmed the right of Pennsylvania to restrict the conditions under which an abortion may be granted. Restrictions that were upheld include a 24-hour waiting period, parental consent for minors, informed consent, and detailed physician reports to the government on each abortion performed. Struck down was the requirement that the husband must be notified before a wife obtains an abortion (Mauro, 1992).

11. 1995—Freedom of Access to Clinic Entrances Act. Enforcement of this act and the Supreme Court's creation of buffer zones surrounding women's health facilities have been credited with the reduction in clinic violence reported in 1995 and 1996 ("Clinic Violence Ebbed in 1996," 1997).

12. 1995–1997—Partial Birth Abortion Legislation. In 1995, Congress passed a bill banning partial birth abortions (dilation and extraction procedures, discussed earlier in the section entitled "Methods of Abortion"). President Clinton, however, vetoed the ban. In 1996, the House voted to override the veto, but the Senate failed to get the necessary two-thirds majority needed to do so. In 1997, the Senate once again began

talks on the banning of dilation and extraction abortion procedures. Clinton aides say that if the bill passes, Clinton will veto it. Clinton has gone on record as saying he would sign a less restrictive bill banning late-term abortions as long as it included exceptions for abortions needed to save the life or protect the health of the woman. In the midst of this ongoing political debate, the American Medical Association released a position paper saying, "The AMA recommends that the [D & X] procedure not be used unless alternative procedures pose materially greater risk to the woman. The physician must, however, retain the discretion to make that judgment" (cited in Hasson, 1997, p. 5A).

In Great Britain, after a bill was introduced in Parliament to ban intact dilation and evacuation abortions, the medical profession objected on the grounds that "such a prohibition would interfere with a physician's ability to act in the patient's best interest" (Chavkin, 1996, p. 1205). The bill was withdrawn.

13. 1996—Abortion restrictions on federal employees and military personnel. President Clinton signed both the Treasury–Postal Service Appropriations Bill, which prohibits insurance coverage of abortion for federal employees, and the Department of Defense Appropriations Bill, which does not allow military personnel or their dependents to obtain abortions in military facilities overseas, even if they pay for the procedure themselves (Chavkin, 1996).

Legislation and policy issues regarding the use of aborted fetal tissue for medical and research purposes is discussed in this chapter's Social Choices section. Later in this chapter, we discuss how restrictive abortion legislation affects the physical and psychological consequences of abortion.

_____ THINK ABOUT IT _____

Do you think that first-trimester abortion will ever be banned in the United States? If abortion were banned, how do you think women with problem pregnancies would be affected? How would society be affected? Do you think there would be fewer unintended pregnancies if abortion were legally banned? Why or why not?

A CROSS-CULTURAL VIEW OF ABORTION

Abortion "is an option to which people at all times and places have resorted, with or without religious consent, legal approval, or medical supervision" (Tribe, 1990, p. 52).

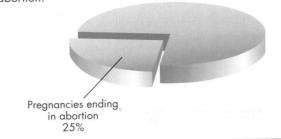

INTERNATIONAL DATA

The World Health Organization estimates that 25% of all pregnancies throughout the world end in abortion.

Pregnancies ending
in abortion
25%

Source: Cited in Miller & Rosenfield, 1996.

Due to the unavailability or expense of using contraceptive technology, many women throughout the world resort to abortion as a form of birth control. Abortion accounts for 10 to 20% of fertility regulation in Africa and 25% of fertility regulation in Latin America. In Central and Eastern European countries, 60% of all fertility regulation is estimated to be due to abortion (cited in Miller & Rosenfield, 1996).

Figure 8.5 presents the countries with the highest known abortion rates. (For many countries, including almost all of the African countries, data on abortion rates are not available.) The U.S. abortion rate is included for comparison purposes.

Abortion Policies Around the World

Policies concerning abortion vary around the world. On one end of the continuum is the Kafir tribe in Central Asia, in which there is no taboo or restriction in regard to abortion. Women are free to choose to terminate their pregnancies. One reason for the Kafirs' approval of abortion is that childbirth in the tribe is associated with high rates of maternal mortality. Since birthing children may threaten the life of significant numbers of women in the community, women may be encouraged to abort, especially when

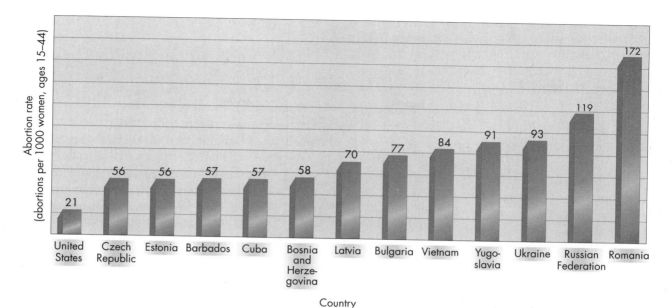

Figure 8.5 Countries with High Abortion Rates (Compared to the U.S. Abortion Rate) **Source:** *World Abortion Policies, 1994, 1997.*

women are viewed as too young, too sick, too old, or too small to bear children.

Abortion may also be encouraged by a tribe or society for other reasons, including practicality, economics, lineage, and honor. Abortion is practical in migratory societies, where women must control their pregnancies because they are limited in the number of children they can nurse and transport. Economic motivations become apparent when resources (such as food) are scarce—the number of children born to a group must be controlled. Abortion for reasons of lineage or honor are encouraged when a woman becomes impregnated in an adulterous relationship. To protect the lineage and honor of her family, she may have an abortion.

While the Kafir tribe has an open policy on abortion, their policy is an exception. In most cultures, abortion is considered 'wrong' (Tribe, 1990).

INTERNATIONAL DATA

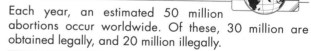

Sixteen countries do not permit abortion under any conditions, not even to save the life of the pregnant woman.

Source: World Abortion Policies, 1994.

Countries that do not permit abortion under any conditions include Egypt, the Philippines, Nepal, the Dominican Republic, Honduras, Chile, and Columbia.

In Nepal, women who abort can be sentenced to 20 years in jail (while men who murder receive sentences of 10 years) (Goodwin, 1997). Figure 8.6 presents the specified conditions under which abortion is allowed in 190 countries.

Legal access to abortion has increased in recent years. In 1996, for example, South Africa's National Assembly passed the Choice on Termination of Pregnancy Bill, which allowed what is virtually abortion on demand in the first 12 weeks of pregnancy, and abortion under specified conditions in the 13th through the 20th week of pregnancy. Also in 1996, the island of Guernsey became the last place in the British Isles to legalize abortion, replacing an old law that made abortion punishable by life imprisonment (Juene, 1996a, 1996b).

INTERNATIONAL DATA

Each year, an estimated 50 million abortions occur worldwide. Of these, 30 million are obtained legally, and 20 million illegally.

Source: Facts in Brief, 1996.

Aside from the United States, most liberal policies on abortion in other Western democracies have been worked out in legislatures rather than handed down by the courts. Nearly all statutes permitting abortion under varying circumstances also contain measures to

SHOULD ABORTED FETUSES BE USED FOR MEDICAL AND RESEARCH PURPOSES?

Fetal tissue is uniquely suitable for medical research in that it is "nonspecific," meaning it can develop into any kind of tissue (such as muscle or organ) if it is transplanted into humans. In the treatment of diseases, fetal tissue takes over the function of damaged tissue. Fetal tissue has been used in the development of immunizations for polio, rubella, and Rh disease. In 1988, the first fetal-cell transplant into a Parkinson's disease patient was performed, whereby neural fetal cells were implanted into the brain of a man suffering from Parkinson's disease. In addition to Parkinson's disease, fetal tissue transplants may help to cure other conditions, including diabetes, leukemia, Huntington's disease, Alzheimer's disease, and spinal cord damage. There are also at least 155 other genetic disorders that could be corrected before birth through fetal tissue transplants (Begley, Hager, Glick, & Foote, 1996). In other words, while still developing in the womb, fetuses with certain genetic disorders can receive transplants from non-defective fetal tissue and subsequently develop into normal, healthy infants and children.

Despite the potential and actual benefits of using fetal tissue for medical and research purposes, many anti-abortion activists oppose the "harvesting" of fetuses for such purposes. Abortion opponents argue that using fetal tissue for medical and research purposes would encourage abortion because many women would be swayed toward having an abortion if they knew the aborted fetus would be used to benefit society. "Women in crisis pregnancies might be persuaded that their abortions would save the lives of others, and thereby make an abortion a self-less, almost noble choice" (DeTurris, 1997, p. 182). Supporters of fetal tissue research and transplantation cite research in which women indicate that medical and research uses of fetal tissue would have little effect on their decision to have an abortion (although many women would feel better about their decision knowing their aborted fetus was contributing to human well-being) (Strong, 1997). Supporters of the scientific and medical use of fetal tissue argue that "whatever wrong might be involved in use of fetal tissue obtained from induced abortions is outweighed by the potential benefits to patients" (Strong, 1997, p. 185). The medical community and the general public have raised concerns over the commercialization of fetal tissue and the potential for using fetal tissue for questionable purposes.

In 1988, President Reagan enacted a ban on the use of federal funds for fetal tissue research. In 1992, President Bush vetoed an attempt by Congress to lift the ban on the grounds that such research has the potential to encourage and legitimize abortions, and taxpayers should not be required to fund research that many Americans find morally unacceptable. Bush did relax the ban to permit research on tissue from miscarriages or ectopic pregnancies. However, fetal tissue from spontaneous abortions and ectopic pregnancies are often unsuitable for medical transplantation because of the high rate of genetic abnormality, decomposition, bacterial contamination, and viral infections. In a study of 1250 spontaneously aborted embryos and 247 products of ectopic pregnancies, less than 1% were potentially useful for human transplantation (Branch et al., 1995). In 1993, President Clinton lifted the ban on government funding of research using fetal tissue transplants from induced abortions. The lifting of this ban has given hope to patients whose otherwise incurable diseases might one day be treated with fetal transplants.

In response to ethical concerns about the medical and research use of fetal tissue, in 1988, a National Institutes of Health ethics advisory panel recommended various guidelines for the scientific use of fetal tissue, including the following (Woodward, Hager, & Glick, 1996): abortion counselors should not discuss the donation of fetuses to science until after clients have decided to undergo an abortion, so that the decision whether to abort or continue the pregnancy would not be influenced by the possible scientific benefit to others; women should not be coerced into providing fetal tissue for

Continued on following page.

scientific or medical purposes; once a woman chooses to abort her fetus, she should not be allowed to designate the beneficiary of the aborted tissue (this guideline would prevent women from conceiving and aborting in order to provide fetal tissue for transplantation for an ailing relative or friend); physicians should not use riskier abortion methods or delay the abortion in order to obtain a better fetal specimen; and in order to prevent women and physicians from seeking abortions for profit, fetal tissue or organs could not be bought or sold. (However, fees could be paid to companies and third parties for the retrieval, preparation, and storage of fetal materials.) These guidelines have not yet been institutionalized, and there still is no organized system to distribute fetal tissue on a nonprofit, equitable basis. Although a Presidential Executive Order of May, 1992, called for the establishment of a "fetal tissue bank" (a network of centers involved in the retrieval, storage, and distribution of fetal tissue) that would follow established guidelines governing medical and research use of fetal tissue, the Department of Health and Human Services decided to abandon plans for developing a fetal tissue bank.

Although the ban on using federal funds for fetal tissue research and medical transplantation has been lifted and fetal tissue is currently being used for these purposes, opposition to using fetal tissue has not subsided. In 1996, the U.S. House of Representatives struggled between two bills that would both increase funding for research on Parkinson's disease. The two bills are virtually identical, except that one bans federal funding for Parkinson's research using fetal tissue from induced abortions (Wadman, 1996). As of this writing, action concerning this bill is pending. The controversy over using aborted fetal tissue for medical and research purposes is likely to continue as long as abortion itself is controversial.

Sources: Begley, S., Hager, M., Glick, D., & Foote, J. (1996). Fetal tissue research will benefit medical science. In C. P. Cozic & J. Petrikin (Eds.), *The abortion controversy* (pp. 221–227). San Diego, CA: Greenhaven Press.

Branch, D. W., Ducat, L., Fantel, A., Low, W. C., Zhou, F. C., Dayton, D. H., & Gill, T. J., III. (1995). Suitability of fetal tissues from spontaneous abortions and from ectopic pregnancies for transplantation. *JAMA, 273*(1), 66–68.

DeTurris, M. (1997). Fetal tissue research is unethical. In T. L. Roleff (Ed.), *Abortion: Opposing viewpoints* (pp. 179–183). San Diego, CA: Greenhaven Press.

Strong, C. (1997). Fetal tissue research is ethical. In T. L. Roleff (Ed.), *Abortion: Opposing viewpoints* (pp. 184–189). San Diego, CA: Greenhaven Press.

Wadman, M. (1996). Rival Parkinson's bills focus U.S. debate on fetal tissue. *Nature, 382*(6589), 286.

Woodward, K. L., Hager, M., & Glick, D. (1996). The ethics of fetal tissue research and transplantation: An overview. In C. P. Cozic & J. Petrikin (Eds.), *The abortion controversy* (pp. 216–220). San Diego, CA: Greenhaven Press.

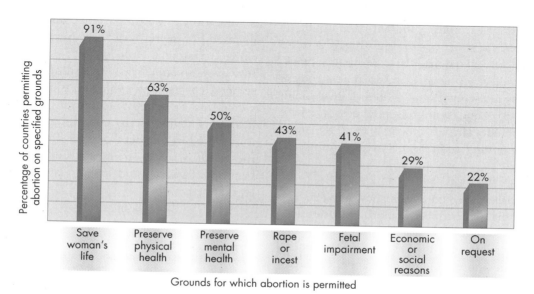

Figure 8.6 Abortion Policies in 190 Countries, 1994 **Source:** *World Abortion Policies, 1994, 1997.*

prevent unplanned pregnancies, promote alternatives to abortion (adoption or assistance in parenting the child), "or otherwise acknowledge and institutionalize the state's concern for life and its interest in supporting childbirth and families" (Maloy & Patterson, 1992, p. 98).

Abortion and Women's Health: A Global View

Access to safe, legal abortion is restricted in many countries throughout the world. Many countries do not have the medical technology and facilities, nor the legal support, for providing women access to safe abortions.

INTERNATIONAL DATA

The World Health Organization estimates that nearly half of all abortions worldwide are performed under unsafe conditions. Most (88%) unsafe abortions occur in developing countries.

Source: Miller & Rosenfield, 1996.

Illegal abortions in less developed countries have an estimated mortality risk of between 100 to 1000 per 100,000 procedures (Miller & Rosenfield, 1996). In comparison, the U.S. mortality risk for legal abortion is 0.6 per 100,000. Chavkin (1996) notes that when abortion is legal and accessible, maternal mortality rates decline.

Unsafe abortion represents a serious health threat to the health and lives of women throughout the world. Between 50,000 to 100,000 deaths result from unsafe abortions each year, "and untold morbidity is caused, in the form of sepsis, hemorrhage, uterine perforation, cervical trauma, pelvic peritonitis, pelvic abscess, jaundice, septicemia, and an almost endless litany of less dire conditions" (Miller & Rosenfield, 1996, p. 375). Long-term consequences of unsafe abortion include chronic pelvic pain, PID, tubal occlusion, infertility, and eventual hysterectomy.

THINK ABOUT IT

Among industrialized countries, the United States has one of the highest rates of abortion. For example, compared to the 1994 U.S abortion rate of 24 (per 1000 women ages 15–44), the abortion rates in Japan, the United Kingdom, France, Canada, and Germany, were 15, 15, 13, 11, and 9, respectively (*World Abortion Policies, 1994*). Why do you think this might be so?

ATTITUDES TOWARD ABORTION

Few issues in human sexuality are as controversial as abortion. Attitudes toward abortion range from fierce opposition to approval of abortion under certain circumstances (including rape and endangerment of a woman's life) to staunch support for legal and affordable access to abortion on request. Before you read further, you may want to complete the Self-Assessment, "Abortion Attitude Scale."

Public and Private Attitudes Toward Abortion

The majority of U.S. adults favor legal availability of abortion.

NATIONAL DATA

A Gallup poll revealed that 83% of U.S. adults believe that abortion should be legal in all or some circumstances.

U.S. adults in favor of legalized abortion 83%

Source: Moore, Newport, & Saad, 1996.

Interestingly, a similar percentage (more than 60%) of a national sample of U.S. adults regard unplanned pregnancy as a "very big problem" in the United States (Mauldon & Delbanco, 1997). However, attitudes vary according to the circumstances. For example, abortion is more likely to be viewed as an acceptable option if the mother's health is endangered by continuing the pregnancy, if a severe birth defect exists, or if the pregnancy is the result of rape or incest (see Table 8.2). The majority of college students also favor availability of legal abortion.

NATIONAL DATA

Fifty-seven percent of college and university first-year students in the United States agree that abortion should be legal.

Source: American Council on Education & University of California, 1996.

ABORTION ATTITUDE SCALE

Directions This is not a test. There are no wrong or right answers to any of the statements, so just answer as honestly as you can. The statements ask you to tell how you feel about legal abortion (the voluntary removal of a human fetus from the mother during the first three months of pregnancy by a qualified medical person). Tell how you feel about each statement by circling one of the choices beside each sentence. Here is a practice statement:

Abortion should be legalized.   SA   A   SlA   SlD   D   SD

(SA = Strongly agree; A = Agree; SlA = Slightly agree;
SlD = Slightly disagree; D = Disagree; SD = Strongly disagree)

Please respond to each statement and circle only one response. No one else will see your responses without your permission.

		SA	A	SlA	SlD	D	SD
1.	The Supreme Court should strike down legal abortions in the United States.	5	4	3	2	1	0
2.	Abortion is a good way of solving an unwanted pregnancy.	5	4	3	2	1	0
3.	A mother should feel obligated to bear a child she has conceived.	5	4	3	2	1	0
4.	Abortion is wrong no matter what the circumstances are.	5	4	3	2	1	0
5.	A fetus is not a person until it can live outside its mother's body.	5	4	3	2	1	0
6.	The decision to have an abortion should be the pregnant mother's.	5	4	3	2	1	0
7.	Every conceived child has the right to be born.	5	4	3	2	1	0
8.	A pregnant female not wanting to have a child should be encouraged to have an abortion.	5	4	3	2	1	0
9.	Abortions should be considered killing a person.	5	4	3	2	1	0
10.	People should not look down on those who choose to have abortions.	5	4	3	2	1	0
11.	Abortion should be an available alternative for unmarried, pregnant teenagers.	5	4	3	2	1	0
12.	Persons should not have the power over the life or death of a fetus.	5	4	3	2	1	0
13.	Unwanted children should not be brought into the world.	5	4	3	2	1	0
14.	A fetus should be considered a person at the moment of conception.	5	4	3	2	1	0

Continued on following page.

Advocacy Groups: Pro-Life, Pro-Choice, and Pro-Dialogue

A dichotomization of attitudes toward abortion is reflected in two opposing groups of abortion activists. Individuals and groups who oppose abortion are commonly referred to as "pro-life," or "anti-abortion." Pro-life groups advocate restrictive abortion policies or a complete ban on abortion. They essentially believe the following:

- The unborn fetus has a right to live and that right should be protected.
- Abortion is a violent and immoral solution to unintended pregnancy.
- The life of an unborn fetus is sacred and should be protected, even at the cost of individual difficulties for the pregnant woman.

People who are over the age of 44, female, mothers of three or more children, married to white-collar workers, and affiliated with a religion are most likely to be pro-life (Luker, 1984; Granberg, 1991). Contrary to common notion, however, not all religious groups oppose the legal availability of abortion. For example, Catholics for Free Choice, a pro-choice organization established in 1973, supports the right to legal abortion and promotes family planning. This organization disagrees with the notion that abortion is necessarily sinful in all circumstances.

> To commit the sin of abortion you have to think that an abortion in your case, with all the circumstances of your life and your pregnancy, is a sin against God. You then have to decide that you are going to do it

TABLE 8.2   Abortion Under What Conditions?

In 1993, the General Social Survey included a question on abortion. Respondents were asked "whether it should be possible for a pregnant woman to obtain a legal abortion if . . ." The percentages of "yes" responses follow.

CONDITION	PERCENTAGE
Health seriously endangered by pregnancy	90%
Pregnancy because of rape	83%
Serious defect in baby	81%
Family has low income, can't afford child	50%
Not married, doesn't want to marry father	48%
Married, wants no more children	47%
Any other reason	45%

Source: Roper, 1993.

anyway, thus going against your conscience. . . . If you carefully examine your conscience and then decide that an abortion is the most moral act you can do at this time, you are not committing a sin. (Catholics for a Free Choice, 1992, p. 1)

The Religious Coalition for Abortion Rights is comprised of 35 mainline Protestant, Jewish, and other faith groups who believe that a woman should be allowed the freedom to "come to a decision that's in harmony with her own moral and religious values—without government intrusion" (Religious Coalition for Abortion Rights, 1992, p. 1).

Pro-choice advocates support the legal availability of abortion for all women. They essentially believe the following:

- Freedom of choice is a central value.
- Those who must personally bear the burden of their moral choices ought to have the right to make these choices.
- Procreation choices must be free of governmental control.

In *Breaking the Abortion Deadlock: From Choice to Consent,* Dr. Eileen McDonagh (1996) argues that if a woman has the right to defend herself against a rapist, she also should be able to defend herself against the invasion of a fetus. While abortion opponents argue that a woman doesn't have the right to terminate the life of a fetus, Dr. McDonagh argues that the fetus doesn't have the right to invade a woman's body. No laws, she says, besides those restricting abortion, allow a person to invade another's body.

People most likely to be pro-choice have the following characteristics: they are under the age of 44, female, mothers of one or two children, have an annual family income of over $50,000, are employed, have some college or postcollege training, and are married to a professional (Luker, 1984). Although many self-proclaimed feminists and women's organizations, such as the National Organization for Women (NOW), have been active in promoting abortion rights, not all feminists are pro-choice, and some feminist philosophies have been used as arguments against abortion. For example, an organization of pro-life feminists called Feminists for Life of America emphasizes that "feminism is part of a larger philosophy that values all life" and that "abortion is incompatible with this feminist vision" (quoted in Muldoon, 1991, p. 146).

Labeling the opposing groups in the abortion controversy is problematic. Some pro-choice advocates object to the use of the term "pro-life" when referring to their opponents because it implies that pro-choice advocates do not value life. They argue that restricting or banning legal abortion lessens the quality of life for women by forcing them to either bear unwanted children or to obtain an illegal, and perhaps unsafe, abortion. The quality of life for children born un-

wanted is also a concern of pro-choice advocates. Pro-choice advocates do not view abortion as desirable, but as a necessary evil, and they often combine their efforts to make and keep abortion available with efforts to reduce abortion by promoting planned parenthood and the use of effective contraception.

Some pro-choice advocates also object to the label "pro-abortion" because some who are pro-choice are personally opposed to abortion. In a study of teenagers' attitudes toward abortion, "most of the participants agreed that it was possible to be anti-abortion and pro-choice at the same time, but felt that the issue was never discussed that way by the press" (Stone & Waszak, 1992, p. 56).

Although "polls show that a majority of Americans are ambivalent about abortion, unwilling to join either faction yet agreeing with some points of each . . . the two extremes [pro-life and pro-choice advocates] have come to rule the public discussion and divide the country by speaking more loudly and passionately than those who find abortion a complex and ambiguous matter" (Maloy & Patterson, 1992, p. 5). Resolving the abortion deadlock would require finding a common ground among two seemingly irrevocably opposed positions.

We use the term *pro-dialogue advocates* to refer to those who seek to explore and focus on concerns that are common to both pro-life and pro-choice advocates. (We have borrowed the term from a group in Fargo, North Dakota.) In 1981, the first abortion clinic in North Dakota, established in the town of Fargo, became the center of fierce opposition between pro-life and pro-choice activists. A number of these activists formed a group called Pro-dialogue, whose purpose was to bring members of both sides of the controversy together to find shared concerns. Anthropologist Faye Ginsburg, who went to Fargo to interview activists on both sides, quotes the minutes of the first meeting of Pro-dialogue:

> As we talked and listened that night, we discovered some very important common ground. We wished that women would not be faced with pregnancies that they couldn't afford, that at times they weren't ready for, by people they didn't love, or for any of the many reasons women have abortions. The common ground gave us something concrete . . . a goal we could work toward together. (Ginsburg, 1989; cited in Maloy and Patterson, 1992, p. 327)

Maloy and Patterson (1992) conducted 95 interviews with women and couples who have faced the dilemma of whether to give birth or have an abortion. The researchers commented that "each of their stories includes something the abortion debate has thus far avoided discussing—some element of ambiguity, complexity, uncertainty, loss, or respect for an opposing view" (p. 9). Although public discourse about abortion is dominated by two opposing views—one advocating the rights of the fetus, the other advocating the rights of women—Maloy and Patterson noted that

> the women and couples to whom we spoke rarely, if ever, mentioned rights. . . . They did not base their actions on an explicit choice between the woman and the fetus. . . . In almost every case, the outcomes of these private dilemmas hung on practical and emotional matters—the quality of the connection between the woman and the man, the financial resources available, the number of other children a woman already had, the state of her self-esteem, the other important options that pregnancy might or might not foreclose. (p. 6)

PHYSICAL AND PSYCHOLOGICAL EFFECTS OF ABORTION

Women who have experienced or are contemplating abortion may be concerned about the potential physical and psychological effects of abortion. Earlier, we discussed the medical health risks associated with illegal abortion (see the section entitled "Abortion and Women's Health: A Global View"); in this section, we discuss the effects of legal abortion.

Physical Effects of Abortion

Legal abortions, performed under safe conditions, are generally considered safe procedures. The earlier in the pregnancy the abortion is performed, the safer it is.

RATES OF MORTALITY AND COMPLICATIONS Mortality rates associated with legal abortion are very low (between 0.4 and 1 woman per 100,000 abortions). This risk is less than the risk of death from an injection of penicillin. Women are ten times more

likely to die from childbirth than from abortion. (The mortality rate of childbirth is 9.1 maternal deaths per 100,000 live births.) Of deaths caused by legal abortion, 23% are due to infection, 23% are caused by embolism, 20% from hemorrhage, and 16% from anesthetic complications (*Facts in Brief,* 1996; Miller, 1996a; Rosenfeld, 1997).

The complication rate of legal abortions is also low. According to the National Abortion Federation, among women obtaining abortions during the first 13 weeks of pregnancy, 97% have no complications or postabortion complaints, 2.5% have minor complications that can be handled at the physician's office or abortion clinic, and less than 0.5% require some additional surgical procedure and/or hospitalization (cited in Miller, 1996a).

Postabortion complications include the possibility of incomplete abortion, which occurs when the initial procedure misses the fetus and a repeat procedure must be done. Other possible complications include uterine infection; excessive bleeding; perforation or laceration of the uterus, bowel, or adjacent organs; and an adverse reaction to a medication or anesthetic.

LONG-TERM EFFECTS Vacuum aspiration abortions, comprising most U.S. abortions, do not increase the risks to future childbearing. However, late-term abortions *do* increase the risks of subsequent miscarriages, premature deliveries, and low birth-weight babies (Council on Scientific Affairs, 1992).

EFFECTS OF LEGAL RESTRICTIONS ON PHYSICAL CONSEQUENCES Some abortion restrictions are in the best interest of women. For example, laws that mandate that abortions be performed by physicians provide women with assurance that their abortion providers have formal medical training. But other laws restricting abortion may compromise a woman's health because "restrictive abortion laws delay abortion, thus posing greater threats to women's health by postponing abortion into later trimesters" (Miller, 1996b, p. 34).

The most common abortion restrictions include parental and spousal notification laws, mandatory counseling and waiting periods, and limitations on public funding. Each of these restrictions causes delays between the time a woman decides to seek an abortion and the time she actually undergoes the procedure. Laws restricting Medicaid funding of abortions create financial hardships for poor women seeking abortion, often causing delays while the woman tries to save or borrow money to pay for the procedure.

NATIONAL DATA

In 1993, the average cost of a nonhospital abortion at ten weeks was $296.

Source: *Facts in Brief,* 1996.

Restrictions on public funding of abortion have a disproportionate impact on poor African American, Hispanic, Native American, and Asian American women, who often cannot afford private medical care. Almost half of the women having abortions beyond 15 weeks of gestation say they were delayed because of problems in obtaining abortion services—either in affording the cost or in finding or traveling to an abortion provider (*Facts in Brief, 1996*). Finally, restrictions on legal abortion may result in some women seeking an unsafe, illegal abortion.

Psychological Effects of Abortion

In 1987, President Reagan asked Surgeon General C. Everett Koop to initiate a study on the effects of legal abortion in the United States. Two years later, Koop (1989, p. 31) concluded that "data do not support the premise that abortion does or does not cause or contribute to psychological problems." The American Psychological Association challenged Koop's conclusion and suggested that the data show that when psychological effects occur, "they are mild and temporary" (Wilmoth, 1989, p. 7).

In a review of studies on the psychological effects of abortion, researchers found that psychological profiles on the Minnesota Multiphasic Personality Inventory of women who have abortions and those who give birth to their babies are very similar (Adler et al., 1990). The researchers also noted that U.S. women obtaining legal abortions experienced the greatest degree of stress *before* the abortion, during the time when the decision-making process was occurring (Adler et al., 1990). In the research review by Adler et al. (1990), only 5 to 10% of women reported severe negative reactions to abortion. Most of those diagnosed with psychiatric illness had suffered from mental illness before the abortion. Other risk factors for psychiatric illness following abortion include genetic fetal health problems, abortion decisions that were pressured or coerced, and extreme ambivalence about the pregnancy. Women who make autonomous, but supported, abortion decisions are likely to experience optimal psychological outcomes after abortion (Stotland, 1996).

For some women, mental health may actually improve after an abortion. Adler et al. (1990) noted that positive reactions following an abortion (such as relief) outweighed negative reactions (such as guilt). Despite the difficulty of making the decision to terminate a pregnancy, for some women, this decision represents their first successful attempt at taking control of the direction of their own lives (Stotland, 1996). Like other major life events, pregnancy and abortion contain the potential for maturation and personal growth. The process of making such a difficult life decision can have positive effects on a woman's self-esteem and sense of autonomy (Minden & Notman, 1991). Data from a longitudinal study of a large national sample showed that after having an abortion, the level of a young woman's self-esteem was best predicted by her self-esteem level prior to the pregnancy (Russo & Dabul, 1997).

IS THERE A "POSTABORTION SYNDROME"? Few would deny that abortion is a stressful experience. But what degree of psychological stress is involved has become a debated issue. Some opponents of abortion, who have been criticized as ignoring the well-being of the women (and focusing only on the interests of unborn fetuses), have changed their tactics by focusing on women's psychological well-being, claiming that women who undergo abortion experience a range of adverse psychological effects referred to as *postabortion syndrome (PAS)*. The symptoms of PAS may include depression, anxiety, shame, helplessness, lowered self-esteem, flashbacks of the abortion, uncontrollable crying, alcohol or drug dependency, eating disorders, and relationship problems. Estimates on the number of women who experience PAS vary from few or none, to one in five, to eight out of ten, to claims that all women who undergo abortion suffer from PAS symptoms (Miller, 1996b).

According to Miller (1996b), postabortion syndrome is a political tool, created to change the legal status of abortion. One strategy associated with PAS involves portraying women who have undergone abortion as "innocent victims."

> The personal testimony of PAS sufferers is framed by a rhetoric of victimization, in which individual women are shown to have suffered either from being forced into having abortions they didn't want, or from being misled by abortion providers . . . into believing that the procedure would be simple and have no aftereffects.
>
> The portrayal of women as victims . . . denies women's rational capacities and places culpability for the act of abortion squarely on the shoulders of the medical establishment, portraying doctors as rational and therefore capable of misleading or mistreating their (less rational or irrational) female patients. . . . Invalidating women as decision makers in this way permits the introduction of laws that remove the locus of choice from women, in the name of their own protection. (p. 37)

Anti-abortion advocates who embrace the concept of a postabortion stress disorder argue that women who report minimal negative (or even positive) psychological outcomes of abortion are in a state of denial (Hopkins, Reicher, & Saleem, 1996). Thus, any psychological outcome, positive or negative, may be explained by PAS.

The concept of postabortion syndrome has little to no validity in the scientific community. Much of the evidence of PAS is anecdotal and not supported by scientific studies.

PSYCHOLOGICAL EFFECTS OF RESTRICTED OR DENIED ACCESS TO ABORTION   Just as abortion legislation increases medical risks due to the delays in the abortion procedure, legislation that restricts abortion also increases the psychological stress associated with abortion. Women whose access to abortion is restricted may be forced to delay the abortion or to carry an unwanted pregnancy to term. According to C. Everett Koop, unwanted births pose a risk of postpartum depression and psychosis, presenting a greater psychological health threat to the woman than would a legal abortion (reported in Miller, 1996a). In one study, 20% of women who would have had a Medicaid-funded abortion carried their pregnancies to term when funding was denied (cited in Henshaw, 1991).

PERSONAL CHOICES

How Do You Choose Whether or Not to Have an Abortion?

Women who are faced with the question of whether or not to have an abortion may benefit by considering the following guidelines:

- Consider all the alternatives available to you, realizing that no alternative may be all good or all bad. As you consider each alternative, think about both the short- and long-term consequences of each course of action.
- Obtain information about each alternative course of action. Inform yourself about the medical, financial, and legal aspects of abortion, childbearing, parenting, and adoption.
- Talk with trusted family members, friends, or unbiased counselors. Talk with the man who participated in the pregnancy. If possible, also talk with women who have had abortions, as well as women who have kept and reared their babies or placed their babies in adoptive homes. If you feel that someone is pressuring you in your decision making, look for help elsewhere.
- Consider your own personal and moral commitments in life. Understand your own feelings, values, and beliefs concerning the fetus, and weigh those against the circumstances surrounding your pregnancy.

_____ THINK ABOUT IT _____

Because abortion decisions typically result from troubled situations, such as lack of resources, relationship unhappiness or instability, sexual coercion, or fetal or maternal health problems, it is often difficult to distinguish the stress of the decision to end the pregnancy from the stress of the surrounding circumstances (Stotland, 1996).

THE REAL CHALLENGE: REDUCING THE NEED FOR ABORTION

More than half of pregnancies among U.S. women are unintended; almost half (44%) of these are terminated by induced abortion, 13% end in miscarriage, and 43% are carried to term resulting in birth (Family Planning Services, 1997). As long as women experience unintended and unwanted pregnancies, they will have abortions, regardless of the legal status and restrictions on abortion. Maloy and Patterson (1992, p. 328) suggest that "the real challenge . . . is how to prevent most unwanted pregnancies and how to deal more positively with the ones that occur." They offer the following suggestions for meeting this challenge:

1. Create laws and policies that demonstrate concern for both women and the value of developing life.

2. Support research for better male and female contraceptives. In addition, make contraceptives more accessible and affordable. While nine in ten managed health care plans routinely cover abortion or provide limited coverage, only four in ten cover all major contraceptive methods (*Facts in Brief,* 1996). Health care reform can include provisions to cover expenses related to contraceptives.

3. Encourage men to share the responsibility for birth control.

4. Promote greater sexual responsibility among men by establishing paternity and enforcing child support.

5. Involve schools, churches, community organizations, and pro-life and pro-choice groups in helping parents talk with their children about sex and sexual responsibility.

6. Provide education to children about the responsibilities of sexuality and parenthood.

7. Implement social policies and services to ease negative family experiences—such as divorce, neglect, abuse, and addiction—that are related to early sexual activity.

8. Encourage more teenage role models to counsel their peers against early sexual activity and birth control misuse.

9. Encourage popular media role models to convey the message that abstinence is okay.

10. Help women proceed with pregnancies they may want to continue through social policies such as subsidized housing, affordable and high quality child care, job training, and perhaps a national health program.

(Maloy & Patterson, 1992).

Reducing the need for abortion is a goal for countries throughout the world. In 1994, representatives from 179 countries attended the International Conference on Population and Development in Cairo and developed a "Programme of Action." The section on abortion in the Programme of Action reads as follows:

> In no case should abortion be promoted as a method of family planning. All Governments and relevant intergovernmental and non-governmental organizations are urged to strengthen their commitment to women's health, to deal with the health impact of unsafe abortion as a major public health concern and to reduce the recourse to abortion through expanded and improved family planning services. Prevention of unwanted pregnancies must always be given the highest priority and all attempts should be made to eliminate the need for abortion. . . . (cited in Miller & Rosenfield, 1996, p. 377)

Sweden has set an example in combining liberal abortion laws with efforts to make abortion a last resort. The Swedish government provides generous maternal benefits, aggressively enforces child support rulings, mandates sex education, promotes available and affordable contraception, requires women seeking second-trimester abortions to meet with a social worker, and prohibits abortion if the fetus was likely to be viable (exceptions are made if the mother's health is endangered by the pregnancy) (Glendon, 1987).

--------- THINK ABOUT IT ---------
Dr. Nafis Sadik, Executive Director of the United Nations Population Fund, advocates reducing the need for abortion by preventing unintended pregnancies. She suggests that "by harnessing the energy expended in debating abortion and using it to prevent unintended pregnancies, we can make enormous progress towards ending the debate altogether" ("Informed Choice, Not Inflamed Rhetoric," 1997, p. 1). Which of the strategies for reducing the need for abortion could be embraced by both pro-life and pro-choice advocates? How can opposition between advocacy groups be transformed into cooperative efforts to reduce the need for abortion?

ADOPTION: AN ALTERNATIVE TO ABORTION

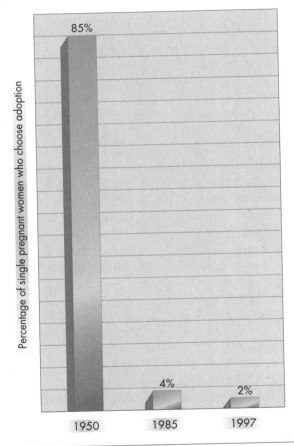

Sources: Lindsay, 1997; Olasky, 1997.

The number of adoptions has decreased, partly because fewer unmarried pregnant women are choosing to place their babies for adoption. Also, with the legalization of abortion, more unmarried pregnant women are choosing to terminate their pregnancies. Increased social acceptance of out-of-wedlock childbearing has also influenced more single pregnant women to parent their own babies.

Who Chooses Adoption?

In one study of 113 pregnant adolescents ages 12 to 19, those who chose to place their babies for adoption tended to be younger than those who chose to keep their babies (Donnelly & Voydanoff, 1996). Placers also were more likely than keepers to be attending school, and the mothers of placing teens were somewhat better educated than those who decided to parent their children. Other researchers have found that the preferences of the biological father are influential in the mother's decision of whether to parent the child or place the child for adoption (Dworkin, Harding, & Schreiber, 1993). Birth mothers are also more likely to follow through with an adoption plan if their own mothers are supportive of their placing the baby for adoption (Dworkin et al., 1993).

Barth (1987, p. 330) found that the adoption decision was positively affected by three factors: "the ability of the birth mother to . . . select the family she wished to raise her child, meetings between the birth and adoptive parents, and placement of the newborn directly from the hospital, with no foster care in the interim."

Barriers to the Adoption Option

Making an adoption plan is an unlikely choice for women who carry their pregnancies to term, because they are likely to have bonded with their baby before birth. During the pregnancy, they may have grown to love their baby, which makes adoption a painful option. In considering what is best for their child, young, unwed pregnant women may wonder about the psychological effects adoption will have on the child. It is a common belief that individuals who have been adopted experience a range of emotional problems in childhood and as adults. However, in a review of studies comparing adopted children and nonadopted children, Bartholet (1993) found no significant disadvantages of adoptive, as opposed to biological, parenting; in fact, some significant advantages were noticed. For example, one study comparing adults who were adopted as children with adults who had not been adopted found that those who had been adopted were more positive about life, perceived their adoptive parents to be more nurturing than the nonadopted adults did, and were more confident (Marquis & Detweiler, 1985).

According to a policy analyst at the Family Research Council, "the most significant barrier to a young black mother's making an adoption decision is that relinquishing a newborn is not readily accepted within the black cultural milieu" (Yoest, 1995, p. 157). Children born to young, unwed African American mothers are often absorbed into the kinship system; they are informally adopted by the pregnant woman's mother, sister, aunt, or other family member. In the traditional African American kinship system, family boundaries are flexible and parenting is a shared and multigenerational responsibility.

Pregnant women and their partners often view adoption as a process that involves "giving your child to strangers" and "never seeing your child again." However, as we discuss later in this chapter, adoption plans now increasingly allow the birth parents to select the adoptive family and include open adoption terms that allow some ongoing contact between the birth family and the adoptive family.

Some proponents of "the adoption option" argue that unmarried pregnant women rarely choose adoption because they view alternatives to adoption—abortion or single parenting—as superior alternatives. Olasky (1997) suggests that "abortion seems to convey an immediate benefit: It makes the problem disappear. . . ." (p. 44). Despite the decreased financial support to single parents due to welfare reform, single-parenting is encouraged by public financial support and its social acceptability. "Adoption, on the other hand, is altruistic—life for a child and a gift to an often-childless couple—but it is also inconvenient and embarrassing, especially when compared to abortions done in secret. Teenagers generally ask not what they can do for others, but what others are thinking about them" (p. 44). Olasky (1997) reflects a segment of conservative America in his conclusion that "for adoption to flourish, the other alternatives [i.e. abortion and single-parenting] need to become shameful once again" (p. 44).

Policies and Processes in Adoption

Women wishing to relinquish their babies to adoptive parents may do so through formal or informal procedures. *Informal adoption,* most common in African American families, involves a woman placing her child with another caregiver, usually within the kinship system, without going through formal court procedures. *Formal adoption* involves a legal agreement consenting to adoption or relinquishing one's parental rights.

Although this chapter focuses on the adoption of infants born to women who do not want—or cannot care for—them, children of all ages may be adopted. For example, parents who abuse, neglect, or abandon their children or commit a felony may lose custody of their children. The state provides institutional or foster care unless (or until) an adoptive home is found. Children whose parents die may also be adopted. Stepparents may adopt their stepchildren, but the biological parent must first relinquish parent status. Even adults can be adopted by other adults! Adult adoptions may be done to make someone a legal relative—a strategy used by some gay couples.

State laws governing adoptions vary widely. In general, the birth parent (or parents) must sign a consent to the adoption or a relinquishment of parental rights, which is not legally binding prior to the birth of the baby. The consent or relinquishment may be revoked for a limited period of time after birth, allowing the birth parents to change their mind. The biological father of the child usually must be notified of the adoption plan, but the procedures for this notification vary from state to state.

The prospective adoptive parent (or parents) must file a petition to adopt. After the child is in the custody of the adoptive parents, the adoptive family undergoes a period of court supervision (usually 6 months to a year), after which the adoption is finalized.

AGENCY VERSUS INDEPENDENT ADOPTIONS Adoptions may be arranged by public agencies, private agencies, or independently. A private adoption agency is supported by private funds and should be licensed or approved by the state in which it operates. A public agency is the local branch of a state social service agency.

In *agency adoption,* birth parents release their child to the adoption agency, which then places the child with a carefully selected family. In an *independent adoption* (arranged without an agency), initial contact can be made directly between a pregnant woman and adoptive parents or the pregnant woman and an attorney, depending on state law. A few states do not permit independent adoptions, but most do (Lindsay, 1997).

NATIONAL DATA

Of the domestic adoptions by nonrelatives in 1993, 39% were arranged by public agencies, 29% by private agencies, and 31% independently.

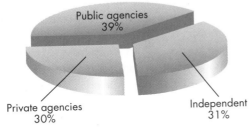

Public agencies
39%

Private agencies
30%

Independent
31%

Source: Merkel-Holguin & Sobel, 1993.

In an independent adoption, it is customary for adoptive parents to pay for the birth mother's medical and legal expenses. Some states also require the adoptive parents to pay for counseling for the birth mother before, and perhaps after, the adoption is final. In some states, the adoptive parents may also help with the birth mother's living or clothing expenses. It is illegal, however, for prospective adoptive parents to offer birth parents any type of payment or "gift" in order to adopt the child. According to law, birth mothers cannot release their child for adoption until after the delivery; therefore, money spent before delivery by prospective adoptive parents is a gamble. If the birth mother decides to keep her baby, she is not legally required to pay back the money the prospective adoptive parents spent on her medical and other bills. However, she, her partner, or her parents may voluntarily choose to repay the money.

OPEN VERSUS CLOSED ADOPTIONS   The practice of adoption has changed in recent decades. In previous generations, unwed pregnant women were hidden and secluded in maternity homes or went to stay with "Aunt Mary" during the pregnancy. Nonmarital pregnancy was considered a shameful sin and a disgrace to the pregnant woman and her family. For nearly a century, the fact that a child was adopted was often hidden from friends, neighbors, and the adopted child. *Closed adoption,* which involved

confidentiality, secrecy, and sealed adoption records, became the norm. After the child was born, the birth parents disappeared and had no further contact with the child or the adoptive family. Traditional, closed adoption procedures "gave birth parents no input into the future of their children. They were encouraged to trust the agency's judgment, accept the agency's rules, agree to sealed records that would preclude any further contact with the child, and get on with their lives" (Hochman & Huston, 1994, p. 3).

Today, open adoption is becoming more common. In an *open adoption,* birth parents and adoptive parents have some knowledge about each other, and the birth parents may even help choose the adoptive parents. Open adoptions can take many forms. Birth parents may choose an adoptive family for their child by reading résumés or descriptions of prospective adopters and looking at their photographs. Birth parents may also meet and interview prospective adopters. This may be the only contact between the two families, or the two families may agree to have ongoing contact throughout the child's life. Some birth mothers use the adoptive mother as their coach during labor and delivery.

Open adoptions allow birth parents to have some control over the adoption process. Birth parents and adoptive parents have the flexibility to create an adoption plan that suits their values and preferences. A typical open adoption involves two to four contacts between the adoptive family and the birth family annually. "In some open adoptions, the adoptive family considers the birth parents an important part of their extended family" (Lindsay, 1997, p. 22).

BIRTH FATHER'S RIGHTS   Years ago, an unmarried father's permission was not required if the pregnant woman made an adoption plan—only the birth mother's consent was required. Today, the father's consent, if he can be found, is usually required before an adoption can be finalized. If the father cannot be located, the court is petitioned to remove the rights of the absent or unknown father.

Psychological Reactions to Placing a Baby for Adoption

Birth mothers usually experience grief, loss, and emotional pain after placing their baby for adoption. In one study of women who placed their babies for adoption, the greater the feelings of guilt and shame regarding the decision to relinquish the child, the higher the levels of unresolved grief (De Simone, 1996). Women who believed that others coerced them into relinquishing their babies felt deep guilt, shame, and regret regarding their decision. Birth mothers who experienced lower levels of grief tended to be more satisfied with their current marital status and family composition (De Simone, 1996). In addition, "birth mothers who had personal achievements of which they felt especially proud since the relinquishment, i.e., raising a family, graduating from college or professional school, or having a career" had lower levels of grief (pp. 72–73). Finally, the study found that birth mothers who had gained information about their child since the placement had lower levels of grief.

Another reaction birth parents may have to placing their baby for adoption is anger—toward themselves, their partner (or other birth parent), their family, and "the system." Birth mothers may feel angry at themselves for getting pregnant or angry at the person who impregnated them. They may feel anger toward family members and professionals who may have pressured them to place their babies for adoption. They may be angry at "the system" for failing to provide them with the emotional or financial support that might have enabled them to keep and parent their babies. Birth mothers may even be angry at the individuals who adopt their child: they "may feel grateful to adopting parents but, at the same time, resent them for their ability to enjoy the child in their stead" (Donnelly & Voydanoff, 1996, p. 427).

Although some women regret their decision to relinquish their children, others, especially those who are not pressured into adoption, accept their decision as painful but necessary. As one birth mother stated, "I knew that something can hurt a lot and still be the right thing to do" (quoted in Olasky, 1995, p. 25).

Birth parents may cope with the emotional pain of relinquishing a child for adoption in a number of ways, including the following (Lindsay, 1997; Smith, 1995):

- Going to counseling
- Attending birth-parent support group meetings
- Writing down their feelings in a story or poem or in a journal
- Being on a panel that talks to pregnant teens about the experience of pregnancy and the decision to place a child for adoption

- Writing letters, even if they are not sent, to their child
- Holding a private ceremony each year on the child's birthday
- Searching for the child (if the adoption was confidential and closed)
- Reading books written for birth parents to help them resolve their grief over placing their child for adoption

PERSONAL CHOICES

How Do You Decide Whether or Not to Place a Baby for Adoption?

A woman experiencing an unintended or unwanted pregnancy who does not want to have an abortion must choose between parenting the child and placing the child for adoption. Teenagers and women faced with this situation get lots of conflicting advice. Friends and family often have different reactions, including "What do you mean, you'll keep the baby?" "You can't raise a baby by yourself," or "How could you think of giving your baby away?" When faced with the decision of keeping a baby versus placing it for adoption, a woman must first realize that her decision may not please everyone. Although being open to the advice of others is important, she must ultimately make the decision for herself based on her best assessment of what is good for her and her baby. Making a decision to please someone else, including family and friends, may result in future resentment and regret over the decision.

Making this type of life-altering decision is best made after considering the short- and long-term advantages and disadvantages of each option. In assessing each option, it is helpful to talk with other birth parents who have placed their babies for adoption, as well as women who have decided to parent their children under less than ideal circumstances (such as still being in school, being young, being single, and having few resources). Birth fathers, as well as birth mothers, play a role in deciding the fate of the child. If possible, both birth parents should be involved in the decision-making process.

Most women in this situation choose to keep their children. Before making the choice to do this, the woman might ask herself how parenting will affect her education, future occupation, dreams, goals, and current and future relationships. She might also investigate the types and amount of social and financial assistance she may receive from the birth father, parents and other family members, and the government. Will her own resources, along with the support she may receive, be enough to provide the kind of life she wants for herself and her child?

If the answers to these questions paint a questionable picture of the future, adoption offers an alternative with several potential advantages. In the words of one woman:

> Adoption can give birth parents a chance to gain control over their lives. It can open up a future that might include pregnancy and parenting experiences for which they will be prepared. In the meantime, adoption enables them to provide their child with the kind of nurturing home that they are not now in a position to offer. (Bartholet, 1995, p. 56)

Researchers have found that unmarried birth mothers who made adoption plans advanced further educationally, were more likely to be employed and have a higher income, were less likely to have a repeat out-of-wedlock pregnancy, were less likely to have an abortion if they did have a repeat out-of-wedlock pregnancy, were more likely to subsequently marry, and were less likely to receive public assistance than birth mothers who chose to parent their children born out of wedlock (National Council for Adoption, 1996). However, those who place their children for adoption are also more likely than those who keep their infants to regret their decision (Donnelly & Voydanoff, 1996). Such regret, however, may be short-term; one study found that regret over the decision to place a child for adoption is most intense one year after the birth but lessens drastically by the end of the second year (Donnelly & Voydanoff, 1996). Finally, it is also important to recognize that "adoption, regardless of how positive the outcome, begins with a traumatic loss for those involved" (Watson, 1996, p. 526).

THINK ABOUT IT

In the past, the phrase "giving up for adoption" was commonly used. Today, the term "making an adoption plan" is preferred, as this phrase implies that the birth parents are involved in the adoption process.

KEY TERMS

abortion rate   194
abortion ratio   194
agency adoption   215
closed adoption   216
dilation and
   curettage (D & C)   197
dilation and
   evacuation
   (D & E)   197
dilation and
   suction (D & S)   197
formal adoption   215
independent
   adoption   215
induced abortion   194
informal adoption   215
intact dilation and
   extraction (D & X)   197
medical abortion   198

open adoption   216
partial birth
   abortion   197
pharmaceutical
   abortion   198
postabortion
   syndrome   211
pro-dialogue
   advocates   209
RU-486   198
spontaneous
   abortion   194
suction curettage   196
therapeutic
   abortion   196
transabdominal first
   trimester selective
   termination   196
vacuum aspiration   196

SUMMARY POINTS

More than half of pregnancies among U.S. women are unintended. How an individual or couple responds to this dilemma is the concern of this chapter.

Abortion in the United States

An estimated 43% of U.S. women will have at least one abortion by the time they are age 45. Most women obtaining abortions are under the age of 25, are single, and want to have children in the future. Women choose abortion for a variety of financial, emotional, interpersonal, and health reasons. Most legal abortions in the United States are performed during the first 12 weeks of pregnancy using suction curettage (vacuum aspiration).

Abortion is a highly controversial political issue. Although women were granted legal abortions in *Roe v. Wade* in 1973, other court rulings and legislation have restricted abortion by mandating parental notification or consent, imposing waiting periods, and limiting public funding of abortion.

A Cross-Cultural View of Abortion

About one-fourth of all pregnancies throughout the world end in abortion. Each year, an estimated 50 million abortions occur worldwide; 20 million are done illegally. Nearly half of all abortions are performed under unsafe conditions, posing a serious threat to women's health.

Attitudes Toward Abortion

Attitudes toward abortion range from fierce opposition to abortion under certain circumstances (including rape and endangerment of a woman's life), to staunch support for legal and affordable access to abortion on request. Abortion is more likely to be viewed as an acceptable option if the mother's health is endangered by continuing the pregnancy, if a severe birth defect exists, or if the pregnancy is the result of rape or incest. Although "pro-life" and "pro-choice" groups dominate public discourse on abortion, most people have views that are mixed. Pro-dialogue advocates attempt to bring both sides of the abortion controversy together to find a common ground and focus on reducing the need for abortion.

Physical and Psychological Effects of Abortion

Legal abortions, performed under safe conditions, are generally considered safe procedures. The earlier in the pregnancy the abortion is performed, the safer it is. Laws restricting abortion may compromise a woman's health because restrictive abortion laws delay abortion, thus posing greater threats to women's health by postponing abortion into later trimesters. According to the American Psychological Association, any adverse psychological effects of abortion are mild and temporary.

The Real Challenge: Reducing the Need for Abortion

Various social policies and strategies have been suggested to reduce the need for abortion by preventing most unwanted pregnancies and dealing more positively with the ones that occur.

Adoption: An Alternative to Abortion

In recent decades, fewer unmarried pregnant women are choosing to place their babies for adoption. With the legalization of abortion, more unmarried pregnant women have chosen to terminate their pregnancies. Increased social acceptance of out-of-wedlock childbearing has also influenced more single, pregnant women to parent their own babies.

Adoption may be formal or informal, through an agency or independent, closed or open. The practice of adoption has changed in recent decades. Instead of closed adoptions, which involve confidentiality, secrecy, and sealed adoption records, more adoptions are open. In an open adoption, birth parents and adoptive parents have some knowledge about each other, and the birth parents may even help to choose the adoptive parents. Birth parents may choose an adoptive family by reading résumés or descriptions of prospective adoptive parents and looking at their photographs. Birth parents may also meet and interview prospective adopters. Birth families and adoptive families may negotiate a plan whereby they have contact with each other throughout the baby's childhood. Open adoptions allow birth parents to have some control over the adoption process. Birth parents and adoptive parents have the flexibility to create an adoption plan that suits their values and preferences.

REFERENCES

Abortion surveillance: Preliminary data—United States, 1994. (1997). *Morbidity and Mortality Weekly Report, 45,* 1123-1127.

Adler, N. E., David, H. P., Major, B. N., Roth, S. H., Russo, N. F., & Wyatt, G. E. (1990). Psychological responses after abortion. *Science, 48,* 41-44.

American Council on Education & University of California. (1996). *The American freshman: National norms for Fall, 1996.* Los Angeles: Los Angeles Higher Education Research Institute.

Barnett, W., Freudenberg, N., & Willie, R. (1992). Partnership after induced abortion: A prospective controlled study. *Archives of Sexual Behavior, 21,* 443-455.

Barth, R. P. (1987). Adolescent mothers' beliefs about open adoption. *Social Casework: The Journal of Contemporary Social Work, 68,* 323-331.

Bartholet, E. (1993). *Family bonds: Adoption and the politics of parenting.* New York: Houghton Mifflin.

Bartholet, E. (1995). Creating more adoption possibilities should be encouraged. In A. Harnack (Ed.), *Adoption: Opposing viewpoints* (pp. 55-62). San Diego, CA: Greenhaven Press.

Blum, R. W., Resnick, M. D., & Stark, T. (1990). Factors associated with the use of court bypass by minors to obtain abortions. *Family Planning Perspectives, 22,* 158-160.

Catholics for a Free Choice. (1992). *You are not alone: Information for Catholic women about the abortion decision.* Washington, DC: Author.

Chavkin, W. (1996). Topics for our times: Public health on the line—abortion and beyond. *American Journal of Public Health, 86*(9), 1204-1206.

Clinic violence ebbed in 1996. (1997). *Family Planning Perspectives, 29,* 50.

Council on Scientific Affairs, American Medical Association. (1992). Council Report: Induced termination of pregnancy before and after *Roe v. Wade:* Trends in mortality and morbidity of women. *Journal of the American Medical Association, 268,* 3231-3239.

De Simone, M. (1996). Birth mother loss: Contributing factors to unresolved grief. *Clinical Social Work Journal, 24*(1), 65-76.

Donnelly, B. W., & Voydanoff, P. (1996). Parenting versus placing for adoption: Consequences for adolescent mothers. *Family Relations, 45,* 427-434.

Dworkin, R. J., Harding, J. T., & Schreiber, N. B. (1993). Parenting or placing: Decision making by pregnant teens. *Youth and Society, 25,* 75-92.

Facts in brief: Induced abortion. (1996). New York: Alan Guttmacher Institute.

Family Planning Services in the United States. (1997). New York: Alan Guttmacher Institute. [On-line] http://www.agi-usa.org/pub/fb-familyplan1.html

Ginsburg, F. D. (1989). *Contested lives: The abortion debate in an American community.* Berkeley, CA: University of California Press.

Glendon, M. A. (1987). *Abortion and divorce in Western law.* Cambridge, MA: Harvard University Press.

Goodwin, J. (1997, January–February). Prisoners of biology: In Nepal, there's no abortion debate, just a life sentence. *Utne Reader, 79,* 66-72.

Granberg, D. (1991). Conformity to religious norms regarding abortion. *Sociological Quarterly, 32,* 267-275.

Hasson, J. (1997, May 15). AMA: Procedure should be rare, up to doctor. *USA Today,* p. 5A.

Henshaw, S. K. (1991). The accessibility of abortion services in the United States. *Family Planning Perspectives, 23,* 246-252.

Henshaw, S. K. (1997). Teenage abortion and pregnancy statistics by state, 1992. *Family Planning Perspectives, 29,* 115-122.

Henshaw, S. K., & Kost, K. (1996). Abortion patients in 1994-1995: Characteristics and contraceptive use. *Family Planning Perspectives 28,* 140-147.

Henshaw, S. K., & Van Vort, J. (1994). Abortion services in the United States, 1991 and 1992. *Family Planning Perspectives, 26,* 100-112.

Hochman, G., & Huston, A. (1994). *Open adoption.* Bockville, MD: National Adoption Information Clearinghouse. [On-line] http://www.adopting.org/open1.html

Holmes, M. M. (1996). Rape-related pregnancy: Estimates and descriptive characteristics from a national sample of women. *American Journal of Obstetrics and Gynecology, 175,* 320-325.

Hopkins, N., Reicher, S., & Saleem, J. (1996). Constructing women's psychological health in anti-abortion rhetoric. *The Sociological Review, 44,* 539-564.

Informed choice, not inflamed rhetoric. (1997). *POPLINE, 19,* 1, 8. Washington, DC: Population Institute.

Jeune, P. (1996a). Sweeping changes made to South Africa's abortion law. *The Lancet, 348,* 1304.

Jeune, P. (1996b). Guernsey approves abortion. *The Lancet, 348,* 1304.

Koop, C. E. (1989). A measured response: Koop on abortion. *Family Planning Perspectives, 21,* 31-32.

Lethbridge, D. J. (1995). Unwanted pregnancy. In C. I. Fogel & N. F. Woods (Eds.), *Women's health care: A comprehensive handbook* (pp. 455-473). Thousand Oaks, CA: Sage.

Lindsay, J. W. (1997). *Pregnant? Adoption is an option.* Buena Park, CA: Morning Glory Press.

Luker, K. (1984). The war between women. *Family Planning Perspectives, 16,* 105-110.

Maloy, K., & Patterson, M. (1992). *Birth or abortion? Private struggles in a political world.* New York: Plenum Press.

Marcus, R. (1991, May 24). Court upholds ban on abortion advice. *News and Observer,* Raleigh, NC, pp. 1-2.

Marquis, K., & Detweiler, R. (1985). Does adopted mean different? An attributional analysis. *Journal of Personality and Social Psychology, 48,* 1054-1066.

Matthews, S., Ribar, D., & Wilhelm, M. (1997). The effects of economic conditions and access to reproductive health services on state abortion rates and birthrates. *Family Planning Perspectives, 29,* 52-60.

Mauldon, J., & Delbanco, S. (1997). Public perceptions about unplanned pregnancy. *Family Planning Perspectives, 29,* 25-29.

Mauro, T. (1992, June 30). High court reigns in 'Roe.' *USA Today,* p. A1.

McDonagh, E. (1996). *Breaking the abortion deadlock: From choice to consent.* Oxford University Press.

Merkel-Holguin, L., & Sobel, A. (1993). *The child welfare state book, 1993.* Washington, DC: Child Welfare League of America.

Millar, W. J., Wadhera, S., & Henshaw, S. K., (1997). Repeat abortions in Canada, 1975-1993. *Family Planning Perspectives, 29,* 20-24.

Miller, D. H. (1996a). Medical and psychological consequences of legal abortion in the United States. In R. L. Parrott & C. M. Condit (Eds.), *Evaluating women's health messages* (pp. 17-32). Thousand Oaks, CA: Sage.

Miller, D. H. (1996b). Abortion rhetoric and media messages. In R. L. Parrott & C. M. Condit (Eds.), *Evaluating women's health messages* (pp. 33–48). Thousand Oaks, CA: Sage.

Miller, K., & Rosenfield, A. (1996). Population and women's reproductive health: An international perspective. *Annual Review of Public Health, 17,* 359–382.

Minden, S. L., & Notman, M. T. (1991). Psychotherapeutic issues related to abortion. In N. L. Stotland (Ed.), *Psychiatric aspects of abortion* (pp. 119–133). Washington, DC: American Psychiatric Press.

Moore, D. W., Newport, F., & Saad, L. (1996, August). Public generally supports a woman's right to abortion. *Gallup Poll Monthly,* 29–35.

Muldoon, M. (1991). *The abortion debate in the United States and Canada: A source book.* New York: Garland.

National Council for Adoption. (1996). NCFA's factsheet on adoption. [On-line] http://www.ncfa-usa.org/factsht.html

Olasky, M. (1995). Adoption is an act of compassion. In A. Harnack (Ed.), *Adoption: Opposing viewpoints* (pp. 24–30). San Diego, CA: Greenhaven Press.

Olasky, M. (1997). Forgotten choice. *National Review, 49*(4), 4345.

Petchesky, R. P. (1990). *Abortion and women's choice: The state, sexuality, and reproductive freedom* (Rev. ed.). Northeastern Series in Feminist Theory. Boston: Northeastern University Press.

Religious Coalition for Abortion Rights. (1992). *No woman is required to build the world by destroying herself* [Public information brochure]. Washington, DC: Author.

Rosenfeld, J. (1997). Postcoital contraception and abortion. In J. Rosenfeld (Ed.), *Women's health in primary care* (pp. 315–329). Media, PA: Williams & Wilkins.

Rubin, E. (1987). *Abortion, politics, and the courts:* Roe v. Wade *and its aftermath* (2nd ed.). Westport, CT: Greenwood Press.

Russo, N. F., & Dabul, A. J. (1997). The relationship of abortion to well-being: Do race and religion make a difference? *Professional Psychology: Research and Practice, 28,* 23–31.

Sapiro, V. (1990). *Women in American society* (2nd ed.). Mountain View, CA: Mayfield.

Smith, D. (1995). *The impact of adoption on birth parents.* Adopt: Assistance Information Support. [On-line] http//www.adopting.org/impact.html#top

Stone, R., & Waszak, C. (1992). Adolescent knowledge and attitudes about abortion. *Family Planning Perspectives, 24,* 52–57.

Stotland, N. L. (1996). Conceptions and misconceptions: Decisions about pregnancy. *General Hospital Psychiatry, 18,* 238–243.

Tribe, L. H. (1990). *The clash of absolutes.* New York: W. W. Norton.

Watson, K. W. (1996). Family-centered adoption practice. *Families in Society: The Journal of Contemporary Human Services, 77,* 523–534.

Wilmoth, G. (1989, Winter). APA challenges Koop's abortion report. *Advancing the Public Interest, 7.*

Winikoff, B. (1995). Acceptability of medical abortion in early pregnancy. *Family Planning Perspectives, 27,* 142–148.

World Abortion Policies, 1994. United Nations Dept. for Economic and Social Information and Policy Analysis. [On-line] gopher://gopher.undp.org:70/00/-ungo phers/popin/wdtrends/charts

Yeost, C. (1995). Informal adoptions should be supported. In A. Harnack (Ed.), *Adoption: Opposing viewpoints* (pp. 154–164). San Diego, CA: Greenhaven Press.

Health Problems and Sexuality

> *S*exual health is the integration of the somatic, emotional, intellectual, and social aspects of sexual beings in ways that are positively enriching and that enhance personality, communication, and love.
>
> World Health Organization

Partners sometimes say things to each other like "I've got a headache," "I'm too tired," or "I'm not feeling well." All of these statements imply a connection between health and engaging in sexual behavior. Physical and psychological health are inextricably tied to sexuality.

More than 12% (approximately 25 million people) of the U.S. population ages 15 and older have what is categorized as a "severe" cognitive or physical disability (*Statistical Abstract of the United States: 1997*, Table 213). An estimated 70% of the U.S. population will suffer from a disability at some point in their lives (Hays, Kraft, & Stolov, 1994). When individuals are born with a disability or develop one later in life, they and their families must contend with many concerns—medical care, finances, social stigma, and quality of life. Illness, disease, and disability may negatively interfere with the quality of life in relationships and sexuality. Unfortunately, the sexuality of these individuals has been traditionally ignored by health care professionals. Recently, however, the sexuality concerns of individuals with disease or disability have received increasing recognition. More and more choices for enhancing sexuality are now available to such individuals.

Myths About Disease, Disability, and Sexuality

Individuals with disease or disability are often stereotyped as asexual beings. However, in the words of Cole and Cole (1983), "Desire does not stop when a disability occurs. . . . Physical disability is not synonymous with sexual inadequacy and sexual enjoyment is not exclusively linked to functional movement" (p. 304). Dr. Thomas Robert H. Ames (1991), who has worked with blind, deaf, and paralyzed individuals, shared his view about the myth that individuals with disabilities are asexual:

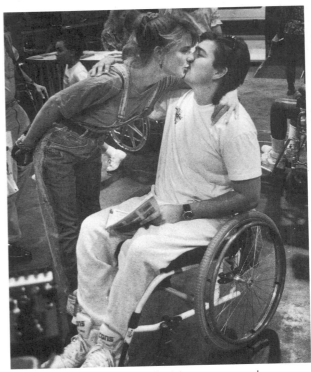

It is a myth that individuals in wheelchairs are asexual.

I have never met a nonsexual client—but I have known numerous men and women who believed that they had no right to their sexuality and others who thought that their lives were over. When freed of these harmful myths, these people blossomed and another door opened for them. (p. 122)

Someone who challenges the idea that people with physical impairments are asexual is Rick Creech. Rick was born with athetoid cerebral palsy and has no oral speech or muscular control of his arms or legs. However, he refuses the label of "disabled"; he communicates by using an augmented communication device that has speech output and goes almost anywhere he wants in his wheelchair. While he was a graduate student in speech, language, and auditory pathology, he published a book, in which he commented on his sexuality.

I am a sexual person. If that shocks you, well, hold on to your seats, you are in for some more shocks . . . Without going into details, I shall say that I have had four or five romances, been engaged three times, and I married my last girlfriend . . . I met my wife, Yolanda, one morning in my apartment in Richmond. The agency had sent her to get me up, bathe, and feed me breakfast . . . Yolanda says that the only thing she saw when she walked into my room were my blue eyes following her everywhere. Thank God for blue eyes! . . . When I met Yolanda, she had a boyfriend, old Georgey, and she thought she was very happy with George. He never knew what happened.

None of the boyfriends of girls I went with could believe that I had taken their girls away from them. Of course, I didn't exactly inform them of my intentions, though I wasn't secretive about it. Really, these men could not believe that I could be any competition, which made things easier for me. And I must admit to taking pleasure in taking these guys' girls.

A challenged person can compete with a physically able person. How you treat a lover, whether you build the person up or tear the person down, whether your lover can find love and trust and gentleness in you—these are the areas in which the challenged person need not be limited. It does take a special woman or man to recognize that these qualities are more important in a relationship than physical beauty and strength or the opinions of others. There are special women and men in the world; we have to keep our hearts opened to them and the possibility of love even though it is dangerous to have open hearts in the world today. (Creech, 1992, pp. 30–33. Used by permission.)

In addition to the myth that individuals with disease or disability are asexual, other common myths about health and sexuality include the following (Schover & Jensen, 1988, pp. 74–75):

- Sex saps one's strength and thus is harmful to anyone not in the best of health.
- Too much sex is unhealthy and causes illness.
- Having sex weakens the potency of medical treatments, such as medication or radiation therapy.
- Strokes and heart attacks are very common during sexual intercourse.
- Diabetic men always develop erection problems.
- Cancer is contagious through sexual activity.
- Psychiatric patients are oversexed.

THINK ABOUT IT

When you see a person in a wheelchair, what assumptions do you make about his or her interest, capacity, and activity related to sexual expression?

PERSONAL CHOICES

Should You Exercise?

One myth about individuals with disabilities is that they cannot engage in exercise. Although a physical disability often restricts the types of activities a person may engage in, "physical disability need not, and indeed should not, mean physical inactivity" (Lockette & Keyes, 1994, p. ix). The benefits of exercise for people with disabilities include improved stamina for activities involved in daily living; enhanced self-esteem and confidence; and minimized muscle atrophy, joint stiffness, pressure sores, and weight gain (Lockette & Keyes, 1994).

Exercise is also beneficial for the prevention and treatment of a variety of illnesses, including heart disease, musculoskeletal disorders, diabetes, and cancer. The prevention benefit of exercise is demonstrated by various studies that have found an association between a sedentary lifestyle and cancer of the colon, lung, prostate, cervix, and breast (Winningham, 1994). Over the last 20 years, the incidence of testicular cancer has risen markedly among men in professional and white-collar occupations, which may be linked to lower levels of exercise among these men (Murphy, Morris, & Lange, 1997).

Regular physical activity is not only important for the promotion and maintenance of our health, it also has benefits for our sexuality. A team of researchers (White, McWhirter, & Mattison, 1990) compared the sex lives of 78 sedentary but healthy men (mean age of 48) who participated in a group aerobic workout for 60 minutes 3.5 days a week with 17 men (mean age of 44) who walked at a moderate pace an average of 4.1 days a week. Participants kept a diary on exercise, diet, smoking, and sexuality the first and last month of a 9-month program. Results showed that those men in the aerobic exercise group reported higher frequencies of various intimate activities and reliability of sexual functioning (erection) and more satisfying orgasms compared with those men in the walking group. Indeed, the more the men improved in their respective health profiles, the greater the benefits in their reported sexuality.

Butt (1990) noted that one's overall well-being is enhanced by exercise and that sexual activity itself is a valuable form of exercise. He noted, however, that health educators rarely emphasize the benefits of exercise on sexuality.

PSYCHOBIOLOGICAL AND PSYCHOSOCIAL EFFECTS OF DISEASE AND DISABILITY

The impact of disease and disability on an individual's sexuality involves more than a physical or biological dimension (Schover & Jensen, 1988). Psychobiological and psychosocial factors also affect sexuality. Psychobiological factors include pain, fatigue, and depression. Psychosocial factors include self-concept, body image, role function and effects on relationships.

Psychobiological Effects

Pain, fatigue, and depression are psychobiological effects of disease and disability that affect one's sexuality.

PAIN   Pain is associated with a number of health problems, including arthritis, migraine headaches, and back problems. The experience of physical pain can have a profound effect on sexuality and sexual functioning. Pain, as well as some medications that are used to control pain, may decrease a person's sexual desire and disrupt the sexual response cycle, resulting in no arousal and no orgasm.

There are various approaches to minimizing the degree to which pain interferes with sexual functioning. For example, patients are encouraged to select sexual positions that minimize pain, engage in sexual behavior when their pain is minimal (such as in the morning or after taking pain medications), and take warm baths before having sex. Open sexual communication is also important because partners need to be told what activities or positions are painful (Rolland, 1994).

FATIGUE   In addition to pain, chronic illness and disease are often accompanied by fatigue. Persons with fatigue feel exhausted, weak, and depleted of energy. Fatigue can cause a marked decrease in sexual interest and functioning.

Fatigue may result from the effects of an illness or disease on the various body organs, as well as from the drugs or other therapy used to treat an illness. Fatigue may also result from the emotional and psychological stress that accompanies chronic illness. People with chronic illness spend a great deal of emotional energy coming to accept their illness.

When fatigue interferes with sexual functioning, several interventions may be helpful. First, the fatigued person should engage in sexual behavior at a time when he or she feels most rested and has the most energy. Second, the person may use different positions for sexual activity that are less demanding. Third, counseling may help a person work through the conflicts of accepting the permanent nature of chronic illness in an effect to reduce psychological fatigue.

DEPRESSION   Depression is a common reaction to becoming chronically ill or disabled. Depression may be related to loss of enjoyable activities, grief over loss of function and aspects of identity, or a perceived social devaluation as an individual with a disability (Brockway, 1994). In writing about women with disabilities, Carol Gill (1996a) suggests that they are at high risk for depression because they "are denied a meaningful role in life, are left without economic power or social supports, and are bombarded with messages that they fall short of society's standards for womanhood" (p. 12).

One of the classic symptoms of depression is a lack of interest in sex. For example, depression is one of the most common causes of sexual problems in people with cancer (Murphy, Morris, & Lange, 1997). In a study of adult amputees, researchers found that higher levels of perceived negative impact of amputation on sexual activity were related to more symptoms of depression (Williamson & Walters, 1996).

People with chronic illness or disabilities who suffer from depression may benefit from assistance in working through their feelings of grief and loss associated with their illness. Such assistance may be obtained through professional counseling and supportive interpersonal relationships.

ⓔ Homosexuals with illness or disabilities may be more vulnerable to depression than heterosexuals. Findings from the National Lesbian and Gay Health Foundation revealed that the most common health problem was depression, that most felt unable to disclose their sexual orientation to their health care provider, and that 80% reported discrimination based on their sexual identity. Some health care providers feel not only that homosexuality is unacceptable, but that it should be illegal (O'Toole, 1996). Experiencing cold or distant professional healers at a time of need can be a particularly poignant rejection (Rolland, 1994). ⓔ

Psychosocial Effects

Self-concept and body image, role function, and intimate relationships are psychosocial factors that are affected by disease and disability. These factors are frequently overlooked in discussions of how health problems affect sexuality.

SELF-CONCEPT AND BODY IMAGE   Self-concept refers to the attitudes, feelings, and perceptions individuals have about themselves. We develop our self-concept through our interactions with others. Persons with chronic illness or disability often develop a negative self-concept, which may interfere with their sexuality. A negative self-concept may create feelings of inadequacy as a sexual partner.

Body image refers to the attitude individuals have toward their bodies, and perceptions they have of how they look to others. Persons with disabilities or disease may view themselves as physically flawed and sexually unattractive. Other aspects of illness and disability that may contribute to a negative body image include loss of control over bodily functions and the use of cold, hard, metallic appliances (such as braces or wheelchairs). In addition, disability may result in loss of mobility, lack of exercise, and consequent weight gain.

Given the cultural emphasis on the physical appearance of women, women with disease or disability may be particularly prone to developing a negative body image. One man described his wife's reaction to having an artificial arm:

> My wife's first response to the accident was not to express concern about her ability to pick up pencils, but to worry if she would still be able to go on a beach in a bikini. Three weeks after the accident, appearance and disguise are her main concerns. (Thomas, 1982, p. 45)

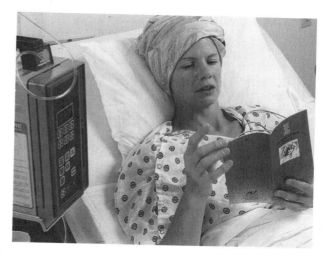

One's physical self is altered by disease, but changes may be made to enhance one's self-image.

Interviews with 31 women with disabilities revealed a preoccupation on the part of many about taking action to enhance their attractiveness. For some, this meant maintaining cleanliness and neatness. For others, it meant makeup and fashionable clothes. "One participant with a severe disability from polio commented that she likes to wear makeup and fashionable clothes so she will look 'less disabled'" (Nosek, 1996, p. 172).

Body-image concerns often lead to avoidance of sexual interaction and problems in sexual response (Murphy, Morris, & Lange, 1997). Conversely, physical limitations on one's ability to be sexually responsive contribute to a negative body image.

ROLE FUNCTION   Some illnesses and disabilities result in role changes for the individual. Such changes may occur in a variety of social roles, including that of lover or spouse, parent, wage earner, and homemaker. For example, a lover or spouse may be abandoned by his or her partner following an illness or disabling injury. Or, the role of an ill or disabled lover or spouse may change in that he or she becomes partially or totally dependent on the care of the partner. Parents who become ill or disabled may no longer be able to fulfill the role of providing care to their offspring. Indeed, some illnesses and disabilities may prohibit individuals from having children, thereby barring them from the role of parent altogether. Such parental role restrictions may affect women more than men because women are traditionally socialized to value the role of parent more than men are. Lastly, disease and disability may interfere with one's occupational role and with one's ability to generate income. One woman who had developed multiple sclerosis in her twenties said:

> You feel yourself insecure as a woman, as well as you're insecure as a mother. You feel the dependence of it all, for somebody who is used to independence. I'd started earning and being a big shot. Then suddenly, never mind being a mother and a big shot, you're physically dependent as well. It takes a lot to survive that. (Quoted in Lonsdale, 1990, p. 67)

INTIMATE RELATIONSHIPS   Establishing intimate relationships is often difficult for individuals with an illness or disability. Compared to the rest of the population, people with disabilities begin dating and experiencing sexual interaction at a later age; they are also less likely to marry (Gill, 1996b). Brockway (1994) explains that "the conspicuously disabled individual may not be seen as a potential sexual partner by a large proportion of the nondisabled population and therefore may have a restricted range of potential partners from which to choose" (p. 109).

Illness or disability can bring a couple closer together or tear them apart. Caring for an ill partner can be an economic, emotional, and physical strain. Combining the role of intimate partner with personal attendant may impair the sexual relationship. Brockway (1994) explains:

> It is often difficult for partners to combine the role of sexual partner with that of attendant, which may include hygiene, dressing, bathing, and bowel and bladder care. This [is] partly due to the level of fatigue involved in providing caretaking. As important, however, appears to be a psychological difficulty in performing personal-care chores—particularly bowel and bladder care—and "switching gears" to an erotic interaction. (p. 108)

In a study of how illness affects marriage relationships, Booth and Johnson (1994) found that spouses of sick partners experienced a greater decline in marital quality than did the spouses who had become ill. Wallerstein and Blakeslee (1995) suggested that confronting the inevitable and unpredictable adversities of life in ways that enhance relationships is a challenge for all couples.

THINK ABOUT IT

Carol Gill (1996b) explains how government policies discourage individuals with severe disabilities from marrying:

> Current public policies penalize persons with extensive disabilities for marrying or even living with the man or woman they love by cutting off government funding for health coverage, adaptive equipment, and personal assistance services and shifting the inflated costs of these life necessities onto the working partner. (p. 122)

Do you think such policies are justified? Should they be changed?

PERSONAL CHOICES

How Do You Use Cognitive Strategies to Cope with Illness or Disability?

Spinal cord injuries, multiple sclerosis, and cancer are physically debilitating illnesses over which we have little control. Choosing to get the best medical treatment and advice available and choosing to follow these recommendation are choices that will help us to minimize the negative impact of such illnesses on our sexuality. Beyond what is possible medically, we might choose to reframe our situation and to view changes in our sexuality in positive rather than negative terms.

Individuals with disabilities often view a disability as something to get rid of:

> Because they are in pain, the preferred treatment, as initially seen through their eyes, is eradication. Trying to "get rid of" problems is actually an ineffective approach to life's challenges since the real issue is not what is happening but how we relate to what is happening. (Hulnick & Hulnick, 1989, p. 167)

Questions that researchers Hulnick and Hulnick (1989) recommend that people coping with a disability consider include (p. 167):

1. How can we use this situation to our advancement?
2. What can we learn from our disability?

3. What might we do that might result in a more uplifting experience for everyone involved?
4. How can we relate to ourselves in a more loving way?

Viewing one's situation in positive terms is a choice. For example, individuals with spinal cord injuries who can no longer function as they did prior to their accident may choose to focus on the enjoyments derived from touch, caressing, and emotional closeness. Without such an accident, such a focus may not have occurred to the individual and no movement in that area would have been achieved. Similarly, the heart attack survivor, after experiencing a close encounter with death, may have a renewed value for the relationship with the partner with whom he or she is involved. Choosing to focus on what is gained rather than what has been lost may provide a different outcome for the way one feels about a physical illness or disability.

DRUGS AND SEXUALITY

Drugs affect the sexual response in both women and men. The term "drugs" includes those used for medication and those used for recreation.

Drugs for Medication

More than 200 types of drugs can influence sexual performance (either positively or negatively), according to drug manufacturers' official product literature (Lieberman, 1988, p. 2). Individuals are not likely to discuss the negative effects. Only 10% of patients on high blood pressure medication spontaneously reported that they had experienced difficulties with erection. When questioned by their physician, the percentage rose to 26%. When the patients were asked to complete a questionnaire in private, the percentage rose again to 47% (DeLeo & Magni, 1983).

Various prescription drugs have been reported to have a negative effect on sexual response:

- Antihypertensive medications, designed to lower blood pressure, are associated with erectile dysfunction in men and decreased vaginal lubrication in women. Both men and women may experience loss of sexual interest, delayed orgasm, or inability

to attain orgasm (Smith & Talbert, 1986). Some types of medications are more likely than others to cause sexual dysfunction (such as diuretics) and should be avoided if a sexual dysfunction is already present (Huws, 1993). Such concerns should be taken into consideration because they are likely to effect medication adherence. A medication change may be a simple intervention, saving the patient time, money, and distress (Finger, Lund, & Slagel, 1997).

- Psychotropic medications (used to improve psychological functioning) may have a negative effect on sexual functioning. Some antidepressant drugs (monoamine oxidase inhibitors and heterocyclic antidepressants) have been reported to cause a variety of effects on sexual functioning, including erectile dysfunction (in a small number of patients), delayed ejaculation, anorgasmia (inability to come to orgasm), priapism (prolonged erection) and increase or decrease in libido (Barnes & Harvery, 1993). These problems sometimes subside with continuation of the drug or can be reversed by switching to another drug. Antianxiety drugs, such as barbiturates and benzodiazepines, have also been associated with depressed sexual interest and orgasmic response (Rogers, 1990).

Other psychotropic medications that are reported to cause sexual dysfunction are antipsychotic drugs. The drug-induced dysfunctions from these drugs are often persistent because most patients receiving antipsychotic medications do so long-term. The possible sexual side effects include loss of sexual interest and drive, erectile and ejaculatory difficulties, priapism, and inhibition of orgasm (Barnes & Harvey, 1993). In some cases, switching to another drug returns sexual functioning to normal. Because of the potential impact on social and intimate relationships, increased attention should be paid to sexual counseling for schizophrenic patients (Barnes & Harvey, 1993).

- Anabolic steroids, endogenous androgens, and testosterone are used in replacement therapy for men with a deficiency or absence of endogenous testosterone. These agents may also be used in women as adjunctive therapy for inoperable metastatic mammary cancer (Rogers, 1990). Both sexes taking these agents have reported both increases and decreases in sexual desire.

Drugs for Recreation

Drugs that are not used for medical purposes under the supervision of a physician are referred to as recreational drugs. (This category includes alcohol.) The Self-Assessment "Alcohol Expectancies Survey" offers an opportunity to assess your expectations of how drinking alcohol might affect your sexual functioning.

A discussion of various drugs and their effects on sexual functioning follows.

ALCOHOL Alcohol is the most frequently used recreational drug in our society and on college and university campuses. Alcohol is a central nervous system depressant that has both psychological and physiological effects on sexual response. In a review of research on the physiological effects of alcohol consumption on sexuality, Crowe and George (1989) noted that alcohol consumption in very low doses appears to enhance male sexual response, as assessed by measurement of penile tumescence. As the level of alcohol consumption increases, a steady decline in sexual responsivity results, as indicated by erectile dysfunction. The point at which there is a significant linear decrease in sexual response has not been precisely determined. However, Crowe and George (1989) cited an estimate of .05 blood alcohol concentration (or about the equivalent of three mixed drinks consumed in 1 to 2 hours by a 150-pound person) as the point at which alcohol may interfere with male sexual functioning. Sexual responsivity in women (orgasmic response) seems to be adversely affected by increased alcohol intake.

In Rosen and Beck's (1988) review of alcohol effects on male sexual function, studies were cited that revealed that moderate drinking was related to some impairment of erection ability. With high doses of alcohol, significant interference occurred. In contrast to the actual experience, most research participants believed that alcohol improved their sexual performance and persisted in this erroneous belief despite knowledge of their laboratory results. Perhaps most important in mediating alcohol's sexual effect are the individual's expectations. If alcohol is expected to heighten sexual arousal, it will.

Long-term heavy use of alcohol causes damage to the hypothalamus, which results in decreased testosterone levels; "the effects are often irreversible" (Munsat, 1990, p. 596). Sexual effects of long-term alcohol use in men include erectile dysfunction, lowered sex drive, infertility, and feminization syndrome (the characteristics of which include varying degrees of breast enlargement and testicular atrophy) (Munsat, 1990; Crowe & George, 1989). In a study of 50 hospitalized alcoholic men, half reported erectile dysfunction (Schiavi, 1990, p. 26). A return to normal sexual functioning has been found in only 50% of the cases after abstinence from alcohol abuse for months of years (Munsat, 1990).

Alcohol abuse also has negative effects on the sexual functioning of women. Munsat (1990) observed that long-term alcohol use in women results in decreased interest in sex and sexual activity, more difficulty in becoming aroused and in having an orgasm, and disturbances in physiological functioning of the reproductive system (menstrual irregularity and infertility).

Alcohol can affect sexual functioning through several mechanisms:

- Anticipated disinhibiting effect of drinking used to justify behavior or influence judgment
- Impact on spinal reflexes and autonomic nerves damaging erection and ejaculation
- Lowered testosterone effecting sexual interest
- Ovarian and testicular atrophy subsequent to prolonged abuse
- Disinhibiting and sedative effects that may impair relationships (Huws & Sampson, 1993)

MARIJUANA Marijuana (cannabis) is also used as a recreational drug, but its effects on sexuality are less predictable than those of alcohol. Although there are numerous self-report studies, "there is a complete absence of direct psychophysiological research comparable to that reported for the effects of alcohol on male and female sexual response" (Rosen & Beck, 1988, p. 312). In one study, researchers found that marijuana in moderate doses enhanced the quality of orgasm for 40% of the women and 68% of the men (Halikas, Weller, & Morse, 1982). In

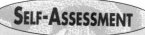

ALCOHOL EXPECTANCIES SURVEY

Here is a list of some effects that many people feel after drinking alcohol. Please circle the letter to describe whether you think alcohol has this effect on you.

DOES ALCOHOL HAVE THIS EFFECT ON YOU?

When you drink enough alcohol to feel its effects, you:

		Not at all	A little	Some	Very much
a.	feel less self-conscious	A	B	C	D
b.	feel closer to a sexual partner	A	B	C	D
c.	are a better lover	A	B	C	D
d.	are more sexually responsive	A	B	C	D
e.	are less nervous about sex	A	B	C	D
f.	are more self-confident	A	B	C	D
g.	become more sexually forward	A	B	C	D
h.	feel less shy	A	B	C	D
i.	get horny (want sex)	A	B	C	D
j.	enjoy sex more	A	B	C	D
k.	have sex with people who you normally wouldn't if you were sober	A	B	C	D
l.	are more likely to do something sexually that is risky	A	B	C	D
m.	lose your inhibitions	A	B	C	D

The Alcohol Expectancies Survey was one of the measures developed in a large study on drinking and sexual behavior (Leigh, 1990). Instead of computing an overall total score to summarize responses, the author examined three dimensions of the scale that were identified through factor analysis. The dimensions (and the items for each) are the following:

- Enhanced sex (feel closer, better lover, more responsive, get horny, enjoy sex more)
- Decreased nervousness (feel less self-conscious, less nervous, more self-confident, more sexually forward, less shy, lose inhibitions)
- Increased riskiness (have sex with people I normally wouldn't have sex with if sober, more likely to do something sexually risky)

In reviewing your responses, did you endorse items in any of the dimensions? The most salient finding reported by Leigh (1990) in her sample of people from San Francisco households was that gay men and lesbians reported stronger expectancies for decreased nervousness and increased sexual riskiness compared to heterosexual men and women. The study also found that heavier drinkers were more likely to strongly endorse the items.

From "Alcohol Expectations Questionnaire," by B. C. Leigh, 1990, *British Journal of Addiction, 85.* Reprinted by permission of the author.

addition, these researchers found that 75% of the men and 90% of the women reported that moderate doses of marijuana increased their sexual pleasure and satisfaction. Perceived effects may be due to expectations of sexual enhancement.

Some studies suggest that chronic use of marijuana in men may cause testosterone levels to drop, thereby decreasing sex drive; other studies find no effect on testosterone levels due to marijuana use (Munsat, 1990). Studies also differ on whether marijuana is associated with lowering sperm count. The National Academy of Sciences, Institute of Medicine (1982) reported that although marijuana was associated with reducing sperm production, there was no evidence that marijuana causes sterility.

The effects of marijuana on the female reproductive system are also unpredictable. Some studies suggest that marijuana is associated with shorter menstrual cycles and has actually been used to reduce menstrual cramps. In lower animals, marijuana has a negative effect on the female reproductive system. However, such a finding may be due to the reduced food and water consumption (malnutrition) that accompanies the use of marijuana in lower animals (Abel, 1985).

OTHER RECREATIONAL DRUGS   Other recreational drugs that effect sexual arousal and performance include barbiturates, opiate narcotics, amphetamines, cocaine, inhalants, and tobacco. Barbiturates have an effect similar to alcohol in that they blunt anxiety and reduce inhibitions. But because barbiturates are primarily sedatives that depress the central nervous system, higher doses may result in loss of sexual ability. As with most sleeping pills, which contain barbiturates, the desire for sleep replaces the desire for sex.

Among the opiate narcotics are morphine, heroin, and methadone. Use of these drugs has been associated with decreased sexual interest and ability. DeLoen and Wexler (1973) found in their study of heroin addicts that all subjects reported decreases in intercourse, masturbation, and nocturnal emissions. Heroin is associated with decreased libido, delayed ejaculation, and erectile dysfunction. Many heroin addicts develop chronic illnesses and relationship problems that affect their sexual functioning. They are particularly at risk for HIV infection. Abstinent addicts often report that a major reason for their abstinence is stable relationships with drug-free partners (Huws & Sampson, 1993).

Amphetamines, such as pep pills and diet pills, are "uppers" that stimulate the central nervous system. The effect of such drugs is to overcome fatigue and to give a feeling of alertness and energy. Prolonged use of amphetamines may make orgasm difficult for men, although they may still have erections. For women, menstrual difficulties have been associated with the use of amphetamines.

Cocaine is a central nervous system stimulant that increases alertness, elevates mood, and produces euphoria. Cocaine use is associated with erectile dysfunction, spontaneous or delayed ejaculation, and priaprism (Finger, Lund, & Slagle, 1997). Cocaine, taken intranasally or smoked as "crack," can lead to psychological dependence. It is sometimes used to prolong intercourse or delay orgasm by applying it to the head of the penis or to the clitoris as a local anesthetic. It has also been used anally as an anesthetic to allow violent sexual behavior to occur. Huws and Sampson (1993) quoted from the 1903 *American Journal of Pharmacy,* which discussed the one redeeming feature of the cocaine habit—due to its suppression of sexual desire and ability, "there is less danger of its transmission by heredity" (p. 204).

Amyl nitrate, also known as "snappers" or "poppers," is used by heart patients to prevent heart pain (angina). It is inhaled from a small ampule that is broken open and causes rapid dilation of the arteries that supply various organs of the body with oxygen. The effect on the brain is to induce a feeling of giddiness and euphoria; the effect on the genitals is to produce a sensation of warmth. When inhaled at the approach of orgasm, the effect is to enhance and prolong the orgasmic experience. The person feels a "rush," along with an altered state of consciousness, a loss of inhibition, a tingling sensation in the head and body, and a sensation of faintness. Negative side effects of amyl nitrate include nasal irritation, nausea, loss of erection, coughing, and dizziness.

Reports from the 1980s suggested a link between amyl nitrate use and Kaposi's sarcoma (which is common in people with AIDS). This has recently been explained to more likely be a result of the fact that

Kaposi's sarcoma is more common when AIDS is sexually acquired, than a direct effect of the drug itself (Huws & Sampson, 1993).

Young teenage boys are the main users of volatile solvents; they are used for their euphoriant and hallucinogenic effects. Their effect on sexuality has not been studied (Huws & Sampson, 1993).

Tobacco is one of the most widely used drugs in the world. "The main psychological effect of nicotine is stimulation of the brain although smokers often feel relaxed. Heart rate is increased and blood pressure is increased whereas blood flow to the extremities is decreased" (Abel, 1985, p. 205). LoPiccolo (1983, p. 55) observed that reduced penile blood pressure in heavy smokers may be accompanied by erectile problems. "In other words, though the Marlboro man may be macho, he may also be impotent." Some argue that nicotine is an aphrodisiac, but others disagree. Abel (1985) concluded that "the evidence that smoking affects male libido is inconclusive" (p. 225).

_____ **THINK ABOUT IT** _____

Since patients are usually not informed about the effects of a particular medication on their sexual response, they often take such medications unaware. For example, Accutane (isotretinoin) is widely marketed in the United States as a treatment for severe acne. Yet, this medication has been found to be associated with vaginal dryness in women, erectile problems in men, and decreased interest in sex for women and men (Lieberman, 1988, pp. 147-148).

_____

Table 9.1 lists some of the effects various drugs have on sexual response.

TABLE 9.1   Illicit and Abused Drugs Associated with Sexual Disorders

SUBSTANCE	SEXUAL DISORDER
alcohol	**Acute effects: erectile disorder,*** desire disorder,*** delayed orgasm;*** Chronic effects: erectile disorder,*** desire disorder*****
amphetamines	Low doses: may increase desire and delay orgasm;* High doses and chronic use: **delayed or no ejaculation,***** erectile disorder,** inhibition of orgasm (men and women)*
amyl nitrate	Decrease in arousal and lubrication; erectile disorder; delayed orgasm or ejaculation*
barbiturates	**Decreased desire, erectile disorder, inhibited ejaculation*****
cocaine	**Erectile disorder,*** spontaneous or delayed ejaculation, priapism***
diazepam (Valium)	**Decreased desire, delayed ejaculation, retarded or no orgasm in women***
marijuana	**Decreased desire, hormonal alteration***
MDMA	**Erectile disorder,**** inhibited ejaculation**** and orgasm,****** decreased desire**
methaqualone	Erectile disorder, inhibited ejaculation, decreased desire in women*
morphine	Decreased desire, erectile disorder, hormonal alteration*
tobacco	Erectile disorder**

*Case reports, package insert, or uncertain frequency; **infrequent side effect; ***frequent side effect; **** very frequent side effect.
Note: Medications and their accompanying side effects that have been cited frequently as causing sexual disorders are in bold type.
Source: Finger et al., 1997.

NEUROLOGICAL DISABILITIES AND SEXUALITY

In the spring of 1995, Christopher Reeve, the star of three *Superman* movies, became paralyzed from the neck down in a horseback riding accident. His accident demonstrated how suddenly one can change from being an able-bodied person to a person in a wheelchair who cannot breathe without the assistance of a respirator.

Neurological disabilities affect the central nervous system—the "switchboard" of the sexual system. Examples of neurological disabilities include spinal cord injury, stroke, multiple sclerosis, and cerebral palsy.

Spinal Cord Injury

A recent study by the Kinsey Institute at Indiana University focused on the sexuality of men and women who have sustained spinal cord injuries. More than 200 quadriplegics (people with complete paralysis from the neck down) and paraplegics (people with complete paralysis of the lower half of the body) were interviewed during the course of the study (Donohue & Gebhard, 1995).

A substantial number reported feeling sensation in the genital-perineal area: 26% of the male quadriplegics, 22% of the male paraplegics, 50% of the female quadriplegics, and 32% of the female paraplegics (p. 15). Orgasm is also possible for some men and women. About half of the men and 60% of the women reported orgasm after their injury. Although orgasm may occur from direct stimulation of the genitals, it may also occur as a consequence of the person focusing on physical sensations that can be felt in other areas of the body, such as stroking the arm and mentally reassigning these sensations to the genitals. Women seem more able to "reassign" sexual sensations than men. ". . . . One cannot escape the impression that before injury male sexuality is strongly genital whereas females are less exclusively genital and can react more than males to stimulation of other body areas" (p. 41). Even women with complete spinal cord injury (SCI) are capable of sexual arousal and orgasm from genital and nongenital self-stimulation (Whipple, Cerdes, & Komisaruk, 1996).

Spinal cord injuries can have profound effects on sexual identity, self-image, role function, and interpersonal relationships. The effect of a spinal cord injury on a person's sex life depends on the extent and location of the injury and the etiology or cause of the injury (such as trauma, infection, or secondary to multiple sclerosis). Depending on these factors, the person with a spinal cord injury may regain varying degrees of his or her functioning abilities within approximately 2 years of the injury. In general, the more severe the spinal cord injury, the greater the damage to sexual functioning. However, whether the cord was severed completely or partially and whether the person has any sensation or movement are also relevant variables. Figure 9.1 shows the connection between the brain and the spinal cord.

Intercourse may take place with the partner sitting down on the erect penis of the spinal cord–injured man. This is usually preceded by a lot of direct stimulation to ensure an erect penis. But intercourse is possible without an erect penis. Some

Christopher Reeve chose to view his accident as a challenge to be overcome.

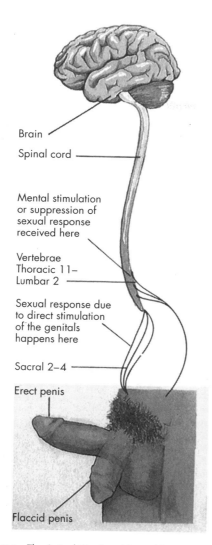

FIGURE 9.1 The Spinal Cord and Sexual Response

Brain

Spinal cord

Mental stimulation or suppression of sexual response received here

Vertebrae Thoracic 11– Lumbar 2

Sexual response due to direct stimulation of the genitals happens here

Sacral 2–4

Erect penis

Flaccid penis

couples use the "stuffing technique," in which partners push the soft penis into the woman's vagina. The woman with strong vaginal muscles can contract them around the penis to hold it inside her. An inflatable penile prosthesis implant (see Chapter 10, "Sexual Dysfunctions and Sex Therapy") is an alternative for some spinal cord-injured men.

Fertility is profoundly affected by spinal cord injury. Only one-seventh of the respondents in the Kinsey survey reported a postinjury pregnancy in either themselves or their partners. However, reproductive technology does make both pregnancy and delivery possible for many spinal cord-injured individuals.

Stroke

Strokes are cerebral malfunctions that are also referred to as cerebrovascular accidents. In most cases, a stroke results in some form of paralysis to certain parts of the body. Strokes may also produce memory loss, impaired language, and mood disorders. About half of all stroke survivors experience at least one major or minor depressive episode (Gitter, 1994). In regard to sexuality, stroke victims report erectile dysfunction, decreased sexual interest, fatigue, bowel or bladder incontinence, and decreased frequency of vaginal intercourse. In a study of poststroke women, the most prominent sexual finding was a decline in desire (Aloni, Schwartz, & Ring, 1997).

Multiple Sclerosis

Multiple sclerosis (MS) is a progressive disease that attacks the central nervous system. Although relatively rare, it occurs in about 1 in 1000 individuals in North America. The age of onset is 20–40, and its symptoms include urological, bowel, and sexual dysfunction (Hatzichristou, 1996).

The most common sexual problem among women with MS is a lack of sexual desire (McCabe, McDonald, Deeks, Vowels, & Cobain, 1996). Women with MS also report difficulty achieving orgasm. Intercourse decreases; this decrease is said to be attributable to practical problems connected with the illness (such as bladder urgency), the partner, and the fact that sex becomes less important (Lundberg & Hulter, 1996). In some cases, patients may be instructed in the use of vibrators, specific coital positions, or alternatives to intercourse.

The most common sexual problem among men with MS is difficulty attaining or maintaining erection (McCabe et al., 1996). About 80% of men with MS report erectile dysfunction (Opsomer, 1996). While injections of vasoactive agents have been the most effective treatment, some patients report pain following an injection. Alternatives to injection therapy include vacuum devices, penile prostheses, and nitroglycerin patches.

Cerebral Palsy

Cerebral palsy refers to a disability resulting from damage to the motor centers of the developing brain. Brain injury can result from illness in the mother during pregnancy (German measles, for example) or from hypoxia (lack of oxygen) during birth, which causes brain cells to die. In the young child, infections and head injuries may also cause cerebral palsy.

The symptoms of cerebral palsy vary according to the area and degree of brain injury but generally include muscular incoordination and speech disturbances. Mental retardation, learning disabilities, and problems with sight and hearing may also occur.

Adolescents with cerebral palsy have difficulty establishing a positive body image because they often face social isolation or rejection by their peers. Adults with cerebral palsy often require counseling and equipment to aid in contraception, intercourse, and masturbation. In regard to the latter, Donnelly (1997) reported the case of a woman in her thirties with severe spasticity who expressed a desire to receive assistance in achieving sexual satisfaction. A specially designed vibrator was developed to accommodate her need, whereby the "woman uses her mouth to operate the vibrator and is thus able to reach orgasm" (p. 17).

THINK ABOUT IT

In some cases, a disabling disease or injury may have positive effects on a person's role function. In a study of women who had spinal cord injury, Bonwich found that many of these women experienced increased self-esteem as a result of having mastered new roles. In addition, many felt that their disability liberated them from the constraints of traditional gender role stereotypes (reported in Lonsdale, 1990).

INTELLECTUAL AND PSYCHOLOGICAL DISTURBANCES AND SEXUALITY

We have been discussing the management of physical disability and illness. But not all illnesses are physical in nature—some are mental. Everyone experiences "problems in living" from time to time, including relationship problems, criminal or domestic victimization, work-related problems, and low self-esteem. However, some conditions or mental disorders are more intense, persistent, and debilitating. The toll of mental illness on a relationship can be immense. Intellectual and emotional qualities are a major part of

the initial attraction between partners. When these are affected, a partner may feel that his or her mate has already died psychologically because they are "not the same person." Spouses of individuals who have Alzheimer's disease emphasize that they are forced to abandon their role of lover and partner to become caretaker of a person who becomes increasingly dependent and childlike (Kaplan, 1996). "It's the end of your dream as a couple," noted one spouse of an Alzheimer's patient. Nancy Reagan, wife of former President Ronald Reagan, has talked publicly about the difficulty of watching one's spouse "slip away."

Intellectual Disability

Intellectual disability, commonly referred to as mental retardation, is defined as significantly subaverage general intellectual functioning, existing concurrently with deficits in adaptive behavior. This disability is manifested during the developmental period. Approximately 3% of the U.S. population is intellectually disabled. In general, intellectual disability may result in limitations in the following areas: self-care, receptive and expressive language, learning, mobility, self-direction, capacity for independent living, and economic self-sufficiency. The extent of these limitations varies according to the level of retardation (mild, moderate, severe, or profound).

Sexual abuse of people with an intellectual disability may be an overlooked problem. Victims may not recognize sexually abusive behaviors or may lack verbal ability or information for making an abuse report. Estimates of the percentage of young people with developmental disabilities who were abused before the age of 18 range from 39 to 83% of girls and 16 to 32% of boys (Golden & Heckrotte, 1995).

Persons with mental retardation "are individuals with sexual feelings who develop physically at a rate comparable to that of normal young adults and respond to many of the same sexual stimuli and situations as do persons without mental retardation" (Scotti, Slack, Bowman, & Morris, 1996, p. 250). Studies suggest that people with mental retardation are sexually active and engage in such behaviors as prolonged kissing, oral sex, and sexual intercourse. However, sexual behavior by them is viewed as less acceptable than that of individuals without retardation (p. 250). The following Social Choices section discusses sexuality of people with mental retardation.

SEXUAL BEHAVIOR AND PEOPLE WITH MENTAL RETARDATION

There is considerable anxiety on the part of caretakers in regard to the sexual behavior of people with mental retardation in institutions. Although both masturbation and mutual sex behavior occur (Scotti et al., 1996) in these institutions, how staff should react to this behavior is unclear. In general, sexual expression by and among people with mental retardation is regarded more negatively than that which occurs among individuals with full mental capacity.

Kaeser (1996b) suggested that the sexual rights of people with mental retardation should include the right to orgasm through masturbation. A human rights committee in the institution where the individual lives could recommend supervised guided masturbation training.

> . . . The person is taught how to identify his or her own particular sexual response pattern. That is, the person is led or guided through each of the different components of masturbation, including holding and manipulating the genitals, by using different motions and a rhythm and rate that gradually builds as the person becomes more and more sexually aroused. (p. 302)

Mutual sexual contact between people with severe mental retardation is more complicated.

> For example, should persons be forced to stop their sexual contacting, no matter how beneficial the behavior might be, because of a legal standard that says one must possess the capacity to render informed consent before participating in sex? Is it morally right to categorically preclude others' ability to voluntarily engage in a sexual act? If so, what would be the positive and negative consequences of such an arrangement and how would these consequences affect the quality of life and overall adjustment of individuals? (Kaeser, 1996a, p. 317)

Sources: Kaeser, F. (1996a). A survey of the perceptions of twenty-three service providing agencies on the sexual behaviors of persons with severe or profound mental retardation. *Sexuality and Disability, 14,* 309–320.

Kaeser, F. (1996b). Developing a philosophy of masturbation training for persons with severe or profound mental retardation. *Sexuality and Disability, 14,* 295–308.

Scotti, J. R., Slack, B. S., Bowman, R. A., & Morris, T. L. (1996). College student attitudes concerning the sexuality of persons with mental retardation: Development of the Perceptions of Sexuality Scale. *Sexuality and Disability, 14,* 249–263.

Psychological Disturbances

The influence of psychological disturbances on sexuality is complex and interactive. For example, depression can affect one's interest in sexual activity and one's capacity to engage in sexual activity and enjoy sexual pleasure (Lustman & Clouse, 1990). However, lack of sexual activity can create depression, and a reciprocal cycle is set in motion. Woods (1981) observed that "there is no consistent relationship between any specific psychiatric illness and disordered sexuality" (p. 200). Hence, intervention requires a detailed knowledge of the patient's background (development of sexual attitudes and values) and a physical examination to rule out organic pathology. Probably the greatest attention to psychological disturbances affecting sexuality has focused on affective disorders, such as depressive disorders.

Depression often affects sexual desire. Compared to people not diagnosed as depressed, depressed people more often report loss of sexual interest (Mathew & Weinman, 1982). One study found that a person's first depressive episode almost always preceded or occurred simultaneously with loss of desire. In their study of men and women with low sexual desire, Schreiner-Engel and Schiavi (1986) found that among those who were not depressed when assessment was done, there was a significant history of depression.

Bipolar disorder, also known as manic-depression, is characterized by alternating periods of severe depression and extreme emotional excitement and activity. During manic periods, some individuals may direct their excessive excitement and activity into increased and often indiscriminate sexual activity.

The individual may masturbate in public, initiate extramarital affairs, and act seductively. In a small percentage of individuals with bipolar illness, decreased sexual interest may occur.

Bancroft (1989) offered several hypotheses to explain the connection between sexual interest and depression. In general, people are more likely to be sexually active when they feel well. It is not surprising that negative cognitions and low self-esteem would be related to a low sense of sexual worth. In addition, there are a number of biochemical theories; a change in cerebral amine function may connect sexuality with mood. Side effects of drug treatment for depression may decrease desire. Depression may also be related to relationship problems; disturbances in the sexual aspect of the relationship may be a cause or an effect of the relationship discord.

Investigators have noted that women are nearly twice as likely as men to experience unipolar depression (depressed affect and mood). Cutler and Nolen-Hoeksema (1991) investigated the hypothesis that this sex difference may be influenced by the high rate of sexual abuse girls experience in childhood. Not only are girls and women at greater risk of being sexually victimized, girls and boys may react differently to sexual abuse. Severity and duration of abuse is a factor: girls seem to experience more serious types of abuse than boys. While Cutler and Nolen-Hoeksema acknowledged that child sexual abuse is not the only contributor to the sex differences in depression, they suggested that it is a very significant factor.

Other investigators have studied the relationship between abuse history and diagnosis of mental disorders. Carmen, Rieker, and Mills (1984) examined the records of 188 men and women who were hospitalized in psychiatric treatment settings. Half of the patients had affective disorders, and the other half had diagnoses that included psychoses, personality disorders, adjustment reactions, and substance abuse. Eighty of the 188 patients (43%) had documented histories of physical or sexual abuse, or both. Female patients were more likely to have been abused, mostly by family members. After retrospectively studying 40 patients with multiple personality disorder, Putnam discovered that 80% had experienced severe abuse during childhood (Abused Child, 1982).

A connection between sexual assault history and certain types of mental health problems has also been found in adults who were not selected on the basis of seeking psychotherapy or psychiatric hospitalization. Burnam et al. (1988) analyzed interview data from a study of over 3000 randomly selected adults in two Los Angeles communities. They compared lifetime diagnoses of nine major mental disorders and the respondent's reports of whether they have ever been sexually assaulted.

> Sexual assault predicted later onset of major depressive episodes, substance use disorders (alcohol and drug abuse or dependence), and anxiety disorders (phobia, panic disorder, and obsessive-compulsive disorder) but was not related to later onset of mania, schizophrenic disorders or antisocial personality. (p. 843)

Recent research suggests that some instances of borderline personality disorder (characterized by unstable, intense personal relationships and impulsivity), multiple personality disorder (now diagnosed as dissociative identity disorder), and posttraumatic stress disorder in adulthood are related to a history of childhood sexual abuse (Murray, 1993). While further research is needed to learn more about the cause of the relationship, it is clear that experiencing sexual assault does increase one's risk of experiencing emotional and psychological problems. As Carmen et al. (1984) said, "From our perspective, a major focus of treatment must be to help victims become survivors" (p. 383).

THINK ABOUT IT

A number of studies have revealed that sexual abuse histories were often not detected when survivors were patients in psychiatric facilities or at mental health agencies. What factors have influenced contemporary recognition of the connection between childhood sexual abuse and some mental health disorders?

Another psychological disturbance that affects sexuality is schizophrenia. This psychotic disorder affects behavior and thought process so severely that it would be surprising if sexual behavior were not affected (Bancroft, 1989). The following examples of sexual effects are from Bancroft's review. The development of schizophrenia, with its onset most likely in young adulthood, is bound to influence social and relationship development. Sexual desire does not seem to be influenced as much by schizophrenia as by other psychological diagnoses, but sexual dysfunctions, such as anorgasmia, were noted in a study of schizophrenic women. The hallucinations and delusions of schizophrenics often have sexual content, including hallucinations involving genitalia, delusions of genital change, and delusions of sex change. Since sexual hallucinations are often gustatory or olfactory in content, a temporal lobe disorder may be involved (Connolly & Gittelson, 1971).

THINK ABOUT IT

The movie *Rain Man* focused on the relationship between two siblings, one of whom was institutionalized. What do you regard as the sexual rights of individuals who are institutionalized? To what degree do you feel that people with mental retardation should be allowed to have sex with each other?

CANCER AND SEXUALITY

Of every five deaths in the United States, one is from cancer. Following heart disease, cancer is the second leading cause of death in the United States (*Statistical Abstract of the United States: 1996*, Table 131).

Cancer of the Breast and Uterus

Cancer of the breast is the most common type of cancer in women. Cancer of the breast and the reproductive system often has a direct influence on the sexuality of the individuals and couples involved.

BREAST CANCER The most important factor that determines a woman's chance of surviving breast cancer is early detection. A *mammography* involves taking an X ray of the breast to look for growths that may be cancerous. Many physicians recommend that women between the ages of 35 and 39 get a mammogram as a baseline for future comparisons. Women ages 40 to 49 with no other signs of breast cancer should have a mammogram every 1 or 2 years; women ages 50 and above should have one each year (American Cancer Society, 1997).

The American Cancer Society also recommends that all women should conduct monthly breast self-examination (BSE) in order to detect any early signs of cancer (see Figure 9.2).

Treatment for breast cancer may involve *lumpectomy* (removal of the tumor) and removal of the lymph nodes under the arm, radiation therapy, chemotherapy, and hormone therapy; or *mastectomy* (surgical removal of the breast) and removal of the lymph nodes under the arm. The most difficult aspects of such surgery are the effects on the woman's self-esteem and body image and the relationship with her partner. In regard to her concern that her partner will be put off by her breastless body, Kaplan (1992) observed:

> Happily, such concerns are largely unfounded. The great majority of husbands and lovers, provided of course that they were attracted to their partners prior to surgery, and that she continues to be sexually responsive, do not lose sexual interest nor do they develop potency problems. In most cases, men 'tune out' their partner's missing breast(s), and focus instead on the pleasurable erotic stimulation of love making. However, some women develop a pattern of sexual avoidance because they anticipate rejection, and this can become destructive to themselves and to their relationships. (p. 5)

Chinese women in Hong Kong subscribing to Taoism who have been told that they have cancer believe that they should reduce or stop having sex to facilitate recovery. They believe that ill health is an

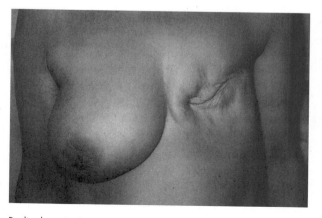

Radical mastectomy

Looking

Stand in front of a mirror with your upper body unclothed. Look for changes in the shape and size of the breast, and for dimpling of the skin or "pulling in" of the nipples. Any changes in the breast may be more noticeable by a change in position of the body or arms. Look for any changes in shape from one breast to the other.

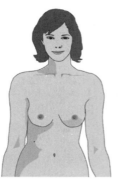 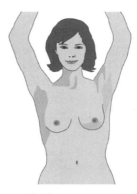 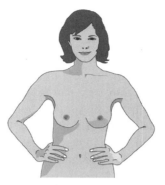

1. Stand with your arms down.

2. Raise your arms overhead.

3. Place your hands on your hips and tighten your chest and arm muscles by pressing firmly.

Feeling

 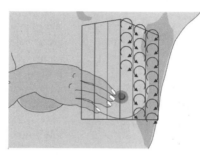 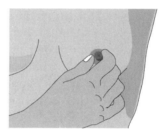

1. Lie flat on your back. Place a pillow or towel under one shoulder, and raise that arm over your head. With the opposite hand, you'll feel with the pads, not the fingertips, of the three middle fingers, for lumps or any change in the texture of the breast or skin.

2. The area you'll examine is from your collarbone to your bra line and from your breastbone to the center of your armpit. Imagine the area divided into vertical strips. Using small circular motions (the size of a dime), move your fingers up and down the strips. Apply light, medium, and deep pressure to examine each spot. Repeat this same process for your other breast.

3. Gently squeeze the nipple of each breast between your thumb and index finger. Any discharge, clear or bloody, should be reported to your doctor immediately.

FIGURE 9.2 Breast Self-Exam. The best time to examine your breasts is after your menstrual period every month.

---

imbalance of the Yang (male) and Yin (female) sources of creative power and that reducing sex will restore the Yin element (Tang, Siu, Lai, & Chung, 1996).

UTERINE CANCER   There are two types of uterine cancer—cancer of the cervix and cancer of the endometrium (lining of the uterus). Cervical cancer is the second most common type of cancer in women. Although vaginal discharge, pain, and bleeding are the typical symptoms, the cancerous cells can be present for 5 to 10 years before being detected. Factors associated with increased risk for developing cervical cancer include young age at time of initial sexual intercourse, having multiple sexual partners, cigarette smoking, and low socioeconomic status (American Cancer Society, 1997). Some types of human papilloma virus, a sexually transmitted virus that causes genital warts (see Chapter 15), have also been associated with cervical cancer (Katchadourian, 1990, p. 109).

Endometrial cancer is less common than cervical cancer. It primarily affects women over the age of 50. Risk factors include history of infertility, failure to ovulate, prolonged estrogen therapy, and obesity (American Cancer Society, 1997).

About 10% of all hysterectomies are performed as treatment for cervical or endometrial cancer (Travis, 1988, p. 171). The best detection method for cervical cancer is the Pap smear test. All women who are or have been sexually active, or have reached the age of 18 should have an annual Pap test and pelvic examination (American Cancer Society, 1997). (See Figure 9.3). The Pap test is only partially effective in detecting endometrial cancer; women at high risk should have an endometrial tissue sample evaluated at menopause. An annual pelvic exam is also useful in early detection of endometrial cancer.

Prostate Cancer

Next to skin cancer, prostate cancer is the most common cancer in men. The chance of getting prostate cancer increases with age; the typical prostatic cancer patient is 65 or older. Symptoms include difficulty with urination, frequent urination, painful urination, and blood in the urine. These symptoms are due to the growth of a tumor that disrupts the normal functioning of the surrounding structures. Some older men may also experience a nonmalignant enlargement of the prostate. This should be treated if it interferes with urination.

Over half of prostate cancers are found during routine digital examinations, before the man has any symptoms (Sackett, 1990). Men over age 40 should have a digital rectal exam yearly. The effects of prostate cancer on sexual functioning are influenced more by the particular treatment regimen than by the disease itself (Sackett, 1990). Treatment options include a *radical prostatectomy* (removal of the prostate), radiation therapy, chemotherapy, hormonal therapy, and orchiectomy (removal of one or both testes). Removal of the testes is a way to reduce testosterone to control tumor growth. These treatments may lead to erectile dysfunction, low sexual

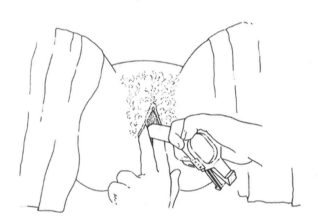

Speculum Examination

Preparation
Usually with the aid of the nurse, your body is draped with a sheet and your feet are placed in stirrups. After routinely examining the breasts, abdomen and groin, your physician inspects the outer genitals. Because good light is important, a lamp may be used during this inspection. Generally, the examiners will place an arm or elbow on your leg or thigh before touching the outer genitals. This is to avoid startling you—in which case your genital muscles might involuntarily contract and interfere with the examination.

Inserting the Speculum
A speculum is an instrument which enlarges the vaginal opening and spreads the vaginal walls so that your physician can "see what is going on" inside the vagina. Your doctor will carefully insert the speculum into the vaginal entrance with one hand, while using the other hand to gently spread the labia. The type or size of the speculum depends on whether the patient is a virgin, has had children, or is postmenopausal. To avoid discomfort, the speculum is inserted slowly and at an angle. But if you feel any distress—which is extremely rare—your doctor may adjust the speculum to make you feel more comfortable.

Continued on following page.

FIGURE 9.3 Pelvic Examination and Pap Test **Source:** Wyeth-Ayerst Laboratories, Philadelphia, PA.

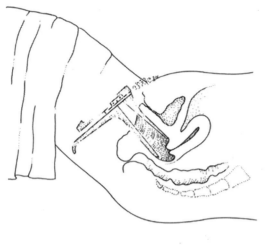

Inspecting the Cervix

As it is gradually rotated, the speculum can be opened to expose the cervix—the "neck" of the lower uterus that connects it with the vagina. Again, this is done with very little discomfort to the patient. By manipulating the speculum, the doctor obtains a clear view of the cervix and can examine it for cysts, tears or other abnormalities.

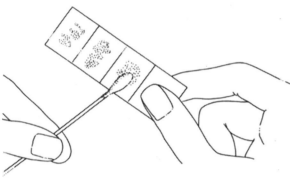

The Pap Smear

Named for its developer, Dr. George N. Papanicolau, the Pap test is a simple procedure which detects precancerous cells. In other words, the Pap test can warn of cancer even before clinical signs of disease are apparent.

You've probably been instructed not to use douches, vaginal creams, or medications for at least 48 hours prior to your pelvic exam. This is important because these substances can distort the appearance of the cells to be studied in the Pap smear.

While the cervix is still exposed by the speculum, cells are taken from the cervix and vagina with a scraper or cotton-tipped applicator. The cells are then smeared on a glass slide and sent to a laboratory for analysis.

With the speculum still in place, your physician may also take appropriate smears to determine the presence or absence of vaginal infection.

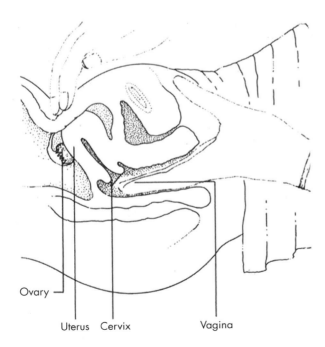

Ovary

Uterus Cervix   Vagina

Digital Examination

After gradually withdrawing the speculum, the examiner will perform the digital examination. This is just what it sounds like: an examination with the fingers or "digits." It is also a "bimanual" examination because both hands are used—one internally and one externally on the abdomen.

Wearing a glove, your physician inserts the index or middle finger of one hand into the vagina. In this way, the cervix can be palpated or "felt" for consistency, shape and position. The cervix may be moved from side to side to determine if it is tender to the touch. The upper vagina is also explored for masses, tenderness, or distortion.

During the digital exam, your physician will also examine the uterus and ovaries. While the finger (or fingers) within the vagina elevate the cervix and uterus, the other hand is gently placed on the abdomen. By "grasping" the upper portion of the uterus between the vaginal fingers and the abdominal hand, the examiner can determine its size, its mobility and the presence or absence of tenderness. The ovaries also can often be located and felt.

Figure 9.3 (Continued)

desire, retrograde ejaculation, lack of orgasm, dry orgasm, and infertility (Murphy, Morris, & Lange, 1997).

Testicular Cancer

Cancer of the testes is rare, accounting for only about 1% of all cancers in men of all ages. However, testicular cancer is the most common cancer in young men between the ages of 15 and 35, and the second most common cancer in men aged 35 to 39 (Murphy, Morris, & Lange, 1997). An increased risk of testicular cancer is found among African American men, men with cryptorchidism (undescended testes), men with a history of hernia, men with extra nipples, and men with history of infertility problems (Murphy, Morris, & Lange, 1997).

Testicular cancer usually affects one testis; about 2 to 3% of testicular cancer affects both testes either at the same time or successively. The most common symptoms of testicular cancer are a lump or nodule on a testicle or swelling of the testicles. The cure rate for testicular cancer is high, exceeding 90% in all stages. As with other cancers, testicular cancer cure rates are higher when the cancer is detected at an early stage. The American Cancer Society recommends that all men perform a monthly testicular self-examination (see Figure 9.4) in addition to having a physician conduct a testicular examination during regular checkups.

Treatment for testicular cancer includes surgical removal of the affected testicle, removal of lymph nodes, radiation therapy, and chemotherapy. After undergoing surgical removal of a testicle, men may seek surgical implantation of a testicular prosthesis—a silicone gel-filled sac that looks and feels like a testicle. When only one testicle is removed, the remaining testicle provides normal levels of testosterone. However, if both testicles are removed, the loss of testosterone production can greatly reduce a man's sexual desire and ability to achieve and maintain erections. Removal of both testicles also leads to infertility and may result in the inability to have an orgasm or to have a dry orgasm or weaker orgasm.

THINK ABOUT IT

What are the various reasons why you might put off being tested for breast or prostate cancer? What fears perpetuate avoidance of such diagnostic procedures?

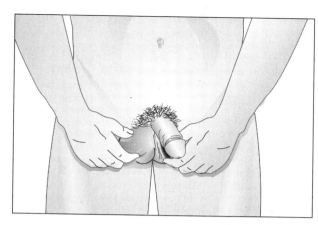

FIGURE 9.4 Method for Testicular Self-Examination, as Recommended by the American Cancer Society. Perform the exam when the scrotum is relaxed, as it is after a warm bath or shower. Simply roll each testicle between the thumb and forefinger, feeling for any lumps or thickening. By performing the exam regularly, you can detect changes early on and discuss them with your physician. As with breast lumps, most such changes are *not* cancer, but only a doctor can make the diagnosis. **Source:** Starr, 1997.

OTHER DISEASES AND SEXUALITY

Aside from cancer, numerous other diseases affect an individual's sexuality. Next, we look briefly at arthritis, cardiovascular disease, diabetes, chronic obstructive pulmonary disease, and endometriosis, and we discuss the effects these diseases have on sexuality.

Arthritis

Arthritis is the painful swelling of joints that results in muscle weakness, limited mobility, and, in some cases, deformity. Arthritis usually begins in mid-life and affects more women than men (four to one).

NATIONAL DATA

More than 33 million Americans suffer from arthritis.

Source: *Statistical Abstract of the United States: 1996*, Table 219.

The joints most often affected by arthritis include the wrist, elbow, shoulder, hip, knee, and ankle. Pain is the predominant symptom, but feeling stiff, fatigued, and weak are common. Individuals also report feeling depressed by the constant pain and embarrassed or shameful because of their altered body image (Palmeri & Wise, 1988). Some men with arthritis complain of erectile dysfunction (Blake, Maisiak, Koplan, Alarcon, & Brown, 1988). Both sexes report that the arthritis affects their sexual mobility, which may inhibit orgasmic enjoyment (Palmeri & Wise, 1988).

Cardiovascular Disease

The various forms of cardiovascular conditions affecting sexuality include hypertension, coronary artery disease, myocardial infarction, and coronary artery bypass surgery.

NATIONAL DATA

Over 22 million Americans have a heart condition, and 28 million have high blood pressure.

Source: *Statistical Abstract of the United States: 1996,* Table 219.

Hypertension (commonly known as high blood pressure) has been associated with less penile rigidity (Hirschkowitz, Karacan, Gurakar, & Williams, 1989). Many medications used to treat hypertension have been linked to erectile dysfunction and decreased sexual desire (Burke, 1990).

Follow-up studies of male heart attack victims demonstrate that about 10% report erectile problems and about two-thirds report a decreased frequency of intercourse. Female heart attack victims also report a decreased frequency of intercourse following a myocardial infarction (MI) (Burke, 1990).

The reduction in frequency of intercourse is most often a function of fear that sexual activity will precipitate another heart attack, initiate angina (tightness in chest, neck, or arm), or cause death. These fears are "based on misconceptions and lack of information regarding the cardiovascular demands of sexual activity" (Burke, 1990, p. 360). While intercourse and orgasm does increase the respiratory rate (from 16 to 60 per minute), the heart rate (from 65 to 170 beats per minute), and blood pressure (120/80 to 220/110), these changes are not sufficient to induce a heart attack. In general, Burke concluded that for middle-aged married men with chronic heart disease, having sexual intercourse with their regular partner involves minimal cardiac risk.

Diabetes

Many diseases of the endocrine system affect sexual functioning, but the most common is diabetes mellitus. *Diabetes mellitus* is a chronic disease in which the pancreas fails to produce sufficient insulin, which is necessary for metabolizing carbohydrates. The symptoms of diabetes include excess sugar in the blood and urine; excessive thirst, hunger, and urination; and weakness. These symptoms may be controlled through injections of insulin.

NATIONAL DATA

Nearly 8 million Americans have diabetes.

Source: *Statistical Abstract of the United States: 1996,* Table 219.

Much more is known about the effects of diabetes on male sexual functioning than on female sexual functioning. Diabetic men may notice a progressive softening of the penis eventually leading to the inability to perform vaginal penetration. Erectile dysfunction may be caused by physiological or psychosocial factors. Physiologically, there is damage to the autonomic nerves that is irreversible, even with the restoration of "normal" blood sugars via insulin. Psychosocial factors include anxiety and depression resulting from the perceived disability and difficulty in functioning. But erectile dysfunction is not inevitable. Using data from 23 prevalence studies published since 1958, it is estimated that between 26 to 35% of diabetic men will develop an erectile disorder. This finding counters the conventional view that an erectile disorder is inevitable for men diagnosed with diabetes (Weinhardt & Carey, 1996).

Research on the effects of diabetes on women is inconclusive. Slob, Radder, and Van Der Werff Ten Bosch (1990) compared diabetic and nondiabetic women and found no differences in sexual desire, arousal, or problems. Diabetic women do complain of vaginitis and vaginal dryness. The former is remedied by controlling blood sugar and taking measures to prevent yeast infections; the latter by using water-soluble lubricants and allowing more time for vaginal lubrication to occur.

Chronic Obstructive Pulmonary Disease

Chronic obstructive pulmonary disease (COPD) is a collective term for diseases that affect the flow of air into the body. The three most common subtypes of COPD are asthma, bronchitis, and emphysema. Persons with COPD may experience fatigue, decreased sexual desire, difficulty in achieving and maintaining erection, and a general decrease in sexual activity (Stockdale-Woolley, 1990).

NATIONAL DATA

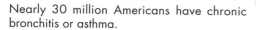

Nearly 30 million Americans have chronic bronchitis or asthma.

Source: *Statistical Abstract of the United States: 1996,* Table 219.

The effects of COPD on sexuality are due to a combination of physical, psychological, and social variables. Physically, COPD patients report feeling easily fatigued and irritated by the frequent wheezing and coughing. Psychologically, they often fear that sexual activity will further deplete their energy reserves and will create a new round of coughing.

Socially, COPD patients may experience other changes: "Shortness of breath and limited energy reserves force activity restriction, decreased socialization and recreation, and early retirement or disability" (Stockdale-Woolley, 1990, p. 373). In a study of COPD in women, Sexton and Munro (1988) noted that primary complaints included shortness of breath, fatigue, loneliness, depression, and restricted activity. Men were primarily affected by the loss of their wage earner role and the necessity to assume a more dependent role. These changes in social roles may decrease self-esteem and sexual desire.

Endometriosis

Endometrial tissue lines the uterus. *Endometriosis* is the presence of this tissue in locations other than the uterus, such as the ovaries or pelvis. Pain is the primary symptom, which results from this misplaced uterine tissue expanding and contracting during the menstrual cycle. Other symptoms include inflammation, scarring, adhesions, and cysts. Infertility often results from endometriosis because of damage to the ovaries and fallopian tubes.

Endometriosis most often occurs during the childbearing years. It is confirmed by surgical removal of suspected tissue, which is examined under the microscope. Treatment involves surgical removal of the tissue and hormonal therapy. Side effects of hormonal treatment of endometriosis include weight gain or loss, nausea, vomiting, headache, and irregular periods (Parker & Rosenfeld, 1997). A decrease in sexual desire is another side effect (Bernhard, 1990).

THINK ABOUT IT

Suppose you were concerned about how a physical condition or treatment was affecting your sexual functioning. Would you discuss your concern with your health care practitioner? Why or why not?

KEY TERMS

arthritis 243
cerebral palsy 235
chronic obstructive
    pulmonary
    disease 245
diabetes mellitus 244
endometriosis 245
intellectual disability 236

lumpectomy 239
mammography 239
mastectomy 239
multiple sclerosis 235
radical
    prostatectomy 241
stroke 235

SUMMARY POINTS

In this chapter, we have emphasized the connection between the body and mind and sexuality. The effects may become profound when there is a physical or psychological disturbance.

Myths About Disease, Disability, and Sexuality

Asexuality is assumed to be normative among individuals who are sick and disabled. Such asexuality is particularly assumed among individuals who are visibly afflicted, such as those with spinal cord injuries, those with cerebral palsy, or those who are bedridden. The reality is that sexual interest, capacity, and activity may remain high in spite of the visible disability.

Psychobiological and Psychosocial Effects of Disease and Disability

Pain, fatigue, and depression may cause a decrease in libido and sexual activity. Such issues may not be easy to manage, since some illnesses and disabilities involve chronic pain and fatigue. Being depressed in the face of such circumstances is not unusual.

Alterations in self-concept, body image, and social roles also accompany acute changes in one's health and ability to be mobile. In some cases, one may develop a renewed sense of accomplishment as a result of adapting positively to a sickness or disability.

Drugs and Sexuality

Prescription drugs and recreational drugs may affect sexual desire, arousal, and orgasm. Drug use may interfere with sexual response and lead to nonadherence to prescribed treatments, so increased communication between the patient and health provider is important. Recreational drugs may affect sexual response, partly based on a person's expectation of their effects.

Neurological Disabilities and Sexuality

Spinal cord injury, stroke, multiple sclerosis, and traumatic brain injury emphasize the importance of the brain and central nervous system in sexual response. Successful adjustment is difficult and most often involves reframing one's disability as a challenge, and discovering alternative ways of deriving emotional and sexual satisfaction.

Intellectual and Psychological Disturbances and Sexuality

Public debate abounds over the sexual rights of individuals who are intellectually challenged. Questions about the capacity to give consent make institutional decisions difficult when considering the conditions under which the intellectually challenged should be allowed to masturbate and have consensual sex. Individuals who are intellectually disabled may be especially vulnerable to sexual abuse. Psychological disturbances may affect sexual functioning, and traumatic sexual history may be a precipitator of some types of psychological disturbances.

Cancer and Sexuality

Cancer not only increases vulnerability to depression ("Am I going to die?"), but it also alters one's self-concept. Breast surgery in women sometimes results in an altered sexual self-concept ("Am I desirable with one breast?"). Men may also question their virility after prostate surgery.

Other Diseases and Sexuality

Arthritis, cardiovascular disease, diabetes, chronic obstructive pulmonary disease, and endometriosis all have different effects on one's sexual self-concept and sexual capacity. Regardless of the physical changes, one may elect to view his or her disease or illness in positive, life-enhancing ways. The perception of the illness, rather than the illness itself, will ultimately affect one's adjustment.

REFERENCES

Abel, E. L. (1985). *Psychoactive drugs and sex.* New York: Plenum Press.

Abused child, multiple personality tied. (1982, September). *Clinical Psychiatry News,* p. 2.

Aloni, R., Schwartz, J., & Ring, H. (1997). Sexual function in post-stroke female patients. *Sexuality and Disability, 15,* 11.

American Cancer Society. (1997). *Cancer facts and figures—1997.* Atlanta, GA: Author.

Ames, T. R. H. (1991). Guidelines for providing sexuality-related services to severely and profoundly retarded individuals: The challenge for the 1990s. *Sexuality and Disability, 9,* 113–122.

Bancroft, J. (1989). *Human sexuality and its problems* (2nd Ed.). Edinburgh: Churchill Livingstone.

Barnes, T. R. E., & Harvey, C. A. (1993). Psychiatric drugs and sexuality. In A. J. Riley, M. Peet, & C. Wilson (Eds.), *Sexual pharmacology* (pp. 176–196). Oxford: Clarendon Press.

Bernhard, L. (1990). Gynecological conditions and sexuality. In C. I. Fogel & D. Lauver (Eds.), *Sexual health promotion* (pp. 436–458). Philadelphia: W. B. Saunders.

Bezkor, M. F., & Canedo, A. (1987a). Physiological and psychological factors influencing sexual dysfunction in multiple sclerosis: Part I. *Sexuality and Disability, 8,* 143–146.

Bezkor, M. F., & Canedo, A. (1987b). Physiological and psychological factors influencing sexual dysfunction in multiple sclerosis: Part II, Emotionality and sexuality in persons with multiple sclerosis. *Sexuality and Disability, 8,* 147–151.

Blake, D. J., Maisiak, R., Koplan, A., Alarcon, G. S., & Brown, S. (1988). Sexual dysfunction among patients with arthritis. *Clinical Rheumatology, 7,* 5–60.

Booth, A., & Johnson, D. R. (1994). Declining health and marital quality. *Journal of Marriage and the Family, 56,* 218–223.

Brockway, J. (1994). Sexuality and physical disability. In R. M. Hays, G. H. Kraft, & W. C. Stolov (Eds.), *Chronic disease and disability* (pp. 105–114). New York: Demos.

Burke, L. E. (1990). Cardiovascular disturbances and sexuality. In C. I. Fogel & D. Lauver (Eds.), *Sexual health promotion* (pp. 360–374). Philadelphia: W. B. Saunders.

Burnam, M.A., Stein, J. A., Golding, J. M., Siegel, J. M., Sorenson, S. B., Forsythe, A. B., & Telles, C. A. (1988). Sexual assault and mental disorders in a community population. *Journal of Consulting and Clinical Psychology, 56,* 843–850.

Butt, D. S. (1990). The sexual response as exercise: A brief review and theoretical proposal. *Sports Medicine, 9,* 330–343.

Carmen, E. H., Rieker, P. P., & Mills, T. (1984). Victims of violence and psychiatric illness. *American Journal of Psychiatry, 141,* 378-383.

Cole, S., & Cole, T. M. (1983). Disability and intimacy: The importance of sexual health. In G. Albee, S. Gordon, & H. Leitenberg (Eds.), *Promoting sexual responsibility and preventing sexual problems* (pp. 297-305). Hanover, England: University Press.

Connolly, F. H., & Gittelson, N. L. (1971). The relationship between delusions of sexual change and olfactory and gustatory hallucinations in schizophrenia. *British Journal of Psychiatry, 119,* 443-444.

Creech, R. (1992). *Reflections from a unicorn.* Greenville, NC: RC Publishing.

Crowe, L. C., & George, W. H. (1989). Alcohol and human sexuality: Review and integration. *Psychological Bulletin, 102,* 374-386.

Cutler, S. E., & Nolen-Hoeksema, S. (1991). Accounting for sex differences in depression through female victimization: Childhood sexual abuse. *Sex Roles, 24,* 425-438.

DeLeo, D., & Magni, G. (1983). Sexual side effects of antidepressant drugs. *Psychosomatics, 24,* 1076-1082.

DeLeon, G., & Wexler, H. K. (1973). Heroin addiction: Its relation to sexual behavior and sexual experience. *Journal of Abnormal Psychology 81,* 36-38.

Donnelly, J. (1997). Sexual satisfaction for a woman with severe cerebral palsy. *Sexuality and Disability 15,* 16.

Donohue, J., & Gebhard, P. (1995). The Kinsey Institute/ Indiana University report on sexuality and spinal cord injury. *Sexuality and Disability 13,* 7-85.

Finger, W. W., Lund, M., & Slagle, M. A. (1997). Medications that may contribute to sexual disorders: A guide to assessment and treatment in family practice. *Journal of Family Practice, 44,* 33-43.

Gitter, A. (1994). Stroke syndromes. In R. M. Hays, G. H. Kraft, & W. C. Stolov (Eds.), *Chronic disease and disability* (pp. 117-129). New York: Demos.

Gill, C. J. (1996a). Becoming visible: Personal health experiences of women with disabilities. In D. M. Krotoski, M. A. Nosek, & M. A. Turk (Eds.), *Women with physical disabilities* (pp. 5-15). Baltimore: Paul H. Brooks.

Gill, C. J. (1996b). Dating and relationship issues. In D. M. Krotoski, M. A. Nosek, & M. A. Turk (Eds.), *Women with physical disabilities* (pp. 117-124). Baltimore: Paul H. Brooks.

Golden, J. A., & Heckrotte, M. L. (1995). Sexual abuse of disabled persons: A case history. *The Journal: North Carolina Crime Prevention,* 6-7.

Halikas, J., Weller, R., & Morse, C. (1982). Effects of marijuana use on sexual performance. *Journal of Psychoactive Drugs, 14,* 1-2.

Hatzichristou, D. G. (1996). Preface to the special issue: Management of voiding, bowel, and sexual dysfunction of multiple sclerosis: Towards a holistic approach. *Sexuality and Disability, 14,* 3-6.

Hays, R. M., Kraft, G. H., & Stolov, W. C. (1994). Preface. In R. M. Hays, G. H. Kraft, & W. C. Stolov (Eds.), *Chronic disease and disability* (p. v). New York: Demos.

Hirshkowitz, M., Karacan, I., Gurakar, A., & Williams, R. L. (1989). Hypertension, erectile dysfunction, and occult sleep apnea. *Sleep, 12,* 223-232.

Hulnick, M. R., & Hulnick, H. R. (1989). Life's challenges: Curse or opportunity? Counseling families of persons with disabilities. *Journal of Counseling and Development, 68,* 16-176.

Huws, R. (1993). Antihypertensive medication and sexual problems. In A. J. Riley, M. Peet, & C. Wilson (Eds.), *Sexual pharmacology* (pp. 146-158). Oxford: Clarendon Press.

Huws, R., & Sampson, G. (1993). Recreational drugs and sexuality. In A. J. Riley, M. Peet, & C. Wilson (Eds.), *Sexual pharmacology* (pp. 197-210). Oxford: Clarendon Press.

Kaplan, H. S.. (1992). A neglected issue: The sexual side effects of current treatments for breast cancer. *Journal of Sex and Marital Therapy, 18,* 3-19.

Kaplan, L. (1996). Sexual and institutional issues when one spouse resides in the community and the other lives in a nursing home. *Sexuality and Disability, 14,* 281-293.

Katchadourian, H. A. (1990). *The biological aspects of human sexuality* (4th Ed.). Fort Worth, TX: Holt, Rinehart & Winston.

Lieberman, M. L. (1988). *The sexual pharmacy.* New York: New American Library.

Litz, B. T., Zeiss, A. M., & Davies, H. D. (1990). Sexual concerns of male spouses of female Alzheimer's disease patients. *Gerontologist, 30,* 113-116.

Lockette, K. F., & Keyes, A. M. (1994). *Conditioning with physical disabilities.* Champaign, IL: Human Kinetics.

Lonsdale, S. (1990). *Women and disability: The experience of physical disability among women.* New York: St. Martin's Press.

LoPiccolo, J. (1983). The prevention of sexual problems in men. In G. W. Albee, S. Gordon, & H. Leitenberg (Eds.), *Promoting sexual responsibility and preventing sexual problems* (pp. 39-65). Hanover, NH: University Press of New England.

Lundberg, P. O., and Hulter, B. (1996). Female sexual dysfunction in multiple sclerosis: A review. *Sexuality and Disability, 14,* 65-72.

Lustman, P. J., & Clouse, R. E. (1990). Relationship of psychiatric illness to impotence in men with diabetes. *Diabetes Care, 13,* 893-895.

Mathew, R. J., & Weinman, M. L. (1982). Sexual dysfunction in depression. *Archives of Sexual Behavior, 11,* 323-328.

McCabe, M. P., McDonald, E., Deeks, A. A., Vowels, L. M., & Cobain, M. J. (1996). The impact of multiple sclerosis on sexuality and relationships. *The Journal of Sex Research, 33,* 241-248.

Miller, J. F. (1983). *Coping with chronic illness: Overcoming powerlessness.* Philadelphia: F. A. Davis.

Munsat, E. M. (1990). Mental illness, substance abuse and sexuality. In C. I. Fogel & D. Lauver (Eds.), *Sexual health promotion* (pp. 578-604). Philadelphia: W. B. Saunders.

Murphy, G. P., Morris, L. B., & Lange, D. (1997). *Informed decisions: The complete book of cancer diagnosis, treatment, and recovery*. New York: Penguin Books.

Murray, J. B. (1993). Relationship of childhood sexual abuse to borderline personality disorder, posttraumatic stress disorder, and multiple personality disorder. *The Journal of Psychology, 126,* 657-676.

Nankervis, A. (1989). Sexual function in chronic disease. *Medical Journal of Australia, 151,* 548-549.

National Academy of Sciences, Institute of Medicine. (1982). *Marijuana and health.* Washington, DC: National Academy Press.

Nosek, M. A. (1996). Wellness among women with physical disabilities. *Sexuality and Disability, 14,* 165-181.

Opsomer, R. J. (1996). Management of male sexual dysfunction in multiple sclerosis. *Sexuality and Disability, 14,* 57-63.

O'Toole, J. (1996). Disabled lesbians: Challenging monocultural constructs. *Sexuality and Disability, 14,* 221-236.

Palmeri, B. A., & Wise, T. N. (1988). Sexual dysfunction in the medically ill. In R. A. Brown & J. R. Field (Eds.), *Treatment of sexual problems in individual and couple therapy* (pp. 81-98). Baltimore: PMA.

Parker, P., & Rosenfeld, J. (1997). Dyspareunia and pelvic pain. In J. Rosenfeld (Ed.), *Women's health in primary care* (pp. 503-514). Baltimore: Williams & Wilkins.

Rogers, A. (1990). Drugs and disturbed sexual functioning. In C. I. Fogel & D. Lauver (Eds.), *Sexual health promotion* (pp. 485-497). Philadelphia: W. B. Saunders.

Rolland, J. S. (1994). In sickness and in health: The impact of illness on couples' relationships. *Journal of Marital and Family Therapy, 20,* 327-347.

Rosen, R. C., & Beck, J. G. (1988). *Patterns of sexual arousal: Psychophysiological processes and clinical applications.* New York: Guilford Press.

Rosen, R. C., & Leiblum, S. R. (1987). Current approaches to the evaluation of sexual desire disorders. *Journal of Sex Research, 23,* 141-162.

Rounds, K. A., Weil, M., & Bishop, K. K. (1994). Practice with culturally diverse families of young children with disabilities. *Families in Society, 75,* 3-15.

Sackett, C. (1990). Genitourinary conditions and sexuality. In C. I. Fogel & D. R. Lauver (Eds.), *Sexual health promotion* (pp. 407-435). Philadelphia: W. B. Saunders.

Schiavi, R. C. (1990). Chronic alcoholism and male sexual dysfunction. *Journal of Sex and Marital Therapy, 16,* 23-33.

Schover, L. R., & Jensen, S. B. (1988). *Sexuality and chronic illness: A comprehensive approach.* New York: Guilford Press.

Schreiner-Engel, P., & Schiavi, R. C. (1986). Lifetime psychopathology in individuals with low sexual desire. *Journal of Nervous and Mental Diseases, 174,* 646-651.

Scotti, J. R., Slack, B. S., Bowman, R. A., & Morris, T. L. (1996). College student attitudes concerning the sexuality of persons with mental retardation: Development of the Perceptions of Sexuality Scale. *Sexuality and Disability, 14,* 249-263.

Sexton, D. L., & Munro, B. H. (1988). Living with a chronic illness: The experience of women with chronic obstructive pulmonary disease. *Western Journal of Nursing Research, 10,* 26-44.

Slob, A. K., Radder, J. K., & Van Der Werff Ten Bosch, J. J. (1990). Sexuality and psychophysiological functioning in women with diabetes mellitus. *Journal of Sex and Marital Therapy, 16,* 59-69.

Smith, P. J., & Talbert, R. L. (1986). Sexual dysfunction with antihypertensive and antipsychotic agents. *Clinical Pharmacology, 5,* 373-384.

Statistical Abstract of the United States: 1996 (116th ed.) (1996). Washington, DC: U.S. Bureau of the Census.

Statistical Abstract of the United States: 1997 (117th ed.). (1997). Washington, DC: U.S. Bureau of the Census.

Stockdale-Woolley, R. (1990). Respiratory disturbances and sexuality. In C. I. Fogel & D. R. Lauver (Eds.), *Sexual health promotion* (pp. 372-383). Philadelphia: W. B. Saunders.

Tang, C. S., Siu, B. N., Lai, F. D., & Chung, T. K. H. (1996). Heterosexual chinese women's sexual adjustment after gynecologic cancer. *The Journal of Sex Research, 33,* 189-195.

Thomas, D. J. (1982). *The experience of handicap.* New York: Methuen.

Travis, C. B. (1988). *Women and heath psychology: Biomedical issues.* Hillsdale, NJ: Erlbaum.

Wallerstein, J. S., & Blakeslee, S. (1995). *The good marriage.* Boston: Houghton Mifflin.

Weinhardt, L. S., & Carey, M. P. (1996). Prevalence of erectile disorder among men with diabetes mellitus: Comprehensive review, methodological critique, and suggestions for future research. *The Journal of Sex Research, 33,* 205-214.

Whipple, B., Cerdes, C. A., & Komisaruk, B. R. (1996). Sexual response to self-stimulation in women with complete spinal cord injury. *The Journal of Sex Research, 33,* 231-240.

White, J. R., McWhirter, D., & Mattison, A. M. (1990). Enhanced sexual behavior in exercising men. *Archives of Sexual Behavior, 19,* 193-209.

Williamson, G. M., & Walters, A. S. (1996). Perceived impact of limb amputation on sexual activity: A study of adult amputees. *Journal of Sex Research, 33*(3), 221-230.

Winningham, M. L. (1994). Exercise and cancer. In L. Goldberg & D.L. Elliot (Eds.), *Exercise for prevention and treatment of illness* (pp. 301-315). Philadelphia: Davis.

Woods, S. M. (1981). Sexuality and mental disorders. In H. Lief (Ed.), *Sexual problems in medical practice* (pp. 199-210). Chicago: American Medical Association.

SEXUAL DYSFUNCTIONS AND SEX THERAPY

Chapter 10

Causes and Contributing Factors in Sexual Dysfunction

Biological Factors
Sociocultural Factors
Intrapsychic Factors
Relationship Factors
SOCIAL CHOICES: Do You Need a Physician and a Psychologist to Cure a Sexual Dysfunction?
Cognitive Factors
SELF-ASSESSMENT: How Much Do You Know About Sexuality?
PERSONAL CHOICES: Should You Have Individual or Conjoint Therapy?

QUESTION Why is it inaccurate to target one specific cause for a sexual dysfunction?

Desire- and Arousal-Phase Dysfunctions

Hypoactive Sexual Desire Disorder
Sexual Aversion Disorder
Sexual Arousal Disorder
Hyperactive Sexual Desire Disorder

QUESTION How might a "male bias" place women at a disadvantage by causing them to be labeled with hypoactive sexual desire (low sexual desire)?

Orgasm-Phase Dysfunctions

Female Orgasmic Disorder
Male Orgasmic Disorder
Premature Ejaculation

QUESTION What are the causes and treatments of female and male orgasmic disorders?

Sexual Pain Dysfunctions

Dyspareunia
Vaginismus
PERSONAL CHOICES: Should You Have Private or Group Therapy?

QUESTION How might dyspareunia (pain during intercourse) be caused by multiple factors?

Approaches Used in Sex Therapy

The Psychoanalytic Approach
Masters and Johnson's Approach
The PLISSIT Model Approach
The Cognitive Therapy Approach
Helen Kaplan's Approach
LoPiccolo's Postmodern Approach
Effectiveness of Sex Therapy
PERSONAL CHOICES: Should You Have a Male-Female Sex Therapy Team or an Individual Therapist?

QUESTION What aspects do all forms of sex therapy have in common?

> *If increased intimacy is the goal of sex therapy, interventions must be designed with this goal in mind and sex therapists need to ensure consistency between desired outcomes and treatment strategies.*
>
> Clark Christensen
> Marriage Therapist

Sex therapist Barry McCarthy (1995) observed, "When sexuality is going well, it is a positive, integral component contributing perhaps 15–20% to the relationship. However, when sexuality is problematic or dysfunctional, it becomes inordinately powerful: 50–70% of the relationship. Sexual problems drain the relationship of good feelings" (p. 37). Although McCarthy's statement may be an oversimplification of the complexity of relationships and an overstatement of the importance of sex in relationships, it emphasizes the association between sexual and relationship satisfaction. Sexual dysfunctions, the subject of this chapter, may certainly interfere with both.

A *sexual dysfunction* is an impairment or difficulty that affects sexual functioning or produces sexual pain. Sexual dysfunctions occur in both heterosexuals and homosexuals. One way to categorize sexual dysfunctions is to conceptualize the various problems that may occur across the sexual response cycle (see Table 10.1). A liability of this categorization is that it emphasizes the physical processes within the genitals more than a person's or couple's overall satisfaction. Throughout the discussion of each sexual dysfunction, it is important to keep in mind the cognitions and feelings of the individuals and their partners. From this point of view, a couple may be incapable of sexual intercourse due to one or more sexual dysfunctions, yet may still be happy with one another and their sexual relationship.

In this chapter, we will review sexual dysfunctions as they are classified in the *Diagnostic and Statistical Manual of Mental Disorders, Fourth Edition* (DSM-IV) (American Psychiatric Association, 1994). This handbook is used by clinicians and researchers from many disciplines, including physicians, psychologists, social workers, nurses, and other health and mental health professionals. Although the title of the handbook implies that mental disorders are distinct from physical disorders, there is much overlap between them, and the term "mental disorders" is used because an appropriate substitute has not been found. "A compelling literature documents that there is much 'physical' in 'mental' disorders and much 'mental' in 'physical' disorders" (American Psychiatric Association, 1994, p. xxi). This is certainly true in reference to sexual problems.

A *sexual disorder* is diagnosed when a disturbance in sexual desire or the psychophysiological components of one's sexual response cycle cause significant distress and interpersonal difficulty. The types of dysfunction—organized according to the component of the response cycle affected—are summarized in Table 10.1

Each of the dysfunctions identified in Table 10.1 may also be classified as being lifelong or acquired. A *lifelong* dysfunction (previously referred to as a primary dysfunction) is one that a person has always experienced; for example, a person may have always lacked sexual desire. An *acquired* or (secondary) dysfunction is one that a person is currently experiencing, but has not always experienced. Dysfunctions may also be *situational,* in that they occur only with one partner or in one situation, or *generalized,* in that they occur with all partners, contexts, and settings. Basic causes for the various sexual dysfunctions follow.

CAUSES AND CONTRIBUTING FACTORS IN SEXUAL DYSFUNCTIONS

There are numerous causes of sexual dysfunctions (Mulcahy, 1997).

Biological Factors

Biological factors are increasingly being considered as causes for sexual dysfunctions. Such factors include physical illness, disease, aging, or disability and its treatment (such as surgery, medication, or chemotherapy). A physical condition (such as diabetes, arthritis, pituitary tumors, or vascular disease) or treatment may directly interfere with physiological or anatomical mechanisms involved in sexual desire, arousal, or orgasm.

TABLE 10.1 Types of Sexual Dysfunctions in Women and Men

ASPECTS OF SEXUALITY AFFECTED	SEXUAL DYSFUNCTION	
	WOMEN	MEN
Sexual desire	Hypoactive sexual desire disorder Sexual aversion disorder	Hypoactive sexual desire disorder Sexual aversion disorder
Arousal	Female sexual arousal disorder	Male erectile disorder
Orgasm	Female orgasmic disorder	Male orgasmic disorder Premature ejaculation
Sexual pain	Dyspareunia Vaginismus	Dyspareunia

Another common physical cause of sexual dysfunction is fatigue. For many people, the persistent demands of career, school, children, and domestic tasks leave little physical energy for sexual activity. Fatigue may affect the sexual desire and arousal phases of the sexual response cycle in both women and men.

Although we discuss drugs and sexuality in detail in Chapter 9, here we note that alcohol, marijuana, barbiturates, and amphetamines, as well as numerous medications used to treat various diseases and illnesses, affect sexuality and may cause or contribute to sexual dysfunction. Finally, sexual dysfunction often results from a combination of biological and psychosocial factors. For example, a woman may experience a lack of sexual desire because she is chronically fatigued (biological factor) from holding a full-time job while taking care of children, a husband, and a house. Compounding her fatigue is resentment (psychosocial factor) toward her husband for not supporting her career, not sharing the housework and child care, and taking care of his mother.

Sociocultural Factors

When diagnosing a sexual dysfunction, clinicians should consider variables such as ethnicity, culture, religion, and social background (American Psychiatric Association, 1994). In addition to physical or biological factors, sociocultural factors may also cause or contribute to sexual dysfunction. These include restrictive upbringing and religious training.

For example, in some families, parents may openly express negative attitudes toward sexuality by teaching their children that "sex is dirty." Some children and adolescents are punished by their parents for engaging in masturbation or other sexual exploration. In many families, sex is never discussed with the children. Children who learn that sex is a taboo subject may come to regard sex as somehow wrong or shameful.

Some religions teach that sex is only for procreation and that sexual pleasure is evil. Such negative attitudes learned in childhood may interfere with a person's ability to experience sexual desire, arousal, and orgasm as an adult. On the island of Inis Beag (discussed in Chapter 17 on cultural diversity), women are not expected to find pleasure in sex. Indeed, women who experience orgasm are viewed as deviant (Messenger, 1971).

Another sociocultural factor that may contribute to sexual dysfunction is society's traditional gender role socialization. Women may be socialized to be sexually passive and to "please their man"; men may be taught to be sexually aggressive and to "be in control" of sexual situations.

Still another sociocultural factor contributing to sexual dysfunction is our society's emphasis on intercourse as "the" sexual act and on orgasm as necessary for satisfaction. Nongenital sexual expressions and sexual experiences that do not result in orgasm are given little recognition. The result is enormous pressure on couples to engage in "the act" and for orgasm to result.

Intrapsychic Factors

Numerous intrapsychic factors play a role in sexual dysfunction.

1. *Anxiety.* Anxiety may be aroused by thoughts and fears about sexual performance or the ability to please the partner. Other sources of anxiety may result from fear of intimacy, concern about the partner's commitment to the relationship, fear of rejection, and uncertainty about the partner's intentions, or sexual expectations.

    One specific type of anxiety related to sexual dysfunction is *performance anxiety,* which refers to excessive concern over adequate sexual performance. The woman or man becomes so anxious about having an orgasm or erection that anxiety interferes with both goals.

2. *Fear.* Impairment in the desire, arousal, or orgasm phases of sexual response may result from fear of any of the following: unwanted pregnancy or STDs, intimacy or commitment, physical pain, displeasing a partner, or losing self-control during sexual arousal or orgasm.

3. *Guilt.* Guilt—which may be related to the enjoyment of sexual activity, choice of sexual partner, or participation in "forbidden" or "sinful" sexual activity—may also interfere with sexual functioning.

4. *Depression and low self-esteem.* Sexual dysfunction may result from depression, which is known to suppress sexual drive. Related to depression is low self-esteem, which may cause an individual to feel unworthy of being loved or experiencing pleasure.

5. *Conflict concerning one's sexual orientation.* Because of the social stigma associated with being homosexual, some gay men and lesbians experience internal conflict about their sexual orientation. Some may deny their homosexuality and seek heterosexual relationships, only to find that sexual activity with other-sex individuals doesn't feel right for them. Internal conflict about being homosexual or the attempt to deny their homosexuality through seeking heterosexual relationships may interfere with sexual response in homosexual individuals.

6. *Sexual abuse.* Women who have been sexually abused report lower sexual satisfaction, inhibited desire, sexual aversion, and inhibited orgasm (Mullen, Martin, Anderson, Romans, & Herbison, 1996). Sexually abused men also report low sexual desire, difficulty in maintaining an erection, and ejaculation problems (Elliott & Briere, 1992).

Relationship Factors

Sexual dysfunction and relationship conflict seldom exist in isolation. Marriage and sex therapists always focus on the relationship between the partners before addressing a specific sexual dysfunction (such as lack of orgasm or erectile dysfunction). MacPhee, Johnson, and Van Der Veer (1995) found that marital therapy enhanced the positive outcome of women who complained of low sexual desire. In some cases, relationship problems, such as anger, lack of trust, lack of intimacy, or lack of communication, can contribute to sexual dysfunctions. In other cases, sexual dysfunctions may contribute to relationship problems.

The fact that sexual dysfunctions may have a biological *and* psychogenic basis raises questions about what the public should assume about treatment, and how they should proceed when seeking treatment. The following Social Choices section addresses the need to provide guidelines for patients and clients.

A good out-of-bed relationship between partners is associated with a good sexual relationship.

DO YOU NEED A PHYSICIAN AND A PSYCHOLOGIST TO CURE A SEXUAL DYSFUNCTION?

Although second opinions are often required for major surgery, there is no public policy that protects individuals in regard to the treatment they receive for sexual dysfunctions. Indeed, some sex therapists feel that sex therapy is becoming too "medicalized." Specifically with regard to the treatment of erectile dysfunction, "comprehensive urology and impotence centers" have emerged to offer medical solutions to psychogenic problems.

> More and more often I speak to organically intact individuals who have been offered surgical or pharmacological treatments for psychogenic sexual disturbances. Only when these men balk at the invasive nature of the recommended interventions do the physicians at these centers refer their patients to mental health professionals trained to treat such individuals. (Bass, 1994, p. 319)

To illustrate this point, Bass notes a man in his fifties (married for 25 years) who had been to a Regional Impotence Center to help alleviate his inability to create and maintain an erection. After $2500 of medical evaluations, two urologists concluded there was no organic pathology but offered to treat the erection difficulty pharmacologically with papaverine injections. Desperate, the man sought consultation with a psychologist, discovered that his erectile dysfunction was caused by performance anxiety, and began appropriate psychological treatment. By the second visit, he had engaged in intercourse three times with no erection difficulties. A 6-month follow-up visit revealed "no recurrence of the symptom" (p. 319).

In their review of new pharmacological therapies for erectile dysfunction, Foreman and Doherty (1993) cautioned that the development of more reliable diagnostic techniques will be critical to the successful use of these therapies. Pharmacological treatments will vary in their efficacy, depending on the factors causing the dysfunction. Treatments need to be tailored to the specific disorder, whether it be a result of psychological, neurological, vascular, or combined etiologies. A summary of six studies from urologic sexual dysfunction clinics that included a total of almost 2000 patients revealed that 34% were diagnosed as having psychogenic dysfunction, 42% as having organic causes, and 36% as having a mixed etiology (Foreman & Doherty, 1993).

Another consideration is that too much emphasis on anatomical functioning is misguided. Tiefer (1994) specifically commented on the erect penis being the focus in male sex therapy.

> For every dollar devoted to perfecting the phallus, let's insist that a dollar be devoted to assisting women with their complaints about partner impairments in kissing, tenderness, talk, hygiene, and general eroticism. Too many men still can't dance, write love poems, erotically massage the clitoris, or diaper the baby and let Mom get her rest. The fundamental problem is with the human sexual response cycle model of sexual relations. If we continue to work within this barren conceptualization, we will have nowhere to go but towards maximizing mechanical, compartmentalized sexual components. (Tiefer, 1994, p. 8)

Sources: Bass, B. A. (1994). In further pursuit of the perfect penis: The comprehensive urology center and the medicalization of male sexual dysfunction. *Journal of Sex and Marital Therapy, 20,* 318–320.

Foreman, M. M., & Doherty, P. C. (1993). Experimental approaches for the development of pharmacological therapies for erectile dysfunction. In A.J. Riley, M. Peet, & C. Wilson (Eds.), *Sexual pharmacology.* Oxford: Clarendon.

Tiefer, L. (1994). Might premature ejaculation be organic? The perfect penis takes a giant step forward. *Journal of Sex Education and Therapy, 20,* 7–8.

Cognitive Factors

What a person learns and believes about sex may be related to sexual difficulties. Consider the following examples:

- A woman in her fifties believes the myth that women her age should not be interested in sex.
- A man in his fifties believes the myth that men his age are unable to achieve an erection that is satisfactory for intercourse.

HOW MUCH DO YOU KNOW ABOUT SEXUALITY?

Take this true-false test to assess how much you know about sexuality.

T F 1. Sexual expression is purely natural, not a function of learning.

T F 2. Foreplay is for the woman; intercourse is for the man.

T F 3. Once a couple establishes a good sexual relationship, they don't need to set aside time for intimacy together.

T F 4. If you love each other and communicate, everything will go fine sexually.

T F 5. Sex and love are two sides of the same coin.

T F 6. Technique is more important than intimacy in achieving a satisfying sexual relationship.

T F 7. Casual sex is more exciting than intimate sex.

T F 8. If you have a good sexual relationship, you will have a fulfilling experience each time you have sex.

T F 9. After age 25 your sex drive dramatically decreases, and most people stop being sexual by 65.

T F 10. It is primarily the man's role to initiate sex.

T F 11. If one or both partners become aroused, intercourse must follow or there will be frustration.

T F 12. Men are more sexual than women.

T F 13. Having a "G" spot and multiple orgasms is a sign you are a sexually liberated woman.

T F 14. Since men don't have spontaneous erections after age 50, they are less able to have intercourse.

T F 15. When you lose sexual desire, the best remedy is to seek another partner.

T F 16. The most common female sexual problem is pain during intercourse.

T F 17. The most common male sexual problem is not having enough sex.

T F 18. Penis size is crucial for female sexual satisfaction.

T F 19. Oral/genital sex is an exciting but perverse sexual behavior.

T F 20. Simultaneous orgasms provide the most erotic pleasure.

T F 21. Married people do not masturbate.

T F 22. Using sexual fantasies during intercourse indicates dissatisfaction with your partner.

T F 23. Clitoral orgasms are superior to vaginal orgasms.

T F 24. Male-on-top is the most natural position for intercourse.

T F 25. People of today are doing much better sexually than the previous generation.

Scoring and Interpretation   Add the number of *trues* you checked. This is the number of sex myths you believe. What you took was a sex-myth test, so all the answers are false. Don't be surprised if you believed several of these myths; the average person thinks nine of these statements are true. Even among college students taking a human sexual-behavior course, the average number of myths believed is seven (McCarthy & McCarthy, 1984)! (Used by permission. Carroll & Graf Publishers.)

- A heterosexual couple believes that the only appropriate way for the woman to have an orgasm is through sexual intercourse.
- A person believes that it is wrong to have sexual fantasies during lovemaking.

These are just a few examples of beliefs or myths that may interfere with sexual desire, arousal, or orgasm. Inadequate sex education can contribute to belief in such myths and to ignorance of sexual anatomy and physiology, which may also be related to sexual difficulties. For example, a woman who does not know where her clitoris is (or that it even exists) may have difficulty experiencing orgasm. This chapter's Self-Assessment is designed to assess one's knowledge about sexuality.

THINK ABOUT IT

How do biological, sociocultural, intrapsychic, interpersonal, and cognitive factors interact in regard to the development of sexual dysfunctions?

PERSONAL CHOICES

Should You Have Individual or Conjoint Therapy?

Should a person experiencing a sexual problem seek therapy alone (individual therapy) or with his or her partner (couple or conjoint therapy)? It depends. Some people prefer to go alone. One woman said:

> If I ask him to go to therapy with me, he'll think I'm more emotionally involved than I am. And since I don't want to encourage him, I'll just work out my problems without him. (authors' files)

Other reasons a person might see a sex therapist alone are if no partner is available, if the partner won't go, or if the person feels more comfortable discussing sex in the partner's absence. In addition, individual therapy might be the best treatment approach when the roots of the sexual conflicts are unconscious, when resistance to therapy is great, and when there is a high level of mistrust in the couple relationship (Strean, 1983).

However, there are also several reasons individuals might want their partners to become involved in the therapy, including the following: to work on the problem with someone, to share the experience, to

prevent one partner from being identified as the "one with the problem," to explore relationship factors that may be contributing to the sexual problem, and to address the difficulties in dealing with the sexual problem. When 356 college students were asked to rate the acceptability and credibility of various marital therapy formats (conjoint, concurrent, group, and individual), the conjoint treatment format (when the therapist sees both partners together at the same time) was consistently rated as the most acceptable and credible. When asked to choose between the four therapy formats, significantly more research participants chose the conjoint format as the most preferred type of therapy (Wilson, Flammang, & Dehle, 1992). However, a study of 80 college women's ratings of sex therapy formats showed that including the identified patient's partner in therapy did not influence acceptability ratings (Wilson & Wilson, 1991).

In a study of sexually nonresponsive women, researchers found that sex therapy for the woman alone was as effective as treating the couple in conjoint therapy (Whitehead, Mathews, & Ramage, 1987). However, the researchers also stated that conjoint therapy was "the treatment of choice" in that it had a more positive outcome for the woman's anxiety and for her perception of her partner (p. 204).

Another treatment alternative is to combine individual therapy with conjoint therapy. For example, one or both partners may receive individual therapy and, either concurrently or subsequently, also receive conjoint therapy. If partners are anxious or uncomfortable about sharing their feelings and concerns with each other, "a one-to-one relationship with the therapist should probably be considered initially, so that each spouse can receive enough protection and understanding while communicating with the therapist to eventually develop the strength to share problems with the mate" (Strean, 1983, p. 208).

Before becoming involved in any type of sex therapy, individuals should be careful in choosing a therapist. A basic concern is training. With rare exceptions, there are no laws preventing a person from advertising that she or he is a sex therapist. Anyone can legally open an office in most communities and offer sex therapy. Academic degrees, therapy experience under supervision, and exposure to other aspects of formal training in human sexuality are not legally required to market oneself as a sex therapist. California is the only state that exercises some legal restraint on sex therapy. To be licensed in California as a physician, psychologist, social worker, or marriage, family, or child counselor, a person must have had training in human sexuality.

To help upgrade the skills of those providing sex therapy, the American Association of Sex Educators, Counselors, and Therapists (AASECT) offers a Certified Sex Therapist certificate to applicants who have a minimum of a master's degree in a clinical field (psychology, social work, nursing, marriage therapy), have conducted sex therapy under supervision for a minimum of 100 hours, and have attended a 2-day workshop on human sexuality (sponsored by AASECT) to sort out their own attitudes and values about human sexuality. AASECT guidelines indicate that the therapist should have a basic understanding of sexual and reproductive anatomy and physiology, sexual development (biological and psychological), interpersonal relationships, gender-related issues, marital and family dynamics, sociocultural factors in sexual values and behavior, medical issues affecting sexuality (including pregnancy, STDs, drugs, illness and disability, contraception, and fertility), sex research, sexual abuse, and personality theories.

The therapists certified by AASECT are expected to conduct their practice in a manner that reflects the organization's Code of Ethics for Sex Therapists. Beyond being knowledgeable about treating sexual dysfunctions, being empathic, and being trained in communication and counseling skills, the certified sex therapist is expected to refrain from engaging in sexual activity with clients.

Desire- and Arousal-Phase Dysfunctions

The DSM-IV classifies two types of desire-phase dysfunctions: hypoactive sexual desire and sexual aversion.

Hypoactive Sexual Desire Disorder

The term *hypoactive sexual desire* refers to a low interest in sexual activity and absence of sexual fantasies. Other terms used to refer to low interest in sex include "inhibited sexual desire," "low sexual desire," and "impaired sexual interest." Like other sex-

ual dysfunctions, hypoactive sexual desire may be lifelong, acquired, situational, or generalized. Some men experience high rates of desire involving paraphilic (or fetish) activity but have no interest in partner sex (McCarthy, 1994).

Assessing whether or not someone has hypoactive sexual desire is problematic. First, there are no clear criteria for determining "abnormal" levels of sexual desire. Two people can vary greatly in the degree to which they experience sexual interest or desire, and each may feel comfortable with their level of desire. Furthermore, sexual desire predictably decreases over time. It is important not to interpret normal declines in sexual interest and activity as a sexual dysfunction.

NATIONAL DATA

Results of a national survey of women and men reporting that "lack of interest in sex" was a sexual problem for at least one of the past 12 months

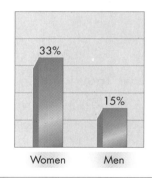

Source: Michael, Gagnon, Laumann, & Kolata, 1994, p. 126.

It is important to keep in mind that the preceding percentages may represent a male bias because a high level of "interest in sex" has become identified as the national norm and the symbol of what is normal. We might ask then, if women were not reared in a society where male norms of sexual performance and interest prevail, to what degree would women list "lack of interest" as a sexual concern?

CAUSES AND CONTRIBUTING FACTORS Lack of interest in sex may be caused by one or more factors, including restrictive upbringing, relationship dissatisfaction, nonacceptance of one's sexual orientation, learning a passive sexual role, and physical factors such as stress, illness, drugs, and fatigue. In

The stress of work and parenting may contribute to hypoactive sexual desire.

addition, abnormal hormonal states have been shown to be associated with low sexual desire. Men with low testosterone may benefit from 5-milligram Androderm testosterone patches (Meyer, 1997).

TREATMENT   Treatment for lack of interest in sex depends on the underlying causes of the problem. Some of the ways in which lack of sexual desire may be treated include the following:

1. *Improvement of relationship satisfaction.*   As noted earlier, "treating the relationship before treating the sexual problem" is standard therapy with any sexual dysfunction, including lack of interest in sex. A common prerequisite for being interested in sex with a partner—particularly from the viewpoint of a woman—is to be in love and to feel comfortable and secure with her partner. Couple therapy focusing on a loving, egalitarian relationship becomes the focus of therapy.

2. *Identification and implementation of conditions for satisfying sex.*   Bass (1985) suggested that many women who believe they have a low sexual drive have mislabeled the problem. In many cases, the "real" problem (according to Bass) is not that the woman has low sexual desire but rather that she has not identified or implemented the conditions under which she experiences satisfactory sex. Bass tells his clients who believe they have a low sex drive that "just as their desire to eat is only temporarily diminished when confronted with certain unappetizing foods, so too their sexual desire is only

temporarily inhibited through their failure to identify and implement their requirements for enjoyable sex" (1985, p. 62).

3. *Sensate focus practice.*   Sensate focus is a series of exercises developed by Masters and Johnson used to treat various sexual dysfunctions. Sensate focus may also be used by couples who are not experiencing sexual dysfunction, but who want to enhance their sexual relationship.

   In doing the *sensate focus* exercise, partners (in the privacy of their bedroom) remove their clothing and take turns touching, feeling, caressing, and exploring each other in ways intended to provide sensual pleasure. In the first phase of sensate focus, genital touching is not allowed. The person being touched should indicate whether he or she finds a particular touching behavior unpleasant, at which point the partner will stop or change what is being done.

   During the second phase of sensate focus, the person being touched is instructed to give positive as well as negative feedback (in order to indicate what is enjoyable as well as what is unpleasant). During the third phase, genital touching can be included, without the intention of producing orgasm. The goal of progressing through the three phases of sensate focus is to help the partners learn to give and receive pleasure by promoting trust and communication and reducing anxiety related to sexual performance.

4. *Openness to reeducation.*   Reeducation involves being open to examining and reevaluating the thoughts, feelings, and attitudes learned in childhood. The goal is to redefine sexual activity so that it is viewed as a positive, desirable, healthy, and pleasurable experience.

5. *Consideration of other treatments.*   Other treatments for lack of sexual desire include rest and relaxation. This is indicated when the culprit is chronic fatigue syndrome (CFS), the symptoms of which are overwhelming fatigue, low-grade fever, and sore throat. Other treatments for lack of sexual desire include hormone treatment and changing medications (if possible) in cases where medication interferes with sexual desire. In addition, sex therapists often recommend that people who are troubled by a low level of sexual desire

engage in masturbation as a means of developing positive sexual feelings. Therapists also recommend the use of sexual fantasies. Woman who do not have sexual fantasies or who report feeling guilty about having them report higher levels of sexual dissatisfaction (Cado & Leitenberg, 1990).

Sexual Aversion Disorder

Another desire-phase disorder is *sexual aversion,* also known as "sexual phobia" and "sexual panic disorder." Sexual aversion is defined as "the aversion to and active avoidance of genital sexual contact with a sexual partner" (American Psychiatric Association, 1994, p. 499). The individual reports anxiety, fear, or disgust when confronted with a sexual opportunity with a partner. Some individuals experience generalized revulsion to all sexual stimuli, including kissing and touching.

NATIONAL DATA

Results of a national survey of women and men reporting that "sex being not pleasurable" was a problem for at least one of the past 12 months

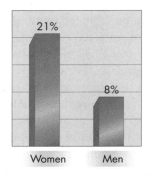

Source: Michael et al., 1994, p. 126.

CAUSES AND CONTRIBUTING FACTORS   The immediate cause of sexual aversion is an intense fear of sex. Such fear may result from negative sexual attitudes acquired in childhood or from sexual trauma, such as rape or incest. Some cases of sexual aversion may be caused by fear of intimacy, intrapsychic conflicts, or hostility toward the other sex.

TREATMENT   Treatment for sexual aversion involves providing insight into the possible ways in which the negative attitudes toward sexual activity developed, increasing the communication skills of the partners, and sensate focus. Understanding the origins of the sexual aversion may enable the individual to view

change as possible. Through communication with the partner and sensate focus exercises, the individual may learn to associate more positive feelings with sexual behavior. Cognitive restructuring, stress inoculation training, systematic desensitization, and other fear reduction tactics may be helpful.

Sexual Arousal Disorder

Even though an individual may feel desire for sexual activity, he or she may have difficulty becoming aroused. As noted in Chapter 3, physiological changes indicating arousal include vaginal lubrication, nipple erection, and genital vasocongestion. Problems of sexual arousal are characterized by failure of the physiological responses that normally occur during this phase and a lack of pleasurable sensations usually associated with sexual arousal. The two types of arousal phase disorders are female sexual arousal disorder and male erectile disorder.

FEMALE SEXUAL AROUSAL DISORDER   The American Psychiatric Association defines *female sexual arousal disorder* as a persistent or recurrent inability to attain, or maintain until completion of sexual activity, an adequate lubrication-swelling response of sexual excitement. Like other sexual dysfunctions, female sexual arousal disorder may be lifelong, acquired, situational, or generalized.

NATIONAL DATA

A national sample of women reporting trouble with lubrication for at least one of the past 12 months

Women having trouble lubricating 19%

Source: Michael et al., 1994, p. 126.

CAUSES AND CONTRIBUTING FACTORS   Factors that may cause sexual arousal difficulties are similar to the factors associated with hypoactive sexual desire. Thus, relationship dissatisfaction, restrictive upbringing, and nonacceptance of one's sexual orientation may contribute to arousal difficulties.

Female sexual arousal dysfunction may also result from estrogen deficiency; the most common cause of estrogen deficiency is menopause. Other biological factors that may be related to lack of sexual arousal in women include neurogenic disorders (such as multiple sclerosis) and some drugs (such as antihistamines and antihypertensives). Strong emotions, such as fear and anger, and stress may also interfere with the autonomic reflex that controls genital vasocongestion (Kaplan, 1974, 1983).

TREATMENT   Treatment for women who have difficulty experiencing sexual arousal is similar to treatment for hypoactive sexual desire. Treatment may involve some combination of the following: efforts to improve the relationship, sensate focus, reeducation, rest and relaxation, hormone treatment, masturbation or fantasy, and medication change. In addition, the problem may not be the woman's inability to become aroused, but her partner's not providing the kind of stimulation required for arousal to occur. Goldsmith (1988, p. 21) notes that "an insensitive partner, whose sexual arousal techniques are too rough or too fast, is thought to contribute greatly to a woman's lack of ability to become aroused." When this is the case, the woman may benefit from identifying and implementing conditions for satisfying sex (the same treatment that Bass, 1985, suggested for hypoactive sexual desire).

MALE ERECTILE DISORDER   The American Psychiatric Association defines *male erectile disorder* as a persistent or recurrent inability to attain, or to maintain until completion of sexual activity, an adequate erection. Like other sexual dysfunctions, erectile dysfunction may be lifelong, acquired, situational, or generalized. Occasional isolated episodes of the inability to attain or maintain an erection are not considered dysfunctional; these are regarded as normal occurrences.

CAUSES AND CONTRIBUTING FACTORS   One factor influencing erectile dysfunction, associated with both psychogenic and organic causes, is the man's age. This is especially true for men beyond 65 years of age, but many younger men are affected as well (Foreman & Doherty, 1993). In a survey of 212 family practice patients (mean age, 35), 27% reported problems with erectile response (Schein et al., 1988). Men between the ages of 40 and 60 are most likely to seek treatment for erectile dysfunction (Foreman & Doherty, 1993).

A national sample of men reporting trouble maintaining an erection for at least one of the past 12 months

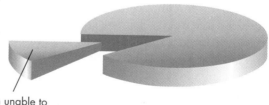

Men unable to
keep an erection
11%

Source: Michael et al., 1994, p. 126.

Up to 70% of all cases of erectile dysfunction may be caused by physiological conditions (Mulcahy, 1995). Such biological causes include blockage in the arteries, neurological disorders, heavy smoking, alcohol or drug abuse, chronic disease (kidney or liver failure), pelvic surgery, and diabetes. All physiological disabilities do not inevitably lead to erectile dysfunction. In Chapter 9, we noted that the percentage of diabetic men who experience erectile dysfunction has been overestimated. This finding counters the conventional view that erectile disorders are inevitable for men diagnosed with diabetes (Weinhardt & Carey, 1996).

Psychiatric and emotional problems, such as depression and hypoactive sexual desire, may interfere with erectile capacity. A number of men have concurrent problems with low sexual drive and erectile dysfunction. Again, the importance of a thorough assessment is apparent, as the success in treating the erectile dysfunction could depend on whether or not hypoactive sexual desire is a primary or secondary cause (Foreman & Doherty, 1993).

Psychosocial factors associated with erectile dysfunction include fear (of unwanted pregnancy, intimacy, HIV, or other STDs), guilt, and relationship dissatisfaction. For example, the man who is having an extradyadic sexual relationship may feel guilty. This guilt may lead to difficulty in achieving or maintaining an erection in sexual interaction with the primary partner or the extradyadic partner.

Anxiety may also inhibit the man's ability to create and maintain an erection. One source of anxiety is performance pressure, which may be self-imposed or imposed by a partner. In self-imposed performance anxiety, the man constantly "checks" (mentally or visually) to see that he is erect. Such self-monitoring (also referred to as spectatoring) creates anxiety, since the man fears that he may not be erect.

Partner-imposed performance pressure involves the partner's communicating that the man must get and stay erect to be regarded as a good lover. Such pressure usually increases the man's anxiety, thus ensuring no erection. Whether self- or partner-imposed, the anxiety associated with performance pressure results in a vicious cycle—anxiety, erectile difficulty, embarrassment, followed by anxiety, erectile difficulty, and so on.

Performance anxiety may also be related to alcohol use. After consuming more than a few drinks, the man may initiate sex but may become anxious after failing to achieve an erection. (Too much alcohol will interfere with erection.) Although alcohol may be responsible for his initial "failure," his erection difficulties may continue because of his anxiety.

Some men are not accustomed to satisfying their partner in any other way (such as cuddling, cunnilingus, digital stimulation) than through the use of an erect penis. Most of the women in one study (86%) who had male partners with erectile dysfunction reported that their partner never engaged in any sexual activities other than intercourse (Carroll & Bagley, 1990). However, when these women were asked, "What is your favorite part of sexual behavior?", 60% said foreplay and 3% said afterplay; only 37% said sexual intercourse was their favorite part of sexual interaction.

TREATMENT Treatment of erectile dysfunction depends on the causes of the problem. When erection difficulties are caused by psychosocial factors, treatment may include improving the relationship with the partner or removing the man's fear, guilt, or anxiety (performance pressure) about sexual activity. These goals may be accomplished through couple counseling, reeducation, and sensate focus exercises. A sex therapist would instruct the man and his partner not to engage in intercourse to remove the pressure to attain or maintain an erection. During this period, the man is encouraged to pleasure his partner in ways (such as oral or manual stimulation) that do not require him to have an erection. Once the man is relieved of the pressure to perform and learns alternative ways to satisfy his partner, his erection difficulties (if caused by psychosocial factors) often disappear.

Treatment for erectile dysfunction related to biological factors can include modification of medication, alcohol, or other drugs, or hormone treatment. Surgery to improve the blood flow in the penis is also an effective treatment for some men with erectile difficulty.

Another option for treating biologically caused erectile dysfunction is a penile prosthesis (or penile implant). These may be inflatable or permanent semi-rigid rods. In a study of 27 men (who had had an implant) and their partners, the majority of the men (72%) and their partners (65%) would recommend penile implants for men with erectile dysfunction (McCarthy & McMillan, 1990). However, restoration of erectile competence may not improve the overall relationship between the man and his partner.

There are three main types of pharmacological therapies used to treat erectile dysfunction: psychopharmacologic, neuropharmacologic, and vascular pharmacologic treatments (Foreman & Doherty, 1993). The psychopharmacologic treatments primarily influence sexual drive by altering neuronal activity within the part of the brain responsible for initiating sexual response (the medical preoptic area). Neuropharmacological approaches affect neuronal activity in the brain-spinal-genitalia pathway. Vascular approaches induce erection by correcting defects in the vascular system of the penis. This is mainly accomplished by controlling relaxation of the corpora cavernosal smooth muscle. Although attempts have been made to deliver the drugs orally, through transdermal patches, or through topical creams, direct intrapenile injections have been the most successful.

In one type of injection therapy, the patient injects premixed solutions of papaverine or prostaglandin E combined with phentolamine into the corpora cavernosa of the penis via a syringe. The injection results in a firm erection 5 to 10 minutes after the injection, which lasts about 15 minutes (Levitt & Mulcahy, 1995). In a study of 42 men who used papaverine hydrochloride and phentolamine mesylate, the quality of erections, sexual satisfaction, and frequency of intercourse were all improved

(Althof et al., 1991). Disadvantages of injection therapy include discomfort and bruising associated with self-injections; side effects, such as sustained or recurring erections; fibrotic nodules; and abnormal liver function values (Althof et al., 1989, 1991). Many individuals stop using the injection method because of their aversion to penile self-injection (Hellstrom et al., 1996).

A new procedure involves administering a drug (Alprostadil) at the tip of the penis to induce erection (Hellstrom et al., 1996). This can be done at home using an applicator containing a semisolid pellet of medication that is inserted 3 cm into the urethra. A button on the end of the applicator is pressed, and the medication is deposited against the urethral mucosa (see Figure 10.1). Of 68 men between the ages of 27 and 76 with erectile difficulties, 64% were able to have intercourse using this procedure. Mild to moderate pain was reported by up to 18% of the men as the primary side effect. In late 1997, three new oral drug treatments for erectile dysfunction were in various stages of FDA review.

Another treatment is the vacuum device, which produces an erection that lasts for 30 minutes. Vacuum devices contain a chamber (large enough to fit over an erect penis), a pump, connector tubing, and tension rings (see Figure 10.2).

When the pump is activated, negative pressure is created within the system, which pulls blood into

the penis to produce either erectile augmentation or an erection-like state. After adequate tumescence is achieved, the tension band is guided from the chamber to the base of the penis to produce entrapment of blood. (Witherington, 1991, p. 73)

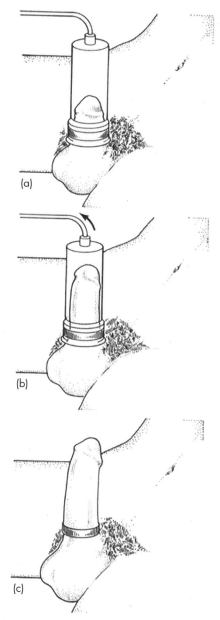

FIGURE 10.2   Vacuum Device
(a) The vacuum chamber is placed over the penis.
(b) Activating the pump draws blood into the penis, enlarging it.
(c) The tension band is placed at the base of the penis to retain the erection.

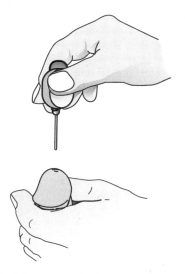

FIGURE 10.1   Applying Transurethral Alprostadil

Of 20 men evaluated for erectile dysfunction for whom vacuum erection, erection devices, or constriction bands were recommended, only 4 experienced improvement in their erection by using the specific suggested method (Shuetz-Mueller, Tiefer, & Melman, 1995). Because of anxiety, social shame, and cognitive rigidity, most of the men did not follow what was recommended, stopped sexual activity, or tried the intracavernosal injection method.

Other medical treatments include the use of trazodone in combination with yohimbine. Although the way this combination works is not clear, some men report developing "abnormally prolonged, rigid erections." (Leslie, 1994).

Hyperactive Sexual Desire Disorder

In Chapter 18, "Paraphilias and Sexuality," we discuss whether the pursuit of sex achieves the magnitude and dimension of other paraphilias and whether the term "sexual addiction" is a valid concept. Although the DSM-IV (American Psychiatric Association, 1994) does not recognize such a concept, here we note that some individuals behave as though they are driven to sexual expression. Such behavior has been defined as **sexual addiction** when the pursuit of sex negatively affects the health, relationships, or career of the individual. Carnes (1991) estimated that up to 6% of Americans suffer from sexual addiction characterized by denial, loss of control, and pathological prioritization. Repetitive extradyadic affairs, the frequenting of massage parlors, and hiring prostitutes are all associated with hyperactive sexual desire.

_____ **THINK ABOUT IT** _____

Cultures differ in terms of how they treat sexual dysfunctions. In China, men with erectile dysfunction are regarded as "suffering from deficiency of Yang elements in the kidney" and are treated by having them drink a solution prepared with water and several chemicals designed to benefit kidney function. They may also be given acupuncture therapy (Skikai, 1990, p. 198).

ORGASM-PHASE DYSFUNCTIONS

Orgasm-phase dysfunctions include female orgasmic disorder and male orgasmic disorder.

Female Orgasmic Disorder

The essential feature of **female orgasmic disorder** is a persistent or recurrent delay in or absence of orgasm following normal sexual excitement. Since normal sexual excitement is typically considered to be sexual intercourse, the problem with labeling the lack of orgasm as a disorder rests on the fact that the majority of women are not capable of orgasm without additional stimulation. (We will discuss this in greater detail later in the chapter.)

Since women vary quite a lot in the type or intensity of stimulation that it takes to trigger orgasm, a clinician making this diagnosis takes into consideration the woman's age, sexual experience, and whether or not the stimulation in sexual activity is adequate. Lifelong orgasmic disorders are more common than acquired ones and are more often diagnosed in younger women than in older women (American Psychiatric Association, 1994).

NATIONAL DATA

A national sample of women reporting trouble achieving orgasm for at least one of the past 12 months

Women unable to
achieve orgasm
23%

Source: Michael et al., 1994, p. 126.

CAUSES AND CONTRIBUTING FACTORS Biological factors associated with orgasmic dysfunction can be related to fatigue, stress, alcohol, and some medications, such as antidepressants and antihypertensives. Over half (61%) of 65 married women identified fatigue as an important reason why they had difficulty achieving orgasm (Davidson & Darling, 1988). Diseases or tumors that affect the neurological system, diabetes, and radical pelvic surgery (for cancer, for example) may also impair a woman's ability to experience orgasm.

Psychosocial and cultural factors associated with orgasmic dysfunctions are similar to those related to lack of sexual desire. Causes of orgasm difficulties in women include a restrictive upbringing and learning a passive female sexual role. Guilt, fear of intimacy, fear of losing control, ambivalence about commitment, and spectatoring may also interfere with the ability to experience orgasm. Other women may not achieve orgasm because of their belief in the myth that women are not supposed to enjoy sex. Experiencing a traumatic event, such as being raped, could interfere with orgasmic capacity.

Relationship factors, such as anger and lack of trust, can also produce orgasmic dysfunction. For some women, the lack of information can result in orgasmic difficulties. (Some women do not know that clitoral stimulation is important for orgasm to occur, for example.) Some women might not achieve orgasm with their partners because they are ashamed and insecure about telling their partners what they want in terms of sexual stimulation (Kelly, Strassberg, & Kircher, 1990).

A woman who does not achieve orgasm because of lack of sufficient stimulation is not considered to have a sexual dysfunction. In one study, 64% of the women who did not experience orgasm during sexual intercourse said that the primary reason was lack of noncoital clitoral stimulation. The type of stimulation most effective in inducing orgasm was manual and oral stimulation and manipulation of the clitoral and vaginal area (Darling, Davidson, & Cox. 1991).

TREATMENT Because the causes for orgasm difficulties vary, the treatment must be tailored to the particular woman. Treatment can include rest and relaxation, change of medication, or limiting alcohol consumption prior to sexual activity. Sensate focus exercises might help a woman explore her sexual feelings and increase her comfort with her partner. Treatment can also involve improving relationship satisfaction and teaching the woman how to communicate her sexual needs.

Masturbation is a widely used treatment for women with orgasm difficulties. LoPiccolo and Lobitz (1972) developed a nine-step program of masturbation for women with orgasm difficulties. The rationale behind masturbation as a therapeutic technique is that masturbation is the technique that is most likely to produce orgasm. Masturbation gives the individual complete control of the stimulation, provides direct feedback to the woman of the type of stimulation she enjoys and eliminates the distraction of a partner. Kinsey, Pomeroy, Martin, and Gebhard (1953) reported that

the average woman reached orgasm in 95% or more of her masturbatory attempts. In addition, the intense orgasm produced by masturbation leads to increased vascularity in the vagina, labia, and clitoris, which enhances the potential for future orgasms.

Not all therapists agree that masturbation is beneficial for the pair-bonded nonorgasmic woman. Schnarch (1991, 1993) suggests that masturbation focuses the individual on personal, individualistic happenings, when intimacy with the partner is the more appropriate focus.

> The essence of sexual intimacy lies not in mastering specific sexual skills or reducing performance anxiety or having regular orgasms but in the ability to allow one's self to deeply know and to be deeply known by the partner. (Schnarch, 1993, p. 43)

Clinicians are admonished to encourage partners to explore and experiment with each other and to stimulate each other (Christensen, 1995, p. 97).

Male Orgasmic Disorder

Difficulty experiencing orgasm also occurs in men. Also known as "inhibited male orgasm" and "retarded ejaculation," *male orgasmic disorder* is defined as a persistent or recurrent delay in or absence of orgasm following a normal sexual excitement phase. The clinician making the judgment about male orgasmic disorder should take into account the man's age and whether the stimulation has been adequate in focus, intensity, and duration. The inability to achieve orgasm is viewed as a problem in modern Western society. But traditional Chinese Taoist philosophy views avoiding ejaculation during intercourse in positive terms, since this vital source of energy needs to be preserved (Tang, Lai, Phil, & Chung, 1997).

Like other sexual dysfunctions, male orgasmic disorder may be lifelong, acquired, situational, or generalized. In most cases of inhibited male orgasm, the man is unable to reach orgasm during sexual intercourse but is able to reach orgasm through other means, such as masturbation. Orgasm difficulties are much less common in men than they are in women. A review of five small survey studies on the incidence of sexual dysfunctions revealed that the rate of orgasm difficulties in men ranged from 0 to 4%. Of 374 men with sexual disorders, only 5% were categorized as having a problem with achieving orgasm (Segraves & Segraves, 1990).

CAUSES AND CONTRIBUTING FACTORS Several medications may interfere with ejaculation, including some hormone-based medications, tranquilizers, barbiturates, antidepressants, and antihypertensives. Injury or disease that impairs the neurological system may also interfere with orgasm in the male.

Most cases of inhibited male orgasm are believed to be caused by psychosocial factors (Kaplan, 1974; Weinstein & Rosen, 1988). Psychosocial causes of male orgasmic disorder include anxiety, fear, "spectatoring," negative attitudes toward sexuality, and conflict or power struggles in the relationship. For example, traumatic experiences or embarrassing ones, such as being discovered by parents while masturbating, can lead to fear, anxiety, and punishment associated with impending orgasm. Thus, the sensation of impending orgasm can become conditioned to produce the response of fear and anxiety, which inhibits orgasm (Kaplan, 1974). Some men are obsessed with trying to become aroused and pleasing their partners, which may lead to anxiety and "spectatoring," which inhibits the ejaculatory reflex (Shaw, 1990). Fear of pregnancy and guilt may also interfere with a man's ability to achieve orgasm and to ejaculate. Learning negative messages about genitals or sexual activities from one's parents or religious training may also lead to ejaculation difficulties. Regarding relationship power struggles, a man's inability to achieve orgasm may be conceptualized as "an expression of the penis's refusal to be commanded interpersonally" (Shaw, 1990, p. 160).

Just as with many women, some men are unable to orgasm because of a lack of sufficient stimulation. Some heterosexual men may have developed a pattern of masturbation that involves vigorous stimulation; they then are unable to obtain sufficient stimulation from the vagina during coitus (Bancroft, 1989).

TREATMENT Treatment for male orgasmic disorder may involve changing medications. More frequently, treatment focuses on the psychosocial origins of retarded ejaculation and may consist of exploring the negative attitudes and cognitions that interfere with ejaculation, and reeducating to change such negative attitudes.

Treatment may also involve sensate focus exercises, which allow the couple to experience physical intimacy without putting pressure on the man to perform sexually. Eventually the man's partner helps him ejaculate through oral or manual stimulation. Research on treating inhibited orgasm has mainly focused on men in heterosexual relationships. After the couple is confident that the man can be brought to orgasm orally or manually, the partner stimulates him to a high level of sexual excitement and, at the moment of orgasm, inserts his penis into her vagina so that he ejaculates inside her. After several sessions, the woman gradually reduces the amount of time she orally or manually manipulates her partner and increases the amount of time she stimulates him with her vagina (Masters & Johnson, 1970). Alternatively, the goal in treating male orgasmic disorder may be to enjoy sexual activities with a partner without the expectation that ejaculation must occur inside the vagina (Leiblum & Rosen, 1989).

Premature Ejaculation

Also known as rapid ejaculation, *premature ejaculation* is defined as the persistent or recurrent onset of orgasm and ejaculation—with minimal sexual stimulation—before, on, or shortly after penetration. Grenier and Byers (1997) identified four criteria that help to identify rapid ejaculation: perceived control over the occurrence of rapid ejaculation, latency from vaginal penetration to ejaculation, satisfaction with perceived degree of ejaculatory control, and concern over the occurrence of rapid ejaculation.

NATIONAL DATA

Twenty-eight percent of a national sample of men reported that, for at least one of the past 12 months, they had a problem with ejaculating too soon.

Source: Michael et al., 1994.

Whether a man ejaculates too soon is a matter of definition, depending on his and his partner's desires. Some partners define a rapid ejaculation in positive terms. One woman said she felt pleased that her partner was so excited by her that he "couldn't control himself." Another said, "The sooner he ejaculates, the sooner it's over with, and the sooner the better." Other women prefer that their partners delay ejaculation. Thirty-one percent of 709 female nurses reported that their partners ejaculated before they had an orgasm, and 23% wanted their partners to delay their ejaculation

(Darling et al., 1991). Some women regard a pattern of rapid ejaculation as indicative of selfishness in their partner. This feeling can lead to resentment and anger. 🖋 On the island of Inis Beag, off the coast of Ireland, men are expected to ejaculate as fast as they can. By doing so, it is believed that they spare the woman as much unpleasantness as possible by getting the sex over with as quickly as possible. Only men are thought to have sexual needs and to enjoy sex (Messenger, 1971). 🖋

CAUSES AND CONTRIBUTING FACTORS While there is disagreement about the cause of rapid ejaculation (Grenier & Byers, 1995), biological causes are increasingly being regarded as more significant than previously thought (Assalian, 1994). Some men may have a constitutionally hypersensitive sympathetic nervous system that predisposes them to rapid ejaculation. "Further research is needed in the area of physiological processes of ejaculation and the role of brain neurotransmitters in human sexual response" (Assalian, 1994, p. 3).

Psychosocial factors associated with premature ejaculation include early learning experiences, anxiety, and conflict or power struggles in the relationship between the man and his partner. Some examples of early learning experiences are with prostitutes who rush their clients, thus resulting in quick ejaculation (Masters & Johnson, 1970). Sex therapists Hartman and Fithian of the Hartman and Fithian Clinic in Long Beach, California, claim that the primary cause of premature ejaculation stems from growing up in a house with not enough bathrooms. With siblings beating on the door while a boy is masturbating, he learns rapid ejaculation, which then turns into a lifetime habit. However, this claim has not been substantiated by research.

TREATMENT A procedure for treating premature ejaculation is the squeeze technique, developed by Masters and Johnson. The partner stimulates the man's penis manually until the man signals that he feels the urge to ejaculate. At the man's signal, the partner places her thumb on the underside of his penis and squeezes hard for 3 to 4 seconds. This causes the man to lose his urge to ejaculate. After 30 seconds, the partner resumes stimulation, applying the squeeze technique again when the man signals. The important rule to remember is that the partner should apply the squeeze technique whenever the man gives the slightest hint of readiness to ejaculate. (The man can also use the squeeze technique during masturbation to teach himself to delay his ejaculation.)

Another technique used to delay ejaculation is known as the pause technique, also referred to as the stop-start technique. This technique involves the man's stopping penile stimulation (or signaling his partner to stop stimulation) at the point that he begins to feel the urge to ejaculate. After the period of preejaculatory sensations subsides, stimulation resumes. This process may be repeated as often as desired by the partners.

Success of the squeeze technique and stop-start technique is disputed. While success rates of Masters and Johnson (1970) are often interpreted to be 98%, subsequent research has shown rates closer to 60%.

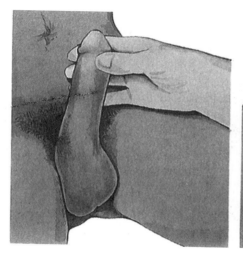
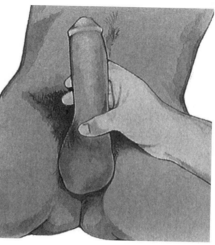

FIGURE 10.3 Squeeze Technique In using the squeeze technique, the man or his partner applies firm pressure for several seconds below the glans or at the base of the penis (front and back, not sides).

And most of the gains are lost at follow-up. "Since it is not entirely clear why the intervention works in the first place, it is difficult to identify why the treatment gains were lost over time," observe Grenier and Byers (1995, p. 465).

Some sex therapists are prescribing medications to slow down ejaculation. Clomipramine, fluoxetine, paroxetine, and sertraline seem to be safe treatment options for patients with premature ejaculation. This is especially true in cases of failed psychological treatment, rejection of psychological treatment, and when partners are unwilling to cooperate in treatment (Balon, 1996). Kaplan (1994) also reported successful use of Prozac in treating premature ejaculation. Paxil has also been shown to delay or retard ejaculation. Currently, the most useful pharmacological treatment for managing premature ejaculation is clomipramine (an antidepressant drug that increases the sensory threshold of the penis) (Riley & Riley, 1993). Some pharmacological interventions that have been employed have not been grounded in studies using control groups and long-term follow-up. Grenier and Byers (1997) suggest that future research should be launched to provide more definitive data on the treatment of this pervasive dysfunction.

_____ THINK ABOUT IT _____

What does the use of numerous techniques to help resolve premature ejaculation suggest about its etiology?

SEXUAL PAIN DYSFUNCTIONS

Two types of pain dysfunctions are dyspareunia and vaginismus.

Dyspareunia

Dyspareunia refers to genital pain that is associated with sexual intercourse. The pain may occur before, during, or after intercourse and may be experienced by either women or men. The symptoms range from mild discomfort to sharp pain.

CAUSES AND CONTRIBUTING FACTORS Dyspareunia in women may be caused by biological factors, such as vaginal or pelvic infections or inflammations, and allergic reactions to deodorant, douches, and contraceptive devices. In rare cases, the woman with dyspareunia is allergic to her partner's semen (Hawton, 1985). Coital pain may also result from tender scarring following an episiotomy, which is a surgical slit sometimes made in the perineal area to ease the childbirth process (Bancroft, 1989). Dyspareunia may also be caused by a lack of lubrication, a rigid hymen, or an improperly positioned uterus or ovary. In men, it may be caused by inflammations of or lesions on the penis (often caused by herpes), Peyronie's disease (which causes a bending in the penis during erection), and urethritis (Kaplan, 1983). Because dyspareunia is often a symptom of a medical problem, a health care provider should be consulted.

Of 58 female patients who complained of "burning, tight, or focused" pain during intercourse and contacted a physician, 61% were told that the problem was psychological. Another physician, however, discovered that the dyspareunia was caused by a rigid hymen, and coital pain was relieved or improved in 90% of the cases following surgery (Brashear & Munsick, 1991).

Dyspareunia may also be caused by psychosocial factors, including guilt, anxiety, or unresolved feelings about a previous trauma, such as rape or childhood molestation. Religious and parental prohibitions against sexual activity and relationship conflicts may also result in dyspareunia. Lazarus (1989) suggested that in 50% of cases, unsatisfactory or unhappy relationships contribute to dyspareunia. The pain may be caused by attempting sexual activity without desire or arousal.

TREATMENT Dyspareunia that is caused by biological factors may be treated by evaluating the medical condition that is causing the coital pain. If medical or surgical procedures cannot resolve the pain, the person with dyspareunia may try different intercourse positions or other sexual activities that provide pleasure with no or minimal pain.

When dyspareunia is caused by psychosocial factors, treatment may involve reeducation to replace negative attitudes toward sexual activity with positive ones. Individual therapy may help the person resolve feelings of guilt or anxiety associated with sexual activity. Couple therapy may be indicated to resolve relationship conflicts. Sensate focus exercises may help the individual relax and enjoy sexual contact.

Vaginismus

Vaginismus is "the recurrent or persistent involuntary contraction of the perineal muscles surrounding the vagina when vaginal penetration with the penis, finger, tampon, or speculum is attempted" (American Psychiatric Association, 1994). Vaginismus may be lifelong or acquired. Lifelong vaginismus means that the vaginal muscles have always constricted to prevent penetration of any object, including tampons. Acquired vaginismus, the more usual variety, suggests that the vagina has permitted penetration in the past, but currently constricts when penetration is imminent.

CAUSES AND CONTRIBUTING FACTORS In women who experience dyspareunia (which may be caused by biological or psychosocial factors), vaginismus may be a protective response to prevent pain. In other words, if a woman anticipates coital pain, she may involuntarily constrict her vagina to prevent painful intercourse.

Vaginismus may also be related to psychosocial factors, such as a restrictive parental and religious upbringing in which the woman learned to view intercourse as dirty and shameful. Other psychosocial factors include rape, incest, and childhood molestation.

TREATMENT Treatment for vaginismus should begin with a gynecological examination to determine if an organic or physical problem is the cause. If the origin is psychological, the treatment may involve teaching the woman relaxation techniques. When relaxation is achieved, the woman is instructed to introduce her index finger into her vagina. The use of lubricants, such as K-Y jelly, may be helpful. After the woman is able to insert one finger into her vagina, she is instructed to introduce two fingers into the vagina, and this exercise is repeated until she feels relaxed enough to contain the penis. Some therapists use graduated dilators. Once the woman learns that she is capable of vaginal containment of the penis, she is usually able to have intercourse without difficulty. Therapy focusing on the woman's cognitions and perceptions about sex and sexuality with her particular partner may precede or accompany the finger exercise.

Shaw (1994) recommended that treatment for primary vaginismus should shift away from cognitive-behavioral treatment described earlier to focus on differentiation, which is defined as the ability to function autonomously with emotional and physical maturity. In effect, the therapist helps the person to learn that it is OK to be intimate with another and that this can occur without a loss of self.

> Primary vaginismus may be an unspoken, somatic boundary, a nonverbal limit, a way to respect one's self. Vaginismus is not a bad symptom, it is a solution, a symbolic description of what needs to happen. Our task as clinicians is to look, listen, question, and give meaning to symptoms. (Shaw, 1994, p. 53)

THINK ABOUT IT

Why might individuals with sexual concerns choose not to seek sex therapy?

PERSONAL CHOICES

Should You Have Private or Group Therapy?

Once an individual has decided to pursue therapy, what is the best option—seeing a therapist alone, or seeing a therapist with others who are experiencing the same problem? Although 80 women who were asked their preferences clearly preferred individual therapy (Wilson & Wilson, 1991), each treatment modality had advantages and disadvantages.

Being seen privately helps to ensure that the therapy will be tailored to fit the specific needs of the client, but the cost is considerably higher for private therapy than for therapy in a group. Private therapy may cost $100 or more an hour; therapy in a group of five members may cost $20 or less for the same amount of time.

Another advantage of group therapy is that being surrounded by others who have similar problems helps to reduce the client's feeling of isolation—that he or she is "the only one." One woman who had difficulty achieving orgasm said, "When I heard the other women discuss their difficulty with climaxing, I knew I wasn't abnormal" (authors' notes). The empathy of a group of peers can be extremely effective in helping a person feel less isolated.

A group setting also furnishes the opportunity to try new behaviors. For example, some sexual problems may be part of a larger problem, such as the lack of social skills to attract and maintain a partner. Fear of rejection can perpetuate being alone. But group members, with the help of their therapist, can practice making requests of each other and getting turned down. Such an exercise helps to develop the social skill of approaching others while learning to cope with rejection. Practicing with other group members is safe and gives a person the necessary confidence to approach someone outside the group.

Group therapy has at least three disadvantages. The first is the possibility that not enough time will be spent on the individual's own problem. The second is the risk to the relationship with the partner, who may not be involved in the group. In one study of women in group therapy for lack of orgasm, one in four reported a negative effect on their partner (Barbach & Flaherty, 1980). Finally, some people are reluctant to try group therapy. In Wilson and Wilson's (1991) study of college women's ratings of therapy formats, the students rated the individual format as more credible and acceptable than the group format.

What is the comparative effectiveness of couples being treated in a group or in private therapy? In one study, when group-couple therapy for early ejaculation and orgasmic dysfunction was compared with therapy for the same problems treated in private, there were no differences in outcome. Both treatment patterns were effective. Men reported satisfaction with their ability to prolong intercourse, and women reported satisfaction with their orgasmic ability (Golden, Price, Heinrich, & Lobitz, 1978). Other researchers have found similar results: couples in groups are as successful in achieving their goals as couples in private therapy (Duddle & Ingram, 1980). But group therapy for individuals may not be as effective as therapy with a partner in private or in a couple's group. However, most individuals in group sex therapy without a partner do benefit from the experience.

These studies suggest that individuals can be treated effectively in either a private or a group setting. The selection of a therapy setting is therefore a matter of preference and perhaps a matter of affordability. As with individual and conjoint therapy, private and group therapy can be combined.

APPROACHES USED IN SEX THERAPY

The previous paragraph illustrates the wide range of treatment available for sexual problems. In this section, we examine the various approaches to sex therapy and the various treatment techniques that have developed from these approaches. We also review the effectiveness of sex therapy.

The Psychoanalytic Approach

Before 1970, most of the treatment for sexual dysfunctions was conducted by psychoanalytically trained psychiatrists who viewed sexual dysfunctions as symptoms of deeply rooted psychological disturbances originating from childhood experiences. Through dream analysis and free association (saying whatever came into the patient's mind), the therapist using the psychoanalytic approach helped patients to relive childhood experiences in order to achieve insight into the causes of their sexual dysfunction, emphasizing instinctual theory and oedipal conflict. More recent applications of psychoanalytically oriented psychotherapy have focused on how personality structures were formed, and how those relate to difficulties in loving and being intimate with another person (Masterson, 1976). Psychotherapy may be "supportive" (in which the client learns conscious control of his or her defense mechanisms) or "reconstructive" (an outgrowth and expansion of supportive therapy).

Masters and Johnson's Approach

Masters and Johnson's approach to sex therapy represented a significant departure from the psychoanalytic approach and a major advance in the treatment of sexual dysfunctions. When the Masters and Johnson Institute in St. Louis began, couples went through an intensive 2-week sex therapy program. Treatment began with assessment procedures, including a physical examination and interviews with therapists who take medical and personal histories. On the third day, the therapists met with the couple to discuss their assessment of the nature, extent, and origin of the sexual problem; to recommend treatment procedures; and to answer any questions. All couples receiving treatment at the Masters and Johnson Institute were instructed to engage in sensate focus exercises (described earlier in this chapter).

The essential elements of the early Masters and Johnson approach to resolving sexual dysfunctions are summarized below.

1. Both partners in a marital or coupled unit are expected to participate in sex therapy.
2. A male and a female sex therapist provide the treatment for heterosexual couples; in this way, each patient has a same-sex role model.
3. Sexual dysfunctions are conceptualized as having been learned. Hence, much of sex therapy is devoted to sex education and information.
4. Performance anxiety, fear of failure, and excessive need to please the partner are regarded as underlying causes of sexual problems and are addressed in therapy.
5. Communication between the partners is regarded as critical to a good sexual relationship. Hence, enhancing communication between the sexual partners becomes a goal.
6. The specific resolution of a sexual dysfunction involves behavioral change that is accomplished through the assignment of progressive tasks and behavioral prescriptions.

The PLISSIT Model Approach

A helpful approach for treating sexual problems and dysfunctions is the *PLISSIT model* (Annon, 1976). The PLISSIT model outlines four treatment levels: permission, limited information, specific suggestions, and intensive therapy. The permission level of the PLISSIT model involves encouraging clients to discuss their sexual problems. The therapist may also assure clients that (in many cases) their thoughts, feelings, behaviors, and concerns are "normal," common, and understandable. The second level of the PLISSIT model involves giving the client limited information, such as educating the client about sexual response, sexual anatomy, or the effects of medications or alcohol on sexual functioning. This level of intervention also involves dispelling sexual myths. The third level of intervention involves specific suggestions. Examples of specific suggestions include instructing couples on how to do sensate focus exercises, instructing women on

masturbation techniques, and instructing men and their partners on how to cope with premature ejaculation (such as using the squeeze technique). The fourth level of treatment involves intensive therapy. This level of intervention is used when the other three have not alleviated the sexual dysfunction or problem. Intensive therapy may consist of any of the other sex therapy approaches described in this chapter, such as Masters and Johnson's approach (or a variation of it) or Kaplan's approach (to be discussed).

The Cognitive Therapy Approach

Cognitive therapy emphasizes that negative thoughts and attitudes about sex interfere with sexual interest, pleasure, and performance. *Cognitive sex therapy* consists of exploring more positive ways of viewing sex and sexuality. For example, a person who has no interest in sex may believe that sex is shameful and sinful and that "good people" regard sex as disgusting. A sex therapist using a cognitive approach might encourage this person to examine the negative consequences of such thoughts and ask the person to consider a different vein of "self-talk." By consciously replacing the old, negative thoughts about sex with positive thoughts like "sex is great, an experience to share, and a fantastic feeling," sexual desire would have a better cognitive context in which to develop. Similarly, a sex therapist may help a couple who thinks masturbation is sinful and selfish to regard it as a means of discovering self-pleasure so as to enhance their sexual relationship.

Negative cognitions may also interfere with personal, partner, and relationship functioning. Firestone (1990) described thoughts as "voices" and suggested that negative voices may interfere with relationship and sexual satisfaction. For example, one woman reported self-deprecating statements, such as "Why should he [her husband] be attracted to me? I'm getting fat; I'm not as young as I used to be." She also tended to have thoughts about her husband, such as "He's so critical of me. He doesn't feel anything for me. He's so insensitive." Both types of negative cognitions (toward self and partner) lead to diminished feelings of sexual attraction and foster the withholding of affectionate and sexual behaviors. The therapeutic process involves each partner in a relationship identifying the negative "voices" they experience, releasing the anger and sadness associated with the voices, developing insight into the origins of the thoughts, and opening up direct communication with their partner.

Negative attitudes and cognitions about sex often result from sexual trauma, such as rape and incest. One way to change these negative attitudes and cognitions is for the therapist to teach the individual to be a survivor, rather than a victim. In addition, the therapist can suggest that "living well is the best revenge" against the person who perpetrated the trauma.

Helen Kaplan's Approach

The late Helen Kaplan (1974) of Cornell Medical Center combined elements of the psychoanalytic, cognitive, and learning approaches (Masters and Johnson) to develop her own approach to sex therapy. Kaplan's approach does not have a rigid 2-week format, nor does it assume that therapy will continue indefinitely. Her goal is to assist the partners in achieving their sexual goals in as short a time as possible. Sessions are usually held once or twice a week (with an occasional phone call during the week) while the partners continue to live at home. Although participation of both partners is seen as a crucial ingredient for successful sex therapy, Kaplan's approach does not require that sexual partners participate equally in the therapy program. For example, in the case of inhibited female orgasm, the therapist may spend most of the time working with the woman in individual sessions.

Like Masters and Johnson, Kaplan assigned behavioral "homework" tasks that are designed to help the individual or couple overcome a sexual dysfunction. However, she suggested that some individuals may not respond to behavioral interventions when the source of the sexual dysfunction is rooted in unconscious intrapsychic conflicts, deep-seated personality traits, or interpersonal dynamics. Thus, an important part of Kaplan's approach to sex therapy is insight therapy, through which the presumed deeper roots of sexual dysfunction are uncovered.

Kaplan also noted that sex therapy clients often resist treatment and that therapists must be aware of such resistance and help clients overcome it. In sex therapy, "resistance" refers to the client's unconscious opposition to or lack of cooperation in treatment. Resistance may involve clients' doing something to interfere with the resolution of their sexual problem. Examples of resistance include "forgetting" therapy appointments, "not finding time" to complete homework assignments, doing homework assignments incorrectly, or antagonizing the partner. Kaplan (1974) observed:

> Resistance is a critical therapeutic issue in all but the simplest cases and must be managed effectively for therapy to succeed. The paradoxical tendency of patients to resist "getting well" was first described by Freud in the early days of psychoanalysis, and it is now known that resistance occurs to all kinds of psychological treatments, including sex therapy. (p. 197)

In order for sex therapy to be effective, the sex therapist must diffuse any resistance on the part of the client. Diffusing resistance may be accomplished by confronting the client directly, exploring unconscious conflicts, or making use of dream material.

LoPiccolo's Postmodern Approach

Building on the contributions of Masters and Johnson's system of modern sex therapy, and drawing from cognitive-behavioral therapy and systems theory, Joseph LoPiccolo (1992) offered a three-part theory he dubbed "postmodern." Although his comments focused on erectile failure, the three theoretical elements he described are applicable to understanding other categories of sexual dysfunction as well.

1. *Systems theory.* LoPiccolo recommended that in assessing sexual dysfunction, the therapist should carefully examine the effect of the dysfunction on the relationship between the partners. Although sexual problems may cause distress, they may also serve a purpose. Unlike Kaplan's approach, in which resistance is examined when standard therapies haven't worked, in LoPiccolo's framework, the therapist begins in the first session to prevent resistance. Clients may be asked to anticipate any possible negative effects on their marital relationship if the husband were to regain erectile functioning. "For example, might a husband feel more powerful and revert to a more authoritarian role with the wife if he became more 'potent' again? Might the wife find his sexual needs burdensome if the husband regained erectile function?" (p. 178).

Ideally, if the systemic value of the problem is discovered during the initial assessment, therapy can immediately begin to meet the needs that the erectile failure serves. LoPiccolo identified a number of frequently occurring systemic issues, including the following: not feeling attracted to one' partner, being unable to combine feelings of love and sexual desire, discrepancies in the extent of "personal space" needed by the partners, and general unhappiness in the marriage.

2. *Integrated (physiological and psychological) planning.* It is often not useful, and may be harmful, to classify people's dysfunctions as organic *or* psychogenic. As noted, *both* organic and psychogenic factors are operating. LoPiccolo suggested that even when organic etiology is clearly established, a thorough psychological evaluation is also indicated.

3. *Sexual behavior patterns.* Finally, as discussed in a number of the previous sections on treatment of specific dysfunctions, it is important to examine the specific sexual behaviors of the couple. Are the behaviors used to cue sexual desire and arousal adequate? Does the couple need to reconsider the methods, sites, or philosophies of stimulation?

Effectiveness of Sex Therapy

The largest series of sex therapy cases for which outcome data have been reported is that of Masters and Johnson (1970). Masters and Johnson did not report success rates for their sex therapy; rather, they reported a "failure" rate of 20% for the 1872 cases they treated at their institute from 1959 through 1977 (Kolodny, 1981). This reported average "failure" rate of 20% is often misinterpreted to mean that the "success" rate was 80%. However, the "failure" category included cases that were actually "improved" (to a greater or lesser degree) as well as cases that showed no improvement whatsoever (Kolodny, 1981).

In 1979, Kaplan estimated the overall average percentage of sex therapy cases that are successfully resolved is about 66%. In a number of treatment outcome studies in the 1980s, with follow-up periods of 3 months to 3 years, researchers have documented clients' increased satisfaction with their sexual relationship, although symptom remission and satisfaction in marital relationships were more variable (DeAmicis, Goldberg, LoPiccolo, Friedman, & Davies,

Many sex therapists emphasize the importance of seeing both partners together in therapy sessions.

1984, 1985). Kilmann et al. (1986) surveyed randomly selected sex therapists who were members of AASECT. In their reports of therapy outcomes, "highest success rates (client satisfaction with sexual functioning) were for premature ejaculation (62%), secondary orgasmic dysfunction (56%), and desire discrepancies (53%). Primary erectile dysfunctions had the lowest success rate (25%)" (p. 116).

Reports of sex therapy effectiveness are highly varied for several reasons. First, the degree to which sex therapy is effective in resolving sexual problems depends on the problem being treated. Some problems are easier to treat than others. In general, acquired problems are easier to treat than lifelong problems, and situational problems are easier to treat than generalized (or global) problems. Premature ejaculation and vaginismus are more likely to respond quickly to therapeutic intervention. Problems of sexual desire may be the most difficult to treat (Schover & LoPiccolo, 1982; Kilmann et al., 1986). Erectile dysfunction, inability to achieve orgasm, and hypoactive sexual desire require more time.

LoPiccolo (1992) identified several factors that influence the effectiveness of sex therapy. For example, LoPiccolo suggested that sex therapy is less likely to be effective under the following conditions.

- Either the patient or his or her partner is unwilling to reconsider how cognitive, behavioral, or systemic factors are contributing to the maintenance of the sexual dysfunction.
- The patient has a sexual deviation in which he or she is aroused by an inappropriate sexual object (such as children) or has a paraphilia (see Chapter 18).

Sexual Dysfunctions and Sex Therapy   271

- The patient's religious beliefs are interfering with sexual performance. LoPiccolo suggested that "these cases are best referred to a pastoral counselor, who may have some credibility in changing or at least helping the patient reexamine these beliefs" (p. 187).
- The patient has severe clinical depression. However, mild to moderate depression due to sexual and relationship issues may respond well to sex therapy.

Sex therapy effectiveness rates may vary because of the methodological problems in determining such rates. For example, who should decide whether treatment has failed or succeeded—the client or the therapist? What criteria should be used in determining success or failure? What if the client is successful in resolving sexual dysfunctions, but is not successful in resolving related nonsexual issues, such as marital conflict, negative body image, and low self-esteem? What if the client is successful in resolving these related nonsexual issues, but is still sexually dysfunctional? What criteria will be used to measure success and failure? Different answers to these questions will yield different results regarding reported success rates of sex therapy.

Finally, sex therapy effectiveness rates based on current studies are likely to be lower than effectiveness rates based on older studies because of differences in the severity of the dysfunctions treated. Newcomb and Bentler (1988) suggested that in previous decades, a higher percentage of people with sexual difficulties lacked information about sexuality. In many cases, sexual difficulties were caused by "ignorance, naivete, and misunderstanding." However, people today are more likely to be informed about matters related to sexuality (through self-help books, sex education, the media, and other educational materials available to the public). Thus, compared to sex therapy clients in previous decades, the sex therapy client today often suffers from more than a simple lack of sexual information. As Newcomb and Bentler (1988) explained, "People presenting now with sexual problems typically have more basic knowledge of sexual functioning and behavior than previously, and thus arrive with more complex and severe sexual disturbances. . . . " (p. 127).

As we end this section on the treatment of sexual dysfunctions, it is important to point out that sex therapy has its downside. Indeed, rather than improving a person's sexuality and a couple's happiness, it can have negative outcomes. McCarthy noted some of the unwanted effects of sex therapy as

increased sexual self-consciousness, increased anticipatory and performance anxiety, an acute problem becoming a chronic sexual dysfunction, therapy resulting in the dissolution of what had been a marginally functional relationship, increased feelings of personal deficit, and vulnerability resulting from shared sexual secrets being used against the person, especially in divorce proceedings. (1995, p. 36)

While the buyer should beware, couples who decide to seek sex therapy should see only a credentialed therapist. The American Association of Sex Educators, Counselors, and Therapists, 11 Dupont Circle, N.W., Suite 220, Washington, DC 20036, maintains a list of certified sex therapists throughout the country.

PERSONAL CHOICES

Should You See a Male-Female Sex Therapy Team or an Individual Therapist?

For heterosexual couples, is it best to see one therapist or a male-female sex therapy team? Masters and Johnson recommend the latter for couple therapy, suggesting that the male client can better relate to a male therapist and a female client can better relate to a female therapist. A dual-sex team also provides a model for appropriate male-female interaction.

Although many sex therapists have adopted the dual-sex team approach, there is no evidence that such a team is more effective than individual male or female therapists (Clement & Schmidt, 1983; LoPiccolo, Heiman, Hogan, & Roberts, 1985). In addition, therapy with a dual-sex therapy team is likely to be more expensive than therapy with an individual therapist. Rather than how many therapists of what sex are in the therapy setting, the quality of the therapy seems to be the important variable.

THINK ABOUT IT

How are different sexual problems conceptualized and what treatments follow from these theoretical views?

SUMMARY POINTS

Masters and Johnson have suggested that as many as one half of all couples experience some form of sexual dysfunction for which sex therapy might be helpful. This chapter reviewed the nature, causes, consequences, and treatments of the major sexual dysfunctions.

Causes and Contributing Factors in Sexual Dysfunctions

A number of factors may cause or contribute to sexual dysfunctions. Biological factors include physical illness, disease, aging, and disability and its treatment (surgery, medication, chemotherapy). Chronic fatigue fostered by the relentless demands of career, school, children, and domestic tasks may leave little physical energy for sexual activity. Drugs, both legal and illegal, may also impair sexual functioning.

Sociocultural factors include negative upbringing (sex is dirty), negative religion (sex is sinful), and traditional gender role socialization (female passivity). Intrapsychic factors include anxiety, fear of intimacy, fear of rejection, and sexual abuse. Relationship factors include negative feelings and lack of trust toward one's partner. Finally, cognitive factors—such as the belief that one is too old to enjoy sex—will affect sexual functioning.

Desire- and Arousal-Phase Dysfunctions

Hypoactive sexual desire (or little interest in sex) occurs in both women and men. Causes may be any or all of those mentioned above, and treatment follows from the most likely culprits. In many cases, improving the relationship is an important prerequisite to increasing one's sexual desire.

Sexual aversion disorder involves anxiety, fear, or disgust when confronted with a sexual opportunity with a partner. Some individuals experience generalized revulsion to all sexual stimuli, including kissing and touching. Insight and cognitive therapies are usually the most helpful.

Sexual arousal dysfunction results in the individual's inability to attain, or to maintain until completion of the sexual activity, an adequate lubrication-swelling response in the female, or erection in the male. The condition may be lifelong, acquired, situational, or generalized. Treatment varies with the cause.

Orgasm-Phase Dysfunctions

Female orgasmic disorder, or difficulty with achieving orgasm, can be lifelong, acquired, situational, or generalized. It is important to be aware that the cause may be inadequate stimulation provided by the partner, rather than a problem with the woman's response. Types of male orgasmic disorder include premature ejaculation and retarded ejaculation. Both psychosocial and biological factors are involved in each of these dysfunctions, and the treatments vary according to the cause.

Sexual Pain Dysfunctions

Dyspareunia refers to genital pain that may occur in both women and men before, during, or after intercourse. Vaginismus is recurrent or persistent involuntary contraction of the vagina when penetration is attempted. These conditions may be lifelong, acquired, situational, or generalized. Treatment is dictated by the psychological or biological cause.

Approaches Used in Sex Therapy

The various approaches used in sex therapy include psychoanalytic, Masters and Johnson, the PLISSIT model approach, cognitive therapy, Helen Kaplan's approach, and LoPiccolo's postmodern approach. Some sex therapists feel that sex therapy is becoming too "medicalized." Specifically with regard to the treatment of erectile dysfunction, "comprehensive urology and impotence centers" have emerged to offer medical solutions to psychogenic problems. Other sex therapists feel that too much emphasis on anatomical functioning is misguided.

REFERENCES

Althof, S. E., Turner, L. A., Levine, S. D., Risen, C., Kursh, D., Bodner, D., & Resnick, M. (1989). Why do so many people drop out of autoinjection therapy for impotence? *Journal of Sex and Marital Therapy, 15,* 121–129.

Althof, S. E., Turner, L. A., Levine, S. D., Risen, C., Kursh, D., Bodner, D., & Resnick, M. (1991). Sexual, psychological and marital impact of self-injection of papaverine and phentolamine: A long-term prospective study. *Journal of Sex and Marital Therapy, 17,* 101–112.

American Psychiatric Association. (1994). *Diagnostic and statistical manual of mental disorders* (4th ed.). Washington, DC: APA.

Annon, J. (1976). The PLISSIT model. *Journal of Sex Education and Therapy, 2,* 1–15.

Assalian, P. (1994). Premature ejaculation: Is it really psychogenic? *Journal of Sex Education and Therapy, 20,* 1–4.

Balon, R. (1996). Antidepressants in the treatment of premature ejaculation. *Journal of Sex and Marital Therapy, 22,* 85–96.

Bancroft, J. (1989). *Human sexuality and its problems* (2nd ed.). New York: Churchill Livingstone.

Barbach, L., & Flaherty, M. (1980). Group treatment of situationally orgasmic women. *Journal of Sex and Marital Therapy, 6,* 19–29.

Bass, B. A. (1985). The myth of low sexual desire: A cognitive behavioral approach to treatment. *Journal of Sex Education and Therapy, 11,* 61–64.

Brashear, D. B., & Munsick, R. A. (1991). Hymenal dyspareunia. *Journal of Sex Education and Therapy, 19,* 27–31.

Cado, S., & Leitenberg, H. (1990). Guilt reactions to sexual fantasies during intercourse. *Archives of Sexual Behavior, 19,* 49–63.

Carnes, P. J. (1991). *Contrary to love: Helping the sexual addict.* Minneapolis: Comprehensive Care.

Carroll, J. L., & Bagley, D. H. (1990). Evaluation of sexual satisfaction in partners of men experiencing erectile failure. *Journal of Sex and Marital Therapy, 16,* 70–78.

Christensen, C. (1995). Prescribed masturbation in sex therapy: A critique. *Journal of Sex and Marital Therapy, 21,* 87–99.

Clement, U., & Schmidt, G. (1983). The outcome of couple therapy for sexual dysfunctions using three different formats. *Journal of Sex and Marital Therapy, 9,* 67–78.

Darling, C. A., Davidson, J. K., & Cox, R. P. (1991). Female sexual response and the timing of partner orgasm. *Journal of Sex and Marital Therapy, 17,* 3–21.

Davidson, J. K., & Darling, C. A. (1988). The stereotype of single women revisited: Sexual practices and sexual satisfaction among professional women. *Health Care for Women International, 9,* 317–336.

DeAmicis, L. A., Goldberg, D. C., LoPiccolo, J., Friedman, J., & Davies, L. (1984). Three year follow-up of couples evaluated for sexual dysfunction. *Journal of Sex and Marital Therapy, 10,* 215–228.

DeAmicis, L. A., Goldberg, D. C., LoPiccolo, J., Friedman, J., & Davies, L. (1985). Clinical follow-up of couples evaluated for sexual dysfunction. *Archives of Sexual Behavior, 14,* 467–489.

Duddle, C. M., Ingram, A. (1980). Treating sexual dysfunction in couple's groups. In R. Forleo & W. Pasini (Eds.), *Medical sexology* (pp. 598–605). Amsterdam: Elsevier.

Elliott, D. M., & Briere, J. (1992). The sexually abused boy: Problems in manhood. *Medical Aspects of Human Sexuality, 26,* 68–71.

Firestone, R. W. (1990). Voices during sex: Application of voice therapy to sexuality. *Journal of Sex and Marital Therapy, 16,* 258–277.

Foreman, M. M., & Doherty, P. C. (1993). Experimental approaches for the development of pharmacological therapies for erectile dysfunction. In A. J. Riley, M. Peet, & C. Wilson (Eds.), *Sexual pharmacology.* Oxford: Clarendon.

Golden, J. S., Price, S., Heinrich, A. G., & Lobitz, W. C. (1978). Group versus couple treatment of sexual dysfunctions. *Archives of Sexual Behavior, 7,* 593–602.

Goldsmith, L. (1988). Treatment of sexual dysfunction. In E. Weinstein & E. Rosen (Eds.), *Sexuality counseling: Issues and implications* (pp. 16–34). Pacific Grove, CA: Brooks/Cole.

Grenier, G., & Byers, E. S. (1995). Rapid ejaculation: A review of conceptual, etiological, and treatment issues. *Archives of Sexual Behavior, 24,* 447–472.

Grenier, G., & Byers, E. S. (1997). The relationships among ejaculatory control, ejaculatory latency, and attempt to prolong heterosexual intercourse. *Archives of Sexual Behavior, 26,* 27–48

Hawton, K. (1985). *Sex therapy: A practical guide.* Oxford: Oxford University Press.

Hellstrom, W. J. G., Bennett, A. H., Gesundheit, N., Kaiser, F. E., Lue, T. F., Padma-Nathan, H., Peterson, C. A., Tam, P. Y., Todd, L. K., Varady, J. C., & Place, V. A. (1996). A double-blind, placebo-controlled evaluation of the erectile response to transurethral alprostadil. *Urology, 48,* 851–856.

Kaplan, H. S. (1974). The classification of the female sexual dysfunctions. *Journal of Sex and Marital Therapy, 2,* 124–138.

Kaplan, H. S. (1983). *The evaluation of sexual disorders.* New York: Brunner/Mazel.

Kaplan, P. M. (1994). The use of serotonergic uptake inhibitors in the treatment of premature ejaculation. *Journal of Sex and Marital Therapy, 20,* 321–324.

Kelly, M. P., Strassberg, D. S., and Kircher, J. R. (1990). Attitudinal and experiential correlates of anaorgasmia. *Archives of Sexual Behavior, 19,* 165–177.

Kilmann, P. R., Mills, K. H., Caid, C., Bella, B., Davidson, E., & Wanlass, R. (1984). The sexual interaction of women with secondary orgasmic dysfunction and their partners. *Archives of Sexual Behavior, 13,* 41–49.

Kinsey, A. C., Pomeroy, W. B., Martin, C. E., & Gebhard, P. H. (1953). *Sexual behavior in the human female.* Philadelphia: Saunders.

Kolodny, R. C. (1981). Evaluating sex therapy: Process and outcome at the Masters and Johnson Institute. *Journal of Sex Research, 17,* 301–318.

Lazarus, A. A. (1989). Dyspareunia: A multimodal psychotherapeutic perspective. In S. R. Leiblum & R. C. Rosen (Eds.), *Principles and practice of sex therapy, 2nd ed. Update for the 1990s* (pp. 89–112). New York: Guilford Press.

Leiblum, S. R., & Rosen, R. C. (1989). Couples therapy for erectile disorders: Conceptual and clinical considerations. *Journal of Sex and Marital Therapy, 17,* 147–159.

Leslie, S. W. (1994). *Impotence: Current diagnosis and treatment.* Birmingham, AL: Vet-Co.

Levitt, E. E., & Mulcahy, J. J. (1995). The effect of intracavernosal injection of papaverine hydrochloride on orgasm latency. *Journal of Sex and Marital Therapy, 21,* 39–56.

LoPiccolo, J. (1992). Postmodern sex therapy for erectile failure. In R. C. Rosen & S. R. Leiblum (Eds.), *Erectile disorders: Assessment and treatment* (pp. 171–197). New York: Guilford Press.

LoPiccolo, J., Heiman, J. R., Hogan, D. R., & Roberts, C. W. (1985). Effectiveness of single therapists versus cotherapy teams in sex therapy. *Journal of Consulting and Clinical Psychology, 53,* 287–294.

LoPiccolo, J., & Lobitz, C. (1972). The role of masturbation in the treatment of orgasmic dysfunction. *Archives of Sexual Behavior, 2,* 163–171.

MacPhee, D. C., Johnson, S. M., & Van Der Veer, M. M. C. (1995). Low sexual desire in women: The effects of marital therapy. *Journal of Sex and Marital Therapy, 21,* 159–182.

Masters, W. H., & Johnson, V. E. (1970). *Human sexual inadequacy.* Boston: Little, Brown.

Masterson, J. F. (1976). *Psychotherapy of the borderline adult: A developmental approach.* New York: Brunner/Mazel.

McCarthy, B. W. (1990). Treating sexual dysfunction associated with prior sexual trauma. *Journal of Sex and Marital Therapy, 16,* 142–146.

McCarthy, B. W. (1994). Sexually compulsive men and inhibited sexual desire. *Journal of Sex and Marital Therapy, 20,* 200–209.

McCarthy, B. W. (1995). Learning from unsuccessful sex therapy patients. *Journal of Sex Therapy, 21,* 31–39.

McCarthy, J., & McMillan, S. (1990). Patient/partner satisfaction with penile implant surgery. *Journal of Sex and Marital Therapy, 16,* 25–37.

Messenger, J. C. (1971). Sex and repression in an Irish folk community. In D. S. Marshall & R. C. Suggs (Eds.), *Human sexual desire: Variations in the ethnographic spectrum* (pp. 3–37). New York: Basic Books.

Meyer, A. (1997, March/April). Patching up testosterone. *Psychology Today,* 54.

Michael, R. T., Gagnon, J. H., Laumann, E. O., & Kolata, G. (1994). *Sex in America: A definitive survey.* Boston: Little, Brown.

Mulcahy, J. L. (1995, Winter). Sexual function and aging. *Foundation Focus,* 1–3.

Mulcahy, J. L. (1997). *Diagnosis and management of male sexual dysfunction.* New York: Igaku-Shoinu.

Mullen, P. E., Martin, J. L., Anderson, J. C., Romans, S. E., & Herbison, G. P. (1996). The long-term impact of the physical, emotional, and sexual abuse of children: A community study. *Child Abuse and Neglect, 20,* 7–21.

Newcomb, M. D., & Bentler, P. M. (1988). Behavioral and psychological assessment of sexual dysfunction: An overview. In R. A. Brown & J. R. Field (Eds.), *Treatment of sexual problems in individual and couples therapy* (pp. 127–166). New York: PMA.

Riley, A. J., & Riley, E. J. (1993). Pharmacotherapy for sexual dysfunction: Current status. In A. J. Riley, M. Peet, & C. Wilson (Eds.), *Sexual pharmacology.* Oxford: Clarendon.

Schein, M., Zyzanski, S. J., Levine, S., Medalie, J. H., Dickman, R. L., & Alemangno, S. A. (1988). The frequency of sexual problems among family practice patients. *Family Practice Research Journal, 7,* 122–134.

Schnarch, D. (1991). *Constructing the sexual crucible: An integration of sexual and marital therapy.* New York: Norton.

Schnarch, D. (1993). Inside the sexual crucible. *Family Therapy Networker, 17,* 40–49.

Schover, L. R., & LoPiccolo, J. (1982). Treatment effectiveness for dysfunctions of sexual desire. *Journal of Sex and Marital Therapy, 8,* 179–197.

Segraves, R. T., & Segraves, K. B. (1990). Categorical and multi-axial diagnosis of male erectile disorder. *Journal of Sex and Marital Therapy, 16,* 208–213.

Shaw, J. (1990). Play therapy with the sexual workhorse: Successful treatment with twelve cases of inhibited ejaculation. *Journal of Sex and Marital Therapy, 16,* 159–164.

Shaw, J. (1994). Treatment of primary vaginismus: A new perspective. *Journal of Sex and Marital Therapy, 20,* 46–53.

Shikai, X. (1990). Treatment of impotence in traditional Chinese medicine. *Journal of Sex Education and Therapy, 16,* 198–200.

Shuetz-Mueller, D., Tiefer, L., & Melman, A. (1995). Follow-up of vacuum and nonvacuum constriction devices as treatments for erectile dysfunction. *Journal of Sex and Marital Therapy, 21,* 229–238.

Strean, H. S. (1983). *Sexual dimension: A guide for the mental health practitioner.* New York: Free Press.

Tang, C. S., Lai, F. D., Phil, M., & Chung, T. K. H. (1997). Assessment of sexual functioning for Chinese college students. *Archives of Sexual Behavior, 26,* 79-90.

Weinhardt, L. S., & Carey, M. P. (1996). Prevalence of erectile disorder among men with diabetes mellitus: Comprehensive review, methodological critique, and suggestions for future research. *The Journal of Sex Research, 33,* 205-214.

Weinstein, E., & Rosen, E. (1988). Introduction: Sexuality counseling. In E. Weinstein & E. Rosen (Eds.), *Sexuality counseling: Issues and implications* (pp. 1-15). Pacific Grove, CA: Brooks/Cole.

Whitehead, A., Mathews, A., & Ramage, M. (1987). The treatment of sexually unresponsive women: A comparative evaluation. *Behavior Research and Therapy, 25,* 195-205.

Wilson, G. L., Flammang, M. R., & Dehle, C. M. (1992). Therapeutic formats in the resolution of relationship dysfunction: An acceptability investigation. *Journal of Sex and Marital Therapy, 18,* 20-33.

Wilson, G. L., & Wilson, L. L. (1991). Treatment acceptability of alternative sex therapies: A comparative analysis. *Journal of Sex and Marital Therapy, 17,* 69-80.

Witherington, R. (1991). Vacuum devices for the impotent. *Journal of Sex and Marital Therapy, 17,* 69-80.

Rape, Child Sexual Abuse, and Sexual Harassment

Chapter 11

Sexual Coercion: Rape and Sexual Assault

Perpetrators of Rape
False Rape Allegations and Unpunished
  Sexual Offenses

QUESTION Why are technical definitions of rape inadequate in assessing the incidence of sexual coercion?

Theories of Rape

Evolutionary and Biological Theories of Rape
Psychopathological Theory of Rape
Feminist Theory of Rape
Social Learning Theory of Rape

QUESTION What explanation do most people give for rape?

Consequences of Rape and Treatment for Rape Survivors

Consequences of Rape
Treatment for Rape Survivors
SELF-ASSESSMENT: Rape Empathy Scale
Treatment for the Rape Perpetrator

QUESTIONS What are some typical reactions to rape? What are some alternative treatment procedures for rape victims?

Patterns and Theories of Child Sexual Abuse

Intrafamilial Child Sexual Abuse
Extrafamilial Child Sexual Abuse
Recovered Memories of Abuse
Theories of Child Sexual Abuse

QUESTIONS What theories are helpful in explaining child sexual abuse? How does the definition of incest vary cross-culturally?

Consequences and Treatment of Child Sexual Abuse

Impact of Child Sexual Abuse
Treatment of Sexually Abused Children
PERSONAL CHOICES: Should Children Testify in
  Cases of Alleged Child Sexual Abuse?

QUESTION How does family background help to explain the association between childhood sexual abuse and psychological problems?

Prevention of Rape and Child Sexual Abuse

Rape Prevention
Prevention of Child Sexual Abuse
SOCIAL CHOICES: Megan's Law

QUESTION What strategies might communities and individuals adopt to help prevent both rape and child sexual abuse?

Sexual Harassment

Definition and Incidence of Sexual Harassment
Consequences of Sexual Harassment
Responses to Sexual Harassment
PERSONAL CHOICES: Should You Confront
  Sexual Harassment?
SOCIAL CHOICES: Sexual Harassment Policy in
  the Workplace

QUESTION What options do victims of sexual harassment have for responding to sexual harassment?

277

I was only nine years of age when I was raped by my 19-year-old cousin. He was the first of three family members to sexually molest me.

Oprah Winfrey
Talk Show Host

Date rape on college campuses, sexual molestation of children, and sexual harassment of women exemplify abuse of power and misuse of sexuality. In this chapter, we examine rape, child sexual abuse, and sexual harassment in terms of their nature, consequences, and prevention. We begin by discussing the concept of sexual coercion.

SEXUAL COERCION: RAPE AND SEXUAL ASSAULT

Sexual coercion involves depriving a person of free choice and using force (actual or threatened) to engage a person in sexual acts against that person's will. The Sex Information and Education Council of the United States takes the position that coerced and exploitative sexual acts and such behaviors as rape, incest, and sexual relations between adults and children "are always reprehensible" (SIECUS, 1996, p. 22). Although sexual coercion has existed for centuries, only in the last couple of decades have social scientists, medical and mental health professionals, and politicians acknowledged the prevalence and seriousness of sexually coercive acts. The turning point associated with ending our society's mass silence about rape and sexual assault occurred with the 1975 publication of Susan Brownmiller's *Against Our Will*.

One of the difficulties in studying rape and sexual assault is that these terms are variously defined in legal codes and research literature. Criminal law distinguishes between forcible rape and statutory rape. Forcible rape usually includes three elements: vaginal penetration, force or threat of force, and nonconsent of the victim. Statutory rape involves sexual intercourse without use of force with a person below the legal age of consent. Marital rape, now recognized in all states, is forcible rape by one's spouse.

The ways in which individual women and men define rape also vary. Some women report that they experienced some event that meets the behavioral definition of rape, even though they do not call what they experienced "rape." Similarly, some men have engaged in behavior that was coercive, but do not define themselves as having committed rape. Hence, what actually happens and the label for it may be very different.

Because legal definitions of rape are varied and restrictive, the term "forced sex" is preferable.

NATIONAL DATA

Single women reporting that they had ever been forced to do something sexual by a man

Women not married and not living with a man reporting having been forced to do something sexual by a man 25%

Source: Michael, Gagnon, Laumann, & Kolata, 1994.

In this chapter, we use the terms *forced sex* and *rape* interchangeably to refer to acts of sex (or attempted sex) in which one party is nonconsenting—regardless of the age and sex of the offender and victim—whether or not the act meets criteria for what legally constitutes rape. When the definition of sexual coercion includes rape, sexual abuse, sexual assault, and intercourse in response to pressure, 39% of women and 16% of men in a study of 1399 youths (ages 19 to 22) reported such coercion (Zweig, Barber, & Eccles, 1997).

As just noted, experiencing forced sex applies not just to women. In a study of 101 male medical students, 7% reported being coerced into sexual activity (McConaghy & Zamir, 1995). In another study of 204 heterosexual college men, 34% reported forced coercive sexual contact, mostly by women. In this study, the pressure the men experienced may have been psychological, such as verbal persuasion or the threat of love withdrawal. Most of the men in this study had no negative reaction, but 20 resented the forced sex and feared telling others about the experience (Struckman-Johnson & Struckman-Johnson, 1994).

Perpetrators of Rape

Strangers, acquaintances (such as dates, lovers, or co-workers), gangs, and husbands can all be perpetrators of rape.

STRANGERS   Although it is assumed that most rapes occur as an attack by a stranger, only about 15% of rapes are perpetrated by strangers (Koss, Dinero, Siebel, & Cox, 1988). Rape by a stranger is known as *predatory rape* or *classic rape,* and may involve a weapon (a gun or knife). Rapes by strangers are taken more seriously by the courts, and rapists who do not know their victims are more often convicted.

ACQUAINTANCES   An acquaintance rapist may be a boyfriend or lover (35%); a friend, co-worker, or neighbor (29%); or a casual date (25%) (Koss et al., 1988). In a random sample of sorority women at Purdue University, 63% reported that while attending college, they had experienced a forced attempt at sexual intercourse by a man; 95% of the women reported that they knew their attacker (Copenhaver & Grauerholz, 1991). Acquaintance rape also occurs in gay relationships. In a study of 29 men who were victims of sexual assault, half of the male-male assaults were acquaintance assaults (Stermac, Sheridan, Davidson, & Dunn, 1996).

Date rape is the most typical form of acquaintance rape; it refers to nonconsensual sex between people who are dating or on a date. The following is the recollection of a woman who was raped by her boyfriend on a date.

> Last spring, I met this guy and a relationship started which was great. One year later, he raped me. The term was almost over and we would not be able to spend much time together during the summer. Therefore, we planned to go out to eat and spend some time together.
>
> After dinner we drove to a park. I did not mind or suspect anything for we had done this many times. Then he asked me into the back seat. I got into the back seat with him because I trusted him and he said

Although neither person shown here is a rapist, statistics show that approximately 85% of rapes occur between acquaintances.

> he wanted to be close to me as we talked. He began talking. He told me that he was tired of always pleasing me and not getting a reward. Therefore, he was going to "make love to me" whether I wanted to or not. I thought he was joking, so I asked him to stop playing. He told me he was serious, and after looking at him closely, I knew he was serious. I began to plead with him not to have sex with me. He did not listen. He began to tear my clothes off and confine me so that I could not move. All this time I was fighting him. At one time, I managed to open the door, but he threw me back into the seat, hit me, then he got on me and raped me. After he was satisfied, he stopped, told me to get dressed and stop crying. He said he was sorry it had to happen that way.
>
> He brought me back to the dorm and expected me to kiss him good night. He didn't think he had done anything wrong. Before this happened, I loved this man very much, but afterward I felt great hatred for him.
>
> My life has not been the same since that night. I do not trust men as I once did, nor do I feel completely comfortable when I'm with my present boyfriend. He wants to know why I back off when he tries to be intimate with me. However, right now I can't tell him, as he knows the guy who raped me. (authors' files)

One-third of 828 university students reported having been told by a woman that she had been raped by a date or acquaintance (Dunn, Vail-Smith, & Knight, 1997). The most common sites for rape incidents were the man's apartment (about 25%), at a party (20%) and the woman's apartment (12%). Ninety percent of the victims were age 19 or younger at the time of the rape: 82% did not report the incident to the police.

Date rapes most often occur in the context of alcohol or drugs. In a study of 217 female high school students, 31% said that they were under the influence of alcohol or other drugs when their partner forced them to have sex (Patton & Mannison, 1995). Aware of the effect alcohol has on the opportunity to take advantage of a woman, three members of a fraternity at a state university wrote a letter to potential pledges implying that their parties create a context in which date rapes may occur:

> The forecast calls for a 99 percent chance of getting sex from one of the many new beautiful sorority pledges as they stumble around the dance floor in a drunken stupor bordering on the brink of alcohol poisoning. (O'Brien, 1995, p. 1b)

Alcohol and sexual activity are commonly linked. Half of 523 university sorority women reported "sometimes" or "always" drinking before intercourse (Sawyer, Schulken, & Pinciaro, 1997). Tyson (1997) assessed date rape expectations of 141 university students and found that both women and men predicted rape most often when the man was intoxicated and the woman was sober. The students predicted that rape was least likely when both the man and women were sober.

Two illegal drugs that have been associated with date rape cases are Rohypnol and gamma hydroxybutyrate (GHB). *Rohypnol* (also known as "the date rape drug") causes profound and prolonged sedation, a feeling of well-being, and short-term memory loss. *GHB*, which is potentially fatal, is used for varied effects, including lowering inhibitions. Police in Los Angeles County routinely test date/rape victims for both Rohypnol and GHB.

Unwanted sexual aggression in dating relationships has also been reported by Chinese students. Tang, Critelli, and Porter (1995) studied sexual aggression and victimization among 74 undergraduate women and 146 undergraduate men at the Chinese University of Hong Kong, and found that nonstranger sexual victimization was common among Chinese female college students. Women were much more likely to report engaging in behaviors against their will. For example, about 20% of the women reported that a hand was placed on their breast or thigh against their will.

GANG Some rapes involve more than one perpetrator, and they may be either strangers or acquain-
tances. Chris O'Sullivan (1991) studied acquaintance gang rapes on campus and found that men who would not rape alone may become rapists in the company of their sexually aggressive buddies. She also noted that athletes and fraternity men were more likely to be sexually aggressive and explained that, in gang rapes, there is often one leader of a closely knit group (athletic team, fraternity, or roommates) who instigates the rape. The other group members follow the leader. Participation in gang rape may be motivated by the quest for recreation, adventure, and acceptance by and camaraderie among the group members.

Three social-psychological factors help explain why group members who individually would not commit rape would do so in a group context. First, the group context allows members to diffuse responsibility for the gang rape by blaming others in the group. Second, a group context may produce a state of deindividuation, or "loss of self-awareness, including awareness of one's beliefs, attitudes, and self-standards" (O'Sullivan, 1991, p. 148). Lastly, in a group setting, modeling of aggression occurs. Not only does watching group members rape a woman convey to other group members that this behavior is considered appropriate and fun, it also demonstrates techniques of how to force someone to have sex.

HUSBAND Marital rape may occur as part of a larger pattern of verbal and emotional abuse by the husband. Ten percent of married women in a Boston survey reported that they had been raped by their husbands (Finkelhor & Yllo, 1988). Estimates from other research range from 7 to 14% (Monson, Byrd, & Langhinrichsen-Rohling, 1996). Such rapes may have included not only vaginal intercourse, but also forced fellatio and anal intercourse. The various types of marital rape identified by the researchers included battering rape, nonbattering rape, and obsessive rape (Finkelhor & Yllo, 1988).

Battering marital rape occurs in the context of a regular pattern of verbal and physical abuse. The husbands yell at their wives, call them names, slap, shove, and beat them. These husbands are angry, belligerent, and frequent alcohol abusers. An example follows:

> One afternoon she came home from school, changed into a housecoat, and started toward the bathroom. He got up from the couch where he had been lying, grabbed her, and pushed her down on

the floor. With her face pressed into a pillow and his hand clamped over her mouth, he proceeded to have anal intercourse with her. She screamed and struggled to no avail. Her injuries were painful and extensive. She had a torn muscle in her rectum, so that for three months she had to go to the bathroom standing up. (pp. 144–145)

Nonbattering marital rape often occurs in response to a long-standing conflict or disagreement about sex. The violence is not generalized to the rest of the relationship, but is specific to the sexual conflict. An example follows:

Their love making on this occasion started out pleasantly enough, but he tried to get her to have anal intercourse with him. She refused. He persisted. She kicked and pushed him away. Still, he persisted. They ended up having vaginal intercourse. The force he used was mostly that of his weight on top of her. At 220 pounds, he weighs twice as much as she. "It was horrible," she said. She was sick to her stomach afterward. She cried and felt angry and disgusted. He showed little guilt. "He felt like he'd won something." (p. 145)

Obsessive marital rape may also be categorized as bizarre. The woman is used as a sex object to satisfy an atypical need of the husband. An example follows:

"I was really his masturbating machine," one woman recalled. He was very rough sexually and would hold a pillow over her face to stifle her screams. He would also tie her up and insert objects into her vagina and take pictures, which he shared with his friends. The interviewee later discovered a file card in her husband's desk which sickened her. On the card, he had written a list of dates—dates that corresponded to the forced sex episodes of the past months. Next to each was a complicated coding system which seemed to indicate the type of sex act and a ranking of how much he enjoyed it. (p. 146)

Historically, husbands could not be prosecuted for rape because the wife was the husband's property and "taking her sexually" was his right. Today, every state recognizes marital rape as a crime. Most wives are reluctant to press charges, but those who do are usually successful in seeing their husbands convicted. Russell (1991) reported that 88% of husbands who were reported to the police and arrested for rape were eventually convicted. One reason for such a high conviction rate is that such rapes are often particularly brutal or deviant.

False Rape Allegations and Unpunished Sexual Offenses

Some men are charged with a rape they did not commit. Nina Shahravan accused Erik Williams of raping her while his Dallas Cowboys' teammate, Michael Irvin, held a gun to her head (Carter, 1997). Both of the accused were taken into custody, and for 10 days, the media linked them with the crime of rape. However, Shahravan later admitted that the incident had never happened.

Kanin (1994) documented 45 disposed, false rape allegations in a small metropolitan community over a 9-year period. There were three reasons the women made the false rape charges: to provide an alibi (a young woman gets pregnant by her boyfriend but claims the rapist did it), for revenge (a woman accuses the boyfriend who rejected her), and for attention or sympathy (a woman claims she was raped in order to get her mother to stop being mad at her). The penalty for false allegations varies. Shahravan faced a maximum $2000 fine and a maximum of 6 months in jail. Damage to the reputation of the innocent person who is accused of rape can be enormous.

False accusations of rape are scandalous and cause great distress and harm to anyone who is falsely accused. They also cause harm to victims of rape and other sexual crimes, as they may lead to skepticism when victims report crimes. In addition, victims may be reluctant to report rape out of fear they will not be believed. Russell (1984) found that only 9.5% of rapes were reported by women in her randomly selected community sample. In fact, unpunished sexual offenses are much more common than convictions due to false accusations. People often engage in sexual offenses and are not apprehended by the law. In a sample of 60 undergraduate college men (who are often used as nonoffender controls in sex research), nearly two-thirds had engaged in some form of sexual misconduct in the past. Over half (52%) had engaged in a sexual offense for which they could be arrested (Templeman & Stinnett, 1991). Some examples of these offenses included voyeurism (42%), frottage (35%), obscene phone calls (8%), and coercive sex (8%). In spite of the relatively high incidence of engaging in punishable sex offenses, only two of the respondents (3%) had been arrested.

Because most rapes of adult women are perpetrated by men with whom the women were acquainted or romantically involved, rape is one of the most underreported violent crimes in the United States. Estimates suggest that between 50 and 90% of completed rapes go unreported (Powers & Rosenfeld, 1997).

THEORIES OF RAPE

Various theories have been suggested in an attempt to explain why rape occurs.

Evolutionary and Biological Theories of Rape

Evolutionary and biological theories explain rape on the basis of anatomy, biologically based drives, and natural selection for reproductive success. It is possible for men to have a penile erection when intercourse is not desired; hence, it is possible for women to rape men. However, the biological difference between women and men is such that the woman's vagina is always in a state of being "rapable," whereas the man's penis is not. (This statement is true only if the definition of rape that is used involves vaginal penetration.)

In addition, men are usually physically taller and stronger than women and are therefore capable of overpowering them. Being aware of the biological advantage men have over women, many women have begun to level the playing field by becoming proficient in karate or other forms of self-defense.

Some biological theories of rape suggest that rape results from a strong biological sex drive in men. This strong sex drive is explained in part by the high level of androgens and other sex hormones to which the male brain is exposed.

Evolutionary (or sociobiological) theory explains that males have a strong sex drive because natural selection favors males who copulate with numerous females. Males achieve reproductive success through copulating with as many females as possible; females achieve reproductive success through limiting their copulation behavior to males who are committed to help care for the female and her offspring.

Although rape is made possible by both men's capacity to rape and their greater physical strength, this does not explain why men want to rape women. Similarly, it does not explain why some men rape and some do not.

Psychopathological Theory of Rape

According to the psychopathological theory of rape, rapists are viewed as having a mental disorder. Most people in the general population agree with this theory and think of rapists as being "crazy." Groth and Birnbaum (1979) developed a typology of rapes, each of which is based on some form of emotional or intrapsychic problem. Groth's typology includes the following: anger rape, which results from the rapist's extreme anger (rape is viewed as the ultimate expression of anger toward another person); power rape, which is motivated by the rapist's desire to sexually possess his victim (this need to possess is often based on the rapist's insecurity regarding his masculinity); and sadistic rape, which involves elements of sexuality and aggression. (In sadistic rape, the offender derives sexual pleasure from inflicting intense pain and humiliation on his victim, who is usually a stranger.)

The psychopathological theory of rape may be criticized on the basis that the subject populations used for studies on rapists have been made up of incarcerated rapists. Also, not all rapists display the same symptomology or show marked deviation on standard psychological tests. Russell (1984) argued that "there is no denying that some rapists are mentally ill; the psychopathological model only becomes objectionable when it is used to apply to all or most rapists, as is done so often" (p. 148).

Feminist Theory of Rape

The feminist theory of rape emphasizes the inequality between men and women in society. Proponents of this theory believe that men dominate women in the political and economic sphere, and that rape is an extension of the dominance, power, and control men exert over women. Through the feminist theory, rape is viewed as an act of aggression and violence perpetrated to establish the man's control over the woman: it is not just an act of sex (Brownmiller, 1975).

Support for the view that rape is essentially a male response associated with the social inequality between the sexes is provided by data that suggest that the incidence and prevalence of rape in different societies varies by the degree of inequality between the women and men in those societies. In one study of 95 societies (Sanday, 1981), rape was either absent or rare in almost half (47%) of the cases. In these societies (the Ashanti of West Africa, for example), women tend to have equal status with men. "In 'rape free' societies women are treated with considerable respect, and prestige is attached to female reproductive and productive roles" (p. 16). Similarly, Lottes and Weinberg (1996) found lower rates of sexual coercion among Swedish students when compared to U.S. students. The researchers pointed out that women in Sweden have more institutional power and social benefits than women in the United States, which means there is greater equality between the sexes in Sweden. 🖉

Societies in which women are viewed as inferior to men tend to be more rape-prone. Women in rape-prone societies are also viewed as property, implying that men may take them by violent means. Research that supports the feminist theory of rape is also provided by Frank (1991), who found that self-reported rapists placed greater emphasis on power and dominance in their relationships with women.

One of the strengths of the feminist view on rape is that it asserts that women should not be blamed for their victimization. Regarding a weakness of this view on rape, Ellis (1989) suggested that "the feminist theory seems to considerably underestimate the degree to which rape is sexually motivated . . ." (p. 31). While domination and power may be primary motivations in predatory rape, sex may be a primary motivation in most date rapes (Kanin, 1957).

Social Learning Theory of Rape

The social learning theory of rape views rape as "behavior that males learn through the acquisition of social attitudes favorable to rape, and through the imitation of depictions of sexuality interlinked with aggression" (Ellis, 1989, p. 16). According to Ellis (1989), men learn aggressive behavior toward women, including rape behavior, through four interrelated processes: the sex-violence linkage effect, the modeling effect, the desensitization effect, and the "rape myth" effect.

1. The sex-violence linkage effect refers to the association of sexuality and violence. For example, many slasher and horror films, some pornography, and even some music videos depict sex and violence together, thus causing the viewer to form a link or association between sex and violence.

2. The modeling effect involves imitating rape scenes and other acts of violence toward women that are seen in real life and in the mass media. Frank (1991) also observed that having sexually aggressive friends is associated with self-reported rape.

3. The desensitization effect involves becoming desensitized to the pain, fear, and humiliation of sexual aggression through repeated exposure to sexual aggression.

4. The "rape myth" effect refers to the perpetuation of stereotyped beliefs about rape, its victims, and its perpetrators.

Table 11.1 lists several rape-tolerant beliefs and the percentage of men and women who agree with these beliefs. Men score higher on rape myths, which tend to justify sexual aggression toward women. A man who thinks that a woman really means "yes" when she says "no" believes he has not raped a woman who repeatedly told him "no."

Burt (1991) suggested that rape myths (also referred to as rape-supportive beliefs) which are learned from family, friends, and mass media, "are the mechanism that people use to justify dismissing an incident of sexual assault from the category of 'real' rape" (p. 27). Belief in rape myths may also predispose rape victims toward blaming themselves for the rape. Research suggests that the rape myth effect, that is, belief in rape myths, both facilitates the act of rape and serves as a subsequent justification for engaging in rape behavior (Check & Malamuth, 1981; Scully, 1990). Scales measuring rape myths and related attitudes predicted college students' reactions to a fictional rape, a report of an actual rape, and men's predictions of their own likelihood of raping (Check & Malamuth, 1985).

More recent studies confirm these findings. In Frank's study (1991) of university men and prison inmates, rape-supportive attitudes was the strongest predictor of raping. He found that such attitudes have a "single core" that centers on the notion that "it is 'OK' to force sex on certain kinds of women who 'deserve it' or in certain kinds of situations," such as when "he has spent a lot of money on her, or if she has a 'loose' reputation" (p. 11).

TABLE 11.1   Percentage of College Men and Women Agreeing with Rape-Tolerant Statements

ITEM	MEN (N=407)	WOMEN (N=422)
1. A man sees sex as an achievement or notch in his belt.	47.9	67.8*
2. Rape really only occurs when a man has a weapon.	2.5	1.2
3. Deep down, a woman likes to be whistled at on the street.	54.8	38.9*
4. If a woman is heavily intoxicated, it is OK to have sex with her.	22.6	1.9*
5. Women frequently cry false rape.	28.3	19.0*
6. In a woman, submissiveness equals femininity.	25.8	14.2*
7. In a man, aggressiveness equals masculinity.	32.4	30.3
8. A prostitute cannot be raped.	81.6	93.8*
9. Some women ask to be raped and may enjoy it.	44.7	20.6*
10. Any woman could prevent rape if she wanted to.	27.3	16.6*
11. Rape is often provoked by the victim.	30.5	14.7*
12. If a woman says "no" to having sex, she means "maybe" or even "yes."	36.9	21.1*

* indicates a statistically significant gender difference.

Source: Holcomb et al., 1991.

_____ **THINK ABOUT IT** _____

Why does the inaccurate stereotype persist that most rapes are committed by strangers?

CONSEQUENCES OF RAPE AND TREATMENT FOR RAPE SURVIVORS

Rape is a traumatic experience, and the success of treatment is slow.

Consequences of Rape

An individual who has been raped has been traumatized. Initial reactions to rape include an acute period of disorganization, helplessness, vulnerability, and anger. The person may also blame himself or herself for the incident.

The most devastating aspect of rape may not be the genital contact, but rather the sense of cognitive and emotional violation. The woman who felt that her environment was safe and predictable, that other people were trustworthy, and that she was competent and autonomous may become someone who is fearful of her surroundings, suspicious of other people, and unsure of her ability to control her life.

Rape trauma syndrome refers to the acute and long-term reorganization process that occurs as a result of forcible rape or attempted rape (Burgess & Holmstrom, 1974). The acute phase involves fear, anxiety, crying, and restlessness. Long-term reorganization may involve moving to another community and changing one's phone number. Nightmares, sexual dysfunctions, and phobias associated with the rape may also occur. Examples of the latter include fear of being alone, being in the dark, or touching a man's penis.

Posttraumatic stress disorder (PTSD), a DSM-IV diagnosis, is characteristic of reactions to military combat or natural disasters. It is also a reaction experienced by some rape victims. The rape survivor may have persistent flashbacks or hallucinations and will attempt to avoid any stimuli associated with the trauma. This may involve efforts to avoid thoughts, feelings, or activities associated with the trauma; a restricted range of affect (such as the inability to have love feelings); feelings of detachment or estrangement from others; and the inability to recall aspects of the trauma (psychogenic amnesia). The person may also report difficulty sleeping, increased irritability, and outbursts of anger. Rothbaum, Foa, Riggs, Murdock, & Walsh (1992) found that 94% of the women they assessed within the first two weeks of a rape experience had symptoms that met the diagnostic criteria for PTSD. At 3 months after the rape, PTSD persisted for almost half (47%).

In a longitudinal study of 1399 youth (women and men)—both college and noncollege—having been raped was associated with anger, social isolation, depressed mood, and lower self-esteem. The more violent the coercion, the more difficult the adjustment (Zweig et al., 1997).

Treatment for Rape Survivors

Not all rape victims experience symptoms of trauma. Some seem to view the event as unfortunate, unavoidable, and something over which they had no control. They are determined that the event will not psychologically immobilize them and it doesn't. Others benefit from both crisis counseling and long-term therapy.

Crisis counseling may last from a few days to 2 or 3 months after the assault. The primary goals of crisis counseling include establishing a therapeutic relationship, encouraging emotional expression, and providing information about reporting rape to the police and symptoms the victim may experience. The therapist may also promote adjustment of immediate role responsibilities, which may take the form of encouraging the person to take time off from work or eliciting the support of others to provide a period for processing the rape experience.

Crisis counselors also discuss with the victim the importance of seeing a physician to take care of medical needs (care for physical injuries, testing for STDs and pregnancy) as well as to document the rape if the victim decides to take legal action. The latter is often a difficult choice for most rape victims as it makes their rape experience public and exposes them to questioning and interrogation by strangers.

Long-term therapy was required for two-thirds of 92 rape victims studied by Burgess and Holmstrom (1974); all 92 victims needed more than a "few months" to recover from their rape experience. Techniques and approaches used to help the rape victim adjust include the following (Becker &

Both short- and long-term therapy may help an individual cope with rape.

Kaplan, 1991; Calhoun & Atkeson, 1991; Resick & Schnicke, 1992; Roth, Dye, & Lebowitz, 1988):

1. *Systematic desensitization.* For the woman overwhelmed with specific fear, systematic desensitization allows her to overcome anxiety and be relaxed while alone or with a man.
2. *Flooding and implosion.* An alternative to systematic desensitization, this procedure involves extended exposure to the upsetting thoughts and situations "until habituation occurs and the cues no longer elicit anxiety" (Calhoun & Atkeson, 1991, p. 66). Systematic desensitization and implosion are usually effective in reducing the frequency of nightmares and flashbacks.
3. *Writing about the trauma.* For many clients, writing about their experience and its meaning to them is therapeutic because it allows them to confront the experience (exposure therapy) in a safe environment where a therapist or group can help them gain information and support in processing the event.

Rape, Child Sexual Abuse, and Sexual Harassment　285

4. *Stress inoculation training.* This technique provides rape victims with a systematic way of framing their rape experience, learning how to relax through deep-muscle relaxation procedures and breathing control, and using covert modeling. The latter involves the rape survivor visualizing a rape encounter and successfully confronting the event.

5. *Cognitive therapy.* This involves recognizing and eliminating dysfunctional thoughts. Cognitive therapy emphasizes reframing the rape experience from one of great horror to one in which the person has benefited—by learning to be more cautious, by recognizing one's vulnerability, and by appreciating the safety of one's close relationships. Cognitive therapy also encourages the person to increase the frequency of positive self-statements so as to enhance self-esteem. For example, persons who have been raped are encouraged to view themselves as survivors rather than as victims.

6. *Sex therapy.* Sexual dysfunctions may occur subsequent to a rape experience. Anxiety responses, lack of trust, fear and avoidance of sexual contact, and the inability to have an orgasm or feel sexual arousal or pleasure are possible outcomes of being raped. A number of sex therapy techniques may be used to remediate these sexual dysfunctions, including systematic desensitization, sensate focus, and graduated assignments (shaping). Initially, all expectations of intercourse are eliminated.

7. *Assertiveness training.* Rape victims often fear being assaulted again. Through assertiveness training, "victims learn to distinguish passive, assertive, and aggressive behavior, so that they more accurately interpret the behavior of others and gain more control in their interactions" (Calhoun & Atkeson, 1991, p. 74). In addition, victims learn that they have a right to be assertive and to have their needs respected.

8. *Group treatment.* Providing therapy to rape survivors in a group context (sometimes called a "support group") allows them to share their experience with others who have had similar experiences. Group treatment is one of the more frequently used modalities in reducing a sense of isolation and alienation. "The common bond allowed for the identification of common issues, the sharing of coping methods, and the attainment of insight" (Roth et al., 1988, p. 85). Therapy techniques for treating fear, anxiety, and depression can also be used in a group setting.

9. *Conjoint therapy.* Conjoint, or couple, therapy helps the rape survivor and his or her partner discuss the impact of the rape on each other and on their relationship.

About half of 87 female victims of rape and incest in the Katz (1991) study reported that they had "completely or nearly completely" recovered. The researcher concluded that "although rape may have lifelong effects, it is also possible to feel recovered from it" (p. 265). Hence, rape victims become rape survivors.

The Rape Empathy Scale in the following Self-Assessment will assess the degree to which you have empathy for rape victims.

Treatment for the Rape Perpetrator

One way to reduce the incidence of repeat rape and sexual assaults is to treat the offender. According to the U.S. Department of Justice, most institutional treatment programs for sex offenders have found that about 15 to 20% of treated offenders will commit a sex offense within 3 years of release; about 60% of those who have not received treatment will commit another sex offense (Interagency Council on Sex Offender Treatment, 1991).

The majority of sex offenders never receive treatment because in most cases, the rapist is neither caught nor convicted. Most often, he is not caught because the rape is not reported. Only 2% of those in Copenhaver and Grauerholz's study (1991) who had been raped or had experienced an attempted rape reported the experience to the police. Among the rapes that are reported where the alleged rapists is apprehended, few cases come to trial. Of nearly 1000 rapes that were reported to the Denver police, less than 5% of the accused were brought to trial and even fewer were convicted (Sheppard, Giacinti, & Tjaden, 1976).

In *Against Our Will*, Susan Brownmiller (1975) said that men rape because they can get away with it. Rapists often escape conviction with the help of

RAPE EMPATHY SCALE

This is a questionnaire designed to find out how different people feel about certain aspects of a rape situation. For the purpose of this questionnaire, rape is defined as an act in which one adult person (a male) compels another adult person (a female) to submit to penile-vaginal sexual intercourse against her will.

Each question consists of a pair of alternative statements lettered a or b. Please select the one statement of each pair which you more strongly *believe* to be the case as far as you are concerned. Be sure to select the one you actually *believe* to be more true rather than the one you think you should choose or the one you would like to be true. This is a measure of personal belief; thus, *there are no right or wrong answers*. Once you have decided which statement you more strongly believe to be the case, write the letter of the statement that indicates how strongly you prefer one statement over the alternative statement.

1 = strongly prefer statement (a) over statement (b)

2 = moderately prefer statement (a) over statement (b)

3 = slightly prefer statement (a) over statement (b)

4 = prefer both statements equally or can't decide between them

5 = slightly prefer statement (b) over statement (a)

6 = moderately prefer statement (b) over statement (a)

7 = strongly prefer statement (b) over statement (a)

For example, if you strongly prefer statement (b) over statement (a), you could write the number 7 on your answer sheet for that pair of statements.

In some rare instances, you may discover that you genuinely prefer both statements or neither one. In such cases, and only in such cases, you may indicate a neutral position by writing the number 4.

1. __1__ a) I feel that the situation in which a man compels a woman to submit to sexual intercourse against her will is an unjustifiable act under any circumstances.

    b) I feel that the situation in which a man compels a woman to submit to sexual intercourse against her will is a justifiable act under certain circumstances.

2. __7__ a) In deciding the matter of guilt or innocence in a rape case, it is more important to know about the past sexual activity of the alleged rape victim than the past sexual activity of the alleged rapist.

    b) It is more important to know about the past sexual activity of the alleged rapist than the past sexual activity of the alleged rape victim in deciding the matter of guilt or innocence in a rape case.

3. __7__ a) In general, I feel that rape is an act that is provoked by the rape victim.

    b) In general, I feel that rape is an act that is not provoked by the rape victim.

4. __6__ a) I would find it easier to imagine how a rapist might feel during an actual rape than how a rape victim might feel.

    b) I would find it easier to imagine how a rape victim might feel during an actual rape than how a rapist might feel.

5. __7__ a) Under certain circumstances, I can understand why a man would use force to obtain sexual relations with a woman.

    b) I cannot understand why a man would use force to obtain sexual relations with a woman under any circumstances.

Continued on following page.

6. ___ **a)** In a court of law, I feel that the rapist must be held accountable for his behavior during the rape.

   b) In a court of law, I feel that the rape victim must be held accountable for her behavior during the rape.

7. ___ **a)** When a woman dresses in a sexually attractive way, she must be willing to accept the consequences of her behavior, whatever they are, since she is signaling her interest in having sexual relations.

   b) A woman has the right to dress in a sexually attractive way whether she is really interested in having sexual relations or not.

8. ___ **a)** I would find it easier to empathize with the shame and humiliation a rapist might feel during a trial for rape than with the feelings a rape victim might have during the trial.

   b) I would find it easier to empathize with the shame and humiliation a rape victim might feel during a trial to prove rape than with the feelings a rapist might have during the trial.

9. ___ **a)** If a man rapes a sexually active woman, he would probably be justified in his actions by the fact that she chooses to have sexual relations with other men.

   b) If a man rapes a sexually active woman, his actions would not be justified by the fact that she chooses to have sexual relations with other men.

10. ___ **a)** I believe that all women secretly want to be raped.

   b) I don't believe that any women secretly want to be raped.

11. ___ **a)** In deciding whether a rape has occurred or not, the burden of proof should rest with the woman, who must prove that a rape has actually occurred.

   b) In deciding whether a rape has occurred or not, the burden of proof should rest with the man, who must prove that a rape has not actually occurred.

12. ___ **a)** I believe that it is impossible for a rape victim to enjoy being raped.

   b) I believe that it is possible for a rape victim to enjoy the experience of being raped, whether she admits it or not.

13. ___ **a)** I can really empathize with the helplessness a rapist might feel during a rape, since he's at the mercy of forces beyond his control.

   b) I can really empathize with the helplessness a victim might feel during a rape if all of her attempts to resist the rape have failed.

14. ___ **a)** After a rape has occurred, I think the woman would suffer more emotional torment in dealing with the police than the man would.

   b) After a rape has occurred, I think the man would suffer more emotional torment in dealing with the police than the woman would.

15. ___ **a)** I feel it is impossible for a man to rape a woman unless she is willing.

   b) I feel it is possible for a man to rape a woman against her will.

16. ___ **a)** If a rape trial were publicized in the press, I feel the rape victim would suffer more emotional trauma from the publicity than the rapist.

   b) If a rape trial were publicized in the press, I feel the rapist would suffer more emotional trauma from the publicity than the rape victim.

17. ___ **a)** Once a couple has had sexual intercourse, then that issue is resolved and it is no longer possible for that man to rape that woman.

Continued on following page.

b) Even if a couple has had sexual intercourse before, if the man forces the woman to have sexual intercourse with him against her will, this should be considered rape.

⌐ **18.** ⊥ **a)** I can understand a wife's humiliation and anger if her husband forced her to have sexual relations with him.

b) A husband has every right to determine when sexual relations with his wife occur, even if it means forcing her to have sex with him.

⌐ **19.** ⊥ **a)** If I were a member of the jury in a rape trial, I would probably be more likely to believe the woman's testimony than the man's, since it takes a lot of courage on the woman's part to accuse the man of rape.

b) If I were a member of the jury in a rape trial, I would probably be more likely to believe the man's testimony than the woman's since rape is a charge that is difficult to defend against, even if the man is innocent.

Scoring and Interpretation   Responses are scored so that an item score of 1 indicates strong empathy for the rapist and 7 indicates strong empathy for the rape victim (Deitz, Blackwell, Daley, & Bentley, 1982). Therefore, reverse the scores (change 1, 2, and 3 to 7, 6, and 5) for the following items: 1, 6, 12, 14, 16, 18, and 19. Then sum the scores.

In Table 1, mean scores for men and women from three studies are presented, so that you may compare your score to those obtained from other students and community members.

Study Population	Women	Men
Deitz, et al. (1982)		
Group 1 (Colorado State University undergraduates)	108.86	98.25
Group 2 (Colorado State University undergraduates)	111.71	100.25
Group 3 (Eligible jurors in county)	112.60	101.91
Borden, Karr, & Caldwell-Colbert (1988)		
Group 1 (small midwest state university undergraduates)	107.88	100.36
Group 2 (small midwest state university undergraduates)	112.04	98.56
Weir & Wrightsman (1990)		
Undergraduates	113.97	102.72

Reliability and Validity   Deitz et al. (1982) reported that respondents were fairly consistent in answering the items within the scale (coefficient alpha for their juror group as 0.89 and 0.84 for the students), with essentially no difference between men and women's reliability scores. The relation between respondent's endorsement of individual items and their total score (item-total correlations) ranged from 0.33 to 0.75 for the juror group and from 0.18 to 0.52 for the student group. Cross-validation was performed on separate juror and student samples.

From "Measurement of Empathy Toward Rape Victims and Rapists," by S. R. Deitz, K. T. Blackwell, P. C. Daley & B. J. Bentley, 1982, *Journal of Personality and Social Psychology, 43*(2), 372-384. Copyright © 1983 by the American Psychological Association. Reprinted by permission.

an attorney who contends that the rape complaint is "unfounded" and requests that the police stop prosecution procedures. A rape complaint may be labeled "unfounded" if the case is seen as weak; for example, if the victim was intoxicated at the time, delayed reporting the alleged attack, refused to submit to a medical examination, had a previous relationship with the rapist, or if there is a lack of physical evidence to document that the rape occurred.

Sex offenders rarely seek treatment prior to any involvement with legal authorities and on their own volition. Most sex offenders in treatment are required to be there by legal authorities, and many therapists in outpatient programs refuse to take voluntary clients.

The timing of therapy is important. Unless therapy occurs when the offender is facing a court hearing or as a condition of probation, the perpetrator usually denies the existence of a problem and has little motivation for treatment. Experienced clinicians typically request a court order before beginning treatment or recommend a period of inpatient treatment (Salter, 1988; Saunders & Awad, 1988). This has proved to be important in keeping offenders in treatment, due to their denial and minimization of their offenses. It also helps reduce the "two-week cure" ("Thank you, doc. That was great. I learned a lot. No, I don't think I need therapy any more. Well, I'll never do that again. So long.") (Salter, 1988, p. 87). When well-meaning people allow offenders to seek voluntary therapy instead of reporting the offender to legal authorities, there is no leverage to maintain participation in treatment or to protect the safety of the community (Salter, 1988).

Multiple modalites are used in the treatment of sex offenders. Such modalites include the following (Saunders & Awad, 1988; Interagency Council on Sex Offender Treatment, 1991; Perkins, 1991):

1. *Group therapy.* In group therapy, peer pressure is used as a means of forcing the offender to abandon his denial, to accept his problem, and to be motivated to change.
2. *Reducing rape interests.* Techniques and medications for reducing deviant arousal interests (such as rape) will be discussed in Chapter 18, "Paraphilias and Sexuality."
3. *Increasing arousal to appropriate stimuli.* This involves orgasmic reconditioning (by having the man masturbate to socially appropriate stimuli) to increase arousal to such stimuli. Social skills training may also be used to provide the perpetrator with the opportunity for emotional, social, and sexual involvement with a partner in a consenting relationship.
4. *Cognitive restructuring.* Sex offenders often have rape-supportive beliefs and attitudes (also called "thinking errors"). Cognitive restructuring involves changing such errors in thinking.
5. *Victim empathy.* Sex offenders may be required to either write an account of the rape or sexual assault from the point of view of the victim or play the role of the victim in a role-play of the rape or sexual assault. These activities are designed to develop empathy for victims of sexual assault.

6. *Additional therapeutic modalities.* Other treatment modalities used in sex offender treatment programs include relaxation and stress management, communication skills training, impulse control, sex education, gender-role stereotyping awareness, values clarification, and dealing with the offender's own past sexual or physical abuse.
7. *After-treatment care.* Some sex offender programs have an after-care component designed to assist the client once he is released from treatment. After-treatment care may include assisting the client in gaining further education or in securing employment.

One special focus in treating sex offenders is the development of programs to identify and treat juvenile perpetrators. In 1982, there were only about 20 specialized programs identified in the United States, but by 1988, there were 520. The growth in these programs reflects recognition of the finding that as many as 60 to 80% of adult offenders began offending during adolescence. Reports reveal that 50% of molested boys and 15 to 20% of sexually abused girls were offended by adolescents (The National Adolescent Perpetrator Network, 1988).

In general, the goals for sex offenders in treatment include the following (Interagency Council on Sex Offender Treatment, 1991, p. 26):

- To accept total responsibility for the crime
- To build empathy for victims and other people
- To identify and understand how he or she exploits others
- To learn how to control and eliminate inappropriate impulses
- To develop socially acceptable ways of interacting with others

--- THINK ABOUT IT ---

The rape survivor's partner also experiences reactions to the rape. "Not only must the partner cope with the victim's psychological distress and emotional needs, but he must also deal with his own reactions to the assault" (Calhoun & Atkeson, 1991, p. 117). Partner reactions include shock, rage, self-blame, concern for the victim, and emotional distress.

PATTERNS AND THEORIES OF CHILD SEXUAL ABUSE

An alarming percentage of adults report having been sexually abused as children.

NATIONAL DATA

In a national survey of adults concerning child sexual abuse, 27% of the women and 16% of the men reported being victims of such abuse.

Source: Finkelhor & Yllo, 1990.

Child sexual abuse is categorized as being either intrafamilial or extrafamilial.

Intrafamilial Child Sexual Abuse

Also referred to as incestuous child abuse, *intrafamilial child sexual abuse* refers to exploitative sexual contact or attempted or forced sex that occurs between relatives when the victim is under the age of 18. Sexual contact or attempted sexual contact includes intercourse, fondling of the breasts and genitals, and oral sex. "Relatives" in this instance include biologically related individuals, stepparents, and stepsiblings.

FATHERS AS PERPETRATORS Parent-child incest, particularly between a father or stepfather and a child in the family, is the type of incest that has received the most attention in society. Such incest is a blatant abuse of power and authority. Stepfathers are much more likely than biological fathers to perpetrate incest. In Russell's 1984 random sample, nearly one in six women (17%) who had a stepfather as a principal childhood figure experienced sexual abuse perpetrated by him. In contrast, the figure for biological fathers was approximately 1 out of every 40 women (2%). Five percent of 9000 15-year-olds in Finland reported that they had been sexually abused by their father or stepfather. The percent of girls who reported sexual experiences with their biological father or stepfather was 0.2% and 3.7%, respectively (Sariola & Uutela, 1996).

The experience of a woman who, as a child, was forced to have sexual relations with her father is described as follows:

I was around 6 years old when I was sexually abused by my father. He was not drinking at the time; therefore, he had a clear mind as to what he was doing. On looking back, it seemed so well planned. For some reason, my father wanted me to go with him to the woods behind our house to help him saw wood for the night. I went without any question. Once we got there, he looked around for a place to sit and wanted me to sit down with him. In doing so, he said, "Susan, I want you to do something for daddy." I said, "What's that, daddy?" He went on to explain that "I want you to lie down, and we are going to play mamma and daddy." Being a child, I said "okay," thinking it was going to be fun. I don't know what happened next because I can't remember if there was pain or whatever. I was threatened not to tell, and remembering how he beat my mother, I didn't want the same treatment. It happened approximately two other times. I remember not liking this at all. Since I couldn't tell mama, I came to the conclusion it was wrong and I was not going to let it happen again.

But what could I do? Until age 18, I was constantly on the run, hiding from him when I had to stay home alone with him, staying out of his way so he wouldn't touch me by hiding in the corn fields all day long, under the house, in the barns, and so on, until my mother got home, then getting punished by her for not doing the chores she had assigned to me that day. It was a miserable life growing up in that environment. (authors' files)

Factors contributing to father-daughter incest include extreme paternal dominance (the daughter learns to be obedient to her father), maternal disability (the mother ceases to function as an emotional and sexual partner for the husband), and imposition of the mothering role on the oldest daughter (she becomes responsible for housework and child care). An added consequence of the oldest daughter taking over the role of the mother is her belief that she is responsible for keeping the family together. This implies not only doing what the father wants, but keeping it a secret because she or her father will be expelled from the family for disclosure (Herman, 1981).

Although some fathers may force themselves on their daughters (as in the example of the 6-year-old girl described earlier), incest may begin by affectionate cuddling between father and daughter. The father's motives may be sexual; his daughter's are typically nonsexual. Indeed, the daughter is often unaware of any sexual connotations of her behavior; her motive is to feel acceptance and love from her father. Ambivalent feelings often result:

> My daddy never touched me unless he wanted to have me play with his genitals. I didn't like touching him there, but he was affectionate to me and told me how pretty I was. I was really mixed up about the whole thing. (authors' files)

Because of her ambivalence, the daughter may continue to participate in sexual activity with her father. Not only may she derive attention and affection from the relationship, but she may also develop a sense of power over her father. As she grows older, she may even demand gifts in exchange for her silence.

What does the mother do when she finds out her husband has been molesting their daughter? In a study of 43 mothers whose daughters were sexually abused by their fathers, 56% sided with their daughters and rejected their mates, 9% denied the incest and took no action, and 35% sided with their mates at the expense of their daughters (Myer, 1985). The latter could have occurred because they believed their daughter was lying, they did not want to threaten the marriage, or they wanted to drive the daughter out of the family.

Father-daughter touching is influenced by culture; what is defined as child sexual abuse varies by the society and culture in which it occurs. Sam and Kathy Kresnidi are an Albanian immigrant couple (now U.S. citizens) who had two children, Tim and Lima. One day in 1989 while Sam was attending his son's karate tournament, Sam was observed to be "molesting" his 4-year-old daughter Lima. The police were called, and he was arrested and taken to jail. Subsequently, his children were taken from him and adopted by a Christian family. The Kresnidis have been forbidden by the courts from any contact with their children (ABC's *20/20*, 1995). In Albanian culture, physical intimacy in the form of kissing and touching are normative and assigned no sexual connotations by either the parent or the child. In the United States, such behaviors are assigned sexual meaning and result in the children's being permanently taken from their parents.

There has been less attention to father-son incest in the literature than to mother-son incest, and some investigators believe it is significantly underreported. Herman (1981) located 32 cases of father-son incest in the professional literature, as well as a report in which one guidance clinic for children identified 10 cases of father-son incest.

WOMEN AS PERPETRATORS   Incest between mothers and sons (or daughters) occurs less frequently than father-daughter incest (Marvasti, 1986). It rarely includes intercourse but is usually confined to various stimulating behaviors. The mother may continue to bathe her son long after he is capable of caring for himself, during which time she stimulates him sexually. Later, she may stimulate her son to ejaculation. The mother may also sleep with her son. Although no specific sexual contact may occur, she may sleep in the nude; this behavior is provocative as well as stimulating.

Russell (1984) noted that mother-daughter incest has been virtually unexamined. She cited Finkelhor's conclusion that mothers are more likely to abuse daughters than sons and that mother-son incest is the least frequently occurring form of parent-child sexual abuse.

Although women are much less likely to sexually abuse their children than men, recent writers have voiced the concern that the incidence of women as perpetrators of child sexual abuse had been underreported and underestimated. The tendency to view mothers as asexual and men as sexual aggressors may be one reason why incidences of maternal sexual abuse are seldom identified (Lawson, 1991). Professional bias against the possibility that women could sexually abuse children may have prevented professionals from seeing it (Allen, 1990). In addition, Allen warns that focusing only on low relative rates of women sexually abusing children (as opposed to abuse by men) may be deceptive in terms of absolute numbers of children abused. "Gender dichotomy theories which cast perpetration into 'men do/women don't' categories divert attention from women who do sexually abuse children" (p. 121). Extrapolating from victimization data collected by Russell and Finkelhor, Allen offered the following projections. Starting from an estimated 29 million U.S. women believed to be survivors of child sexual abuse, if 5% were abused by adult women, that results in 1.5 million female victims abused by women. And of the estimated 5.4 million male victims of child sexual abuse, if 20% were sexually abused by women, then there are 1.1 million male victims abused by women. So even though rates of male and female victimizing are quite disproportionate, the absolute numbers are striking, and we need to be sensitive to the experiences of these survivors.

SIBLING INCEST   Sibling incest is more common than parent-child incest; in fact, it is probably the most common type of incest (Adler & Schutz, 1995). Pierce and Pierce (1990) identified two categories of sibling activities. One type usually begins early as mutual exploration. It may end when the children realize the behavior is not acceptable. If, however, the behavior continues into adolescence, the siblings may have distress in later sexual relationships, although this is not always the case. The other type of activity involves one sibling forcing another to participate in sexual activities. Such offenders may be imitating the sexually precocious acts of abused siblings, participating in a promiscuous family lifestyle, or acting out other problems within the family.

Canavan, Meyer, and Higgs (1992) presented four case histories of sibling incest victims and emphasized that the victims felt powerless, angry, depressed, and anxious. One such case involved Anne, who was abused by her brother:

> He would usually offer her some kind of bribe (such as candy) to have sex and then threaten to tell mother how bad she had been if she refused. Anne believed that she, rather than her brother, would be punished for all that went on. Therefore, she never told; the secret persisted. Sexual intercourse occurred on a fairly regular basis until Anne became old enough to spend most of her free time outside the home. (p. 135)

Adler and Schutz (1995) studied 12 male sibling sex offenders (a very small sample) and noted that they came from intact middle-class homes with no previous victimization. The researchers also noted considerable parental denial and minimization. In almost 60% of the cases, sibling incest had been previously reported to the parents, but the incest continued. The mean age difference between the offending sibling and the victim sibling was 5 years; a mean of 16 or more incidents were involved (mostly oral sex and vaginal penetration); and the average duration of the incest was 22 months. Verbal threats were used to maintain the secrecy.

Although brother-sister incest taboos are nearly universal across cultures, there are exceptions. Royalty siblings in ancient Egypt, Hawaii, and the Incas of Peru were permitted to have sex to keep power invested in a small group.

OTHER RELATIVES   In Russell's study (1984), 60% of incestuous child sexual abuse occurred outside the nuclear family. Abuse by uncles was slightly more prevalent than abuse by fathers. Nearly 5% of the 930 women reported abuse by an uncle, and 4.5% reported paternal abuse. Other familial perpetrators included first cousins (reported by 3% of respondents), brothers (2%), other relatives (2%), grandfathers (1%), in-laws (1%), and sisters and mothers (less than 0.5%).

Extrafamilial Child Sexual Abuse

Another pattern of child sexual abuse is *extrafamilial child sexual abuse,* which includes sexual abuse by adults in day care contexts, caretakers in institutional settings, same- or opposite-sex peers, and strangers. Technically, extrafamilial child sexual abuse is defined as attempted or completed forced sex, before a child reaches the age of 14, by a person who is unrelated to the child by blood or marriage. The nature of the sexual behavior may range from touching breasts and genitals to rape. In some states, any forced or attempted sex with an unrelated child before the age of 17 (in Japan it is age 13) constitutes extrafamilial child sexual abuse. In Russell's study (1984), the perpetrators of extrafamilial child sexual abuse were acquaintances (42%), friends (of the family, of the respondent, dates, or boyfriends) (41%), and strangers (15%).

Recovered Memories of Abuse

Before leaving this section on childhood sexual abuse, it is important to comment on the issue of false memory syndrome. Indeed, some individuals "recall" incidents of sexual molestation that never happened. There is debate among professionals as well as the general public as to whether some sexual molestation charges are the product of a therapist's suggestion or the client's imagination. Melchert and Parker (1997) observed that "human memory is imperfect and sometimes completely inaccurate" (p. 134). Judges and law enforcement personnel are also sometimes skeptical. Ten percent of these professionals, in contrast to 2% of mental health professionals in the Everson, Boat, Bourg, and Robertson study (1996), reported that they felt children frequently lie about sexual abuse.

There has been vigorous scientific debate on the reality of repressed memories of childhood trauma. Laboratory research on memory has shown that children can be persuaded to "remember" a traumatic event that did not actually happen to them (such as being separated from a parent on a shopping trip) (Loftus, 1993). Although such studies of suggestibility and memory have documented that there can be problems with the memories of children and adults, the generalizability of these results to the topic of adult survivors of child sexual abuse has been challenged.

Ornstein (1995) summarized studies designed to explore children's memories of medical experiences that involved touching their genitals—situations that would somewhat approximate aspects of sexual abuse experiences. A routine checkup in which genitalia were checked was used as the stimulus event in one study. In another study, the stimulus event was a voiding cystourethrogram (VCUG), an invasive radiological procedure that involves catheterization of the bladder. Results showed that following the medical checkup, children were able to reliably report salient medical events, with 3-year-olds not as good as 5- and 7-year-olds at recalling and differentiating between events that did and did not happen. Following the VCUG, even the younger children showed a clear memory over a 6-week period with little suggestibility. Although children can be reliable in their accounting of events, Ornstein cautioned that conditions established by interviewers (police, attorneys, and clinicians) can profoundly influence the types of reports that children make.

Williams (1994) studied 129 women with documented histories (in hospital emergency departments) of childhood sexual abuse. When the women were interviewed 17 years after their abuse, 38% did not seem to recall the abuse, revealing that it is not uncommon for women to have no memory of abuse. Williams conducted a subsequent analysis (1995) of 75 women who recalled the abuse to examine recovery of memories. Twelve (16%) of the women who recalled the documented abuse reported that they had experienced a time in which they did not

remember it. Women with recovered memories were less likely to have experienced physical force during the molestation and were more likely to have been abused by someone with whom they had a close relationship. These women were younger at the time of the abuse, received weak support from their mothers, and were somewhat less likely to have received counseling as compared to women who always remembered their abuse. Although this study certainly does not document the veracity of all recovered memories of child sexual abuse, it does affirm that recovered memories reported by adults can be consistent with documentation of the abuse at the time it occurred and "should not be summarily dismissed by therapists, lawyers, family members, judges or the women themselves" (p. 670).

Theories of Child Sexual Abuse

A number of theories have been suggested as to why child sexual abuse occurs (Russell, 1984).

FREUDIAN THEORY   Freudian theory maintains that humans are naturally capable of sexual arousal from a variety of stimuli, including children. For most people, cultural taboos and socialization act to repress any sexual interest that adults have in children. Chodorow (1989) identified family constellation factors that may predispose mother-son incest, such as the father's absence. If the father is absent or inadequate, the son may perceive his mother's seductiveness as an oedipal victory.

SOCIAL LEARNING THEORY   Social learning theory suggests that adults learn to regard children as sexual objects. Such learning may result from being exposed to child pornography or from being inadvertently sexually stimulated by a child. For example, the grandfather who bounces his grandchild on his lap could have an erection while doing so and could learn to associate sexual feelings with the child. Or a brother hugging his sister may discover that her body feels good against his.

MALE SEX ROLE SOCIALIZATION   Male sex role socialization teaches men to be sexually aroused by sexual activities independent of the interpersonal context. Hence, some men find it easier to disregard that the sex they are enjoying is with a child. In addition, men are socialized to be attracted to partners who are "smaller, younger, and less powerful than themselves" (Russell, 1984). Finally, fathers are socialized to be the controlling parent in families and use their power to take what they want sexually from the children in the home.

HISTORY OF CHILDHOOD SEXUAL ABUSE Some fathers who sexually abuse their children were sexually abused themselves. Repeating the experience of their own victimization is said to be an expression of trying to control or master the hurt (Araji & Finkelhor, 1986). By being the aggressive parent, they are in control of what is happening (unlike the feeling of helplessness they experienced as a child).

CHILDHOOD SEXUAL EXPERIENCES Engaging in preadolescent sex play with younger children may be associated with subsequent sexual activity with children in adulthood. It is believed that such sex play in one's youth may weaken age and sex distinctions in adult life so that the man associates sex with children.

─────── THINK ABOUT IT ───────
Since no single factor can explain all child sexual abuse, which theories do you think are most applicable to intrafamilial abuse? To extrafamilial abuse?

CONSEQUENCES AND TREATMENT OF CHILD SEXUAL ABUSE

In this section, we look at the impact of—and the treatment alternatives for—child sexual abuse.

Impact of Child Sexual Abuse

Child sexual abuse is associated with negative outcomes. Chandy, Blum, and Resnick (1996a) studied 1011 female teenagers with a history of sexual abuse and compared them with an equal number of randomly selected female teenagers from a group who did not report a history of child sexual abuse. Lower school performance, suicidal involvement, eating disorder behavior, pregnancy risk, and chemical use were associated with the former. When compared with boys, girls had higher tendencies of suicidal behavior, eating disorders, and drinking problems. Boys showed higher tendencies of delinquent activities and sexual risk-taking (Chandy, Blum, & Resnick, 1996b).

A team of researchers (Rodriguez, Ryan, Rowan, & Foy, 1996) studied 117 adult survivors who sought help for sex abuse and found that 72% met the current criteria, and 86%, the lifetime criteria, for posttraumatic stress disorder. Mullen, Martin, Anderson, Romans, and Herbison (1996) also observed serious long-term negative consequences of child sexual abuse. Effects of father-daughter incest can include low self-esteem, difficulty in intimate relationships, and repeated victimization (Herman, 1981). Low self-esteem results from repeatedly engaging in behavior society labels as bad. Difficulty in intimate relationships results from the generalization of negative feelings from the incestuous relationship to other relationships, and repeated victimization results from a feeling of entrapment and accommodation: the child feels trapped by her father's control, and her only perceived alternative is to accommodate the situation.

The age at which a child experiences sex abuse is relevant to the effects of the experience. Children who experience sex abuse between the ages of 7 and 13, when they are old enough to be aware of cultural taboos, experience the highest incidence of psychopathology (Browne & Finkelhor, 1986). In addition, those women who had suffered forceful, prolonged, or highly intrusive sexual abuse (penetration) or who had been abused by their fathers or stepfathers were the most likely to report long-lasting negative effects of incest (Herman, Russell, & Trocki, 1986: Beitchman et al., 1992).

Two researchers (Morrow & Sorrell, 1989) studied adolescent girls who had been sexually abused and observed that the most devastating effects occurred when the sexual behavior was intercourse. Not only were sexually abused girls more likely to have a teenage pregnancy (Boyer, Fine, & Killpack, 1991), they were likely to have lower self-esteem, higher levels of depression, and greater numbers of antisocial (running away from home, illegal drug use) and self-injurious (attempted suicide) behaviors. "This finding supports the contention that sexual intercourse in a tabooed incestuous relationship, which is likely to involve the loss of virginity, is viewed as extremely negative by adolescent incest victims" (p. 683). Sarwer and Durlak (1996) also found that penetration in child sexual abuse was significantly associated with sexual dysfunction in adult women.

Case studies of eight adult men who were molested as children by their nonpsychotic mothers revealed several problems the men had as adults. These problems included difficulty establishing intimate relationships with significant others (100%), depression (88%), and substance abuse (63%) (Krug, 1989). Elliott and Briere (1992), in their review of the literature, observed that abused men develop negative self-perceptions, anxiety disorders, sleep and eating disturbances, and gastrointestinal problems. They further noted an increased incidence of sexual dysfunctions in the form of decreased sexual desire, early ejaculation, and anorgasmia.

Boys who are sexually abused by men (including relatives) also tend to develop concerns about their sexual identities for years afterwards. Myers (1989) described a man who had been victimized as a child and developed a "profound and unrelenting homophobia way out of proportion to social norms and adopted hypermasculine behavior in his community including a 'tough guy image,' excessive drinking, frequent fighting and brawls, and aggressive behavior toward women" (p. 213).

Summit (1983) identified a child sexual abuse accommodation syndrome that characterizes what children experience as victims of incest. Children are threatened into secrecy and feel entrapped and helpless with no other choice other than to accommodate the situation. Disclosure of the incest is delayed and often disbelieved by the nonoffending parent. Being disbelieved by the mother and feeling the extreme impending disorganization of the family, the child usually retracts the allegations of abuse. Hence, in the case of father-daughter incest, "unless there is immediate support for the child and immediate intervention to force responsibility on the father, the girl will follow the normal course and retract her complaint" (p. 82). It is usually only when men are in treatment that they concede that the child told the truth (p. 190).

Long-term consequences of child sexual abuse are associated with various negative outcomes for adults. These include the following (Jackson, Calhoun, Amick, Maddever, & Habif, 1990; Browne & Finkelhor, 1986): depression, low self-esteem, distorted body image, suicide attempts, sleep disturbances, eating disorders, substance abuse, sexual guilt, marital problems, a greater number of sexual partners, and abuse

of their own children. When 344 male pedophiles were compared with men who had not been similarly convicted, the pedophiles were almost twice as likely to have been victims of child sexual abuse (Freund, Watson, & Dickey, 1990).

Whether brother-sister incest is a problem for siblings depends on a number of factors. If the siblings are young (4 to 8 years of age), of the same age, have an isolated sexual episode, engage only in exploratory, nonintercourse behavior, and both consent to the behavior, there may be little to no harm. However, as we have noted, a change in any of these factors increases the chance that sibling incest may have negative consequences for the individual (depression) and her or his subsequent relationships (unsatisfying sexual relationships) (Canavan et al., 1992).

Negative consequences of adult-child sex are not inevitable (Rind, 1995). Variables influencing the outcome include the use of force by the adult, the perception of willingness of participation by the child, and the child's knowledge about and values related to sex. The degree to which one feels self-blame for the sexual abuse is also associated with adjustment (McMillen & Zuravin, 1997). Hence, individuals who have experienced sex as a child with an adult should not assume dire consequences for the future.

Previous sexual abuse has been blamed as a contributing cause of teenage pregnancy. However, Roosa, Tein, Reinholtz, and Angelini (1997) analyzed data from 2003 young women and concluded that sexual abuse was not related to the incidence of teenage pregnancy. Sexual precocity, alone and in combination with child sexual abuse, was found to be related to teenage pregnancy.

Finally, it is important to keep in mind that sexual abuse is often not the only hardship young people endure. Considering this fact, it is difficult to distinguish the impact of sexual abuse from other family problems. Pierce and Pierce (1990) noted in their study of 43 sibling offenders who were reported to the Illinois Department of Child and Family Services that all but three had been reported as abused. "Eleven percent were exposed to inappropriate sexual behavior, 63% were physically abused, and 70% were neglected" (p. 102). Parental problems included mental illness (54% of the juveniles' parents), substance abuse problems (24%), and imprisonment (14%). Financial problems were a concern for more than half of the parents, and almost half needed better housing. Murray (1993) also notes that "childhood sexual abuse often occurs in the context of other family problems including parental alcoholism, depression, physical handicaps, or death of a parent" (p. 670). Thus, the association between childhood sexual abuse and psychiatric disorders may be due to family background.

Treatment of Sexually Abused Children

Since father-daughter sexual abuse is the most frequent type of child sexual abuse reported to professionals, we will follow the case of a girl who tells a school nurse or counselor that she is being sexually molested by her father. The counselor calls the designated child protection agency to report the suspected abuse. The child protection agency will probably involve the local law enforcement agency and an officer may be sent to obtain an initial statement from the girl. If the community has an interdisciplinary child abuse investigation team, this reduces the number of times the child must be interviewed. If the investigation suggests there is sufficient evidence to warrant an arrest and referral to the district attorney for prosecution, the father is arrested and placed in jail or released on his own recognizance. Ideally, he is not allowed to make contact with the daughter or to return to the home until legal disposition of the case is completed and progress in therapy has been made.

Incest is viewed as a family problem in terms of assessment and intervention (McCarthy, 1990). Counseling begins immediately; the individuals are first seen alone and then as a family. The focus of the counseling is to open channels of communication between all family members and to develop or reestablish trust between the husband and the wife. Another aspect of the program involves the confrontation between the father and the daughter, in which the father apologizes and takes full responsibility for the sexual abuse (Herman, 1981).

In discussing the emphasis on family therapy used in treating incestuous fathers, Finkelhor (1986) noted that some family analyses have exaggerated the role of family dynamics, especially the contribution of the mother to the child's abuse. Finkelhor recommended not limiting attention to the matrix of family dynamics. He observed that many incestuous abusers "have characteristics of pedophiles and other sex offenders who have a rather autonomous proclivity to abuse"

(p. 56). Finkelhor cited data from a unique study in which abusers were given absolute confidentiality; 45% of incestuous abusers of girls were sexually involved with children outside their family. These findings suggest deviant arousal patterns that could not be adequately treated without individual and group work with the offender.

Depending on the circumstances and the recommendation of the social worker, the father might face criminal proceedings. If he is convicted (usually for child molestation or statutory rape), a presentencing evaluation may be completed in order to assess whether incarceration or treatment are indicated. He may be sent to prison or receive a suspended sentence if he agrees to participate in a treatment program of individual, group, and family counseling. Treatment is usually prescribed to last anywhere from 18 months to 5 years (Ballard, Williams, Horton, & Johnson, 1990).

A resolution model for treating incest suggested by Orenchuk-Tomiuk, Matthey, and Christensen (1990) is described in Table 11.2.

Bass and Davis (1988), in their book *The Courage to Heal,* noted that a basic step in healing from sex abuse is to have compassion for one's previous choices. "Even if you didn't make the wisest, healthiest choices, you took the options you saw at the time. And now you're making better choices. Focus on that "(p. 174). Lew (1990), in *Victims No Longer,* emphasized the importance of forgiving oneself:

> Without question, this is the most important need of all. As long as you continue to accept blame for what happened to you—as long as you buy any part of the lies that you have been told—the abuse is continuing. Although having been abused does not call for forgiveness of others, it is necessary for you to "forgive yourself." (p. 258)

Finally, help for sex abuse victims is available nationwide through Childhelp USA (1-800-422-4453).

PERSONAL CHOICES

Should Children Testify in Cases of Alleged Child Sexual Abuse?

Robert Kelly was the owner and operator of the Little Rascals Day Care Center in Edenton, North Carolina. In the spring of 1992, he was found guilty on 99 counts of sexual abuse of the children in his center.

TABLE 11.2 A Resolution Model for Treating Incest

CHILD	NONOFFENDING PARENT	OFFENDING PARENT
Beginning Stage	**Beginning Stage**	**Beginning Stage**
• feels totally responsible for the sex abuse and the stress to self and family • exhibits denial, anxiety, and posttraumatic stress	• refuses to accept that sex abuse has occurred • blames the child for the disclosure of the sex abuse • refuses to be an ally for the child • protects the offending parent	• refuses to accept responsibility for the sex abuse • does not view the child as a victim • will not agree to treatment • continues physical and verbal abuse
Resolution Stage	**Resolution Stage**	**Resolution Stage**
• no longer feels responsible for the sex abuse • accepts the fact that he or she was victimized • most symptoms have subsided	• accepts the fact that sex abuse occurred • reinforces the child for disclosure • becomes an ally for the child • agrees to have the offending parent prosecuted	• accepts responsibility for the sex abuse • accepts that the child was victimized • agrees to treatment • stops physical, verbal, and emotional abuse

Source: Orenchuck-Tomiuk et al., 1990.

Parents agonized over whether to subject their children to testifying in court, to cross-examination, and to the disruption of their schedules for the 6-month trial. After the verdict was read, they sighed with relief that the man charged with abusing their children had not been allowed to escape with impunity.

In a study by Burgess, Hartman, Kelley, Grant, & Gray (1990), parents whose children testified in trials against defendants charged with committing sexual abuse in day care centers were compared with parents whose children were also alleged to have been sexually abused but who decided not to encourage their children to testify. The parents' motivation for encouraging their child to testify was "to create safety for their child as well as other children. Safety was defined in terms of the child feeling safe to know the perpetrator was 'locked up' and that the child would be believed and protected during testifying" (Burgess et al., 1990, p. 402). When parents who encouraged their children to testify were asked if they had made the right decision, 70% said "yes."

However, for some parents, the cost of their decision was high. Parents whose children testified presented higher symptoms of psychological distress than parents whose children did not testify. Such distress involved decreased income (legal expenses, time in court), job changes, alcohol or drug abuse, and separation or divorce (Burgess et al., 1990).

Peters, Dinsmore, and Toth (1989) emphasized the importance of prosecuting alleged child sexual abuse perpetuated by family members. Although the argument for not prosecuting is to "keep the family together," there are at least two reasons to pursue prosecution vigorously:

1. Criminal prosecution clearly establishes that children are innocent victims and that the perpetrators are solely responsible for their wrongful behavior.
2. Successful prosecutions educate the public and provide community visibility for the unacceptability of child sex abuse.

Peters et al. (1989) also noted that "in the great majority of cases that are criminally prosecuted, children do not have to testify at trial" (p. 657). But if they do, the benefits may far outweigh the discomfort for the children or the family.

What factors are associated with less trauma in child sexual abuse? What treatment outcomes do therapists work toward in helping children cope with sex abuse?

PREVENTION OF RAPE AND CHILD SEXUAL ABUSE

While both rape and child sexual abuse cannot be completely prevented, their frequency can be reduced.

Rape Prevention

Effective rape prevention must address the multiple and overlapping causes. In their three-tier approach to rape prevention, Rozee, Bateman, and Gilmore (1991) recommended intervention at three levels: social responsibility, individual awareness to avoid high-risk situations, and self-protection when confronted by an assailant.

SOCIETAL RESPONSIBILITY   Several groups of professionals were asked to evaluate which strategies would reduce rape. The option most frequently endorsed by social service personnel was to use educational strategies to encourage a new way of perceiving women in our society (Feldman-Summers & Palmer, 1980). This would be compatible with educating people to reduce acceptance of rape-supportive beliefs and interpersonal violence.

Preventing rape involves men making new choices in regard to how they view having sex with a woman. In a random sample of U.S. adults (conducted for *Time* magazine), almost one-fifth (17%) of the men said that it is not "rape" when a man has sex with a woman who has passed out after drinking too much alcohol (Gibbs, 1991). Even when alcohol is not involved, most men (59%) in the random sample felt that the use of emotional pressure to get a woman to have sex does not constitute rape. What is needed is respect for the preferences of another and the value that sexual aggression is wrong. Taking "no" for an answer is both important and necessary.

Rozee et al. (1991) suggested,

Men must begin to protest rape as actively as women do by setting a nonaccepting standard for other men; by refusing to engage in rape jokes or

victim-blaming and discouraging other men from doing so; and by joining with women in making the social and institutional changes that will eliminate rape. (pp. 350–351)

One way to change knowledge and attitudes about rape myths is through rape education. In a study of 582 students enrolled in introductory sociology classes at Ohio State University, researchers randomly assigned students to one of three groups: those seeing a rape education video, those participating in a rape education workshop, and those serving as a control (no rape education) (Fonow, Richardson, & Wemmerus, 1992). Students who received rape education had lower rape-myth acceptance scores than students who were given no education. The researchers concluded that rape education was effective in changing students' false beliefs about rape.

HIGH-RISK SITUATIONS   One way to prevent rape is to avoid situations in which it is likely to occur. Although most rapes (85%) are acquaintance rapes, those by strangers can be reduced by minimizing the time the woman is out alone at night. The choice for many women is how mobile they want to be versus how much they want to reduce their rape exposure. Hitchhiking and picking up hitchhikers should be avoided. Opening the door to strangers is also dangerous. If a stranger comes to a woman's door and asks to use the phone to call an ambulance, she should not let him in, but offer to call the ambulance for him.

Avoiding the abuse of alcohol may also be associated with preventing rape. In a study of 407 male college students, over one-fifth (22.6%) agreed that "if a woman is heavily intoxicated, it is OK to have sex with her" (Holcomb et al., 1991, p. 436).

Rozee et al. (1991) noted that most women perform dozens of rape-preventive behaviors every day. "But women tend to be torn between what they must do for their safety and what they want to do in order to enjoy a certain quality of life." While locking their doors doesn't challenge quality of life, "many balk, understandably, at treating friends as potential threats. Women must therefore find ways of protecting themselves without having to isolate themselves" (p. 342).

USE SELF-PROTECTION DURING CONFRONTATION   When a woman is actually confronted with being raped, what might she do? There are several alternatives, none of which is foolproof, but all of which work some of the time.

Trying to talk the rapist out of his plan is one alternative. There are a number of different strategies, such as the following:

- "Get the hell away from me." (attack)
- "You don't really want to do this. Let's be friends and talk." (interpersonal liaison)
- "My boyfriend will be here any moment." (distraction)
- "Please don't. I've got AIDS." (disease, illness)
- "Let's go out for a couple of drinks first." (distraction)
- "I'm going to be married Saturday. I've never had sex before. Please don't do this to me." (virginity)
- "It's wrong to do this. You'll go to hell if you do this." (moral appeal)

A woman who screams, kicks, and bites may, indeed, discourage a rapist because the encounter may be more trouble than he anticipated. But her screaming may also frighten him and cause him to knock her unconscious to stop her screaming. (However, he will also hurt her if he rapes her, so avoiding physical injury may not be possible; Bart & O'Brien 1985.) Quinsey and Upfold (1985) found that resistance of any kind on the part of the victim was associated with an uncompleted attack. Bart and O'Brien (1985) noted that both words and physical resistance seemed to be the most effective in thwarting a rape. Sixty-four percent of the sorority women in Copenhaver and Grauerholz's (1991) study reported that reasoning and pleading was the mechanism they used for extricating themselves from being raped; 48% physically struggled.

Strategies to avoid rape depend on the situation. Rozee et al. (1991) suggested that avoiding and resisting rape

> requires each individual to choose methods that will be consistent with her own life-style and values rather than to adopt some standard set of safety measures. Each individual is faced with making choices that will maximize her resources for both avoidance and resistance. (p. 349)

Prevention of Child Sexual Abuse

Incest and sexual abuse of children are best prevented through using a number of measures (Daro, 1991). These include information on sex abuse and healthy sexuality provided for both teachers and children in the public schools at regular intervals,

The sexual molestation and murder of JonBenet Ramsey in 1996 prompted a surge of public outrage and sympathy.

parenting classes to foster bonding between parents and children, and public awareness campaigns.

From a larger societal preventive perspective, Edwin Schur (1988) emphasized that traditional male gender role socialization may perpetuate child sexual abuse. Schur suggested that "our culture promotes sexual victimization of women and children when it encourages males to believe that they have overpowering sexual needs that must be met by whatever means available" (p. 173). Schur said that this belief, and the association of sexual conquest with masculinity, enable men to think of using women and children for their own sexual gratification. The implication here is that one way to discourage child sexual abuse is to change traditional notions of masculinity and male sexuality so that men take responsibility for their sexual behavior and respect the sexuality of women and children.

The Committee for Children (P.O. Box 15190, Wedgewood Station, Seattle, WA 98115; 206-322-5050) is an organization that helps children acquire specific knowledge and skills to protect themselves

MEGAN'S LAW

In 1994, Jesse Timmendequas lured 7-year-old Megan Kanka into his Hamilton Township house in New Jersey to see a puppy. He then raped and strangled her and left her body in a nearby park. Prior to his rape of Megan, Timmendequas had two prior convictions for sexually assaulting girls. Megan's mother, Maureen Kanka, argued that she would have kept her daughter away from her neighbor if she had known about his past sex offenses. She campaigned for a law, known as *Megan's Law,* that requires that communities be notified of a neighbor's previous sex convictions. New Jersey and 45 other states have enacted similar laws. President Clinton signed a federal version in 1996.

The law requires that convicted sexual offenders register with local police in the communities in which they live. It also requires the police to go out and notify residents and certain institutions (such as schools) that a dangerous sex offender has moved into the area. It is this provision of the law that has been challenged on the belief that individuals should not be punished forever for past deeds. Critics of

the law argue that convicted child molesters who have been in prison have paid for their crime. To stigmatize them in communities as sex offenders may further alienate them from mainstream society and increase their vulnerability for repeat offenses. In many states, Megan's Law is not operative because it is on appeal. Although parents ask, "Would you want a convicted sex offender, even one who has completed his prison sentence, living next door to your 8-year-old daughter?" the reality is that little notification is afforded parents in most states. Rather, the issue is tied up in court and will likely remain so until the Supreme Court decides.

In the meantime, some cities are providing a way for residents to ascertain the presence of sex offenders in their neighborhoods. In Los Angeles, a computerized list of serious sex offenders is available in the police office. Concerned residents can go to the police station and look up the presence of sex offenders in their neighborhoods themselves.

In addition to alerting residents to the existence of sex offenders, some counties in some states (such as Maricopa County in

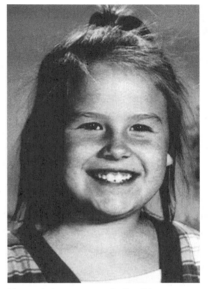

Megan's Law is named after Megan Kanka, a 7-year-old who was raped and murdered by a man who had two prior sex offense convictions.

Arizona) assume that sex offenders must be permanently "managed" by lifetime probation. A released sexual felon must pass regular polygraph tests about his fantasies and behavior as well as periodic tests that use a plethysmograph (an instrument that measures penile reactions to various stimuli, such as prepubescent girls). Regular individual and group therapy are also required, and "surveillance officers" can stop by sex offenders' homes at any time.

from sexual abuse. Through various presentations in the elementary schools, children are taught how to differentiate between appropriate and inappropriate touching by adults or siblings, to understand that it is OK to feel uncomfortable if they do not like the way someone else is touching them, to say "no" in poten-

tially exploitative situations, and to tell other adults if the offending behavior occurs.

In spite of the worthwhile goals of this and other preventive programs, Reppucci and Haugaard (1989) questioned whether preschool children are capable of conceptualizing sex abuse, discriminating what is and isn't abuse, and being assertive where indicated. Some evaluations question whether such programs have accomplished the goal of preventing child sexual abuse (Tharinger et al., 1988). Furthermore, prevention programs may have unwanted negative side effects, such as making children feel uncomfortable with nonsexual contact (such as tickling) with their parents and teaching them that "sexuality is essentially secretive, negative, and even dangerous" (p. 629).

One aspect of prevention programs that may be inadvertently effective is the increased fear perpetrators may have that children will tell on them if they engage in sexual behavior with them (Reppucci & Haugaard, 1989). However, some men also report that fear of being accused of child sexual abuse prevents them from engaging in nonsexual physical affection with children.

Another line of defense in the prevention of child sexual abuse is Megan's Law, which we discussed in the Social Choices section.

THINK ABOUT IT

Assume that you have a young child. A convicted child molester has been released from prison and now lives in your neighborhood. What do you feel your rights are as a parent in terms of knowing about the presence of this person? What about this person's right to privacy?

SEXUAL HARASSMENT

Like rape or child sexual abuse, sexual harassment is another form of sexual coercion.

Definition and Incidence of Sexual Harassment

People sometimes use the term "sexual harassment" to describe behaviors ranging from telling a sexual joke to sexual assault. We use the term *sexual harassment* to refer to deliberate or repeated unwanted sexual comments or behaviors that affect one's performance at work or school. Some behaviors that have been considered sexual harassment include the following:

- Sexual comments about a woman's body or attire
- Rumoring—spreading sexual gossip behind a target's back
- Sexual graffiti or material placed on a target's desk

- Personal questions
- Sexual posturing
- Sexual touching
- Pressure for dates or relationships
- Sexual bribery

About half of all working women in the United States and Canada are affected by sexual harassment in the workplace (Gruber, 1997). About 3% of U.S. women and 6% of Canadian women reported having experienced the most severe forms of harassment—assault and bribery. The most frequent forms of harassment are sexual comments and posturing.

Although sexual harassment of men does occur, it is less common (Fitzgerald, Swan, & Magley, 1997). The majority of sexual harassment is directed toward young unmarried women in traditionally all-male organizations. The United States military is a contextual haven for sexual harassment that has recently been exposed. In 1997, 50 female recruits at the army's training base in Aberdeen, Maryland, filed sexual harassment or sexual abuse complaints. Staff Sergeant Delmar Simpson was sentenced to 25 years in prison for raping female trainees at the army's training base (Komarow, 1997). Police stations provide another context for sexual harassment of women. In these traditionally all-male organizations, sexual harassment may serve the functions of preserving male dominance and facilitating male bonding.

Sexual harassment is difficult to define.

Consequences of Sexual Harassment

Regardless of its context or form, sexual harassment may be devastating for its victims. Direct experiences with victimization can lead to a shattering of victims' core assumptions about the world and themselves, which, in turn, can result in considerable psychological distress (Dansky & Kilpatrick, 1997). Victims complain of decreased self-esteem, depression, isolation, irritability, anxiety, anger, fear, guilt, helplessness, sexual dysfunction, and substance abuse. Sexual harassment may also become a "threat to an individual's resources by threatening financial resources . . . losses can occur in terms of a lost job, lost status among coworkers, failure to gain a raise or promotion, lost interpersonal supports, and lost esteem regarding one's work" (Dansky & Kilpatrick, 1997, p. 156).

Responses to Sexual Harassment

The most frequent response victims have to sexual harassment is to ignore it. Unfortunately, ignoring harassment does not make it go away. Many victims try to avoid the harasser by dropping a class, changing a position, or quitting a job. Why don't many targets of sexual harassment voice their complaints about the harassment? Many victims fear retaliation if they do complain. In a sample of almost 3000 women, over half (57%) of those who had been harassed reported they felt that their chances of promotions or pay raises would be hurt if they complained (Dansky & Kilpatrick, 1997). As a result of feeling that there will be limited gains from complaining, less than 15% of victims file formal sexual harassment complaints.

PERSONAL CHOICES

Should You Confront Sexual Harassment?

Aside from ignoring or avoiding the sexual harasser, a victim has at least three choices: verbal, written, or institutional/legal action. The verbal choice consists of telling the harasser what behavior he or she is engaging in that creates discomfort and asking the person to stop. The victim could soften the accusation by saying something like, "You may not be aware that some of the things you say and do make me uncomfortable. . . ." Some harassers will respond with denial

("What are you talking about? I was just joking."); others will apologize and stop the behavior.

If direct communication is not successful in terminating the harassment, a written statement of the concerns is the next level of intervention. Such a letter should detail the sexual harassment behaviors (with dates of occurrence) and include a description of the consequences (personal distress, depression, sleeplessness). The letter should end with a statement of what the victim would like to happen in the future. For example, "I ask that our future interaction be formal and professional."

The letter should be sent immediately after it becomes clear that the offender did not take the verbal requests for change seriously. If the desired behavior is not forthcoming, the letter can be used as evidence of an attempt to alert the offender of the sexual harassment problem. Use of this evidence may be internal (inside the organization) or external (a formal complaint filed with the Equal Employment Opportunity Commission).

Due to increased visibility of sexual harassment suits in our society, various policies have been instituted for dealing with such harassment. These policies are the topic of the following Social Choices section.

THINK ABOUT IT

Suppose Carl, the manager of a restaurant, likes Shirly, a waitress at the restaurant. Carl wants to pursue a relationship with Shirly, but is afraid that any suggestive comments he might make may be construed as harassment. How can Carl "flirt" with Shirly without risking an accusation of harassment? How can Shirly communicate to Carl that his behavior makes her uncomfortable and that she wants him to stop?

KEY TERMS

classic rape 279	posttraumatic stress disorder 284
date rape 279	
extrafamilial child sexual abuse 293	predatory rape 279
forced sex 278	rape 278
GHB 280	rape trauma syndrome 284
intrafamilial child sexual abuse 291	Rohypnol 280
	sexual coercion 278
Megan's Law 301	sexual harassment 302

SEXUAL HARASSMENT POLICY IN THE WORKPLACE

Over 10,000 complaints of sexual harassment are filed with the Equal Employment Opportunity Commission (EEOC) annually. In response to such complaints, major companies, governmental agencies, and academic institutions have developed sexual harassment policies. The formal goals of these policies are to go on record as being against sexual harassment, to discourage employees from engaging in sexually harassing behavior, and to provide a mechanism through which harassment victims can inform management. The informal goals are to provide the organization with guidelines for reacting to allegations of harassment, and to protect the organization from being taken to court and being forced to pay punitive damages. Most policy statements are restatements of EEOC guidelines.

> Unwelcome sexual advances, requests for sexual favors, and other verbal or physical conduct of a sexual nature constitute sexual harassment when (1) submission to such conduct is made either explicitly or implicitly a term or condition of an individual's employment or academic advancement, (2) submission to or rejection of such conduct by an individual is used as the basis for employment decisions or academic decisions affecting such individuals, or (3) such conduct has the purpose or effect of reasonably interfering with an individual's work or academic performance or creating an intimidating, hostile or offensive working or academic environment. (EEOC, 1993)

Organizations and schools also offer educational programs about sexual harassment by developing and distributing brochures and conducting training workshops. "Training may be designed mostly for managers and focus narrowly on the laws and the organization's legal liability, or it may be broader in scope in attempting to explain why it exists, to change men's thinking about women at work, or to alter both men's and women's behavior" (Gutek, 1997, p. 194). Increasingly, policies emphasize the rights of the harassed and the responsibility of the organization to prevent harassment and provide mechanisms for dealing with it when it occurs.

Persons who file sexual harassment suits may encounter empathy for their experiences, or they may discover that the full weight of the organization is being used against them. Both the institution and the alleged harasser may be willing, and have the resources to be able, to launch a full-scale attack on the professional, personal, and sexual life of the complainant (Schultz & Woo, 1994). Many persons who file sexual harassment complaints end up withdrawing them.

Sources: Equal Employment Opportunity Commission. (1993). 29 CFR 1609.1. Washington, DC.

Gutek, B. A. (1997). Sexual harassment policy initiatives. In W. O'Donohue (Ed.), *Sexual harassment: Theory, research, and treatment* (pp.185–198). Needham Heights, MA: Allyn & Bacon.

Schultz, E. E., & Woo, J. (1994, September 19), Plaintiffs' sex lives are being laid bare in harassment cases. *Wall Street Journal*, pp. A1, A9.

SUMMARY

Sexual coercion in the form of rape, child sexual abuse, and sexual harassment exemplify abuse of power and misuse of sexuality. This chapter has examined the nature, consequences, and prevention aspects of these behaviors.

Sexual Coercion: Rape and Sexual Assault

Sexual coercion involves depriving a person of free choice and using force (actual or threatened) to engage that person in sexual acts against that person's will. The term "forced sex" is preferable to "rape" because it is more inclusive than the legal definition of rape, which must meet certain age and behavior restrictions. About 25% of women report having experienced "forced sex," while only 15% report having been raped. Women report being victims of forced sex more often than men, with the perpetrators being acquaintances more often than strangers. Different theories of rape include biological (men are driven to rape), psychopathological (men are mentally sick), feminist (men express their dominance over women), and social learning (men learn rape-supportive attitudes and violence toward women).

Consequences of Rape and Treatment for Rape Survivors

Rape is usually a traumatic experience involving an acute period of disorganization, helplessness, vulnerability, and anger. Long-term problems may involve nightmares, sexual dysfunctions, and phobias associated with the rape. The rape survivor may also have persistent flashbacks and hallucinations (posttraumatic stress disorder). Most rape survivors benefit from both short-and long-term therapy. Therapeutic techniques which are used include systematic desensitization, stress inoculation training, cognitive therapy, sex therapy, and assertiveness training.

Patterns and Theories of Child Sexual Abuse

Child sexual abuse is categorized as intrafamilial (forced sex where the perpetrator is related to the child) or extrafamilial (forced sex where the perpetrator is not related to the child). Although father-daughter incest has received the most public attention, sibling incest is the most common type of intrafamilial child sexual abuse. Theoretical explanations of child sexual abuse include that it is "natural" (Freudian theory), "learned" (social learning theory), or "socialized" (male role socialization theory).

Consequences and Treatment of Child Sexual Abuse

Consequences of child sexual abuse are usually serious and long-term. Child sexual abuse victims tend to have low self-esteem, difficulty in intimate relationships, and higher incidences of depression and suicide. However, family background variables may explain the association between child sexual abuse and psychological problems. Treatment involves the child's acceptance that she or he is not responsible for the abuse and realization that he or she was victimized. Treatment programs also exist for the offender.

Prevention of Rape and Child Sexual Abuse

Rape prevention involves socializing men to reject rape jokes and rape myths, encouraging women to avoid high-risk situations, and alerting women to the various strategies they can use to avert a rape. Prevention of sexual abuse of children involves information on sex abuse and healthy sexuality provided in the public schools at regular intervals, parenting classes to foster bonding between parents and children, and public awareness campaigns.

Sexual Harassment

Sexual harassment refers to unwanted sexual comments or behaviors that affect one's performance at work or school. Sexual harassment is experienced by about 50% of women in the U.S. workforce. Consequences are devastating and include depression, loss of self-esteem, sleeplessness, and substance abuse. While most individuals who are sexually harassed ignore or avoid the harasser, others confront the harasser verbally or in writing. Most schools, workplaces, and organizations have policies concerning sexual harassment and educational and training programs to prevent it from occurring.

REFERENCES

ABC (American Broadcasting Company). (1995, August 19). The death of a family. In *20/20*. New York.

Adler, N. A., & Schutz, J. (1995). Sibling incest offenders. *Child Abuse and Neglect, 19,* 811–819.

Allen, C. M. (1990). Women as perpetrators of child sexual abuse: Recognition barriers. In A. L. Horton, B. L. Johnson, L. M. Roundy, & D. Williams (Eds.), *The incest perpetrator: A family member no one wants to treat.* Newbury Park, CA: Sage.

Araji, S., & Finkelhor, D. (1986). Abusers: A review of research. In D. Finkelhor (Ed.), *A sourcebook on child sexual abuse* (pp. 89–118). Newbury Park, CA: Sage.

Ballard, D. T., Williams, D., Horton, A. T., & Johnson, B. L. (1990). Offender identification and current use of community resources. In A.L. Horton, B. L. Johnson, L. M. Roundy, & D. Williams (Eds.), *The incest perpetrator: A family member no on wants to treat* (pp. 150–163). Newbury Park, CA: Sage.

Bart, P. B., & O'Brien, P. H. (1985). *Stopping rape.* Oxford: Pergamon Press.

Bass, E. and Davis, L. (1988). *The courage to heal.* New York: Harper and Row.

Becker, J. V., & Kaplan, M. S. (1991). Rape victims: Issues, theories, and treatment. *Annual Review of Sex Research, 2,* 267–292.

Beitchman, J. H., Zucker, K. J., Hood, J. E., daCosta, G. A., Akman, D., & Cassavia, E. (1992). A review of the long-term effects of child sexual abuse. *Child Abuse and Neglect, 16,* 101–119.

Berliner, L., & Conte, J. R. (1990). The process of victimization: The victim's perspective. *Child Abuse and Neglect, 14,* 29–40.

Boyer, D., Fine, D., & Killpack, S. (1991, summer). Sexual abuse and teen pregnancy. *The Network,* 1–2.

Bridgeland, W. M., Duane, E. A., & Stewart, C. S. (1995). Sexual victimization among undergraduates. *College Student Journal, 29,* 16–25.

Browne, A., & Finkelhor, D. (1986). Initial and long-term effects: A review of the research. In D. Finkelhor (Ed.), *A sourcebook on child sexual abuse* (pp. 143–179). Newbury Park, CA: Sage.

Brownmiller, S. (1975). *Against our will: Men, women, and rape.* New York: Simon and Schuster.

Burgess, A. W., Hartman, C. R., Kelley, S. J., Grant, C. A., & Gray, E. B. (1990). Parental response to child sexual abuse trials involving day care settings. *Journal of Traumatic Stress, 3,* 395–405.

Burgess, A. W., & Holmstrom, L. L. (1974). Rape trauma syndrome. *American Journal of Psychiatry, 131,* 981–986.

Burt, M. R. (1991). Rape myths and acquaintance rape. In A. Parrot & L. Bechhofer (Eds.), *Acquaintance rape: The hidden crime* (pp. 26–40). New York: Wiley.

Calhoun, K. S., & Atkeson, B. M. (1991). *Treatment of rape victims: Facilitating psychological adjustment.* New York: Pergamon Press.

Canavan, M. M., Meyer, W. J., III, & Higgs, D. C. (1992). The female experience of sibling incest. *Journal of Marital and Family Therapy, 18,* 129–142.

Carter, K. (1997). Police charge woman who accused Cowboys. *USA Today,* p. A1.

Chandy, J. M., Blum, R. W., & Resnick, M. D. (1996a). Female adolescents with a history of sexual abuse. *Journal of Interpersonal Violence, 11,* 503–518.

Chandy J. M., Blum, R. W., & Resnick, M. D. (1996b). Gender specific outcomes for sexually abused adolescents. *Child Abuse and Neglect, 20,* 1219–1231.

Check, J. V. P., & Malamuth, N. (1985). An empirical assessment of some feminist hypotheses about rape. *International Journal of Women's Studies, 8,* 414–433.

Check, J. V. P., & Malamuth, N. M. (1981). Feminism and rape in the 1980's: Recent research findings. In P. Caplan, C. Larson, & L. Cammaert (Eds.), *Psychology changing for women.* Montreal: Eden Press Women's Publications.

Chodorow, N. (1989). Parameters of sexual contact of boys with women. In S. Condy, D. Temler, R. Brown, & L. Veaco (Eds.), *Feminism & psychoanalytic theory.* New Haven, CT: Yale University Press.

Copenhaver, S., & Grauerholz, E. (1991). Sexual victimization among sorority women: Exploring the link between sexual violence and institutional practices. *Sex Roles, 24,* 31–41.

Dansky, B. S., & Kilpatrick, D. G. (1997). Effects of sexual harassment. In W. O'Donohue (Ed.), *Sexual harassment: Theory, research, and treatment* (pp. 152–174). Needham Heights, MA: Allyn & Bacon.

Daro, D. (1991). Prevention programs. In C. R. Hollin & K. Howell (Eds.), *Clinical approaches to sex offenders and their victims* (pp. 285-313). New York: Wiley.

Dunn, P., Vail-Smith, K., Knight, S. (1997). Date/acquaintance rape: What friends tell friends. Poster presentation. American Public Health Association, Annual Meeting. Used by permission.

Elliott, D. M., & Briere, J. (1992). The sexually abused boy: Problems in manhood. *Medical Aspects of Human Sexuality, 26,* 68–71.

Ellis, L. (1989). *Theories of rape: Inquiries into the causes of sexual aggression.* New York: Hemisphere.

Everson, M. D., Boat, B. W., Bourg, S., & Robertson, K. R. (1996). Beliefs among professionals about rates of false allegations of child sexual abuse. *Journal of Interpersonal Violence, 11,* 541–553.

Feldman-Summers, S., & Palmer, G. C. (1980). Rape as viewed by judges, prosecutors, and police officers. *Criminal Justice and Behavior, 7,* 19–40.

Finkelhor, D. (1986). Sexual abuse: Beyond the family systems approach. In T. S. Trepper & M. J. Barrett (Eds.), *Treating incest: A multiple systems perspective* (pp. 55–65). New York: Haworth.

Finkelhor, D., Hotaling, G., Lewis, I. A., & Smith, C. (1990). Sexual abuse in a national survey of adult men and women: Prevalence, characteristics, and risk factors. *Child Abuse and Neglect, 14,* 19–28.

Finkelhor, D., & Yllo, K. (1988). Rape in marriage. In M. B. Straus (Ed.), *Abuse and victimization across the life span* (pp. 140–152). Baltimore: Johns Hopkins University Press.

Fitzgerald, L. F., Swan, S., & Magley, V. J. (1997). But was it really sexual harassment? In W. O'Donohue (Ed.), *Sexual harassment: Theory, research, and treatment* (pp. 5–28). Needham Heights, MA: Allyn & Bacon.

Fonow, M. M., Richardson, L., & Wemmerus, V. (1992). Feminist rape education: Does it work? *Gender & Society,* 6 (1), 108–121.

Frank, J. G. (1991, August 16). *Risk factors for rape: Empirical confirmation and preventive implications.* Poster session presented at the 99th annual convention of the American Psychological Association, San Francisco.

Freund, K., Watson, R., & Dickey, R. (1990). Does sexual abuse in childhood cause pedophilia? An exploratory study. *Archives of Sexual Behavior, 19,* 557–568.

Gibbs, N. (1991, June 3). When is it rape? *Time,* pp. 48–55.

Groth, A. N., & Birnbaum, H. J. (1979). *Men who rape: The psychology of the male offender.* New York: Plenum Press.

Gruber, J. E. (1997). An epidemiology of sexual harassment: Evidence from North America and Europe. In W. O'Donohue (Ed.), *Sexual harassment: Theory, research, and treatment* (pp. 84–98). Needham Heights, MA: Allyn & Bacon.

Herman, J. (1981a). Father-daughter incest. *Professional Psychology, 12,* 76–91.

Herman, J. (1981b). *Father-daughter incest.* Cambridge, MA: Harvard University Press.

Herman, J., Russell, D., & Trocki, K. (1986). Long-term effects of incestuous abuse in childhood. *American Journal of Psychiatry, 143,* 1293–1296.

Holcomb, D. R., Holcomb, L. C., Sondag, K. A., & Williams, N. (1991). Attitudes about date rape: Gender differences among college students. *College Student Journal, 25,* 434–439.

Interagency Council on Sex Offender Treatment. (1991) *Treatment brings control: Breaking the cycle.* Austin, TX: Author.

Jackson, J. L., Calhoun, K. S., Amick, A. E., Maddever, H. M., & Habif, V. L. (1990). Young adult women who report childhood intrafamilial sexual abuse: Subsequent adjustment. *Archives of Sexual Behavior, 19,* 211–221.

Kanin, E. J. (1957). Male aggression in dating-courtship relations. *American Journal of Sociology, 63,* 197–204.

Kanin, E. J. (1994). False rape allegations. *Archives of Sexual Behavior, 23,* 81–92.

Katz, B. L. (1991). The psychological impact of stranger versus nonstranger rape on victim's recovery. In A. Parrot & L. Bechhofer (Eds.), *Acquaintance rape: The hidden crime* (pp. 251–269). New York: Wiley.

Komarow, S. (1997, May 7). Army sergeant sentenced to 25 years for raping trainees. *USA Today,* p. 4A.

Koss, M. P., Dinero, T. E., Siebel, C. A., & Cox, S. L. (1988). Stranger and acquaintance rape. *Psychology of Women Quarterly, 12,* 1–24.

Krug, R. S. (1989). Adult male report of childhood sexual abuse by mothers: Case descriptions, motivations, and long-term consequences. *Child Abuse and Neglect, 13,* 111–119.

Lawson, C. (1991). Clinical assessment of mother-son sexual abuse. *Clinical Social Work Journal, 19,* 391–403.

Lew, M. (1990). *Victims no longer: Men recovering from incest and other sexual child abuse.* New York: Harper and Row.

Loftus, E. F. (1993). The reality of repressed memories. *American Psychologist, 48,* 518–537.

Lottes, I. L., & Weinberg, M. S. (1996). Sexual coercion among university students: A comparison of the United States and Sweden. *The Journal of Sex Research, 34,* 67–76.

Marvasti, J. (1986). Incestuous mothers. *American Journal of Forensic Psychiatry, 8,* 63–69.

McCarthy, B. W. (1990). Treatment of incest families: A cognitive-behavioral model. *Journal of Sex Education and Therapy, 16,* 101–114.

McConaghy, N., & Zamir, M. R. (1995). Heterosexual and homosexual coercion, sexual orientation and sexual roles in medical students. *Archives of Sexual Behavior, 24,* 489–502.

McMillen, C., & Zuravin, S. (1997). Attributions of blame and responsibility for child sexual abuse and adult adjustment. *Journal of Interpersonal Violence, 12,* 30–48.

Melchert, T. P., & Parker, R. L. (1997). Different forms of childhood abuse and memory. *Child Abuse and Neglect, 21,* 125–135.

Meyers, M. H. (1989). A new look at mothers of incest victims. *Journal of Social Work and Human Sexuality, 3,* 47–58.

Michael, R. T., Gagnon, J. H., Laumann, E. O., & Kolata, G. (1994). *Sex in America: A definitive survey.* Boston: Little, Brown.

Monson, C. M., Byrd, G. R., & Langhinrichsen-Rohling, J. (1996). To have and to hold: Perceptions of marital rape. *Journal of Interpersonal Violence, 11,* 410–424.

Morrow, R. B., & Sorrell, G. T. (1989). Factors affecting self-esteem, depression, and negative behaviors in sexually abused, female adolescents. *Journal of Marriage and the Family, 51,* 677–686.

Mullen, P. E., Martin, J. L., Anderson, J. C., Romans, S. E., & Herbison, G. P. (1996). The long-term impact of the physical, emotional, and sexual abuse of children: A community study. *Child Abuse and Neglect, 20,* 7–21.

Murray, J. B. (1993). Relationship of childhood sexual abuse to borderline personality disorder, posttraumatic stress disorder, and multiple personality disorder. *The Journal of Psychology, 127,* 657–676.

Myer, M. H. (1985). A new look at mothers of incest victims. *Journal of Social Work and Human Sexuality, 3,* 47–58.

Myers, M. F. (1989). Men sexually assaulted as adults and sexually abused as boys. *Archives of Sexual Behavior, 18,* 203–215.

The National Adolescent Perpetrator Network. (1988). Preliminary report from the National Task Force on Juvenile Sexual Offending. *Juvenile and Family Court Journal, 39*(2), 1–67.

O'Brien, C. (1995, November 16). Phi Gamma Delta offers public apology for lewd letter. *The News and Observer,* p. 1B.

Orenchuk-Tomiuk, N., Matthey, G., & Christensen, C. P. (1990). The resolution model: A comprehensive treatment framework in sexual abuse. *Child Welfare, 69,* 417–431.

Ornstein, P. A. (1995). Children's long-term retention of salient personal experience. *Journal of Traumatic Stress, 8,* 581-605.

O'Sullivan, C. S. (1991). Acquaintance gang rape on campus. In A. Parrot & L. Bechhofer (Eds.), *Acquaintance rape* (pp. 368-380). New York: Wiley.

Patton, W., & Mannison, M. (1995). Sexual coercion in high school dating. *Sex Roles, 33,* 447-457.

Perkins, D. (1991). Clinical work with sex offenders in secure settings. In C. R. Hollin & K. Howells (Eds.), *Clinical approaches to sex offenders and their victims* (pp. 151-171). New York: Wiley.

Peters, J. M., Dinsmore, J., & Toth, P. (1989). Why prosecute child abuse? *South Dakota Law Review, 34,* 649-659.

Pierce, L. H., & Pierce, R. L. (1990). Adolescent/sibling incest perpetrators. In A. L. Horton, B. L. Johnson, L. M. Roundy, & D. Williams (Eds.), *The incest perpetrator: A family member no one wants to treat.* Newbury Park, CA: Sage.

Powers, Z. L., & Rosenfeld, J. (1997). Rape. In J. Rosenfeld (Ed.), *Women's health in primary care* (pp. 257-276). Baltimore: Williams & Wilkins.

Quinsey, V. L., & Upfold, D. (1985). Rape completion and victim injury as a function of female resistance strategy. *Canadian Journal of Behavioral Science, 17,* 40-49.

Reppucci, N. D., & Haugaard, J. J. (1989). Prevention of child sexual abuse. *American Psychologist, 44,* 1266-1275.

Resick, P. A., & Schnicke, M. K. (1992). Cognitive processing therapy for sexual assault victims. *Journal of Consulting and Clinical Psychology, 60,* 748-756.

Rind, B. (1995). An analysis of human sexuality textbook coverage of the psychological correlates of adult-nonadult sex. *The Journal of Sex Research, 32,* 219-233.

Rodriguez, N., Ryan, S. W., Rowan, A. B., & Foy, D. W. (1996). Posttraumatic stress disorder in a clinical sample of adult survivors of childhood sexual abuse. *Child Abuse and Neglect, 20,* 943-952.

Roosa, M. W., Tein, J., Reinholtz, C., & Angelini, P. J. (1997). The relationship of childhood sexual abuse to teenage pregnancy. *Journal of Marriage and the Family, 59,* 119-130.

Roth, S., Dye, E., and Lebowitz, L. (1988). Group therapy for sexual assault victims. *Psychotherapy, 25,* 82-93.

Rothbaum, B. O., Foa, E. B., Riggs, D. S., Murdock, T., & Walsh, W. (1992). A prospective examination of posttraumatic stress disorder in rape victims. *Journal of Traumatic Stress, 5,* 455-475.

Rozee, P. D., Bateman, P., & Gilmore, T. (1991). A personal perspective of acquaintance rape prevention: A three-tier approach. In A. Parrot & L. Bechhofer (Eds.), *Acquaintance rape: The hidden crime* (pp. 337-354). New York: Wiley.

Russell, D. E. H. (1984). *Sexual exploitation: Rape, child sexual abuse and workplace harassment.* Beverly Hills, CA: Sage.

Russell, D. E. H. (1991). Wife rape. In A. Parrot & L. Bechhofer (Eds.), *Acquaintance rape: The hidden crime* (pp. 129-139). New York: Wiley.

Sanday, P. R. (1981). The socio-cultural context of rape: A cross-cultural study. *Journal of Social Issues, 37,* 5-27.

Salter, A. (1988). *Treating child sex offenders and victims: A practical guide.* Newbury Park, CA: Sage.

Sariola, H., & Uutela, A. (1996). The prevalence and context of incest abuse in Finland. *Child Abuse and Neglect, 20,* 834-850.

Sarwer D. B., & Durlak, J. A. (1996). Childhood sexual abuse as a predictor of adult female sexual dysfunction: A study of couples seeking sex therapy. *Child Abuse and Neglect, 20,* 693-972.

Saunders, E. B., & Awad, G. A. (1988). Assessment, management, and treatment planning for male adolescent sexual offenders. *American Journal of Orthopsychiatry, 58,* 571-579.

Sawyer, R. G., Schulken, E. D., & Pinciaro, P. J. (1997). A survey of sexual victimization in sorority women. *College Student Journal, 31,* 387-395.

Schur, E. (1988). *The Americanization of sex.* Philadelphia: Temple University Press.

Scully, D. (1990). *Understanding sexual violence: A study of convicted rapists.* Boston: Unwin Hyman.

Sheppard, D. I., Giacinti, T., & Tjaden, C. (1976). Rape reduction: A citywide program. In M. J. Walker & S. L. Brodsky (Eds.), *Sexual assault* (pp. 169-173). Lexington, MA: Lexington Books.

SIECUS. (1996, February/March). SIECUS position statements on human sexuality, sexual health, and sexuality education and information, 1995-96. *SIECUS Report,* 21-23.

Solomon, J. C. (1992). Child sexual abuse by family members: A radical feminist perspective. *Sex Roles, 27,* 473-485

Stermac, L., Sheridan, P. M., Davidson, A., & Dunn, S. (1996). Sexual assault of adult males. *Journal of Interpersonal Violence, 11,* 52-64.

Struckman-Johnson, C., & Struckman-Johnson, D. (1994). Men pressured and forced into sexual experience. *Archives of Sexual Behavior, 23,* 93-114.

Summit, R. C. (1983). The child sexual abuse accommodation syndrome. *Child Abuse and Neglect, 7,* 177-192.

Tang, C. S., Critelli, J. W., & Porter, J. F. (1995). Sexual aggression and victimization in dating relationships among Chinese college students. *Archives of Sexual Behavior, 24,* 47-54.

Templeman, T. L., & Stinnett, R. D. (1991). Patterns of sexual arousal and history in a "normal" sample of young men. *Archives of Sexual Behavior, 20,* 137-150.

Tharinger, D. J., Tharinger, D. H., Krivacska, J. J., Laye-McDonough, M., Jamison, L., Vincent, G. G., & Hedlund, A. D. (1988). Prevention of child sexual abuse: An analysis of issues, educational programs, and research findings. *School Psychology Review, 17,* 614–634.

Tyson, A. (1997). Students' expectations for rape when alcohol is involved. Master's thesis. Greenville, NC: Department of Psychology, East Carolina University. Used by permission.

Williams, L. M. (1994). Recall of childhood trauma: A prospective study of women's memories of sexual abuse. *Journal of Consulting and Clinical Psychology, 62,* 1167–1176.

Williams, L. M. (1995). Recovered memories of abuse in women with documented child sexual victimization histories. *Journal of Traumatic Stress, 8,* 649–673.

Wylie, M. S. (1993, September/October). The shadow of a doubt. *Networker,* 19–29.

Zweig, J. M., Barber, B. L., & Eccles, J. S. (1997). Sexual coercion and well-being in young adulthood. *Journal of Interpersonal Violence, 12,* 291–308.

DIVERSITY OF
SEXUAL CHOICES

VALUES, EMOTIONS, AND SEXUALITY

We should exercise our right to choose among our sexual options with informed discrimination, and with respect for the basic values of honesty, equality, and responsibility for ourselves and others.

Ira L. Reiss
Harriet M. Reiss
Sex Researchers

Consider the following situations that require a choice in sexual values.

Two people are dancing at a party. Although they just met only 2 hours ago, they feel a strong attraction to each other. Each is wondering how much sexual intimacy will be appropriate when they go back to one of their apartments later that evening. How much sex in a new relationship is appropriate?

A couple is involved in a commuter marriage, and they see each other only on weekends. During the interim, each is vulnerable to feeling lonely and sexually frustrated. Each spouse has been asked out by other-sex colleagues for dinner and a video at the colleagues' apartments. Where do spouses draw the line about what is and what is not appropriate with others?

While one partner in a pair-bonded relationship was visiting a relative, the other had sex with a previous lover on a chance meeting. The individual felt guilty, confessed, and apologized, promising never to be unfaithful again. If this were your partner, how would you respond?

The preceding scenarios involve the issues of emotion, fidelity, and forgiveness. We are continually making sexual choices based on our emotions and sexual values, but knowledge also affects the sexual decisions we make. In this chapter, we will examine all three of these issues. We begin with a look at how knowledge affects our sexual choices.

SEXUAL KNOWLEDGE IN THE UNITED STATES

Despite the wide availability of information about sex, many individuals in the United States lack accurate information on this topic. An extreme but true example is a couple who "shared" the responsibility of taking birth control pills (she took a pill one day, he took one the next day), thinking that this would protect the woman from getting pregnant. In effect, they had made the choice to avoid pregnancy, but their ignorance resulted in a pregnancy. Effective sexual decision making requires accurate knowledge.

In a study of the sexual knowledge of 1033 high school students on the West Coast, researchers found that students correctly answered an average of only 11 items on a 20-item test about general sexual knowledge (Leland & Barth, 1992). Another study looked at the level of knowledge of female and male adolescents and mothers of adolescents regarding general sexual development terms (Hockenberry-Eaton, Richman, Dilorio, Rivero, & Maibach, 1996). Researchers interviewed 90 adolescents and 73 mothers of adolescents, asking participants to define seven terms related to sexual development: ejaculation, hormones, menstruation, ovulation, puberty, semen, and wet dreams. Results indicated that the adolescents and mothers were unable adequately to define most of the seven sexual development terms (see Table 12.1).

Do young adults who are misinformed about sexual matters know they are misinformed? Do they want additional information to correct their misconceptions? Based on a study of 698 Flemish students ages 17 to 20, the answer to these questions is "no." A researcher in Belgium administered a survey to Flemish students to assess their knowledge of AIDS and other sex-related matters, as well as their perceived need for additional information about sex in general and safe sex in particular (Buysse, 1996). Although answers on the knowledge questions revealed important misconceptions, the "respondents reported being rather unconcerned about additional information" (p. 269).

Many individuals learn from experience the importance of accurate information about sexuality. When a sample of individuals ranging in age from 9 to 73 were asked if inaccurate sexuality information had ever had a negative effect on their emotional or physical well-being, 69% answered in the affirmative (Ansuini, Fiddler-Woite, & Woite, 1996).

TABLE 12.1 Percentage of Adolescent Males, Adolescent Females, and Mothers of Adolescents Who *Incorrectly* Defined Sexual Development Terms

Term	Adolescent Males % Incorrect	Adolescent Females % Incorrect	Mothers % Incorrect
Puberty	36	17	25
Ovulation	98	71	30
Wet dreams	76	85	66
Menstruation	74	19	6
Ejaculation	71	63	33
Semen	57	42	29
Hormones	74	71	56

Source: Hockenberry-Eaton et al., 1996.

THINK ABOUT IT

Are U.S. citizens adequately informed about sexuality-related issues? What are some of the potential consequences of being uninformed or misinformed about matters regarding sexuality?

ALTERNATIVE SEXUAL VALUES

Values, simply defined, are attitudes or behaviors that represent something important. Raths, Merrill, and Simon (1996) identified seven criteria of a value. According to them, a value must be chosen freely, chosen from among alternatives, chosen after thoughtful consideration of the consequences of each action, something prized and cherished, something affirming, something that results in acting on choices, and something that is repeating. Sexual values can be thought of as having each of these characteristics. ℮ Of course, sexual values are operative in nonmarital, marital, heterosexual, and homosexual relationships. ℮ After discussing the functions of sexual values, we will compare three perspectives that describe sexual values and choices: absolutism, relativism, and hedonism.

Functions of Sexual Values

Sexual values serve to guide our sexual behavior and sexual choices. For example, a person who believes in being in a stable, monogamous love relationship before having intercourse may choose not to have a one-night encounter of casual sex. By making this choice, this person would be truly acting through his or her values. A belief becomes a value when a person acts on his or her belief system; a value is a value only when one acts. If it does not involve any action, then it is an attitude or a belief, which are both precursors to a value.

For example, one's sexual behavior is not always consistent with one's beliefs. Although most spouses say they believe in fidelity, 20% of wives and 15 to 35% of husbands report having engaged in extramarital sex, thereby demonstrating a discrepancy between what they believe and how they act (Michael, Gagnon, Laumann, & Kolata, 1994). In effect, some spouses seemed to value infidelity, according to their behavior.

In a study on the influence of religion on women's sexuality, researchers found that women who frequently attended church were more likely to believe that masturbation is both a sin and an unhealthy practice (Davidson, Darling, & Norton, 1995). However, church attenders were just as likely to participate in masturbation as nonchurch attenders. The discrepancy between beliefs and behavior is also illustrated in the sex education parents provide for their children. In one study, all of the parents reported that they believed "open and honest communication" about sex was important for their children. However, only a few participants reported behavior that reflected this value (Geasler, Dannison, & Edlund, 1995).

Sexual values also serve as a factor in mate selection as people tend to bond with partners who have similar values. ✒ In an effort to ascertain the importance of sexual values in mate selection in China, Palestine, Zambia, Sweden, and the United States, two researchers asked college students in these countries: "How desirable is chastity in potential long-term mates or marriage partners?" Respondents were asked to indicate the degree to which they were concerned that their future spouse be a virgin on a scale from zero (irrelevant or unimportant) to three (indispensable). Chinese students were the most concerned (2.5 out of 3), and Swedish students were the least concerned (less than one-half of 1%). U.S. male students rated their concern at slightly less than 1, with women reporting a 0.5 level of concern (Buss & Schmitt, 1993). ✒

————— **THINK ABOUT IT** —————

Have you ever made a sexual decision that was not consistent with your sexual values? If so, what influenced you to do so? How did you feel about your decision then? How do you feel about it now?

PERSONAL CHOICES

Should You Be Tolerant of the Sexual Values of Others?

Regardless of our own sexual values, we can choose to either be accepting or critical of those who have sexual values that are different from our own. Choosing to accept that others have different sexual values reflects a perspective that recognizes that "there is, in sum, no one right way to be" (Tavris, 1992, p. 333). ✒ For example, although most Swedish college men in one study reported that their first intercourse experience was with a steady partner, they reported an accepting attitude toward individuals whose first intercourse was with a nonsteady partner (Weinberg, Lottes, & Shaver, 1995). ✒ The choice to accept individuals whose values differ from our own must be balanced by the social responsibility to protect the rights and well-

being of others. In choosing whether or not to be accepting of another person's sexual values, we might think about whether or not that person's values result in behavior that may be harmful to others.

Absolutism

Absolutism refers to a belief system that is based on the unconditional power and authority of religion, law, or tradition. Many religions teach that sexual intercourse between spouses is morally correct and that nonmarital, extramarital, and homosexual sex acts are sins against the self, God, and the community. Some religions also view masturbation, the use of contraception, the use of pornography, and abortion as sins. The federal government has taken an absolutist position against sex before marriage. In 1997, Congress authorized $250 million in funds for state sex education programs that would emphasize abstinence.

People who are guided by absolutism in their sexual choices have a clear notion of what is right and wrong. In the United States, the people most likely to have absolutist sexual values are women, people over the age of 50, married individuals, people affiliated with conservative Protestant religion, and African Americans (Michael et al., 1994).

Media emphasis on unwed parenthood gives the impression that most African American adolescent women are having intercourse. But national data on African American females aged 15 to 21 revealed that 38% were virgins. Half of those who were not virgins reported waiting until after the age of 16 to have intercourse (Murry, 1994).

Data from 14,396 individuals over a 14-year period revealed that conservative Protestants remained steadfast in their belief that premarital sex is always wrong (Petersen & Donnenwerth, 1997).

A subcategory of absolutism is *asceticism*—a belief system that is based on the conviction that giving into carnal lust is wrong and that one must rise above the pursuit of sensual pleasure to live a life of self-discipline and self-denial. Asceticism is reflected in the sexual values of Catholic priests, monks, nuns, and other celibates.

Relativism

Relativism is a value system emphasizing that sexual decisions should be made in the context of a particular situation. Whereas an absolutist might feel that it

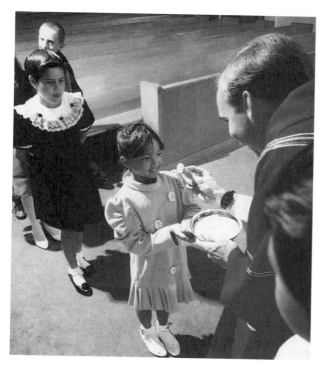

Our sexual values are often strongly influenced by the religious doctrines we learned early in life.

is wrong for unmarried people to have intercourse, a relativist might feel that the moral correctness of sex outside of marriage depends on the particular situation. For example, a relativist might feel that in some situations, sex between casual dating partners is wrong (such as when one individual pressures the other into having sex or lies in order to persuade the other to have sex). In other cases—when there is no deception or coercion and the dating partners are practicing "safer sex"—intercourse between casual dating partners may be viewed as acceptable.

Sexual values and choices that are based on relativism often consider the degree of love, commitment, and relationship involvement important factors. In a sample of undergraduates who reported never having had intercourse, the most frequent reason given from both women and men was that they had not been in a relationship long enough or had not been in love (Sprecher & Regan, 1996). A relativist might feel that although sex between casual dating partners is wrong, nonmarital sex between two individuals who have a committed, monogamous relationship is acceptable. As shown in Figure 12.1, college students are more likely to view sexual behavior between seriously

involved and engaged couples as acceptable than sexual behavior between couples who are on a first date or couples who are casually dating.

The Reiss Premarital Sexual Permissiveness Scale (see this chapter's Self-Assessment) allows you to assess whether the degree of love or affection in a premarital relationship influences your attitude about the acceptability of premarital intercourse.

The *sexual double standard*—the view that encourages and accepts sexual expression of men more than women—reflects a relativistic perspective on sexuality. In the United States, college men are more likely than college women to adhere to the sexual double standard. In a study of American and Swedish university students, U.S. university men reported more disapproval toward 15-year-old girls having sexual intercourse with a nonsteady partner than 15-year-old boys having intercourse with a nonsteady partner (Weinberg et al., 1995). They also reported more disapproval toward 18-year-old women having many sex partners than toward 18-year-old men having many sex partners. The sexual double standard was less evident among U.S. university women, Swedish university women, and Swedish university men.

Hedonism

Hedonism suggests that the ultimate value and motivation for human behavior is the pursuit of pleasure and the avoidance of pain. The hit song "All By Myself," sung by Celine Dion, reflects a hedonistic

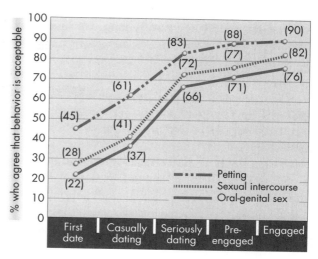

FIGURE 12.1 Acceptance of Sexual Activity by Relationship Stage **Source:** Sprecher et al., 1988.

REISS PREMARITAL SEXUAL PERMISSIVENESS SCALE (UPDATED 4-ITEM VERSION)

The following four questions concern *your* attitude regarding premarital sexual intercourse. First, decide whether you agree or disagree with the view expressed. Then indicate the level of your agreement or disagreement by circling the number that best represents *your* view. To answer, use the following 6-point scale.

Strongly Agree	Moderately Agree	Slightly Agree	Slightly Disagree	Moderately Disagree	Strongly Disagree
1	2	3	4	5	6

1. I believe that premarital sexual intercourse is acceptable if one is in a love relationship.

   1   2   3   4   5   6

2. I believe that premarital sexual intercourse is acceptable if one is in a relationship involving strong affection.

   1   2   3   4   5   6

3. I believe that premarital sexual intercourse is acceptable if one is in a relationship involving moderate amounts of affection.

   1   2   3   4   5   6

4. I believe that premarital sexual intercourse is acceptable even if one is in a relationship without much affection.

   1   2   3   4   5   6

Note: The scale was given to 217 university students in New Jersey, Ohio, Louisiana, and California. The percentage endorsing each item is as follows: 1 = 96.7%, 2 = 80.2%, 3 = 46.7%, and 4 = 12.3%.

From "The Scaling of Premarital Sexual Permissiveness Revisited: Test Results of Reiss's New Short Form Version," by I. M. Schwartz and I. L. Reiss, *Journal of Sex and Marital Therapy*, 21, pp. 78–86. Copyright © 1995 by Tayor & Francis. Reprinted by permission.

view of sex: ". . . When I was young, I never needed anyone . . . and making love was just for fun . . . those days are gone."

The hedonist's sexual values are reflected in the creed "If it feels good, do it." Hedonists are sensation seekers; they tend to pursue novel, exciting, and optimal levels of stimulation and arousal. Their goal is pleasure.

In Chapter 1, we noted that alcohol and drug use is related to high-risk sexual behavior. One explanation for this relationship is that both substance use and high-risk sexual behavior are related to sensation seeking (Kalichman, Heckman, & Kelly, 1996). In other words, people who are motivated by the need for high levels of sensory stimulation and arousal (a trait often characteristic of a hedonist) are more likely to use drugs and engage in high-risk sexual practices. Substance use, for the sensation-seeking hedonist, may be a corollary to, rather than a cause of, high-risk sexual behavior.

Sexual Values of U.S. Adults

What percent of U.S. adults have the sexual values of absolutism, relativism, and hedonism? Michael and his colleagues (1994) collected national data on U.S. sexual values using value categories similar to those we have discussed. The category of "traditional" (similar to absolutism) included those who say their religious beliefs always guide their sexual behavior, homosexuality is always wrong, and nonmarital sex, teenage sex, and extramarital sex are wrong. The "relational" category (similar to relativism) included those who believe that sex should be part of a loving relationship but not always reserved for marriage. Finally, the "recreational" (similar to hedonism) category characterized those who feel that sexual activity and interaction does not require the context of a marital, committed, or even a loving relationship; sex need not have anything to do with love.

Individuals' sexual values and choices often reflect a combination of absolutism, relativism, and hedonism. For example, an individual may be absolutist (or traditional) regarding extramarital sex, relativistic (or relational) regarding nonmarital sex, and hedonistic (recreational) regarding masturbation or pornography. Based on interviews with 2843 U.S. adults,

77% reported that extramarital sex is always wrong, but only 20% reported that premarital sex is always wrong. This suggests that most U.S. adults have absolutist values concerning extramarital sex, but relativistic values concerning premarital sex (Michael et al., 1994, p. 234).

NATIONAL DATA

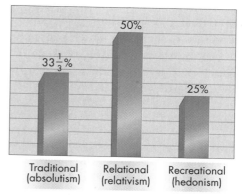

Percentage of U.S. adults representing three broad categories of sexual values

Traditional (absolutism)	Relational (relativism)	Recreational (hedonism)
$33\frac{1}{3}$%	50%	25%

Note: Respondents could be in more than one category.

Source: Michael et al., 1994.

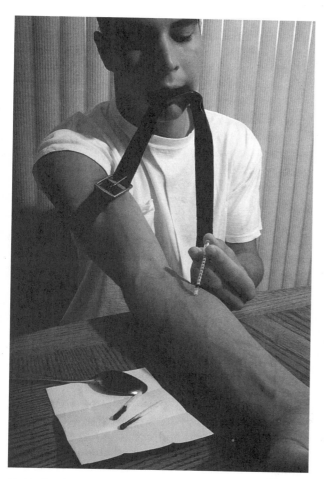

High-risk sexual behavior is associated with drug use because both are motivated by hedonism (or sensation-seeking).

THINK ABOUT IT

What choices would you make in the following situations?

- Your 17-year-old daughter tells you she wants to begin using birth control pills.
- While your partner is out of town, an old flame contacts you and suggests meeting at a motel.
- At a weekend outdoor concert, you meet someone to whom you are intensely attracted. It seems like the interest is mutual, but you find out that this person is married.
- You and your dating partner are celebrating your first anniversary by having dinner at your place. After dinner, you both want and agree to have sexual intercourse, but neither of you has a condom or any other form of birth control.

Based on your choices in these four situations, would you say that your sexual values reflect absolutism, relativism, hedonism, or a combination of these?

RELIGIOUS ROOTS OF SEXUAL VALUES

For some individuals, spirituality or religion serves as a basis for sexual values and decision making. Over half (52.3%) of the respondents in a nationwide study agreed with the statement "My religious beliefs have guided my sexual behavior" (Michael et al., 1994, p. 234). Not surprisingly, church attendance and religiosity are related to delaying the first experience of intercourse (Udry, Kovenock, Morris, & Van den Berg, 1995; Heaton & Jacobson, 1994). Although we live in a pluralistic society in which people have different sexual values, many of the roots of our values are religious. The Jewish and Christian influences have been the most prominent.

Jewish Heritage

Many of our values concerning sexuality can be traced to the laws and customs of Mosaic Judaism. The Old Testament, written between 800 and 200 B.C., reflects the society of the Jewish people at the that time and should be viewed in its historical context. The Jews were a small, persecuted group. Although they believed in God and believed that their sexual values were God-given, from a sociological perspective, their goal was to increase their numbers as rapidly as possible and to minimize defections. From this need to solidify their position as a group and a nation, they developed the following sexual norms.

MARRIAGE IS GOOD Marriage (to a person of one's faith) was a way to encourage the birth of new members into the Jewish faith and to control their upbringing in this communal faith. Men were permitted to marry at 15; women, even younger. Eighteen was considered the maximum age a man could remain single before he would have to explain to the elders of the community why he was still unmarried. Hence, singlehood was regarded as unnatural and immoral. Even widows and widowers were encouraged to remarry as soon as possible. In the case of a widow, her husband's brother could marry her.

CHILDREN ARE EXPECTED Once married, the couple was expected to "be fruitful and multiply." Sexual intercourse was encouraged. During the first year of marriage, the husband was exempt from military service so he could be with his wife. "When a man hath taken a new wife, he shall not go out to war, neither shall he be charged with any business; but he shall be free at home one year, and shall cheer up his wife which he hath taken" (Deut. 24:5).

ADULTERY IS WRONG The couple was restricted to having intercourse with each other. The Jewish society did not tolerate adultery. "And the man that committeth adultery with another man's wife, even he that committeth adultery with his neighbor's wife, the adulterer and the adulteress shall surely be put to death" (Lev. 20:10).

OTHER SEXUAL ADMONITIONS Homosexuality, bestiality (sex with animals), and masturbation were forbidden because they did not involve marriage or procreation. As in many other societies, incest was prohibited. Indeed, any form of sexual expression outside of heterosexual marriage was regarded as immoral. The absolutist sexual value prevailed (Nelson, 1983). In addition, transvestitism was disapproved of because it was a pagan practice and, as such, it was seen as a threat to the community.

Judaism has had a major impact on our view of sexual values. Our feelings about marriage (more than 90% of us marry), children (more than 90% of us express a desire to have children), and sex in marriage (most U.S. adults regard infidelity as something to be ashamed of) have been significantly influenced by the ancient Hebrews. But Christianity has also strongly affected our sexual values.

Christian Heritage

While Judaism was based on the teachings of Moses in the Old Testament, Christianity was based on the teachings of Jesus in the New Testament. Because early Christian congregations were geographically scattered, interpretations differed; "there were hundreds of competing groups with different and contradictory doctrines" (Bullough, 1987, p. 52).

TEACHINGS OF JESUS Most of Jesus's teachings were about salvation and living positively. He said very little about sex, although in one instance, he equated thoughts about having intercourse with the act itself. "But I say unto you that whosoever looketh on a woman to lust after her hath committed adultery with her already in his heart" (Matt. 5:28).

TEACHINGS OF ST. PAUL   After the death of Jesus, his followers continued to preach the message of Christianity. Among these was St. Paul, who added his own interpretations of sexuality. He felt that marriage was the most desirable context for sex. His writings should be viewed in their historical context. Paul and others of his day believed that the return of Christ (the "second coming") was imminent. Sex and marriage were seen as unnecessary uses of a person's time when there was so much to do in preparation for Christ's return (such as recruit new members) and so little time.

St. Paul's ideas about sex reflected the impact of Greco-Roman culture and its Hellenistic philosophy, spiritualistic dualism. The body and spirit or mind were seen as being at odds with each other. The body was "temporal, material, corruptible and corrupting," while the spirit was pure and responsible for delivering the body from sin (Nelson, 1983, p. 122). "Sex was particularly bad because it was not only pleasurable but because it might lead to procreation and the imprisonment of other souls" (Bullough, 1987, p. 50).

This preoccupation with the body-spirit dichotomy continues today. "Much sex-negativity in this culture displays this spiritualistic distortion, which generates both fear of and, simultaneously, fixation with sex and the body" (Special Committee on Human Sexuality, 1991, p. 29).

TEACHINGS OF ST. AUGUSTINE   Around 386 A.D., at the age of 32, Augustine read the writings of St. Paul. Before this time, he had lived a promiscuous life that included fathering a son outside of marriage, cohabiting with his son's mother while becoming engaged to another woman, and being unfaithful to his fiancée. Frustrated with his inability to control his sexual desires, he converted to Christianity, broke off his engagement, stopped his affairs, and never married.

His own writings, particularly *The City of God*, reflect a very negative view of sex and sexuality. He felt that sexual desires, emotions, and passions, expressed through sexual intercourse, were sinful. While the only justification or purpose for intercourse was procreation, even in marriage, the act itself was tainted with shame. This shame, according to St. Augustine, was a result of the lust Adam and Eve felt for each other, their disobedience to God by engaging in sexual intercourse, and their expulsion from the Garden of Eden.

St. Augustine rose to be a bishop in the Roman Catholic Church, and his views became widespread. The ritual for infant baptism grew out of the belief that children were conceived in an impure act (original sin) and must be cleansed of this sin. This sacrament is still practiced and recognized by many Christian faiths.

Early Christian interpretations of sexuality as evil led to the adoption of a reward-punishment model to control believers. People who controlled their sexual appetites were rewarded by the knowledge that they were like Christ, who was essentially asexual. Those who gave in to their lusts would be punished in Hell's fires after death. However, a way to avoid such threats was to confess one's sins to members of the clergy. Such confession helped the church monitor the sexual behavior of its members and ensure compliance (Bullough, 1987, p. 53).

OTHER INFLUENTIAL RELIGIOUS LEADERS   St. Thomas Aquinas is another important writer whose thinking influenced sexual values in Western culture. A 13th-century Roman Catholic, Aquinas specified in *Summa Theologica* that any sexual act that did not lead specifically to procreation was sinful and against the will of God. Masturbation, bestiality, and homosexuality headed the list. Even sexual caresses were sinful if engaged in solely for pleasure. Also, face-to-face intercourse was the only acceptable position.

Martin Luther and John Calvin, in their break from the Roman Catholic Church, adopted a more positive view of sexuality. According to Luther (who married and had more than ten children), marriage was a good and positive relationship and not second to singlehood. He also regarded sexual desires as normal appetites, much like hunger and thirst. Calvin, too, saw sex, at least in marriage, as holy, honorable, and desirable. Hence, marital sex was for more than procreation (Carswell, 1969).

The Puritans

The Puritans who settled along the coast of New England in the 17th century were radical Protestants who had seceded from the Church of England. We can trace many of our sexual values to their beliefs and social norms. Tannahill (1982) noted that the forcefulness and power of the Puritans in imposing their ways on others and the fact that new immigrants were predominantly Protestant explain why the Puritans influenced several generations of later colonists. In fact, Tannahill suggested that the Puritan ethic has had a disproportionate influence in the history of the United States. "Senators and Congressmen today, struggling (whatever the state of their faith and/or marital relationships) to project an image of dedicated family men, at work, at rest, at church, at play, owe this particular electoral hazard to the early New England settlers who wove the public demonstration of family solidarity into the American ethos" (p.330).

The Puritans wanted their members to get married and stay married. Religious values (avoiding temptation), social values (being a member of a close-knit community), and economic values (working hard for material reward) helped to emphasize the importance of the marital relationship. The Puritan woman had little choice of an adult role other than wife and mother. Only in marriage could she achieve status in the community. Men and women were taught that their best chance for survival was to find a spouse to satisfy their needs for clothing, food, companionship, and sex.

The Puritans approved of sex only within marriage. Like Augustine and Aquinas, they viewed sex as a passion to conquer or control and marriage as the only safe place for its expression. Rigid codes of dress helped to discourage sexual thoughts.

Any discussion of sex among the Puritans would not be complete without reference to bundling, also called tarrying. Not unique to the Puritans, bundling was a courtship custom in which the would-be groom slept in the prospective bride's bed in her parents' home. But there were rules to restrict sexual contact. Both partners were fully clothed, and a wooden bar was placed between them. In addition, the young woman might be encased in a long bag up to her armpits, her clothes might be sewn together at strategic points, and her parents might be sleeping in the same room.

The justifications for the bundling were convenience and economics. Aside from meeting at church, bundling was one of the few opportunities a couple had to get together to talk and learn about each other. Because daylight hours were consumed by heavy work demands, night became a time for courtship. But how did the bed become the courtship arena? New England winters were cold. Firewood, oil for lamps, and candles were in short supply. By talking in bed, the young couple could come to know each other without wasting valuable sources of energy.

Although bundling flourished in the middle of the 18th century, it provoked a great deal of controversy. "Jonathan Edwards attacked it from the pulpit, and other ministers, who had allowed it to go unnoticed, joined in its suppression" (Calhoun, 1960, p. 71). By about 1800, the custom had virtually disappeared.

Taoism, Hinduism, and Islam

While Western culture often has a negative view of sexuality, Eastern religions are quite positive.

TAOISM   Instead of prohibiting sexual behaviors that could interfere with fertility, Taoism (a dominant religion in China for thousands of years) actively encourages sexual behaviors, not only to promote conception, but also to contribute to spiritual growth. Tannahill (1982) noted that

> Just as the European of early medieval times knew, without quite understanding why, that sex was sinful but occasionally permissible, so his contemporary in China knew, without quite understanding why, that sex was a sacred duty and one that he must perform frequently and conscientiously if he was truly to achieve harmony with the Supreme Path, the Way, *Tao.* (p. 168)

Chinese sexual attitudes were shaped by Confucianism, Taoism, and Buddhism, which all included the concept of yin-yang (Hatfield & Rapson, 1996). Yin (the female force) was seen as negative, passive, weak, and destructive. Yang (the male force) was the opposite—positive, active, strong, and constructive. The longer a man prolonged intercourse, the more *yin* essence he would absorb. The woman's yin essence was believed to be in generous supply. However, the man's *yang* essence (semen) was seen as limited and not to be squandered. The man was encouraged to nourish his yin with a number of women. "If in one night he can have intercourse with more than ten women it is best" (Tannahill, 1982, p. 172). Noncoital activities were allowed as long as no precious yang essence was lost. These values persisted until the late 17th century, when Chinese sexual attitudes resembled those of the Puritans.

HINDUISM   Between the third and fifth centuries, the *Kama Sutra* was compiled as an interpersonal code of conduct as well as a sex manual (Tannahill, 1982). Hinduism viewed sexuality as being an integral part of nature having cosmic importance; it was not separated from the rest of life as it was in Western religions. The doctrine of Karma (transmigration of souls) taught that, through correct behavior, one could be reincarnated at a higher level. Sex was one of a Hindu Indian's religious duties, "not one that would put him straight in tune with the infinite, but certainly one of the least taxing and most pleasurable ways of improving the state of his Karma" (p. 201).

ISLAM   Prophet Mohammed was born in 570 A.D. He received his first revelation from God through the angel Gabriel at the age of 40. The beginning of Islam coincides with this divine revelation (which continued for 23 years) known as Qur`an. The Qur`an is God's final message to man—a reconfirmation of the eternal message and a summary of all that has gone before. Islam as a religion reaffirms the beliefs that the previous prophets—including Abraham, Moses and Jesus—propounded, namely submission to the will of the one, and only, unique, incomparable God.

Islam emphasizes and allows sexual fulfillment only in marriage. Sexual intercourse between husband and wife is considered desirable, and both have a full right to enjoyment (except through anal intercourse, which is forbidden). "There is an emphasis on tenderness with words of love and always a sense of holiness and reverence" (Al Bustan, El Tomi, Faiwalla, & Manav, 1995). Individuals who have intercourse outside of marriage are thought to be committing a major sin. According to Islamic law, the penalty for premarital and extramarital intercourse is a public whipping and stoning to death. Anything that leads to illegal sex is also illegal. This includes dating, free mixing of the sexes, provocative dress, nudity, obscenity, and pornography. The dress code both for men and women protects them from temptation and desires (Haeri, 1992). Muslim women are required to cover their heads and body in public as a mark of chastity. They are also required to avoid all physical contact with men.

————— THINK ABOUT IT —————
How spiritual or religious are you? What sexual values do you have today that you would attribute to religious roots? How would your views of sexuality be different if you had been socialized in the Taoist, Hindu, or Islamic traditions?

HISTORICAL AND SCIENTIFIC ROOTS OF SEXUAL VALUES

The Victorian era and the rise of science have both influenced the sexual values we have today.

Victorian Influence

The Victorian era (which took its name from Englands' Queen Alexandria Victoria, who reigned from 1837 to 1901) is popularly viewed as a time of prudery and propriety in sexual behavior. However, there was a great disparity between expressed middle-class morality and actual practices. In his study of this era, Wendell Johnson (1979) wrote:

> What were the Victorians actually doing? One might reply "Just about everything." Free love, adultery, male homosexuality and (in spite of the Queen's disbelief) lesbianism, nymphetism, sadism, and masochism, exhibitionism—the Victorians practiced them all . . . the number of whores per acre in mid-Victorian London and the consumption of pornography . . . would put today's Times Square to shame. (p. 11)

But the official view of sexuality during the Victorian era was that sexual behavior and the discussion of it should be suppressed. Some specific Victorian notions of sexuality are discussed below.

MARITAL SEXUALITY   Sex was a passion that should be channeled into marriage. Uncontrollable sexual desires were believed to be characteristic only of men. Women were thought to be asexual and nonorgasmic. William Hammond, the surgeon general of the United States Army during the 1860s, wrote that it was doubtful that women experienced the slightest degree of pleasure in even one-tenth of the occasions of sexual intercourse. (Of course, such lack of pleasure may have been related to the insensitivity of their husbands, who were not concerned about creating pleasure for their partners during intercourse.)

PRUDISHNESS   Examples of Victorian prudishness include skirts to the ankle and discreet references to anything sexual. Women were not pregnant, they were "in an interesting way." Ladies delicately nibbled their "bosom of chicken," and librarians shelved books by male and female authors separately.

FEMALE TYPES   There were "good" women and "bad" women in Victorian society. The latter were whores or women who practiced no social graces in expressing their sexuality. Women who were not whores but who did enjoy sexual feelings were in conflict. Some felt degraded, even insane. "If I love sex, I must be like a whore" was an inescapable conclusion. Some women even had clitoridectomies (surgical removal of the clitoris) performed to eliminate the "cause" of their sexual feelings.

Tannahill (1982) traced how the Victorian reincarnation of courtly love, which cast women in the role of untouchable moral guardians, fueled "an explosive increase in prostitution, an epidemic spread of venereal disease, and a morbid taste for masochism" (p. 347). The subsequent attempts of women to "set society to rights" was the foundation of their struggle for suffrage. In the 20th century, the dissemination of scientific ideologies and discoveries, the industrial revolution, and economic reality presented a challenge to the artificial ideal of the Victorian family. The rise of scientific approaches is described in the following section.

Scientific Ideologies

Beyond the religious ideology that the mind must control the corrupt body, science has also influenced the way we think about sexuality. Several early 20th-century scientists were instrumental in shifting society's ideas about sex from a sacred to a scientific perspective, including Richard von Krafft-Ebing, Sigmund Freud, Havelock Ellis, Magnus Hirschfeld, and Hendrick van de Velde. Richard von Krafft-Ebing (1840–1902) was a Viennese psychiatrist and sexologist who focused on the study of abnormal or pathological sexuality. *Psychopathia Sexualis* (1886) contains Krafft-Ebing's case histories of over 200 individuals. He described the most lurid details in Latin, and according to Tannahill (1982, p. 382), the work "soon became the bible of all pornographers who could afford a good Latin dictionary."

Theories developed by the Austrian physician Sigmund Freud (1885–1939) are described in Chapter 2. Freud described stages of psychosexual development in terms of the erogenous zones (areas of the body that can bring pleasure). Personality formation was shaped by one's negotiation of predictable developmental crises, such as the oedipal conflict with its castration anxiety and the electra complex with its penis envy. Even those who advocate psychoanalytic theory, however, allow that "it is difficult to prove Freudian contentions empirically. Much of the difficulty here lies in the fact that we are dealing in the realm of fantasy and infant fantasy to boot!" (Cameron & Rychlak, 1985, p. 47). Nevertheless, this did not prevent Freud's ideas from being widely disseminated and influential in our thinking about sex roles and sexual expectations.

Havelock Ellis (1859–1939) emphasized that sexual behavior was learned social behavior, that "deviant" sexual behavior was merely that which society labeled as abnormal, and that an enjoyable sex life (a desirable goal) was not something that just happened but had to be achieved. About the sex education of children, Ellis (1931) wrote, "No doubt is any longer possible as to the absolute necessity of taking a deliberate and active part in this sexual initiation, instead of leaving it to chance or to revelation of ignorant and perhaps vicious companions or servants" (p.43).

The work of Magnus Hirschfeld (1868–1935) on homosexuality and transsexualism was not translated into English until recently. Perhaps this is because the scholarly community felt that he could not be objective, given that he was openly homosexual (and possibly transvestite, inferred from his empathy for transvestites and his campaign for acceptance of them). However, his book, *Transvestites,* is considered to be "an outstanding classic that, while often cited, has been rarely read" (Bullough, 1991, p. 13).

Theodore Hendrik van de Velde (1873–1937) was a Dutch gynecologist, who, in 1926, published a guide to sex, *Ideal Marriage,* which became a bestseller. Like Ellis, van de Velde believed that sexual response was not automatic. He prescribed specific sexual techniques whereby his patients—and readers—could translate their emotional commitments into delightful orgasms. He also emphasized that sex is an interpersonal experience, and he considered lack of orgasm and impotence a couple's problem, rather than the wife's or husband's problem.

While a scientific emphasis contributed a valuable approach to understanding sexuality, it is important to recognize that even "objective" observations of scientists are framed and interpreted by cultural and historical context. For example, since the days of Aristotle, semen was emphasized as the essential element in reproduction. Although the ovaries had been discovered by the start of the Christian era, they were seen as an unimportant feminine replica of the testes. Tannahill (1982) quoted a 16th-century Spanish anatomist as reluctantly reporting their existence, hoping that "women might not become all the more arrogant for knowing that they also, like men, have testicles" (p. 344).

Following the discovery of the ovum in 1672, there were decades of debate over the relative contributions of the ovum and sperm (first seen under a microscope by Antony van Leeuwenhoeck in 1675). By the mid-1800s, observation of the fusion of a frog ovum and sperm confirmed what botanical study implied, that children derived characteristics as much from their mother as from their fathers. This information was applied with dire social consequences. Racially mixed marriages were seen as dangerous, especially in anti-Semitic Germany and a conflicted United States grappling with the abolition of slavery. Race mixing would dilute the superior strain, according to prominent zoologist and geneticist C. B. Davenport. In 1929, Davenport published his comparison of white, brown, and black people from Jamaica and concluded that "the browns had a larger number who were 'muddled and wuzzle-headed.' What these engaging terms signify was not made clear, nor was any statistical evidence offered" (Thomas & Sillen, 1972, pp. 109–110). The term "miscegenation" (race mixing) wore the cloak of scientific authenticity, but was actually coined by two journalists in an attempt to discredit Abraham Lincoln and antislavery forces by presenting abolitionists as promoting systematic race mixing.

In addition to being used in acts of deliberate political trickery, science has been used to promote social agendas. LoPiccolo (1983) noted, "Indeed, it would appear that many of the pronouncements on sexual-

ity made by experts (psychiatrists, psychologists, and sexologists) over the years have been little more than translation of cultural biases into pseudoscientific jargon" (p. 51). For example, the dire warnings of the dangers of masturbation, although presented as medical wisdom, were based on moral concerns. Krafft-Ebing described applying a white-hot iron to the clitoris of young girls brought in by their parents for "treatment" of masturbation.

Freud's work has been especially criticized for his pronouncements regarding the sexuality of women. "A large volume of empirical evidence has been accumulated to indicate that virtually all of Freud's inspired guesses about sexuality were wrong. . . . Yet we continue to see couples applying for sex therapy with concerns that reflect this Freudian view of female sexuality" (LoPiccolo, 1983, p. 52). Freud's views of male sexuality, judging that any sexual behavior other than penile penetration of the vagina implied arrested sexual development, were simply reflecting traditional Jewish attitudes, according to sexuality educator Sol Gordon. "'Infantile,' 'immature,' 'personality defect' is just name calling and the substitution of Freudian pseudoscientific language for the prohibitions of the Talmud" (LoPiccolo, 1983, p. 52).

Nevertheless, early sexology pioneers set a precedent for studying sexuality from the perspective of a more scientific ideology. One historian (Johnson, 1979) offered the analogy that Havelock Ellis was to modern sexual theory what Albert Einstein was to modern physics, in that he offered a paradigm that has influenced modern sexual theory. These early theorists paved the way for the next quantum leap. The works of Alfred Kinsey and Masters and Johnson (discussed in Chapter 2) have added scientific credibility to the study of sexuality and have served as a foundation for further research. Indeed, it was said of Kinsey's research that he did for sex what Columbus did for geography (Ernst & Loth, 1948).

OTHER SOURCES OF SEXUAL KNOWLEDGE AND VALUES

In addition to religion, the Victorians, and science, the media, parents, and schoolteachers are major influences on our sexual knowledge and values.

Television

Although television is the leading media source of sex information in the United States (Strasburger, 1995), rarely do we see mature discussions on contraception, condom usage, abstinence, or sexual consequences and responsibility on television. The television viewer learns that sex is romantic and exciting but learns nothing about discussing the need for contraception or HIV and STD protection. With few exceptions (such as the character Donna on *Beverly Hills 90210,* who remained a virgin until the last semester of her senior year in college), viewers are inundated with role models who engage in casual sex. Of 50 soap opera episodes, only one specific mention was made of the potential for AIDS from unprotected sex (Greenberg & Busselle, 1996). Recommendations for improving this aspect of television programming include depicting "situations which show planned mature relationships as opposed to spur-of-the-moment responses to passion" (Edwards, 1996, p. 5). Safer-sex depictions should also permeate television.

Parents

Parents influence their children's sexual knowledge by what they teach—and don't teach—their children about sexuality. Parents continuously send signals about sexuality through their verbal and nonverbal behavior toward each other and their children. It is impossible to not communicate (teach), and parents are persistent models.

Traditionally, parents have been inadequate sources of sexual information for their children. Less than 15% of over 8000 students reported that they received a "meaningful sex education" from their parents (Gordon, 1986, p. 22). In a study of 700 individuals ranging in age from 9 to 73, none of the participants identified parents as their primary source of sexuality information (Ansuini, Fiddler-Woite, & Woite, 1996).

Parental reluctance to talk to their children about sex is often based on their own insecurity about their level of sexual knowledge, as well as the fear that telling their children about sex will promote sexual activity. Many parents also feel that their children will learn about sex and birth control from other sources (such as school-based sex education programs), so the parents feel little need to talk about it. Even when parents do talk to their children about sexuality, they do

not always convey accurate information. In a study referred to earlier (Hockenberry-Eaton et al., 1996; see Table 2.1), more than half of the mothers of adolescents in the sample were unable to correctly define wet dreams and hormones; and about one-third could not accurately define semen, ejaculation, and ovulation. The researchers concluded that "mothers . . . may be ill-prepared to teach their children about sex" (p. 35).

Parents also influence their children's sexual values, not only by what they teach their children, but also by what they do in their own sexual lives. For example, one study found that the permissive sexual values of divorced mothers influenced their adolescent daughters' sexual attitudes and behaviors in the same direction (Whitbeck, Simons, & Kao, 1994). In another study, researchers questioned 224 Latino and 160 Anglo teens about their sexual behavior and family background and found that conservative maternal attitudes about sex were associated with a delay in sexual behavior in teens (Hovell et al., 1994).

Schoolteachers

Over 80% of parents want sexuality education taught in high schools, and only about 75% of the states require their public schools to provide either sexuality or STD and HIV prevention education (Daley, 1996). Sex education is usually taught as part of another subject, such as health education, home economics, biology, or physical education. Because each state, rather than the federal government, is responsible for sex education in the public school system, there is considerable variation among the states in terms of the sex education they offer. Kirby (1992) identified and examined evaluation research for sex education curricula implemented in junior and senior high schools over the past 15 to 20 years. He categorized sexuality education efforts into the following groups (or "generations") of programs.

- First-generation programs emphasized increasing knowledge, especially about the risk and consequences of pregnancy. Unfortunately, evaluation studies showed that having greater knowledge (knowing that unprotected sex can result in pregnancy or STDs) does not measurably change risk-taking behavior. "Ignorance is not the solution, but knowledge is not enough" (Kirby, 1992, p. 285).

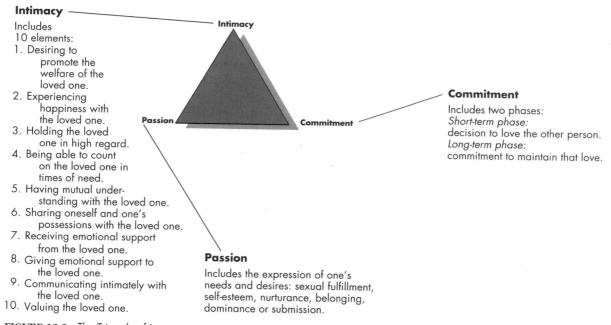

Intimacy
Includes
10 elements:
1. Desiring to promote the welfare of the loved one.
2. Experiencing happiness with the loved one.
3. Holding the loved one in high regard.
4. Being able to count on the loved one in times of need.
5. Having mutual understanding with the loved one.
6. Sharing oneself and one's possessions with the loved one.
7. Receiving emotional support from the loved one.
8. Giving emotional support to the loved one.
9. Communicating intimately with the loved one.
10. Valuing the loved one.

Commitment
Includes two phases:
Short-term phase: decision to love the other person.
Long-term phase: commitment to maintain that love.

Passion
Includes the expression of one's needs and desires: sexual fulfillment, self-esteem, nurturance, belonging, dominance or submission.

FIGURE 12.2 The Triangle of Love
Psychology professor Robert Sternberg's research shows that love is the interaction between intimacy, passion, and commitment.
Source: Based on Sternberg, 1986.

level of passion is felt between companionate lovers (companionate love). However the predominate focus of romantic love is passion, and the predominate quality of companionate love is commitment.

Individuals bring different love triangles to the table of love. One lover may bring a predominance of passion with some intimacy but no commitment (romantic love), while the other person brings commitment but no passion or intimacy (empty love). The triangular theory of love allows lovers to see the degree to which they are matched in terms of the three basic elements of passion, intimacy, and commitment.

Hendrick and Hendrick (1992) described and studied another schema for looking at types of love relationships or orientations toward love (based on the theory of Canadian sociologist John Alan Lee). Although a person may show characteristics of more than one love style, people are often characterized as exhibiting one of six different love styles:

1. *Eros:* Passionate love, not limited to physical passion
2. *Ludus:* Game-playing love—for mutual enjoyment—without serious intent
3. *Storge:* Friendship; companionate love
4. *Pragma:* Pragmatic and practical love
5. *Mania:* Manic, jealous, obsessive love
6. *Agape:* Selfless, idealistic love

Hendrick and Hendrick (1992) offered weather analogies to depict the six love styles. Eros lovers, they suggested, get hit by a bolt of lightning. Ludic lovers like rainstorms but don't like getting wet. Storgic lovers like to stay inside during the lightning and thunder but will go outside in soft, gentle rain showers. Pragma lovers will always have an umbrella in case of rain, Mania lovers don't mind getting wet, and Agape lovers will give their umbrella to their partner.

Montgomery and Sorell (1997) observed that love styles associated with the lowest relationship satisfaction are Ludus and Mania styles. Conversely, Eros and Agape love styles are associated with the highest relationship satisfaction. We await research on the relationship between love style and sexual satisfaction, although we might predict greater sexual satisfaction with Eros and Agape.

🍂 The connection between love styles, marital satisfaction, and acculturation was studied in Mexican American and Anglo American couples (Contreras, Hendrick, & Hendrick, 1996). For all groups, passionate love scores best predicted marital satisfaction. Hispanic-oriented participants were more pragmatic and less idealistic about love and sex than bicultural Hispanic couples and Anglo Americans. Some theorists have argued that passionate love is a Western phenomenon because of our emphasis on individualism, but studies from Europe, Russia, Japan, China, and the Pacific Islands confirm that men and women in a variety of cultures are as romantic as Americans (Hatfield & Rapson, 1996).

Love and affection are important motives for sexual engagement (Hill & Preston, 1996). In general, women are more likely than men to require love and affection in a relationship as a prerequisite for having sex. In one study, only half of U.S. men, compared to about three-quarters of U.S. women, reported that their first sexual intercourse experience was with a steady partner with whom they were significantly involved (Weinberg, Lottes, & Shaver, 1995). In another study of 163 college students, 31% of the women in contrast to 68% of the men reported that "low emotional intimacy" characterized their last intercourse experience (Brigman & Knox, 1992).

PERSONAL CHOICES

Should You Have Sex With or Without Love?

Most sexual encounters occur on a continuum from love involvement to no love involvement. Opinions vary with regard to whether an emotional relationship is a worthy prerequisite for sexual involvement.

> Sex is good and beautiful when both parties want it, but when one person wants sex only, that's bad. I love sex, but I like to feel that the man cares about me. I can't handle the type of sexual relationship where one night I spend the night with him and the next night he spends the night with someone else. I feel like I am being used. There are still a few women around like me who need the commitment before sex. (authors' files)

Other people feel that love is not necessary for sexual expression. "Some of the best sex I've had," remarked one person, "was with people I was not in love with." The ideal that sex with love is wholesome and sex without love is exploitative may be an untenable position. For example, two strangers can meet, share each other sexually, have a deep mutual admiration for each other's sensuous qualities, and then go their separate ways. Such an encounter is not necessarily an example of sexual exploitation. Rather, it may be an example of two individuals who have a preference for independence and singlehood rather than emotional involvement, commitment, and marriage. Given the risk of contracting STDs and HIV, we suggest that sex with numerous anonymous partners may have fatal consequences.

Each person in a sexual encounter will undoubtedly experience different degrees of love feelings, and the experience of each may differ across time. One woman reported that the first time she had intercourse with her future husband was shortly after they had met in a bar. She described their first sexual encounter as "raw naked sex" with no emotional feelings. But as they continued to see each other over a period of months, an emotional relationship developed, and "sex took on a love meaning for us."

Sex with love can also drift into sex without love. One man said he had been deeply in love with his wife, but that they had gradually drifted apart. Sex between them was no longer sex with love. Similarly, some women report being in relationships with men who feign love but actually use them for sex. Bepko and Krestan (1991) emphasized the importance of individuals' breaking from these co-dependent relationships and establishing their own self-love as a secure base for making choices in relationships with others. Both love and sex can be viewed on a continuum. Love feelings can range from nonexistent to intense, and relationships can range from limited sexual interaction to intense interaction. Hence, rarely are sexual encounters completely with or without love; rather, they will include varying degrees of emotional involvement. Also, rarely are romantic love relationships completely with or without sex. Rather, they display varying degrees of sexual expression. Where on the continuum one chooses to be—at what degree of emotional and sexual involvement—will vary from person to person and from time to time.

Sexual Guilt

Sexual guilt involves the feeling that sexual behavior violates personal sexual values. One study of college students found that 75% of U.S. women, compared to 44% of U.S. men, felt guilty after their first intercourse experience (Weinberg, Lottes, & Shaver, 1995).

Reflecting on their most recent intercourse experience, 44% of men, but only 31% of women, reported feeling guilty afterward. Men may feel less guilty after their first intercourse experience because losing one's virginity is traditionally regarded as more significant for women. The lower percentage of women reporting guilt in their most recent intercourse experience may reflect a more stable emotional relationship context, which is the condition needed for cultural approval for female sexual expression.

Absolutist religious sexual values are associated with sexual guilt. One study found that women who frequently attended religious services were more likely to feel guilty about masturbation (Davidson, Darling, & Norton, 1995). Table 12.2 reflects the average level of guilt on a four-point continuum for various sexual situations reported by 249 undergraduate university students. You might compare your answers with theirs.

Sexual guilt can be a tool that helps us to make choices consistent with our values and sexual well-being. If you imagine that a particular sexual behavior or choice would result in considerable guilt, then that behavior or choice probably violates your sexual values and may compromise your sexual well-being. If you feel guilty after engaging in a particular sexual behavior, that behavior probably violated your sexual values, and you may want to rethink whether or not you will choose to engage in that behavior in the future.

TABLE 12.2   Contexts Conducive to Sexual Guilt

How Guilty Would You Feel If . . .	Average Score
1. You have intercourse with someone 18 years older than you. Both of you are unmarried.	2.04
2. You decide not to tell the person you are about to marry any information concerning your previous affectional relationship because you believe it will have no bearing on your marriage.	2.18
3. The person you are about to marry learns of a previous sexual affair with another person you did not particularly care for prior to your present relationship.	2.29
4. You reveal to an associate that a person who had invited you to dinner was gay and there were to be no other guests.	2.48
5. Your mother discovers that you, at age 16, are having intercourse with a member of the other sex.	2.76
6. You concealed from the person you are about to marry that you had earlier contracted and were cured of gonorrhea.	2.88
7. Your parents learn of your sexual relationship with someone of another race, and you know they disapprove.	3.03
8. As a student, you are in love with a teacher who is fired because your sexual relationship has been brought to the attention of the instructor's dean.	3.51
9. You are in a committed relationship with a person, yet you had intercourse with someone else.	3.52
10. Your fiancé learns that you had a sexual encounter with your fiancé's best friend while your fiancé was away visiting his or her grandmother.	3.66

Scoring   1 = No guilt; 2 = Little guilt; 3 = Moderate guilt; 4 = Considerable guilt

Source: Knox et al., 1991.

In some cases, however, sexual guilt may interfere with a person's sexual well-being. For example, some women feel guilty about experiencing sexual pleasure because they have been taught that "sex is bad" and "good women do not enjoy sex." In this situation, sexual guilt may interfere with a woman's ability to become sexually aroused and experience orgasm, even within a loving and committed relationship.

—————— THINK ABOUT IT ——————

How do you think the HIV/AIDS epidemic has affected the level of sexual guilt experienced by individuals who engage in high-risk sexual behaviors?

CONTROVERSIES INVOLVING SEXUAL VALUES

Thus far in this chapter, we have focused on personal sexual values. But societies develop their own sexual values and express them in the form of laws. Following is a discussion of the law and sexuality. We then look at two controversial social issues—prostitution and pornography.

Sex and the Law

An unending debate in U.S. society exists around the issue of private rights versus social morality. For example, should consenting adults be permitted to engage in any sexual behaviors they choose, or should the law define morally acceptable parameters? As of May 1995, 22 states (and Puerto Rico) had laws banning sodomy (oral or anal intercourse) between consenting adults. In 11 states, the sodomy laws apply to both gay and straight couples. Any violation of these laws is considered a felony. By a 5–4 decision, the Supreme Court has held that there is no federal constitutional right to engage in private, consensual, same-sex sodomy.

John Stuart Mill (1859) emphasized the rights of the individual by arguing that the only purpose of government should be to protect its citizens from harm by others. He also advocated

> liberty of taste and pursuits . . . of doing as we like, subject to such consequences as may follow: Without impediment for our fellow creatures so long as what we do does not harm them even though they should think our conduct foolish, perverse, or wrong.

In contrast, Lord Devlin (1965) argued that no private morality should operate outside the concern of criminal law. He felt that the health of society was defined by its adherence to a binding moral code and recommended that legal definitions of morality be identified and enforced. A modern version of legislating morality was reflected by the Meese Commission Report on pornography. The commission took the position that the protection of society's moral environment is a legitimate purpose of government and recommended more restrictive laws on pornography.

Private citizens also "praise sex laws as an expression of a collective conscience" (Sachs, 1990, p. 98). Rebecca Hagelin of Concerned Women for America, speaking of adultery laws, noted, "If these laws had been enforced with regularity in this country, then a lot more people would think twice about participating in sexually immoral acts" (p. 98).

One of the ways society has achieved compromise and balance between the radically opposing views of private versus public morality has been to view certain sexual behaviors on a continuum of offensiveness, and to assign relative penalties for engaging in them. For example, child sexual abuse and rape are regarded as severely offensive and are subject to strong sanctions. However, frottage (touching or rubbing a nonconsenting person; see Chapter 18) may go unrecognized in criminal statistics because such behavior is likely to be prosecuted under a more generalized category, such as assault.

The following are five categories of sexual acts according to criminal classification (MacNamara & Sagarin, 1977):

- Category I—Criminal acts that require enforcement to protect society. Rape and child molestation are examples.
- Category II—Sexual acts with potential victimization. Exhibitionism and voyeurism are examples. Although these behaviors themselves may not be regarded as morally severe, they may create harm to the victims, who deserve protection.
- Category III—Sexual acts midway between those considered morally reprehensible and those creating victims. Prostitution and adultery are examples. Both are said to reflect immorality, and both have the potential to produce victims (the prostitutes in the case of prostitution and the spouse or children of the adulterer).

- Category IV—Sex acts between consenting adults, including homosexual behavior and behaviors within marriage.
- Category V—Behaviors that do not involve sexual contact, but are either criminalized or considered to be sex crimes. Abortion (in countries where it is illegal) and the sale and distribution of child pornography are examples.

It is commonly assumed that most people have not committed criminal sexual acts. However, people often engage in sexual activities (or have the desire to do so) and are not apprehended by the law. In a sample of 60 undergraduate college men (who are often used as nonoffender controls in sex research), nearly two-thirds had engaged in some form of sexual misconduct in the past. Over half (52%) had engaged in a sexual offense for which they could be arrested (Templeman & Stinnett, 1991). Some examples included voyeurism (42%), frottage (35%), obscene phone calls (8%), and coercive sex (8%) (p. 142). In spite of the relatively high incidence of having engaged in punishable sex offenses, only two of the 60 respondents (3%) had been arrested.

Prostitution

Prostitution has been defined as attending to the sexual desires of a particular individual (or individuals) with bodily acts in exchange for payment of money (Zatz, 1997, p. 279). Prostitution is also referred to as sex work. Money may be exchanged for various types of services, including erotic dancing, stripping, modeling for pornographic material, and serving as a phone sex partner (Overall, 1992).

NATIONAL DATA

The National Task Force on Prostitution estimates that over 1 million people in the United States have worked as prostitutes.

Source: National Task Force on Prostitution, 1997.

Prostitution is a controversial topic, with some individuals viewing it as a form of sexual abuse and exploitation and others viewing it as a legitimate activity that adults have the right to engage in. Proponents of the prostitution-as-abuse perspective argue that prostitutes are physically and morally exploited. Dangers of prostitution include rape, beatings and injury, robbery, psychological abuse, and emotional pain (Overall, 1992). Vulnerability to diseases—particularly AIDS—is a substantial risk. A study of imprisoned prostitutes in the Czech Republic (Malinova, 1995) documented histories of frequent abortions, unwanted children, and STDs. Critics of prostitution have questioned whether economic coercion is the main lure of prostitution for women (and some men) who have limited social and economic opportunities (Overall, 1992).

Finally, some critics argue that survivors of childhood sexual abuse are more likely to turn to prostitution because of attitudes about themselves and sexual acts fostered by their abuse. One U.S. study of adolescent runaways and homeless women found that early sexual abuse increased involvement in prostitution beyond the influence of factors such as running away from home or substance abuse (Simons & Whitbeck, 1991).

Alternatively, many prostitutes say that their occupation is simply a way of earning an income and argue that they are abused by the courts and the police who harass them. Prostitutes are more often women than men, and are more often arrested than the men they serve (Zatz, 1997). COYOTE, an acronym for Call Off Your Old Tired Ethics, was formed in San Francisco by an ex-prostitute, Margo St. James. COYOTE has promoted the idea of a prostitutes' union to change the public image of prostitutes and to fight the moral and legal discrimination to which they are subjected. Rather than viewing prostitution as the use of a woman's body by a man for his satisfaction, Zatz (1997) has suggested, "What's wrong with the description, 'Prostitution is about the use of a man's desire by a woman for her own profit?'"

Prostitution occurs worldwide. Russian women in particular have come into demand lately (Pope, 1997). "Traffickers rustle up false papers, assumed identities, and phony marriage partners so that the women can work abroad. Young, pretty women are told they have modeling jobs, only to be forced into the sex industry" (p. 38). Israel is said to have a $450 million per year prostitution ring. "Young Russian women described hostagelike conditions, severe beatings, and rape as punishment by their captors. 'These women are kept like dogs,' a senior vice officer on the Tel Aviv police force told *U.S. News*" (Pope, 1997, p. 44).

Two million girls (5 to 15 years old) are introduced into the commercial sex market each year.

Source: United Nations Population Fund, 1997.

🖋 Epidemiologists in Thailand have traced occurrences of HIV from a southern fishing port, along a heavily traveled truck route, into Bangkok. Prostitution fuels the epidemic; Thai men typically have their first sexual experience with a prostitute, and 95% of men over the age of 21 have slept with a prostitute. Thailand has instituted vigorous educational campaigns to promote condom use (Handley, 1992). 🖋

Over the past decade, analysis of prostitution has been transformed from conceptualization as a "victimless crime" to an examination of its sociopolitical reality (Davis, 1993). In her edited volume, Davis collected articles examining female prostitution in 16 countries from Australia to Yugoslavia. The social problems that are addressed include the following: AIDS as a public health epidemic, child prostitution, victimization of prostitutes, self-help political movements, international tourism, and social policy changes.

In the following Social Choices section, we discuss the controversy over whether or not prostitution should be legalized or decriminalized.

Pornography and Erotica

The term *pornography*—derived from the words *porne* ("prostitute") and *graphein* ("to write")—originally meant "stories of prostitutes." Steinem (1983) observed that pornography "is about an imbalance of male-female power that allows and even requires sex to be used as a form of aggression" (p. 222). In contrast, Steinem emphasized that the term *erotica* comes from the Greek "eros," meaning "sexual desire or passionate love" and "contains the idea of love, positive choice, and the yearning for a particular person" (p. 222).

There is debate over what is pornography and what is erotica. One viewpoint suggests that the perception of what is "pornographic" or what is "erotic" is subjective. Whatever the label, this type of material takes various forms, including novels, magazines, X-rated movies or videos, and live nude or seminude shows. The percentage of men and women in one study who spent money on various erotic materials is presented in the following National Data chart.

Percentage of U.S. adults purchasing erotic materials in the past twelve months

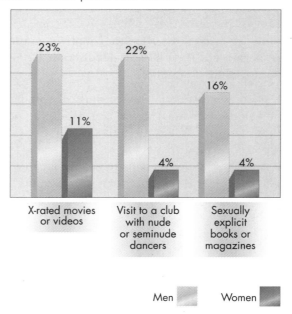

Source: Adapted from Michael et al., 1994.

Although some people enjoy viewing pornography or erotica, others view it as offensive and obscene. *Obscenity* has been legally defined by meeting three criteria. First, the dominant theme of the material must appeal to a prurient interest in sex. Such interest implies that the material is sexually arousing in a lewd way. Second, the material must be patently offensive to the community. In general, a community can dictate what its standards are regarding the sale, display, and distribution of sexual materials. Third, the sexual material must have no redeeming social value. If the material can be viewed as entertaining or educational (if it helps with the sexual communication of couples, for example), a case can be made for its social value. More recently, obscenity has been defined as "sexually explicit visual, printed, or recorded material or a live performance that is found beyond a reasonable doubt to be material that is not protected under the First Amendment" (Bullis, 1995, pp. 13-14). College students who have less favorable attitudes toward pornography are more likely to be women, those affiliated with religious organizations, those who report less sexual behavior, and those who have never seen such materials (Lottes, Weinberg, & Weller, 1993).

SHOULD WE LEGALIZE OR DECRIMINALIZE PROSTITUTION?

Sex researchers, enforcement officials, politicians, and prostitutes continue to debate the issue of whether prostitution should be legalized or decriminalized in the United States. Arguments for the legalization of prostitution include that it would permit the taxation of the billions of currently untaxed dollars spent on prostitution, help control and regulate the criminal activity associated with prostitution, help prevent teenage prostitution, and help protect prostitutes against abuse by pimps and clients (by enabling prostitutes to report abuse without fear of being arrested). Furthermore, if prostitution were legal, public health regulations could require prostitutes to use condoms and have regular gynecological exams to ensure they are not infected with a sexually transmitted disease, and to treat any diseases they may acquire. Just as restaurants must pass a health inspection and display a rating certificate, prostitutes could be required to obtain a similar certificate of health.

Prostitution has been legalized in some districts of Nevada and in other countries (including West Germany, where prostitutes work in large dormitories and are checked regularly by a physician for sexually transmitted diseases). Clients make their selection by observing the available women on closed-circuit television monitors. These bordellos are advertised as creating a safer and healthier environment for both prostitutes and clients (Rio, 1991).

Some opponents of legalized prostitution feel that it is wrong to condone any type of sexual behavior that occurs outside of a marital relationship. Other opponents feel that prostitution perpetuates the sexual objectification of women. Surprisingly, even some prostitutes oppose legalizing their trade. In Nevada, where there is legalized prostitution, some prostitutes resent the legal conditions of their

Prostitution flourishes in the tourism industry in many developing countries.

employment. Legal prostitutes cannot discriminate against certain customers by refusing to service them: they must service whoever comes in the door. They also feel that the law interferes with their private lives. For example, legal prostitutes can go to town only during certain hours and cannot appear in the company of a client in a restaurant. The stigmatization of the profession through fingerprinting and registration makes it difficult for prostitutes to leave the profession and enter another.

Source: Rio, L. M., (1991). Psychological and sociological research and the decriminalization or legalization of prostitution. *Archives of Sexual Behavior, 20,* 205–218.

The effects of pornography have been studied extensively. In 1967, the U.S. Commission on Obscenity and Pornography found no evidence that explicit sexual material played a significant role in causing individual or social harm. Rather, such material seemed to be sought for entertainment and educational purposes and seemed to enhance sexual communication. Further, the commission recommended that all federal, state, and local legislation prohibiting the sale, exhibition, and distribution of sexual material to adults be repealed. The U.S. Senate and President Nixon rejected the committee's recommendations.

To update the commission's findings, President Reagan established the Meese Commission on Pornography in 1985. This 11-person commission concluded that pornography is harmful to both individuals and society, and called for more stringent law enforcement regulation. Linz, Donnerstein and Penrod (1987) examined the same data as did the commission and concluded "we can find no consistent evidence for these specific conclusions" (p. 951). Critics of the Meese Commission argued that it was biased against pornography. Of the 11 members, six had previously gone on record prior to the conference as opposed to pornography because they believed it had harmful effects. For example, one of these was Dr. James Dodson, the president of *Focus on the Family,* a conservative publication.

In the summer of 1986, the Surgeon General's Workshop on Pornography and Public Health was convened in Arlington, Virginia, with 19 specialists in the area of pornography. Conclusions about the workshop's presentations and discussions (C. Everett Koop, 1987) follow:

1. Prolonged exposure to pornography results in people believing that less common sexual practices are more common than they are.
2. Pornography depicting sexual aggression as pleasurable to the victim increases the acceptance of the use of coercion in sexual relations.
3. Such acceptance may increase the chance of engaging in sexual aggression.
4. In laboratory studies measuring short-term effects, exposure to violent pornography increases punitive behavior toward women. In regard to this latter conclusion, Linz et al. (1987) noted, "What is conspicuously absent from the Surgeon General's summary is an endorsement of the view that exposure to sexually violent material leads to aggressive or assaultive behavior outside the confines of the laboratory" (p. 950). Fisher and Grenier (1994) failed to find consistent negative effects of violent pornography on men's fantasies, attitudes, and behaviors toward women.
5. Children who participate in the production of pornography experience adverse and enduring effects.

In regard to child pornography, also referred to as "kiddie porn" and "chicken porn," there is a strong cultural value that views the use of children in sex films as immoral and abusive. These children, it is believed, do not have the right of free choice and are manipulated or forced into participation. Congress has passed legislation that provides a maximum penalty of 15 years in prison and a fine of $15,000 for the trafficking of child pornography.

Beyond child pornography, legislative attempts are being made to restrict the flow of sexually explicit material. The Pornography Victims Compensation Act of 1992 permits suits by alleged victims of pornography against the manufacturers and distributors of erotic material. The bill has been submitted to Congress and reflects an attempt to "chill" the production and distribution of pornography. The primary motive behind the Communications Decency Act of 1996 (which made it a crime—punishable by a $250,000 fine or up to 2 years in prison—for anyone to make "indecent" material available to children on the Internet), was to protect children from pornography. The courts are still trying to figure out how to protect children without censoring the content available to adults (Mauro, 1997).

Although consistent proof of a causal link between sexually explicit material and "harm" is lacking, attacks against such material continue (Bullis, 1995). In fact, some sex researchers have found neutral to positive effects from exposure to sexually explicit material. In one study, over 7000 adults who had been exposed to sexually explicit materials in sex education seminars or workshops were asked about the effects of such exposure. Almost all of the research participants reported experiencing these media as not harmful, and most reported positive responses to the explicit visual material (Rosser et al., 1995). This conclusion is not surprising, however, given that all the participants had volunteered to view the films.

THINK ABOUT IT

What would the absolutist, relativist, and hedonist say about prostitution and pornography, and what would they recommend as public policy?

KEY TERMS

absolutism 316
asceticism 316
erotica 334
hedonism 317
obscenity 334
pornography 334

prostitution 333
relativism 316
sexual double
    standard 317
sexual guilt 330
sexual values 315

SUMMARY POINTS

Sexual expression occurs on the basis of our values and emotions. This chapter emphasized how values, emotions, and knowledge influence sexual behavior.

Sexual Knowledge in the United States

Several research studies assessing sexual knowledge among individuals in the United States show that Americans are surprisingly uninformed and misinformed about sexuality issues. In one study, almost 70% of the respondents said that they had experienced negative effects from inaccurate sexuality information.

Alternative Sexual Values

Sexual values are beliefs about what sexual behaviors are right (or appropriate) and what sexual behaviors are wrong (or inappropriate). Sexual values guide sexual choices, influence one's self-concept, and affect one's choice of a mate. A person's sexual behavior is not always consistent with his or her beliefs—he or she may say one thing but do another. A person's behavior reflects that person's values.

Three value perspectives that describe sexual values and choices include absolutism (based on religion), relativism (based on what seems right in a particular situation), and hedonism (based on what feels good). Research suggests that the sexual values of most Americans are based on relativism, then absolutism, and finally, hedonism. However, individuals' sexual values and choices often reflect a combination of absolutism, relativism, and hedonism.

Religious Roots and Sexual Values

Many contemporary sexual values (such as the beliefs that masturbation, adultery, and homosexuality are wrong) have their roots in Jewish and Christian religious influences that emphasize sexuality within marriage. In contrast to Western societies, which view sex as sinful, Eastern sexual views focus more on sexuality as a positive force. The Chinese encourage sexual activity as promoting spiritual growth. The Hindu view sex as one of the ways to become in tune with the infinite. Islamics emphasize sexual fulfillment in marriage.

Historical and Scientific Roots of Sexual Values

The Victorian era is known for its prudery and propriety about sexual behavior. While private sexual behavior included "just about everything," the public norms emphasized sex only within marriage, suppression of talking about sex, and the labeling of "good" and "bad" women in reference to their sexual behavior. Scientific ideologies shifted the view of sex from the sacred to the scientific, whereby sexuality was dissected and explained.

Other Sources of Sexual Knowledge and Values

Media, parents, and teachers continue to be important sources of sexual knowledge and values. Media exposure to sexuality can be faulted because it emphasizes romance and excitement but does not promote responsible sexual decision making. Parents typically promote various sexual values, but as sources of sexual information, they are often inadequate. Parental reluctance to talk to their children about sex is often based on their own insecurity about their level of sexual knowledge, as well as the fear that telling their children about sex will promote sexual activity. Teachers are variable sources of sex information and values because each state, rather than the federal government, is responsible for sex education in the public school system. Local school boards may also influence the content with some programs emphasizing "value-free" sex education focusing on the biology of sex and reproduction. Other programs emphasize absolutist sexual values and urge "abstinence only."

Emotions and Sexual Values

Love and guilt are two emotions that interact with sexual values. These emotions affect and are affected by sexual choices. Regarding love, some individuals—more often women—require love as a context for sexual involvement. Hedonists feel that love is irrelevant when choosing to engage in sexual behavior. Sexual guilt affects one's sexual choices. The more guilty an individual feels, the less likely that individual is to engage in sexual behavior.

Controversies Involving Sexual Values

There is debate in our society over whether there should be laws to ensure private rights or social morality. While there is agreement that clear laws with strong sanctions should exist for child sexual abuse, there is less agreement for the legal regulation of private adult consenting sexual behavior.

Our society is also ambivalent about whether prostitution and pornography should be allowed. Arguments for the legalization of prostitution in the United States include that it would permit the taxation of the billions of currently untaxed dollars spent on prostitution, help control and regulate the criminal activity associated with prostitution, help prevent teenage prostitution, and help protect prostitutes against abuse by pimps and clients by enabling prostitutes to report abuse without fear of being arrested. Legalizing prostitution could also allow public health agencies to impose and enforce health guidelines in the prostitution trade.

References

Al Bustan, M. A., El Tomi, N. F., Faiwalla, M. F., & Manav, V. (1995). Maternal sexuality during pregnancy and after childbirth in Muslim Kuwaiti women. *Archives of Sexual Behavior, 24,* 207-215.

Ansuini, C. G., Fiddler-Woite, J., & Woite, R. S. (1996). The source, accuracy, and impact of initial sexuality information on lifetime wellness. *Adolescence, 31*(122), 283-289.

Bepko, C., & Krestan, J. (1991). *Too good for her own good: Searching for self and intimacy in important relationships.* New York: HarperCollins.

Brigman, B., & Knox, D. (1992). University students' motivations to have intercourse. *College Student Journal, 26,* 406-408.

Bullis, R. K. (1995). From gag rules to blindfolds: The Pornography Victims Compensation Act. *Journal of Sex Education and Therapy, 21,* 11-21.

Bullough, V. L. (1987). A historical approach. In J. H. Greer & W. T. O'Donohue (Eds.), *Theories of human sexuality* (pp. 49-63). New York: Plenum Press.

Bullough, V. L. (1991). Introduction. In M. Hirschfeld (Ed.), *Transvestites: The erotic drive to cross-dress* (M. A. Lombardi-Nash, Trans.). Buffalo: Prometheus Books.

Buss, D. M., & Schmitt, D. P. (1993). Sexual strategies theory: An evolutionary perspective on human mating. *Psychological Review, 100,* 204-232.

Buysse, A. (1996). Adolescents, young adults and AIDS: A study of actual knowledge vs. perceived need for additional information. *Journal of Youth and Adolescence, 25*(2), 259-271.

Calhoun, A. (1960). *A social history of the American family.* New York: Barnes and Noble.

Cameron, N., & Rychlak, J. F. (1985). *Personality development and psychopathology* (2nd ed.). Boston: Houghton Mifflin.

Carswell, R. W. (1969). Historical analysis of religion and sex. *Journal of School Health, 39,* 673-684.

Contreras, R., Hendrick, S. S., & Hendrick, C. (1996). Perspectives on marital love and satisfaction in Mexican American and Anglo-American couples. *Journal of Counseling & Development, 74,* 408-415.

Coyle, K., Kirby, D., Parcel, G., Basen-Engquist, K., Banspach, S., Rugg, D., & Weil, M. (1996). Safer choices: A multicomponent school-based HIV/STD and pregnancy prevention program for adolescents. *Journal of School Health, 66,* 89-94.

Daley, D. (1996). Fact sheet on sexuality in education. *SIECUS Report, 24*(6), 22-25.

Davidson, K. J., Darling, C., & Norton, L. (1995). Religiosity and the sexuality of women: Sexual behavior and sexual satisfaction revisited. *The Journal of Sex Research, 32*(3), 235-243.

Davis, N. J. (1993). *Prostitution: An international handbooks on trends, problems, and policies.* Westport, CT: Greenwood Press.

Devlin, P. (1965). *The enforcement of morals.* Oxford: Oxford University Press.

Edwards, M. (1996, June/July). We have a responsibility to dialogue with the media. *SIECUS Report,* 5.

Ernst, M. L., & Loth, D. (1948). *American sexual behavior and the Kinsey Report.* New York: Greystone Press.

Fisher, W. A., & Grenier, G. (1994). Violent pornography, antiwoman thoughts, and antiwoman acts: In search of reliable effects. *The Journal of Sex Research, 31,* 23-38.

Geasler, M. J., Dannison, L. L., & Edlund, C. J. (1995). Sexuality education of young children: Parental concerns. *Family Relations, 44,* 184-188.

Gordon, S. (1986, October). What kids need to know. *Psychology Today,* October. 22-26.

Greenberg, B. S., & Busselle, R. (1996). What's old, what's new: Sexuality on the soaps. *SIECUS Report, 24*(5), 14-16.

Haeri, S. (1992). Temporary marriage and the state in Iran: An Islamic discourse on female sexuality. *Social Research, 59,* 210-223.

Handley, P. (February 13, 1992). Thailand moves to stanch the virus: Catch if catch can. *Far Eastern Economic Review, 29*-30.

Hatfield, E., & Rapson, R. L. (1996). *Love and sex: Cross-cultural perspectives.* Boston: Allyn & Bacon.

Heaton, T. B., & Jacobson, C. K. (1994). Race differences in changing family demographics in the 1980s. *Journal of Marriage and the Family, 15,* 290-308.

Hendrick, S. S., & Hendrick, C. (1992). *Romantic love.* Newbury Park, CA: Sage.

Hill, C. A., & Preston, L. K. (1996). Individual differences in the experience of sexual motivation: Theory and measurement of dispositional sexual motives. *The Journal of Sex Research, 33,* 27-45.

Hockenberry-Eaton, M., Richman, M. J., Dilorio, C., Rivero, T., & Maibach, E. (1996). Mother and adolescent knowledge of sexual development: The effects of gender, age, and sexual experience. *Adolescence, 31*(121), 35-47.

Hovell, M., Sipan, C., Blumberg, E., Atkins, C, Hofstetter, C. R., & Kreitner, S. (1994). Family influences on Latino and Anglo adolescents' sexual behavior. *Journal of Marriage and the Family, 56,* 973-986.

Jacobs, C. D., & Wolf, E. M. (1995). School sexuality education and adolescent risk-taking behavior. *Journal of School Health, 65,* 91-95.

Johnson, W. S. (1979). *Living in sin: The Victorian sexual revolution.* Chicago: Nelson-Hall.

Kalichman, S. C., Heckman, T., & Kelly, J. A. (1996). Sensation seeking as an explanation for the association between substance use and HIV-related risky sexual behavior. *Archives of Sexual Behavior, 25*(2), 141-154.

Kirby, D. (1992). School-based programs to reduce sexual risk-taking behaviors. *Journal of School Health, 62,* 280-287.

Koo, H. P., Duntemann, G. H., George, C., Green, Y., & Vincent, M. (1994). Reducing adolescent pregnancy through school- and community-based intervention: Denmark, South Carolina revisited. *Family Planning Perspectives, 26,* 206-217.

Koop, C. E. (1987). Report of the Surgeon General's Workshop on Pornography and Public Health. *American Psychologist, 42,* 944-945.

Leland, M. L., & Barth, R. P. (1992). Gender differences in knowledge, intentions, and behaviors concerning pregnancy and sexually transmitted disease prevention among adolescents. *Journal of Adolescent Health, 13,* 589-599.

Linz, D., Donnerstein, E., & Penrod, S. (1987). The findings and recommendations of the Attorney General's Commission on Pornography: Do the psychological 'facts' fit the political fury? *American Psychologist, 42,* 946-953.

LoPiccolo, J. (1983). The prevention of sexual problems in men. In G. Albee, S. Gordon, & H. Leitenberg (Eds.), *Promoting sexual responsibility and preventing sexual problems* (pp. 39-65). Hanover, NH: University Press of New England.

Lottes, I., Weinberg, M., & Weller, I. (1993). Reactions to pornography on a college campus: For or against? *Sex Roles, 29,* 69-89.

MacNamara, D., & Sagarin, E. (1977). *Sex, crime, and the law.* New York: Free Press.

Malinova, H. (1995). The recent rise in prostitution in the Czech Republic. *Journal of Community Health, 20,* 213-218.

Mauro, T. (1997, March 18). Taming the Internet. *USA Today,* p. 1A.

Michael, R. T., Gagnon, J. H., Laumann, E. O., & Kolata, G. (1994). *Sex in America: A definitive survey.* Boston: Little, Brown.

Mill, J. A. (1859). *On liberty.* New York: Penguin.

Montgomery, M. J., & Sorell, G. T. (1997). Differences in love attitudes across family life stages. *Family Relations, 46,* 55-61.

Muehlenhard, C. L., & Cook, S. W. (1988). Men's self-reports of unwanted sexual activity. *Journal of Sex Research, 24,* pp. 58-72.

Murry, V. M. (1994). Early versus late coital initiation: A study of African American adolescent females. *Family Relations, 48,* 342-348.

National Task Force on Prostitution. (1997). [On-line]: http://www.creative.net/~penet/stats.html

Nelson, J. B. (1983). Religious dimensions of sexual health. In G. W. Albee, S. Gordon, & H. Leitenberg (Eds.), *Promoting sexual responsibility and preventing sexual problems* (pp. 121-132). Hanover, NH: University Press of New England.

Overall, C. (1992). What's wrong with prostitution? Evaluating sex work. *Signs: Journal of Women in Culture and Society, 17,* 705-724.

Petersen, L. R., & Donnenwerth, G. V. (1997). Secularization and the influence of religion on beliefs about premarital sex. *Social Forces, 75*(3), 1071-1089.

Pope, V. (1997, April 7). Trafficking in women. *U.S. News and World Report,* p. 38.

Raths, L., Merrill, H., & Simon, S. (1996). *Values and teaching.* Columbus, OH: Charles E. Merrill.

Rosser, B. R. S., Dwyer, M., Coleman, E., Miner, M., Metz, M., Robinson, B. E., & Bockting, W. O. (1995). Using sexually explicit material in adult sex education: An eighteen-year comparative analysis. *Journal of Sex Education and Therapy, 21,* 117-128.

Sachs, A. (1990, October 1). Handing out scarlet letters. *Time,* 98.

Simons, R. L., & Whitbeck, L. B. (1991). Sexual abuse as a precursor to prostitution and victimization among adolescent and adult homeless women. *Journal of Family Issues, 12,* 361-379.

Special Committee on Human Sexuality. (1991). *Part I: Keeping body and soul together: Sexuality, spirituality, and social justice.* Louisville, KY: General Assembly, Presbyterian Church (USA).

Sprecher, S., & Regan, P. C. (1996). College virgins: How men and women perceive their sexual status. *The Journal of Sex Research, 33,* 3-15.

Steinem, G. (1983). *Outrageous acts and everyday rebellions.* New York: Holt, Rinehart, and Winston.

Sternberg, R. J. (1986). A triangular theory of love. *Psychological Review, 93,* 119-135.

Strasburger, V. C. (1995). *Adolescents and the media.* Thousand Oaks, CA: Sage.

Tannahill, R. (1982). *Sex in history.* New York: Stein and Day.

Task force enters sex education debate. *(1996, July 21). CQ Researcher,* 534-535.

Tavris, C. (1992). *The mismeasure of woman.* New York: Simon & Schuster.

Templeman, T. L., & Stinnett, R. D. (1991). Patterns of sexual arousal and history in a "normal" sample of young men. *Archives of Sexual Behavior, 20,* 137-150.

Thomas, A., & Sillen, S. (1972). *Racism and psychiatry.* New York: Brunner/Mazel.

Udry, J. R., Kovenock, J., Morris, N. M., & Van den Berg, B. J. (1995). Childhood precursors of age at first intercourse for females. *Archives of Sexual Behavior, 24,* 329-337.

United Nations Population Fund. 1997 State of World Population Report. (1997, May/June). The right to choose: Reproductive rights and health. *POPLINE,* 4-5.

Weinberg, M. S., Lottes, I. L., & Shaver, F. M. (1995). Swedish or American heterosexual college youth: Who is more permissive? *Archives of Sexual Behavior, 24*(4), 409-437.

Whitbeck, L. B., Simons, R. L., & Kao, M. (1994). The effects of divorced mothers' dating behaviors and sexual attitudes on the sexual attitudes and behaviors of their adolescent children. *Journal of Marriage and the Family,* 615-621.

Zatz, N. D. (1997). Sex work/sex act: Law, labor, and desire in constructions of prostitution. *Signs, 22,* 277-308.

INDIVIDUAL AND INTERPERSONAL SEXUAL BEHAVIORS

Erotophilia and Erotophobia

Sexual Celibacy

Autoerotic Behavior

Sexual Fantasy

Interpersonal Sexual Behaviors

*T*he price is exorbitant, the pleasure is transitory, and the position is ridiculous.

Lord Chesterfield (on sex)

Intimate relationships shape sexuality.

Philip Blumstein
Pepper Schwartz
Sociologists

In one of his stand-up comedy routines, Robin Williams mused, "In the '90s, it's sex with you and you." His statement reflects the fear of STD and HIV infection that surrounds sexual choices and emphasizes the safety of sex with oneself ("you and you"). Individual sexual decisions include whether to be celibate, masturbate, and fantasize about sex. Interpersonal sexual choices include whether to engage in a wide range of behaviors, including intercourse, clitoral and penile stimulation, and touching. In this chapter, we explore individual and interpersonal sexual behaviors and choices.

EROTOPHILIA AND EROTOPHOBIA

Although much of a person's sexual energy is expressed in interpersonal relationships, the longest sexual relationship an individual has is with himself or herself. How an individual experiences sexuality is influenced by individual variables, such as self-concept and body image. Those with a positive self-concept and body image are more likely to enjoy the sexual aspect of their lives. Those with a negative self-concept and body image are more likely to experience some anxiety and discomfort about the sexual aspect of their lives.

In the Sexual Behavior Sequence Model, Fisher (1983) hypothesized that the way we evaluate a sexual topic or behavior, and our expectations related to it, influence our preparations for engaging in a behavior and our performing it. One of these intervening variables is the erotophilic-erotophobic continuum.

The propensity to have positive emotional responses to sexuality is referred to as *erotophilia*. Individuals who are erotophilic tend to enjoy and seek out sexual experiences. The propensity to have negative emotional responses to sexuality is known as *erotophobia*. Individuals who are erotophobic tend to

feel uncomfortable with sexuality and avoid sexual experiences. Erotophobic individuals participate in less masturbation and interpersonal sexual behavior and report briefer, less explicit sexual fantasies. Compared to erotophilic individuals, erotophobics have more difficulty learning, talking, or teaching about sexuality and may be less likely to acquire or use contraception (Fisher, 1988).

This chapter's Self-Assessment provides a way for you to assess where your beliefs fall on the erotophilic/erotophobic continuum.

Fisher (1988), who developed the Revised Sexual Opinion Survey, found men to be more erotophilic than women. Other researchers have confirmed this finding. For example, Purnine, Carey, and Jorgensen (1994) found that men are significantly more likely than women to agree strongly with the following statements:

- I would prefer to have sex every day.
- I would enjoy having sex outdoors.
- Swimming in the nude with my partner would be a turn-on.

Erotophobia is associated with high sexual guilt and having parents who were strict in their attitudes toward sex (Fisher, Byrne, White, & Kelly, 1988). Although erotophobic individuals are less likely than erotophilic individuals to be sexually active, those who do engage in sexual relations have a higher risk of pregnancy and HIV/STD transmission because they feel uncomfortable discussing or using contraception or condoms.

SEXUAL CELIBACY

Early sexual dogma linked marriage with having intercourse and, conversely, being unmarried with not having intercourse. The term used for those who chose to remain single—and by implication, to not

342   Chapter 13

REVISED SEXUAL OPINION SURVEY

Please respond to each item as honestly as you can. There are no right or wrong answers.

Place an X in the space on the scale that describes your feelings about each statement.

1. I think it would be very entertaining to look at erotica (sexually explicit books, movies, etc.).
   I strongly agree __:__:__:__:__:__:__ I strongly disagree

2. Erotica (sexually explicit books, movies, etc.) is obviously filthy and people should not try to describe it as anything else.
   I strongly agree __:__:__:__:__:__:__ I strongly disagree

3. Swimming in the nude with a member of the opposite sex would be an exciting experience.
   I strongly agree __:__:__:__:__:__:__ I strongly disagree

4. Masturbation can be an exciting experience.
   I strongly agree __:__:__:__:__:__:__ I strongly disagree

5. If I found out that a close friend of mine was a homosexual it would annoy me.
   I strongly agree __:__:__:__:__:__:__ I strongly disagree

6. If people thought I was interested in oral sex, I would be embarrassed.
   I strongly agree __:__:__:__:__:__:__ I strongly disagree

7. Engaging in group sex is an entertaining idea.
   I strongly agree __:__:__:__:__:__:__ I strongly disagree

8. I personally find that thinking about engaging in sexual intercourse is arousing.
   I strongly agree __:__:__:__:__:__:__ I strongly disagree

9. Seeing an erotic (sexually explicit) movie would be sexually arousing to me.
   I strongly agree __:__:__:__:__:__:__ I strongly disagree

10. Thoughts that I may have homosexual tendencies would not worry me at all.
    I strongly agree __:__:__:__:__:__:__ I strongly disagree

11. The idea of my being physically attracted to members of the same sex is not depressing.
    I strongly agree __:__:__:__:__:__:__ I strongly disagree

12. Almost all erotic (sexually explicit) material is nauseating.
    I strongly agree __:__:__:__:__:__:__ I strongly disagree

13. It would be emotionally upsetting to me to see someone exposing himself publicly.
    I strongly agree __:__:__:__:__:__:__ I strongly disagree

14. Watching a stripper of the opposite sex would not be very exciting.
    I strongly agree __:__:__:__:__:__:__ I strongly disagree

15. I would not enjoy seeing an erotic (sexually explicit) movie.
    I strongly agree __:__:__:__:__:__:__ I strongly disagree

16. When I think about seeing pictures showing someone of the same sex as myself masturbating it nauseates me.
    I strongly agree __:__:__:__:__:__:__ I strongly disagree

17. The thought of engaging in unusual sex practices is highly arousing.
    I strongly agree __:__:__:__:__:__:__ I strongly disagree

18. Manipulating my genitals would probably be an arousing experience.
    I strongly agree __:__:__:__:__:__:__ I strongly disagree

19. I do not enjoy daydreaming about sexual matters.
    I strongly agree __:__:__:__:__:__:__ I strongly disagree

20. I am not curious about explicit erotica (sexually explicit, books, movies, etc.).
    I strongly agree __:__:__:__:__:__:__ I strongly disagree

Continued on following page.

21. The thought of having long-term sexual relations with more than one sex partner is not disgusting to me.

I strongly
agree   __:__:__:__:__:__:__   disagree   I strongly

Scoring

1. Score responses from 1 = I strongly agree to 7 = I strongly disagree.
2. Add scores from Items 2, 5, 6, 12, 13, 14, 15, 16, 19, and 20.
3. Subtract from this total the sum of Items 1, 3, 4, 7, 8, 9, 10, 11, 17, 18, and 21.
4. Add 67 to this quantity.

Interpreting Your Score: The Sexual Opinion Survey (SOS) measures erotophobia/erotophilia, a personality dimension reflecting negative or positive emotional reaction to sexual cues. The possible scores range from 0 (most erotophobic) to 126 (most erotophilic). You may want to compare your score with those of a group of Canadian undergraduate students who completed this revised version of the SOS in a human sexuality course. The mean score of the men was 77.81 ($n = 107$, $SD = 15.16$). For women, the mean score was 67.11 ($n = 216$, $SD = 18.59$). The difference between the men and the women was statistically significant ($t = 0.05$) (Fisher, 1988).

have intercourse—was "celibate." The condition of being unmarried was known as *celibacy*. Because most celibates (singles) today do choose to have intercourse, we use the term *sexual celibacy* to refer to the condition of abstaining from sexual intercourse. Technically, sexual celibacy has two levels. One level involves no sexual behavior with another person but permits the option of masturbation. Another level of celibacy is engaging in no sexual behavior at all, including masturbation. Sexual celibacy may be characterized as voluntary or involuntary.

Voluntary Sexual Celibacy

A person might choose to be sexually celibate for a number of reasons. Some individuals have little to no interest in sex and, therefore, have no desire to engage in sexual activity. Although some of these individuals are nevertheless sexually active, others choose to be celibate.

Some individuals choose to be celibate for religious reasons. Members of Heaven's Gate, a California-based cult group whose 39 members planned and enacted a mass suicide in 1997, were expected to be celibate. The official position of the Catholic Church maintains that priests, nuns, and monks are expected to be celibate (unmarried) so they may have the maximum freedom and energy for the work of the church. Other religious people choose celibacy because they, too, want to be available to do God's will and work (which may not involve having an official position in the church).

Sexual celibacy may become a lifestyle through which a person witnesses the priority of God in his or her life. Still others may regard sexual celibacy as a spiritually pure state and may seek to avoid sexual activity as a means to achieve that goal.

NATIONAL DATA

Results of a national sample of men and women who reported that they "never" think about sex or do so "less than once a month"

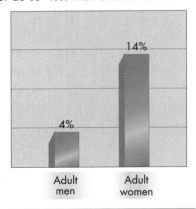

Source: Michael, Gagnon, Laumann, & Kolata, 1994, p. 156.

Other reasons for choosing to be sexually celibate include previous negative sexual experiences, alternative focus, depression, relationship enhancement, therapy for sexual dysfunctions, therapy for sex addiction, and the desire to avoid pregnancy or the transmission of sexually transmissible diseases.

Regarding previous negative sexual experiences, some women who never achieve orgasm and some men who ejaculate too soon or are incapable of creating and maintaining an erection feel inadequate during sexual encounters. As a result, they avoid relationships with others that involve sexual expectations. Their negative feelings about partner sex may or may not generalize to individual sex. Prior sexual abuse (rape, molestation) may also cause some individuals to choose to refrain from sexual activity.

Involvement in work or other activity is another reason some people elect to be sexually celibate, at least temporarily. They may derive major satisfaction from their work and feel too exhausted or uninterested in sex.

Others choose to be sexually celibate because they are too depressed to choose otherwise. They feel no sexual desire and have no interest whatsoever in sexual or erotic activity or involvement.

Still others choose sexual celibacy because they want to explore relationships without the sexual dimension. They feel that avoiding sex permits the relationship to develop without becoming focused on sex. Based on the data from 1275 of her respondents, Rubin (1991) noted:

> After years of experience with relationships that never grew beyond the sexual connection, many people now wonder whether it's better to wait until they know each other better, until they have established some basis besides sex for moving ahead. "When you jump into bed like that, I think things get stuck there," explained 35-year-old Brad, a New Jersey salesman. (p. 154)

Individuals may also choose to follow the recommendations of a sex therapist who suggests a period of no partner sex as part of the treatment program for erectile dysfunction. As we discussed in Chapter 10, "Sexual Dysfunctions and Sex Therapy," the inability to create and maintain an erection may be intensified by performance anxiety, which is reduced by the directive to refrain from genital sex. Once partners choose to be sexually celibate, the man is no longer anxious about getting an erection, and the capability of an erection returns. In one study of 61 elderly (average age, 71) men in a nursing home, those without sexual partners reported less emotional stress over sexual issues than those with partners "possibly because of lesser expectations" (Mulligan & Palguta, 1991, p. 203).

One aspect of the treatment program for "sex addiction" recommended by Patrick Carnes (1983) is sexual abstinence on the premise that one must totally break his or her dependency on sex before getting control of the addiction. Like the alcoholic who must abstain from using alcohol to maintain sobriety, the "sex addict" must become completely "sex sober" for a period of at least 6 months.

Some individuals elect to be abstinent so they do not create a pregnancy. Those favoring the "natural" method of contraception abstain from having intercourse during those times when they feel they (or their partner) are most likely to get pregnant. The term for this type of celibacy is "periodic abstinence."

Finally, some men are celibate so as to enhance the chance of impregnating their partners. A team of researchers (Sauer, Zeffer, Buster, & Sokol, 1988) compared the ejaculates of ten fertile donors who were abstinent for increasingly longer periods of time. The longer the donors went between ejaculations, the greater the volume and concentration of the sperm. (Sperm motility was not affected.)

Choosing to be sexually celibate requires a positive view about the decision. Zilbergeld (1978) cautioned:

> Another problem (with celibacy) is the meaning that you and those close to you put on your behavior. You may find yourself wondering if there is something wrong with you, especially when you realize that staying away from sex isn't terribly difficult. And, your friends may wonder along with you. Sex has been so oversold that many people can't even conceive of not having it regularly. So you'll probably have to put up with some questions and astonishment. (p. 154)

Involuntary Sexual Celibacy

Although some people may choose to be sexually celibate, others may have little choice. The lack of an available partner is a major reason for involuntary sexual celibacy. This situation is common to many of us at different times in our lives. We may be between relationships, separated, divorced, or widowed. Sexual celibacy may also be induced by separation of partners due to military service, work-related travel, or prison. Hospital, nursing, and retirement home residents are also vulnerable to involuntary sexual celibacy (see the following Social Choices section).

ARE INSTITUTIONS TOO RESTRICTIVE OF SEXUAL EXPRESSION?

Hospitals are notorious for encouraging or enforcing sexual celibacy. It is assumed that if you are in the hospital, you should have no sexual experience of any kind. There is no discussion of sexual activity, no privacy for masturbation (the nurse or physician can walk in at any time), and no accommodations for engaging in sexual relations with one's partner.

Nursing homes also institutionalize sexual celibacy. Added to the hospital atmosphere of a nursing home is the belief that the elderly are sexless. Some nursing homes do not even allow spouses to occupy the same room. Over 1.4 million patients (5% of the elderly population) live in about 15,000 nursing homes in the United States (*Statistical Abstract of the United States: 1997,* Table 199). Sexual expression among nursing home residents is restricted as a result of chronic illness, the lack of willing partners, a loss of interest, the negative attitudes of physicians and staff toward sexual expression among the elderly, feelings of unattractiveness, and an insufficient understanding of sexuality. Some of these factors are related to the physiological effect of aging on sexual interest and behavior; other factors are under the

control of physicians and staff. Barriers to sexual activity among nursing home residents may be removed by educating staff about sexuality in the elderly, providing privacy ("do not disturb" signs, closed doors, private rooms designated for intimacy), allowing conjugal visits or home visits, changing medications that may impair sexual function, and providing information and counseling about sexuality to interested residents (Richardson & Lazur, 1995).

Retirement homes, in which the residents are physically healthy, may also cause involuntary celibacy. In one study, 202 residents between the ages of 80 and 102 responded to a 117-item questionnaire about their sexual experiences in retirement homes. Thirty percent reported that living in the home definitely prevented them from engaging in sexual activity at least some of the time (Bretschneider & McCoy, 1988).

Sources: Bretschneider, J. G., & McCoy, N. L. (1988). Sexual interest and behavior in healthy 80- to 102-year-olds. *Archives of Sexual Behavior, 17,* 109–129.

Richardson, J. P., & Lazur, A. (1995). Sexuality in the nursing home patient. *American Family Physician, 51,* 121–124.

Statistical Abstract of the United States: 1997 (117th ed.). Washington, DC: U.S. Bureau of the Census.

AUTOEROTIC BEHAVIOR

More commonly called *masturbation, autoerotic behavior* is "a natural, common, and nonharmful means of sexual self-pleasuring that is engaged in by individuals of all ages, sexual orientations, and levels of functioning" (SIECUS Position Statements, 1996). Masturbation has been referred to as "having sex with the one you love most" and "having sex with the only person whose sexual history you can trust completely." Other terms for masturbation include self-pleasuring, solo sex, and sex without a partner. Several older, more pejorative terms for masturbation are self-pollution, self-abuse, solitary vice, sin against nature, voluntary pollution, and onanism. The negative connotations associated with these terms are a result of various myths (which we may no longer

choose to accept) about masturbation. These myths originated in religion, medicine, and traditional psychotherapy. Parents have also traditionally transmitted a negative view of masturbation to their children.

Table 13.1 lists some of the myths and truths about masturbation.

Historical Origins of Negative Attitudes Toward Masturbation

During the World AIDS Day Conference at the United Nations in December 1994, former Surgeon General Joycelyn Elders spoke to an audience of 200 members about the spread of STDs. After her presentation, a psychologist in the audience asked if she would consider promoting masturbation to discourage school-age children from engaging in riskier forms of sexual

TABLE 13.1 Myths and Truths About Masturbation

Myths	Truths
Masturbation causes insanity, headaches, epilepsy, acne, blindness, nosebleeds, "masturbator's heart," tenderness of the breasts, warts, nymphomania, undesirable odor, hair on the palms.	There is no evidence that masturbation impairs physical or mental health.
Masturbation is an abnormal, unnatural behavior.	Masturbation is a normal function.
Masturbation is immature.	Masturbation is an effective way to experience sexual pleasure.
Masturbation is practiced mostly by simple-minded people.	Many people masturbate throughout their lives. Many sexually active people with available partners masturbate for additional gratification.
Masturbation is a substitute for intercourse.	Intercourse and masturbation can be viewed as complementary sexual experiences, not necessarily as mutually exclusive.
Masturbation is antisocial.	Masturbation may be an effective way to learn about your own sexual responses so you can communicate them to a partner.

activity. Elders replied that masturbation "is something that is a part of human sexuality and . . . that perhaps should be taught" ("The Politics of Masturbation," 1994, p. 1714). Partly due to the public and political taboo on discussing, let alone advocating masturbation, President Clinton asked for and received Elders's resignation. Why did Elders's comments about masturbation send shock waves through the U.S. conservative population? Throughout American history, masturbation has been viewed as being both the cause and result of sin and sickness. Religion, medicine, traditional psychotherapy, and parents have contributed to the negative views toward masturbation.

RELIGION AND MASTURBATION Although the Jewish and Catholic religions have been most severe in their stand against masturbation, Protestants have also been negative about this issue. Ancient Jews considered masturbation to be a sin. Catholics also regarded masturbation as a mortal sin that, if not given up, would result in eternal damnation. Protestants felt that neither death nor eternal hellfire was an appropriate consequence for masturbation, but that hell on earth was. The basis for these indict-

ments was the belief that masturbation is nonprocreative sex, and any sexual act that cannot produce offspring is morally wrong. The antidote for this evil behavior was abstinence and prayer (Money, Prakasam, & Joshi, 1991).

However, some Protestant denominations have adopted the view that masturbation may be good or bad, depending upon one's reason for deciding to masturbate. For example, a curriculum developed for Presbyterian Youth (Bartosch et al., 1989) asserted that masturbation could be bad if it was used as a way to avoid relationships with other people or was done out of fear of becoming involved with someone else. Masturbation could be a good choice if it was practiced by those who were not married or those whose spouses were not available for sexual relations due to absence, disability, or illness. This curriculum states that masturbation is a normal part of growing up.

In ancient Chinese religious thought, life was viewed as a balance between the active and passive forces of yin and yang. Sex represented this harmonious balance; the essence of sexual yang was the male's semen and the essence of sexual yin was the woman's vaginal fluids. Female masturbation was virtually ignored, as vaginal fluids (yin) were thought to be inexhaustible. However, semen (yang) was viewed as precious, and masturbation was regarded as a waste of vital yang essence (Bullough, 1976; Tannahill, 1982).

MEDICINE AND MASTURBATION The *semen-conservation doctrine* (from early Ayurvedic teachings in India) held that general good health in both sexes depended on conserving the life-giving power of "vital fluids" (Money et al., 1991, p. 10). These fluids, which include both semen and vaginal fluids, were believed to be important for intelligence and memory and derived from good nutrition. Wastage or depletion of semen (regarded as more important) was discouraged because it might result in loss of resistance to all illnesses and in a decrease in well-being. Agniversa and Susruta are believed to be two of the earliest teachers in India (1500 B.C.) who spoke of the semen-conservation doctrine (Money et al., 1991).

The Western medical community helped reinforce the negative associations of masturbation by bringing "scientific validity" to bear on its description of the hazards of masturbation. In 1758, Samuel Tissot, a Swiss physician, published a book on the diseases produced by "Onanism," in which he implied that the loss of too much semen, whether by intercourse or masturbation, was injurious to the body and would cause debility, disease, and death (Tissot, 1758/1766). What Tissot did not recognize, as it had not yet been discovered at that time, was that it is the loss of testosterone, not the loss of semen, that causes the devirilizing effects of castration.

Adding to the medical bias against masturbation was John Harvey Kellogg, M.D., who believed, as did the Reverend Sylvester Graham, that masturbation resulted in the loss of fluids that were vital to the body. In 1834, Graham wrote that an ounce of semen was equal to the loss of several ounces of blood. Graham believed that every time a man ejaculated, he ran the risk of contracting a disease of the nervous system. Among his solutions were graham crackers, which would help prevent the development of carnal lust that resulted from eating carnivorous flesh (Graham, 1848). Kellogg suggested his own cure—corn flakes. Kellogg's Corn Flakes were originally developed as a food to extinguish sexual desire and curb masturbation desires.

By the mid-19th century, Tissot's theories had made their way into medical textbooks, journals, and books for parents. With no data, physicians added to the list of disorders resulting from masturbation: pimples, hair loss, weak eyes, and suicidal tendencies. However, as belief in these myths declined toward the end of the 19th century, they were "quickly replaced by a new set of beliefs that did little to ease the anxiety that most people had about masturbation. The conviction grew that masturbation was a common cause of neurotic disorders and marital sexual problems, a view shared by Freud" (Zilbergeld, 1978, p. 136).

Kinsey and his colleagues contributed the greatest challenge to the existing myths about masturbation through their disclosure that 92% of the men in their sample reported having masturbated (Kinsey, Pomeroy, & Martin, 1948). Yet the researchers found no evidence of the dire consequences that had been earlier predicted for those who masturbate.

In spite of the documentation that masturbation was not physically, emotionally, or socially debilitating, negative attitudes toward masturbation continued. One explanation for this is that physicians continued to look upon masturbation negatively and continued to convey this to their patients. Dr. David Reuben, in his best-seller *Everything You Ever Wanted to Know About Sex,* noted that masturbation was OK, but that it was less preferable to intercourse and that the practice was mostly enjoyed by "children, the aged, the infirm, and the incarcerated" (Zilbergeld, 1978, p. 138).

TRADITIONAL PSYCHOTHERAPY AND MASTURBATION In the early 20th century, psychotherapy joined medicine and religion to convince people of the negative effects of masturbation. Psychotherapists, led by Freud, suggested that masturbation was an infantile form of sexual gratification. People who masturbated "to excess" could fixate on themselves as a sexual object and would not be able to relate to others in a sexually mature way. The message was clear: If you want to be a good sexual partner in marriage, don't masturbate; if you do masturbate, don't do it too often.

The result of religious, medical, and therapeutic professions denigrating masturbation was devastating. Those who masturbated felt the shame and guilt they were supposed to feel. The burden of these feelings was particularly heavy because there was no one with whom to share the guilt. In the case of a premarital pregnancy, responsibility could be shared. But with masturbation, the "crime" had been committed alone.

PARENTS AND MASTURBATION   While parents can opt to counter the negative religious, medical, and psychotherapeutic attitudes toward masturbation, they have rarely done so. Rather, the tendency for parents to be silent on the subject communicates agreement that masturbation is shameful. Rubin (1991) observed:

> Children who may witness all kinds of emotional expression and sexual innuendo between their parents never see or hear anything that even suggests that this thing they do is something anyone else knows about, let alone engages in. In such a setting, parents don't have to frown upon the masturbatory activities of the child; they have only to avoid noticing and labeling it for it to become suspect. By singling it out with silence, they send a message that the child interprets to mean that this nameless activity is something we don't talk about, one that calls for guilt and concealment. (p. 22)

Understandably, it may be difficult for parents to choose to be open about the topic of masturbation with their children. Even though they may regard masturbation in positive terms, they may have had no model to emulate when discussing sexual issues, including masturbation. Hence, the choice of being open with one's children about masturbation or any sexual issue may necessitate seeking a context where one might learn to talk with one's children about sex. Such contexts include therapy or sex education courses for parents. Additional options are available in the form of books, pamphlets, and programs sponsored by local parent-teacher associations, churches, or family planning agencies.

Benefits of Masturbation

Due to traditional negative attitudes toward masturbation, shame, guilt, and anxiety continue to be common feelings associated with masturbation in our society. But new attitudes are emerging. Although the attitudes of some religious leaders are still negative, most physicians and therapists are clearly positive about masturbation. Masturbation is not only

approved but may be recommended. Specific benefits of masturbation include the following:

1. *Self-knowledge.* Masturbation can provide immediate feedback about what one enjoys. Self-knowledge about what turns one on may benefit one's relationship in that one may teach one's partner how to provide pleasure. Without such self-knowledge, one may feel incapable of providing pleasure to one's self or teaching a lover to do so.

2. *Increased body comfort.* Barbach (1976) emphasized that masturbation increases an individual's comfort with her or his own body. Such comfort is associated with less anxiety in interpersonal sexual contexts, which may be related to overall satisfaction. Not all individuals (particularly women) are comfortable when they begin masturbating, but most usually develop such comfort with continued trials. Masturbation may also increase an individual's physical, as well as psychological, body comfort. Students in the authors' classes report that they masturbate to relieve tension, to get to sleep, and to help abate menstrual cramps.

3. *Orgasm more likely for women.* Masturbating to orgasm before marriage seems to have a positive effect on having an orgasm during intercourse after marriage. Forty-four percent of the women in Kinsey, Pomeroy, Martin, and Gebhard's (1953) study who had not had an orgasm before marriage failed to have a climax during their first year of marriage. But of those who had experienced orgasm before marriage, only 13% had not had an orgasm during intercourse in their first year of marriage.

    Aware of the link between masturbation and orgasm, therapists often encourage female clients who want to experience an orgasm to learn how to masturbate. LoPiccolo and Lobitz (1972) have developed a treatment program that is designed to help women experience orgasm through masturbation. (See Chapter 10 for a description of this treatment program.)

4. *Pressure taken off partner.* Inevitably, partners in a relationship will vary in their desire for having sex. During such time, the partner wanting more sex may feel frustrated, and the partner wanting less sex may feel guilty for not wanting to be accommodating. Masturbation might provide an alternative of sexual satisfaction for the partner

wanting more sex while taking the pressure off the other partner to provide a sexual experience. The result may be less interpersonal stress for both people.

5. *No partner necessary.* In one study (Darling, Davidson, & Cox, 1991) the most frequently reported reason women gave for masturbating was that a partner was not available.

Choosing to masturbate provides a way to enjoy a sexual experience or an orgasm when no partner may be available. Even if a partner is available, the individual may choose to have a quick release that can be accomplished with no need to interact. Since masturbation does not involve a partner, the risk of contracting HIV and other STDs is also eliminated. As an alternative to heterosexual involvement, masturbation also eliminates the risk of unintended pregnancy.

6. *Unique experience.* Masturbation is a unique sexual experience, different from petting, intercourse, mutual stimulation of the genitals, and other sexual behaviors. As we will note later, many people who have sexual experiences on a regular basis with their respective partners masturbate because they regard masturbation as a unique experience that partner sex cannot duplicate.

7. *Extradyadic entanglements avoided.* When away from their usual partner, some individuals choose to masturbate as a means of relieving sexual tension rather than risk emotional involvement with or contracting STDs from another person. Otherwise, the person may feel driven to obtain sexual release that might result in a regrettable interpersonal entanglement or a breech of trust in the primary relationship.

8. *Improved self-image.* Masturbation may also help a woman improve her body image and her perception of herself as a woman. Betty Dodson in her book, *Sex for One: The Joy of Self Love* (1987), emphasized that masturbation is a meditation of self-love. She suggested that people are often confronted with bad body images, shame about body functions, and confusion about sex and pleasure. In contrast, masturbation is—and should be—an intense love affair with one's self.

9. *Useful in treatment of sexual offenders.* Behavior therapy treatments of sex offenders use masturbation in reconditioning techniques. By shifting the timing and sequence of erotic fantasies and images during masturbation, deviant arousal is weakened, and arousal to appropriate stimuli is strengthened (Maletzky, 1991).

In spite of the benefits of masturbation, there are disadvantages. We have already made reference to the enormous guilt sometimes associated with masturbation. Related to such guilt is the feeling that some people have of being abnormal because they fear they masturbate too frequently. In addition, masturbation to an inappropriate stimulus (such as children) may strengthen erotic feelings toward that stimulus. Some sexual abusers "have cultivated aberrant sexual fantasies and deviant masturbatory behaviors for years" (Maletzky, 1991, p. 40). Finally, some partners interpret their lover's masturbation as evidence that they are inadequate and undesirable.

PERSONAL CHOICES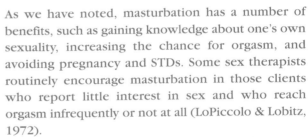

Should You Masturbate?

As we have noted, masturbation has a number of benefits, such as gaining knowledge about one's own sexuality, increasing the chance for orgasm, and avoiding pregnancy and STDs. Some sex therapists routinely encourage masturbation in those clients who report little interest in sex and who reach orgasm infrequently or not at all (LoPiccolo & Lobitz, 1972).

However, not all therapists agree with this viewpoint. Psychiatrist Thomas Szasz (1980) noted that some clients who feel very uncomfortable about masturbating are, nevertheless, browbeaten into masturbating. In the hope of therapeutic success, therapists induce them into something they do not want to do. Dr. Szasz feels that therapists should recognize that opting not to masturbate is a viable and acceptable choice.

> Masturbation—like any sexual activity uninjurious to others—is a matter of private, personal conduct. It expresses and reflects, as does all behavior, the individual's medical and moral convictions about the nature of human sexuality and its proper role in her or his own life. The fact that a particular act is unpleasant or bad does not make it a disease; nor does the fact that it is pleasant or good make it a treatment. (p. 69)

PERSONAL CHOICES

Should You Use a Vibrator?

Using a vibrator is also a choice. Such a choice should involve a number of considerations. First, a vibrator should never be used near water because it may produce a deadly shock. Also, some people report a feeling of pain or a sensation that is too intense when the vibrator is placed directly on the clitoris or the head of the penis. To avoid this, the vibrator should not be in direct contact with these areas. A piece of material, such as a thin towel, placed between the clitoris or penis and the vibrator will eliminate these unpleasant sensations.

Virginia Johnson also recommended caution in using a vibrator (Masters & Johnson, 1976). She suggested that if a woman uses intense mechanical stimulation over a long period of time, she may lose her appreciation of the various stages of buildup and diminish her ultimate joy. In other words, since the vibrator will usually produce an orgasm quickly, it may short-circuit erotic fantasies, slow buildup, and eventual release so that some of the emotional and cognitive aspects of orgasm are lost. Of course, these admonitions are also appropriate to men.

A final caveat to consider in deciding whether to use a vibrator is to be sensitive to a partner's feelings about such use. Some partners encourage the use of a vibrator, but others may be threatened by them. One man, who said that his fiancée had gotten "hooked" on her vibrator, stated "I think she prefers it to me." The vibrator should be integrated with caution into an existing sexual relationship.

Social and Psychological Correlates of Masturbation

Frequency of masturbation tends to be associated with several factors: gender, age, education, religion, and locus of control.

GENDER AND AGE   Men are more likely to report having masturbated than women. Of 280 undergraduates, 81% of the men and 45% of the women reported ever having masturbated (Leitenberg, Detzer, & Srebnik, 1993). The average age they first masturbated was 13.45 and 12.75 for men and

women, respectively. Most (over 80%) learned to masturbate through self-exploration. National studies have also reported higher rates of male masturbation.

NATIONAL DATA

Americans aged 18 to 59 who reported having masturbated in the past year

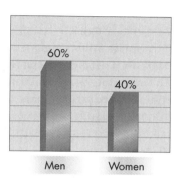

Source: Michael et al., 1994.

The pattern of men masturbating more frequently than women is true at all ages (Michael et al., 1994), and the pattern begins early. Kinsey and his associates (1948, 1953) observed that 21% of 12-year-old boys, in contrast to 12% of 12-year-old girls, masturbated.

The discrepancy is also evident between the sexes in other countries. In a study of more than 20,000 Japanese high school and university students, 98% of the boys and 39% of the girls reported having masturbated (Hatano, 1991). In another study, students at Anadolu University in Eskisehir, Turkey, were asked about their masturbatory behavior. Of the 166 female subjects, 11.5% reported that they had masturbated; of the 172 male subjects, 87.2% professed to having done so (Erkmen, Dilbaz, Serber, Kaptanoglu, & Tekin, 1990). In still another study, the discrepancy between women and men was evident, although it was not as large. Seventy percent of 147 Colombian university women, compared to 99% of 144 university men, reported having masturbated (Alzate, 1989).

A study of masturbation among a sample of Chinese college students also revealed a higher incidence among men. Of 305 undergraduates, twice as many men reported having masturbated as women (43.8 and 21.4%, respectively) (Tang, Lai, Phil, & Chung, 1997).

Several explanations have been suggested as to why men masturbate more than women (Leitenberg, Detzer, & Srebnik, 1993). One is greater genital availability. A man's penis is easy to touch or rub; a woman's genitals are more hidden. Most of the more than 7000 men in Hite's (1981) sample reported that they learned about masturbation through self-discovery. Other possible explanations for greater masturbation among men include the desire for release of periodic seminal buildup, traditional male social scripts that emphasize the physical release and pleasure aspects of sexuality rather than the relationship aspect, and greater social support for sexual expression among men than women. In regard to the latter, traditionally, "good girls" (particularly in adolescence) were not sexual. As women reach their twenties and thirties, they are much more likely to masturbate.

In spite of the high percentage of men who masturbate, some men never choose to masturbate. Kinsey et al. (1948) suggested that a low sex drive, dependency on nocturnal emissions, and the regular availability of a sexual partner may account for this. Another explanation may be that these men have strong religious beliefs against masturbation.

With advancing age, masturbation frequency among men decreases. In a study of 61 men who were in nursing homes (average age, 71.3), only 10% reported that they masturbated. These men also reported that their interest in sex was at a level of 5.4 on a 10-point scale, with 10 being high interest (Mulligan & Palguta, 1991). In Chapter 14, "Sexuality Across the Life Span," we note a decrease in all forms of sexual activity, including masturbation, as a person becomes elderly.

Elderly women are less likely to report having every masturbated than middle-aged women. In a study of 625 Danish women born in three generations (1910, 1936, and 1958), the percentages of those who reported ever having masturbated were 38%, 47%, and 81%, respectively (Lunde, Larsen, Fog, & Garde, 1991). These findings suggest that the cohort in which women are born is related to self-reported prevalence of masturbation. As the Lunde et al. (1991) study suggests, contemporary cohorts of women are more likely to report having masturbated than earlier cohorts. This may be due to the fact that contemporary cohorts have been reared in a less sexually restrictive society.

EDUCATION AND RELIGION The less education a person has, the less often that person reportedly masturbates. Among a national sample of adults, more than half of all men and more than three-quarters of all women with less than a high school education reported that they did not masturbate in the last year (Michael et al., 1994). Among those with advanced degrees, only one out of five men and six out of ten women reported that they did not masturbate (Michael et al., 1994). Conversely stated, the more educated the individual, the more likely she or he reports having masturbated.

It is not clear from these data whether less educated individuals have lower rates of masturbatory behavior or whether they are less willing to report such behavior due to embarrassment, guilt, or fear of disapproval.

Those who attend religious services and regard themselves as devout are also less likely to report having masturbated than those who do not attend religious services or regard themselves as devout (Kinsey et al., 1948, 1953). This is not surprising in view of the traditional attitude of religion toward masturbation.

LOCUS OF CONTROL We discussed locus of control in Chapter 1. Recall that people who believe in internal control view outcomes (events and rewards) as being dependent on their own abilities, while people who believe in external control view outcomes as being dependent on chance, fate, or other people. In one study (Catania & White, 1982), 30 elderly persons (average age, 68.5) completed a scale that revealed the degree to which they tended to be internally or externally controlled. They also indicated how frequently they masturbated. Results showed that those who felt in control of their lives (internally controlled) had higher masturbatory frequencies than those who felt out of control (externally controlled). The researchers concluded that "internal control in a sexual context may reflect a person's perceptions of self-regulation with regard to his/her body and sexuality" (p. 243).

Masturbation in Relationships

It is sometimes assumed that married people and those in on-going relationships do not masturbate because they have a sexual partner. To the contrary, individuals with partners have the highest frequency of masturbation. Based on data from a national sample, 85% of men and 45% of women who were living with a partner reported that they had masturbated in the last year. Married people were significantly more likely to report engaging in masturbation than people who were living alone (Michael et al., 1994).

Spouses who masturbate do so for a variety of reasons. In some cases, the partner is away for extended periods of time and is not available for sexual activity. Other spouses masturbate for the unique experience it provides, or because it relieves stress or helps them to fall asleep. Some spouses masturbate because they find their sexual relationship with their partner unfulfilling. Perhaps their desired frequency of sex exceeds that of their partner, or their partner does not provide the type of stimulation they desire. Some couples masturbate during the later stages of pregnancy when intercourse is uncomfortable.

Masturbation may have positive effects on a relationship. For some couples, watching each other masturbate is a turn-on that adds another dimension to the couple's sex life. Also, differences in desire for sexual interaction can be reduced if the partner with the greater desire masturbates some of the time. Individuals who masturbate aren't totally dependent on their partners to satisfy them sexually, which can provide a sense of freedom for both partners.

Masturbation may also help spouses remain faithful. While masturbation isn't cheating, it nevertheless provides an opportunity for fantasy and sexual arousal outside the relationship. Sex and marital therapist Michael Perelman commented that "wives who perceive masturbation as a form of 'mental adultery' aren't recognizing its value in maintaining monogamy by providing variety in thought rather than deed" (cited in Rae, 1995, p. 74).

Since women who masturbate are better able to teach their partners how to pleasure them, they may be more satisfied in their relationships. Their partners may also derive satisfaction from being able to provide them with pleasure.

Finally, masturbation is associated with finding various sexual activities with one's partner "very appealing." Michael et al. (1994) found that individuals who reported masturbating also reported being interested in vaginal sex, oral sex, and anal sex, as well as watching a partner undress.

Masturbation can also have negative consequences for a relationship. An individual may regard his or her partner's masturbation as rejection. A person may feel that his or her partner masturbates because he or she is not a good lover. Other spouses may feel that their partner masturbating is a form of cheating in the relationship. Some spouses feel fine that their partner masturbates, but are troubled by their partner keeping their masturbation a secret.

Another way masturbation may hurt a couple's relationship is through the guilt it may produce. About half of the men and women in a national sample who reported having masturbated said that they felt guilty (Michael et al., 1994, p. 166). In some cases, individuals who have negative feelings about masturbation may unconsciously displace these feelings onto their partners.

PERSONAL CHOICES

Should You Masturbate with Your Partner?

Some partners regard masturbation as a personal and private experience, while others view it as an experience to share. Regarding the latter, Rubin (1991) noted that couples under 35 were particularly likely to share the experience: "We love to watch each other masturbate; it's a great turn on" (p. 186).

A positive view of masturbating with one's partner is reflected in the following (Boston Women's Health Book Collective, 1984, p. 178):

> When my fiancé asked if he could help me masturbate I thought it was kinky at first. Then I showed him how I do it and he showed me how he does. We watch each other to see what feels good. . . .

> My lover rubbed her breasts and clitoris while I made love to her yesterday. After I got over feeling a little inadequate (I should be able to do it all!), I found it was like having another pair of hands to make love to her with. It was a turn-on to both of us.

Choosing to avoid masturbating together should not be interpreted negatively. Rather, one's need for privacy may create discomfort with mutual masturbation and be independent of the positive feelings one has for the partner and the quality of the relationship.

THINK ABOUT IT

Taking a college sexuality education course has been shown to influence attitudes toward masturbation. Compared to scores from a survey administered the first day of class, scores from the last day of class revealed a more permissive attitude toward masturbation (Weis, Rabinowitz, & Ruckstuhl, 1992). Has your experience with this college sexuality course influenced your attitudes toward masturbation? If so, how?

SEXUAL FANTASY

When thoughts are considered behavior, sexual fantasies are the most common form of sexual behavior. A *sexual fantasy* may be defined as "a dynamic intrapsychic process which contains imaginal sexual content and is sexually arousing" (Mednick, 1980, p. 684). Sexual fantasies are commonly experienced by both women and men throughout the day, as well as during masturbation and sexual activity with a partner. About 95% of both women and men say they have had sexual fantasies (Leitenberg & Henning, 1995). Sexual fantasies may be unintended (daydreaming or dreaming while asleep), or intended (deliberately conjuring up sexual images).

Individuals may fantasize about events they do not actually want to occur (Gold, Balzano, & Stamey, 1991). For example, women who have fantasies of being overpowered and forced to have sexual relations do not want to be raped in reality. Indeed, although 17% of the 79 women in one study reported having at least one fantasy about forced sexual activity, they were the most likely to report that they did not want the fantasy to come true. Wilson (1978) observed that women may fantasize about being raped because it would relieve them of guilt they would feel about consenting to sexual relations with someone who is desirable but socially taboo. For example, "conscience would not allow most women to have sex with the husband of their best friend, but how could they be blamed if taken against their will?" (p. 52).

Functions of Sexual Fantasy

A primary function of fantasy is to heighten sexual arousal. Sexual fantasies often accompany masturbation. Jones and Barlow (1990) asked 49 men and 47 women to monitor the frequency with which they employed sexual fantasy during masturbation. They found that men reported a greater frequency of masturbatory fantasies than women. This is not surprising in view of the fact that men masturbate more than women. ✍ In a study of 625 Danish women, sexual fantasies "were most often used to increase sexual desire and to facilitate orgasm (while masturbating)" (Lunde et al., 1991). ✍ Due to the arousal function of sexual fantasy, sex therapists routinely encourage women who have difficulty experiencing arousal and orgasm to use sexual fantasies during masturbation and interpersonal sexual activity.

Both women and men are capable of achieving an orgasm through fantasy alone. Eleven percent of the women in Clifford's 1978 study on masturbation reported that they had fantasy-induced orgasms. These most often occurred in a state of semisleep or on waking from a sexual dream.

Sexual fantasies also permit the individual to have sex with unattainable partners. Elliot and Brantley (1997) found in their study of college students that Elisabeth Shue and Brad Pitt were favorite sexual fantasies of men and women, respectively.

Fantasies may also serve the purpose of escape. While driving, working out, or preparing dinner, individuals may fantasize at will. Several students in the authors' classes wrote that when they get bored in class, they switch to a favorite fantasy.

Finally, sexual fantasies provide excitement with safety and convenience. There is no embarrassment, no risk of acquiring or transmitting HIV or other STDs, and no hassle involved in conjuring up one's sexual fantasy.

Sexual fantasy does not seem to serve as a substitute for sexual activity. Some research suggests that sexual fantasies are more often reported by individuals with high rates of sexual activity and sexual experience. Indeed, "it is now considered a sign of pathology not to have sexual fantasies rather than to have them" (Leitenberg & Henning, 1995, p. 477). For example, infrequent sexual fantasy is one of the symptoms of hypoactive sexual desire disorder (discussed in Chapter 11).

Fantasies, however, can sometimes involve guilt. About 25% of the respondents in one study reported feeling strong guilt associated with their fantasies (Leitenberg & Henning, 1995). Those who felt most guilty tended to believe that such fantasizing was abnormal, socially unacceptable, uncommon, and immoral.

Gender Differences in Sexual Fantasy

In a study of the sexual fantasies of undergraduate women and men, Ellis and Symons (1990) found significant sex differences (see Table 13.2). Leitenberg and Henning (1995) summarized research findings on gender differences in sexual fantasies:

- Men more than women imagine doing something sexual to their partner, whereas women more than men imagine something sexual being done to them.

- Men tend to have more explicit and visual imagery in their fantasies, whereas women tend to have more emotional and romantic imagery.

- Men are more likely than women to fantasize about having sex with multiple partners at the same time.

- Women are more likely than men to have fantasies in which they are submissive and are forced or overpowered.

- Men are more likely than women to have fantasies in which they are dominant over their partner.

PERSONAL CHOICES

Should You Share Your Sexual Fantasies with Your Partner?

The respondents in Rubin's 1991 study (who were all under the age of 35) reported that they enjoyed sharing their fantasies. One respondent noted, "It's very exciting to tell our fantasies to each other while we're making love" (p. 186). Other people may be less comfortable. To them, hearing the sexual fantasies of a partner may engender feelings of insecurity, jealousy, and rage—particularly in those cases where the sexual fantasies of a partner involve a previous lover.

In the Davidson and Hoffman (1980) study, about 20% of the respondents reported that their sex partners were aware of their sexual fantasies. Those who

TABLE 13.2 Gender Differences in Sexual Fantasies

FANTASY	WOMEN (N = 182)	MEN (N = 125)
Taking into consideration all of your fantasies, have you fantasized a sexual encounter with over 1000 different people?	Yes, 8%	Yes, 32%
Are your sexual fantasies typically about someone with whom you are or have been romantically/sexually involved?	Yes, 59%	Yes, 28%
During sexual fantasy, do you typically focus on visual images?	Yes, 43%	Yes, 81%
During sexual fantasy, do you typically focus on emotional feelings?	Yes, 57%	Yes, 19%
Would any person in your sexual fantasy be acceptable as long as he or she were physically attractive (emotional involvement not relevant)?	Yes, 25%	Yes, 62%

Source: Ellis & Symons, 1990.

disclosed their sexual fantasies to the partners tended to be as satisfied with their current sex life as those who did not. However, more respondents felt that revealing their personal sexual fantasies would have potentially negative (rather than positive) effects on their sex partners. Wilson (1978) suggested that

> Fantasies may play a constructive role in adding spice to love-making that threatens to become dull. This positive benefit is more likely to be gained if the fantasies are openly shared and discussed with the partner. We should be aware of our own fantasies and what they tell us. We should also recognize those of our partner, so we can take account of them in developing a truly satisfying relationship. (pp. 148–149)

INTERPERSONAL SEXUAL BEHAVIORS

Most adult sexual behavior occurs in the context of a relationship. In this section, we discuss a variety of interpersonal sexual behaviors, including vaginal intercourse; anal intercourse; clitoral, penile, and breast stimulation; kissing; and touching.

Vaginal Intercourse

Sexual intercourse, or *coitus*, refers to the sexual union of a man's penis and a woman's vagina (see Figure 13.1). The world's earliest known and most detailed sex manuals were produced by the Chinese (Tannahill, 1982). The manuals, intended for women as well as men, typically included "introductory remarks on the cosmic significance of the sexual encounter" (p. 169), foreplay recommendations, and techniques and positions for intercourse (illustrated for bedside reference). And to prevent these encounters from being boring, the handbooks listed a variety of positions, "really only 30 basic ones" (p. 175). Many of these were poetically named and acrobatically described, such as Dragon in Flight, Tiger in the Forest, Swinging Monkey, Cicadas Mating, and Flying Through the Clouds (Humana & Wu, 1984).

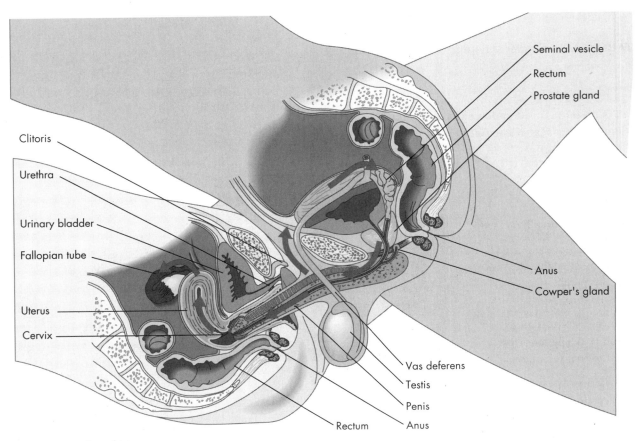

FIGURE 13.1 Sexual Intercourse

Between the third and fifth centuries A.D., the *Kama Sutra,* the most famous of the Indian sex manuals, was compiled (Tannahill, 1982). The doctrine of *Karma* (transmigration of souls) held that through correct behavior, one could be reincarnated at a higher level. Sex was one of a Hindu Indian's religious duties—"not one that would put him straight into tune with the infinite, but certainly one of the least taxing and most pleasurable ways of improving the state of his *Karma*" (p. 201).

Following is a brief description of six sexual positions: man-on-top, woman-on-top, side-by-side, rear-entry, sitting, and standing.

MAN-ON-TOP POSITION   The man-on-top position is the most frequently used position during intercourse (see Figure 13.2). This position is also referred to as the "missionary position," because the Polynesians observed that the British missionaries had intercourse with the man on top. The woman reclines on her back, bends her knees, and spreads her legs. The man positions himself between her legs, supporting himself on his elbows and knees. The man or woman may guide his penis into her vagina. This position may be preferred because of the belief that this is the way most people have intercourse and, therefore, it is "normal." In addition, it permits maximum male thrusting and facilitates kissing and caressing.

But there are disadvantages to the missionary position. Some women experience pain from the deep penetration. Unless such a woman closes her legs after penetration, she is likely to feel the penis thrusting against her cervix. The man-above position also makes clitoral contact difficult. Although a woman can move her buttocks in a circular fashion to achieve some clitoral friction, some women find it almost impossible to achieve clitoral stimulation in this position. However, the woman's clitoris may be stimulated by either the man's or the woman's hand or finger during man-on-top intercourse. A final disadvantage of the man-on-top position is the muscle tension produced by the man having to support his weight and control thrusting. This added tension may hasten ejaculation, which may be problematic for both the woman and the man.

WOMAN-ON-TOP POSITION   This is an alternative position that couples frequently use (see Figure 13.3). The woman may either lie lengthwise, so that her legs are between her partner's, or kneel on top with her knees on either side of him. The primary advantage of this position is that it permits maximum freedom of movement for the woman to ensure clitoral stimulation. Many women report that they have an orgasm most often in this position. "I like to be on top," wrote one woman, "because I can better control the amount of friction in the right places." In addition, both partners may have their hands free, and either the man or woman may stimulate her clitoris during intercourse.

Some women report drawbacks to the woman-above position. Some feel too shy in this position and do not enjoy "being on display." Others complain that the penis keeps falling out because the woman may lift too high before the downward stroke on the penis. Still others say there is a "lot of work when you're on top" and prefer the more passive role.

SIDE-BY-SIDE POSITION   A relaxing position for both partners is the side-by-side position (see Figure 13.4). The partners lie on their sides, with one leg touching the bed. The top legs are lifted and positioned to accommodate easy entry of the penis. Neither partner

FIGURE 13.2 Man-on-Top Position

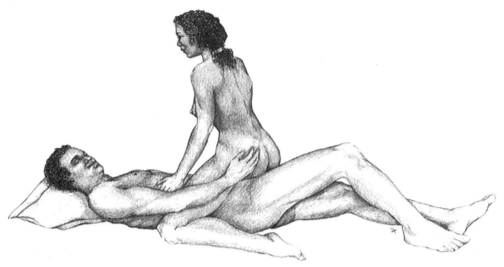

FIGURE 13.3 Woman-on-Top Position

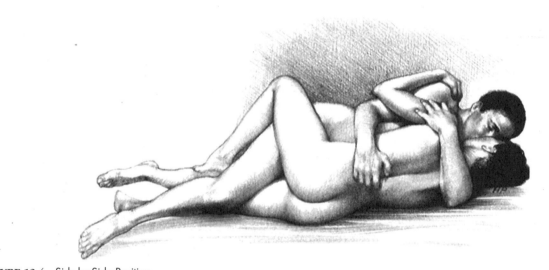

FIGURE 13.4 Side-by-Side Position

FIGURE 13.5 Rear Entry During Pregnancy

FIGURE 13.6 Rear Entry, Kneeling

bears the strain of "doing all the work," and the partners have relative freedom to move their body as they wish to achieve the desired place of contact and rhythm of movement.

REAR-ENTRY POSITION   There are several ways to achieve a rear-entry intercourse position. The woman may lie on her side with her back to her partner (see Figure 13.5). She may also support herself on her knees and hands (see Figure 13.6), or she may lie on her stomach and tilt her buttocks upward while the man enters her vagina from behind. In another rear-entry variation, the man may lie on his back and the woman may kneel or squat above him with her back toward her partner.

Many of the rear-entry intercourse positions permit the man or the woman to manually stimulate her breasts or clitoris or caress her legs and buttocks. Some women are unable to achieve orgasm using the rear-entry position. Although some women enjoy the deep penetration that results from rear-entry intercourse, others find it painful. Other disadvantages of rear-entry intercourse include a tendency for the penis to slip out and the loss of face-to-face contact.

SITTING POSITION   In the sitting position, the man sits on a chair or the edge of the bed with his partner sitting across his thighs (see Figure 13.7). She can lower herself onto his erect penis or insert his penis after she is sitting. She may be facing him, or her

FIGURE 13.7 Sitting Position

back may be turned to him. The face-to-face sitting position involves maximum freedom to stimulate the breasts (manually or orally), to kiss, and to hug.

STANDING POSITION   In the standing position, the woman raises one leg, or the man picks hers up and places her onto his erect penis. She puts her legs around his waist and her arms around his neck while he is holding her. Both must be well-coordinated and in good physical condition for this position.

An easier variation of the standing position is for the man to stand while the woman sits or reclines on a raised surface (a high bed, a table, or a chair). The woman's legs are spread, and the man inserts his penis into her vagina while standing between her legs.

VARIATIONS   There are innumerable variations to the basic positions described here. For example, in the man-above position, the woman's legs may be closed or open, bent or straight, over his shoulders or around his neck. The woman may be on her back or raised on her elbows. The partners may face each other or be head-to-toe. Although couples may choose different positions to add variety to their love-making, pregnancy and health concerns may be other motivations for doing so.

PERSONAL CHOICES

Should You Have Intercourse with a New Partner?

Issues to consider in deciding whether to have intercourse with a new partner include personal consequences, partner consequences, relationship consequences, contraception, and HIV and other STDs.

PERSONAL CONSEQUENCES   How do you predict you will feel about yourself after you have intercourse? Will you feel guilty or used? Will you regret your decision? The effect intercourse will have on you personally will be influenced by your personal and religious values and the emotional involvement you have with your partner. Some people feel it is important to wait until they are married or in a committed relationship before having intercourse. There is often a religious basis for this value. Strong personal and religious values against nonmarital or casual intercourse will cause guilt and regret following nonmarital or casual intercourse. In contrast, values that regard intercourse as acceptable within the context of a love relationship or among any two consenting adults will allow feelings of satisfaction and contentment after intercourse.

PARTNER CONSEQUENCES   How will having intercourse affect your partner? Whereas intercourse may be a pleasurable experience for you, your partner may react differently. What are your partner's feelings about nonmarital intercourse? Does he or she have the ability to handle the experience? If you suspect that your partner will regret having intercourse, you might reconsider whether intercourse would be appropriate with this person. One man reported that after having intercourse with a woman he had just met, he awakened to the sound of her sobbing as she sat on the end of the bed. She felt guilty and regretted the experience. He said of the event, "If I had known how she was going to respond, we wouldn't have had intercourse." One woman reported that she made a mistake in having intercourse with a friend. "To me," she said, "it was just a friendship and I knew that there was no romantic future. For him it was different. He fell in love and wanted us to get married. It destroyed him when he learned I had no such interest."

RELATIONSHIP CONSEQUENCES   How intercourse affects a relationship is largely influenced by how it affects each of the partners in the relationship. If one of the partners (or both) feels guilty or used, those negative feelings are going to affect how the partners feel about each other. The effect of having intercourse with a new partner also depends on how each of the partners defines the experience. Ideally, both partners should have the same definition. But, if their definitions of having intercourse differ, the relationship may suffer. For example, suppose one partner views having intercourse as meaning that they have entered into a committed, monogamous love relationship, but the other partner defines their intercourse experience as simply having a good time. These different views or definitions of the intercourse experience are going to create some conflict and hurt feelings in the relationship.

CONTRACEPTION   Another potential consequence of intercourse is pregnancy. Once a couple decides to have intercourse, a separate decision must be made as to whether intercourse should result in pregnancy. Some couples want children and make a mutual commitment to love and care for their offspring. Other couples do not want children. If the couple wants to avoid pregnancy, they must choose and effectively use a contraceptive method. But many do not. Six percent of 672 sexually active first-year university students in the Phillips survey (1992) reported that they used no method of birth control. Six percent of these sexually active students also reported that they had become pregnant at least once. In many cases, pregnancy comes as a surprise. One woman recalled:

> It was the first time I had intercourse, so I didn't really think I would get pregnant my first time. But I did. And when I told him I was pregnant, he told me he didn't have any money and couldn't help me pay for the abortion. He really wanted nothing to do with me after that. (authors' files)

HIV AND OTHER SEXUALLY TRANSMISSIBLE DIS-EASES Avoiding HIV infection and other sexually transmissible diseases is an important consideration in deciding whether to have intercourse in a new relationship. Increasing numbers of people having more partners results in the rapid spread of the bacteria and viruses responsible for numerous varieties of STDs.

In addition to selectivity in choosing one's sexual partner and an awareness of potential dishonesty with regard to information about a chosen partner's previous sexual partners, looking for sores or discharges before sex and washing exposed areas after contact may help to reduce exposure. A critical precaution is the use of a latex reservoir tip condom lubricated with nonoxynol-9 (shown to kill HIV in laboratory animals). Read the label on condoms to ensure that nonoxynol-9 is included.

This may be good advice, but only 63% of a sample of 4000 university students said that they always used protection during penile/vaginal intercourse, and only 3% said that they used protection when participating in oral sex (Latman & Latman, 1995)

Deciding to have sexual intercourse in a new relationship is a complex issue. Allgeier (1985) summarized some of the issues individuals might consider before deciding to have intercourse: feeling guiltless and comfortable with your present level of involvement; feeling confident that you will not be humiliated and that your reputation will not be hurt; feeling free to choose not to have intercourse, rather than feeling pressure to have intercourse; not using intercourse as an attempt to improve a poor relationship; and not being motivated to have intercourse for inappropriate reasons, such as to prove love to the other person, to prove that you are desirable, to gain affection, or to rebel against your parents.

Anal Intercourse

While vaginal intercourse was reported as "very appealing" by 78% of women and 83% of men ages 18 to 44 (national sample), only 1% of women and 5% of men reported that anal sex was "very appealing" (Michael et al., 1994, pp. 146–147).

NATIONAL DATA

In the last 12 months, about 10% of both women and men in a national sample reported having engaged in anal sex.

Source: Michael et al., 1994, p. 140.

Anal intercourse is the sexual behavior associated with the highest risk of HIV infection (Brody, 1995). The person receiving anal intercourse is at higher risk than the man who inserts his penis into his partner's rectum. This is because anal intercourse often tears the rectum, allowing HIV-infected semen to come in contact with the bloodstream. In addition, the first 1½ inches of the anus provide darkness, warmth, and moisture in the mucous membranes, which is a prime host for transmitting HIV. Couples who engage in anal intercourse should always use condoms to protect against transmission of HIV and other STDs. The use of water-based lubrication products, such as K-Y jelly, may also enable the penis to enter the partner's rectum more easily and, thus, minimize tearing of the rectal tissue. Vaginal intercourse should never follow anal intercourse without a thorough washing.

Another risk associated with anal intercourse (as well as with manual or oral stimulation of the woman's anus) is cystitis (bladder infection). Cystitis may result from bacteria from the anal region being spread to the urethral opening. Symptoms of cystitis may include a persistent urge to urinate, pain during urination, and fever. Cystitis is treated with antibiotics; if left untreated, a serious kidney infection could develop. Women are much more prone to developing cystitis than men. To avoid cystitis, use a condom. If you do not use a condom, clean the anal area before engaging in anal stimulation, urinate immediately after sex, and clean the anal and genital area after sex. Also, once a penis, mouth, or finger has come in contact with the anal area, avoid contact with the vagina and clitoris until the penis, mouth, or finger has been washed thoroughly.

Clitoral Stimulation

"Please take me clitorally" is the message most women would like their lovers to act on (Hite, 1977). Again and again, the women in Hite's study, when asked how men made love to them, said that their partners spent too little time (sometimes none at all) stimulating their clitoris and that they needed such stimulation to derive maximum pleasure from the sexual experience. The clitoris may be stimulated by the hand, mouth, or penis.

MANUAL CLITORAL STIMULATION   Ninety-six percent of 128 university males reported that they had actively manually stimulated their partner's genitals (Alzate, 1989). Such stimulation may be to ready the woman for intercourse or as an end in itself, and the style of stimulation may vary. Some partners rub the mons veneris area, putting indirect pressure on the clitoris (see Figure 13.8). Others may apply direct clitoral pressure. Still others may insert one or several fingers into the vagina, with gentle or rapid thrusting, at the same time they stimulate the clitoris.

Not all women enjoy the insertion of the man's fingers in their vagina during petting. Some women permit it because their partners want to do it, and often the man wants to do it because he assumes that the woman wants something in her vagina. But the key to sexual pleasure for many women is pressure on and around their clitoris, not necessarily insertion.

ORAL CLITORAL STIMULATION   *Cunnilingus,* translated from the Latin, means "he who licks the vulva." Specifically, cunnilingus involves the stimulation of the clitoris, labia, and vaginal opening of the woman by her partner's tongue and lips. As noted earlier, the clitoris is an extremely sensitive organ. The technique many women enjoy is gentle teasing by the tongue, with stronger, more rhythmic sucking movements when orgasm approaches. While the partner's mouth is caressing and licking the clitoral shaft and glans, some women prefer additional stimulation by a finger or vibrator in the vagina or anus.

Three-fourths of the almost 600 college students in Rubin's study (1991) reported that they had engaged in oral sex. The women reported that cunnilingus was one of two ways they were able to have an orgasm (being on top during intercourse was the other way) (p. 121).

FIGURE 13.8 Manual Clitoral Stimulation

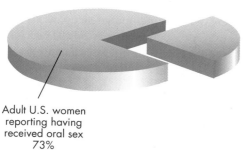

Adult U.S. women
reporting having
received oral sex
73%

Source: Michael et al., 1994.

In regard to their "last sexual event," 20% of women report that the last time they had sex, their partner performed cunnilingus on them (Michael et al., 1994).

Almost 70% of a national sample of U.S. women aged 18 to 44 reported that "receiving oral sex" was "very" or "somewhat" appealing to them. About 30% reported that receiving oral sex was either "not appealing" or "not at all appealing" (Michael et al., 1994, p. 146). Those who find it unpleasant or repulsive often view their vaginal area as dirty and oral sex as obscene and unnatural.

How do men feel about cunnilingus? In a study of 4000 men, less than 3% said that cunnilingus was unpleasant or boring (Pietropinto & Simenauer, 1977). Some men perform cunnilingus because they want to, rather than because their partners ask them to. Their enjoyment in cunnilingus may spring from doing something forbidden, from their enhanced self-image as a good lover, or from just wanting to please their partner.

In order to reduce risk of STD transmission, the woman receiving oral sex should use a *dental dam,* which is a thin piece of latex that covers the vulva during cunnilingus. A piece of household plastic wrap or a latex condom that is cut into a flat piece may act as a substitute for a dental dam.

PENILE CLITORAL STIMULATION   In addition to stimulating the clitoral area by hand and mouth, some women rub their partner's penis across and around their clitoris. Such stimulation may or may not be followed by penetration. Although rubbing the penis on or near the clitoris is not the same as intercourse, it

can have the same outcome—pregnancy. If the man ejaculates near the woman's vaginal opening during penile-clitoral stimulation, pregnancy may occur. Even if the man does not ejaculate, his penis may emit a small amount of fluid that contains sperm.

Penile Stimulation (Manual and Oral)

Aside from stimulating the penis through intercourse, a man's partner may stimulate his penis manually or orally.

MANUAL STIMULATION   Eighty-six percent of university women in one study reported that they had manually stimulated their partner's genitals (Alzate, 1989). Manual penile stimulation may provide a means of arousing the man in order to produce erection. After achieving erection, manual stimulation may continue as either a precursor to or substitute for intercourse. Use of a personal lubrication product or saliva may also provide pleasure during manual penile stimulation.

ORAL STIMULATION   Oral stimulation of the man's genitals is known as *fellatio.* The term comes from the Latin *fellare,* meaning "to suck." Although fellatio most often involves sucking the penis, fellatio may also include licking the shaft, glans, frenulum, and scrotum. Some partners take only the head of the penis in their mouth while alternating sucking and blowing motions. The partner's hands also may caress the scrotum and perineum during fellatio. Fellatio may be enjoyed as a precursor to or substitute for intercourse. If fellatio results in orgasm, the semen may be swallowed without harm (in the absence of HIV infection) if the partner desires to do so. However, to reduce risk of HIV and other STD transmission, the man's penis should be covered with a condom during fellatio.

In regard to their "last sexual event," 28% of men report that the last time they had sex, they experienced fellatio (Michael et al., 1994).

In spite of the reported high incidence of fellatio, it remains a relatively taboo subject for open discussion. In some states, legal statutes regard fellatio as a "crime against nature." "Nature" in this case refers to reproduction, and the "crime" is sex that does not produce babies.

People engage in fellatio for a number of reasons. Pleasure is a central one. Next to kissing and hugging, oral sex was reported as the most pleasurable form of petting by more than 4000 men (Pietropinto & Simenauer, 1977). It is the interpretation of the experience, as well as the physical sensations, that may produce the pleasure. One man said that his partner fellating him meant that she really loved him and enjoyed his body.

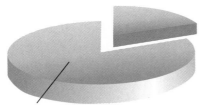
Dominance may be another reason for the enjoyment of fellatio. A common theme in pornographic movies is forcing the woman to perform fellatio. In this context, the act implies sexual submission, which may give the male an ego boost. Aware of this motive, some women refuse to fellate their partners. One woman said that her partner viewed her as a prostitute when she fellated him, that she did not like such a perception, and that she had stopped doing so.

Variety is another motive for fellatio. Some lovers complain that penis-in-vagina intercourse is sometimes boring. Fellatio adds another dimension to a couple's sexual relationship. The greater the range of sexual behaviors a couple has to share, the less likely they are to define their sexual relationship as routine and uninteresting.

As noted earlier, fellatio may also be used as a means of avoiding intercourse. Unmarried couples who feel that intercourse outside marriage is wrong may view oral sex, including fellatio, as an acceptable alternative. Although there may be clear social and religious prohibitions against premarital intercourse, little or nothing is said about oral sex. So any sexual activity that is not intercourse may carry only limited guilt.

Some couples engage in fellatio and cunnilingus simultaneously (see Figure 13.9). The term "69" has been used to identify the respective position of the couple engaging in mutual oral-genital stimulation. Sixty-nine may be enjoyed as a prelude to intercourse or as an end in itself. However, some people find it difficult to be a giver and a receiver at the same time.

Touching

Our skin contains about 900,000 sensory receptors (Montagu & Matson, 1979); it is a primary mechanism for experiencing pleasure. Many regard touching as the most significant aspect of sex. The 3000 women in Hite's (1977) study stated repeatedly that touching, holding, caressing, being close to, lying next to, and pressing bodies together were more important to them than intercourse or orgasm. For many, such physical closeness gives a feeling of emotional closeness that is satisfying whether or not intercourse or orgasm follows. "Long, gentle passionate encounters, with much touching and enthusiasm, give me a feeling of being loved all over and are all I need most of the time," said one woman (p. 556).

Masters and Johnson (1976) echoed the feeling of many women: "It is important to avoid the fundamental error of believing that touch is a means to an

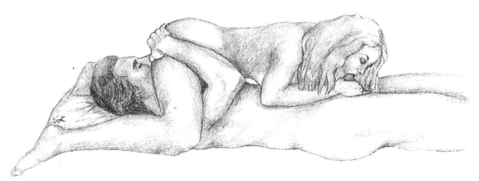

FIGURE 13.9 Simultaneous Oral-Genital Stimulation

end. It is not. Touch is an end in itself. It is a primary form of communication, a silent voice that avoids the pitfall of words while expressing the feelings of the moment" (p. 253).

While women delight in the experience of touching (and often get less touching than they want), they may feel that men do not share their enthusiasm. Most women feel that men engage in foreplay only as a means of priming them for intercourse, and many resent it. (Some say that while women fake orgasm, men fake foreplay.) Their suspicions are mostly accurate. In a study of 7000 men, the majority said that physical affection should always lead to intercourse and orgasm (Hite, 1981).

Kissing is a frequent behavior among lovers.

Kissing

There are different types of kissing. In one style of kissing, the partners gently touch their lips together for a short time with their mouths closed. In another, there is considerable pressure and movement for a prolonged time when the closed mouths meet. In still another, the partners kiss with their mouths open, using gentle or light pressure and variations in movement and time. Kinsey referred to the latter as deep kissing (also known as soul kissing, tongue kissing, or French kissing).

Desmond Morris, a noted zoologist with an interest in the behavior of humans, suggested that mouth kissing had its origins in mother-infant interactions of early human history:

> In early human societies, before commercial baby-food was invented, mothers weaned their children by chewing up their food and then passing it into the infantile mouth by lip-to-lip contact—which naturally involved a considerable amount of tonguing and mutual mouth-pressure. This almost bird-like system of parental care seems strange and alien to us today, but our species probably practiced it for a million years or more, and adult erotic kissing today is almost certainly a Relic Gesture stemming from these origins. . . . Whether it has been handed down to us from generation to generation . . . or whether we have an inborn predisposition towards it, we cannot say. But, whichever is the case, it looks rather as though, with the deep kissing and tonguing of modern lovers, we are back again at the infantile mouth-feeding stage of the far-distant past. . . . If the young lovers exploring each other's mouths with their tongues feel the ancient comfort of

parental mouth-feeding, this may help them to increase their mutual trust and thereby their pair-bonding. (quoted in Ackerman, 1990, p. 112)

When writing a letter to a loved one, we sometimes write a row of "XXXXXXXXs" to represent kisses. This custom stems from the Middle Ages, when there were so many illiterate people that a cross (X) was acceptable as a signature on a legal document. The cross (X) stood for "St. Andrew's mark," and people vowed to be honest by writing a cross that represented his sacred name. To pledge their sincere honesty, people would kiss their signature. Thus in time, the "X" became associated with the kiss (Ackerman, 1990, p. 113).

Breast Stimulation

Breast stimulation, both manual and oral, was reported by over 95% of female and male students in a study on sexuality at a Colombian university (Alzate, 1989). In our society, the female breasts are charged with erotic potential. A billion-dollar pornographic industry encourages viewing women's breasts in erotic terms. *Playboy, Penthouse,* and an array of other adult magazines feature women with naked breasts in seductive, erotic poses.

Not all women share men's erotic feelings about breasts. Women may or may not manually stimulate their own breasts and often neglect the breasts of their male partners, even though male breasts have the same potential for erotic stimulation as female breasts. For some men, breast stimulation by their partners is particularly important.

Other Noncoital Sexual Behaviors

Another form of experiencing intense physical stimulation without having intercourse is *genital apposition,* or pressing the genitals close together while clothed or unclothed. The couple lies together, entwines their legs, and "grinds." An orgasm may or may not result.

Anal stimulation is still another means of noncoital stimulation. This may consist of manual or oral stimulation (*rimming*) of the anus and surrounding area. The anal area is particularly sensitive, and some couples routinely stimulate each other during foreplay or intercourse.

_____ THINK ABOUT IT _____

Whereas any sexual behavior that is not vaginal intercourse is often referred to as "foreplay," this term suggests that touching, kissing, stroking, and licking behaviors are merely precursors to the "main act"—intercourse. How does this assumption affect the sexual interaction and satisfaction of women and men?

KEY TERMS

autoerotic behavior 346	genital apposition 366
celibacy 344	masturbation 346
coitus 356	rimming 366
cunnilingus 362	semen-conservation doctrine 348
dental dam 363	
erotophilia 342	sexual celibacy 344
erotophobia 342	sexual fantasy 354
fellatio 363	sexual intercourse 356

SUMMARY POINTS

Sexuality differs in the same individual and couple across time, and between individuals and couples. In this chapter, we have examined the range of individual and interpersonal sexual behaviors and fantasies.

Erotophilia and Erotophobia

How we respond to erotic stimuli and how we behave sexually are influenced not only by arousal mechanisms, but also by affective and cognitive processes. The propensity to have positive emotional responses to sexuality is referred to as erotophilia.

Individuals who are erotophilic tend to enjoy and seek out sexual experiences. The propensity to have negative emotional responses to sexuality is known as erotophobia. Individuals who are erotophobic tend to feel uncomfortable with sexuality and avoid sexual experiences. Although erotophobic individuals are less likely to be sexually active, those who do engage in sexual relations have a higher risk of pregnancy and HIV or STD transmission because they feel uncomfortable discussing or using contraception or condoms.

Sexual Celibacy

Some adults are celibate because they have little to no interest in sex and, therefore, have no desire to engage in sexual activity. Others are celibate for religious reasons. While some people may choose to be sexually celibate, others are involuntarily celibate because they do not have a partner or are separated from their partner due to military service, work-related travel, or prison. Hospital, nursing, and retirement home residents are also vulnerable to involuntary sexual celibacy.

Autoerotic Behavior

It is sometimes assumed that married people and those in ongoing relationships do not engage in autoerotic behavior because they have a sexual partner. To the contrary, individuals with partners have the highest frequency of masturbation. Based on data from a national sample, 85% of men and 45% of women who were living with a partner reported that they had masturbated in the last year.

Negative attitudes toward masturbation stem from religion, parents, and false beliefs about masturbation promoted by early medicine and psychoanalytic theorists. Most health care professionals today agree that masturbation is a normal and healthy sexual behavior.

Sexual Fantasy

Research reveals that sexual fantasies occur most often in individuals who exhibit the least number of sexual problems and the least sexual dissatisfaction. The function of sexual fantasy is not to serve as a substitute for an absence of sexual activity; in fact, more sexual fantasies are reported by individuals with higher rates of sexual activity.

Interpersonal Sexual Behaviors

The sexual intercourse position reported by many women as the one most likely to produce orgasm is the woman-on-top position. The most common position is the man-on-top, or "missionary" position. Other intercourse positions include side-by-side, sitting, standing, and rear-entry. Although many people equate "sex" with "intercourse," interpersonal sexual activity involves many other behaviors, including clitoral and penile stimulation by the hand or mouth, breast stimulation, anal intercourse, kissing, and touching.

REFERENCES

Ackerman, D. (1990). *A natural history of the senses.* New York: Random House.

Allgeier, E. R. (1985, July). Are you ready for sex? Informed consent for sexual intimacy. *SIECUS Report,* 8–9.

Alzate, H. (1989). Sexual behavior of unmarried Colombian university students: A follow-up. *Archives of Sexual Behavior, 18,* 239–250.

Barbach, L. (1976). *For yourself: The fulfillment of female sexuality.* Garden City, NY: Doubleday.

Bartosch, J., Berry, W., Maodush-Pitzer, D., Hunter-Geboy, C., Thompson, P. M., & Woodard, L. (1989). *God's gift of sexuality: A study for young people in the reformed tradition in the Presbyterian church (U.S.A.) and reformed church in America.* Louisville, KY: Presbyterian Publishing House.

Boston Women's Health Book Collective. (1984). *The new our bodies, ourselves.* New York: Simon & Schuster.

Brody, S. (1995). Lack of evidence for transmission of human immunodeficiency virus through vaginal intercourse. *Archives of Sexual Behavior, 24,* 383–394.

Bullough, V. L. (1976). *Sexual variance in society and history.* New York: Wiley.

Carnes, P. (1983). *Out of the shadows: Understanding sexual addiction.* Minneapolis: CompCare.

Catania, J. A., & White, C. B. (1982). Sexuality in an aged sample: Cognitive determinants of masturbation. *Archives of Sexual Behavior, 11,* 237–245.

Cate, R. M., Long, E., Angera, J. J., & Draper, K. K. (1993). Sexual intercourse and relationship development. *Family Relations, 42,* 158–164.

Clifford, R. E. (1978). Development of masturbation in college women. *Archives of Sexual Behavior, 7,* 559-573.

Darling, C. A., Davidson, J. K., Sr., & Cox, R. P. (1991). Female sexual response and the timing of partner orgasm. *Journal of Sex and Marital Therapy, 17,* 3–21.

Davidson, J. K., Sr., & Hoffman, L. E. (1980). *Sexual fantasies and sexual satisfaction: An empirical analysis of erotic thoughts.* Unpublished paper, University of Wisconsin, Eau Claire and University of Notre Dame, IN. Used with permission.

Dodson, B. (1987). *Sex for one: The joy of self love.* Glendale, CA: Crown.

Elliott, L., & Brantley, C. (1997). *Sex on campus: The naked truth about the real sex lives of college students.* New York: Random House.

Ellis, B. J., & Symons, D. (1990). Sex differences in sexual fantasy: An evolutionary psychological approach. *Journal of Sex Research, 27,* 527–555.

Erkmen, H., Dilbaz, N., Serber, G., Kaptanoglu, C., & Tekin, D. (1990). Sexual attitudes of Turkish university students. *Journal of Sex Education and Therapy, 16,* 251–261.

Fisher, W. A. (1983). A psychological approach to human sexuality: The sexual behavior sequence. In D. Byrne & K. K. Kelly (Eds.), *Alternative approaches to the study of sexual behavior* (pp. 131–171). London: Lawrence Erlbaum.

Fisher, W. A. (1988). The sexual opinion survey. In C. M. Davis, W. L. Yarber, & S. L. Davis (Eds.), *Sexuality-related measures: A compendium* (pp. 34–38). Lake Mills, IA: Graphic.

Fisher, W. A., Byrne, D., White, L. A., & Kelley, K. (1988). Erotophobia-erotophilia as a dimension of personality. *Journal of Sex Research, 25,* 123-151.

Gold, S. R., Balzano, B. F., & Stamey, R. (1991). Two studies of females' sexual force fantasies. *Journal of Sex Education and Therapy, 17,* 15–26.

Graham, S. (1848). *Lecture to young men on chastity, intended also for the serious consideration of parents and guardians* (10th ed.). Boston: C. H. Price.

Hariton, E. B., & Singer, J. L. (1974). Women's fantasies during sexual intercourse. *Journal of Consulting and Clinical Psychology, 42,* 313–322.

Hatano, Y. (1991). Changes in the sexual activities of Japanese youth. *Journal of Sex Education and Therapy, 17,* 1–14.

Hite, S. (1977). *The Hite report: A nationwide study of female sexuality.* New York: Dell.

Hite, S. (1981). *The Hite report on male sexuality.* New York: Knopf.

Humana, C., & Wu, N. (1984). *Chinese sex secrets: A look behind the screen.* New York: Gallery Books.

Jones, J. C., & Barlow, D. H. (1990). Self-reported frequency of sexual urges, fantasies and masturbatory fantasies in heterosexual males and females. *Archives of Sexual Behavior, 19,* 269–280.

Kinsey, A., Pomeroy, W., & Martin, C. (1948). *Sexual behavior in the human male.* Philadelphia: W. B. Saunders.

Kinsey, A., Pomeroy, W., Martin, C., & Gebhard, P. (1953). *Sexual behavior in the human female.* Philadelphia: W. B. Saunders.

Latman, N. S., & Latman A. I. (1995). Behavioral risk of human immunodeficiency virus/acquired immunodeficiency syndrome in the university student community. *Sexually Transmitted Diseases, 22,* 104-109.

Leitenberg, H., Detzer, M. J., & Srebnik, D. (1993). Gender differences in masturbation and the relation of masturbation experience in preadolescence and/or early adolescence to sexual behavior and sexual adjustment in young adulthood. *Archives of Sexual Behavior, 22,* 87-98.

Leitenberg, H., & Henning, K. (1995). Sexual fantasy. *Psychological Bulletin, 117,* 469-496.

LoPiccolo, J., & Lobitz, W. C. (1972). The role of masturbation in the treatment of orgasmic dysfunction. *Archives of Sexual Behavior, 2,* 163-171.

Lunde, I., Larsen, G. K., Fog, E., & Garde, K. (1991). Sexual desire, orgasm, and sexual fantasies: A study of 625 Danish women born in 1910, 1936, and 1958. *Journal of Sex Education and Therapy, 17,* 111-116.

Maletzky, B. M. (1991). *Treating the sexual offender.* Newbury Park: Sage.

Masters, W. H., & Johnson, V. E. (1976). *The pleasure bond.* New York: Bantam.

Mednick, R. A. (1980). Sexual fantasy. In R. Woody (Ed.), *Encyclopedia of clinical assessment* (Vol. 2, pp. 684-696). San Francisco: Jossey-Bass.

Michael, R. T., Gagnon, J. H., Laumann, E. O., & Kolata, G. (1994). *Sex in America: A definitive survey.* Boston: Little, Brown.

Money, J., Prakasam, K. S., & Joshi, V. N. (1991). Semen-conservation doctrine from ancient Ayurvedic to modern sexological theory. *American Journal of Psychotherapy, 45,* 9-13.

Montagu, A., & Matson, F. (1979). *The human connection.* New York: McGraw-Hill.

Mulligan, T., & Palguta, R. F., Jr. (1991). Sexual interest, activity, and satisfaction among male nursing home residents. *Archives of Sexual Behavior, 20,* 199-204.

Phillips, J. C. (1992). *Self-reported health behaviors of college freshmen.* Unpublished thesis. Department of Health, Physical Education, Recreation, and Safety. East Carolina University, Greenville, NC. Used by permission.

Pietropinto, A., & Simenauer, J. (1977). *Beyond the male myth.* New York: Quadrangle.

The politics of masturbation. (1994, December 24). *The Lancet, 344,* 1714-1715.

Purnine, D. M., Carey, M. P., & Jorgensen, R. S. (1994). Gender differences regarding preferences for specific heterosexual practices. *Journal of Sex and Marital Therapy 20,* 271-287.

Rae, S. (1995, September). Party of one. *Men's Health,* 72-74.

Rubin, L. B. (1991). *Erotic wars: What happened to the sexual revolution?* New York: HarperCollins.

Sauer, M. V., Zeffer, K. B., Buster, J. E., & Sokol, R. Z. (1988). The effect of abstinence on sperm motility in normal men. *American Journal of Obstetrics and Gynecology, 158,* 604-607.

SIECUS Position Statements on Human Sexuality, Sexual Health and Sexuality Education and Information, 1995-1996. (1996). *24*(3), 21-23. New York.

Szasz. J. T. (1980). *Sex by prescription.* New York: Doubleday.

Tang, C. S., Lai, F. D., Phil, M., & Chung, T. K. H. (1997). Assessment of sexual functioning for Chinese college students. *Archives of Sexual Behavior, 26,* 79-90.

Tannahill, F. (1982). *Sex in history.* New York: Scarborough.

Tissot, S. A. (1766). *Onania, or a treatise upon the disorders produced by masturbation* (A. Hume, Trans.). London: J. Pridden. (Original work published 1758)

Weis, D. L., Rabinowitz, B., & Ruckstuhl, M. F. (1992). Individual changes in sexual attitudes and behavior within college-level human sexuality courses. *The Journal of Sex Research, 29,* 43-59.

Wilson, G. (1978). *The secrets of sexual fantasy.* London: Dent.

Zilbergeld, B. (1978). *Male sexuality.* Boston: Little, Brown.

Zilbergeld, B. (1992). *The new male sexuality.* New York: Bantam.

SEXUALITY ACROSS THE LIFE SPAN

Chapter 14

Just remember, once you're over the hill you begin to pick up speed.

Charles Schulz
Cartoonist

Just as a baseball game is not the same in all of its innings, life is different as we pass through the various stages. A person's sexuality varies depending on whether that person is a child, an adolescent, an adult, or a senior citizen. At each life stage, an individual may experience different emotions, motivations, and patterns of expression. In this chapter, we examine sexuality across the life span and take a look at some of the choices individuals face at different stages in their lives.

SEXUALITY FROM INFANCY THROUGH ADOLESCENCE

A life cycle view of sexuality emphasizes that early experiences are important influences in subsequent sexual development.

Infancy

Infancy is defined as the first year of life following birth. Just as infants are born with digestive and respiratory systems, they are born with a sexual response system that begins to function very early in life. In 1983, Calderone commented on the use of ultrasound to document fetal erection of the penis. She noted that evidence of fetal erection confirmed that, with the exception of the reproductive system (which remains "on hold" until puberty), all of the human bodily systems begin functioning prenatally. It is now known that almost immediately after birth, boys often have erections and girls may have clitoral erections or vaginal lubrication. This knowledge is important because it allows the conclusion that a person's sexual *response* system literally functions throughout the entire life span (Calderone, 1983).

The sexual response system functions prior to birth, and sexual behavior occurs in infancy. Both boys and girls in the nursery have been observed engaging in genital play (boys begin this behavior at

about 6 months of age; girls, at about 11 months). Obvious masturbation has been observed in boys at about 15–16 months. Girls tend to stimulate themselves less directly by rocking or through thigh pressure. Both boys and girls have been observed masturbating to the point of orgasm as early as 6 months of age (Bancroft, 1989).

Because sexual pleasure is an unconditioned positive stimulus, infants are capable of learning associations via classical conditioning processes. As such, infants may learn to associate sexual pleasure with a particular cloth bunny—hence the beginning of a fetish—or they may learn the positive or negative emotions associated with their bodies. In regard to the latter, parents who slap their infants for touching their own body parts and label such behaviors as "dirty" may teach their children to associate anxiety and guilt with sexuality. As noted, it is normal for babies to find pleasure in their bodies. Calderone and Johnson (1989) emphasize that it is an essential part of the baby's growth and development, and Leight (1990) stressed the importance of parents not overreacting.

Psychologists and child development specialists have suggested that parent-infant bonding is important for the establishment of intimate physical and emotional relationships as an adult. The more positive the emotional experiences of infants, the better the potential for positive adult sexual experiences.

Childhood

Childhood extends from age 2 to age 12 and involves physical, cognitive, social, and sexual development. As the child moves through this period, he or she becomes more physically autonomous, becomes capable of more complex thought processes, and develops increased skill in interacting with others and the environment.

As with infants, children experiment with their own bodies as sources of physical pleasure. Genital self-pleasuring may occur at any time throughout childhood. In addition, children are interested in the bodies of others. A favorite game among preschool children is "doctor." This game, which may be played between boys, between girls, or between boys and girls, involves one child assuming the role of patient and the other the role of doctor. The patient undresses, and the doctor examines the patient both visually and by touching his or her body, including the genitals. Some parents, believing such exploration is wrong, punish their children for playing "doctor." Alternatively, parents might respond by saying something nonpunitive, such as "It is interesting to find out how other people's bodies look, isn't it?"

Developmental psychologists suggest that parents should be concerned, and should intervene, if one child is unwilling or coerced, if the children are not the same age (within a couple of years), or if the activity is potentially harmful, such as inserting objects into themselves or each other (Packer, 1995). In such situations, parents might say something like "Bodies are wonderful things, and I know you're curious. But your body is delicate and you hurt it if you put things inside. Also, your body is private, and only you should touch yourself in your private places" (p. 57).

Bancroft (1989) summarized studies of children's self-report of masturbation and sex play. By age 10, half the boys had masturbated and engaged in sex play with other boys, and one-third had engaged in sex play with girls. Comparison data were provided for 8-year-old girls; 30% had masturbated, 37% had engaged in sex play with boys, and 35% had participated in sex play with girls. Both boys and girls who masturbated were likely to continue doing so into adolescence, but girls and middle-class boys were likely to discontinue the prepubertal play with other children. In a study of children's knowledge and thinking about sex, Goldman and Goldman (1982) interviewed 5- to 15-year-olds in Australia, England, Sweden, and the United States. They found no evidence of a latency period (in which children refrained from sexual activity and interest), but they did find support for a developmental process in sexual thinking that was consistent with Piagetian cognitive development stages and Kohlberg's description of moral development. The Swedish children were ahead of the English-speaking children in terms of the developmental stage of their sexual thinking.

The "family bed" seems to have no significant negative consequences for children.

PERSONAL CHOICES

Parental Nudity and the Family Bed?

Some parents are concerned about the effects parental nudity may have on their children. "Will it traumatize my children or affect their sexual development negatively if I allow them to see me nude?" they ask. Others enjoy occasionally sleeping with their children in the "family bed." This is particularly true on weekends, when some parents like to lie in the bed and doze off with their children. Will their choice to do so have negative developmental effects on their children? Other parents are concerned that they may have already damaged their children, who walked in on the parents and observed them having intercourse. (This is known as the "primal scene.") To what degree should parents be concerned about these issues?

Research suggests that there is no cause for alarm. Okami (1995) reviewed the literature on each of these issues and concluded:

A number of commentators have characterized behaviors such as exposure to parental nudity, parent-child co-sleeping, and exposure to 'primal scenes' as forms of sexual abuse. . . . Surprisingly then—especially considering the vehemence with which these behaviors have been condemned in much of the clinical literature—there is little evidence to support dire predictions. (pp. 59–60)

Parents should be careful not to overreact to a child who walks in when they are having sex. To do so is to give the event an emotional valence unwarranted in the child's mind. Parents should bring the child back to his or her room and explain that they (the parents) were loving each other, which adults do in private. Parents should also remind the child that a closed door means he or she should knock and wait to be invited in (Packer, 1995).

Adolescence

Researchers disagree over when *adolescence* begins and ends. Some suggest that it begins at age 12 and ends at age 22. This time is further broken into different categories of adolescence: early adolescence (ages 12–15), middle adolescence (ages 15–18), and late adolescence (ages 18–22).

Numerous changes occur during adolescence. The most noticeable are the physical changes.

PHYSICAL CHANGES   The adolescent's body is undergoing rapid physiological and anatomical change. The very term *puberty* comes from the Latin *pubescere,* which means to be covered with hair. Pubic hair and underarm hair in young girls and pubic hair and facial hair in young boys are evidence that the hypothalamus is triggering the pituitary gland to release gonadotropins into the bloodstream. These are hormones that cause the testes in the male to increase testosterone production and the ovaries in the female to increase estrogen production.

Further physical changes in adolescence include the development of *secondary sex characteristics,* such as breasts in the female and a deepened voice in the male. A growth spurt also ensues, with girls preceding boys by about 2 years. The growth spurt is characterized by girls becoming taller than boys their age. Genitals of the respective sexes also enlarge (the penis and testes in the male and the labia in the female).

Internally, the prostate gland and seminal vesicles begin to function to make it possible for the young adolescent male to ejaculate. (Sperm is present in the ejaculate at about age 14.) First ejaculation usually occurs around age 13 or 14 but is variable.

Girls are experiencing their own internal changes. The uterus, cervix, and vaginal walls respond to hormone changes to produce the first menstruation, or menarche. This usually occurs between the ages of 12 and 13, but the timing is highly variable. Age of first menstruation and sexual maturity are important because they are associated with earlier dating and coital onset (Phinney, Jensen, Olsen, & Cundick, 1990).

A recent study of more than 17,000 girls seen in U. S. pediatric offices suggests that early puberty may be more common than previously realized (Herman-Giddens et al., 1997). A small number (3% of African Americans and 1% of whites) of girls as young as 3 years of age had breast or pubic hair development. The average age for breast development was 8.9 for African American girls and 10 for white girls, with similar ages for the development of pubic hair. Menstruation occurred at ages 12.2 and 12.9, respectively.

Male adolescents report various reactions to their changing bodies (Bell, 1987). Regarding erections:

> I get a hard-on in drama class almost every time I have to go up onstage. I can never tell if they are laughing at my performance or at my bulging cock. (p. 14)

Regarding first ejaculation:

> I heard everyone talking about coming and jacking off, and at fifteen I hadn't experienced it yet. It was real mysterious to me. I would try and try, masturbating every night, and even though it felt good, it didn't bring results. Finally one night, bang. It happened. (p. 15)

Regarding first wet dream:

> I was about thirteen. I felt like I had this total sexual experience in my dream and I woke up and thought, Wow, did this really happen or not? It blew my mind it felt so real. After a second I realized my pajamas were wet. I sort of knew what it had to be, but still I was a little surprised. (p.16)

Female adolescents are also responding to the physical changes in their bodies (Bell, 1987).

Regarding pubic hair:

> Me and my friends (age 11) go swimming at the center every week. In the shower there aren't any doors, so we kind of check each other out. Well, a couple of weeks ago, Amy showed me these hairs that were starting to grow down there, and I thought. Oh my God, that isn't going to happen to me, is it? Then I examined myself closer and I had three hairs there too. Three little dark hairs. (p. 25)

Regarding vaginal awareness:

> I figure it's a part of my body, just like any other part, except it's not right out there like your boobs are. Anyway, I sure as hell don't want someone else playing with it if I don't know what it is myself. (p. 26)

Regarding breast development:

> My mom and I are really close, and when I first started getting breasts she took me out to celebrate. It was around my tenth birthday, and I remember feeling very grown-up about it. (p. 21)

> When my breasts first started growing I used to wear really supertight shirts—to flatten me. Then I'd wear another shirt over that because I was really self-conscious. I was only in third grade and every other girl in the class was flat as a board. (p. 21)

A team of researchers (Duncan, Ritter, Dornbusch, Gross, & Carlsmith, 1990) reviewed the literature on pubertal timing and body image and found that early maturing in males is associated with being rated as more popular, relaxed, good-natured, and poised. However, data on girls have been inconsistent; some studies show that early maturing girls enjoy greater prestige and self-confidence, and others show that they are more self-conscious and less popular.

Duncan et al. (1990) also studied the effect of weight gain on self-image in adolescence. Girls regard it as getting fat, whereas boys view it as becoming more muscular. Data on over 5000 adolescents revealed that 69% of the early maturing girls, and only 27% of the late maturers, wanted to be thinner. In contrast, most early maturing boys (67%) were satisfied with their weight (Duncan et al., 1990).

Adolescents are particularly concerned about the degree to which their bodies match the cultural image and are unhappy about it when it does not. Girls are more likely to be dissatisfied with their body image than boys. Among female adolescents ages 13 to 19, 54% report being dissatisfied with their bodies; 41% of male adolescents the same age are dissatisfied (Garner, 1997).

PSYCHOLOGICAL CHANGES   In addition to physical changes, psychological changes also occur in adolescence. Psychological changes include moving from a state of childish dependence to a state of relative independence, resolving sexual identity issues, and feeling secure that one is normal. An example of adolescent ambivalence about growing up is the adolescent female who has a bottle of blow bubbles and a bottle of perfume on her bedroom dresser. Adolescents often want the freedom of adults but still have the dependence of children.

Resolving sexual identity issues requires becoming comfortable with one's sexual orientation. There are an estimated 2.9 million gay or lesbian adolescents in the United States. They have been described as an "invisible" minority within the schools that is just beginning to be acknowledged (Bailey & Phariss, 1996). Although we explore sexual orientation diversity in Chapter 16, it is important to emphasize the additional burden homosexual adolescents feel when they discover that they are not part of the heterosexual mainstream (Mercier & Berger, 1989).

Adolescents want to feel that they are normal (Campbell & Campbell, 1990). Part of this quest is to be normal in their sexual thoughts, feelings, and behaviors. Forty percent of 61 undergraduate men reported that they had "concerns about the normalcy of their sexual thoughts, feelings, or behaviors" (Metz & Seifert, 1990, p. 82).

So far, we have discussed the physical and psychological changes (dependence to independence, sexual identity, desire to be normal) that adolescents experience. Another significant occurrence during adolescence is the emerging importance of peers over parents in regard to language, dress, drugs, and sexual behavior. Researchers using data from the Carolina Population Center's Adolescent Sexuality Project observed that adolescents were more likely to engage in mildly deviant behavior (premarital intercourse, drinking, smoking, cheating) if their best friend of the same sex did (Rogers & Rowe, 1990). In addition, peers also become the major source of information about sex during adolescence (Andre, Frevert, & Schuchmann, 1989).

NEW SEXUAL BEHAVIORS   In addition to physical and psychological changes, adolescence is a time of sexual unfolding. Sarrel and Sarrel (1979) referred to "unfolding" as a process

> by which a person becomes aware of himself or herself as a sexual being, a male or female, who relates to oneself and others, sexually, in some characteristic ways. When unfolding is successful the person becomes capable of satisfying sexual and psychological intimacy with another (nonfamily) person (or persons). (p. 19)

The first kiss and first intercourse are primary experiences involved in the process of sexual unfolding. Kissing may occur in the context of a "sex game" (Markov, 1991). Such games are socially structured contexts for physical and sexual exploration. An example of a kissing game is spin-the-bottle, which is played by young adolescents at mixed-sex parties. There are three versions:

> In the first version, one member of the group is chosen as "it" and leaves the room. The remaining members gather in a circle and spin the bottle. Whomever the neck of the bottle points to when it stops spinning is to join the other person outside the room and "kiss." In the second version, the spinner is one of the kissing partners and the person the bottle stops spinning on is the other. They both leave the room and "kiss." In the third version, there are two circles, one of boys and one of girls. The bottle is spun twice so as to select the kissing partners. (Markov, 1991, p. 4)

As adolescence continues, mixed-sex group interactions give way to encounters between individuals in dating contexts. By age 16, over 85% of adolescents report having had their first date (Thornton, 1990). In his probability sample of adolescents, Thornton (1990) observed that the younger individuals were at the time they began to date, the more likely they were to develop steady dating relationships and to have intercourse.

First intercourse experiences are often characterized by anxiety, pain, fear and awkwardness. The following are descriptions of first intercourse experiences from the authors' classes:

> I was 15 and my partner was 16. I had two fears. The first was my fear of getting her pregnant the first time. The second was of "parking" in dark and desolate areas. Therefore, once we decided to have intercourse, we spent a boring evening waiting for my parents to go to sleep so we could move to the station wagon in the driveway.
>
> After near hyperventilation in an attempt to fog the windows (to prevent others from seeing in), we commenced to prepare for the long-awaited event. In recognition of my first fear, I wore four prophylactics. She, out of fear, was not lubricating well, and needless to say, I couldn't feel anything through four layers of latex.
>
> We were able to climax, which I attribute solely to sheer emotional excitement, yet both of us were later able to admit that the experience was disappointing. We knew it could only get better.
>
> My first intercourse was actually very nice—both physically and emotionally. I dated the same guy for four years in high school, and it wasn't until my senior year when we actually made love. I was nervous and we did not use any contraception, which doubled my nervousness. Also, for years my mother preached, "Nice girls don't." My philosophy is that nice girls do because they are the ones with the steady boyfriends.
>
> I had been dating this guy for almost a year when we first made love. The first time was not the best. It was quite painful physically, and I couldn't understand how people could find such enjoyment from sex.
>
> My first time I really felt nothing. I didn't know what to expect. I didn't feel guilty or sad or happy. I wasn't sorry it happened. I was not forced into the situation, and the guy was not in just for sex because we are still dating.
>
> My first intercourse experience was a disaster. Both the girl and I were virgins and had no idea what we were doing. Actually, we really didn't have intercourse the first time: she was so tight that I couldn't get inside of her. We gave up after 15 minutes.
>
> My first intercourse experience was simply terrible. There was no romance involved. He just came like a bull. He was the worst lover, ever. I was very hurt when he left me, but now I'm glad he did.
>
> My spouse and I waited until we were married to have intercourse. We felt that it would mean something special for us to wait and we are glad that we did. It was a "spiritual high" for both of us.

Deciding to engage in sexual intercourse during adolescence is influenced by one's closest peers. Two researchers observed that adolescents were more likely to engage in intercourse if their best friend of the same sex had engaged in intercourse (Rodgers & Rowe, 1990).

Average age at first intercourse in adolescence is related to race and gender, with African American men reporting intercourse shortly after age 15 and African American women around age 17. White men and women have intercourse at the average age of 17 (Michael, Gagnon, Laumann, & Kolata, 1994). A study of junior high school students revealed that adolescent females are more likely than males to believe that the sex urge can be controlled and to report having had fewer sex partners (DeGaston, Weed, & Jensen, 1996). Factors associated with sexual activity among both female and male high school students are alcohol use and high levels of stress (Harvey & Spigner, 1995). Adolescents who had their first sexual experience before age 14 were more likely to use controlled substances, have mothers who were sexually active as teens, and have mothers who worked extensively (Mott, Fondell, Hu, Kowaleski-Jones, & Menaghan, 1996).

Condom use is influenced by the type of relationship the adolescent has with his or her partner. In a study of 75 sexually experienced adolescents (mean age 16.6), condom use was highest with one-night-stand partners (61%) and lowest with steady partners (57%) (Ellen, Cahn, Eyre, & Boyer, 1996). In another study, adolescents were most likely to use condoms if they felt their partners supported condom use (Santelli et al., 1996). 🍂 In contrast to U.S. data, a national survey in Japan showed that Japanese students do not begin having intercourse until they are at least 20 years old, and most use a contraceptive method ("Most Japanese Students," 1997). 🍂

In this chapter's Social Choices section, we address the issue of whether or not adolescents are competent to make independent choices concerning abortion.

THINK ABOUT IT

How might the experiences of infants and young children influence their sexuality during adolescence? How might a negative parental reaction to masturbation, being overweight as a child, and having sexually conservative or permissive parents contribute to a child's sexual development?

SEXUALITY IN EARLY ADULTHOOD

Early adulthood can be defined as the period from age 23 (late adolescence ending at age 22) to age 40 (the beginning of middle age). A number of theorists who have proposed stage models of life-span development have identified the early to middle adult years as focusing on intimate partnerships. Erikson (1968) conceptualized the developmental crisis of intimacy versus isolation. In her description of adult passages, Sheehy (1976) named crises from the twenties to the forties: "the urge to merge," "the couple knot, the single spot, the rebound," and "switch-40s and the couple." Bancroft (1989, p. 149) defined "marriage (or the establishment of a stable sexual relationship)" as the fourth basic stage of sexual development. However, people do not necessarily follow the maps of popular stage theories. For example, for young

women, the intimacy developmental focus cede the identity crisis (Fischer, 1981)—an "no right or only time" (Tavris, 1992, p. 38) to experience developmental milestones. Nevertheless, intimate relationships are important in early adulthood.

Most individuals (93% of young men and 78% of young women) move into adulthood (age 20 and beyond) as never-marrieds, most (90% of both sexes) eventually marry, over half divorce, and most (particularly women—66% by age 75) become widows. Not all relationships are heterosexual or marriage-focused. Sexuality among adults may also be among homosexuals in casual dating or committed relationships.

Sexuality Among the Never-Married

One of the basic choices during young adulthood is whether to remain single. An increasing percentage of young adults are opting to remain single into their late 20s.

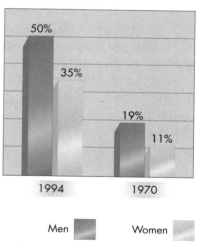

NATIONAL DATA

Adult men and women in the U.S. who had never been married

50% | 35% | 19% | 11%

1994 | 1970

Men | Women

Source: Saluter, 1996.

Although most people eventually marry, social support for singlehood is stronger today than it has ever been in the United States.

> At the most basic level, more people today can choose if, who, and when to marry. There is less pressure to marry, and less, if any stigma to living alone or cohabiting. Choosing not to marry does not prevent people from being sexually active. . . . (Jones, Tepperman, & Wilson, 1995, p. 14)

ARE ADOLESCENTS COMPETENT TO MAKE ABORTION DECISIONS?

In most states, parental consent must be obtained before medical services can be delivered to minors (adolescents under the age of 18). However, in many states, an exception is made for services related to sensitive health care concerns, such as sexuality, substance abuse, and mental health. Health professionals recognize that minors may be reluctant to seek health care if they are required to tell their parents or obtain parental consent.

An adolescent's capacity to independently make decisions regarding abortion has been the focus of legislation in many states. Most states have enacted laws requiring parental involvement. Parental consent is required before a minor can obtain an abortion in 26 states; 12 states require parental notification. Connecticut and Wisconsin require counseling, and Maine requires either counseling or consent from a parent or an adult relative. Only 11 states and the District of Columbia have not restricted minors' access to abortion (Haffner, 1992). In some states, a judicial bypass procedure is available, in which a judge can rule to bypass the parental involvement if the minor is judged sufficiently mature to give her own consent, or if it is judged that parental notification is not in her best interests (Greenberger & Connor, 1991).

Legislation that restricts adolescents' access to abortion is based on the assumption that "adolescents are less likely than adults to make sound decisions when they are faced with an unintended pregnancy" (Interdivisional Committee on Adolescent Abortion, 1987, p. 73). A number of psychologists have challenged this assumption. A review of child development and psychological research does not reveal evidence of the belief that adolescents lack decision-making skills (Lewis, 1987). For example, Lewis (1987) reported several studies affirming that minors

with low self-perceived competence and high conflict regarding the pregnancy decision were more likely to involve their parents in the abortion decision. In another study, 75 young women who were seeking a pregnancy test completed an audiotaped interview that was scored on four criteria of legal competence. All of the adolescents who considered abortion appeared as competent as legal adults. Only adolescents who were age 15 or younger who did not consider abortion appeared less competent (Ambuel & Rappaport, 1992). Lewis (1987) cited another study revealing that although high school students generate fewer alternative solutions to hypothetical stories than college students, the high school students were better able to generate potential consequences. Lewis argued that minors may be as competent as adults in reasoning about decisions, but the social circumstances in which they function may limit their ability to implement their reasoning.

As policymakers continue to struggle with the issue of adolescent access to abortion, they may choose either to consider or to ignore Lewis's (1987) conclusion: "At present, psychological research gives no basis for restrictions on minors' privacy in decision making on the ground of competence alone" (p. 87).

Ambuel, B., & Rappaport, J. (1992). Developmental trends in adolescents' psychological and legal competence to consent to abortion. *Law and Human Behavior, 16*(2), 129–154.

Greenberger, M. D., & Connor, K. (1991). Parental notice and consent for abortion: Out of step with family law principles and policies. *Family Planning Perspectives, 23*, 31–35.

Haffner, D. W. (1992). Report card on the states: Sexual rights in America. *SIECUS Report, 20*(3), 1–7.

Interdivisional Committee on Adolescent Abortion. (1987). Adolescent abortion: Psychological and legal issues. *American Psychologist, 42*, 73–78.

Lewis, C. C. (1987). Minors' competence to consent to abortion. *American Psychologist, 42*, 84–88.

The primary advantage of remaining single is freedom and control over one's life. Once a decision has been made to involve another person in one's life, it follows that one's choices become vulnerable to the influence of the other. The person who chooses to

remain single views such restrictions on freedom as something to avoid.

Freedom to have sex with whomever one chooses is another perceived advantage of remaining single. One hundred percent of men and 100% of women in

Benefits of Singlehood	Limitations of Marriage
• Freedom to do as one wishes • Responsible for oneself only • Close friends of both sexes • Spontaneous lifestyle • Feeling of self-sufficiency • Spend money as wish • Freedom to move as career dictates • Avoid being controlled by spouse • Avoid emotional and financial stress of divorce	• Restricted by spouse or children • Responsible for spouse and children • Pressure to avoid close other-sex friendships • Routine, predictable lifestyle • Potential to feel dependent • Expenditures influenced by needs of spouse and children • Restrictions on career mobility • Potential to be controlled by spouse • Possibility of divorce

a random sample of heterosexual undergraduates at a Midwestern university reported having engaged in vaginal intercourse. The average age of the first experience was 17 for both sexes, with men reporting eight partners and women reporting six (Reinisch et al., 1995). Although the never-married report having intercourse, there may be considerable time between occasions of intercourse. In one study, about 25% of adult men and 30% of adult women not living with a partner reported not having had intercourse in the last year (Michael et al., 1994).

Some individuals who decide to remain single also decide to live together. Indeed, over 3.6 million unmarried couples live together (Saluter, 1996). By the time they reach their thirties, almost half of the U.S. adult population report having cohabitated with

Individuals not involved in a relationship report the least frequent and least satisfying sex life.

someone (Nock, 1995). The various types of never-married couples who live together can be categorized as follows:

• Adventurers—new partners who have an affectionate relationship and want to live together because they enjoy each other. They are focused on the here and now, not the future of the relationship.
• Testers—couples involved in a good relationship who want to assess if staying together and getting married would be right for them.
• Engaged—couples in love and planning to marry.
• Alternative avoiders—couples who don't like the idea of living alone, dating an array of partners, or getting married. Living together is their best alternative.
• Career seekers—couples who enjoy each other for now but are on respective career paths that will probably separate them eventually.
• Money savers—couples who live together primarily out of economic convenience. They are open to the possibility of a future together but regard such a possibility as unlikely.
• Teenagers—some young couples feel that they are not developmentally ready to take on the social expectations of marriage as an institution. They are most likely in their teens and want to wait until they are older to marry. In the meantime, they enjoy living together.

- Cohabitants forever—couples who view living together as a permanent alternative to marriage. They plan to stay together but never marry. They regard marriage as a relationship defined by the couple rather than as an institution defined by society and culture.

Living with a partner (*cohabitation*) is associated with a higher frequency of intercourse than not living with a partner. In a national sample, among those who were living together, none of the men and only 1% of the women reported no intercourse in the last 12 months (Michael et al., 1994, p. 116).

Although there may be long intervals between partners, a higher number of partners is reported by those who are not married and not living together. Nine percent of the never-married and not living together reported having had five or more sexual partners in the last 12 months; 5% and 1% of the cohabitants and marrieds reported the same (Michael et al., 1994, p. 102).

Condom use among the unmarried has also been studied. Among a nationally representative sample of 932 sexually experienced unmarried women aged 17 to 44, 41% reported using condoms for protection against sexually transmitted diseases; 30% reported using condoms specifically to prevent STDs. Only 4% said that prevention of pregnancy was their sole reason for using a condom (Anderson, Brackbill, & Mosher, 1996).

The never-married may be particularly vulnerable to engaging in high-risk sexual behavior with multiple partners. This chapter's Self-Assessment allows you to determine the degree to which you engage in behavior that involves a high risk for HIV infection.

Sexuality Among the Married

In spite of the perceived benefits of singlehood or living together, more than 90% of both women and men eventually marry (*Statistical Abstract of the United States: 1997,* Table 48). More than five million individuals decide to marry each year (National Center for Health Statistics, 1997).

Marital sex is characterized by its social legitimacy, declining frequency, and physical and emotional satisfaction.

SOCIAL LEGITIMACY   In our society, marital intercourse is the most legitimate form of sexual behavior. Homosexual, premarital, and extramarital intercourse do not enjoy similar social approval. It is not only OK to have intercourse when married, it is expected. People assume that married couples make love and that something is wrong if they do not.

DECLINING FREQUENCY   The frequency of marital intercourse declines across time. In a study of 100 well-educated, middle-class couples, 59% of those who had been married less than 10 years reported having intercourse more than once a week. In contrast, 20% of those who had been married 20 years or longer reported having intercourse more than once a week (Frank & Anderson, 1989).

Reasons for declining frequency are employment, children, and satiation. Regarding the impact of employment, one spouse said:

> Exhaustion is a very big problem. I never thought it could happen. When I'm working and running my business, it is totally absorbing and it takes me a long time to decompress at night, by which time Jerry is usually sound asleep! And I guess Jerry, unlike when we first got married, has a lot of responsibility in his position—so it's work that's taking its toll on our sex life! (Greenblat, 1983, p. 296)

Children also decrease the frequency of intercourse by their presence and by the toll they take on the caregiver's energy. Frank and Anderson (1989) noted, "The never-ending responsibilities and interruptions of child-caring may be a much greater distraction from sexual pleasure than holding a full-time job" (p. 193).

Psychologists use the term *satiation* to mean that repeated exposure to a stimulus results in the loss of its ability to reinforce. For example, the first time you listen to a new recording, you derive considerable enjoyment and satisfaction from it. You may play it over and over during the first few days. But after a week or so, listening to the same music is no longer new and does not give you the same level of enjoyment that it first did. So it is with intercourse. The thousandth time that a person has intercourse with the same partner is not as new and exciting as the first few times. Although intercourse can remain very

STUDENT SEXUAL RISKS SCALE (SSRS)

The following self-assessment allows you to evaluate the degree to which you may be at risk for engaging in behavior that could lead to HIV infection. Safer sex means sexual activity that reduces the risk of HIV transmission. Using condoms is an example of safer sex. Unsafe, risky, or unprotected sex refers to sex without a condom or to other activity that might increase the risk of HIV transmission. For each of the following items, check the response that best characterizes your opinion.

A = Agree   U = Undecided   D = Disagree

A U D

1. If my partner wanted me to have unprotected sex, I would probably give in.
2. The proper use of a condom can enhance sexual pleasure.
3. I may have had sex with someone who was at risk for HIV and AIDS.
4. If I were going to have sex, I would take precautions to reduce my risk of HIV and AIDS.
5. Condoms ruin the natural sex act.
6. When I think that one of my friends might have sex on a date, I ask them if they have a condom.
7. I am at risk for HIV and AIDS.
8. I would try to use a condom if I had sex.
9. Condoms interfere with romance.
10. My friends talk a lot about safer sex.
11. If my partner wanted me to participate in risky sex and I said that we needed to be safer, we would still probably end up having unsafe sex.
12. Generally, I am in favor of using condoms.
13. I would avoid using condoms if at all possible.
14. If a friend knew that I might have sex on a date, he or she would ask me if I had a condom.
15. There is a possibility that I might be HIV-positive.

A U D

16. If I had a date, I would probably not drink alcohol or use drugs.
17. Safer sex reduces the mental pleasure of sex.
18. If I thought that one of my friends had sex on a date, I would ask them if they used a condom.
19. The idea of using a condom doesn't appeal to me.
20. Safer sex is a habit for me.
21. If a friend knew that I had sex on a date, he or she wouldn't care if I had used a condom or not.
22. If my partner wanted me to participate in risky sex and I suggested a lower-risk alternative, we would have the safer sex instead.
23. The sensory aspects (smell, touch, texture) of condoms make them unpleasant.
24. I intend to follow safer-sex guidelines within the next year.
25. With condoms, you can't really "give yourself over" to your partner.
26. I am determined to practice safer sex.
27. If my partner wanted me to have unprotected sex and I made some excuse to use a condom, we would still end up having unprotected sex.

Continued on following page.

28. If I had sex and I told my friends ___ ___ ___ that I did not use a condom, they would be angry or disappointed.

29. I think safer sex would get boring ___ ___ ___ fast.

30. My sexual experiences do not put ___ ___ ___ me at risk for HIV and AIDS.

31. Condoms are irritating.   ___ ___ ___

32. Before dates, my friends and I en- ___ ___ ___ courage each other to practice safer sex.

33. When I socialize, I usually drink ___ ___ ___ alcohol or use drugs.

34. If I were going to have sex in the ___ ___ ___ next year, I would use condoms.

35. If a sexual partner didn't want to ___ ___ ___ use a condom, we would have sex without using one.

36. People can get the same pleasure ___ ___ ___ from safer sex as they can from unprotected sex.

37. Using condoms interrupts sex play. ___ ___ ___

38. It is a hassle to use condoms.   ___ ___ ___

Scoring: Begin by giving yourself 80 points. Subtract one point for every undecided response. Subtract two points every time that you agreed with an odd-numbered item or with item number 38. Subtract two points for each time you disagreed with even-numbered items 2 through 36.

Interpreting Your Score:

Research shows that students who get higher scores on the SSRS are more likely to engage in risky sexual activities, such as having multiple sex partners and failing to consistently use condoms during sex. In contrast, students who practice safer sex tend to endorse more positive attitudes toward safer sex, and tend to have peer networks that encourage safer sexual practices. These students usually plan on making sexual activity safer, and feel confident in their ability to negotiate safer sex—even when a dating partner pushes for riskier sex. Students who practice safer sex often refrain from using alcohol or drugs (which may impede negotiation of safer sex) and report having engaged in lower-risk sexual activities in the past. How do you measure up?

Lower Risk (Below 15)   Of the 200 students surveyed by DeHart and Birkimer (1997), 16% were in this category. If your score falls into this category, congratulations! Your score on the SSRS indicates that relative to other students, your thoughts and behaviors are more supportive of safer sex. Is there any room for improvement in your score? If so, you may want to examine items for which you lost points and try to build safer sexual strengths in those areas. You can help protect others from HIV transmission by educating your peers about how to make sexual activity safer.

Average Risk (15 to 37)   Of the 200 students surveyed by DeHart and Birkimer, 68% were in this category. Your score on the SSRS is about average in comparison to other college students. Though it is good that you don't fall into the higher risk category, be aware that people with an average risk can get HIV, too. In fact, a recent study indicated that the rate of HIV among college students is 10 times that of the general heterosexual population. Thus, you may want to enhance your sexual safety by figuring out where you lost points and working toward safer sexual strengths in those areas.

Higher risk (38 and above)   Of the 200 students surveyed by DeHart and Birkimer, 16% were in this category. Relative to other students, your score on the SSRS indicates that your thoughts and behaviors are less supportive of safer sex. Such high scores tend to be associated with riskier sexual behavior and a higher risk for HIV transmission. Rather than simply giving in to riskier attitudes and behaviors, you may want to empower yourself and reduce your risk by critically examining areas for improvement. On which items did you lose points? Think about how you can strengthen your sexual safety in these areas. Reading more about safer sex can help, and sometimes colleges and health clinics offer courses or workshops on safer sex. You can get more information about resources in your area by contacting the CDC's HIV and AIDS Information Line at 1-800-342-2437.

Scale developed specifically for this text by Dana D. DeHart, University of South Carolina; John C. Birkimer, University of Louisville. Reproduced by permission of Dr. Dana DeHart.

satisfying for couples in long-term relationships (Frank & Anderson, 1989), satiation may result in decreased frequency of intercourse.

Some spouses do not have intercourse at all. One percent of husbands and 3% of wives in a nationwide study of sexuality reported that they had not had intercourse in the past 12 months (Michael et al., 1994, p. 116). Ill health, age, sexual orientation, stress, depression, and conflict are some of the reasons for not having intercourse with one's spouse. Such an arrangement may be accompanied by either limited or extensive affection.

EMOTIONAL AND PHYSICAL SATISFACTION In spite of the declining frequency, marital sex remains physically and emotionally satisfying (Michael et al., 1994). Contrary to the popular belief that unattached singles have the best sex, it is the married and pair-bonded adults who enjoy the most satisfying sexual relationships. Eighty-eight percent of married people said they received great physical pleasure from their sexual lives, and almost 85% said they received great emotional satisfaction (Michael et al., 1994). Individuals least likely to report being physically and emotionally pleased in their sexual relationships were those who were not married, not living with anyone, and not in a stable relationship with one person.

One study found that the most important variable affecting a woman's satisfaction with her sexual relationship was her marital adjustment; age was not related to sexual satisfaction (Hawton, Gath, & Gay, 1994). Other research has also found that positive sexual relations are associated with perceptions of psychological intimacy for both women and men (although more so for women) (Oggins, Leber, & Veroff, 1993).

Sexuality Among the Divorced

Between 40 to 50% of individuals who marry will eventually divorce. Of the more than 2 million who divorce each year, most will have intercourse within one year of being separated from their spouse. The meanings of intercourse for the separated or divorced vary. For many, intercourse is a way to reestablish—indeed, repair—their crippled self-esteem. Questions like "What did I do wrong?' 'Am I a failure?" and "Is there anybody out there who will love me again?" loom in the minds of the divorced. One way to feel loved, at least temporarily, is through sex. Being held by another and being told that it feels good gives people some evidence that they are desirable. Because divorced people may be particularly vulnerable, they may reach for sexual encounters as if for a lifeboat. "I felt that as long as someone was having sex with me, I wasn't dead and I did matter," said one recently divorced person.

NATIONAL DATA

Individuals who reported having had between two and four sexual partners in the past 12 months

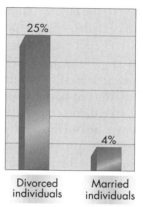

Source: Michael et al., 1994, p. 102.

Whereas some divorced people use sex to mend their self-esteem, others use it to test their sexual adequacy. The divorced person may have been told by the former spouse that he or she was an inept lover. One man said his wife used to make fun of him because he was occasionally impotent. Intercourse with a new partner who did not belittle him reassured him of his sexual adequacy, and his impotence ceased to be a problem. A woman described how her husband would sneer at her body and say no man would ever want her because she was so fat. After the divorce, she found a man who thought she was attractive and who did not consider her weight to be a problem. Other divorced men and women say that things their spouses did not like, their new partners view as turn-ons. The result is a renewed sense of sexual desirability.

Beyond these motives for sexual interactions, many divorced people simply enjoy the sexual freedom their divorced state offers. Freed from the guilt that spouses who have extramarital intercourse experience, the divorced can have intercourse with whomever they choose.

Before getting remarried, most divorced people seem to go through predictable stages of sexual expression. The initial impact of the separation is followed by a variable period of emotional pain. During this time, the divorced may turn to sex for intimacy to soothe some of the pain, although this is rarely achieved.

This stage of looking for intimacy through intercourse overlaps with the divorced person's feeling of freedom and the desire to explore a wider range of sexual partners and behaviors than marriage provided. "I was a virgin at marriage and was married for 12 years. I've never had sex with anyone but my spouse, so I'm curious to know what other people are like sexually," one divorced person said.

Divorced women are often perceived as more sexually experienced than single women. Apt and Hurlbert (1995) assessed the perceptions men had of a photograph of a woman who was identified either as being single or as being divorced. When the woman was identified as being divorced, she was perceived as having greater "sexual experience" and "sexual knowledge" and as being more "sexually assertive" and "promiscuous."

Because divorced people are usually in their thirties, they may not be as sensitized to the danger of contracting HIV as persons in their twenties. Yet HIV is not a youth disease. In the United States, 60% of male HIV diagnoses (reported through 1996) were among men ages 30 and older; 51% of female HIV diagnoses were among women ages 30 and older (Centers for Disease Control and Prevention, 1996). Divorced individuals who are sexually active with a number of partners should always use a condom.

THINK ABOUT IT

Why do you think married individuals are more likely than singles or divorced individuals to report high levels of emotional and physical satisfaction in their sexual relationships?

SEXUALITY IN THE MIDDLE YEARS

Age, like sexuality, is largely socially defined. Cultural definitions of "old" and "young" vary from society to society, from time to time, and from person to person. For example, the older a person is, the less likely it is that he or she will define a particular age as old. In a national study of 2503 men and women ages 18 to 75, 30% of those under 25 believed that 40 to 64 years of age is considered "old." But, among those over the age of 65, only 8% reported that 65 was old (Clements, 1993). With an average life expectancy of 20 years in ancient Greece or Rome, a person was old at the age of 18; a person was old at 30 in medieval Europe; and in 1850, a person was old at the age of 40 in the United States.

Middle age is commonly thought to occur between the ages of 40 and 60. The U.S. Census Bureau regards a person at age 45 as middle-aged. Family life specialists define middle age as beginning when the last child leaves home and continuing until retirement or the death of either spouse. Regardless of how middle age is defined, it is a time of transition for women, men, and their sexuality. In general, beginning at age 50, there appears to be a gradual continuous decline in sexual interest and activity. Some of this decline is a function of normal aging, and some may be related to age-related disease processes. A major change in the sexuality of women is the experience of going through menopause. For men, sexual changes are associated with a decrease in testosterone.

Women and Menopause

Menopause is the primary physical event for middle-aged women. Defined as the permanent cessation of menstruation, menopause is caused by the gradual decline of estrogen produced by the ovaries. It occurs around age 50 for most women but may begin much earlier or later. Signs that the woman may be nearing menopause include decreased menstrual flow and a less predictable cycle. After 12 months with no period, the woman is said to be through menopause. During this time, the woman should use some form of contraception. Women with irregular periods may remain at risk for pregnancy for up to 24 months following their last menstrual period.

While the term *climacteric* is often used synonymously with menopause, it refers to changes that both men and women experience. The term menopause refers only to the time when the menstrual flow permanently stops, whereas climacteric refers to the whole process of hormonal change induced by the ovaries or testes, pituitary gland, and hypothalamus. Reactions to such hormonal changes may include hot flashes, in which the woman feels a sudden rush of heat from the waist up. Hot flashes are often accompanied by an increased reddening of the skin surface and a drenching perspiration. Other symptoms may include heart palpitations, dizziness, irritability, headaches, backache, and weight gain. Wing, Matthews, Kuller, Meilahn, and Plantinga (1991) noted that weight gain is a normal occurrence for women during menopause, which increases their risk of coronary heart disease.

For 85% of women, the symptoms associated with decreasing levels of estrogen will stop within one year of their final period. "But for those who are in too much misery to wait it out, estrogen can do wonders" (Wallis, 1995, p. 51).

To minimize the effects of decreasing levels of estrogen, some physicians recommend estrogen replacement therapy (ERT), particularly to control hot flashes, night sweats, and vaginal dryness. Researchers do not agree on the advisability of women's taking such therapy, also referred to as HRT (hormone replacement therapy) or postmenopausal hormone therapy. Although HRT reduces the risk of heart attacks, colon cancer, and osteoporosis and keeps the skin looking plumped up and moist, it is associated with an increased risk of breast and ovarian cancer (Folsom, Mink, Sellars, Hong, & Potter, 1995). Although a new drug, Raloxifene, appears to help protect women's bones from osteoporosis without increasing the risks of heart disease and cancer, women who have a high risk for breast or uterine cancer or have clotting problems should not take estrogen. A woman considering hormonal therapy should be counseled regarding the potential risks and benefits—in consideration of her symptoms and risk factors—so that she may make an informed choice regarding its use. One community survey found that 32% of women ages 50 to 65 reported taking hormones (Fogel & Woods, 1995).

While studies have documented the incidence of depression and anxiety in women during mid-life, research that blames its incidence on menopause has been criticized for being based on samples of women seeking medical help. The effect of hormonal alterations on mood has not been clearly delineated. However, the mood changes that are reported by some women during menopause may be due to a combination of factors, including hormonal changes, normal aging processes, dietary and lifestyle habits, social and psychological transitions, and cultural beliefs and expectations (Fogel & Woods, 1995).

A cross-cultural look at menopause suggests that a woman's reaction to this phase of her life may be related to the society in which she lives. For example, among Chinese women, fewer menopausal symptoms have been observed. Researchers have suggested that this may be true because older women in China are highly respected, as are older people generally. Researchers Karen Matthews and Nancy Avis conducted a longitudinal study of 541 women as they progressed through menopause and found that the negative expectations our society has of the menopausal years "may cause at least some of the problems women experience" (quoted in Adler, 1991, p. 14).

Men and the Decrease in Testosterone

The climacteric for men is usually less profound. It involves a decrease in testosterone production that begins at about age 40 and continues until age 60, when it levels off. A 20-year-old man usually has twice the amount of testosterone in his system as a 60-year-old man (Young, 1990). The decline is not inevitable but is related to general health status.

The consequences of lowered testosterone include more difficulty in getting and maintaining a firm erection; greater ejaculatory control, with the possibility of more prolonged erections; less consistency in achieving orgasm; fewer genital spasms during orgasm; a qualitative change from an intense, genitally focused sensation to a more diffused and generalized feeling of pleasure; and an increase in the length of the refractory period—the period after orgasm during which the man is unable to ejaculate again or have another erection.

These physiological changes in the middle-aged man, along with psychological changes, have sometimes been referred to as male menopause. During this period, the man may experience nervousness, hot flashes, insomnia, and lack of interest in sex. But these changes most often occur over a long period of time, and the anxiety and depression some men experience seem to be as much related to their life situation (lack of career success) as to hormonal alterations.

A middle-aged man who is not successful in his career is often forced to recognize that he will never achieve what he had hoped but instead will carry his unfulfilled dreams to the grave. This knowledge may be coupled with his awareness of diminishing sexual vigor. For the man who has been taught that masculinity is measured by career success and sexual prowess, middle age may be particularly difficult.

─────── **THINK ABOUT IT** ───────

What cultural and social factors influence the psychological effects of menopause in women and lower testosterone in men? How might Chinese and American women differ in their response to menopause?

EXTRADYADIC SEXUAL INVOLVEMENTS

The public crisis Kathie Lee and Frank Gifford endured over his extramarital encounter with a flight attendant in 1997 emphasized that such experiences do occur and that they often are very difficult events for individuals, couples, and families. Extradyadic sexual involvements (external to the dyad) may occur at any point in the life cycle (from late adolescence through the later years) and between individuals of any sexual orientation. Individuals who are involved with one partner sometimes find themselves emotionally and sexually attracted to others. It is a myth that people in stable love relationships are no longer attracted to others. Indeed, because of the reality of such potential attraction, partners in a relationship can benefit from addressing this issue.

The term *extradyadic* includes sexual involvement with someone other than the person one is involved with in an emotional and sexual relationship. While the term *extramarital* refers to the attraction of a spouse to someone other than the mate, extradyadic refers to all pair-bonded individuals who are attracted to someone other than the partner.

The terms "cheating," "unfaithfulness," and "infidelity" reflect societal disapproval in reference to extramarital sexual involvements.

NATIONAL DATA

Based on a national sample of adults in the United States, men and women who agreed that extramarital sex is "always wrong"

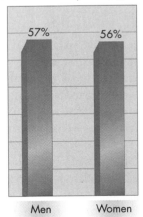

Source: Wiederman, 1997, p. 171.

Studies disagree on the extent of extramarital sex. Although earlier studies on nonrandom convenience samples found that about 50% of husbands and wives had extramarital sex (Thompson, 1983), large, national, random samples have shown much smaller percentages.

NATIONAL DATA

Based on a national sample of adults in the United States, currently married men and women who have had extramarital sex

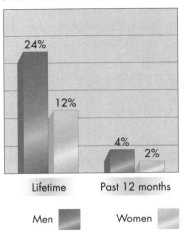

Source: Wiederman, 1997, pp. 170–171.

Types of Extradyadic Sexual Involvements

Extradyadic encounters include brief sexual encounters, romantic affairs, open marriages, swinging, and computer affairs.

BRIEF SEXUAL ENCOUNTERS   Extradyadic involvements that are brief and involve little to no emotional investment are referred to as brief sexual encounters. The lyrics to the song "Strangers in the Night" describe two people exchanging glances who end up having sex "before the night is through." Although the partners may see each other again, more often than not, their sexual encounter is a one-night stand. Sexual involvement with prostitutes or with women who offer sex in massage parlors may also be viewed as a brief sexual encounter.

ROMANTIC AFFAIRS   Intense reciprocal emotional feelings characterize many romantic affairs. The affair between Francesca Johnson and Robert Kincaid, as personified in the novel and movie *The Bridges of Madison County,* depicted a romantic affair. One condition of such love affairs is restriction. The "Bridges" couple was restricted by marriage and children (hers) and by time (he would be with her only 4 days). Such limited access makes the time that romantic lovers spend together very special. In addition, the lover in a romantic affair is not associated with the struggles of marriage—bills, child care, washing dishes, cleaning house, mowing the lawn—and so may experience the affair from a more romantic perspective. The Personal Choices feature at the end of this section considers the effects of extramarital affairs on marriage relationships.

OPEN MARRIAGES   *Open marriages* are those in which the spouses regard their own relationship as primary but agree that each will have sexual relationships with others. Unlike affairs, extramarital sex in open marriages involves no dishonesty because each spouse is aware of the partner's having sex with someone else. The concept of open marriage may also apply to cohabiting couples.

When 35 couples in sexually open marriages were compared with 35 married couples who did not have sexually open marriages, the open-marriage couples reported greater satisfaction with their marital sexual relationship. The researchers (Wheeler & Kilmann, 1983) commented that for some couples

engaging in recreational sexual activities with outside partners apparently does not interfere with each member's perception of a positive marital sexual relationship; for these couples, it may be that their marital sexual relationship is enhanced by agreed-on sexual contact with outside partners. This may not be the case for couple members who engage in covert extramarital sexual relationships, often as an "escape" from a dysfunctional marital relationship. (p. 304)

Although a motivation for becoming involved in an open marriage is to enhance the couple's sexual and marital relationship, most of these relationships do not last. Even the originators of the concept of open marriage, Nena and George O'Neill, have since divorced. Because most individuals in our society are socialized to emphasize fidelity as important in marriage, including others sexually (even with the knowledge and approval of the mate) in one's marriage is unacceptable and problematic for oneself, one's partner, and one's marriage.

SWINGING   *Swinging,* also referred to as comarital sex, exists when the partners of one marriage or committed relationship have sexual relations with the partners of another relationship. Swinging is similar to sexually open relationships in that it involves mutual consent between the partners for extradyadic sexual activity. However, swinging is unique in that it is a more couple-oriented activity. Bringle and Buunk (1991) describe swinging as

extramarital sexual relationships [that] occur with both persons present and only within specified times and settings. The actual sexual contact may be open (occurs in the presence of others) or closed (occurs in separate rooms); in either case, the participants most typically arrive as a couple and depart as a couple. Furthermore, the sexual activity is, to a greater extent than with open marriages, engaged in for its own sake. The philosophy is one of recreational, body-oriented sexuality rather than emotional involvement and personal growth. (p. 148)

COMPUTER AFFAIRS   Although, legally, two individuals must have physical sex before their relationship is defined as adultery, an on-line computer affair can be just as disruptive to a marriage or a couple's relationship (Fletcher, 1996). Computer friendships that move to feelings of intimacy involve secrecy (one's partner does not know the level of involvement), include sexual tension (even though there is no overt sex), and take the time, attention, energy, and affection away from one's partner. "There is really another person there, and that person can move you in various ways, emotionally and sexually" (Turkle, 1996). One New Jersey husband sued his wife for divorce, claiming that his wife committed infidelity during dozens of sexually explicit exchanges on America Online (Peterson, 1996).

Motivations for Extradyadic Sexual Encounters

Partners involved in committed relationships report a number of reasons why they become involved in extradyadic sexual relationships. Some of these reasons are discussed in the following subsections.

VARIETY, NOVELTY, AND EXCITEMENT   Extradyadic sexual involvement may be motivated by the desire for variety, novelty, and excitement (Bringle & Buunk, 1991). One of the characteristics of sex in long-term committed relationships is the tendency for it to become routine. Early in a relationship, the partners seemingly cannot have sex often enough. But with constant availability, the partners may achieve a level of satisfaction, and the attractiveness and excitement of sex with the primary partner seem to wane. The *Coolidge effect* is a term used to describe this waning of sexual excitement and the effect of novelty and variety on sexual arousal:

> One day President and Mrs. Coolidge were visiting a government farm. Soon after their arrival, they were taken off on separate tours. When Mrs. Coolidge passed the chicken pens, she paused to ask the man in charge if the rooster copulated more than once each day. "Dozens of times," was the reply. "Please tell that to the President," Mrs. Coolidge requested. When the President passed the pens and was told about the rooster, he asked, "Same hen every time?" "Oh no, Mr. President, a different one each time." The President nodded slowly, and then said, "Tell that to Mrs. Coolidge." (Bermant, 1976, pp. 76–77)

The Coolidge effect illustrates the effect of novelty and variety on the copulation behaviors of roosters, not humans. Varying levels of sexual novelty and variety may, indeed, be important for achieving sexual satisfaction for many individuals. However, unlike roosters, humans need not have multiple sexual partners to experience novelty and variety. Rather,

Work provides a context where people meet and become involved.

humans may create sexual novelty and variety within a monogamous relationship by having sex in novel places, exploring different intercourse positions, engaging in a variety of noncoital petting behaviors, wearing a variety of erotic clothing, watching erotic films, and utilizing sexual fantasies.

FRIENDSHIP   Extradyadic sexual involvements may develop from friendships. The extramarital involvements of women are more likely to develop out of friendships than those of men (Atwater, 1979). Friendships that develop into extradyadic sexual relationships often begin in the workplace. Co-workers share the same world 8 to 10 hours a day and, over a period of time, may develop good feelings for each other that eventually lead to a sexual relationship. The skill of having a nonsexual relationship with a close and intimate friend may be useful in a variety of contexts.

RELATIONSHIP DISSATISFACTION   It is commonly believed that people who have affairs are not happy in their marriage, but this is more likely to be true of wives than of husbands. Men who have affairs often are not dissatisfied with the quality of their marriage or their sexual relationship with their wife (Yablonsky, 1979). Rather, men often seek extramarital relationships as an additional life experience.

One source of relationship dissatisfaction is an unfulfilling sexual relationship. Some people engage in extradyadic sex because their partner is not interested in sex. Others may go outside the relationship because their partners will not engage in the sexual behaviors they want and enjoy. The unwillingness of the spouse to engage in oral sex, anal intercourse, or a variety of sexual positions sometimes results in the other partner looking elsewhere for a more cooperative sexual partner.

REVENGE   Some extradyadic sexual involvements are acts of revenge against one's partner for engaging in extradyadic sexual activity. When partners find out that their mate has had or is having an affair, they are often hurt and angry. One response to this hurt and anger is to have an affair to get even with the unfaithful partner.

DESIRE FOR HOMOSEXUAL RELATIONSHIP   Some individuals in heterosexual committed relationships engage in extradyadic sex because they desire a homosexual relationship. Some gay individuals marry as a way of denying their homosexuality or creating a social pretense that they are heterosexual. These individuals are likely to feel unfulfilled in their marriage and may seek involvement in an extramarital homosexual relationship. Other individuals may marry and then discover later in life that they desire a homosexual relationship. Such individuals may feel that they have been homosexual or bisexual all along; their sexual orientation has changed from heterosexual to homosexual or bisexual; they are unsure of their sexual orientation and want to explore a homosexual relationship; or they are predominately heterosexual but wish to experience a homosexual relationship for variety.

Spouses in heterosexual marriages who engage in extramarital homosexual relationships may or may not be happy with their marital partner. Blumstein and Schwartz (1990) provide an example of a woman

> unhappily married for 23 years but feeling a profound absence of a real "soul mate." She met a woman at her son's college graduation ceremony, and over a long period of time, the two women gradually fell in love and left their husbands. Not only did the respondent's sense of self change but so did her sexual habits and desires. (p. 314)

AGING   A frequent motive for intercourse outside of marriage is the desire to reexperience the world of youth. Our society promotes the idea that it is good to be young and bad to be old. Sexual attractiveness

is equated with youth, and having an affair may confirm to an older partner that he or she is still sexually desirable. Also, people may try to recapture the love, excitement, adventure, and romance associated with youth by having an affair.

One writer (Gordon, 1988) interviewed men who had left their wives for a younger woman. The men focused not on the physical youth of their new partners, but on the youthful attitude—the openness, innocence, unscarred emotions. They also emphasized the uncritical love they felt from their younger partner. Gordon labeled these men as having "Jennifer Fever"—they had developed a pattern of denying the aging process by seeking a youthful partner to create the illusion that they were not getting older. Gordon suggested the term "Jennifer" because she found that the name of the younger woman was often Jennifer. Gordon further warned that these men would seek another "Jennifer" as the current one aged.

ABSENCE FROM PARTNER   One factor that predisposes a person to an extradyadic sexual encounter is prolonged separation from the partner. Some spouses whose partners are away for military service report that the loneliness can become unbearable. Some partners who are away say it is difficult to be faithful. Partners in commuter relationships may also be vulnerable to extradyadic sexual relationships.

The spouse who chooses to have an affair is often judged as being unfaithful to the vows of the marriage, as being deceitful to the partner, and as inflicting enormous pain on the partner (and children). What is often not considered is that when an affair is defined in terms of giving emotional energy, time, and economic resources to something or someone outside the primary relationship, other types of "affairs" are equally devastating to a relationship. Spouses who choose to devote their lives to their children, careers, parents, friends, or recreational interests may deprive the partner of significant amounts of emotional energy, time, and money and create a context in which the partner may choose to become involved with a person who provides more attention and interest.

Before ending this section on extradyadic involvements, we note that some societies and cultures "encourage or at least allow extramarital relations under 'appropriate conditions'" (Hatfield &

Rapson, 1996, p. 144). The Toda of India do not even have a word for adultery. Some Korean marriages today involve a "second wife" who may live in the home with the first wife. (This wife may even have a child by the husband, but her status is clearly secondary to that of the first wife.) And in Spain, married men have mistresses that are culturally condoned. 🍂

PERSONAL CHOICES

Should You Participate in Extradyadic Sex?

Beginning in adolescence, individuals are confronted with the decision to be monogamous and faithful.

No to Extradyadic Sex

When 672 spouses were asked if they had been monogamous during the last 12 months, 96% reported affirmatively (Greeley, Michael, & Smith, 1990). While not all spouses have the opportunity (an available partner) and a context (out of town or away from the spouse) for extradyadic sex, regardless of the reason, the overwhelming majority are faithful in any given year.

Some of those deciding not to have extramarital sex feel that it causes more trouble to themselves and to their partners than it is worth. "I can't say I don't think about having sex with other women, because I do—a lot," said one husband, "but I would feel guilty as hell, and if my wife found out, she would kill me." Spanier and Margolis (1983) found that more women who engaged in extradyadic sex reported guilt feelings than did men (59% versus 34%).

Partners who engage in sex with someone else risk hurting their mate emotionally. Extradyadic intercourse not only involves a breach of intimacy by having sex with someone else, it also involves deceit. As a result, the partner may develop a deep sense of distrust, which often lingers in the relationship long after the affair is over.

Another reason why having an affair hurts the partner and the relationship is that "it represents a regressive transformation from the person considering the couple's joint outcomes to decisions being made on appraisals that are based on individualistic outcomes" (Bringle & Buunk, 1991). In other words, choosing to engage in sex with someone other than the primary partner is a decision based on what the individual wants (individualism), not on what the couple wants (familism).

In addition to guilt, distrust, and emotional pain as potential outcomes of an affair, another danger is the development of a pattern of having affairs. "Once you've had an affair, it's easier the second time," said one spouse. "And the third time, you don't give it a thought." Increasingly, the spouse looks outside the existing relationship for sex and companionship.

Engaging in extradyadic sex may result in the termination of the primary relationship. In a study on how dating partners would cope with learning their partner had been unfaithful, respondents revealed they would (in descending order of frequency) terminate the relationship, confront and find out the reason, talk it over, consider terminating the relationship, and work to improve the relationship (Roscoe, Cavanaugh, & Kennedy, 1988). Another study found that extramarital affairs played a role in one-third of divorces (Burns, 1984). Regardless of who has the affair, Pitman (1993) observed, "However utopian the theories, the reality is that infidelity, whether it is furtive or blatant, will blow the hell out of a marriage" (p. 35).

If the partner finds out the spouse wants a divorce because of an affair, the "adulterer" may also pay an economic price. In some states, adultery is grounds for alimony.

Another potential danger in having extradyadic sex is the potential to contract a sexually transmitted disease. The HIV epidemic has increased the concern over this possibility. Spouses who engage in extradyadic sex may not only contract a sexually transmitted disease, but may also transmit the disease to their partners (and potentially their unborn offspring). In some cases, extradyadic sex may be deadly.

Finally, spouses who engage in extradyadic sex relationships risk the possibility of their partner finding out and going into a jealous rage. Jealousy may result in violence and even the death of the unfaithful spouse or the lover involved. Another possible tragic outcome of extramarital relationships is that the spouse who has been "cheated on" becomes depressed and commits suicide.

Partners who decide to avoid extradyadic encounters might focus on the small choices that lead to a sexual encounter. Since extradyadic sex occurs in certain relationships and structural contexts, the person can choose to avoid these. For example, choosing not to become involved in intimate conversations and choosing not to have lunch or a drink in a bar with someone to whom you are attracted decreases the chance a relationship will develop or that a context will present itself where a sexual encounter becomes a possibility. The person who chooses to allow these situations to occur is increasing the chance that an extramarital relationship will develop.

Yes to Extradyadic Sex

A small percentage of spouses who have had an affair feel it had positive consequences for them, their marriages, or their partners. In one instance, a woman whose husband constantly criticized her said of her extramarital relationship, "He made me feel loved, valued, and worthwhile again." This woman eventually divorced her husband and said that she never regretted moving from an emotionally abusive relationship to one in which she was loved and nurtured.

In a study by Atwater (1982), 60% of women reported that they enjoyed sex more with their extramarital partners than with their husbands. In addition to good sex, other potential positive consequences of engaging in extradyadic sex include personal growth and self-discovery.

For some spouses who have an affair and stay married, the marriage may benefit. Some partners become more sensitive to the problems in their marriage. "For us," one spouse said, "the affair helped us to look at our marriage, to know that we were in trouble, and to seek help." Couples need not view the discovery of an affair as the end of their marriage; it can be a new beginning.

Another positive effect of a partner's discovering an affair is that the partner may become more sensitive to

the needs of the spouse and more motivated to satisfy them. The partner may realize that if the spouse is not satisfied at home, he or she will go elsewhere. One husband said his wife had an affair because he was too busy with his work and did not spend enough time with her. Her affair taught him that she had alternatives—other men who would love her emotionally and sexually. To ensure that he did not lose her, he cut back on his work hours and spent more time with his wife.

T. Britton (personal communication, 1984) interviewed 276 spouses who had an affair and noted the conditions under which extradyadic sex is likely to have the least negative consequences. These included having a solid marriage relationship, being able to compartmentalize one's life, not telling the partner, having infrequent contacts with the lover, and having extradyadic sex for recreation (not emotion) only.

SEXUALITY IN THE LATER YEARS

In the United States today, one is not usually considered elderly until he or she reaches the age of 65. The elderly are stereotyped as having little to no interest in sexual expression (or as being "dirty old men or women"). However, a minority of individuals remain sexually active on a once-a-week to a once-a-month basis into their eighties and nineties (Segraves & Segraves, 1995). Next, we discuss the sexuality of elderly men and elderly women.

Sexuality of Elderly Men

Numerous studies have shown that the man's sexual capacity, interest, and activity decrease with age. Absence of good health or an available partner account for some of the decline. Physiological changes also occur in elderly men during the sexual response cycle:

- Excitement Phase—As men age, it takes them longer to get an erection. While the young man may get an erection within 10 seconds, elderly men may take several minutes (10 to 30). During this time, he usually needs intense stimulation (manual or oral). Unaware that the greater delay in becoming erect is a normal consequence of aging, men who experience this for the first time may panic and have erectile dysfunction.

The need for intimacy never stops.

- Plateau Phase—The erection may be less rigid than when the man was younger, and there is usually a longer delay before ejaculation. This latter change is usually regarded as an advantage by both the man and his partner.
- Orgasm Phase—Orgasm in the elderly man is usually less intense, with fewer contractions and less fluid. However, orgasm remains an enjoyable experience; over 70% of older men in one study reported that having a climax was very important when having a sexual experience (Starr & Weiner, 1981).
- Resolution Phase—The elderly man loses his erection rather quickly after ejaculation. The refractory period is also increased. Whereas the young man needs only a short time after ejaculation to get an erection, the elderly man may need considerably longer (Boskin, Graf, & Kreisworth, 1990).

In regard to sexual activity, Spector and Fremeth (1996) studied 40 elders (mean age, 82.5) in a long-term care institution and found that sexual activity was infrequent for both males and females. Men reported more sexual desire than women. Higher levels of testosterone in men than women and more social approval for sexual interest among males may account for the difference.

Bullard-Poe, Powell, and Mulligan (1994) studied 45 men, ages 44 to 99, in a nursing home. Social, nonsexual-physical, intellectual, emotional, and sexual-physical intimacy were rated in that order as most important to the residents. These findings were true whether the men were married or not. Indeed, although capacity may decrease as well as behavior, social, emotional, and intellectual intimacy continue. Schlesinger (1996) stated that the main reason elderly men do not have intercourse is "fear of impotency and the ensuing self-devaluation" (p. 121).

Sexuality of Elderly Women

Elderly women experience a variety of physiological changes during the sexual response cycle:

- Excitement Phase—Vaginal lubrication takes several minutes or longer, as opposed to 10 to 30 seconds. Both the length and the width of the vagina decrease. Considerable decreased lubrication and vaginal size are associated with pain during intercourse. Some women report decreased sexual desire and unusual sensitivity of the clitoris (Sarrel, 1990).
- Plateau Phase—Little change occurs as the woman ages. During this phase, the vaginal orgasmic platform is formed, and the uterus elevates.
- Orgasm Phase—Elderly women continue to experience and enjoy orgasm. Of women aged 60 to 91, almost 70% reported that having an orgasm made for a good sexual experience (Starr & Weiner, 1981). With regard to their frequency of orgasm now as opposed to when they were younger, 65% said "unchanged," 20% "increased," and 14% "decreased."
- Resolution Phase—Defined as a return to the preexcitement state, the resolution phase of the sexual response phase happens more quickly in elderly than in younger women. Clitoral retraction and orgasmic platform disappear quickly after orgasm. This is most likely a result of less pelvic vasocongestion to begin with during the arousal phase (Boskin et al., 1990).

Aside from the Spector and Fremeth (1996) study, few studies have been conducted on the sexuality of elderly women. However, Bretschneider and McCoy (1988) collected data from 102 white women and 100 white men ranging in age from 80 to 102. Some of the findings follow:

- Thirty-eight percent of the women and 66% of the men reported that sex was currently important to them.
- Thirty percent of the women and 62% of the men reported they had sexual intercourse sometimes.
- Of those with sexual partners, 64% of the women and 82% of the men said that they were at least mildly happy with their partners as lovers.
- Forty percent of the women and 72% of the men reported that they currently masturbated.
- Touching and caressing without sexual intercourse was the most frequently engaged-in behavior by women (64%) and by men (82%).

These findings suggest that declines in sexual enjoyment and frequency are greater for women in the later years than for men.

Other studies confirm that sexual frequency decreases with age.

NATIONAL DATA

Women who reported having intercourse between two and four times a week in the past 12 months

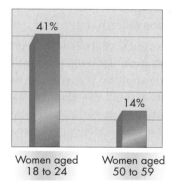

41%

14%

Women aged 18 to 24   Women aged 50 to 59

Source: Michael et al., 1994, p. 116.

Indeed, about 95% of women and 55% of men over the age of 80 report not having had sex with anyone in the past 12 months. The following figure reflects that the elderly, particularly widows, are very limited in terms of available sexual partners. This, in part, accounts for declines in sexual enjoyment and frequency.

NATIONAL DATA

U.S. adults with no sexual partner in the past 12 months

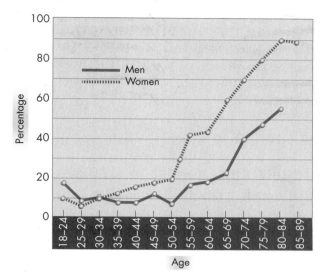

Source: Michael et al., 1994.

A woman in her 80s commented on the changes in sexuality in old age and the feelings of passion that endure.

> The longing to belong with somebody, to love somebody, to have somebody, and to feel the touch of somebody near us remain equally young, fresh and intact as always. The need for love and intimacy does not change as we get older. Even when our physical capacity for sex wanes slightly, we still have overwhelming feelings of desire, passion and love. As a person in her eighties, I remind everyone of the importance of feeling—with your heart, body and mind. My feelings won't disappear when I turn ninety just as they didn't evaporate when I turned eighty or seventy or sixty. (Reti, 1995, p. 215)

THINK ABOUT IT

How is the sexuality of elderly women and men affected by physiological changes associated with aging? How is their sexuality affected by cultural stereotypes and expectations? How might a generation of today's young women, who have grown up in a sexually open and permissive era, differ when they become elderly (in terms of their sexuality) from elderly women of today who were reared in a more conservative, restrictive era?

SUMMARY POINTS

Sexuality changes throughout one's life span.

Sexuality from Infancy through Adolescence

Infants are born with a sexual response system that begins to function early in life. At birth, some boys are born with erections and some girls are born with a vaginal discharge equivalent to lubricating fluid. Early emotional bonding experiences are important for the development of intimate physical and emotional relationships as an adult.

Children often experiment with their own bodies as sources of physical pleasure and also show an interest in the bodies of other children. Parents might be careful not to punish their children for normal sexual exploration, as doing so teaches children that sex is "bad." Research suggests that children who are exposed to parental nudity, the "family bed," or the "primal" scene do not suffer negative consequences.

Adolescents experience considerable physical and psychological changes. They are concerned about their bodies matching the cultural ideal. They are also making sexual choices about first intercourse, preventing pregnancy and STDs, and abortion.

Sexuality in Early Adulthood

Never-married young adults who live alone and those who live with someone report different sexual lives. Those who are unattached report having less frequent sex but report more partners than those who are living with someone. However, those who cohabit report a higher quality of sexual experience, similar to those who are married.

Marital sex is the most socially legitimate, physically pleasurable, and emotionally satisfying sex that people report. Divorced individuals report more sexual partners than never-marrieds or marrieds.

Divorced women are stereotyped as having greater sexual experience and sexual knowledge and being more sexually assertive and promiscuous. Divorced people may be more vulnerable to contracting STDs because they are less sensitized to the danger of contracting HIV than people in their twenties.

Sexuality in the Middle Years

Sexuality is affected by the aging process. Women experience menopause around age 50, and some experience hot flashes, irritability, and headaches. Hormone replacement therapy to relieve the symptoms is an alternative that a woman must consider carefully with her physician. Men in the middle years experience decreasing levels of testosterone, which results in more difficulty in getting and maintaining an erection and a greater amount of time between erections.

Extradyadic Sexual Involvements

Although most Americans do not approve of extramarital sex, about 20% of wives and 15 to 35% of husbands have at least one sexual partner other than their spouse during the marriage. Motivations for extradyadic sexual involvements include variety, a desire to return to youth, or dissatisfaction with the partner. Although there are exceptions, the relationship consequences of extramarital sex are usually negative. Rebuilding the lost trust is a major challenge.

Sexuality in the Later Years

As individuals age, sexual capacity, interest, and activity tend to decrease. However, many elderly women and men value the physical and emotional pleasure and intimacy associated with sexual expression. Although genital expression may decrease, the need for touch and love do not.

REFERENCES

Adler, T. (1991, July). Women's expectations are menopause villains. *APA Monitor,* p. 14.

Anderson, J. E., Brackbill, R., & Mosher, W. D. (1996). Condom use for disease prevention among unmarried U.S. women. *Family Planning Perspectives, 17,* 25–28.

Andre, T., Frevert, R. L., & Schuchmann, D. (1989). From whom have college students learned about sex? *Youth and Society, 20,* 241–268.

Apt, C., & Hurlbert, D. F. (1995). Male cognitive schemata in the sexual perceptions associated with the marital status of women. *Journal of Sex Education and Therapy, 21,* 1–10.

Atwater, L. (1979). Getting involved: Women's transition to first extramarital sex. *Alternative Lifestyles 2,* 33–68.

Atwater, L. (1982). *The extramarital connection.* New York: Irvington.

Bailey, N. J., & Phariss, T. (1996, January). Breaking through the wall of silence: Gay, lesbian, and bisexual issues for middle level educators. *Middle School Journal,* 338–346.

Bancroft, J. (1989). *Human sexuality and its problems* (2nd ed.). Edinburgh: Churchill Livingstone.

Bell, R. (1987). *Changing bodies, changing lives: A book for teens on sex and relationships.* New York: Vintage Books.

Bermant, G. (1976). Sexual behavior: Hard times with the Coolidge effect. In M. H. Siegel & H. P. Zeigler (Eds.), *Psychological research: The inside story.* New York: Harper and Row.

Blumstein, P., & Schwartz, P. (1990). Intimate relationships and the creation of sexuality. In D. P. McWhirter, S. A. Sanders, & J. M. Reinish (Eds.), *Homosexuality/heterosexuality: Concepts of sexual orientation* (pp. 307–320). New York: Oxford University Press.

Boskin, W., Graf, G., & Kreisworth, V. (1990). *Health dynamics: Attitudes and behaviors.* St. Paul, MN: West.

Bretschneider, J. G., & McCoy, N. L. (1988). Sexual interest and behavior in healthy 80 to 102 year olds. *Archives of Sexual Behavior, 17,* 109–129.

Bringle, R. G., & Buunk, B. T. (1991). Extradyadic relationships and sexual jealousy. In K. McKinney & S. Sprecher (Eds.), *Sexuality in close relationships* (pp. 135–152). Hillsdale, NJ: Lawrence Erlbaum.

Bullard-Poe, L., Powell, C., & Mulligan, T. (1994). The importance of intimacy to men living in a nursing home. *Archives of Sexual Behavior, 23,* 231–236.

Burns, A. (1984). Perceived causes of marriage breakdown and conditions of life. *Journal of Marriage and the Family, 46,* 551–562.

Calderone, M. S. (1983). Fetal erection and its message to us. *SIECUS Report, II,* 5–6.

Calderone, M. S., & Johnson, E. W. (1989). *The family book about sexuality.* New York: Harper and Row.

Campbell, T. A., & Campbell, D. E. (1990). Considering the adolescent's point of view: A marketing model for sex education. *Journal of Sex Education and Therapy, 16,* 185–194.

Centers for Disease Control and Prevention. (1994). *HIV/AIDS Surveillance Report,* 6(2), 1–39. Atlanta, GA.

Centers for Disease Control and Prevention. (1996). *HIV/AIDS Surveillance Report,* 8(2), 1–39. Atlanta, GA.

Clements, M. (1993, August 7). Sex in America today. *Parade Magazine,* 4–6.

DeGaston, J. F., Weed, S., & Jensen, L. (1996). Understanding gender differences in adolescent sexuality. *Adolescence, 31,* 217–231.

Duncan, P. D., Ritter, P. L., Dornbusch, S. M., Gross, R. T., & Carlsmith, J. M. (1990). The effects of pubertal timing on body image, school behavior, and deviance. In R. E. Muuss (Ed.), *Adolescent behavior and society* (pp. 51–56). New York: McGraw-Hill.

Ellen, J. M., Cahn, S., Eyre, S. L., & Boyer, C. B. (1996). Types of adolescent sexual relationships and associated perceptions about condom use. *Journal of Adolescent Health, 18,* 417–421.

Erikson, E. (1968). *Identity: Youth and crisis.* New York: Norton.

Fischer, J. L. (1981). Transitions in relationship style from adolescence to young adulthood. *Journal of Youth and Adolescence, 10,* 11–24.

Fletcher, S. D. (1996). E-mail: *A love story.* New York: Fine.

Fogel, C. I., & Woods, N. F. (1995). Midlife women's health. In C. I. Fogel & N. F. Woods (Eds.), *Women's health care: A comprehensive handbook.* Thousand Oaks, CA: Sage.

Folsom, A. R., Mink, P. J., Sellars, T. A., Hong, C. P., & Potter, J. D. (1995). Hormonal replacement therapy and morbidity and mortality in a prospective study of postmenopausal women. *American Journal of Public Health, 85,* 1128–1132.

Frank, E., & Anderson, C. (1989). The sexual stages of marriage. In J. M. Henslin (Ed.), *Marriage and family in a changing society* (pp. 190–196). New York: Free Press.

Garner, D. M. (1997). The 1997 Body Image Survey results. *Psychology Today, 30,* 31.

Goldman, R., & Goldman, J. (1982). *Children's sexual thinking.* London: Routledge & Kegan Paul.

Gordon, B. (1988). Jennifer fever. New York: Harper and Row.

Greeley, A. M., Michael, R. T., & Smith, T. W. (1990, July/August). Americans and their sexual partners. *Society,* 36–42.

Greenblat, C. S. (1983). The salience of sexuality in the early years of marriage. *Journal of Marriage and the Family, 4,* 289–299.

Harvey, S. M., & Spigner, C. (1995). Factors associated with sexual behavior among adolescents: A multivariate analysis. *Adolescence, 30,* 253–264.

Hatfield, E., & Rapson, R. L. (1996). *Love and sex: Cross-cultural perspectives.* Boston: Allyn and Bacon.

Hawton, K., Gath, D., & Gay, A. (1994). Sexual function in a community sample of middle-aged women with partners: Effects of age, marital, socioeconomic, psychiatric, gynecological, and menopausal factors. *Archives of Sexual Behavior, 23,* 375–395.

Herman-Giddens, M. E., Slora, E. J., Wasserman, R. C. Bourdony, C. J., Bhapkar, M. V., Koch, G. G., & Hasemeier, C. M. (1997). Secondary sexual characteristics and menses in young girls seen in office practice: A study from the pediatric research in office settings network. *Pediatrics, 99,* 505–512.

Jones, C. L., Tepperman, L., & Wilson, S. J. (1995). *The futures of the family.* Englewood Cliffs, NJ: Prentice Hall.

Leight, L. (1990). *Raising sexually healthy children.* New York: Avon.

Markov, T. (1991). *Sex games and folklore.* Unpublished manuscript. East Carolina University, Greenville, NC.

Mercier, L. R., & Berger, R. M. (1989). Social service needs of lesbian and gay adolescents: Telling it their way. *Journal of Social Work and Human Sexuality, 8,* 75–98.

Metz, M. E., & Seifert, M. H., Jr. (1990). Men's expectations of physicians in sexual health concerns. *Journal of Sex and Marital Therapy, 16,* 79–88.

Michael, R. T., Gagnon, J. H., Laumann, E. O., & Kolata, G. (1994). *Sex in America: A definitive survey.* Boston: Little, Brown.

Most Japanese students do not have intercourse until after adolescence. (1997). *Family Planning Perspectives, 29,* 145–146.

Mott, F. L., Fondell, M. M., Hu, P. N., Kowaleski-Jones, L., & Menaghan, E. G. (1996). The determinants of first sex by age 14 in a high-risk adolescent population. *Family Planning Perspectives, 28,* 13–18.

Murstein, B. I., Case, D., & Gunn, S. P. (1985). Personality correlates of ex-swingers. *Lifestyles, 8,* 21–34.

National Center for Health Statistics. (1997). Births, marriages, divorces, and deaths for August 1997. *Monthly Vital Statistics Report, 45*(8), Hyattsville, MD: National Center for Health Statistics.

Nock, S. L. (1995). A comparison of marriages and cohabiting relationships. *Journal of Family Issues, 54,* 686–698.

Oggins, J., Leber, D., & Veroff, J. (1993). Race and gender differences in black and white newlyweds' perceptions of sexual and marital relations. *Journal of Sex Research, 30,* 152–160.

Okami, P. (1995). Childhood exposure to parental nudity, parent-child co-sleeping, and 'primal scenes': A review of clinical opinion and empirical evidence. *The Journal of Sex Research, 32,* 51–64.

Packer, A. J. (1995, September). Everything your kids want to know about sex and aren't afraid to ask. *Child,* 56–58, 60.

Peterson, K. S. (1996, February 6). On-line adultery. *USA Today,* p. 4D.

Phinney, V. G., Jensen, L. C., Olsen, J. A., & Cundick, B. (1990). The relationship between early development and psychosexual behaviors in adolescent females. *Adolescence, 25,* 321–332.

Pittman, F. (1993, May/June). Beyond betrayal: Life after infidelity. *Psychology Today, 33.*

Reinisch, J. M., Hill, C. A., Sanders, S. A., & Ziemba-Davis, M. (1995). High risk sexual behavior at a Midwestern university: A confirmatory survey. *Family Planning Perspectives, 27,* 79–82.

Reti, L. (1995). Golden age and love: An insider's report. In R. Neugebauer-Visano (Ed.), *Seniors and sexuality: Experiencing intimacy in later life* (pp. 215–216). Toronto: Canadian Scholars Press.

Rodgers, J. L., & Rowe, D. C. (1990). Adolescent sexual activity and mildly deviant behavior. *Journal of Family Issues, 11,* 274–293.

Roscoe, B., Cavanaugh, L. E., & Kennedy, D. R. (1988). Dating infidelity: Behavior, reasons, and consequences. *Adolescence 13,* 35–43.

Saluter, A. F. (1996). *Marital status and living arrangements: March 1994 U.S. Bureau of the Census.* (Current Population Reports, Series P20-484). Washington, DC: U.S. Government Printing Office.

Santelli, J. S., Kouzis, A. C., Hoover, D. R., Polacsek, M., Burwell, L. G., & Celantano, D. D. (1996). Stage of behavior change for condom use: The influence of partner type, relationship and pregnancy factors. *Family Planning Perspectives, 28,* 101–107.

Sarrel, L. J., & Sarrel, P. M. (1979). *Sexual unfolding: Sexual development and sex therapies in late adolescence.* Boston: Little, Brown.

Sarrel, P. M. (1990). Sexuality and menopause. *Obstetrics and Gynecology, 75,* (4 Suppl), 26s–30s.

Schlesinger, B. (1996). The sexless years or sex rediscovered. *Journal of Gerontological Social Work, 26,* 117–131.

Segraves, R. T., & Segraves, K. B. (1995). Human sexuality and aging. *Journal of Sex Education and Therapy, 21,* 88–102.

Sheehy, G. (1976). *Passages: Predictable crises of adult life.* New York: Dutton.

Smith, T. W. (1994). American sexual behavior: Trends, socio-demographic differences, in risk behavior. *General Social Survey* (updated version). New York: Springer-Verlag.

Spanier, G. B., & Margolis, R. L. (1983). Marital separation and extramarital sexual behavior. *Journal of Sex Research, 19,* 23–48.

Spector, I. P., & Fremeth, S. M. (1996). Sexual behaviors and attitudes of geriatric residents in long-term care facilities. *Journal of Sex and Marital Therapy, 22,* 235–246.

Starr, B., & Weiner, M. (1981). *The Starr-Weiner report on sex and sexuality in the mature years.* New York: Stein and Day.

Statistical Abstract of the United States: 1997 (117th ed.). (1997). Washington, DC: U.S. Bureau of the Census.

Tavris, C. (1992). *The mismeasure of woman.* New York: Simon & Schuster.

Thompson, A. P. (1983). Extramarital sex: A review of the research literature. *Journal of Sex Research, 19,* 1–22.

Thornton, A. (1990). The courtship process of adolescent sexuality. *Journal of Family Issues, 11,* 239–273.

Turkle, S. (1996). *Life on the screen: Identity in the Age of the Internet.* New York: Simon & Schuster.

Wallis, C. (1995, June 26). The estrogen dilemma. *Time,* 46–53.

Wheeler, J., & Kilmann, P. R. (1983). Comarital sexual behavior: Individual and relationship variables. *Archives of Sexual Behavior, 12,* 295–306.

Wiederman, M. W. (1997). Extramarital sex: Prevalence and correlates in a national survey. *The Journal of Sex Research, 34,* 167–174.

Wing, R. R., Matthews, K. A., Kuller, L. H., Meilahn, E. N., & Plantinga, P. L. (1991). Weight gain at the time of menopause. *Archives of Internal Medicine, 151,* 97–102.

Yablonsky, L. (1979). *The extra-sex factor: Why over half of America's married men play around.* New York: Times Books.

Young, W. R. (1990). Changes in sexual functioning during the aging process. In F. J. Bianoco & R. H. Serrano (Eds.), *Sexology: An independent field* (pp. 121–128). New York: Elsevier Science.

GENDER DIVERSITY IN SEXUALITY

Chapter 15

When a video segment depicting U.S. marines in Camp LeJeune, North Carolina, pounding spiked "wings" into the chests of paratrooper cadets was aired on national television, the American public watched with horror. The scenes in the video were so graphic and violent that some television viewers, disgusted and sickened by what they saw, turned their heads or closed their eyes. Americans asked themselves why any self-respecting individual would allow himself to be subjected to such a painful and brutal ritual. They also wondered why any sane individual would inflict such unnecessary pain on another person. Defending the practice, James Perry, a United States Marine Corps first lieutenant, said that the "blood wings" are a symbol of masochism that reflects membership in an elite unit that takes on dangerous assignments. Perry felt that such a ritual was important and noted that he couldn't even remember the puncture he received when he got his "wings" (Associated Press, 1997). Although public reaction to the televised video included shock and disbelief, another reaction was, "well, boys will be boys." The wing-pounding ritual is consistent with traditional male gender role socialization, which teaches men to be tough and stoical.

The influence of gender and gender roles is evident not only in dramatic examples like this, but also in the everyday lives of women and men. In this chapter, we focus on the influences gender has on one's sexuality and sexual choices.

TERMINOLOGY

In common usage, the terms "sex" and "gender" are often used interchangeably. To psychologists, sociologists, health educators, sexologists, and sex therapists, however, these terms are not synonymous. After clarifying the distinction between "sex" and "gender," we discuss other relevant terminology, including gender identity, gender role, sexual identity, and gender role ideology.

Sex

Sex refers to the biological distinction between being female and being male. The primary sex characteristics that differentiate women and men include external genitalia (vulva and penis), gonads (ovaries and testes), sex chromosomes (XX and XY), and hormones (estrogen, progesterone, and testosterone). Secondary sex characteristics include the larger breasts of women and the deeper voice and presence of a beard in men.

Even though we commonly think of biological sex as consisting of two dichotomous categories (female and male), current views suggest that biological sex exists on a continuum. This view is supported by the existence of individuals with mixed or ambiguous genitals (hermaphrodites and pseudohermaphrodites, or intersexed individuals). Evidence of overlap between the sexes is also found in the fact that some normal males produce fewer male hormones (androgens) than some females, just as some females produce fewer female hormones (estrogens) than some males (Morrow, 1991) (see Figure 15.1).

Gender

Gender refers to the social and psychological characteristics associated with being female or male. Characteristics typically associated with the female gender include being gentle, emotional, and cooperative; characteristics typically associated with the male gender include being aggressive, rational, and competitive. In popular usage, gender is dichotomized as an either/or concept (masculine or feminine), but gender may also be viewed as existing along a continuum of femininity and masculinity.

Traditional gender expectations are changing. Almost 2000 undergraduate women at a large metropolitan university said that their ideal man had both compassion and intellect. More than 1000 undergraduate men at the same university identified compassion, intellect, sexuality, and power as the most important preferences for their ideal woman (Street, Kimmel, & Kromrey, 1995).

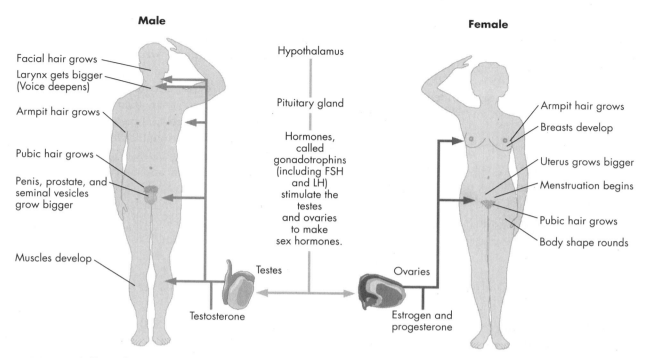

FIGURE 15.1 Effects of Hormones on Sexual Development During Puberty
The body's endocrine system produces hormones that trigger body changes in males and females.

An ongoing controversy revolves around gender differences being innate versus learned or socially determined. Just as sexual orientation (discussed in Chapter 16) may be best explained by an interaction of biological and social/psychological variables, gender differences may be explained as a consequence of both biological and social/psychological influences. However, social scientists tend to emphasize the role of social variables in gender differences.

Gender Identity

Gender identity is the psychological state of viewing oneself as a girl or a boy and later, as a woman or a man. Gender identity is largely learned and is a reflection of society's conceptions of femininity and masculinity. *Transsexuals* have the gender identity that is different from their biological sex. A transsexual person may have the self-concept of a woman but the biological makeup of a man (or vice versa). We will discuss transsexuals in greater detail later in the chapter.

Gender Role

Gender roles are the set of social norms that dictate what is socially regarded as appropriate female and male behavior. All societies have expectations of how boys and girls, or men and women, should behave. Gender roles influence women and men in virtually every sphere of life, including family and occupation. For example, traditional gender roles have influenced women to be the primary child caregivers and housekeepers and to enter "female" occupations, such as nursing, secretarial work, and teaching. Traditional gender roles have influenced men to be the primary breadwinners and decision makers and to enter "male" occupations, such as engineering, construction, and mechanical repair work. The concentration of women in certain occupations and men in other occupations is referred to as *occupational sex segregation.* Some gender scholars suggest that "while there has been a reduction of strict gender-role adherence, traditional gender roles continue to predominate in the United States of America today" (Denmark, Nielson, & Scholl, 1993, p. 455).

Sexual Identity

Sexual identity refers to a number of factors, including one's biological sex, gender identity, gender role, and sexual orientation. As we will discuss in Chapter 16, one's sexual orientation includes one's thoughts, feelings, sexual behaviors, and self-identification.

Gender Role Ideology

Gender role ideology refers to the socially prescribed role relationships between women and men in any given society.

> All human societies consist of men and women who must interact with one another, usually on a daily basis, and who have developed customs embracing prescriptive beliefs about the manner in which men and women are to relate to one another. (Williams & Best, 1990, p. 87)

In the United States and throughout the world, gender role ideology has perpetuated and reflected male dominance in social, economic, and political spheres.

INTERNATIONAL DATA

According to the United Nations, although women constitute one-half of the world's population, they perform two-thirds of its work, receive one-tenth of its income, and own less than one-hundredth of its property.

Source: Reported in Russo, 1993.

The Human Development Report (1997) concludes that "no society treats its women as well as its men" (p. 39). Although many countries have laws that prohibit discrimination against women in a variety of arenas, "archaic laws and discriminatory practices continue to undermine women's access to and advancement in education, employment, and the political process, deprive them of assets, deny them liberty and dignity, and violate their physical and mental integrity and autonomy" (Russo, 1993, p. x). Such practices include female infanticide, female genital operations, child marriage, prostitution, and prohibitions against birth control and abortion.

While traditional heterosexual relationships have reflected male dominance, homosexual relationships tend to be more equal, with greater gender role flexibility. When gender role ideology in homosexual relationships is assessed, lesbian relationships are more egalitarian and flexible than gay male relationships (Green, Bettinger, & Zacks, 1996).

THINK ABOUT IT

On many types of forms, including insurance applications, job applications, and credit card applications, individuals are asked to indicate their sex or gender. On such forms, are the terms "sex" and "gender" being used interchangeably? Based on the distinction between these terms, what term do you think is most appropriate in this context?

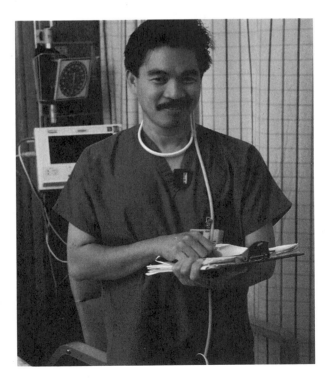

Occupational roles are increasingly being opened to both women and men.

Should You Pursue a Nontraditional Occupational Role?

As noted earlier, women and men often choose occupations that are consistent with traditional gender role expectations. But there are personal and social advantages to choosing nontraditional occupational roles. On the individual level, women and men can make career choices on the basis of their personal talents and interests, rather than on the basis of arbitrary social restrictions regarding who can and cannot have a particular job or career. Because traditional male occupations are generally higher paying than traditional female occupations, women who make nontraditional career choices can gain access to higher paying and higher status jobs (Steiger & Wardell, 1995). In entering traditional female occupations, such as nursing and elementary school teaching, men can develop their capacity for nurturing. Men are also likely to be promoted to supervisors and administrators in traditional female professions.

Lack of acceptance may be a disadvantage of entering a nontraditional role. Women in traditional all-male military careers or schooling (such as Citadel cadets) have reported undue harassment. Data on female acceptance of men in traditional female occupations are lacking.

On the societal level, an increase in nontraditional career choices reduces occupational sex segregation, thereby contributing to social equality between women and men. In addition, women and men who enter nontraditional occupations may contribute greatly to the field they enter. For example, traditional male-dominated occupations, such as politics, science and technology, and medicine, may benefit greatly from increased involvement of women in these fields. Similarly, the field of public school teaching, which is currently a female-dominated occupation, has not provided enough male role models for children. Additionally, when men enter a profession, broad-based salary increases tend to occur.

Choosing nontraditional occupations may also help to eliminate gender stereotypes. Women are stereotyped as being nurturing in part because of their service-oriented jobs, whereas men are believed to be more technically proficient and more competent decision makers because of the kinds of jobs

they hold. Williams (1995) noted that "if equal numbers of men and women were employed as mechanics, managers, and airplane pilots, as well as nurses, librarians, and secretaries, these stereotypes would be far more difficult to sustain" (p. 146).

THEORIES OF GENDER ROLE DEVELOPMENT

A number of theories attempt to explain why women and men exhibit different characteristics and behaviors. After reviewing biological beginnings, we examine the major theories of gender role development.

Biological Beginnings

The distinction between the female and the male sexes begins at the moment of fertilization when the man's sperm and the woman's egg unite to form a zygote. Both chromosomal and hormonal factors contribute to the development of the zygote.

Chromosomes are threadlike structures located within the nucleus of every cell in a person's body. Each cell contains 23 pairs of chromosomes, a total of 46 chromosomes per cell. Chromosomes contain genes, the basic units of heredity, which determine not only such physical characteristics as eye color, hair color, and body type, but also predispositions for such characteristics as baldness, color blindness, and hemophilia.

One of these 23 pairs of chromosomes is referred to as sex chromosomes because they determine whether an individual will be female or male. There are two types of sex chromosomes, called X and Y. Normally, females have two X chromosomes, while males have one X and one Y chromosome.

When the egg and sperm meet in the fallopian tube, each contains only half the normal number of chromosomes (one from each of the 23 pairs). The union of sperm and egg results in a single cell called a zygote, which has the normal 46 chromosomes. The egg will always have an X chromosome, but the sperm will have either an X or Y chromosome. Since the sex chromosome in the egg is always X (the female chromosome), the sex chromosome in the sperm will determine the sex of a child. If the sperm contains an X chromosome, the match with the female chromosome will be XX, and the child will be genetically female. If the sperm contains a Y chromosome (the male chromosome), the match with the female chromosome will be XY, and the child will be genetically male.

The fact that chromosomes control the biological sex of a child has led some parents to select the sex of their offspring. Whether or not this should be an option is discussed in the Social Choices section.

CHROMOSOMAL ABNORMALITIES   As we have seen, normal development in males and females requires that the correct number of chromosomes be present in the developing fetus. Chromosomal abnormalities may result in atypical sexual development of the fetus. For every sex chromosome from the mother (X), there must be a corresponding sex chromosome from the father (X or Y) for normal sexual development to occur. Abnormalities result when there are too many or too few sex chromosomes. Two of the most common of these abnormalities are Klinefelter's syndrome and Turner's syndrome.

Klinefelter's syndrome occurs in males and results from the presence of an extra X sex chromosome (XXY); it occurs in 1 out of 500 male births. The result is abnormal testicular development, infertility, low interest in sex (low libido), and, in some cases, mental retardation. Males with an extra X chromosome often experience language deficits, neuromaturational lag, academic difficulties, and psychological distress (Mandoki, Sumner, Hoffman, & Riconda, 1991).

Early identification of Klinefelter's syndrome is crucial to treating many of the developmental, behavioral, and emotional problems associated with the syndrome. Treatment may include psychiatric treatment, modified educational placement, testosterone supplementation, and corrective surgery in adolescence.

Turner's syndrome occurs in females and results from the absence of an X chromosome (XO); it occurs in 1 out of 2500 female births. It is characterized by abnormal ovarian development, failure to menstruate, infertility, and the lack of secondary sexual characteristics (such as minimal breast development). In addition, Turner's syndrome results in short stature and a predisposition to heart and kidney defects (Orten, 1990). Treatment for Turner's syndrome includes hormone replacement therapy to develop secondary sexual characteristics and the use of a biosynthetic human growth hormone to promote growth.

HORMONES   Hormones are also important in the development of the fetus. Male and female embryos are indistinguishable from one another during the first several weeks of intrauterine life. In both males and females, two primitive gonads and two paired duct systems form about the 5th or 6th week of development. While the reproductive system of the male (epididymis, vas deferens, ejaculatory duct) develops from the Wolffian ducts and the female reproductive system (fallopian tubes, uterus, vagina) from the Mullerian ducts, both ducts are present in the developing embryo at this stage (see Figure 15.2.).

If the embryo is genetically a male (XY), a chemical substance controlled by the Y chromosome (H-Y antigen) stimulates the primitive gonads to develop into testes. The testes, in turn, begin secreting the male hormone testosterone, which stimulates the development of the male reproductive and external sexual organs. The testes also secrete a second substance, called Mullerian duct-inhibiting substance, which causes the potential female ducts to degenerate or become blind tubules. Thus, development of male anatomical structures depends on the presence of male hormones at a critical stage of development (Wilson, George & Griffin, 1981).

The development of a female requires that no additional testosterone be present. Without the controlling substance from the Y chromosome, the primitive gonads will develop into ovaries and the Mullerian duct system into fallopian tubes, uterus, and vagina; and without testosterone, the Wolffian duct system will degenerate or become blind tubules. Animal studies have shown that if the primitive gonads are removed prior to differentiation into testes or ovaries, the organism will always develop anatomically into a female, regardless of genetic composition.

Although the infant's gonads (testes and ovaries) produce the sex hormones (testosterone and estrogen), these hormones are regulated by the pituitary gland, which is located at the base of the brain about 2 inches behind the eyes. The pituitary releases hormones into the blood that determine the amount of testosterone released by the testes and the amounts of estrogen and progesterone released by the ovaries. Production of sex hormones in males is relatively constant; production of female hormones is cyclic. Does this mean the

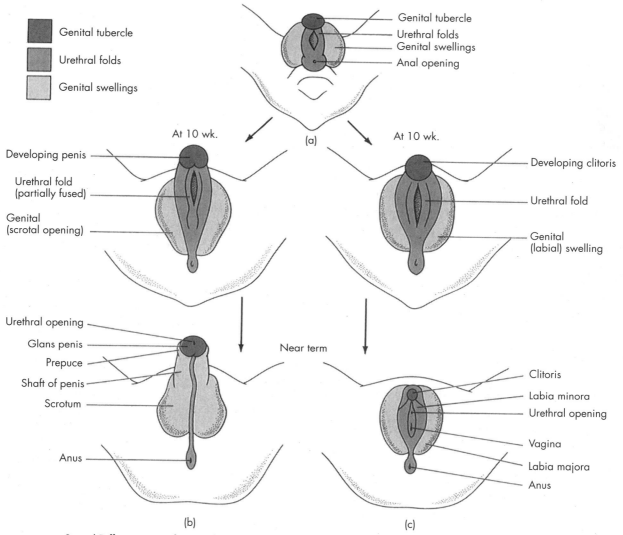

FIGURE 15.2 Sexual Differentiation of External Genitalia
(a) Undifferentiated stage (7 wk.). (b) Male development. (c) Female development.

pituitary glands of males and females are different? In animal studies in which the pituitaries of male organisms have been transplanted into female organisms (and vice versa), the production of sex hormones remains cyclic in females and constant in males. The release of pituitary hormones, as it turns out, is controlled by additional hormones (also called releasing factors) from the hypothalamus, a part of the brain just above the pituitary. It is the hypothalamus that differs in males and females in both the connections between cells and the size of various groups of cells. The presence of testos-

terone before birth not only stimulates the development of the male reproductive system, but also apparently stimulates the development of a male hypothalamus. A female hypothalamus develops in the absence of testosterone.

At puberty, the hormones released by the testes and ovaries are necessary for the development of secondary sex characteristics. Higher levels of testosterone account for the growth of facial hair in men and pubic and underarm hair in both men and women. Breast development, on the other hand, results from increasing levels of estrogen.

SHOULD A COUPLE BE ABLE TO SELECT THE SEX OF THEIR UNBORN CHILD?

Through modern reproductive technology, couples are now able to select the biological sex of their child. Although the practice is highly controversial, *prenatal sex selection* may be achieved through prenatal diagnosis (amniocentesis or chorionic villi sampling) and abortion. Amniocentesis (which is best performed in the 16th or 17th week of pregnancy) involves inserting a needle into the pregnant woman's uterus to withdraw fluid, which is then analyzed to see if the cells carry XX (female) or XY (male) chromosomes. Chorionic villi sampling (CVS), a newer fetal diagnostic technique, can be used to detect fetal sex as early as 8 weeks' gestation. Depending on the position of the fetus, ultrasound may reveal the fetus' genital area, but it is not considered a reliable test to determine the sex of the fetus. If the fetus is the biological sex that is desired by the parents, it is allowed to develop. Otherwise, the parents may choose to abort the child.

An alternative to prenatal sex selection is *preconceptual sex selection;* this involves selecting the sex of a child before it is conceived. One method separates sperm carrying the X and Y chromosomes. Using artificial insemination, the woman's egg is then fertilized with the sperm carrying the chromosome of the desired sex. This technique has a success rate of 69 to 75% (Busch, 1993).

Selecting the sex of one's child is highly controversial. The strongest argument for sex selection is that it can prevent the birth of an infant with a serious and fatal sex-linked genetic disease. Another argument is that aborting a fetus of the "undesired sex" is less objectionable than killing the infant after it is born. The practice of female infanticide—the killing of female infants by drowning, strangling, or exposure—has been well-documented in Eastern countries, including China and India. This practice occurs because of the cultural value that is placed on having male children. In China, India, and many other Eastern countries, boys are seen as an asset because they provide labor in the fields and take care of elderly parents. Girls are considered economic liabilities because they require a dowry and then leave the family to care for their husbands and children. In India, amniocentesis clinics advertise with slogans like, "Better 500 rupees now than 500,000 later," referring to the contrasting costs of abortion now or a dowry at a later date. While less adamant, many couples in Western countries also want a "balanced" family—one that includes a child of each sex. Sex selection technology allows parents to achieve this balance.

Opposition to sex selection is strongest when abortion is used. Not only does abortion for sex selection outrage individuals who are against abortion for any reason, it also offends many individuals who support women's right to choose abortion for other reasons. Many pro-choice individuals view abortion for the purpose of sex selection as morally unjustifiable and are concerned that using abortion for sex selection may generate so much public opposition, that the freedom to choose abortion when there are strong moral reasons to do so may be jeopardized.

Preconceptual methods of sex selection, which do not involve abortion, are less objectionable than prenatal sex selection. However, the widespread acceptance of preconceptual methods of sex selection could have serious social consequences. For instance, the cultural preference for male children would influence couples who want only one child to select a male child, thereby creating an imbalance in the sex ratio. In Eastern countries (where female infanticide and abortion of female fetuses occur on a large scale), the sex ratio is already unbalanced. As of 1996, there were 36 million more boys than girls in China; by the end of 1999, there will be an estimated 70 million more boys than girls (Cardarelli, 1996).

Should individuals and couples be allowed to select the sex of their child through prenatal sex diagnosis and abortion? The Fujian province of China has implemented a ban on prenatal testing for the purposes of sex determination. India has also passed a law prohibiting elective abortion of female fetuses. Although the majority of U.S. adults oppose sex selection through abortion, preconceptual sex

Continued on following page.

selection could gain widespread acceptance. Wertz and Fletcher (1989) suggest that social policy concerning preconceptual sex selection will set a precedent for future policies regarding the acceptability of parents selecting other characteristics, such as eye and hair color, height, weight, skin color, and straight teeth.

Sources: Busch, L. (1993, May 31). Designer families, ethical knots. *U.S. News & World Report, 114*(21), 73.

Cardarelli, L. (1996, May/June). The lost girls. *Utne Reader,* 13–15.

Wertz, D. C., & Fletcher, J. C. (1989, May/June). Fatal knowledge? Prenatal diagnosis and sex selection. *Hastings Center Report,* 21–27.

To summarize, several factors determine the biological sex of an individual:

- *Chromosomes:* XX for female; XY for male
- *Gonads:* ovaries for female; testes for male
- *Hormones:* greater proportion of estrogen and progesterone than testosterone in the female; greater proportion of testosterone than estrogen and progesterone in the male
- *Internal sex organs:* fallopian tubes, uterus, and vagina for female; epididymis, vas deferens, and seminal vesicles for male
- *External genitals:* vulva for female; penis and scrotum for male

HORMONAL ABNORMALITIES   Too much or too little of the wrong kind of hormones can also cause abnormal sex development. Two conditions that may result from hormonal abnormalities are hermaphroditism and pseudohermaphroditism.

Hermaphroditism is an extremely rare condition in which individuals are born with both ovarian and testicular tissue. These individuals, called hermaphrodites, may have one ovary and one testicle, feminine breasts, and a vaginal opening beneath the penis. They are generally genetic females (XX), and while their internal reproductive systems are usually mixed and incomplete as well, many hermaphrodites menstruate. Hermaphrodites may be reared as either males or females, depending largely on their appearance.

More common than hermaphroditism is *pseudohermaphroditism,* which refers to a condition in which an individual is born with gonads matching the sex chromosomes, but genitals resembling those of the other sex. There are numerous causes of pseudohermaphroditism. Two syndromes that we will discuss here are androgenital syndrome in women and testicular feminization syndrome in men.

You will recall that for the female fetus to develop normally, it must avoid unusually high doses of androgen ("male" hormones). Androgens, however, are produced not only by the testes, but also by the adrenal glands. Exposure to high levels of androgen can result from a malfunction of the mother's adrenal glands or from the mother's ingestion of synthetic hormones (such as progestin) that have an androgen effect on the fetus. (In the 1950s, progestin was often prescribed for pregnant women to prevent premature delivery.) Sometimes a genetic defect causes the adrenal glands of the XX fetus to produce excessive amounts of androgens, which results in *androgenital syndrome.* Excessive androgen causes the clitoris to greatly enlarge and the labia majora to fuse together to resemble a scrotum, resulting in genitals that resemble those of a male. Because individuals with this syndrome are genetically female, they are referred to as *female pseudohermaphrodites.* Genetically female infants whose genitals appear to be male are usually reared as males. During adolescence, the male-reared female may notice lack of facial hair growth, failure of the voice to deepen, and enlargement of the breasts. Chromosomal tests would reveal the XX genetic makeup of the individual, at which point it is usually recommended that the individual retain his male gender identity and have surgery to remove female internal organs (ovaries and uterus). In addition, hormone therapy is provided to deepen the voice, produce facial hair growth, and minimize breast growth.

Another hormonal fetal abnormality that results in pseudohermaphroditism—testicular feminization syndrome (TFS)—involves the lack of development of male genitals in the body of a person who is genetically male (a person who has XY chromosomes). In TFS, also known as *androgen-insensitivity syndrome,* the external tissues of the fetus fail to turn into male genitals. Even though normal amounts of androgen are produced, the tissues do not respond to the male hormones, and female external genitals are formed (labia, clitoris, and vaginal opening). The production of Mullerian duct–inhibiting substance is not impaired, so the fallopian tubes and uterus do not develop, and the vagina is quite short. Hence, while the newborn infant has the external genital appearance of a female (and is therefore reared as a female), the infant has testes embedded in the abdomen. These individuals are called *male pseudohermaphrodites.*

Parents are usually unaware of this hormonal abnormality until they realize at mid-adolescence that their daughter has not menstruated. She cannot do so because she has no uterus. Surgery can remove the testes and increase the depth of the vagina.

Sometimes infants are born with ambiguous genitals; they are neither clearly male nor female. These infants are called *intersexed infants.* When ambiguous genitals are detected at birth, physicians face the decision of assigning either the male or female gender to the intersexed infant.

In the past, infants with ambiguous genitals were reared in the gender most closely approximating the appearance of a particular sex. For example, if the infant's genitals were more similar to those of a female's, then it was assigned a female gender, regardless of its chromosomal makeup. Or, if there was a surgical mishap—during circumcision, for example—the genitals were reconstructed, and the "male" was reared as a "female" (Gorman, 1997). The practice of assigning sex on the basis of external appearance was based on the assumption that the environment was more important in determining a person's gender than one's biological sex (Money, Hampson, & Hampson, 1995). This assumption, however, has come into question (Kessler, 1990). Milton Diamond (1996), a specialist in intersexed infants, emphasizes "an inherent predisposition or bias toward a male or female identity which is inferred by prenatal influences" and suggests rearing the child in the biological (chromosomal) sex and performing genital reconstruction if necessary. He referred to an XY individual whose penis had been accidentally ablated and who was subsequently reared as a female. At puberty, however, the individual rejected his sex of rearing and switched to living as a male. Diamond and Sigmundson (1997) conclude:

> Considering this case follow-up, and as far as an extensive literature review can attest, there is no known case where a 46 chromosome, XY male, unequivocally so at birth, has ever easily and fully accepted an imposed life as an androphilic female regardless of physical and medical intervention. (p. 303)

Similarly, Diamond (1997a) recommended:

> . . . if the child is clearly 46, XX, even with a clitoral hypertrophy, raise it as a girl, but do not do a clitoral reduction. . . . A female with a large clitoris may be at some psychological and social disadvantage, but there are no data to show she would be worse off than being raised as a male. (p. 208)

Zucker (1996) examined both sides of the issue and pointed out that "there are clearly cases in the literature in which reassignment as a girl has been successful and cases in which it has not, and cases in which rearing in the male social role has also been problematic" (p. 156). While Zucker calls for more research and information, McKain (1996) calls for cultural acknowledgment and acceptance of mixed-sexed people. Rather than force intersexed individuals into one gender category of "male" or "female," intersexed individuals should be accepted as they are—a unique variation of the human population.

Some individuals experience *gender dysphoria,* which is a condition in which one's gender identity does not match one's biological sex. These individuals, known as transsexuals, have the genetic and anatomical characteristics of one sex but the self-concept of the other. "I am a woman trapped in a man's body" (or the reverse) reflects the feeling of being a transsexual.

> Most transsexual individuals, at first, seem to just have an amorphous feeling of being different quite early in life. Then slowly they *know* they are different from others in how they view themselves. Transsexual males . . . brought up as boys and transsexual females . . . reared as girls see this as a cruel mistake of fate. In their own minds there is no doubt they are of the opposite sex and should be reared accordingly . . . The TS [transsexual] then eventually presents to a physician or other professional with the urge to have sex reassignment surgery (SR). (Diamond, 1997b, p. 105)

At least one in 50,000 individuals over the age of 15 is likely to be a transsexual (Pauly, 1990). Men outnumber women by two or three times in adult clinical samples (American Psychiatric Association, 1994).

The transsexual does not have the self-concept of a homosexual. Both may be attracted to others of their own biological sex, but for different reasons. Whereas a homosexual male is attracted to other

This male-to-female transsexual demonstrates the degree to which some individuals can adopt the sexual and gender characteristics of the other sex.

For many years, gender dysphoria and transsexualism have been viewed as "conditions" that were "cured" by sex reassignment surgery. However, a new paradigm is emerging that recognizes a category of individuals who transcend the gender dichotomy. These individuals, referred to as *transgenderists,* live in a gender role that does not match their biological sex. Kymberleigh Richards (1997), who has the physical body of a man and the social identity of a woman, notes:

> The key difference between a transsexual and a transgenderist is that the latter has no burning desire to alter his or her birth genitalia in order to live in society in a role with which he or she feels comfortable . . . If anything, a transgenderist is the absolute best proof that sex does not equal gender. . . . (p. 503)

There is an important distinction between transvestites and transsexuals. *Transvestites* dress in the clothing of the other gender. They may experience erotic stimulation from wearing clothing of the other sex that is often a prelude to heterosexual sexual activity. But they retain their anatomical sexual orientation and are not interested in sex reassignment surgery. Hence, a male transvestite has a penis and enjoys dressing up as a woman but wants to keep his

This cross-dresser, shown here with his daughter on a family trip, is heterosexual.

males, the transsexual male is attracted to other men because he sees himself as a woman. Likewise, the transsexual woman is attracted to other women because she sees herself as a man. The homosexual's gender identity is consistent with his or her biological sex.

Cole, O'Boyle, Emory, and Meyer (1997) studied 435 transsexuals (318 male to female; 117 female to male) to assess the presence of major psychopathology. They concluded that "gender dysphoric individuals appear to be relatively 'normal' in terms of an absence of diagnosable, comorbid psychiatric problems" (p. 21). About 7 to 10% of the group did have identifiable psychiatric problems, but this is consistent with the general population (p. 21). Some transsexuals try to label themselves as transvestites as a way of denying their transsexual nature (Mason-Schrock, 1996).

penis. A male transsexual has a penis but dresses as a woman because he sees himself as a woman and wants to have his genitals changed so that he can become anatomically female.

Transvestites are usually heterosexual. Bullough and Bullough (1997) surveyed 372 cross-dressers. Sixty-seven percent identified themselves as heterosexual, 11% as bisexual, and 2% as homosexual. Twenty percent reported that "sex is not a part of my life now" (p. 6).

Sociobiology

Sociobiological explanations of gender roles emphasize that biological differences (such as hormonal and chromosomal differences) between men and women account for the social and psychological differences in female and male characteristics, behaviors, and roles. Testosterone is a male hormone associated with aggression; progesterone is a female hormone associated with nurturance. When female rats are given large doses of testosterone, they become aggressive; when male rats are given large doses of progesterone, they become nurturing (Arnold, 1980). The same hormonal reversal patterns have been observed in monkeys (Goy & McEwen, 1980).

Some research suggests that sexual thoughts and desires may be influenced by physiological factors. One study found that hypogonadal men, whose gonads produce limited amounts of androgen (testosterone), reported having few to no sexual thoughts (Bancroft, 1984). When they were administered androgen (androgen replacement therapy), they reported rapid increases in the frequency with which they thought about sex within 2 weeks of receiving the androgen. When the androgen replacement therapy was stopped for a 3-week period, the men reported rapid decreases in the frequency with which they thought about sex. This study was a placebo-controlled study, which means the men did not know if they were in the group receiving the androgen or the placebo, so the effects were not attributed to expectation.

Women's sexual thoughts are also influenced by androgen. Young surgically menopausal women (following removal of the ovaries) who received androgen reported increases in desire, arousal, and frequency of sexual fantasies (Sherwin, Gelfand, & Brender, 1985).

In mate selection, heterosexual men tend to value women who are youthful and physically attractive, whereas heterosexual women tend to value men who are economically stable. The pattern of men seeking physically attractive young women and women seeking economically ambitious men was observed in 37 groups of women and men in 33 different societies (Buss, 1989). This pattern is also evident in courtship patterns in the United States (Davis, 1990). An evolutionary explanation for this pattern argues that men and women have different biological agendas in terms of reproducing and caring for offspring (Symons & Ellis, 1989; Symons, 1987).

The term *parental investment* refers to any investment by a parent that increases the offspring's chance of surviving and thus increases reproductive success. Parental investments require time and energy. Women have a great deal of parental investment in their offspring (9 months' gestation, taking care of dependent offspring) and tend to mate with men who have high status, economic resources, and a willingness "to invest their resources in a given female and her offspring" (Ellis & Symons, 1990, p. 533). Men, on the other hand, focus on the importance of "health and youth" in their selection of a mate because young, healthy women are more likely to produce healthy offspring (Ellis & Symons, 1990, p. 534). Men also "have an aversion to invest in relationships with females who are sexually promiscuous" because men want to ensure that the offspring is their own (Grammer, 1989, p. 149).

The sociobiological explanation for mate selection is extremely controversial. Critics argue that women may show concern for the earning capacity of a potential mate because women have been systematically denied access to similar economic resources, and selecting a mate with these resources is one of their remaining options. In addition, it is argued that both women and men, when selecting a mate, think more about their partners as companions than as future parents of their offspring. Finally, the sociobiological perspective fails to acknowledge the degree to which social and psychological factors influence our behavior.

Identification Theory

Freud was one of the first researchers to study gender role acquisition. Freud suggested that children acquire the characteristics and behaviors of their same-sex parent through a process of identification. Boys identify with their fathers, and girls identify with their mothers. Freud (1925/1974, 1933/1965) said that children identify with the same-gender parent out of fear. Freud felt this fear could be one of two kinds: fear of loss of love or fear of retaliation. Fear of loss of love, which results in both girls and boys identifying with their mother, is caused by their deep dependence on her for love and nurturance. Fearful that she may withdraw her love, young children try to become like her to please her and to ensure the continuance of her love.

According to Freud, at about age 4, the child's identification with the mother begins to change, but in different ways for boys than for girls. Boys experience what Freud called the *"Oedipal complex."* Based on the legend of the Greek youth Oedipus, who unknowingly killed his father and married his mother, the Oedipal complex involves the young boy's awakening sexual feelings for his mother as he becomes aware he has a penis and his mother does not. He unconsciously feels that if his father knew of the intense love feelings he has for his mother, the father would castrate him (which may be what happened to his mother, because she has no penis). The boy resolves the Oedipal struggle—feeling love for his father but wanting to kill him because he is a competitor for his mother's love—by becoming like his father by identifying with him. In this way, the boy can keep his penis and take pride in being like his father. According to Freud, the successful resolution of this Oedipal situation marks the beginning of a boy's appropriate gender-role acquisition.

The *"Electra complex"* is based on the Greek myth in which Electra assists her brother in killing their mother and her lover to avenge their father's death. In Freudian terms, the Electra complex refers to unconscious sexual feelings a daughter develops for her father. These feelings develop when 3- to 6-year-old girls become aware that they do not have a penis. Freud believed that girls blame their mothers for cutting off their penis or causing it to be severed and that they develop "penis envy" and wish that they had a penis. To retaliate, girls take their love away from their mothers and begin to focus on their fathers as love objects. Girls feel that they can be fulfilled by being impregnated by their fathers as love objects. Girls feel that they can be fulfilled by

being impregnated by their fathers, who will give them a baby to substitute for the penis they do not have. To become impregnated by their fathers, girls recognize that they must be more like their mother. So they identify again with the mother. A modern interpretation of penis envy is that women do not desire to have a penis, but rather, they desire the economic and social advantages that men have (Chafetz, 1988).

The view that at least some gender role behaviors are biologically based is deeply ingrained in our culture. For example, we tend to think of mothers as naturally equipped and inclined to perform the role of primary child caregiver. Chodorow (1978) argued that the role of child caregiver has been assigned to women, although there is no biological reason why fathers cannot be the primary caregiver or participate in child-rearing activities.

In *The Reproduction of Mothering,* Chodorow (1978) used Freudian identification theory as a basis for her theory that gender role specialization occurs in the family because of the "asymmetrical organization of parenting" (p. 49).

> Women, as mothers, produce daughters with mothering capacities and the desire to mother. These capacities and needs are built into and grow out of the mother-daughter relationship itself. By contrast, women as mothers (and men as not-mothers) produce sons whose nurturant capacities and needs have been systematically curtailed and repressed. (p. 7)

In other words, all activities associated with nurturing and child care are identified as female activities because women are the primary caregivers of young children. This one-sidedness (or asymmetry) of nurturing by women increases the likelihood that females, because they identify with their mother, will see their own primary identities and roles as mothers. According to Chodorow, "the social structure produces gendered personalities that reproduce the social structure" (Hare-Mustin & Marecek, 1988).

Chodorow sees the "asymmetrical organization of parenting" as the basis for the continuing unequal social organization of gender. In order to change this social inequality, we must recognize "the need for a fundamental reorganization of parenting, so that primary parenting is shared between men and women" (Chodorow, 1978, p. 215).

Social Learning Theory

Derived from the school of behavioral psychology, social learning theory emphasizes the role of reward and punishment in explaining how a child learns gender role behavior. For example, two young brothers enjoyed playing "lady." Each of them would put on a dress, wear high-heeled shoes, and carry a pocketbook. Their father came home early one day and angrily demanded they "take those clothes off and never put them on again." "Those things are for women," he said. The boys were punished for playing "lady" but rewarded with their father's approval for playing "cowboys," with plastic guns and "Bang! You're dead!" dialogue.

Reward and punishment alone are not sufficient to account for the way in which children learn gender roles. Direct instruction ("girls wear dresses," "men walk on the outside when walking with a woman") is another way children learn through social interaction with others. In addition, many of society's gender rules are learned through modeling. In modeling, the child observes another's behavior and imitates that behavior. Gender role models include parents, peers, siblings, and characters portrayed in the media.

The impact of modeling on the development of gender-role behavior is controversial. For example, a modeling perspective implies that children will tend to imitate the parent of the same sex, but children are usually reared mainly by women in all cultures. Yet this persistent female model does not seem to interfere with the male's development of the behavior that is considered appropriate for his gender. One explanation suggests that boys learn early that our society generally grants boys and men more status and privileges than girls and women; therefore, they devalue the feminine and emphasize the masculine aspects of themselves.

Women also do not strictly model their mothers' behavior. Although women who work outside the home usually have mothers who did likewise, their mothers may also be traditional homemakers.

The fact that gender roles differ across societies provides evidence that gender roles are learned. Mead (1935) visited three New Guinea tribes in the early 1930s and observed that the Arapesh socialized both men and women to be feminine by Western standards. The Arapesh person was taught to be cooperative and responsive to the needs of others. In contrast, the Tchambuli were known for their dominant women and submissive men—just the opposite of our society. Both of these societies were unlike the Mundugumor, which socialized only ruthless, aggressive, "masculine" personalities. The inescapable conclusion of this cross-cultural study is that human beings are products of their social and cultural environment and that gender roles are learned. (However, Mead's 1928 book, *Coming of Age in Samoa,* was disputed by Freeman in 1983.)

A modern-day cross-cultural example of gender role is witnessed in subservient Hindu and Muslim women. In the presence of others, a young wife in either of these cultures must not speak to her husband or stare at him. At meals, a woman eats only after the men have been served, and a wife walking with her husband is expected to follow a few steps behind him. Although we tend to think of the United States as having very liberal gender roles, it was only 40 years ago that women were "refused the right to serve on juries, sign contracts, take out credit cards in their own names, or establish legal residence" (Coontz, 1995, p. 13).

Cognitive-Developmental Theory

The cognitive-developmental theory of gender role acquisition reflects a blend of biological and social learning views. According to this theory, the biological readiness (in terms of the cognitive development of the child) influences how the child responds to gender cues in the environment (Kohlberg, 1966, 1976).

For example, gender discrimination (the ability to identify social and psychological characteristics associated with being female and male) begins at about age 30 months. At that age, toddlers are able to assign a "boy's toy" to a boy and a "girl's toy" to a girl (Etaugh & Duits, 1990). However, at this age, children do not view gender as a permanent characteristic. Thus, while young children may define people who wear long hair as girls and those who never wear dresses as boys, they also believe they can change their gender by altering their hair or changing clothes.

Not until age 6 or 7 does the child view gender as permanent (Kohlberg, 1966, 1969). In Kohlberg's view, this cognitive understanding is not a result of social learning. Rather, it involves the development of a specific mental ability to grasp the idea that certain basic characteristics of people do not change. Once children learn the concept of gender permanence, they seek to become competent and proper members of their gender group. For example, a child standing on the edge of a school playground may observe one group of children jumping rope while another group is playing football. That child's gender identity as either a girl or a boy connects with the observed "gender-appropriate" behavior, and she or he joins one of the two groups. Once in the group, the child seeks to develop the behaviors that are socially defined as appropriate for her or his gender.

Some cognitive-developmental theories suggest that the moral development of men and women may be different. Gilligan (1982) observed that many men make judgments on the basis of competing rights and abstract principles, whereas women often make judgments on their assessments of competing responsibilities. Gilligan's point is to demonstrate not only that men and women have different conceptions of morality, but that the male conception is regarded as the universal standard by which both men and women are evaluated, and to point out that an alternative moral "voice"—the "care" perspective—is as legitimate as the "rights" perspective. However, while Gilligan's work made an important contribution in calling attention to an ethic of care in moral decision making, subsequent research has not confirmed that men and women consistently differ in their patterns of moral reasoning (Tavris, 1992).

Gender Schema Theory

Gender schema theory, a more recently developed theory of gender role acquisition, combines aspects of cognitive-developmental theory and social learning theory. The term "schema" refers to a "network of associations that organizes and guides an individual's perception" (Bem, 1983, p. 603). A *gender schema* is a network of associations with the concepts of male and female (or masculinity and femininity) that organizes and guides perception.

Consistent with social learning theory, the male and female associations that comprise the content of gender schemas are learned through interaction with the social environment. The gender schema then influences how an individual processes information by structuring and organizing perception. A gender schema influences how incoming information, including information about the self, is evaluated with regard to gender norms. This aspect of gender schema theory, which emphasizes the role of cognitive frameworks in processing information, reflects cognitive-developmental theory.

Gender schema theory suggests that people follow gender schemas to different degrees and in different ways.

> Some people, for example, organize many of their thoughts, perceptions, and evaluations around concepts of male and female, masculine and feminine. These people, whom we might describe as highly sex-typed, rely heavily on gender stereotypes and symbols to understand the social world. They see a wide variety of human characteristics, behavior, roles, and jobs as decidedly masculine or feminine and evaluate themselves and others according to how well they conform to gender norms and stereotypes.
>
> Other people follow gender schemas less closely or not at all. This does not necessarily mean that they lack what the highly sex-typed person might regard as appropriate masculine or feminine characteristics. Gender may simply not be the central means by which they organize their perceptions of themselves and the social world. Whereas the highly sex-typed person might immediately understand words such as *pink, nurturant, blushing, librarian,* and *curved,* as "feminine," these words might not have any immediate gender connotation to the person with no gender schema. (Sapiro, 1990, p. 88)

The various theories on gender role development reflect differing views on whether gender differences are biologically based or are the result of social and cognitive factors. While debate about the source of sex differences continues, another debate centers around the degree to which women and men are different and the degree to which they are similar. Unger (1990) commented that "the fact that the sexes are more similar than they are different is not considered noteworthy either by psychology as a discipline or by society as a whole" (p. 104).

Which of the theories of gender role development best reflects popular views on gender differences? Which of the theories might contribute to the perpetuation of social inequality between women and men?

AGENTS OF GENDER ROLE SOCIALIZATION

Three of the four theories discussed in the preceding section emphasize that gender roles are learned through interaction with the environment. Indeed, although biology may provide a basis for some roles (being 7'5" is helpful for a basketball player), cultural influences in the form of various socialization agents (parents, peers, teachers, religion, and the media) shape the individual toward various gender roles. These powerful influences in large part dictate what a person thinks, feels, and does in his or her role as a woman or a man.

Parents

Parents are one of the most important influences in a child's life, but mothers and fathers influence their children in different ways. In a nationally representative sample of about 2000 children and one of their parents, Starrels (1994) found that fathers spend more time with sons than with daughters and provide more instrumental attention (such as giving gifts or money) to their children than do mothers. In contrast, mothers provide more affective nurturance in the form of love and interest, affection, and verbal praise to daughters and sons equally.

Both parents tend to assign chores to their children depending on whether the child is a boy or a girl (McHale, Bartko, Crouter, & Perry-Jenkins, 1990). Boys tend to be assigned maintenance chores, such as mowing lawns, while girls tend to be assigned domestic tasks, such as cooking, laundry, and taking care of siblings. Such differential chore assignment may encourage the development of different personal qualities. For example, girls required to take care of their younger siblings may be more likely to develop nurturing behaviors than boys who are

required to cut the grass (Basow, 1992). Parents should be aware that the chores they assign to their children will affect what they learn.

Peers

While parents are usually the first socializing agents that influence a child's gender role development, peers become increasingly important during the school years. The gender role messages from adolescent peers call for traditional traits.

> For adolescent boys, such traits include being tough (through body build or athletic achievement), being cool (not showing emotions, not fearful of danger, staying reasonable under stress), being interested in girls and sex, being good at something, being physically attractive and having an absence of any trait or characteristic that is female or feminine. (Harrison & Pennell, 1989, p. 32)

Female adolescents are under tremendous pressure to be physically attractive, popular, and achievement-oriented. The latter may be traditional (cheerleading) or nontraditional (sports or academics). Adolescent females are sometimes in great conflict in that high academic success may be viewed as being less than feminine.

Peer disapproval for failure to conform to traditional gender stereotypes is reflected in the terms _sissy_ and _tomboy_. These terms are used pejoratively to refer to children who exhibit behaviors stereotypically associated with the other gender.

Teachers and Educational Materials

Although parents have the earliest influence on a child, and adolescent peers have the most significant influence during the teen years, teachers are another important socialization influence. Research suggests that teachers provide differential treatment to boys and girls:

> . . . Elementary and secondary teachers give far more active teaching attention to boys than girls. They talk to boys more, ask them more lower- and higher-order questions, listen to them more, counsel them more, give them more extended directions, and criticize and reward them more frequently.
>
> This pattern of more active teacher attention directed at male students continues at the post-

secondary level. In general, women are rarely called on; when female students do participate, their comments are more likely to be interrupted and less likely to be accepted or rewarded (Sadker & Sadker, 1990, p. 177).

Gender role stereotypes are also conveyed through educational materials. In a study of 1883 stories used in schools, Purcell and Stewart (1990) found that males were more often presented as clever, brave, adventurous, and income-producing, while females were more often presented as passive and as victims. Females were also more likely to be in need of rescue and were depicted in fewer occupational roles than were males.

Children's books more often show women holding domestic household artifacts (such as a skillet), while men are more often shown holding nondomestic production products (such as a wrench) (Crabb & Bielawski, 1994).

Religion

Traditional and conservative interpretations of the Bible reflect the patriarchal nature of family roles. Basow found that "to the extend that a child has any religious instruction, he or she receives further training in the gender stereotypes" (1992, p. 156). The following passages are commonly cited.

> Wives be subject to your husband, as to the Lord. . . . Husbands, love your wives, even as Christ also loved the church. (Ephesians 5:22–25) (See also Colossians 3:18-19.)

> . . . that both male and female are created in the image of God (Genesis 1:27).

While the Bible has been interpreted in both sexist and nonsexist terms, male dominance is indisputable in the hierarchy of religious organizations, where power and status have been accorded mostly to men. Until recently, only men could be priests, ministers, and rabbis. Basow (1992) noted that the Catholic church does not have female clergy, and men dominate the 19 top positions in the U.S. dioceses.

Male bias is also reflected in terminology used to refer to God in Jewish, Christian, and Islamic religions. For example, God is traditionally referred to as "He," "Father," "Lord," and "King." Two researchers observed that individuals who attend religious services frequently are more likely to have traditional gender role ideologies than individuals who do not attend church frequently (Willetts-Bloom & Nock, 1994).

In response to an interest in removing sexist language from religious works, hymns are being rewritten. The 1865 hymn, "Rejoice, You Pure in Heart" no longer speaks of "strong men and maidens meek" but speaks of "strong souls and spirits meek." And "The Father, Son, and Holy Ghost" has been changed to "Praise God the Spirit, Holy Fire."

Media

In reference to media, the phrase "you are what you eat" might be replaced with "you are what you see and read" (Doyle, 1995, p. 96). Media, such as movies, television, magazines, newspapers, books, and music, both reflect and shape gender roles. Gender role relationships in movies reflect those of male dominance (Hedley, 1994). Media images of women and men typically conform to traditional gender stereotypes, and media portrayals depicting the exploitation, victimization, and sexual objectification of women are common.

What the media fail to address are the political, economic, cultural, and social structures that exist to freeze women into a narrow range of roles to ensure their continued dependence (Baxter & Kane, 1995). The real issues of limited female representation in Congress and sexism in employment and wages are avoided. Rather, the media exist to sell products, not to press political agendas. And men, who control media content, would not allow it anyway. As Rapping (1994) asserts, "we are not allowed to rock the political or economic boat of television by suggesting that things could be different. That would rightly upset the sponsors and network heads" (p. 196).

THINK ABOUT IT

What do you regard as the most significant socialization agents of gender role behavior?

Effects of Traditional Gender Role Socialization on Relationships and Sexuality

Gender role socialization influences virtually every sphere of life, including self-concept, educational achievement, occupation, income, and health. Traditional gender role socialization has different outcomes for women and men and has different effects on their relationships and sexuality.

Socialization Effects on the Relationships and Sexuality of Women

Traditional female gender role socialization affects women in various ways and to different degrees (as listed below). The sexuality and relationships of some women may be more or less influenced by traditional gender role socialization, depending in part on whether the woman accepts or rejects traditional gender roles.

1. *Body image.* The participation of young children in beauty pageants brings into cultural focus the degree to which even very young girls are socialized to emphasize beauty and appearance. The effect for many women who do not match the cultural ideal is to have a negative body image. In the *Psychology Today's* 1997 Body Image Survey, 56% of women, in contrast to 43% of men, reported body image dissatisfaction (Garner, 1997). Women who feel unattractive report that negative feelings about their body have a negative effect on their desire for sex (Garner, 1997). Women are also more likely than men to have eating disorders (Seid, 1994), and to report going on diets. In regard to the latter, 96% of college women in a nonrandom sample reported dieting, in contrast to 59% of college men (Elliott & Brantley, 1997).

    Dissatisfaction with one's body image is not unique to American women. In their study of 305 Chinese college students, Tang, Lai, Phil, and Chung (1997) found that women were significantly more likely to have negative body images than men. They also found that having a better body image was related to being more sexually active.

2. *Sexual thoughts.* Women report thinking about sex less often than men. Nineteen percent of women, in contrast to 54% of men, in a national sample reported thinking about sex "every day" or "several times a day" (Michael, Gagnon, Laumann, & Kolata, 1994, p. 156). Women are also less likely to have sexual fantasies (Hsu et al., 1994) and be interested in watching erotica (Purnine, Carey, & Jorgensen, 1994). In effect, it is more socially acceptable for men in our society to express interest in sex, to fantasize about it, and to watch erotica. Tang et al. (1997) also found that male Chinese college students express more interest in sex and fantasize more about it than female college students. Erotica is much less available in China, so it was not assessed in this study.

3. *Masturbation.* Women are less likely to report masturbation than men. Among Americans aged 18–59, about 40% of women and 60% of men reported having masturbated in the previous 12 months (Michael et al., 1994, p. 60). Traditional female socialization has taught women that it is "dirty" to touch themselves "down there." Tang et al. (1997) reported that twice as many Chinese college men reported having masturbated than college women (44 versus 21%).

4. *Perception of genitals.* Women have more negative perceptions of their own and their partners' genitals than men (Reinholtz & Muehlenhard, 1995). In addition, data from 364 undergraduates studied by Reinholtz and Muehlenhard revealed that women felt more degraded when participating in oral sex than men.

5. *Love and sexuality.* Women are more likely than men to report that their first intercourse experience was in the context of a dating relationship rather than a casual sexual experience. In a sample of college students, 25% of the women, in contrast to 16% of the men, said that they were dating the person they lost their virginity with (Sprecher, Barbee & Schwartz, 1995). These data reflect the larger issue of women being more likely to require a

context of love for sexual involvement. In another sample of college students, Townsend (1995) found that 40% of women and 12% of men reported that they "should be emotionally involved" before having sex. Furthermore, Greer (1996) compared 51 female and 47 male undergraduates and found that sex is more relationship focused for women and more genitally focused for men. Finally, Regan and Berscheid (1996) concluded that "sexual desire represents a more romantic interpersonal experience for women than for men" (p. 110). These findings are not surprising since women have been socialized to associate love and sex, while men have been socialized to associate sex and pleasure.

6. *Sexual guilt.* Women are more likely than men to report feeling guilty after their first intercourse experience (Sprecher et al., 1995). Considerable masturbatory guilt is also characteristic of women (Davidson & Moore, 1994). Most societies exert more social control over the sexuality of women, and guilt inducement is one mechanism of such control.

7. *Orgasm.* Women are less likely than men to experience orgasm. This is particularly true at first intercourse. Seven percent of women, in contrast to 79% of men, reported orgasm during their first intercourse experience (Sprecher et al., 1995). Lower orgasmic frequency is not only related to sexual technique (less contact with the clitoris), but also to traditional female role socialization that discourages women from seeking sexual pleasure.

8. *Age of partners.* Women are more likely than men to be sexually involved with partners older than themselves. Traditional cultural norms suggest that it is more acceptable for women to date and marry men who are older than it is for men to date and marry women who are older.

NATIONAL DATA

The median age of first-married women and men is 24.5 and 26.7, respectively.

Source: Saluter, 1996.

Sometimes the age discrepancy between the woman and her partner is dramatic. Some celebrities are a substantial number of years older than their spouses, including Tony Randall, who is 50 years older; Tony Bennett, who is 40 years older; and Johnny Carson, who is 26 years older. Women report that financial security, maturity, and dependability are the primary advantages of involvement with an older man (Knox, Britton, & Crisp, 1997).

9. *Number of partners.* Women report having fewer sexual partners than men. Six percent of adult women in a national sample, in contrast to 16% of men, reported having between 10 and 20 sexual partners since age 18 (Michael et al., 1994). Traditional female role socialization teaches women to limit the number of sexual partners so they will not be perceived as being "loose" or immoral. In many traditional societies (such as in Palestine), women are expected to have only one sexual partner (their husband) during their lifetime.

10. *Economic dependency.* Although women are more economically independent today than in previous generations, many women are still dependent on their husband's income. Therefore, some women may stay with a male partner out of economic need. Although women earn slightly more than half of all bachelor's and master's degrees, they are less likely to earn advanced degrees, such as degrees in dentistry, medicine, and law (*Statistical Abstract of the United States: 1996,* Tables 302–304). The strongest explanation for why women earn fewer advanced degrees than men is that women are socialized to value motherhood over career preparation. More than half (53%) of 821 undergraduate women selected "graduation, full-time work, marriage, children, stop working at least until youngest child is in school, then pursue a full-time job" as their most preferred lifestyle preference. Only 6% of 535 undergraduate men selected this same pattern (Schroeder, Blood, & Maluso, 1993). Even when women and men have equivalent academic degrees, women still earn about two-thirds of what men earn (*Statistical Abstract of the United States: 1996,* Table 728).

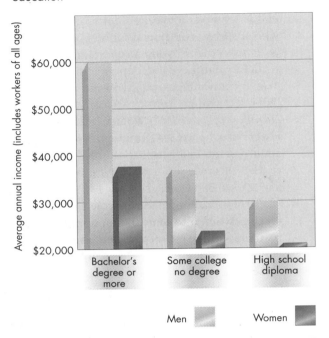

Income of women and men with similar education

Average annual income (includes workers of all ages)

Men ▦   Women ▦

Source: *Statistical Abstract of the United States: 1996*, Table 728.

🍃 The economic inequality between women and men is not unique to the United States. Women in Canada, Australia, Norway, and Sweden also earn about 75% of what men earn (Baxter & Kane, 1995). In China, women earn 60% of what men earn (Cox, 1995). 🍃

11. *Initiation of relationships.* According to traditional expectations of gender role dating behavior, women are expected to be passive and to rely on the man to initiate a relationship (Laner, 1995). Women who are passive and rely on men to make the first move may miss out on potentially rewarding relationships.

12. *Resentment and anger in sexual relationships.* Women who are socialized to accept that they are solely responsible for taking care of their aging parents, their young children, and their husbands are likely to experience role overload. Potentially, this may result in feelings of anger and resentment toward the partner who does not share the workload of caring for others. Hochschild (1989) noted that the term

superwoman or *supermom* is a cultural label that allows women to regard themselves as "unusually efficient, organized, energetic, bright, and confident" (p. 32). However, Hochschild noted that this is a "cultural cover up" for an overworked and frustrated woman. As we noted in Chapter 4, anger and resentment can have a negative effect on sexual interest.

13. *Nonegalitarian relationships. Egalitarian relationships* are those in which partners relate to each other as equals (Schwartz & Jackson, 1989). Although most women would be happier in relationships that are egalitarian, many tolerate nonegalitarian relationships because they have been influenced by traditional gender role socialization that is based on the idea that husbands are dominant in the family. Many women defer to their husbands or male partners because they have been taught to view men as more competent. In a study of first-year students at a southeastern university, compared to men, women reported having less intellectual and social self-confidence (Smith, 1995).

PERSONAL CHOICES

Should You Seek Egalitarian Relationships?

Egalitarian relationships are those in which partners have mutual respect for each other, share the power, and share the work of the relationship. Mutual respect translates into each acknowledging the credibility of the other's thoughts, feelings, and perspectives. Relationships with mutual respect are those in which the power is also shared. Neither partner is dominant but discusses the options to arrive at a mutual decision with the other.

Partners in egalitarian relationships also share the work of their relationship. Either may cook, clean the house, or change the oil in the car. For pair-bonded couples, egalitarian relationships provide an opportunity for empathy unknown in traditional relationships. When only the man was employed outside the home and the woman stayed home to take care of the house and children, each partner had a set of experiences that was unknown to the other partner. He might be tired at the end of the day from working at the office; she might be tired from cleaning the house, preparing the meals, and taking care of two young children. Each was sure that he or she was more tired than the other and regarded his or her own role as the more difficult role and the partner's role as "nothing to complain about." Alternatively, when couples decide to share the generation of income, food preparation, housecleaning, and child care, each has an experiential understanding of what the other feels.

Research findings suggest that being in a relationship of mutual respect, power, and work sharing is associated with high relationship satisfaction. In one study, of the wives who reported that they had "excellent marriages," 88% reported that they shared the decision making equally with their husbands (Schwartz & Jackson, 1989, p. 72). In another study based on 349 college students, those involved in equitable dating relationships reported more contentment and commitment than those in inequitable dating relationships (Winn, Crawford, & Fischer, 1991).

Socialization Effects on the Relationships and Sexuality of Men

Men are also affected by their socialization in the following ways.

1. *Less emotional intimacy.* In general, men are socialized to restrict emotional experience and expression. Men are less emotional than women because traditional male socialization teaches that being emotional is not "manly"; it is a sign of weakness. In addition, men are taught to believe that task accomplishment is an important goal and that emotional control is one general strategy for facilitating that goal. Men who restrict their emotional experience and expression limit their opportunity to discover the rewards of emotional intimacy.

2. *Performance anxiety.* Two researchers compared 119 men and 56 women on an array of sexual concerns and found that men were significantly more concerned about sexual performance than women (Cowden & Koch, 1995). Given that men are socialized to be concerned about penis size (Lee, 1996) and being positively perceived in the bedroom, this finding is not surprising. Men in countries such as Saudi Arabia, where potency expectations are particularly high, have enormous anxiety over sexual performance (Osman & Al-Sawaf, 1995).

3. *Restriction of potential partners.* Heterosexual men who focus on cultural definitions of female beauty overlook potential partners who may be compatible emotional and sexual life companions. Heterosexual men also tend to seek younger women. For example, a sample of 50-year-old men advertising for partners preferred partners who were almost 9 years younger; 70-year-old men preferred women 15 years younger (Hayes, 1995). Focusing on younger women eliminates a large pool of potential partners closer to the men's ages.

4. *Sexual aggression and coercion.* Men are more likely than women to engage in sexually aggressive and coercive behavior. Hence, women are more likely than men to be victims of sexual aggression and coercion. Twenty-two percent of adult women in a national sample, in contrast to 2% of the men, reported being forced to do something sexual at some time in their lives (Michael et al., 1994). Men are more likely than women to believe in "rape myths"—beliefs that promote the acceptance of sexual coercion. For example, men are more likely than women to believe that "women who say 'no' to sex really mean 'yes' or 'maybe.'" Men are also more likely than women to use interpersonal pressure and tell lies in order to achieve sexual ends (Cochran & Mays, 1990; Patton & Mannison, 1995).

5. *Purchase of sex.* Men are more likely than women to buy erotic material and purchase sexual services (such as prostitution and phone sex). Sixteen percent of adult women and 41% of adult men in a national sample reported spending money on erotic material (X-rated videos, sex magazines, sex phone numbers, etc.) in the last 12 months (Michael et al., 1994). To be interested in sex solely for physical gratification is less taboo for men than for women (Leitenberg, Detzer, & Srebnik, 1993). Also, the parental investment required of men to produce offspring is much less than that of women, which translates into their greater involvement in casual, short-term sexual encounters (Malamuth, 1996).

6. *Lack of domestic skills.* Men have traditionally learned that their role in the family is to be the primary breadwinner and that women take care of the children, prepare food, and perform household chores. Lack of domestic participation

among men may create unhappiness in their partners, who feel unfairly burdened with household and child care responsibilities.

7. *Involvement in group sex.* Almost half (46%) of a national sample of men ages 18–44 (in contrast to 9% of women the same age) reported that group sex was "very" or "somewhat" appealing to them (Michael et al., 1994). In terms of actual behavior, 13% of men and 10% of women in a nonrandom sample of 2000 college students reported having engaged in a threesome (Elliott & Brantley, 1997).

8. *Sexual double standard.* Men are more likely than women to believe in the sexual double standard. By completing the Sexual Double Standard Scale in the following self-assessment, you can measure the degree to which you have identical or different sexual standards for women and men.

In effect, traditional gender role socialization may have negative outcomes for the sexuality and intimate relationships of women and men. Individuals should be aware of the potential effects of their socialization and make deliberate choices to their own benefit.

_____ THINK ABOUT IT _____

How have your own relationship and sexual choices been influenced by your gender role socialization?

ANDROGYNY AND GENDER ROLE TRANSCENDENCE

Androgyny

Androgyny refers to a blend of traits that are stereotypically associated with masculinity and femininity. Street et al. (1995) reported a preference on the part of more than 1800 university women and more than 1000 university men for the ideal woman to be "androgynous." In reality, Twenge (1995) observed that U.S. college women are becoming more "masculine" in terms of being assertive, action-oriented, and goal-driven but that U.S. college men are no more "feminine" in terms of being nurturing and empathic than they were 20 years ago.

This person has androgynous physical features.

Androgyny also implies flexibility of traits; for example, an androgynous individual may be emotional in one situation, logical in another, assertive in another, and so forth.

> Thus, each androgynous individual has the opportunity to develop his or her potential to its fullest, without the restriction that only gender-appropriate behaviors are allowed. (Basow, 1992, p. 326)

Although some studies have found that androgyny is associated with high self-esteem, social competence, flexibility, and fewer psychological problems, others had found androgyny to be associated with increased work stress, difficulty in directing behavior effectively, and less overall emotional adjustment (Harrison & Pennell, 1989).

Androgyny may be viewed as an alternative to traditional gender roles, but gender scholars have noted several problems concerning the concept of androgyny. One problem is that "androgyny has come to be seen as a combination of the traits of the two sexes rather than as a transcendence of gender categorization itself" (Unger, 1990, p. 112).

SEXUAL DOUBLE STANDARD SCALE

R ank each statement according to the following scale: (A) agree strongly, (B) agree mildly, (C) disagree mildly, (D) disagree strongly.

		A	B	C	D
1.	It's worse for a woman to sleep around than it is for a man.	__	__	__	__
2.	It's best for a guy to lose his virginity before he's out of his teens.	__	__	__	__
3.	It's OK for a woman to have more than one sexual relationship at the same time.	__	__	__	__
4.	It is just as important for a man to be a virgin when he marries as it is for a woman.	__	__	__	__
5.	I approve of a 16-year-old girl's having sex just as much as a 16-year-old boy's having sex.	__	__	__	__
6.	I kind of admire a girl who has had sex with a lot of guys.	__	__	__	__
7.	I kind of feel sorry for a 21-year-old woman who is still a virgin.	__	__	__	__
8.	A woman's having casual sex is just as acceptable to me as a man's having casual sex.	__	__	__	__
9.	It's okay for a man to have sex with a woman with whom he is not in love.	__	__	__	__
10.	I kind of admire a guy who has had sex with a lot of girls.	__	__	__	__
11.	A woman who initiates sex is too aggressive.	__	__	__	__
12.	It's okay for a man to have more than one sexual relationship at the same time.	__	__	__	__
13.	I question the character of a woman who has had a lot of sexual partners.	__	__	__	__
14.	I admire a man who is a virgin when he gets married.	__	__	__	__
15.	A man should be more sexually experienced than his wife.	__	__	__	__
16.	A girl who has sex on the first date is "easy."	__	__	__	__
17.	I kind of feel sorry for a 21-year-old man who is still a virgin.	__	__	__	__
18.	I question the character of a guy who has had a lot of sexual partners.	__	__	__	__
19.	Women are naturally more monogamous (inclined to stick with one partner) than are men.	__	__	__	__
20.	A man should be sexually experienced when he gets married.	__	__	__	__
21.	A guy who has sex on the first date is "easy."	__	__	__	__
22.	It's okay for a woman to have sex with a man she is not in love with.	__	__	__	__
23.	A woman should be sexually experienced when she gets married.	__	__	__	__
24.	It's best for a girl to lose her virginity before she's out of her teens.	__	__	__	__
25.	I admire a woman who is a virgin when she gets married.	__	__	__	__
26.	A man who initiates sex is too aggressive.	__	__	__	__

Scoring   Convert A's to 0's, B's to 1's, C's to 2's, and D's to 3's. Compute the total = #4 + #5 + #8 + (3 − #1) + (3 − #15) + (3 − #19) + (#24 − #2) + (#3 − #12) + (#6 − #10) + (#7 − #17) + (#22 − #9) + (#26 − #11) + (#18 − #13) + (#14 − #25) + (#21 − #16) + (#23 − #20)

Interpreting your score   A score of 0 indicates identical sexual standards for women and men. Scores greater than 0 reflect more restrictive standards for women than for men; the highest possible score is 48. Scores less than 0 reflect more restrictive standards for

Continued on following page.

men than for women; the lowest possible score is –30. In a study of students from Texas A&M University, the men's mean score was 13.15 ($n = 255$), and the women's mean was 11.99 ($n = 461$) (Muehlenhard & Quackenbush, 1988). (When used in a research study, the title would not be at the top of the scale!) When asked to rate their partner's acceptance of the sexual double standard, female students rated their partners as more accepting of it than the women rated themselves. In fact, the women believed that men adhere to the double standard even more than the men reported (Muehlenhard & McCoy, 1991).

Reliability and validity   Muehlenhard and Quackenbush (cited in Muehlenhard & McCoy, 1991) reported a coefficient alpha of 0.726 for women's reports of their own acceptance of the sexual double standard and 0.817 for their ratings of their partners' beliefs. Correlations of the measure with other variables (traditional gender roles, erotophobia-erotophilia, self-monitoring) have been in the predicted directions.

In their study of 403 female general psychology students at the University of Kansas, Muehlenhard and McCoy (1991) examined the relationship between women's acceptance of the double standard (and their rating of their partners' acceptance) with the women's willingness to acknowledge their desire for sexual intercourse. The women were asked if they had ever been in the following situation:

> You were with a guy you'd *never* had sexual intercourse with before. He wanted to engage in sexual intercourse and you wanted to also, but for some reason you indicated that you didn't want to, although *you had every intention to and were willing to engage in sexual intercourse.* In other words, you indicated "no" and meant "yes." (p. 451)

They were also presented a scenario in which they had wanted to engage in intercourse and "made it clear to the guy that you wanted to have sexual intercourse" (p. 452) and were asked if they had ever been in that situation. The women completed the Sexual Double Standard Scale (self and inferences about partner), the Attitudes Toward Women Scale, the Sexual Opinion Survey, and the Self-Monitoring Scale. Of these five variables, only the women's beliefs about their partner's acceptance of the double standard predicted whether the women had ever said "no" when they meant "yes" (scripted refusal) or said "yes" and meant "yes" (open acknowledgment). The researchers found that "women who had offered scripted refusals were more likely to believe that their partners accepted the sexual double standard than women who had openly acknowledged their desire for sexual intercourse" (p. 457).

Meuhlenhard and McCoy observed that the sexual double standard puts women in a double bind. If they are open about their sexual desires, they risk being negatively labeled. So, is the safest (for one's reputation) course of action to be reluctant to acknowledge wanting to have sex? Muehlenhard and McCoy suggested that the sexual double standard could be decreased by pointing out its unfairness to both men and women. Men may feel pressured to push for sex whether or not they desire it (and whether or not they have a willing partner).

The majority of women had never engaged in scripted refusal (and those who had, reported doing so infrequently). Muehlenhard and McCoy emphasized that men should always take a "no" at face value. This may be even better advice in view of recent information obtained by Muehlenhard and her colleagues. Although these researchers thought the scenario for scripted refusal was clearly indicating a situation in which the woman wanted to have sex, more recent examples from women asked to describe the situation reflect *ambivalence* about having sex more than *willingness.* The situations that were described often indicated that the respondents had misinterpreted the researchers' questions. The number of respondents who engaged in "token resistance" (as evaluated by trained raters)—only 2 to 14% of women and 2 to 10% of men—was much smaller than the 35% indicated in previous studies (Rodgers & Muehlenhard, 1992). Therefore, despite the sexual double standard and stereotypes about women offering token resistance to intercourse, for the vast majority of men and women "no" really does mean "NO!"

From a paper presented at an annual Society for the Scientific Study of Sexuality (SSSS) meeting in San Francisco, "Can the Sexual Double Standard Put Women at Risk for Sexually Transmitted Disease? The Role of the Double Standard in Condom Use Among Women," by Charlene Muehlenhard, Ph.D., and Debra M. Quackenbush, Ph.D., 1988. Reprinted by permission of the authors.

The androgyny model continues to acknowledge and even depend on the conventional concepts of femininity and masculinity. Thus, in spite of its emancipatory promise, the model retains the classic dualism and, hence, the assumption of some real gender difference. (Morawski, 1990, p. 154)

In other words, while androgyny represents a broadening of gender role norms, it still implies two differing sets of gender-related characteristics (masculine = active-instrumental; feminine = expressive-nurturant). One solution to this problem is to simply describe characteristics such as active-instrumental and expressive-nurturant without labeling these traits as masculine or feminine. Another solution is to go beyond the concept of androgyny and focus on gender role transcendence.

Gender Role Transcendence

As noted earlier, we tend to impose a gender-based classification system on the world. Thus, we associate many aspects of our world, including colors, foods, social and occupational roles, and personality traits, with either masculinity or femininity. The concept of *gender role transcendence* involves abandoning gender schema or becoming "gender aschematic" (Bem, 1983) so that personality traits, social and occupational roles, and other aspects of our life become divorced from gender categories.

One way to transcend gender roles is to be reared that way because gender schema develop at an early age. For example, parents can foster non-sex-typed functioning in their children by encouraging emotional expression and independence in both boys and girls. Parents can also deemphasize the importance of gender in children's lives with respect to choosing clothes, toys, colors, and activities.

Even though many individuals may move toward gender role transcendence as they reach and pass middle age, few if any individuals completely reach this stage. As long as gender stereotypes and gender inequalities are ingrained in our social and cultural ideologies and institutions, gender role transcendence will remain unrealized.

THINK ABOUT IT

To what degree do you think gender role transcendence will be achieved in the United States? In any society? Why?

KEY TERMS

SUMMARY POINTS

Women and men have different biological wirings and socializations that influence differences in their sexuality.

Terminology

In common usage, the terms "sex" and "gender" are often used interchangeably. But these terms are not synonymous. "Sex" refers to the biological distinction between females and males. "Gender" refers to the social and psychological characteristics often associated with being female or male. For example, characteristics typically associated with the female gender include being gentle, emotional, and cooperative; characteristics associated with the male gender include being aggressive, rational, and competitive. Other terminology related to sex and gender include gender identity, gender role, sexual identity, and gender role ideology.

Theories of Gender Role Development

Most researchers acknowledge an interaction of biological and environmental factors in gender role behaviors. Sociobiology emphasizes biological sources of social behavior, such as sexual aggression on the part of males due to higher levels of testosterone. Identification theory focuses on the influence of the same-sex parent when children are learning gender roles. Social learning theory discusses how children are rewarded and punished for expressing various gender role behaviors. Cognitive-developmental theorists are concerned with the developmental ages at which children are capable of learning social roles.

Agents of Socialization

Parents, peers, schoolteachers, religion, and the media project and encourage traditional gender roles for women and men. The cumulative effect is the perpetuation of gender stereotypes. Each agent of socialization reinforces gender roles that are learned from other agents of socialization, thereby creating a gender role system that is deeply embedded in our culture.

Effects of Traditional Gender Role Socialization on Sexuality and Relationships

Traditional gender role socialization affects the sexuality and relationships of women and men in many ways. For example, gender socialization affects body image and the perception of genitals; the frequency of sexual thoughts, masturbation, and orgasm; the importance of love in sexual relationships; sexual guilt; age and number of sexual partners; initiation of relationships; emotional intimacy; and sexual aggression, coercion, and victimization.

Androgyny and Gender Role Transcendence

Androgyny refers to the blend of traits stereotypically associated with masculinity and femininity. Evidence suggests that women are more androgynous than men. Gender role transcendence involves abandoning gender schema so that personality traits, social and occupational roles, and other aspects of life are not viewed as "masculine" or "feminine."

References

American Psychiatric Association. (1994). *Diagnostic and statistical manual of mental disorders* (4th ed., revised). Washington, DC: American Psychiatric Association.

Arnold, A. P. (1980, March/April). Sexual differences in the brain. *American Scientist, 68,* 165-173.

Associated Press. (1997, February 2). Hazing video gets range of reactions. *The Daily Reflector,* p. 1.

Bancroft, J. (1984). Hormones and sexual human behavior. *Journal of Sex and Marital Therapy, 10,* 3-27.

Basow, S. A. (1992). *Gender: Stereotypes and roles* (3rd ed.). Pacific Grove, CA: Brooks/Cole.

Baxter, J., & Kane, E. W. (1995). Dependence and independence: A cross-national analysis of gender inequality and gender attitudes. *Gender and Society, 9,* 193-215.

Bem, S. (1983, Summer). Gender schema theory and its implications for child development: Raising gender-aschematic children in a gender-schematic society. *Signs, 8,* 596-616.

Bullough, B., & Bullough, V. (1997). Are transvestites necessarily heterosexual? *Archives of Sexual Behavior, 26,* 1-12.

Buss, D. M. (1989). Sex differences in human mate preferences: Evolutionary hypotheses tested in 37 cultures. *Behavioral and Brain Sciences, 12,* 1-13.

Chafetz, J. S. (1988). *Feminist sociology: An overview of contemporary theories.* Itasca, IL: F. E. Peacock.

Chodorow, N. (1978). *The reproduction of mothering.* Berkeley, CA: University of California Press.

Cochran, S., & Mays, V. (1990). Sex, lies and HIV. *New England Journal of Medicine, 322,* 774-775.

Cole, C. M., O'Boyle, M., Emory, L. E., & Meyer, W. J. (1997). Comorbidity of gender dysphoria and other major psychiatric diagnoses. *Archives of Sexual Behavior 26,* 13-26.

Coontz, S. (1995). The way we weren't: The myth and reality of the "traditional" family. *Phi Kappa Phi Journal, 75,* 11-14.

Cowden, C. R., & Koch, P. B. (1995). Attitudes related to sexual concerns: Gender and orientation comparisons. *Journal of Sex Education and Therapy, 21,* 78-87.

Cox, J. (1995, August 29). China's women make small strides. *USA Today,* p. A1.

Crabb, P. B., & Bielawski, D. (1994). The social representation of material culture and gender in children's books. *Sex Roles, 30,* 69-79.

Davidson, J. K., & Moore, N. B. (1994). Masturbation and premarital sexual intercourse among college women: Making choices for sexual fulfillment. *Journal of Sex and Marital Therapy, 20,* 178-199.

Davis, S. (1990). Men as success objects and women as sex objects: A study of personal advertisements. *Sex Roles, 23,* 43-50.

Denmark, F. L., Nielson, K. A., & Scholl, K. (1993). United States of America. In L. L. Adler (Ed.), *International handbook on gender roles* (pp. 452-467). Westport, CT: Greenwood Press.

Diamond, M. (1996). Prenatal predisposition and the clinical management of some pediatric conditions. *Journal of Sex and Marital Therapy, 22,* 139-147.

Diamond, M. (1997a). Sexual identity and sexual orientation in children with traumatized or ambiguous genitalia. *The Journal of Sex Research, 34,* 199-211.

Diamond, M. (1997b). Self-testing: A check on sexual identity and other levels of sexuality. In B. Bullough, V. Bullough, & J. Elias (Eds.), *Gender blending,* (pp. 103-125). Amherst, NY: Prometheus Books.

Diamond, M., & Sigmundson, K. (1997). Sex reassignment at birth. *Archives of Pediatric Adolescent Medicine, 151,* 298-304.

Doyle, J. A. (1995). *The male experience.* Madison, WI: WCB Brown and Benchmark.

Elliott, L., & Brantley, C. (1997). *Sex on campus: The naked truth about the real sex lives of college students.* New York: Random House.

Ellis, B. J., & Symons, D. (1990). Sex differences in sexual fantasy: An evolutionary psychological approach. *Journal of Sex Research, 27,* 527-556.

Etaugh, C., & Duits, T. (1990). Development of gender discrimination: Role of stereotypic and counter-stereotypic gender cues. *Sex Roles, 23,* 215-222.

Freeman, D. (1983). *Margaret Mead and Samoa: The making and unmaking of an anthropological myth.* Cambridge, MA: Harvard University Press.

Freud, S. (1965). *New introductory lectures in psychoanalysis* (J. Strachey, Ed. and Trans.). New York: W. W. Norton. (Original work published in 1933)

Freud, S. (1974). Some psychological consequences of an anatomical distinction between the sexes. In J. Strouse (Ed.), *Women and analysis.* New York: Grossman. (Original work published in 1925)

Garner, D. M. (1997, February). The 1997 Body Image Survey results. *Psychology Today,* 30.

Gilligan, C. (1982). *In a different voice.* Cambridge, MA: Harvard University Press.

Gorman, C. (1997, March 24). A boy without a penis. *Time,* 83.

Goy, R. W., & McEwen, B. S. (1980). *Sexual differentiation of the brain.* Cambridge, MA: MIT Press.

Grammer, K. (1989). Human courtship behavior: Biological basis and cognitive processes. In A. E. Rasa, C. Vogel, & E. Voland (Eds.), *Sociobiology of sexual and reproductive strategies* (pp. 147-169). London: Chapman and Hall.

Green, R. J., Bettinger, M., & Zacks, E. (1996). Are lesbian couples fused and gay male couples disengaged? In J. Laird & R. J. Green (Eds.), *Lesbians and gays in couples and families* (pp. 185-230). San Francisco: Jossey-Bass.

Greer, J. H. (1996). Gender differences in the organization of sexual information. *Archives of Sexual Behavior, 25,* 91-107.

Hare-Mustin, R. T., & Marecek, J. (1988). The meaning of difference: Gender theory, postmodernism, and psychology. *American Psychologist, 43,* 455-464.

Harrison, D. F., & Pennell R. C. (1989). Contemporary sex roles for adolescents: New options or confusion? *Journal of Social Work and Human Sexuality, 8,* 27-45.

Hayes, A. R. (1995). Age preferences for same and opposite sex partners. *The Journal of Social Psychology, 135,* 125-133.

Hedley, M. (1994). The presentation of gendered conflict in popular movies: Affective stereotypes, cultural sentiments, and men's motivation. *Sex Roles, 31,* 721-740.

Hochschild, A. (1989). *The second shift.* New York: Viking Press.

Hsu, B., Kling, A., Kessler, C., Knape, K., Diefenbach, P., & Elias, J. E. (1994). Gender differences in sexual fantasy and behavior in a college population: A ten-year replication. *Journal of Sex and Marital Therapy, 20,* 103-118.

Human Development Report. (1997). United Nations Development Programme. New York: Oxford University Press.

Kessler, S. J. (1990). The medical construction of gender: Case management of intersexed infants. *Signs: Journal of Women in Culture and Society, 16,* 3-26.

Knox, D., Britton, T., & Crisp, B. (1997). Age discrepant relationships reported by university faculty and their students. *College Student Journal, 31,* 290-292.

Kohlberg, L. (1966). A cognitive-developmental analysis of children's sex-role concepts and attitudes. In E. E. Maccoby (Ed.), *The development of sex differences.* Stanford, CA: Stanford University Press.

Kohlberg, L. (1969). State and sequence: The cognitive-developmental approach to socialization. In D. A. Goslin (Ed.), *Handbook of socialization theory and research* (pp. 347-480).Chicago: Rand McNally.

Kohlberg, L. (1976). Moral stages and moralization: The cognitive-developmental approach. In T. Lickona (Ed.), *Moral development and behavior.* New York: Holt, Rinehart, & Winston.

Laner, M. R. (1995). *Dating: Delights, discontents, and dilemmas* (2nd ed.). Salem, WI: Sheffield.

Lee, P. A. (1996). Survey report: Concept of penis size. *Journal of Sex and Marital Therapy, 22,* 131-135.

Leitenberg, H. (1983). Transsexuality: The epitome of sexism and homosexual denial. In G. Albee, S. Gordon, & H. Leitenberg (Eds.), *Promoting sexual responsibility and preventing sexual problems* (pp. 183-219). Hanover, NH: University Press of New England.

Leitenberg, H., Detzer, M. J., & Srebnik, D. (1993). Gender differences in masturbation and the relation of masturbation experience in preadolescence and/or early childhood to sexual behavior and sexual adjustment in young adulthood. *Archives of Sexual Behavior, 22,* 87-98.

Malamuth, N. M. (1996). Sexually explicit media, gender differences, and evolutionary theory. *Journal of Communication, 46,* 8-31.

Mandoki, M. W., Sumner, G. S., Hoffman, R. P., & Riconda, D. L. (1991). A review of Klinefelter's syndrome in children and adolescents. *Journal of the American Academy of Child and Adolescent Psychiatry, 30,* 167-172.

Mason-Schrock, D. (1996). Transsexual's narrative construction of the 'True Self.' *Social Psychology Quarterly, 59,* 176–192.

McHale, S. M., Bartko, W. T., Crouter, A. C., & Perry-Jenkins, M. (1990). Children's housework and psychosocial functioning: The mediating effects of parents' sex-role behaviors and attitudes. *Child Development, 61,* 1413–1416.

McKain, T. (1996). Acknowledging mixed-sex people. *Journal of Sex and Marital Therapy, 22,* 265–274.

Mead, M. (1928). *Coming of age in Samoa.* New York: Morrow. (Republished in 1973).

Mead, M. (1935). *Sex and temperament in three primitive societies.* New York: Morrow.

Michael, R. T., Gagnon, J. H., Laumann, E. O., & Kolata, G. (1994). *Sex in America: A definitive survey.* Boston: Little, Brown.

Money, J., Hampson, J. G., & Hampson, J. L. (1995). Hermaphroditism: Recommendations concerning assignment of sex, change of sex, and psychologic management. *Bulletin of Johns Hopkins Hospital, 97,* 284–300.

Morawski, J. G. (1990). The troubled quest for masculinity, femininity, and androgyny. In P. Shaver & C. Hendrick (Eds.), *Sex and gender.* Newbury Park, CA: Sage.

Morrow, F. (1991). *Unleashing our unknown selves: An inquiry into the future of femininity and masculinity.* New York: Praeger.

Orten, J. L. (1990). Coming up short: The physical, cognitive, and social effects of Turner's syndrome. *Health and Social Work, 15,* 100–106.

Osman, A. K. A., & Al-Sawaf, M. H. (1995). Cross-cultural aspects of sexual anxieties and the associated dysfunction. *Journal of Sex Education and Therapy, 21,* 174–181.

Patton, W., & Mannison, M. (1995). Sexuality attitudes: A review of the literature and refinement in a new measure. *Journal of Sex Education and Therapy, 21,* 268–295.

Pauly, I. B. (1990). Gender identity disorders: Evaluation and treatment. *Journal of Sex Education and Therapy, 16,* 2–24.

Purcell, P., & Stewart, D. (1990). Dick and Jane in 1989. *Sex Roles, 22,* 177–185.

Purnine, D. M., Carey, M. P., & Jorgensen, R. S. (1994). Gender differences regarding preferences for specific heterosexual practices. *Journal of Sex and Marital Therapy, 20,* 271–287.

Rapping, E. (1994). *Mediations: Forays into the culture and gender wars.* Boston: South End Press.

Regan, P. C., & Berscheid, E. (1996). Beliefs about the state, goals, and objects of sexual desire. *Journal of Sex and Marital Therapy, 22,* 110–120.

Reinholtz, R. K., & Muehlenhard, C. L. (1995). Genital perceptions and sexual activity in a college population. *The Journal of Sex Research, 32,* 155–165.

Richards, K. (1997). What is a transgenderist? In B. Bullough, V. Bullough, & J. Elias (Eds.), *Gender blending* (pp. 503–504). Amherst, NY: Prometheus Books.

Rodgers, C., & Muehlenhard, C. (1992). *Token resistance: New perspectives on an old stereotype.* Unpublished manuscript.

Russo, N. F. (1993). Foreword. In L. L. Adler (Ed.), *International handbook on gender roles* (pp. ix–xv). Westport, CT: Greenwood Press.

Sadker, M., & Sadker, D. (1990). Confronting sexism in the college classroom. In S. L. Gabriel & I. Smithson (Eds.), *Gender in the classroom: Power and pedagogy* (pp. 176–187). Chicago: University of Illinois Press.

Saluter, A. F. (1996). *Marital status and living arrangements: March 1994.* U.S. Bureau of the Census, Current Population Reports (Series p20-484). Washington, DC: U.S. Government Printing Office.

Sapiro, V. (1990). *Women in American society* (2nd ed.). Mountain View, CA: Mayfield.

Schroeder, K. A., Blood, L. L., & Maluso, D. (1993). Gender differences and similarities between male and female undergraduate students regarding expectations for career and family roles. *College Student Journal, 27,* 237–249.

Schwartz, P., & Jackson, D. (1989, February). How to have a model marriage. *New Woman,* 66–74.

Seid, R. P. (1994). Too 'close to the bone': The historical context for women's obsession with slenderness. In P. Fallon, M. A. Katzman, & S. C. Wooley (Eds.), *Feminist perspectives on eating disorders* (pp. 3–16). New York: Guilford Press.

Sherwin, B. B., Gelfand, M. M., & Brender, W. (1985). Androgen enhances sexual motivation in females: A prospective, crossover study of sex steroid administration in surgical menopause. *Psychosomatic Medicine, 47,* 339–351.

Smith, K. M. (1995). *First-year student survey* (Report 9596-1). Greenville, NC: East Carolina University, Research, Assessment, and Testing.

Sprecher, S., Barbee, A., & Schwartz, P. (1995). 'Was it good for you, too?' Gender differences in first sexual intercourse experiences. *The Journal of Sex Research, 32,* 3–15.

Starrels, M. E. (1994). Gender differences in parent-child relations. *Journal of Family Issues, 15,* 148–165.

Statistical Abstract of the United States: 1996 (116th ed.). (1996). Washington, DC: U.S. Bureau of the Census.

Steiger, T. L., & Wardell, M. (1995). Gender and employment in the service sector. *Social Problems, 42*(1), 91–123.

Street, S., Kimmel, E. B., & Kromrey, J. D. (1995). Revisiting university student gender role perceptions. *Sex Roles, 33,* 183–201.

Symons, D. (1987). An evolutionary approach: Can Darwin's view of life shed light on human sexuality?

In J. H. Greer & W. T. O'Donohue (Eds.), *Theories of human sexuality* (pp. 91–125). New York: Plenum.

Symons, D., & Ellis, B. (1989). Human male-female differences in sexual desire. In A. E. Rasa, C. Vogel, & E. Voland (Eds.) *Sociobiology of sexual and reproductive strategies* (pp. 131–146). London: Chapman and Hall.

Tang, C. S., Lai, F. D., Phil, M., & Chung, T. K. H. (1997). Assessment of sexual functioning for Chinese college students. *Archives of Sexual Behavior, 26,* 79–90.

Tavris, C. (1992). *The mismeasure of woman.* New York: Simon & Schuster.

Townsend, J. M. (1995). Sex without emotional involvement: An evolutionary interpretation of sex differences. *Archives of Sexual Behavior, 24,* 173–206.

Twenge, J. M. (1995, August). *Changes in masculinity and femininity over time: A quantitative analysis.* Paper presented at the American Psychological Association Conference, New York, NY.

Unger, R. K. (1990). Imperfect reflections of reality: Psychology constructs gender. In R. T. Hare-Mustin & J. Marecek (Eds.), *Making a difference: Psychology and the construction of gender* (pp. 102–149). New Haven, CT: Yale University Press.

Willetts-Bloom, M. C., & Nock, S. L. (1994). The influence of maternal employment on gender role attitudes of men and women. *Sex Roles, 30,* 371–389.

Williams, C. L. (1995). *Still a man's world: Men who do women's work.* Berkeley, CA: University of California Press.

Williams, J. E., & Best, D. L. (1990). *Sex and psyche: Gender and self viewed cross-culturally.* London: Sage.

Wilson, J. D., George, F. W., & Griffin, J. E. (1981). The hormonal control of sexual development. *Science, 211,* 1278–1284.

Winn, K. I., Crawford, D. W., & Fischer, J. L. (1991). Equity and commitment in romance versus friendship. *Journal of Social Behavior and Personality, 6,* 301–314.

Zucker, K. J. (1996). Commentary on Diamond's "Prenatal predisposition and clinical management of some pediatric conditions." *Journal of Sex and Marital Therapy, 22,* 148–160.

SEXUAL ORIENTATION DIVERSITY

Chapter
16

Conceptual Models of Sexual Orientation

Dichotomous Model
Unidimensional Continuum Model
Multidimensional Model
LesBiGay/Transgender Affirmative Model

QUESTION Why has bisexuality been largely
overlooked, ignored, and invalidated in
sexuality research and U.S. culture?

Prevalence of Homosexuality, Heterosexuality, and Bisexuality

QUESTION Why is it difficult to categorize an
individual as gay, lesbian, bisexual, or
heterosexual?

Heterosexism and Homonegativity

SELF-ASSESSMENT: Homophobia Scale
Homonegativity
Discrimination Against Homosexuals
SOCIAL CHOICES: Should Homosexual
    Marriage Be Legal?
Biphobia

QUESTION What are the cultural roots of negative
views toward homosexuality and bisexuality?

Theories of Sexual Orientation

Biological Explanations
Environmental Explanations

QUESTION On which part do most researchers agree
regarding the "cause" of homosexuality?

Gay and Bisexual Identity Development

Coming Out to Oneself
Coming Out to Others
PERSONAL CHOICES: Would You Accept or
    Reject a Gay Son or Daughter?
Coming Out as a Bisexual
Developing a Positive Gay or Bisexual Identity
SOCIAL CHOICES: Should the Military Allow or
    Ban Homosexuals from Service?

QUESTION What differences do women and men
experience in the development of a gay identity?

Homosexual and Bisexual Relationships

Gay Male Relationships
Gay Female Relationships
Bisexual Relationships
Sexual Orientation and HIV Infection

QUESTION What are the similarities and differences
in lesbian, gay male, bisexual, and heterosexual
relationships?

I know what it feels like to try to blend in so that everybody else will think that you are OK and they won't hurt you.

Ellen DeGeneres
Actress

In a 1997 landmark television event, a character on the sitcom *Ellen* inadvertently blurted out the words "I am gay" over a microphone in an airport. The actress portraying this character, Ellen DeGeneres, then made appearances on ABC's *20/20* and *Primetime Live* revealing that she herself was gay and involved in a stable love relationship with actress Anne Heche. Ellen's "coming out" as both a television character and as herself focused the nation's attention on gay individuals and the issues they face.

In the 1996 comedy *Birdcage,* actor Robin Williams played the role of a gay father whose son was engaged to be married. The comedy revolved around how the son introduces the father's gay companion to his fiancée's homophobic father. In real life, the challenges faced by gay and bisexual individuals living in an antigay social climate extend beyond those addressed on television and in the movies. Unlike the scenarios shown on *Ellen* and in *Birdcage,* the interplay between gays and bisexuals and the larger heterosexual society is far from comedic. To the contrary, issues concerning sexual orientation diversity represent serious concerns not only for gay and lesbian individuals, but for society as a whole. In this chapter, we will explore diversity in sexual orientation, focusing on models of sexual

The "coming out" of Ellen, both as a character on television and in real life, brought national attention to the issues confronting homosexuals.

orientation and how each model conceptualizes homosexuality, heterosexuality, and bisexuality. We will also examine the causes and consequences of homonegativity, the process of developing a gay or bisexual identity, and characteristics of homosexual and bisexual relationships.

THINK ABOUT IT

Although the terms "sexual preference" and "*sexual orientation*" are often used interchangeably, many sexuality researchers and academicians (including the authors of this text) prefer to use the term "sexual orientation." Do you think it matters? What are the implications of each term?

CONCEPTUAL MODELS OF SEXUAL ORIENTATION

Conceptual models of sexual orientation include the dichotomous model, the unidimensional continuum model, and the multidimensional model. In addition, a new paradigm for conceptualizing sexual orientation referred to as the LesBiGay/Transgender affirmative model is emerging.

Dichotomous Model

According to the *dichotomous model of sexual orientation,* people are either heterosexual or homosexual. This model makes a number of inaccurate assumptions, including the following (Firestein, 1996):

1. Individuals exhibiting bisexual feelings and behavior are, in actuality, either homosexual or heterosexual and are masking or denying their true sexual orientation.
2. Individuals who identify themselves as bisexual do so as a means of avoiding the full stigma of a homosexual label.
3. Bisexuality is no more than a transitional orientation, temporarily embraced as an individual moves from a heterosexual to a homosexual identification.

4. The biological sex of a partner is always the critical variable in determining an individual's selection of a sexual and romantic partner.
5. Sexual behavior and sexual self-identity are concordant; therefore, gay and lesbian individuals have only same-sex sexual desires and experiences, and heterosexuals have only other-sex sexual desires and experiences.
6. Heterosexuals and homosexuals constitute discrete, nonoverlapping, unchanging populations.

The dichotomous, or "either-or" model of sexuality prevails not only in views on sexual orientation, but also in cultural understandings of biological sex (male versus female) and gender (masculine versus feminine). Kinsey Institute researchers Sanders, Reinisch, and McWhirter (1990) emphasized that "dichotomous categories such as heterosexual and homosexual fail to reflect adequately the complex realities of sexual orientation and human sexuality in general" (p. xx). The major criticism of the dichotomous model of sexual orientation is that it fails to affirm the existence of *bisexuality*—a sexual orientation that involves a bisexual self-identity and cognitive, emotional, and sexual attractions to both women and men. Bennett (1992) refers to bisexuality as a "both/and option for an either/or world." Because the dichotomous model suggests that true bisexuals do not exist, bisexual concerns have largely been ignored by sexuality researchers and clinicians, as well as by gay rights activists.

Unidimensional Continuum Model

In early research on sexual behavior, Kinsey and his colleagues (1948, 1953) found that a substantial proportion of respondents reported having had same-sex sexual experiences. The data revealed that 37% of men and 13% of women had at least one homosexual experience since adolescence. Yet, very few of the individuals in Kinsey's research reported exclusive homosexual behavior. These data led Kinsey to conclude that, contrary to the dichotomous model of sexual orientation, most people are not exclusively heterosexual or homosexual. Rather, Kinsey suggested a *unidimensional continuum model of sexual orientation.* Kinsey and his colleagues (1953) developed the Heterosexual-Homosexual Rating Scale in order to assess where on the continuum of sexual orientation an individual is (see Figure 16.1).

The "Kinsey scale" was originally a unidimensional measure that assessed sexual orientation by assessing lifetime erotic attractions and sexual behavior.

Unlike the dichotomous model, the unidimensional continuum model recognizes that heterosexual and homosexual orientations are not mutually exclusive and that an individual's sexual orientation may have both heterosexual and homosexual elements. However, this model, as represented by the Heterosexual-Homosexual Rating Scale, is criticized for assuming that an individual's sexual behavior and feelings are synchronous (Paul, 1996). Although Bell and Weinberg (1978) later used separate Kinsey scale continua to measure sexual experiences and sexual feelings, these measures of sexual orientation still did not consider the social context of such behavior or the self-identity of the individual. Thus, the unidimensional continuum model fails to incorporate some important aspects of sexuality, such as self-identity, lifestyle, and social group preference.

Although Kinsey's proposal of a unidimensional continuum model of sexual orientation had a tremendous impact on subsequent sexuality research and

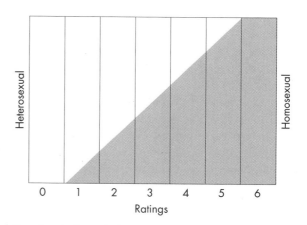

Based on both psychologic reactions and overt experience, individuals rate as follows:

0. Exclusively heterosexual with no homosexual
1. Predominantly heterosexual, only incidentally homosexual
2. Predominantly heterosexual, but more than incidentally homosexual
3. Equally heterosexual and homosexual
4. Predominantly homosexual, but more than incidentally heterosexual
5. Predominantly homosexual, but incidentally heterosexual
6. Exclusively homosexual

FIGURE 16.1 The Heterosexual-Homosexual Rating Scale
Source: Kinsey et al., 1953.

contributed to the emergence of the multidimensional model of sexual orientation, Firestein (1996) believes that the dichotomous model of sexual orientation continues to prevail in U.S. culture.

Multidimensional Model

Since Kinsey's early sexual research, our understanding of sexual orientation has become more complex and multidimensional. The *multidimensional model of sexual orientation* suggests that orientation consists of various independent components (including emotional and social preferences, lifestyle, self-identification, sexual attraction, fantasy, and behavior) and that these components may change over time. The "multidimensional model of sexual orientation has evolved out of the need to more accurately represent the diverse factors involved in the development and expression of human sexuality" (Fox, 1996, p. 9).

For example, The Klein Sexual Orientation Grid (Klein, 1990) includes seven scales measuring distinct dimensions of sexual orientation: sexual behavior, sexual fantasies, erotic attraction, emotional preference, social group preference, self-identification, and lifestyle preference. Individuals rate themselves on a 7-point heterosexual-bisexual-homosexual scale for each variable for past, present, and ideal time frames, yielding a total of 21 self-ratings. An individual's satisfaction with these dimensions is measured by the present versus ideal ratings.

Coleman (1987) developed a sexual orientation assessment tool that expands the focus on sexual relationship experiences. For example, Coleman's assessment tool includes items to assess whether sexual relationships are exclusive versus nonexclusive and primary versus secondary. In Coleman's assessment measure, instead of locating themselves on a horizontal line, individuals represent aspects of sexual orientation within circles, like slices of a pie. This type of representation "implies integration of male and female aspects of sexual identity into a conceptual whole" (Coleman, 1990, p. 274). Coleman suggests that using this measure can help individuals define themselves, examine and affirm the complexity of their sexual orientation, and promote their sexual identity development and satisfaction.

Perhaps the most important contribution of the multidimensional model is its incorporation of self-identity as a central element of sexual orientation. As sexuality researchers began to include self-identity as a variable in their studies, they found that attractions and sexual behavior are not always consistent with one's sexual self-identity. For example, in a study of 52 men who labeled themselves as heterosexual, almost one-quarter (23%) reported that they had had sex with both women and men in the last 2 years; 6% had had sex exclusively with men (Doll et al., 1992). Thus, adult homosexual or bisexual attractions or behaviors do not necessarily imply a homosexual or bisexual self-identity. Also, prior homosexual, bisexual, or heterosexual experiences are not required to label one's self as homosexual. These insights have led researchers to move away from describing individuals simply as "gay," "lesbian," "heterosexual," or "bisexual." Instead, researchers are more explicit about how individuals experience their sexuality, how they identify themselves, and how they behaviorally express their sexual orientation identity.

In sum, the multidimensional model of sexual orientation has broadened the construct of sexual orientation and its assessment to include self-identity, social and relationship aspects of sexual behavior, and temporal changes in sexual attractions, behaviors, and identity.

LesBiGay/Transgender Affirmative Model

The term *LesBiGay* (or lesbigay) is used as a way of abbreviating the phrases "lesbians, bisexuals, and gay men." The term *LesBiGay/Transgender* includes transgendered and transsexual people. Essentially, the *LesBiGay/Transgender affirmative model of sexual orientation* incorporates the insights of the multidimensional model, but also affirms variations in sexual diversity and identity, and differences in the way individuals experience and express gender. Firestein (1996) describes various elements of this emerging model:

1. "Under a LesBiGay/Transgender affirmative paradigm . . . there will be the deep recognition that [sexual orientation labels] do not denote entirely discrete populations, but rather represent the self-identification of individuals whose feelings and experiences contain substantial overlap . . ." (Firestein, 1996, p. 281).

2. Sexual self-identification involves both choice and constraint. "Identification choices are influenced as much by sociopolitical considerations and the heterosexism of the broader society as by

reference to their actual sexual behavior and feelings" (Firestein, 1996, p. 281). Esterberg (1997) explains that "people do not select freely from a menu of identities; rather, cultural ideals and social institutions shape the identities that may be chosen. For those who experience same-sex desire in the United States today, it is difficult to resist a lesbian, gay, or bisexual identity" (p. 26).

3. "The existence and impact of biphobia will be taken as seriously as the existence and impact of homophobia" (Firestein, 1996, p. 281). (Homophobia and biphobia are discussed later in this chapter.)

4. It is important to acknowledge differences of race, ethnicity, and social class in sexual behavior, feelings, and identity.

5. Traditional notions of what constitutes psychological maturity and health among bisexual, gay, and lesbian individuals must be rethought. Firestein (1996) suggests that "imitating the 1950s-style nuclear family, with the substitution of gender-role equality for the gender-role inequality present in most heterosexual relationships, still offers a far too narrow model for what constitutes optimal relational functioning" (p. 282). Rather than base standards of the mental health on the dominant culture's heterosexual norms, the LesBiGay/Transgender model recognizes "the appropriateness and value of diverse choices, such as the choice not to be partnered, to have loving relationships with more than one person at the same time, to parent singly or as part of a community of single and partnered parents, [and] to relate to individuals who are alternatively gendered or not defined in their gender" (Firestein, 1996, p. 282).

6. Finally, this model "challenges us to examine . . . the similarities and differences between different-sex and same-sex desire as these exist across individuals and also within the same individual" (Firestein, 1996, p. 282).

> As we recognize the existence of same- and other-sex desires within the same person, the distance between heterosexuals and homosexuals is narrowed, and eventually closed. Ultimately, there is the recognition that no meaningful line can be drawn that distinguishes all heterosexually oriented individuals from all homosexually oriented individuals.

This recognition undermines discrimination, which is predicated on the ability to differentiate "us" from "them." . . . We recognize ourselves in the *other*, and the *other* within ourselves, and this becomes the basis for acceptance, understanding, and a full appreciation of both *other* and *self*. (p. 283)

A major strength of the LesBiGay/Transgender affirmative model is that it can account for the diversity of ways in which individuals experience and express their sexual attractions, behavior, relationships, and gender. But this model is not only descriptive—it is aspirational in promoting affirmation of sexual orientation diversity. As such, it is the most controversial of sexual orientation models. Perhaps the most controversial aspect of this model is its view that the choice to have "loving relationships with more than one person at the same time" may be appropriate. Given the current societal concern about HIV and AIDS, "family values," and monogamy, this suggestion is sure to elicit criticism.

THINK ABOUT IT

Which conceptual model of sexual orientation best matches your own view of sexual orientation?

PREVALENCE OF HOMOSEXUALITY, HETEROSEXUALITY, AND BISEXUALITY

The prevalence of homosexuality, heterosexuality, and bisexuality is difficult to determine. Due to embarrassment, a desire for privacy, or fear of social disapproval, many individuals are not willing to answer questions about their sexuality honestly. In addition, estimates of the prevalence of sexual orientations vary due to differences in the way researchers define and measure homosexuality, bisexuality, and heterosexuality. Classifying individuals as heterosexual, homosexual, or bisexual is not as clear-cut as some people believe. A person's self-identity as a gay man, lesbian, bisexual, or heterosexual may not correspond with his or her behavior. For example, substantial numbers of individuals who view themselves as heterosexual have had same-sex attractions and relations. Definitional problems also arise due to the considerable overlap between people with different sexual orientation self-identities, and the fact that sexual attractions, behavior, and self-identity may change over time. "Many bisexuals have in the past considered themselves to be lesbian or gay, and many lesbians and gay men have in the past considered themselves to be bisexual" (Ochs, 1996, p. 223).

Nevertheless, research data have yielded rough estimates of prevalence rates of homosexuality and bisexuality. In a national study of U.S. adults ages 18–59, researchers focused on three aspects of homosexuality: sexual attraction to persons of the same sex, sexual behavior with people of the same sex, and homosexual self-identification (Michael et al., 1994). The results, presented in Table 16.1, confirm what other researchers have found: In general, "more people have homosexual feelings than engage in homosexual behavior, and more engage in homosexual behavior than develop lasting homosexual identification" (Lever, Kanouse, Rogers, Carson, & Hertz, 1992, p. 144).

Note that in Table 16.1, data on bisexual and homosexual individuals are grouped together. Even though the researchers asked individuals "Do you think of yourself as . . . heterosexual, homosexual, bisexual, something else?" (p. 175), the data reported in *Sex in America* (Michael et al., 1994) reflect the grouped responses of both homosexual- and bisexual-identified individuals.

TABLE 16.1 Three Dimensions of Same-Sex Orientation

	WOMEN	MEN
Sexually attracted to individuals of the same sex	4%	6%
Had sexual relations with same-sex partner after age 18	4%	5%
Identifies self as homosexual or bisexual	1.4%	2.8%

Source: Data from Michael et al., 1994.

INTERNATIONAL DATA

Men and women reporting having had sexual contact with someone of the same sex in the previous 5 years

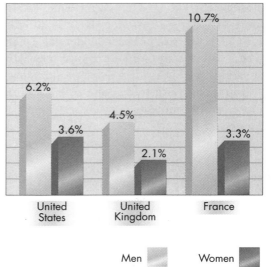

Men   Women

Source: Sell, Wells, & Wypij, 1995.

Same-sex attractions were reported by 16 to 20% of men and women respondents in the United States, United Kingdom, and France.

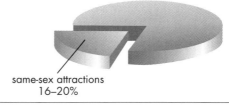

same-sex attractions
16–20%

Source: Sell, Wells, & Wypij, 1995.

A research review by Diamond (1993) suggests that in Denmark, Japan, the Netherlands, the Philippines, and Thailand, exclusive homosexuality is characteristic of about 5% of men and substantially less than that for women.

A frequently cited estimate of gay persons in the U.S. population is 10%. This figure was derived from the Kinsey 1948 and 1953 studies, which reported that 13% of men and 7% of women had more homosexual than heterosexual experience or psychological response for at least three years between the ages of 16 and 55. When the data were reanalyzed to include only "experience," the tabulations yielded a similar combined average of 9.13% of the total population (13.95% of men and 4.25% of women) (Voeller, 1990).

Reviews of sexuality research reveal that same-sex behavior is more prevalent among men than women (Ellis, 1996; Fox, 1996). Also, self-identified homosexuals and bisexuals are more prevalent in urban areas than in rural or suburban areas (Ellis, 1996; Michael et al., 1994).

THINK ABOUT IT

According to the dichotomous model of sexual orientation, what is the prevalence of bisexuality? According to the unidimensional continuum model, what is the prevalence of bisexuality? Which conceptual model of sexual orientation is reflected in the study by Michael and his colleagues? (Refer to Table 16.1.) Based on the LesBiGay/Transgender Affirmative model of sexual orientation, criticize the presentation of data in Table 16.1.

HETEROSEXISM AND HOMONEGATIVITY

Attitudes toward same-sex sexual behavior and relationships vary across cultures and across historical time periods (see Chapter 17). Today, most countries throughout the world, including the United States, are predominantly heterosexist. *Heterosexism* refers to the systematic degradation and stigmatization of any nonheterosexual form of behavior, identity, or relationship. Heterosexism involves the belief that heterosexuality is superior to homosexuality and results in prejudice and discrimination against homosexuals and bisexuals. Before reading further, you may wish to complete this chapter's Self-Assessment: the Homophobia Scale.

Homonegativity

SIECUS, the Sex Information and Education Council of the United States, affirms the sexual orientation of all persons. "Individuals have a right to accept, acknowledge, and live in accordance with their sexual orientation, be they bisexual, heterosexual, gay, or lesbian" (SIECUS, 1996, p. 22). Nevertheless, negative attitudes toward homosexuality are reflected in the high percentage of the U.S. population that disapproves of homosexuality. A *Newsweek* poll revealed that more than half (53%) of the respondents do not believe that homosexuality is an acceptable lifestyle; 41% of respondents believe that it is an acceptable alternative lifestyle (Turque, 1992).

Homonegativity, the construct that refers to antigay responses, is multidimensional and includes at least three components: affective, cognitive, and behavioral (Hudson & Ricketts, 1980). The affective component, *homophobia,* refers to an emotional response of fear, disgust, anger, discomfort, or aversion to homosexuals. In popular usage, the term homophobia is often used to refer to all three components of homonegativity. Hudson and Ricketts distinguished between homophobia ("personal affective responses to gay people") and "intellectual attitudes toward homosexuality as a phenomenon" (p. 358). Homophobia is not necessarily a clinical phobia (that is, one involving a compelling desire to avoid the feared object in spite of recognizing that the fear is unreasonable). However, Weinberg (1973), who coined the term "homophobia," observed that it often involves the phobic characteristic of experiencing distress that spreads from the original source to related objects or situations. Thus, homophobics often feel discomfort not only with homosexuals, but also with traits or behaviors they associate with gay men or lesbians (such as effeminate behavior in men). Homophobics are also often reluctant to express affection toward someone of the same sex for fear of being labeled gay.

Data on 1718 undergraduate students analyzed by McCormack (1997) suggest that men are more homophobic than women. The data also suggest that homophobia among undergraduates may be decreasing. Although 37% of students in 1987 thought homosexuality should be illegal, only 14% thought so in 1995 (p. 358). As expected, positive contact with homosexuals or having homosexuals as friends is associated with less homophobia (Simon, 1995).

In understanding attitudes toward homosexuality, it is essential to distinguish between attitudes toward lesbians and attitudes toward gay men (Kite & Whitley, 1996). In a study of heterosexual college students, Louderback and Whitley (1997) replicated previous research showing that heterosexual women and men hold similar attitudes toward lesbians, but men are more negative toward gay men. The researchers explained that heterosexual men attribute a high

HOMOPHOBIA SCALE

Directions: Indicate the extent to which you agree or disagree with each statement by placing a check mark on the appropriate line.

	Strongly agree	Agree	Undecided	Disagree	Strongly disagree
1. Homosexuals contribute positively to society.	✓				
2. Homosexuality is disgusting.		✓			
3. Homosexuals are just as moral as heterosexuals.		✓			
4. Homosexuals should have equal civil rights.	✓				
5. Homosexuals corrupt young people.				✓	
6. Homosexuality is a sin.	✓				
7. Homosexuality should be against the law.			✓		

Scoring: **Assign scores of 0, 1, 2, 3, and 4 to the five choices respectively ("strongly agree" through "strongly disagree"). Reverse-score items 2, 5, 6, and 7 (0 = 4; 1 = 3; 2 = 2; 3 = 1; 4 = 0). All items are summed for the total score. The possible range is 0 to 28; high scores indicate greater homophobia.**

Comparison Data: **The Homophobia Scale was administered to 524 students enrolled in introductory psychology courses at the University of Texas. The mean score for men was 15.8; for women, it was 13.8. The difference was statistically significant.**

From "Scales for Measuring Fear of AIDS and Homophobia," by Richard A. Bouton, P. E. Gallagher, P. A. Garlinghouse, T. Leal, et al., 1987, *Journal of Personality Assessment, 67*(1), p. 609. Copyright © 1987 by Lawrence Erlbaum Associates, Inc. Reprinted by permission.

erotic value to lesbianism and that this erotic value lessens their negative view of lesbians. The erotic value placed on lesbianism most likely stems from female-female sexual themes in erotic materials marketed to heterosexual men.

Why is homosexuality viewed so negatively in the United States? Affective and attitudinal negativity against homosexuals has its roots in various aspects of U.S. culture:

1. *Religion.* One study of college students' beliefs (VanderStoep & Green, 1988) found that religiosity predicted ethical conservatism, which was related to homonegativity. Although some religious groups (such as the Quakers) accept homosexuality, many religions teach that homosexuality is sinful and prohibited by God. "God made Adam and Eve, not Adam and Steve" is a phrase commonly cited by individuals whose homophobia is rooted in religion. The Roman Catholic Church rejects all homosexual expression (just as it rejects all sex outside of marriage) and resists any attempt to validate or sanction the homosexual orientation. Some fundamentalist churches regard AIDS as God's punishment for homosexuality.

On the other hand, some theologians argue that homosexual expression is consistent with a biblical perspective of Christianity (Scanzoni & Mollenkott, 1980). Many lesbian and gay people of faith refuse to acquiesce in being excluded from their religious traditions and communities. In response, some religious figures are speaking out on behalf of their lesbian and gay constituents. Rabbi Yoel Kahn (1997) made the following plea at a conference for American rabbis:

Deep, heartfelt yearning for companionship and intimacy is not an abomination before God. God does not want us to send the gays and lesbians among us into exile—either cut off from the Jewish community or into internal exile, living a lie for a lifetime. I believe that the time has come, I believe that God summons us to affirm the proper and rightful place of the homosexual Jew—and her or his family—in the synagogue and in the Jewish people. (p. 73)

2. *Marital and procreative bias.* Many societies have traditionally condoned sex only when it occurs in a marital context that provides for the possibility of reproducing and rearing children. Although laws prohibiting homosexuals from marrying have been challenged in the courts (see this chapter's Social Choices section), homosexuals are currently denied legal marriage in the United States. In a report of the Hawaii Commission on Sexual Orientation and the Law (Gill et al., 1997), the commission challenged the argument that same-sex marriage should be barred because it cannot lead to procreation. The commission pointed out that "state law does not require that opposite-sex couples prove that they are capable of procreation before they can be married, and many are obviously not, because of age, medical, or other reasons" (pp. 213–214). Furthermore, even though new reproductive technologies, such as artificial insemination and in vitro fertilization, make it possible for gay individuals and couples to have children, many people believe that these technological advances should be used by heterosexual married couples only

3. *Concern about HIV and AIDS.* Although most cases of HIV and AIDS worldwide are attributed to heterosexual transmission, the rates of HIV and AIDS in the United States are much higher among gay and bisexual men than among other groups. Because of this, many people in the United States associate HIV and AIDS with homosexuality and bisexuality. Lesbians, incidentally, have a very low risk for sexually transmitted HIV—a lower risk than heterosexual women.

4. *Rigid gender roles.* Antigay sentiments also stem from rigid gender roles. When Cooper Thompson (1995) was asked to give a guest presentation on male roles at a suburban high school, male students told him that the most humiliating put-down was being called a "fag." The boys in this school gave Thompson the impression they were expected to conform to rigid, narrow standards of masculinity in order to avoid being labeled in this way.

Lesbians are perceived as "stepping out of line" by relinquishing traditional female sexual and economic dependence on men. Both gay men and lesbians are often viewed as betrayers of their gender who must be punished. Louderback and Whitley (1997) confirmed previous research that found that individuals with traditional sex-role attitudes tend to hold more negative attitudes toward homosexuality. The researchers explained that men tend to hold more negative attitudes toward homosexuality than women because men tend to have more traditional attitudes toward the social roles of women and men in such areas as employment and household management.

> Men may be more heavily invested in the gender belief system because society views sex-role violations as more serious for men than for women. . . . Because these rigidly enforced norms require men to avoid feminine traits and activities, and because gay persons are commonly viewed as deviants from appropriate sex roles . . . men may feel more pressured to display antigay attitudes. (Louderback & Whitley, 1997, p. 180)

5. *Psychiatric labeling.* Prior to 1973, the American Psychiatric Association defined homosexuality as a mental disorder. When the third edition of the *Diagnostic and Statistical Manual* (DSM-III) was published, homosexuality was no longer included as a disorder. However, persistent and marked distress over one's sexual orientation (formerly referred to as "ego-dystonic homosexuality") is listed in the DSM-IV (American Psychiatric Association, 1994) as a sexual disorder. Critics argue that such classifications have succeeded only in getting homosexuality reclassified, not declassified, as a mental disorder (DeCecco, 1987).

There is controversy over "conversion" and "reversion" therapies that strive to help homosexual and bisexual people become heterosexual, or resume practicing heterosexuality. Some therapists assert that gay and bisexual people who seek such therapies do so because of pressures from society

Which of these individuals is homosexual, heterosexual, or bisexual?

and that attempts to "cure" homosexuality are another attempt to repathologize it (Gonsiorek, 1996). In 1990, the APA stated that scientific evidence does not support the effectiveness of conversion therapy in changing sexual orientation (Blommer, undated). Changing sexual orientation involves more than modifying sexual behavior; it requires alterations in a person's emotional, romantic, and sexual feelings, as well as a person's self-concept and social identity.

6. *Myths and negative stereotypes.* Homonegativity may also stem from some of the unsupported beliefs and negative stereotypes regarding homosexuality. For example, many people believe that gays are child molesters, even though the ratio of heterosexual to homosexual child molesters is approximately 11:1 (Moser, 1992). Further, lesbians are stereotyped as women that want to be (or at least look and act like) men, while gay men are stereotyped as men who want to be (or at least look and act like) women. In reality, the gay population is as diverse as the heterosexual population not only in appearance, but also in social class, educational achievement, occupational status, race, ethnicity, and personality.

Like members of other minority groups, gays and lesbians often feel misunderstood and unjustly stigmatized. Some homosexual individuals experience stress, depression, fear, and low self-esteem as a result of living in an antigay social climate. Homophobia and heterosexism also have

serious negative consequences for the larger society; some cases of rape and sexual assault are related to homophobia and compulsory heterosexuality. For example, college men who participate in gang rape, also known as "pulling train," entice each other into the act "by implying that those who do not participate are unmanly or homosexual" (Sanday, 1995, p. 399).

Homonegativity also encourages early sexual activity among adolescent men. Adolescent male virgins are often teased by their male peers, who say things like "You mean you don't do it with girls yet? What are you, a fag or something?" Not wanting to be labeled and stigmatized as a "fag," some adolescent boys "prove" their heterosexuality by having sex with girls.

Discrimination Against Homosexuals

Behaviorial homonegativity involves *discrimination,* or behavior that involves treating categories of individuals unequally. Discrimination against lesbians and gays can occur at the individual level, such as when a college student asks for a dorm room reassignment because his or her roommate is homosexual. The most severe form of behavioral homonegativity is antigay violence, in which gay men and lesbians are physically attacked, injured, tortured, and even killed because of their sexual orientation (Comstock, 1991). A study of harassment on university and college campuses documented gay and lesbian students' reports of verbal insults, threats and perpetration of physical violence, and damage to their personal property (D'Augelli, 1992). The Southern Poverty Law Center, which collects hate crime (offenses committed because of one's perceived sexual orientation, race, and so on) data from media sources and police reports, cited seven assaults against gays and lesbians from January to June, 1997 (For the Record, 1997). Victim service agencies in six U.S. cities (Boston, Chicago, Denver, Minneapolis/St. Paul, New York City, and San Francisco) documented 1813 antigay incidents in 1993 (reported in Ochs, 1996, p. 221). Such incidents included bomb threats, physical assaults, arson, vandalism, telephone harassment, police abuse, and murder. Studies investigating motives and correlates of negative behaviors against gays and lesbians have identified high adherence to traditional masculine roles, homophobia, and personality characteristics of impulsivity and social maladjustment (Patel, Long, McCammon, & Wuensch, 1995; Roderick, McCammon, Long, & Allred, in press).

Discrimination also occurs at the legal level. For example, many states have sodomy laws that criminalize sexual relations between persons of the same sex. Federal law allows military forces to discharge individuals who are discovered to be lesbian or gay (although the military can no longer ask its members if they are gay). In 1993, several federal agencies—including the White House, the Department of Justice, and the FBI—issued policies banning discrimination against employees on the basis of their sexual orientation. These policies, however, are not legally enforceable. To date, there are no federal laws that ban discrimination in employment, housing, and education on the basis of sexual orientation, but some states, cities, towns, and counties have outlawed sexual orientation discrimination. It is projected that by the end of the decade, nearly half of the states will enact civil rights laws against sexual orientation discrimination (Ettelbrick, 1995).

Finally, lesbians and gay men are also discriminated against in family matters. In many states, it is legal to take children out of the home of a lesbian mother or a gay father, even though research studies show that the children of lesbian mothers are just as likely to be well-adjusted as those of straight mothers (no data have been reported yet on children of gay fathers) (Patterson, 1997). Gay and lesbian couples have also been denied the option of being legally married in the United States. Without legal marital status, gay couples are denied many benefits and rights that are granted to married couples. This chapter's Social Choices section discusses the controversy over granting homosexual couples the right to be legally married.

Biphobia

Just as the term "homophobia" is used to refer to negative attitudes and emotional responses and discriminatory behavior toward gay men and lesbians, *biphobia* refers to "the parallel set of negative beliefs about and stigmatization of bisexuality and those identified as bisexual" (Paul, 1996, p. 449). Bennett (1992) defines biphobia as "the denigration of bisexuality as a valid life choice" (p. 207). Biphobia includes negative stereotyping of bisexuals; the exclusion of bisexuals from social and political organizations of lesbians and gay men; and fear and distrust of, as well as anger and hostility toward, people who identify themselves as bisexuals (Firestein, 1996). Aspects of biphobia mentioned earlier in this chapter include the belief among some gay men and lesbians that self-identified bisexuals are really homosexuals afraid to acknowledge their real identity or homosexuals maintaining heterosexual relationships to avoid rejection by the heterosexual mainstream. In addition, bisexual individuals are sometimes viewed as heterosexuals who are looking for exotic sexual experiences.

Although both homosexual- and bisexual-identified individuals are often rejected by heterosexuals, bisexual-identified women and men also face rejection from many homosexual individuals. Thus, bisexuals experience "double discrimination." Gorlin (1991) describes feeling unaccepted by both the heterosexual and homosexual communities:

> When I think of being bisexual, I am reminded of my Jewish ancestors who, kicked out of different countries, tried to find a place called home. I, too, have wandered, in the gay and straight worlds. (p. 252)

Gay women seem to exhibit greater levels of biphobia than do gay men. This is because many lesbian women associate their identity with a political stance against sexism and patriarchy. Some lesbians view heterosexual and bisexual women who "sleep with the enemy" as traitors to the feminist movement. One bisexual woman currently in a relationship with a man explains:

SHOULD HOMOSEXUAL MARRIAGE BE LEGAL?

In late 1996, Hawaii circuit court judge Kevin Chang made history when he ruled (in *Baehr v. Miike*) that Hawaii's refusal to grant marriage licenses to same-sex couples violated the state's constitution. This decision made Hawaii the first state to recognize homosexual marriages. Judge Chang based his ruling on the state's failure to show that the well-being of children and families would be adversely affected by same-sex marriages. Immediately after Judge Chang's decision was released, Kerry Lobel, Executive Director of the National Lesbian, Gay, and Bisexual Task Force, said, "This decision is one small but crucial step forward in a long march toward civil equality for lesbian, gay, bisexual, and transgendered people. . . . We seek the same rights and responsibilities of marriage that heterosexual people enjoy. Marriage is an important personal choice and a basic human right. Whether gay people decide to get married or not, it should be our choice" (quoted in Baird & Rosenbaum, 1997, p. 9). Although the matter has been sent back to the state Supreme Court for further deliberation, Hawaii is expected to be issuing marriage licenses to homosexual couples by the year 2000.

Advocates of same-sex marriage argue that banning homosexual marriage is a form of sex discrimination and a violation of the U.S. Constitution, which says that every person is entitled to equal protection under the law. Banning homosexual marriages, or refusing to recognize gay marriages granted in other states, denies gay and lesbian couples the many legal and financial benefits that are granted to heterosexual married couples. For example, married couples have the following rights: to inherit from a spouse who dies without a will; to avoid inheritance taxes between spouses; to make crucial medical decisions in the event of a partner's critical injury or illness; immunity from having to testify against a spouse in a criminal proceeding; to visit one's partner in prison or in the hospital; to collect Social Security survivor's benefits; to benefit from tax advantages, including deductions, improved rates, credits, and exemptions; to bring a wrongful death suit; to live in neighborhoods zoned "single family only"; to obtain residency status for a noncitizen partner; to seek child custody, support, and equitable property distribution in the event of divorce; to include a partner on his or her employee health insurance coverage; and to be regarded as "family" in reference to family leave policies. Married couples also enjoy tuition benefits, family membership benefits in such organizations as AAA (American Automobile Association) and AARP (American Association of Retired Persons), and purchase discounts on everything from local health club memberships to airline tickets. In addition, as long as gay and lesbian couples cannot be legally married, they will not be regarded as legitimate "families" by the larger society. Domestic partnership laws help, but these apply only to certain areas of the couple's life, and only about 10% of firms offer such benefits (Neuborne, 1997).

Hawaii's movement toward recognizing homosexual marriage has created a conservative backlash. Opponents used the Hawaii case as a rallying cry to pass the federal *Defense of Marriage Act,* which was passed by Congress and signed into law by President Clinton in September, 1996. This law asserts that marriage is a "legal union between one man and one woman" and denies federal recognition of homosexual marriage. The law also permits states not to recognize homosexual marriages that are licensed in other states. In effect, if Hawaii legalizes same-sex marriages, other states can ignore these marriages because federal law does not require individual states to recognize them. However, states wishing to recognize same-sex marriages may do so. As of fall 1997, 25 states had declared—either by law or through executive action—that they will not accept same-sex marriages granted in Hawaii or any other state.

Continued on following page.

Opponents of homosexual marriage point out that most Americans oppose it; almost 70% of a national sample of adults said they would vote against a law making homosexual marriages legal in their state (Lawrence, 1996). Many people fear that if states recognize homosexual marriage, churches that do not perform homosexual weddings may be subjected to civil suit for sexual discrimination. Opponents who view homosexuality as unnatural and as going against our country's moral standards do not want their children to learn that homosexuality is an accepted, "normal" lifestyle.

The most common argument against same-sex marriage is that it subverts the stability and integrity of the heterosexual family. However, Sullivan (1997a) suggests that homosexuals are already part of heterosexual families:

> [Homosexuals] are sons and daughters, brothers and sisters, even mothers and fathers, of heterosexuals. The distinction between "families" and "homosexuals" is, to begin with, empirically false; and the stability of existing families is closely linked to how homosexuals are treated within them. (p. 147)

The discussion presented here represents only a few of the arguments for and against same-sex marriage. The literature on the debate about same-sex marriage includes diverse arguments, including those based on legal and civil rights; moral, ethical, and religious values; emotional and psychological aspects; and political considerations. Sullivan (1997b) notes that the debate about same-sex marriage is "typical of the kind of argument that will increasingly define the way we conduct political affairs. . . . Should the law reflect our common moral values—or our widening moral pluralism?" (p. xxvi).

If the Hawaii ruling is upheld, a confusing legal situation is expected. A same-sex couple can be considered married in one state and not married in another. Further, a homosexual couple married in Hawaii may be considered married when they file their joint state tax return and unmarried when they file their federal tax return.

In July, 1997, Hawaii passed legislation allowing unmarried couples (heterosexual or homosexual) to receive health and family leave benefits (Zimmerman, 1997). The law, which refers to cohabiting couples as "reciprocal beneficiaries" (or RBs), gives cohabiting couples some of the same rights as married couples. However, it is not clear "whether domestic partnership legislation is a steppingstone or a distracting impediment to gay marriage" (Mohr, 1997, p. 100).

Sources: Baird, R.M., & Rosenbaum, S.E. (1997). Introduction. In R.M. Baird & S.E. Rosenbaum (Eds.), *Same-sex marriage: The moral and legal debate* (pp. 9–14). Amherst, NY: Prometheus Books.

Lawrence, J. (1996, July 15). Gay issue sizzles in the Senate. *USA Today*, p. 4A.

Mohr, R.D. (1997). The case for gay marriage. In R.M. Baird & S.E. Rosenbaum (Eds.), *Same-sex marriage: The moral and legal debate* (pp. 84–104). Amherst, NH: Prometheus Books.

Neuborne, E. (1997, January 24). One in 10 firms extend benefits to life partners. *USA Today*, p. B1.

Patterson, C. (1997). Children of lesbian and gay parents: Summary of research findings. In A. Sullivan (Ed.), *Same-sex marriage: Pro and con* (pp. 240–245). New York: Vintage Books.

Sullivan, A. (1997a). The conservative case. In A. Sullivan (Ed.), *Same-sex marriage: Pro and con* (pp. 146–154). New York: Vintage Books.

Sullivan A. (1997b). Introduction. In A. Sullivan (Ed.), *Same-sex marriage: Pro and con* (pp. xvii–xxvi). New York: Vintage Books.

Zimmerman, J. (1997, July 8). Hawaii OKs benefits to same-sex couples. *USA Today*, 2A.

> I have to be in the closet around straight people because they don't like that I like girls . . . In the same way I've got to be kind of in the closet around lesbians because they're really quite put off by this man. . . . I can get shot down from both sides. It's a weird sensation. (quoted in Esterberg, 1997, p. 147)

Biphobia from heterosexual communities often stems from negative stereotypes of bisexual individuals. For example, Ochs (1996) suggests that

> In the minds of many heterosexual Americans, bisexuality has come to be strongly identified with images of married, dishonest, closeted men sneaking out on their unsuspecting wives, contracting AIDS through unsafe sex with other men, then infecting their innocent wives and children. (p. 227)

Ochs (1996) notes that the view of bisexual men as "untrustworthy conduits of the HIV virus from the gay to the straight community [perpetuates] a stigma that drives bisexual behavior and identity even further underground and thereby discourages honesty" (p. 227).

Monica McGoldrick, Director of the Family Institute of New Jersey, suggests that heterosexuals are responsible for many of the problems gays and lesbians experience in society. McGoldrick urges heterosexuals to take the lead in confronting prejudice and ignorance:

> Those of us who identify or are identified as White have left it to African-Americans and others identified as "people of color" to confront the horrors of racism, which is a White construction and therefore a problem to be addressed by Whites. In this case we have left it to lesbians and gays, White or of color, to discuss issues that pertain to homophobia, a problem of heterosexual society. Heterosexuals must begin to take responsibility for their own consciousness-raising, for overcoming their own pervasive ignorance. . . . (1996, p. xii)

Similarly, how might homosexual individuals take responsibility for and confront the biphobia that affects bisexual women and men?

THEORIES OF SEXUAL ORIENTATION

One of the prevailing questions raised regarding homosexuality centers on its origin or "cause." Gay people are often irritated by the fact that heterosexual people are so concerned about finding the cause of homosexuality. The same question is rarely asked about heterosexuality, since it is assumed that this sexual orientation is normal and needs no explanation. Questions about the cause of homosexuality imply that something is "wrong" with homosexuality. Perhaps one reason people are so interested in determining the cause of homosexuality is that public opinion studies show that those who hold a biological view of the development of sexual orientation tend to have more positive attitudes toward homosexuals (Greenberg & Bailey, 1993). However, Greenberg and Bailey argue that it is unreasonable to base moral, legal, and policy consequences on evidence related to biological causality because all behavior is ultimately biologically caused—by mediation of environmental and all other factors—through the brain.

Despite the growing research on this topic, a concrete cause of homosexuality and knowledge on whether its basis is derived from "nature or nurture" have yet to be discovered. Most researchers agree that an interaction of biological, psychological, and social or cultural forces is involved in the development of one's sexual orientation. Any explanation that does not acknowledge the interaction of these components is incomplete (DeCecco & Parker, 1995). McGuire (1995) recommends that the nature-nurture dichotomy should be retired once and for all:

> As a culture, the West is obsessed with causality and dichotomy. Just as many researchers persist in asserting a homosexual/heterosexual dichotomy, most people want to have homosexuality attributed either to a genetic or an environmental factor. At best, they wish to know how much of the trait is genetic and how much is environmental. This nature-nurture dichotomy can never be resolved because it is false. Genetically identical animals reared in identical laboratory environments are often very different . . . even if we knew absolutely everything about genes and absolutely everything about environments, we still could not predict the final phenotype of any individual. (p. 143)

Before the end of the 19th century, most efforts to understand homosexuality were based on religious thinking. Scientific theories on the development of sexual orientation and homosexuality can be organized into those emphasizing biological, and those emphasizing environmental, factors. Theories focusing on biological factors include genetic, perinatal hormonal, and postpubertal hormonal. Environmental theories emphasize the following: parent and child interaction, sexual interaction, and gender role (Ellis, 1996).

Biological Explanations

Biological explanations usually focus on genetic or hormonal differences between heterosexuals and homosexuals. Gooren (1995) pointed out that "Workers in the 'soft' sciences like psychology and sociology are often overly impressed with the so-called 'hard' data of the natural sciences" (p. 244). A discussion of three biological explorations for sexual orientation follows.

GENETIC THEORIES   Is sexual orientation an inborn trait that is transmitted genetically, like eye color? Bailey and Pillard (1991) provided support of a genetic basis for sexual orientation in their study of 56 gay men who were twins or had adoptive brothers. In their study, 52% of the identical twins, 22% of the fraternal twins, and 11% of adoptive brothers were homosexual. This finding "provided some support for the view that sexual orientation is influenced by constitutional factors . . . and emphasizes the necessity of considering causal factors arising within the individual, and not just his psychosocial environment" (p. 1095). Research on female twins also concludes that if one twin is gay, there is an increased chance that the other is also gay (Bailey et al., 1993). However, other research on twins provides no evidence of a genetic basis for homosexuality (King & McDonald, 1992).

Some evidence has also been presented that a homosexual orientation among men is related to the presence of a gene on the X chromosome inherited from the mother. In one study, two-thirds of the gay siblings shared a distinctive pattern along a segment of their X chromosome. "Scientists say the possibility is remote that this genetic pattern would appear by chance" (Park, 1995, p. 95). Turner (1995) also presented evidence that male homosexuality has a genetic basis in the gene at the Xq28 region. Still other research suggests that male homosexual and heterosexual brains reveal some differences (Reite, Sheeder, Richardson, & Teale, 1995). These differences, however, may be due to the effects of environmental and psychosocial factors on the brain (Swaab, Gooren, & Hofman, 1995).

As these data suggest, biological research remains tentative and ongoing. McGuire (1995) concluded, "The evidence for a genetic component for homosexuality is hardly overwhelming. Numerous studies that purport to prove the existence of a genetic aspect to homosexuality are either anecdotal or seriously flawed" (p. 141).

PERINATAL HORMONAL THEORIES   Ellis and Ames (1987) concluded that hormonal and neurological factors operating prior to birth, between the second and fifth month of gestation, are the "main determinants of sexual orientation" (p. 235). Money (1987) suggested that sexual orientation is programmed into the brain during critical prenatal periods and early childhood.

POSTPUBERTAL HORMONAL THEORIES   Endocrinology (the study of hormones) research to determine if the levels of sex hormones of gay men and lesbians resemble the other sex has yielded mixed results (Ellis, 1996). Although some studies of circulating testosterone levels in men have found slightly lower levels in gay men, most studies have not found significant differences. About half of the studies of women have found no differences; the other half have found higher levels of testosterone in lesbians (although the levels are still well below the normal level for men). Ellis concluded that the connection between postpubertal sex hormone levels and homosexuality is complex and is probably applicable only to some subgroups of gay men and lesbians.

In contrast to these observations, Banks and Gartrell (1995) reviewed the studies on sex hormones and the development of sexual orientation and concluded, "Overall, the data do not support a causal connection between hormones and human sexual orientation" (p. 248). They cited methodological problems as well as the questionability of generalizing animal studies to humans. Moreover, Fausto-Sterling (1995) emphasized the need to understand how physiological influences on the brain are affected by experience. Gooren (1995) concluded his review of homosexuality and hormones with the following:

> If I were asked whether there is a biology of homosexuality, my answer would be yes. It is, however, a biology that allows multifarious expressions of sexuality. It is not true that biology causes people to have certain sexual encounters. It is more likely that other levels of human existence shape sexual expression (p. 245).

The belief in biological determinism of sexual orientation among homosexuals is strong. In a national study of homosexual men, 90% believe that they were born with their homosexual orientation (Lever, 1994); only 4% believe that environmental factors are the sole cause (Lever, 1994). However, the general public believes that homosexuality is more of a choice. Based on a *U.S. News & World Report* poll, 46% of U.S. adults believe that homosexuals choose to be gay or lesbian; only 32% think that homosexuals are born that way (Shapiro, Cook, Krackov, & Cook, 1993, p. 48).

Environmental Explanations

According to Doell (1995), ". . . we all probably develop, from infancy, the capacity to have heterosexual, homosexual, or bisexual relationships" (p. 352). Environmentally weighted theories suggest that parent-child interaction, sexual experiences, and adoption of sex roles and self-labels are especially influential.

PARENT-CHILD INTERACTION THEORIES Freud's psychoanalytic theory has been described as one of the first scientific explanations of homosexuality (Ellis, 1996). His theories suggested that the relationship individuals have with their parents may predispose them toward heterosexuality or homosexuality. While heterosexual men identified closely with their fathers and had more distant relationships with their mothers, homosexual men had close emotional relationships with their mothers and were distant with their fathers (Freud had little to say about the development of sexual orientation of women) (Isay, 1990).

The presumed script for the development of a homosexual male follows: The overprotective mother seeks to establish a binding emotional relationship with her son. But this closeness also elicits strong sexual feelings on the part of the son toward the mother, which are punished by her and blocked by the society through the incest taboo. The son is fearful of expressing sexual feelings for his mother. He generalizes this fear to other women, with the result that they are no longer viewed as potential sexual partners.

The son's distant relationship with his father prevents identification with a male role model. For example, the relationship between playwright Tennessee Williams and his father was one of mutual rejection—the father was contemptuous of his "sissy" son, and Williams was hostile to his father because of his father's arrogance.

This theory of male homosexuality is not supported by the scientific community. First, it does not resolve the question "Is the absent or distant father relationship a result or a cause of the child's homosexuality?" Second, sons with overprotective mothers and rejecting fathers also grow up to be heterosexual, just as those with moderate mothering and warm fathering grow up to be homosexual. Third, two sons growing up in the same type of family may have different sexual orientations. A study of family backgrounds of 979 homosexual and 477 heterosexual people confirmed that parent-child relationships as the "cause" for homosexuality is highly questionable and highly suspect (Bell, Weinberg, & Hammersmith, 1981). The researchers concluded that the relationship individuals have with their parents "cannot be said to predict much about sexual orientation" (p. 62). It may be that some maternal protection and parental rejection are reactions to effeminate behaviors of "pre-gay" male children (Ellis, 1996).

SEXUAL INTERACTION THEORIES Sexual interaction theories propose that such factors as availability of sexual partners, early sexual experiences, imprinting, and sexual reinforcement influence subsequent sexual orientation. Since homosexuality is more prevalent among men than women, shortages of women and an emphasis on chastity of women have been hypothesized to be conducive to male homosexuality (Ellis, 1996). The degree to which early sexual experiences have been negative or positive has been hypothesized as influencing sexual orientation. Having pleasurable same-sex experiences would be likely to increase the probability of a homosexual orientation. By the same token, early sexual experiences that are either unsuccessful or traumatic have been suspected as causing fear of heterosexual activity. However, one study that compared sexual histories of lesbian and heterosexual women found no difference in the incidence of traumatic experiences with men (Brannock & Chapman, 1990).

SEX-ROLE THEORIES Sex-role theories include self-labeling theory and inappropriate sex role training. How people perceive themselves and the reactions of others to their sex role behavior are important in a child's development. The self-labeling theory is supported by a number of studies finding that gay men are more likely than heterosexual men to have exhibited effeminate behavior in childhood (Ellis, 1996). In a study comparing the recalled childhood experiences of heterosexual and lesbian women, lesbian women were much more likely to have imagined themselves as male characters, to have a preference for boys' games, and to have considered themselves tomboys as children (Phillips & Over, 1995).

However, some heterosexual women reported much the same childhood experiences as the majority of lesbian women, and some lesbian women reported much the same childhood experiences as the majority of heterosexual women.

According to labeling theorists, "through a process of socialization, lesbians and gays incorporate ideas about what it means to be lesbian or gay into their own identities. The labeling of an individual's acts as homosexual—both by other lesbians and gays and by the straight world—and the stigmatization of that identity, over time, lead to the adoption of a homosexual identity" (Esterberg, 1997, p. 20). Although labeling theory is useful in emphasizing the fact that the labels "homosexual" and "heterosexual" are socially constructed categories, "it does not appear that individuals become lesbian or gay simply by a process of labeling by others" (Esterberg, 1997, p. 21).

The recently proposed Exotic Becomes Erotic (EBE) theory provides an explanation of the development of sexual orientation that combines biological and environmental components (Bem, 1996). Bem suggests that a child's biological inheritance influences temperament (including characteristics such as aggressiveness and activity level), which predisposes him or her to prefer some activities more than others. Gender-conforming children (who enjoy sex-typical activities) will feel different from peers of the other sex and perceive them as dissimilar and exotic. Likewise, gender-nonconforming children (who enjoy atypical activities for their sex) will perceive same-sex peers as unfamiliar and exotic. These feelings result in autonomic arousal, which is transformed into erotic or romantic attraction. Bem observes that as natives of a gender-polarizing culture, we have learned to view the world through the lens of gender. He also notes that culture influences the way biological and behavioral scientists think about sexual orientation.

THINK ABOUT IT

Is homosexuality a choice? Whether one can choose to be lesbian, gay, or bisexual is hotly contested, not only among scientists, but also among lesbians, gays, bisexuals, and heterosexuals (Esterberg, 1997; Whisman, 1996). The lesbians and gay men interviewed by Whisman stated that the idea of choosing to be gay "overrationalizes sex" (p. 122). But Esterberg and Whisman noted that their respondents deliberate this question and debate its significance and effect on their self-definitions and functioning in society.

GAY AND BISEXUAL IDENTITY DEVELOPMENT

Gay and bisexual identity development is usually a gradual process that progresses through various stages. In a review of six theories of gay identity development, Sophie (1985–1986) synthesized four essential stages of identity development:

Stage 1: First awareness or realization that one is "different." This awareness often begins before puberty. Girls and boys may feel different in their lack of interest in the other sex. An awareness of being different from others may also involve a vague feeling of not fitting in with one's peers, without knowing why. Troiden (1989) quoted a gay adolescent who experienced these feelings: "I never felt as if I fit in. I don't know why for sure. I felt different. I thought it was because I was more sensitive" (p. 363).

Stage 2: Test and exploration. At this stage, which often occurs in the teenage years, individuals may suspect they are homosexual but may not be sure. This stage involves exploring one's feelings and attractions, as well as initiating limited contact with other nonheterosexual individuals.

Stage 3: Identity acceptance. In this stage, individuals come to define themselves as homosexual or bisexual. For women, developing a homosexual identity often occurs after developing an emotionally intimate, loving same-sex relationship. One woman declared, "It never occurred to me that I might be a lesbian until I met this woman, fell in love, and thought, 'Oh! That's why I didn't like kissing the guys!'" (quoted in Esterberg, 1997, p. 31). For men, identity acceptance often occurs after having an initial same-sex sexual experience. Troiden (1989) reported that gay men arrive at homosexual self-definitions between the ages of 19 and 21, whereas women arrive at homosexual self-definitions between the ages of 21 and 23. Bisexual self-identification typically occurs at later ages due to the difficulties bisexual women and men have in arriving at an identity that is not affirmed in either the heterosexual or the homosexual community.

Stage 4: Identity integration. The final stage of developing a gay or bisexual identity involves developing pride in and commitment to one's sexual orientation. This stage also involves disclosing one's sexual orientation to others.

Not all homosexual and bisexual individuals go through identity development stages in an orderly, predictable fashion. In a study of 76 lesbian or bisexual female youths and 80 gay or bisexual male youths (age range, 14–21), the pattern of psychosexual development was first, to become aware of attractions to those of the same sex, then to consider a homosexual or bisexual identity, and finally to feel certain about a gay or bisexual identity (Rosario, Meyer-Bahlburg, Exner, Gwadz, & Keller, 1996).

Some researchers have criticized stage identity models on the basis of their small samples, their narrow focus on sexuality, and their lack of attention to the larger sociohistorical context (Eliason, 1996). A more comprehensive model of identity development would put sexual identity into a context that includes other important facets of identity, such as gender, race, and class.

Gay and bisexual identity development also occurs through the process of "coming out." The issue of "coming out" received nationwide attention in 1997 with the disclosure of Ellen DeGeneres's character on the hit television show *Ellen* that she is a lesbian. GLAAD (Gay and Lesbian Alliance Against Defamation) gave her an award for the program, emphasizing the importance of such content on television for the gay rights movement. Indeed, there are 22 recurring gay and lesbian characters on prime-time television (Szymanski, 1997).

The term *coming out* (a shortened form of "coming out of the closet") refers to "the sequence of events through which individuals recognize their own homosexual [or bisexual] orientation and disclose it to others" (Garnets, Herek, & Levy, 1990). Coming out helps to solidify commitment to a homosexual or bisexual identity. Although it is difficult to ascertain the percentage of gay people who "stay in the closet," some data suggest that the majority of gay individuals eventually come out. In one study, only 4% of 317 self-identified gay people had come out to no one (Savin-Williams, 1989).

—————— **THINK ABOUT IT** ——————
Can you describe the development of your own sexual identity as a process consisting of various stages? For example, when did you first become aware of and define your own sexual orientation?

Coming Out to Oneself

For some, coming out to oneself is a confusing and difficult process. At age 12, Kate had her first crush on a girl. Throughout her teenage years, Kate struggled against her attractions to women. At age 18, she experienced her first passionate kiss with another woman: "My reaction to that first encounter . . . was to get up out of bed, brush my teeth vigorously, walk back to bed, and say, 'I'm not that kind of girl.' And the next night I was that kind of girl all over again" (quoted in Esterberg, 1997, p. 2). Kate describes her continuing struggle to acknowledge her sexual orientation:

> Between the age of nineteen and twenty there was a year-and-a half to two-year period in which I was quite convinced that my affair with M. had been just a mistake, one of those biological bleeps that occur. I did not doubt that I was heterosexual and felt that I simply, for whatever reason, had gotten my sexual orientation slightly confused. I did not at that time discredit my feelings about M., but was convinced that once she was gone and I was over that breakup that I would pick up and go on my merry heterosexual way, which I proceeded to do. It was only when I realized that I was attracted to women other than M. that I could no longer ignore the fact that I was in fact probably predominantly attracted to women. . . . And from that point on with rare exception I considered myself homosexual. (quoted in Esterberg, 1997, p. 2)

Others may feel that they have always known and accepted their sexual orientation. One woman, for example, claimed: "I have never *not* felt that I was bisexual" (quoted in Esterberg, 1997, p. 38).

Developing acceptance of oneself is important for one's happiness. Adelman (1990) interviewed 52 self-identified gay men and lesbians and asked them about the importance of coming out to oneself. One respondent said:

I don't think that anybody, if they cannot accept with good grace whatever they are, can be happy . . . that is important. It's not just important; it's basic. I have fully accepted my homosexuality and embrace it. (p. 22)

Most gays eventually accept themselves and enjoy their lives. Sixty percent of 52 gay women and men in their sixties reported that they were "very satisfied with being gay" (Adelman, 1990, p. 14). Kate, the woman described earlier in the identity acceptance section, struggled for years against acknowledging her homosexuality. Finally she declared, "At this point in my life, my lesbian identity is absolutely clear. It's as much a part of me as having brown eyes" (quoted in Esterberg, 1997, p. 3).

Coming Out to Others

Coming out to others involves disclosing one's homosexual or bisexual identity to parents and other family members, friends and peers, employers, partners or spouses, and children. In coming out, some homosexual and bisexual individuals do not directly reveal their sexual orientation to others. Rather, they make no effort to hide their orientation from others. Esterberg (1997) found that women who view their sexual orientation as private are likely to agree with the statement: "I don't usually tell people about my sexual orientation, but I don't hide it either. I just live my life and let people figure it out" (p. 33).

COMING OUT TO PARENTS AND SIBLINGS Sixty-two percent of 104 lesbians reported that they had come out to their mothers, and 39% had come out to their fathers (Green, Bettinger, & Zacks, 1996). Coming out to one's parents is a major decision. Before deciding to tell one's family that one is homosexual, it is recommended that the person feel personally secure with his or her homosexuality, have a support group of friends who are also secure and who have experienced coming out to their parents, and have a relatively good relationship with his or her parents. Even if all of these factors exist, however, the reactions of parents are unpredictable (Cohen & Savin-Williams, 1996).

Deciding to tell or not to tell one's parents is very difficult. Not to do so is to hide one's true self from parents and to feel alienated, afraid, and alone. To tell them is to risk rejection and disapproval. Some parents of homosexuals suspect that their children are gay, even before they are told. Of 402 parents of gay and lesbian children, 26% stated that they suspected their offspring's homosexuality (Robinson, Walters, & Skeen, 1989). In general, youths are more likely to come out to mothers than to fathers (Cohen & Savin-Williams, 1996).

Parents may be told face-to-face, through an intermediary (a sibling, another relative, or a counselor), or in a letter. The following is a letter written by a 21-year-old lesbian college student disclosing her homosexuality to her parents (authors' files).

Dear Mom and Dad:

I love you very much and would give you the world if I could. You've always given me the best. You've always been there when I needed you. The lessons of love, strength, and wisdom you've taught me are invaluable. Most importantly, you've taught me to take pride and stand up for what I believe. In the past six months I've done some very serious thinking about my goals and outlook on life. It's a tough and unyielding world that caters only to those who do for themselves. Having your help and support seems to make it easier to handle. But I've made a decision that may test your love and support. Mom and Dad, I've decided to live a gay lifestyle.

I'm sure your heads are spinning with confusion and disbelief right now but please try to let me finish. As I said before, I've given this decision much thought. First and foremost, I'd like for you to know that I'm happy. All my life as a sexual being has been spent frustrated in a role I could not fulfill. Emotionally and mentally, I'm relieved. Believe me, this was not an easy decision to make. (What made it easier was having the strength to accept myself.) Who I choose to sleep with does not make me more or less of a human being. My need for love and affection is the same as anyone else's; it's just that I fulfill this need in a different way. I'm still the same person I've always been.

It's funny I say I'm still the same person, yet society seems to think I've changed. They seem to think that I don't deserve to be treated as a respectable citizen. Instead, they think I should be treated as a deranged maniac needing constant supervision to prevent me from molesting innocent children. I have the courage and strength to face up to this opposition, but I can't do it alone. Oh, what I would give to have your support!

I realize I've thrown everything at you rather quickly. Please take your time. I don't expect a response. And please don't blame yourselves, for there is no one to blame. Please remember that I'm happy and I felt the need to share my happiness with two people I love with all my heart.

Your loving daughter,
Maria

Maria offers these suggestions to other gay people who want to tell their parents of their sexual orientation:

1. Avoid speaking from a defensive point of view. Too often, gay people are forced to defend their lifestyle as if it is wrong. If you approach your parents with the view that your homosexuality is a positive aspect of your personality, you will have a better chance of evoking a positive response from them.
2. Avoid talking about your current relationship. Homosexuality is often labeled as a phase rather than a permanent facet of one's life. Your parents may feel, as mine did, that your current partner is the cause of your lifestyle. Thus, when your relationship ends (so they hope), so will your homosexuality. Deal with the subject as it affects you as an individual.
3. Try to maintain a constant flow of positive reinforcement toward your parents. Reiterate your love for them as you would like them to do to you.
4. Be confident in your views and outlook on homosexuality. Before you begin to explain your position to anyone else, you must have it clear in your own mind.

Parental reactions to the discovery that their child is gay often include shock and anger (Robinson et al., 1989). Most of the 52 gay respondents in one study said that their parents rejected them when they learned that they were gay. One 68-year-old man bitterly reported, "My father was very hostile when I told him I was homosexual. I was 21. We didn't have a positive relationship after that" (Adelman, 1990, p. 29).

Among 37 homosexual or bisexual male high school seniors (ages 16–18), only 2 reported having a positive relationship with their families over the issue of being gay (Uribe & Harbeck, 1992). For the remaining 35 males in this study, coming out to parents resulted in situations that "varied from extreme family disruption to forcible expulsion from home" (p. 22). Over half of the young gay men in this sample lived with either friends, lovers, or in a residential or foster home for gay adolescents. Eight out of 13 lesbian high school seniors in this study told their parents of their sexual orientation. "In each case, their parents told them that it was a passing phase that would go away" (Uribe & Harbeck, 1992, pp. 24–25).

PERSONAL CHOICES

Would You Accept or Reject a Gay Son or Daughter?

Whereas young adults are confronted with the decision to tell their parents they are gay, parents are confronted with the decision of accepting or rejecting the homosexuality of their offspring. It is helpful to keep in mind that, just as homosexuals live in an antihomosexual society that encourages a negative self-concept (and are therefore victims of social forces that influence them), parents live in the same society, which encourages rejection of homosexuals (and are, therefore, also influenced by negative social forces). If parents want to maintain the relationship with their children, they must decide to override society's antigay bias. One parent said:

I can't say that I like it. In fact, I am sad that my child is homosexual. But I can't let that come between us and have decided to make it clear that I still love Chris to the fullest.

Some parents are unwilling to accept their child's homosexuality:

I'm not the kind to put up with such behavior. I told my kid that what he was doing was wrong and that I wouldn't tolerate it. I haven't seen my son in four years. I'm sad about that but I'd be more sad having a faggot in my house.

Some parents who have rejected their offspring because of their homosexuality have regretted doing so because they missed the relationship with their offspring more than they hated the fact that they were gay. Alternatives available to parents include the following:

1. Outright rejection and attempts to force the child to change.
2. Continuing the relationship with the child but denying the child's lifestyle. "We never talk about it," said one parent, "but he is always welcome here and brings his lovers, too. I'd rather have my son as a homo than have no son at all."
3. Complete acceptance. The child's lifestyle is openly acknowledged and supported. The parents may become members of PFLAG—Parents and Friends of Lesbians and Gays. Most parents need time to accept their child's homosexuality. Parental acceptance and support is important for a person's sense of self-worth—no matter what his or her sexual orientation may be. Parental support may be particularly important for gay individuals, as it may provide a buffer against the difficulties of living in a heterosexist society.

When parents were asked what they would tell other parents who had just learned that their child was gay, some responded (Robinson et al., 1989, p. 74):

Love her or him, simply love her or him. Respect your child's right and wisdom to make his own choices. Affirm his honesty and courage. Celebrate his sexuality as a gift from God. (a 50-year-old mother)

They have gone through so much within themselves, just be there to listen and continue to love them. (a 52-year-old mother)

Take care, go easy, try to understand (easier said than done). (a 55-year-old father)

Most parents struggle to find ways to look beyond the cultural prejudices, to recognize their offspring's homosexuality, and to accept it. While few parents fully accept it (Ben-ari, 1995), involvement with other parents of gay offspring seems to help. One parent who became aware that her son was gay said:

I had my suspicions, but when he told me he was gay I cried anyway. It was over the phone and I think this was more difficult because I couldn't hug

him. At the time I think the tears shed were more for me and the dreams I was losing than for him and the prejudice and battles he would have to endure.

I found an organization called PFLAG—Parents and Friends of Lesbians and Gays—to be a lifesaver to both my husband and myself. It's a support group mostly of parents but it is also attended by siblings, friends, and gays themselves. They meet once a month and make you feel safe there to share your feelings and concerns about being a parent of a gay. They say when the child comes out of the closet, the parent goes in and there is some truth to that. They have a speaker and group discussions and also work toward changing legislation that is anti-gay. PFLAG also helped us to realize that it wasn't anything we said or did that made our son gay—it is how he was born. Needless to say, we love our son just as much now as before we knew. (authors' files)

Homosexuals usually disclose their sexual orientation to their siblings before they tell their parents. The reactions of siblings influence whether and when parents are told. Sibling reactions are often similar to those of parents. However, unlike parents, siblings do not experience guilt or self-blame (Strommen, 1989).

COMING OUT TO A HETEROSEXUAL PARTNER OR SPOUSE AND CHILDREN Gay and bisexual people become involved in heterosexual relationships and marriages for a variety of reasons (Strommen, 1989). These include genuine love for a spouse, wanting to have children, family pressure to marry, the desire to live a socially approved heterosexual lifestyle, and belief that marriage is the only way to achieve a happy adult life. In a probability sample of gay and bisexual men, 42% reported that they were currently married (Harry, 1990). Other researchers estimate that 20% of gay men are married (Strommen, 1989). Some individuals do not realize that they are gay or bisexual until after they are married.

Many homosexuals and bisexuals in heterosexual relationships do not disclose their sexual identity to their partners out of fear that their partners will reject them and that there may be legal consequences (getting custody of the children would be jeopardized). The immediate and long-term consequences for coming out to one's partner vary widely from couple to couple. In general, "acknowledging homoerotic feelings, or even occasional same-sex activity, is less threatening to a spouse than admitting to an ongoing sexual relationship in which there is some degree of emotional commitment" (Paul, 1996, p. 451).

Some gay individuals also confront the issue of coming out to their children. About 10% of gay men are fathers (Strommen, 1990). Children who learn of their fathers' homosexuality usually do so without great trauma. Gay fathers report that the reaction of their children is "none" or "tolerant and understanding" (Bozett, 1989). However, daughters tend to be more accepting than sons, although most children feel their father's honesty brings them closer together (p. 143).

Some children experience embarrassing situations or trauma because of the reactions of other children. Some children are physically or verbally abused, and in one case, a child was subjected to a "mock faggot trial" at school (Hays & Samuels, 1989).

COMING OUT TO FRIENDS AND EMPLOYERS Disclosing one's homosexuality to friends produces reactions that vary from acceptance to termination of the relationship. One friend who could not accept her girlfriend's disclosure of lesbianism said:

> I was shocked and I didn't know how to handle it. It changed how I viewed her—as something awful that I didn't want to be around any longer. I was also ashamed of myself for the way I felt about my friend. But I couldn't change and we didn't see each other again. (authors' class notes)

Some heterosexuals particularly value and enjoy friendships with homosexuals. Several female heterosexual students in the authors' classes have indicated that it is easier to develop close friendships with gay men because the element of sexual attraction does not get in the way.

In regard to employers, Etringer, Hillerbrand, and Hetherington (1990) found that compared to heterosexual men, gay men are more likely to be anxious about their career choices. This is because homosexuals must consider factors related to their sexual orientation and the implication of its potential public exposure. One study of 52 homosexuals found that those who reported high life satisfaction had "low disclosure at work" of their homosexuality (Adelman, 1990).

Some employment firms have policies forbidding discrimination in hiring or advancement based on affectional or sexual orientation. American Telephone and Telegraph (the nation's largest corporate employer); Bank of America; IBM; the radio and television networks ABC, NBC, and CBS; and McDonald's are examples.

Coming Out as a Bisexual

Bisexual individuals face a unique set of concerns in coming out to themselves and to others. For example, they often experience uncertainty about how to interpret concurrent sexual attractions to both women and men. For many bisexual women and men, the process of coming out to one's self is complicated by the feeling that their sexual identity is fluid and evolving, rather than stable and fixed. Many bisexual individuals resist developing an identity that is fixed by a label. In interviews with bisexual women, Esterberg (1997) noted that, "for a number of women, what was important was not taking on a label and an identity, but having the freedom to define themselves and live their lives as they please" (p. 157).

Coming out is also more difficult for bisexual individuals because they have few role models and support networks to affirm their bisexuality. Some bisexual women and men have looked to the gay and lesbian communities for support and acceptance. But due to biphobic attitudes, many bisexual individuals have experienced rejection from the lesbian and gay communities. Fox (1996) notes that an important difference historically between coming out as a bisexual and coming out as a homosexual has been the relative lack of access for bisexual women and men to a community of similar others.

Developing a Positive Gay or Bisexual Identity

Because of massive societal homonegativity and rejection of homosexuals, gay individuals must cope with social rejection in order to overcome a negative self-concept. 🖉 The greater the stigmatization of homosexuality and the greater the antihomosexual bias of a country, the greater the negative impact on homosexuals. For example, Ireland and Australia are less accepting of homosexuality than Sweden and Finland. Homosexual youth in Ireland and Australia have more negative self-concepts and are more likely to believe that "being gay is wrong" than homosexual youth in Sweden and Finland (Ross, 1989). 🖉

Gay and bisexual individuals may develop more positive feelings about their sexual identities through a

SHOULD THE MILITARY ALLOW OR BAN HOMOSEXUALS FROM SERVICE?

One controversial social policy issue regarding sexual orientation involves gays in the military. According to a directive issued in 1982 by the Department of Defense, "homosexuality is incompatible with military service" (Tielman & Hammelburg, 1993, p. 337). This directive was implemented in the army, air force, navy, and Marine Corps and has been applied to enforce dishonorable discharges of gay members in the military.

In 1992, a gay navy serviceman was fired after revealing his homosexuality but was reinstated by orders of a federal judge. In 1993, President Clinton moved to lift the ban on homosexuals in the military. The government adopted a "don't ask, don't tell" policy, in which recruiting officers are not allowed to ask about sexual orientation, and homosexuals are encouraged not to volunteer such information. Some people feel that the "don't ask, don't tell" policy is oppressive to gays. Eric Marcus (1993) comments:

> But my life as a gay man isn't something that takes place only in the privacy of my bedroom. It affects who my friends are, whom I choose to share my life with, the work I do, the organizations I belong to, the magazines I read, where I vacation and what I talk about. I know it's the same for heterosexuals because their sexual orientation affects everything, from choice of senior-prom date and the finger on which they wear their wedding band to the birth

announcements they send and every emotion they feel. . . . So the reality of the "don't ask, don't tell" solution for . . . dealing with gays in the military means having to lie about or hide almost every aspect of your life. It's not merely as simple as just not saying, "I'm gay." (p. 10)

In effect, the "don't ask, don't tell" policy is a subtle message of disapproval. The "not asking" implies that if the answer is "gay" (and, therefore, the "wrong" answer), negative consequences will follow. Hence, most gay people feel the new policy forces them further into the closet. Under the new policy, for example, gay people are forbidden to discuss their sexuality at work or to participate in any gay community activities. To do so is to "act on" their homosexuality, which may lead to legal military consequences.

The debate over the military's "don't ask, don't tell" policy is ongoing. In 1995, federal judge Eugene Nickerson ruled that the "don't ask, don't tell" policy is unconstitutional because it discriminates against homosexuals and violates free speech rights. His decision has been appealed by the Department of Justice and is pending before the U.S. Supreme Court.

Sources: Marcus, E. (1993, July 5). Ignorance is not bliss. *Newsweek*, 10.

Tielman, R., & Hammelburg, H. (1993). World survey on the social and legal position of gays and lesbians. In A. Hendriks, R. Tielman, & E. van der Veen (Eds.), *The third pink book: A global view of lesbian and gay liberation and oppression.* Buffalo, NY: Prometheus Books.

combination of procedures. They are encouraged to view negative feelings they may have about themselves as resulting from the societal rejection of homosexuals. This rejection is based on prejudice and the perpetuation of negative stereotypes regarding homosexuals.

In addition, developing a positive gay or bisexual self-concept is facilitated by labeling one's identity and disclosing one's sexual orientation to others (Cohen and Savin-Williams, 1996; Miranda & Storms, 1989). Gay people are encouraged to establish close relationships with other gay people who feel good about themselves and can serve as positive models.

Developing a positive self-concept may be particularly difficult for gay and bisexual youth. Uribe and Harbeck (1992) observed that among gay and lesbian students who attended a high school in Los Angeles, "low self-esteem, feelings of isolation, alienation, and inadequacy were common" (p. 19). Uribe and Harbeck suggested that

> it is clear from the information available on suicide rates, drop-out risk, low self-esteem, health risks, substance abuse, and the plethora of other problems often experienced by gay, lesbian, and bisexual adolescents that intervention must occur immediately in every school in this nation. (1992, p. 27)

An example of school-based intervention that is being implemented in Los Angeles is PROJECT 10—a counseling and educational program for gay and bisexual youth. PROJECT 10, named after Kinsey's estimate that 10% of the population is homosexual, was also designed to "heighten the school community's acceptance of and sensitivity to gay, lesbian, and bisexual issues" (Uribe & Harbeck, 1992, p. 11).

─────── **THINK ABOUT IT** ───────

Esterberg (1996) notes that "unlike heterosexuals, who are defined by their family structures, communities, occupations, or other aspects of their lives, lesbians, gay men, and bisexuals are often defined primarily by what they do in bed. Many lesbians, gay men, and bisexuals, however, view their identity as social and political as well as sexual" (p. 377). Despite the numerous aspects of individuals' identities, why do heterosexuals tend to focus on the sexual aspect of homosexual and bisexual individuals?

This couple has been in a stable monogamous relationship for 23 years.

HOMOSEXUAL AND BISEXUAL RELATIONSHIPS

Richard Mohr (1995) points out that "the country is profoundly ignorant of the actual experience of gay people" (p. 412). Next, we look at one aspect of the experience of being gay or bisexual: the nature of homosexual, lesbian, and bisexual relationships. Based on a review of research on gay and lesbian relationships, Peplau, Veniegas, and Campbell (1996) concluded that there are many similarities in the relationship experiences of same-sex and different-sex couples. They noted, "That which most clearly distinguishes same-sex from heterosexual couples is the social context of their lives. Whereas heterosexuals enjoy many social and institutional supports for their relationships, gay and lesbian couples are the object of prejudice and discrimination" (p. 268).

Gay Male Relationships

One common stereotype about gay men is that they have no interest in long-term monogamous relationships. However, most gay men prefer such relationships.

NATIONAL DATA

In a national survey of homosexual men, 71% reported that they preferred long-term monogamous relationships to other arrangements.

Source: Lever, 1994.

When sex outside the relationship does occur, it is usually infrequent and not emotionally involving (Green et al., 1996). Edmund White (1994) described the typical long-term gay couple:

If all goes well, two gay men will meet through sex, become lovers, weather the storms of jealousy and diminution of lust, develop shared interests (a hobby, a business, a house, a circle), and end up with a long-term . . . camaraderie that is not as disinterested as friendship or as seismic as passion. . . . Younger couples feel that this sort of relationship, when it happens to them, is incomplete, a compromise, and they break up in order to find total fulfillment (i.e. tireless passion) elsewhere. But older gay couples stay together, cultivate their mild, reasonable love, and defend it against the ever-present danger of the sexual allure exercised by a newcomer. . . . They may have. . . . regular extracurricular sex partners or even beaux, but . . . with an eye attuned to nuance . . . at a certain point will intervene to banish a potential rival. (p. 164)

Another common stereotype is that gay men do not develop close, intimate relationships with their partners. A team of researchers (Green, Bettinger, & Zacks, 1996) compared 50 gay male couples with 218 married couples and found the former almost twice as likely to report the highest levels of cohesiveness (closeness) in their relationships. Gay male couples also report having more flexibility in their roles than heterosexual couples, and their level of relationship satisfaction is roughly similar to heterosexual couples. Contrary to stereotypical beliefs, same-sex couples (male or female) do not typically adopt "husband" and "wife" roles (Peplau, Veniegas, & Campbell, 1996).

One unique aspect of gay male relationships in the United States involves coping with the high rate of HIV and AIDS. Many gay men have lost a love partner to this disease; some have experienced multiple losses.

Some lesbian couples choose to rear a child together.

Gay Female Relationships

Like many heterosexual women, most gay women value stable monogamous relationships that are emotionally as well as sexually satisfying. Transitory sexual encounters among gay women do occur, but they are the exception, not the rule. In a study of long-term gay relationships, 5 years was the average length of the relationship of 706 lesbian couples; 18% reported that they had been together 11 or more years. Ninety-one percent reported that they were sexually monogamous ("National Survey Results," 1990). The majority (57%) of the women in these lesbian relationships noted that they wore a ring to symbolize their commitment to each other. Some (19%) acknowledged their relationship with a ceremony. Most had met through friends or at work. Only 4% had met at a bar.

Women in our society, gay and "straight," are taught that sexual expression "should" occur in the context of emotional or romantic involvement. Ninety-three percent of 94 gay women in one study said their first homosexual experience was emotional; physical expression came later (Corbett & Morgan, 1983). Hence, for gay women, the formula is love first; for gay men, sex first—just as for their "straight" counterparts.

While gay female relationships normally last longer than gay male relationships, long-term relationships (20 years or more) are rare. Of 706 lesbian couples, only 1% had been in relationships lasting more than 20 years ("National Survey Results," 1990). Serial monogamy—one relationship at a time—was the predominant pattern, and 6.6 years was the average relationship duration.

When lesbians engage in extrapartner sexual relations, they (like heterosexual women) are likely to have emotional and sexual affairs rather than just sexual encounters. Nonmonogamy among lesbian couples is also likely to be related to dissatisfaction with the primary relationship. In addition, both lesbians and gay men are more likely than heterosexual couples to be open with their partners about their extrapartner activity (Nichols, 1987).

Kurdek (1995) reviewed the literature on lesbian and gay couples and concluded, "The most striking finding regarding the factors linked to relationship satisfaction is that they seem to be the same for lesbian couples, gay couples, and heterosexual couples" (p. 251). These factors include having equal power and control, being emotionally expressive, perceiving many attractions and few alternatives to the relationship, placing a high value on attachment, and sharing decision making. Also, as is true with heterosexual couples, relationship satisfaction among gay couples largely depends on the emotional intimacy of the partners (Deenen, Gijiis, & Van Naerssen, 1994).

Green et al. (1996) compared 52 lesbian couples with 50 gay male couples and 218 heterosexual married couples. They found that the lesbian couples were the most cohesive (closest), the most flexible in terms of their roles, and the most satisfied in their relationships.

Bisexual Relationships

Contrary to the common myth that bisexuals are, by definition, nonmonogamous, some bisexuals prefer monogamous relationships (especially considering the widespread concern about HIV). In one study, 16.4% of bisexuals reported being in monogamous relationships with no desire to stray (Rust, 1996). In the same study, lesbians and gay men were more likely than bisexual women and men to report that they were in monogamous relationships. Further, the study revealed that 29.5% of bisexual women and 15.4% of bisexual men reported that they would like to have a lifetime committed relationship, compared to 46.7% of lesbians and 75.9% of gay men (the high rate of desire for monogamy among gay men might be a response to the fear of HIV) (Rust, 1996).

Monogamous bisexual women and men may find that erotic attractions can be satisfied through fantasy and affectional needs through nonsexual friendships (Paul, 1996). Even in a monogamous relationship, "the partner of the bisexual person may feel that a bisexual person's decision to continue to identify as bisexual . . . is somehow a withholding of full commitment to the relationship. The bisexual person may be perceived as holding onto the possibility of other relationships by maintaining a bisexual identity and, therefore, not fully committed to the relationship" (Ochs, 1996, p. 234). However, this perception overlooks the fact that one's identity is separate from one's choices about relationship involvement or monogamy. Ochs (1996) notes that "a heterosexual's ability to establish and maintain a committed relationship with one person is not assumed to falter, even though the person retains a sexual identity as 'heterosexual' and may even admit to feeling attractions to other people despite her or his committed status" (p. 234).

In relationships in which one or more partners is bisexual, some couples attempt an "open" relationship that allows for extradyadic involvements. However, it is important for such couples to discuss and establish a mutually satisfactory set of ground rules. These ground rules should "recognize the acceptable limits of both partners, be readily subject to revision and renegotiation, and provide guidelines that are as explicit as possible with regard to that which is and is not acceptable in outside relationships" (Paul, 1996, p. 453).

Sexual Orientation and HIV Infection

As noted earlier, most worldwide HIV infection occurs through heterosexual transmission. However, in the United States, HIV infection remains the most threatening STD for male homosexuals and bisexuals. Men who have sex with men account for more cases of AIDS in the United States than persons in any other transmission category (Council on Scientific Affairs, 1996). (The reasons for the high rate of HIV and AIDS in gay and bisexual men are discussed in Chapter 5.)

Women who have sex exclusively with other women have a much lower rate of HIV infection than men (both gay and "straight") and women who have sex with men. However, "female-to-female transmission of HIV can occur through exposure to cervical and vaginal secretions of an HIV-infected woman. The amount of shedding from these secretions likely increases the risk of HIV exposure" (Council on Scientific Affairs, 1996, p. 1355). In addition, lesbians and bisexual women may also be at risk for HIV due to having sex with high-risk male partners (bisexuals) and injecting drugs (Norman et al., 1996).

THINK ABOUT IT

Same-sex couples face many obstacles and struggles that heterosexual couples do not. However, Ochs (1996) points out that same-sex relationships also offer benefits, such as freedom from unwanted pregnancy, the absence of scripted gender roles, and the comfort and ease of being with someone with a more similar social conditioning.

KEY TERMS

biphobia   435
bisexuality   427
coming out   442
Defense of Marriage Act   436
dichotomous model of sexual orientation   426
discrimination   434
heterosexism   431
homonegativity   431
homophobia   431

LesBiGay   428
LesBiGay/Transgender   428
LesBiGay/Transgender affirmative model of sexual orientation   428
multidimensional model of sexual orientation   428
sexual orientation   426
unidimensional continuum model of sexual orientation   427

Summary Points

With the "coming out" of Ellen DeGeneres on nation-wide television, the political debate on gay marriage, and the continued threat of HIV, homosexuality and bisexuality are no longer being ignored.

Conceptual Models of Sexual Orientation

Conceptual models of sexual orientation include the dichotomous model, the unidimensional continuum model, the multidimensional model, and the LesBiGay/Transgender affirmative model.

Prevalence of Homosexuality, Heterosexuality, and Bisexuality

Estimating the prevalence of various sexual orientations is difficult because categorizing a person as either heterosexual, homosexual, or bisexual is not as clear-cut as most people assume. Sexual identity may change over time, and attractions and sexual behavior are not always consistent with sexual self-identity. Adult homosexual or bisexual experiences do not necessarily result in the acquisition of a homosexual or bisexual self-identity. Also, prior homosexual or bisexual experience is not required to label oneself as homosexual or bisexual.

Heterosexism and Homonegativity

Most societies embrace heterosexism—the view that heterosexuality is the only valid form of sexual behavior, identity, and relationships. Heterosexism and homophobia—negative attitudes toward homosexuality—are rooted in various aspects of the culture. Biphobia refers to negative attitudes and discrimination toward bisexual individuals. Bisexuals are subjected to rejection in both the lesbian and gay, as well as heterosexual, communities.

Theories of Sexual Orientation

Theories of sexual orientation focus on biological and environmental influences. Most researchers agree that sexual orientation is a result of the interaction of biological, social, and cultural forces.

Gay and Bisexual Identity Development

The development of a gay or bisexual identity involves becoming aware of attractions to those of the same sex, considering a homosexual or bisexual iden-tity, and then feeling certain about a gay or bisexual identity. Commitment to the lifestyle may involve join-ing gay rights organizations and coming out. Coming out refers to the recognition of a homosexual or bisexual orientation to oneself, parents, siblings, friends, and employers. Coming out is especially diffi-cult for bisexuals because they have few role models and support networks to affirm their bisexuality.

Homosexual and Bisexual Relationships

Homosexual, bisexual, and heterosexual relationships are more similar than different. However, unlike het-erosexual couples (who receive social support for long-term relationships), same-sex couples receive lit-tle social support. Lack of social support contributes to the difficulty some same-sex couples have in main-taining committed relationships. Some bisexuals pre-fer monogamous relationships; others prefer "open" relationships that permit emotional and sexual involvement with more than one partner. Bisexuality is not, however, synonymous with nonmonogamy.

References

Adelman, M. (1990). Stigma, gay lifestyles, and adjustment to aging: A study of later-life gay men and lesbians. *Journal of Homosexuality, 20,* 7–32.

Ames, L. J., Atchinson, A. B., & Rose, D. T. (1995). Love, lust, and fear: Safer sex decision making among gay men. *Journal of Homosexuality, 30,* 53–73.

Bailey, J. M., & Pillard, R. C. (1991). A genetic study of male sexual orientation. *Archives of General Psychiatry, 48,* 1089–1096.

Bailey, J. M., Pillard, R. C., Neale, M. C., & Agyei, Y. (1993). Heritable factors influence sexual orientation in women. *Archives of General Psychiatry, 50,* 217–223.

Banks, A., & Gartrell, N. K. (1995). Hormones and sexual orientation: A questionable link. *Journal of Homosexuality, 28,* 247–268.

Bell, A. P., & Weinberg, M. S. (1978). *Homosexualities: A study of diversity among men and women.* New York: Simon and Schuster.

Bell, A. P., Weinberg, M. S., & Hammersmith, S. K. (1981). *Sexual preference: Its development in men and women: Statistical appendix.* Bloomington: Indiana University Press.

Bem, D. J. (1996). Exotic becomes erotic: A developmen-tal theory of sexual orientation. *Pyschological Review, 103,* 320–335.

Ben-ari, A. (1995). The discovery that an offspring is gay: Parents', gay men's, and lesbians' perspectives. *Journal of Homosexuality, 30,* 89–112.

Bennett, K. (1992). Feminist bisexuality: A both/and option for an either/or world. In E. R. Weise (Ed.), *Closer to home: bisexuality and feminism* (pp. 205-232). Seattle, WA: Seal.

Berliner, A. K. (1987). Sex, sin, and the church: The dilemma of homosexuality. *Journal of Religion and Health, 26,* 137-142.

Bier, M. (1990). *A comparison of the degree of racism, sexism, and homophobia between beginning and advanced psychology classes.* Unpublished master's thesis. Greenville, NC: Department of Psychology, East Carolina University.

Blommer, S. J. (undated). *Answers to your questions about sexual orientation and homosexuality.* Washington, DC: American Psychological Association.

Blumenfeld, W. J., & Raymond, D. (1989). *Looking at gay and lesbian life.* Boston: Beacon Press.

Bouton, R. A., Gallaher, P. E., Garlinghouse, P. A., Leal, T., Rosenstein, L. D., & Young, R. K. (1987). Scales for measuring fear of AIDS and homophobia. *Journal of Personality Assessment, 51*(4), 606-614.

Bozett, F. W. (1989). Gay fathers: A review of the literature. *Journal of Homosexuality, 18,* 137-162.

Brannock, J. C., & Chapman, B. E. (1990). Negative sexual experiences with men among heterosexual women and lesbians. *Journal of Homosexuality, 19,* 105-110.

Cohen, K. M., & Savin-Williams, R. C. (1996). Developmental perspectives on coming out to self and others. In R. C. Savin-Williams & K. M. Cohen (Eds.), *The lives of lesbians, gays, and bisexuals: Children to adults* (pp. 113-151). Fort Worth, TX: Harcourt Brace.

Coleman, E. (1990). Toward a synthetic understanding of sexual orientation. In D. P. McWhirter, S. A. Sanders, & J. M. Reinisch (Eds.), *Homosexuality/heterosexuality: Concepts of sexual orientation* (pp. 267-276). New York: Oxford University Press.

Coleman, E. (1997). Assessment of sexual orientation. *Journal of Homosexuality, 14*(1, 2), 9-24.

Comstock, G. D. (1991) *Violence against lesbians and gay men.* New York: Columbia University Press.

Corbett, S. L., & Morgan, K. D. (1983). The process of lesbian identification. *Free Inquiry in Creative Sociology, 11,* 81-83.

Council on Scientific Affairs. (1996). Health care needs of gay men and lesbians in the United States. *Journal of the American Medical Association, 275,* 1354-1359.

D'Augelli, A. R. (1992). Lesbian and gay male undergraduates' experiences of harassment and fear on campus. *Journal of Interpersonal Violence, 7,* 383-395.

DeCecco, J. P. (1987). Homosexuality's brief recovery: from sickness and health and back again. *The Journal of Sex Research, 23,* 106-129.

DeCecco, J. P., & Parker, D. A. (1995). The biology of homosexuality: Sexual orientation or sexual preference? *Journal of Homosexuality, 28,* 1-28.

Deenen, A. A., Gijiis, L., & Van Naerssen, A. X. (1994). Intimacy and sexuality in gay male couples. *Archives of Sexual Behavior, 23,* 421-431.

Diamond, M. (1993). Homosexuality and bisexuality in different populations. *Archives of Sexual Behavior, 22,* 291-310.

Doell, R. G. (1995). Sexuality in the brain. *Journal of Homosexuality, 28,* 345-356.

Doll, L. S., Petersen, L. R., White, C. R., Johnson, E. S., Ward, J. W., & the Blood Donor Study Group. (1992). Homosexuality and nonhomosexuality identified men: A behavioral comparison. *Journal of Sex Research, 29,* 1-14.

Eliason, M. J. (1996). Identity formation for lesbian, bisexual, and gay persons: Beyond a "minoritizing" view. *Journal of Homosexuality, 30,* 31-58.

Ellis, L. (1996). Theories of homosexuality. In R. C. Savin-Williams & K. M. Cohen (Eds.), *The lives of lesbians, gays, and bixsexuals: Children to adults* (pp. 11-34). Fort Worth, TX: Harcourt Brace.

Ellis, L., & Ames, M. A. (1987). Neurohormonal functioning and sexual orientation: A theory of homosexuality-heterosexuality. *Psychological Bulletin, 101,* 233-258.

Ernulf, K. E., Innala, S. M., & Whitam, F. L. (1989). Biological explanation, psychological explanation, and tolerance of homosexuals: A cross-national analysis of beliefs and attitudes. *Psychological Reports, 65,* 1003-1010.

Esterberg, K. (1996). Gay cultures, gay communities: The social organization of lesbians, gay men, and bisexuals. In R. Savin-Williams & K. M. Cohen (Eds.), *The lives of lesbians, gays, and bisexuals: Children to adults* (pp. 377-390). Forth Worth, TX: Harcourt Brace.

Esterberg, K. (1997). *Lesbian and bisexual identities: Constructing communities, constructing selves.* Philadelphia: Temple University Press.

Etringer, B. D., Hillerbrand, E., & Hetherington, C. (1990). The influence of sexual orientation on career decision-making: A research note. *Journal of Homosexuality, 19,* 103-111.

Ettelbrick, P. L. (1995). The law and the lesbian and gay community. In P. S. Rothenberg (Ed.), *Race, class, and gender in the United States* (3rd ed., pp. 358-366). New York: St. Martin's Press.

Fausto-Sterling, A. (1995). Animal models for the development of human sexuality: A critical evaluation. *Journal of Homosexuality, 28,* 217-236.

Firestein, B. A. (1996). Bisexuality as paradigm shift: Transforming our disciplines. In B. A. Firestein (Ed.), *Bisexuality: The psychology and politics of an invisible minority* (pp. 263-291). Thousand Oaks, CA: Sage.

For the Record. (1997, Summer). *Intelligence Report, 87,* 19-27.

Fox, R. C. (1996). Bisexuality in perspective: A review of theory and research. In B. A. Firestein (Ed.), *Bisexuality: The psychology and politics of an invisible minority* (pp. 3-50). Thousand Oaks, CA: Sage.

Garnets, L., Herek, G. M., & Levy, B. (1990). Violence and victimization of lesbians and gay men: Mental health consequences. *Journal of Interpersonal Violence, 5,* 366-383.

Gelman, D., & Foote, D. (1992, February 24). Born or bred. *Newsweek,* 46-53. (Also see Marcia Barinaga's article, "Is Homosexuality Biological?" in *Science, 253,* 956-957, which details LeVay's study.)

Gill, T. P., Britt, M., Gomes, L. K., Hochberg, L. J., Jr., Kreidman, N., Sheldon, M. A., & Stauffer, B. (1997). Report of the Hawaii Commission on Sexual Orientation and the Law. In R. M. Baird & S. E. Rosenbaum (Eds.), *Same-sex marriage: The moral and legal debate* (pp. 211-226). Amherst, NY: Prometheus Books.

Gonsiorek, J. C. (1996). Mental health and sexual orientation. In R. C. Savin-Williams & K. M. Cohen (Eds.), *The lives of lesbians, gays, and bisexuals: Children to adults* (pp. 462-478). Fort Worth, TX: Harcourt Brace.

Gooren, L. J. G. (1995). Biomedical concepts of homosexuality: Folk belief in a white coat. *Journal of Homosexuality, 28,* 237-246.

Gorlin, R. (1991). The voice of a wandering Jewish bisexual. In L. Hutchins & L. Kaahumanu (Eds.), *Bi any other name: Bisexual people speak out* (pp. 252-253). Boston: Alyson.

Green, R. J., Bettinger, M., & Zacks, E. (1996). Are lesbian couples fused and gay male couples disengaged? In J. Laird & R. J. Green (Eds.), *Lesbians and gays in couples and families* (pp. 185-230). San Francisco: Jossey-Bass.

Greenberg, A. S., & Bailey, J. M. (1993). Do biological explanations of homosexuality have moral, legal, or policy implications? *The Journal of Sex Research, 30,* 245-251.

Harry, J. (1990). A probability sample of gay males. *Journal of Homosexuality, 19,* 89-104.

Hart, J. (1984). Therapeutic implications of viewing sexual identity in terms of essentialist and constructionist theories. *Journal of Homosexuality, 9,* 39-51.

Hays, D., & Samuels, A. (1989). Heterosexual women's perceptions of their marriages to bisexual or homosexual men. *Journal of Homosexuality, 19,* 81-100.

Heron, A. (Ed.). (1983). *One teenager in ten.* Boston: Alyson.

Hudson, W. W., & Ricketts, W. A. (1980). A strategy for the measurement of homophobia. *Journal of Homosexuality, 5,* 357-372.

Isay, R. A. (1990). Psychoanalytic theory and the therapy of gay men. In D. P. McWhirter, S. A. Sanders, & J. M. Reinish (Eds.), *Homosexuality/heterosexuality: Concepts of sexual orientation* (pp. 283-303). New York: Oxford University Press.

Kahn, Y. H. (1997). The Kedushah of homosexual relationships. In A. Sullivan (Ed.), *Same-sex marriage: Pro and con* (pp. 71-77). New York: Vintage Books.

King, M., & McDonald, E. (1992). Homosexuals who are twins. A study of 46 probands. *British Journal of Psychiatry, 160,* 407-409.

Kinsey, A. C., Pomeroy, W. B., & Martin, C. E. (1948). *Sexual behavior in the human male.* Philadelphia: W. B. Saunders.

Kinsey, A. C., Pomeroy, W. B., Martin, C. E. & Gebhard, P. H. (1953). *Sexual behavior in the human female.* Philadelphia: W. B. Saunders.

Kite, M. E., & Whitley, B. E., Jr. (1996). Sex differences in attitudes toward homosexual persons, behaviors and civil rights: A meta-analysis. *Personality and Social Psychology Bulletin, 22,* 336-352.

Klein, F. (1990). The need to view sexual orientation as a multivariable dynamic process: A theoretical perspective. In D. P. McWhirter, S. A. Sanders, & J. M. Reinisch (Eds.), *Homosexuality/heterosexuality: Concepts of sexual orientation* (pp. 277-282). New York: Oxford University Press.

Kurdek, L. A. (1995). Lesbian and gay couples. In A. R. D'Augelli & C. J. Patterson (Eds.), *Lesbian, gay, and bisexual identities over the lifespan: Psychological perspectives* (pp. 243-261). New York: Oxford University Press.

Lever, J. (1994, August 23). The 1994 *Advocate* survey of sexuality and relationships: The men. *The Advocate,* pp. 16-24.

Lever, J., Kanouse, D. E., Rogers, W. H., Carson, S., & Hertz, R. (1992). Behavior patterns and sexual identity of bisexual males. *The Journal of Sex Research, 29,* 141-167.

Louderback, L. A., & Whitley, B. E. (1997). Perceived erotic value of homosexuality and sex-role attitudes as mediators of sex differences in heterosexual college students' attitudes toward lesbians and gay men. *Journal of Sex Research, 34,* 175-182.

Marcus, E. (1993, July 5). Ignorance is not bliss. *Newsweek,* 10.

McCormack, A. S. (1997). Revisiting college student knowledge and attitudes about HIV/AIDS: 1987, 1991, and 1995. *College Student Journal, 31,* 356-361.

McGoldrick, M. (1996). Foreword. In J. Laird & R.J. Green (Eds.), *Lesbians and gays in couples and families* (pp. xi-xiv). San Francisco: Jossey-Bass.

McGuire, T. R. (1995). Is homosexuality genetic? A critical review and some suggestions. *Journal of Homosexuality, 28,* 115-146.

McNaught, B. (1983). Overcoming self-hate through edu- cation. In G. Albee, S. Gordon, & H. Leitenberg (Eds.), *Promoting sexual responsibility and preventing sex- ual problems* (pp. 133-145). Hanover, NH: University Press of New England.

Michael, R. T., Gagnon, J. H., Laumann, E. O., & Kolata, G. (1994). *Sex in America: A definitive survey.* Boston: Little, Brown.

Miranda, J., & Storms, M. (1989). Psychological adjustment of lesbians and gay men. *Journal of Counseling and Development, 68,* 41-45.

Mohr, R. D. (1995). Anti-gay stereotypes. In P. S. Rothenberg (Ed.), *Race, class, and gender in the United States,* (3rd ed., pp. 402-408). New York: St. Martin's Press.

Money, J. (1987). Sin, sickness, or status? Homosexual gen- der identity and psychoneuroendocrinology. *American Psychologist, 42,* 384-399.

Moser, C. (1992). Lust, lack of desire, and paraphilias: Some thoughts and possible connections. *Journal of Sex and Marital Therapy, 18,* 65-69.

National survey results of gay couples in long-lasting relationships. (1990, May/June). *Partners: Newsletter of Gay and Lesbian Couples* (pp. 1-16). (Available from Stevie Bryant & Demian, Box 9685, Seattle, WA 98109).

Neuborne, E. (1997, January 24). One in 10 firms extend benefits to life partners. *USA Today,* p. B1.

Nichols, M. (1987). Lesbian sexuality: Issues and develop- ing theory. In Boston Lesbian Psychologies (Eds.), *Lesbian psychologies: Explorations and challenges* (pp. 97-125). Chicago: University of Illinois Press.

Norman, A. D., Perry, M. J., Stevenson, L. Y., Kelly, J. A., & Roffman, R. A. (1996). Lesbian and bisexual women in small cities—at risk for HIV. *Public Health Reports, 111,* 347-352.

Ochs, R. (Ed.). (1995). *The bisexual resource guide.* Cambridge, MA: Bisexual Resource Center.

Ochs, R. (1996). Biphobia: It goes more than two ways. In B. A. Firestein (Ed.), *Bisexuality: The psychology and politics of an invisible minority* (pp. 217-239). Thousand Oaks, CA: Sage.

Park, A. (1995, November 13). New evidence of a "gay gene." *Time,* p. 95.

Patel, S., Long, T. E., McCammon, S. L., & Wuensch, K. L. (1995). Personality and emotional correlates of self- reported antigay behaviors. *Journal of Interpersonal Violence, 10,* 354-366.

Patterson, C. J. (1996). Lesbian and gay parents and their children. In R. C. Savin-Williams & K. M. Cohen (Eds.), *The lives of lesbians, gays, and bisexuals: From children to adults* (pp. 274-304). Fort Worth, TX: Harcourt Brace.

Paul, J. P. (1996). Bisexuality: Exploring/exploding the boundaries. In R. Savin-Williams and K. M. Cohen (Eds.), *The lives of lesbians, gays, and bisexuals: Children to adults* (pp. 436-461). Fort Worth, TX: Harcourt Brace.

Peplau, L. A., Veniegas, R. C., & Campbell, S. N. (1996). Gay and lesbian relationships. In R. C. Savin-Williams & K. M. Cohen (Eds.), *The lives of lesbians, gays, and bisexuals: From children to adults* (pp. 250-273). Fort Worth, TX: Harcourt Brace.

Phillips, G., & Over, R. (1995). Differences between het- erosexual, bisexual, and lesbian women in recalled childhood experiences. *Archives of Sexual Behavior, 24,* 1-20.

Reite, M., Sheeder, J., Richardson, D., & Teale, P. (1995). Cerebral laterality in homosexual males: Preliminary communication using magnetoencephalography. *Archives of Sexual Behavior, 24,* 585-593.

Robinson, B. E., Walters, L. H., & Skeen, P. (1989). Response of parents to learning that their child is homosexual and concern over AIDS: A national study. *Journal of Homosexuality, 18,* 59-80.

Roderick, T., McCammon, S. L., Long, T. E., & Allred, L. J. (in press). Behavioral aspects of homonegativity. *Journal of Homosexuality.*

Rosario, M., Meyer-Bahlburg, H. F. L., Exner, T. M., Gwadz, M., & Keller, A. M. (1996). The psychosexual develop- ment of urban, lesbian, and bisexual youths. *The Journal of Sex Research, 33,* 113-126.

Ross, M. W. (1989). Gay youth in four cultures: A compara- tive study. *Journal of Homosexuality, 17,* 299-314.

Rust, P. (1996). Monogamy and polyamory: Relationship issues for bisexuals. In B. A. Firestein (Ed.), *Bisexuality: The psychology and politics of an invis- ible minority* (pp. 127-148). Thousand Oaks, CA: Sage.

Sanday, P. R. (1995). Pulling train. In P. S. Rothenberg (Ed.), *Race, class, and gender in the United States* (3rd ed., pp. 396-402). New York: St. Martin's Press.

Sanders, S. A., Reinisch, J. M., & McWhirter, D. P. (1990). An overview. In D. P. McWhirter, S. A. Sanders, & J. M. Reinisch (Eds.), *Homosexuality/heterosexuality: Concepts of sexual orientation* (pp. xix-xxvii). New York: Oxford.

Savin-Williams, R. C. (1989). Coming out to parents and self-esteem among gay and lesbian youths. *Journal of Homosexuality, 18,* 1-35.

Scanzoni, L., & Mollenkott, V. R. (1980). *Is the homosex- ual my neighbor? Another Christian view.* San Francisco: Harper & Row.

Sell, R. L., Wells, J. A., & Wypij, D. (1995). The prevalence of homosexual behavior and attraction in the United States, the United Kingdom, and France: Results of national population-based samples. *Archives of Sexual Behavior, 24,* 235-248.

Shapiro, J. P., Cook, G. G., Krackov, A. A., & Cook, G. (1993, July 5). Straight talk about gays. *U.S. News & World Report,* 42-48.

Shyer, C., & Shyer, M. (1996). *Not like other boys.* New York: Houghton Mifflin.

SIECUS Position Statements on Human Sexuality, Sexual Health and Sexuality Education and Information, 1995-96. (1996). *SIECUS Report, 24,* 21-23.

Simon, A. (1995). Some correlates of individuals' attitudes toward lesbians. *Journal of Homosexuality, 29,* 89-103.

Sophie, J. (1985/1986). A critical examination of stage theories of lesbian identity development. *Journal of Homosexuality, 12,* 39-51.

Strommen, E. F. (1989). You're a what? Family member reactions to the disclosure of homosexuality. *Journal of Homosexuality, 18,* 37-58.

Swaab, D. F., Gooren, L. J. G., & Hofman, M. A. (1995). Brain research, gender, and sexual orientation. *Journal of Sex Research, 28,* 238-302.

Szymanski, M. (1997, March 18). GLAAD to see "Ellen" coming out. *USA Today,* p. 2D.

Thompson, C. (1995). A new vision of masculinity. In P. S. Rothenberg (Ed.), *Race, class, and gender in the United States,* (3rd ed., pp. 475-481). New York: St. Martin's Press.

Tielman, R., & Hammelburg, H. (1993). World survey on the social and legal position of gays and lesbians. In A. Hendriks, R. Tielman, & E. van der Veen (Eds.), *The third pink book: A global view of lesbian and gay liberation and oppression.* Buffalo, NY: Prometheus Books.

Troiden, R. R. (1989). The formation of homosexual identities. *Journal of Homosexuality, 17,* 43-73.

Turner, W. J. (1995). Homosexuality, type 1: An Xq28 phenomenon. *Archives of Sexual Behavior, 24,* 109-134.

Turque, B. (1992, September 14). Gays under fire. *Newsweek,* 35-40.

Uribe, V., & Harbeck, K. M. (1992). Addressing the needs of lesbian, gay, and bisexual youth: The origins of PROJECT 10 and school-based intervention. In K. Harbeck (Ed.), *Coming out of the classroom closet: Gay and lesbian students, teachers and curricula* (pp. 9-27). New York: Haworth Press.

VanderStoep, S. W., & Green, C. W. (1988). Religiosity and homonegativism: A path-analytic study. *Basic and Applied Social Psychology, 9*(2), 135-147.

Voeller, B. (1990). Some uses and abuses of the Kinsey scale. In D. P. McWhirter, S. A. Sanders, & J. M. Reinisch (Eds.), *Homosexuality/heterosexuality: Concepts of sexual orientation* (pp. 32-38). New York: Oxford.

Weinberg, G. (1973). *Society and the healthy homosexual.* New York: Anchor Books.

Weinberg, M., Williams, C., & Pryor, D. (1994). *Dual attraction: Understanding bisexuality.* New York: Oxford University.

White, E. (1994). Sexual culture. In D. Bergman (Ed.), *The burning library: Essays by Edmund White* (pp. 157-167). New York: Knopf.

Wisman, V. (1996). *Queer by choice: Lesbians, gay men, and the politics of identity.* New York: Routledge.

CULTURAL DIVERSITY IN SEXUALITY

Cross-Cultural Research in Human Sexuality: Ethnography and Ethnology

QUESTION What problems do ethnographers and ethnologists encounter in conducting research on human sexuality in different cultures?

What Is "Normal" Sexual Behavior?

Criteria Used to Define "Normal" Sexual Behavior
Historical Variations in Definitions of "Normal" Sexual Behavior

QUESTION What are the three criteria most cultures use for defining a sexual behavior as "normal"?

Ethnocentrism Versus Cultural Relativism

Ethnocentrism
Cultural Relativism
PERSONAL CHOICES: Should You View Sexual Expression from a Cultural-Relativistic Perspective?

QUESTION Must one accept, without passing moral judgment, the sexual beliefs, values, and practices of other cultures in order to fully understand them?

Cultural Variations in Sexuality

Central Elements of Culture
PERSONAL CHOICES: Should You Conform to Cultural Sexual Norms?
SELF-ASSESSMENT: Sex Knowledge and Attitude Test, Part I
Conceptions of Sexuality
Permissive and Repressive Cultural Contexts
Age at First Sexual Intercourse
Premarital Sex
Positions and Frequency of Intercourse
Extramarital Sex
Incest
Homosexual Sex
Female Genital Operations
SOCIAL CHOICES: U.S. Policies Involving Female Genital Operations
Male Genital Operations

QUESTION What are three elements of culture that underlie cultural variations in sexuality? Discuss how these elements apply to premarital sex, extramarital sex, and homosexual sex.

Sexuality in Nonhuman Primates

Social Versus Hormonal Influences
Grooming
Homosexuality
Mating Patterns
Monogamy

QUESTION How is the study of sexuality among nonhuman primates relevant to the study of human sexuality?

hile human biology is the ultimate basis for our sexual behavior, culture and society are the most important influences on how individuals experience and express their sexuality.

J. Patrick Gray and Linda Wolfe
Anthropologists

Suppose that as a 7- to 15-year-old-boy, you learned that fellating older males was necessary in order to become a man, develop your own sperm, and become capable of fertilizing a woman. Or suppose that as a preadolescent girl, you learned that one of the ways to get God (Allah) to approve of you was to submit eagerly to having your clitoris cut off. Sambian boys (in New Guinea) and Muslim girls (in some parts of the Middle East) have willingly engaged in fellatio and clitoridectomy (respectively) in response to cultural influences (Elliston, 1995). As these examples illustrate, the cultural context in which a person is reared dictates what sexual behavior the person may engage in and the attitude that person is expected to have toward the behavior.

After discussing cross-cultural research in human sexuality, we examine the issue of what is "normal" sexual behavior and review how sexual behaviors are viewed differently in different cultures. We emphasize that sexual choices are often influenced by cultural contexts and forces.

CROSS-CULTURAL RESEARCH IN HUMAN SEXUALITY: ETHNOGRAPHY AND ETHNOLOGY

Early studies (pre-1920s) of human sexuality in non-European cultures largely consisted of unsystematic observations and anecdotal reports from a variety of sources, including missionaries, government officials, and travelers. Despite the fact that these early observations were unreliable, they nonetheless suggested that many aspects of human sexuality were shaped by culture.

In the 1920s, anthropologist Bronislaw Malinowski published *Sex and Repression* (1927), which compared psychosexual development in the Trobriand culture with the segment of European society that Freud had studied. In 1929, Malinowski published

Sexual Life of Savages in North-Western Melanesia, which described sexuality in that culture. These two landmark studies led to the development of two types of cross-cultural research in human sexuality—ethnography and ethnology.

Ethnography refers to the descriptive study of cultures or subcultures. Ethnographic studies of sexuality describe the sexual patterns of behavior and beliefs in various cultures or subcultures. To investigate human sexuality in other cultures, researchers often use field research methods whereby they collect data by interviewing members of a certain community. In his early ethnographic study of sexuality in the Trobriand Islands, Malinowski (1929) described various aspects of sexual behavior among the natives:

> (As told by a native:) When we go on a lovemaking expedition we . . . walk, we arrive at a large tree, we sit down, we search each other's heads and consume the lice, we tell the woman that we want to copulate. (p. 336)

> The more usual position . . . is for the man to squat in front of the woman and, with his hands resting on the ground, to move towards her or, taking hold of her legs, to pull her towards him. When the sexual organs are close to each other the insertion takes place . . . The woman may stretch her legs and place them directly on the man's hips, with his arms outside of them, but a far more usual position is with her legs embracing the man's arms, and resting on the elbow. (pp. 336–337)

> Another element of lovemaking . . . [is] . . . the biting off of eyelashes. As far as I could judge from descriptions and demonstrations, a lover will tenderly or passionately bend over his mistress's eyes and bite off the tip of her eyelashes . . . I was never quite able to grasp either the mechanism or the sensuous value of this caress. (p. 334)

> Altogether the natives are certain that white men do not know how to carry out intercourse effectively. . . . Indeed, to the native idea, the white man achieves orgasm far too quickly. (p. 338)

Ethnology refers to the comparative study of two or more cultures or subcultures. Ethnological studies of sexuality compare the sexual patterns of behavior and beliefs of two or more cultures or subcultures. In an early ethnological study, Malinowski (1927) offered the following comparison of sexuality in Melanesia and European society:

> [In Melanesia,] the facts are different from those found among our educated classes. . . . The early sexual indecencies, clandestine games and interests are absent. In fact, it might be said that for [Melanesian] children the categories of decent-indecent, pure-impure, do not exist. . . . In Melanesia there is no taboo on sex in general. . . . When we consider that these children run about naked, that their excretory functions are treated openly and naturally, that there is no general taboo on bodily parts or on nakedness in general; when we further consider that small children at the age of three and four are beginning to be aware of . . . genital sexuality, and of the fact that this will be their pleasure quite soon . . . we can see that social factors rather than biological explain the difference between the two societies. (pp. 54–55)

Researchers conducting ethnographic or ethnological studies on human sexuality must contend with several problems. First, the researcher must either be fluent in the language of the culture being studied, or must have a translator or interpreter. Also, researchers often rely on informants—persons who live in the culture being studied—as a source of data. Since some sexual behavior occurs in private, informants are only able to give reliable reports of their own experiences and observations, which are limited and biased. Informants may also provide inaccurate information in order to make a good impression on the researcher and present themselves in a way they feel is socially desirable.

Another problem in doing cross-cultural research stems from the fact that every culture is composed of different cultures or subpopulations. In studying the same culture, one ethnographer may focus on people of a particular gender, social class, age, occupation, or sexual orientation, whereas another ethnographer may focus on a different group. Formulating a description of an entire culture based on the observation of one particular subset of the population is misleading. In an edited book of cross-cultural studies on pregnancy loss, Cecil (1996) notes that "the dearth of ethnographic writing on pregnancy loss is

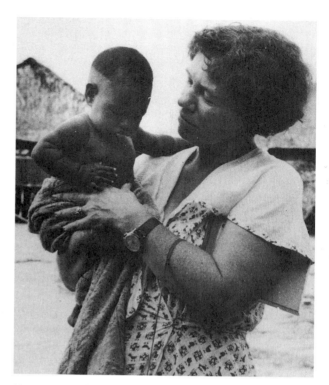

Margaret Mead studied human sexuality in Pacific Island cultures.

not perhaps surprising, for many aspects of women's lives have escaped thorough documentation" (p. 2). Cecil explains that women's lives are often ignored in cross-cultural studies because ethnographers have restricted access to women informants.

Finally, culture is not static but changes over time. Ethnographic or ethnological research conducted years ago may not accurately reflect current cultural practices and beliefs. For example, Margaret Mead (1928) described adolescent Samoan females as sexually relaxed, carefree, and free of psychological conflict. But Freeman (1983) studied young women in the same culture years later and described them as aggressive, impulsive, and sexually hung up. The differences between Mead's and Freeman's observations reflect the cultural changes that occurred in Samoan culture over a 50-year period.

THINK ABOUT IT

If you were a researcher conducting cross-cultural research on human sexuality, what cultures would you want to study, and why? What problems might you encounter in conducting your study?

WHAT IS "NORMAL" SEXUAL BEHAVIOR?

People of all cultures are born into the world without values or beliefs about what is "normal." Through family, school, peers, media, religion, and government, we learn what our culture defines as normal sexual behavior. With no standard of comparison and no knowledge of alternatives, children accept the things their society teaches them. For example, most U.S. children learn that they must wear clothes. Unless they have been reared by nudists (who take their children to family nudist retreats [see the Resources and Organizations section; American Association for Nude Recreation]), they will feel that nudism is "not normal." Otherwise, they may well adopt the norm of most nudists—"clothed when practical, nude when possible."

Criteria Used to Define "Normal" Sexual Behavior

Cultures use various criteria to define what is normal. For example, a specific sexual behavior may be considered normal if it is prevalent, considered to be morally correct, or is viewed as natural.

PREVALENCE   We tend to assume that if most people engage in a sexual behavior, it is normal. Conversely, sexual behaviors that rarely occur are considered not normal. Seventy-three percent of adult U.S. women report having received oral sex (Michael, Gagnon, Lauman, & Kolata, 1994), so we say that a U.S. woman receiving cunnilingus at some time in her life is normal. But, since only 20% of U.S. women report that the last time they had sex, their partner performed cunnilingus on them (Michael et al., 1994), we say that the woman's experiencing cunnilingus every time she has sex is not normal. Prevalence rates also vary by culture. For example, rates of sexual behaviors (intercourse, masturbation, and oral sex) of Chinese college students are lower than those of U.S. students (Tang, Lai, Phil, & Chung, 1997).

MORAL CORRECTNESS   Sexual behaviors are also considered normal if they are viewed as morally correct. According to many religions, penile-vaginal intercourse between husband and wife is the only morally correct form of sexual behavior. Other forms of sexual expression, including oral sex, masturbation, and homosexuality, are considered abnormal because they are viewed as immoral. One of the

reasons some homosexuals seek the approval of the church is because religion is such a powerful gatekeeper of definitions of sexual normality.

NATURALNESS   Finally, sexual behaviors are viewed as natural or unnatural, depending on whether they result in procreation. Since masturbation, homosexuality, oral sex, and anal sex do not result in pregnancy and childbearing, these acts are sometimes viewed as unnatural (and, by implication, abnormal).

Historical Variations in Definitions of "Normal" Sexual Behavior

Within the same culture, sexual behaviors may be labeled as normal in one historical time and abnormal in another. For example, although kissing in public is acceptable normal behavior today, in the American colonial era, kissing in public was considered unacceptable and punishable by being "lodged in the stocks" in public. During this era, unmarried persons who were discovered to have engaged in intercourse were viewed as individuals who had succumbed to the temptations of the flesh. Once discovered, they had to make a public confession and were also subject to fines and a public lashing. Public kissing in Taiwan and in mainland China today is not illegal, but it is frowned upon—there is social disapproval for kissing one's beloved in public.

THINK ABOUT IT

Which of the three criteria used to define what is "normal" sexual behavior carries the most weight in your own personal view? What other criterion might you use to define the acceptability of sexual beliefs and behaviors?

ETHNOCENTRISM VERSUS CULTURAL RELATIVISM

Ethnocentrism and cultural relativism are central concepts in understanding human sexuality from a cross-cultural perspective.

Ethnocentrism

Members of every society learn to view the cultural norms of their own social group as appropriate and the norms of other cultures as strange. Judging other cultures according to the standards of one's own culture and viewing one's own culture as superior is called *ethnocentrism*. Most people are ethnocentric in that they assume that their cultural norms, beliefs, and values are natural, universal, and correct and that other cultures are strange or wrong.

Cultural Relativism

An alternative to viewing others' sexual behavior and beliefs as inferior and abnormal is to view them as different and as "normal" according to the standards of the culture in which the behaviors and beliefs exist. This perspective on cultural differences, known as *cultural relativism,* involves understanding other cultures according to their own standards. Those who adopt the principle of cultural relativism view the beliefs and practices of another culture according to the values and standards of that culture.

PERSONAL CHOICES

Should You View Sexual Expression from a Cultural-Relativistic Perspective?

Cultural relativism has been criticized as being an amoral perspective that accepts and tolerates all forms of cultural practices and beliefs. However, a cultural-relativistic view of human sexuality *does not* imply that all cultural variations in sexuality must be accepted; it merely means that sexual behaviors and beliefs are viewed from the perspective of the cultures that practice the behavior and hold the beliefs. The sexual choices you make do affect you as an individual and do affect your relationship with your partner. Your decisions also affect your community. For example, as a parent on the local school board, you can influence the content of sex education classes in the schools in your community.

According to U.S. cultural values and standards, some sexual practices and beliefs are viewed as "wrong" because they endanger the health and well-being of individuals. For example, most Americans view female infanticide and female genital cutting (discussed later in this chapter) as "wrong." Most Americans would also disagree with the belief that "intercourse helps young girls to mature" (which, among the Lepcha people of India, means that by the age of 12, most Lepcha girls are engaging in regular

intercourse). Viewing such practices and beliefs from a cultural-relativistic perspective involves trying to understand why some cultures accept and promote these practices and beliefs and why these beliefs and practices are important to the people in these cultures. Understanding sexual practices and beliefs according to the perspective of other cultures does not mean that one must abandon one's own moral judgment.

THINK ABOUT IT

Do you think that cultural relativism is advocated equally in traditional societies and modern societies? Could the claim that "cultural relativism is a better perspective than ethnocentrism" itself be an ethnocentric view?

CULTURAL VARIATIONS IN SEXUALITY

Culture refers to the meanings and ways of living that characterize a society. Three central elements of culture include beliefs, values, and norms.

Central Elements of Culture

Beliefs refer to definitions and explanations about what is true. Cultural beliefs influence sexual attitudes and behaviors. The common belief among U.S. men that, when a woman says "no," she really means "yes" or "maybe" contributes to men's forcing themselves sexually on women. The belief that HIV and AIDS is a homosexual disease may result in heterosexuals viewing safer sex as unnecessary and engaging in high-risk sexual behavior (such as sex with more than one partner with no use of condoms). *Values,* another central element of culture, are standards regarding what is good and bad, right and wrong, or desirable and undesirable. Individuals' personal values are greatly influenced by societal values.

NATIONAL DATA

A survey of first-year students at 494 colleges and universities revealed that their top two values were being well-off financially (72.2%) and raising a family (72.1%).

Source: American Council on Education & University of California, 1996.

Norms are socially defined rules of behavior. Norms serve as guidelines for our behavior and our expectations of the behavior of others. Sociologists have identified three types of norms—folkways, laws, and mores. *Folkways* refer to the customs and traditions of society. Most U.S. women, for example, wear bras to support their breasts. Although there is no law requiring women to wear bras, most do so because it is expected of them; it is part of the cultural folkways of U.S. society. *Laws* are norms that are formalized and backed by political authority. Virtually every society has laws concerning sexual behavior. *Mores* are norms that have a moral basis. Mores reflect a sense of what is moral and immoral. Mores may also be laws. For example, child sexual abuse is a violation of the law and a violation of our mores because we view such behavior as immoral. Some behaviors may violate mores but may be legally permitted. For example, among some segments of society, intercourse before marriage is considered immoral and therefore a violation of mores; however, sex before marriage between consenting adults is not illegal.

PERSONAL CHOICES

Should You Conform to Cultural Sexual Norms?

Reiss (1986) emphasized that one of the benefits of knowing that different cultures have different rules regarding sex is that most any form of sexual behavior can be normal or abnormal. Given this truism, he noted that "one can choose to be out of line on this or any issue with the dominant ideological positions" (p. 133). That people choose to be sexual nonconformists is evident from the number of guests on talk shows such as *Geraldo, Montel, Oprah,* and *Yolanda.* Examples of nonconformity to our culture's sexual norms include people in open marriages, as well as those who choose celibate lives. Such choices emphasize the right of people to pursue their own pattern or relationships and sexuality.

As this chapter emphasizes, there are many cultural variations in sexuality. These variations are primarily due to the cultural variations in beliefs, values, and norms. This chapter's Self-Assessment enables you to compare your sexual attitudes to those of people from other cultures.

Conceptions of Sexuality

Cross-cultural variations are also evident in how an individual views sexuality and its importance in the individual's life. Western conceptions of sexuality tend to focus on sexual performance, orgasm, and physical satisfaction. In contrast, some Eastern cultures view sexuality as a vehicle for spiritual development and personal transformation. Tantric sex, described in Hindu and Buddhist Tantric scriptures, reflects the essence of Asian sexuality. The Sanskrit term *Tantra* means "integration," suggesting full involvement of the natural human drives in the pursuit of a fully realized existence. One technique in Tantric practice is to be still and motionless during intercourse so as not to have an orgasm. The purpose of such an exercise is to intensify sexual-spiritual energy.

> Chinese sexuality is based primarily on Confucian and Taoist traditions. According to Confucian sexual philosophy, which emphasizes procreation and social order, sex for pleasure and outside wedlock is prohibited for both genders. The Taoist tradition, on the other hand, focuses on the balance between Yin and Yang, personal health, and longevity. Semen is valued as a source of vitality and needs to be preserved by avoiding ejaculation during intercourse. Masturbation and excessive sexual activities are viewed as causes of men's illnesses, as they lead to excessive waste of semen. (Tang, Lai, Phil, & Chung, 1997, p. 80)

Permissive and Repressive Cultural Contexts

The sexual beliefs, values, and norms of the Mangaians and the inhabitants of Inis Beag represent two extremes on the continuum of sexual permissiveness and sexual repressiveness.

MANGAIANS   Anthropologist Donald Marshall (1971) studied the sexual patterns of the Mangaians of Mangaia (southern Polynesian Islands) and observed the extreme sexual openness with which its members are reared. Adult Mangaians copulated in the same room with all kin. Their doing so was not regarded as particularly significant because household members (including children) were busy with work or play. Masturbation by both sexes at 7 to 10 years of age was advocated and practiced (Marshall, 1971).

Beyond early exposure to parental intercourse and masturbation, childhood sex play with the same- or other-sex individuals was encouraged. Premarital sex was also encouraged, with no stigma for the experienced bride or groom. In marriage, partners were expected to mutually enjoy sex, and orgasm was a goal for both wife and husband. Extramarital sex also was tolerated.

A major theme of sexuality among the Mangaians was active participation on the part of the woman. She was to be sexually active beginning in childhood, to be orgasmic, and to be an active participant. Sexual passivity was viewed as deviant. In addition, affectional feelings usually followed, rather than preceded, sexual behavior with others in adult relationships.

INHABITANTS OF INIS BEAG   In contrast to the sexual openness of the Mangaians is the restrictive society of Inis Beag. John Messenger (1971, 1993) studied every member (350) of the small agrarian Irish island community (which he called "Inis Beag" to protect its identity) from 1958 to 1966. From birth, members were segregated by sex in the family, church, and school. Men bonded with men and women with women. Marriage was for economic and reproductive reasons only, with women marrying around age 25 and men around age 36. This latter age for men was necessary because they had to own land before they could ask a woman to marry them.

Unlike the Mangaian women who were taught to be assertive and to enjoy sex, women of Inis Beag were taught to be sexually passive and to endure the sexual advances of men. Female orgasm was not in the vocabulary of the islanders, and nudity was avoided. Even though the economic livelihood of the community depended on the men catching fish from canoes, they could not swim because they were embarrassed to be without clothing and thus had never learned. Even bathing was to be done in absolute privacy.

Male masturbation seemed to be common, but premarital coitus was unknown. Marital copulation was limited; it was initiated by the husband, was performed using only the male-superior position, and took place without the underclothes being removed. Because sex was rarely discussed, sexual myths permeated the community. Women believed that menopause caused insanity, and men believed that sex debilitated them. Hence, they would avoid sex the night before a strenuous event. Messenger

viewed this sexual puritanism as one of the most important reasons for the dwindling population of Inis Beag.

As the comparison between the Mangaians and the inhabitants of Inis Beag illustrates, sexual beliefs, values, and norms vary widely. Other examples of cultural variations in sexuality follow.

Age at First Sexual Intercourse

Age at first intercourse is partly determined by cultural norms. Among a national sample of U.S. adults, the age at first intercourse was 17.5 (Michael et al., 1994). The mean age at first intercourse among 1659 undergraduates at a large Midwestern university was 16.5, with no significant differences between women and men (Sprecher, Barbee, & Schwartz, 1995). In contrast, Japanese youth report having first intercourse around age 21 (Hatano, 1991). A major factor affecting the expression of sexual behavior among Japanese youth is the emphasis in the culture on academic preparation.

Japanese students typically have their first intercourse experience at a later age than Western students.

SEX KNOWLEDGE AND ATTITUDE TEST, PART I

Please indicate your reaction to each of the following statements on sexual behavior in our culture, using the following alternatives:

A. Strongly agree   D. Disagree
B. Agree   E. Strongly disagree
C. Uncertain

D **1.** The spread of sex education is causing a rise in premarital intercourse.

E **2.** Mutual masturbation among boys is often a precursor of homosexual behavior.

A **3.** Extramarital relations are almost always harmful to a marriage.

C **4.** Abortion should be permitted whenever desired by the woman.

D **5.** The possession of contraceptive information is often an incitement to promiscuity.

A **6.** Relieving tension by masturbation is a healthy practice.

____ **7.** Premarital intercourse is morally undesirable.

____ **8.** Oral-genital sex play is indicative of an excessive desire for physical pleasure.

____ **9.** Parents should stop their children from masturbating.

____ **10.** Women should have coital experience prior to marriage.

____ **11.** Abortion is murder.

____ **12.** Girls should be prohibited from engaging in sexual self-stimulation.

____ **13.** All abortion laws should be repealed.

____ **14.** Strong legal measures should be taken against homosexuals.

____ **15.** Laws requiring a committee of physicians to approve an abortion should be abolished.

____ **16.** Sexual intercourse should occur only between married partners.

____ **17.** The lower-class male has a higher sex drive than others.

____ **18.** Society should offer abortion as an acceptable form of birth control.

____ **19.** Masturbation is generally unhealthy.

____ **20.** A physician has the responsibility to inform the husband or parents of any female [on whom he or she performs an abortion].

____ **21.** Promiscuity is widespread on college campuses today.

____ **22.** Abortions should be disapproved of under all circumstances.

____ **23.** Men should have coital experience prior to marriage.

____ **24.** Boys should be encouraged to masturbate.

____ **25.** Abortions should not be permitted after the twentieth week of pregnancy.

____ **26.** Experiences of seeing family members in the nude arouse undue curiosity in children.

____ **27.** Premarital intercourse between consenting adults should be socially acceptable.

____ **28.** Legal abortions should be restricted to hospitals.

____ **29.** Masturbation among girls is a frequent cause of frigidity.

____ **30.** Lower-class women are typically quite sexually responsive.

____ **31.** Abortion is a greater evil than bringing an unwanted child into the world.

____ **32.** Mutual masturbation in childhood should be prohibited.

____ **33.** Virginity among unmarried girls should be encouraged in our society.

____ **34.** Extramarital sexual relations may result in a strengthening of the marriage relationship of the persons involved.

____ **35.** Masturbation is acceptable when the objective is simply the attainment of sensory enjoyment.

Continued on following page.

The Sex Knowledge and Attitude Test (SKAT; Lief & Reed, 1972) was developed as a teaching aid for courses on human sexuality, as well as a social science research instrument. It was designed to describe *groups* of students, not to assess the attitudes of individuals (*Preliminary Technical Manual,* undated). Its components include measures of attitudes, knowledge, personal background, and frequencies of sexual behaviors. Part I, Attitudes, is reproduced in this Self-Assessment. Lief and Reed have made the SKAT available to researchers from a number of countries. Comparative data from four countries are presented here. Designed for post-high school use, data are available mainly from medical and nursing students. The SKAT norming sample was composed of 850 medical students from 16 medical schools in the United States.

Scoring: The attitude component of the SKAT yields four subscales.

1. Heterosexual Relations (HR) focuses on attitudes toward pre- and extra-marital encounters. High scores indicate an accepting, even encouraging, attitude toward premarital and extramarital relations, while low scores indicate a conservative or disapproving attitude.
2. Sex Myths (SM) deals with one's acceptance or rejections of mistaken yet commonly held beliefs. High scores indicate rejection and low scores acceptance of the misconceptions.

3. Autoeroticism (M) addresses attitudes toward masturbation. High scorers view masturbation as a healthy way to relieve tension and obtain pleasure. They believe that parents should not prohibit their children from masturbating. In contrast, low scorers view masturbation as unhealthy and a practice that parents should prohibit.
4. Abortion (A) focuses on medical, legal, and social judgments on abortion. High scorers view abortion as an acceptable practice that should be permitted whenever the woman desires. Low scores indicate an orientation in which abortion is viewed as a form of murder that should be strictly medically supervised.

To compute your scores, assign the following values: Strongly Agree (A) = 1, Agree (B) = 2, Undecided (C) = 3, Disagree (D) = 4, and Strongly Disagree (E) = 5 for all items except the following which should be scored in reverse (A = 5, B = 4, C = 3, D = 2, E = 1): 4, 6, 10, 13, 15, 18, 23, 27, 34, and 35.

Then, total the scores for the items in each scale:
HR: 3, 7, 10, 16, 23, 27, 33, 34.
SM: 1, 2, 5, 8, 14, 17, 26, 29, 30.
A: 4, 11, 13, 15, 18, 25, 31.
M: 6, 9, 12, 19, 24, 32, 35.

Interpreting your Score You may wish to compute the average scores for your class and compare them to those of Chinese medial students from Hong Kong. In Table 1, data are presented from Chan's (1990) study comparing Chinese medical students with U.S. medical students (from the SKAT validation sample collected in 1972). Chinese students consistently scored more conservatively than the U.S. students. The two groups were more similar in attitudes toward autoeroticism but more dissimilar in attitudes toward premarital and extramarital sex.

TABLE 1 Comparing SKAT Raw Scores of Chinese and U.S. Medical Students

Scale	Chinese Students			U.S. Students*			
	$\overline{X}$	SD	n	$\overline{X}$	SD	nz	z
Heterosexual relations	20.34	5.23	83	28.10	6.41	420	11.87
Sexual myths	29.34	4.26	83	34.72	4.62	422	10.37
Abortion	24.45	4.72	83	29.70	6.08	423	8.80
Autoeroticism	22.04	4.03	83	25.65	4.20	424	7.41

*SKAT scores of U.S. students were those reported for the original validation sample.

The unnecessarily tight pressure of university entrance examinations (admission to which university of which rank) is often considered to be the decisive factor for the whole life of a Japanese; senior high school students are particularly oppressed in their heterosexual behaviors in lieu of the preparatory studies. Based on the same logic, parents, and perhaps classroom teachers too, are eager to require that the children concentrate only on school works, and therefore they definitely discourage the sexual activity of the children. (pp. 12–13)

Sprecher and Hatfield (1996) noted that once Japanese students go to college, they evidence more sexual freedom.

Chinese college students report having first intercourse later than U.S. college students but earlier than Japanese students. Tang et al. (1997) collected data on 305 Chinese students. The age at first intercourse was 17.14 and 18.13 for men and women, respectively. But only 11% of the respondents reported that they had had intercourse, even though their average age was 20.1. Tang et al. (1997) suggested that preoccupation with academic preparation, strong preference for emotional commitment, and living with parents (only 20% of college students live in a college dorm) accounted for lower rates of early premarital experience.

Premarital Sex

Wide variations in sexual values exist in different societies with regard to premarital and extramarital intercourse. A team of researchers (Meston, Trapnell, & Gorzalka, 1996) compared the petting and intercourse behaviors as well as the number of previous partners and "one-night stands" of 356 Asian and 346 non-Asian undergraduate students and found that on all measures, the Asian students reported lower frequencies. In general, Asian cultures promote more conservative sexual values and have greater restrictions on the access of young men and women to each other.

Premarital sexual behavior may be punished in one society, tolerated in a second, and rewarded in a third (see Table 17.1). In the Gilbert Islands, virginity until marriage is an exalted sexual value, and violations are not tolerated. Premarital couples who are discovered to have had intercourse before the wedding are put to death. Our society tolerates premarital intercourse,

TABLE 17.1 Premarital Sex in Four Cultures

CULTURE	NORM REGARDING PREMARITAL SEX
United States	Tolerated
China	Prohibited
India	Prohibited
Pokomo (Kenya, East Africa)	Expected

Source: Bunger, 1996.

particularly if the partners are "in love." In contrast, the Marquesans on Juku Hiva Island in Eastern Polynesia encouraged premarital sexual exploration (homosexual and heterosexual) in both men and women at an early age (10). To ensure proper sexual instruction, young men have their first intercourse with a woman in her thirties or forties, and young women have intercourse with elder tribal leaders.

Most societies communicate disapproval to the woman who has premarital intercourse by shunning her and making it difficult for her to marry (her reputation is ruined). In some societies, women who have had premarital sex also risk divorce. In traditional China,

Newlyweds were expected to wear a special white suit or sleep on a special cloth, which provided visible evidence of "deflowering" and loss of virginity. In the morning after consummation, the blood-stained evidence was produced for inspection by the groom's mother. . . . Virginity of the bride (but not the groom) was an implied condition of the marriage contract. Failure to provide proof of virginity could result in dismissal, divorce, or reclamation of the bride-price. (Engel, 1982, p. 8)

Positions and Frequency of Intercourse

While sexual intercourse is a universal act, its expression is influenced by culture. Societies have different beliefs, values, and norms about intercourse positions and frequency. While the preferred coital position in most cultures is face-to-face with the woman lying on her back, due to crowded sleeping arrangements in many cultures, some couples adopt the side position because they feel it is less conspicuous.

The frequency of intercourse also varies with the culture. In the United States, couples have intercourse, on average, two times a week (Michael et al., 1994). But among the Basonge in the Sasai province of Zaire, couples (even in their fifties and sixties) report that they have intercourse every night (Merriam, 1972). In contrast, a man of the Cayapa Indians of Ecuador may go for several years without having intercourse. Their term for intercourse, *medio trabajo,* means "a little work."

Extramarital Sex

In Chapter 14, "Sexuality Across the Life Span," we discussed extradyadic and extramarital sex as an issue confronting most couples. In that chapter, we also discussed the various types of extradyadic relationships and the motivations individuals report for becoming involved in them. In this section, we note that extramarital sexuality is an issue that societies view differently.

Most societies are less tolerant of extramarital than premarital sexuality. Frayser (1985) observed that three-quarters of 58 societies forbade extramarital intercourse for one or both sexes.

The rules of marriage in some societies permit extramarital partners. For example, an Aleut husband may "lend" his wife to a houseguest as a symbol of hospitality. And in the traditional Chinese family, wealthy men were allowed to have concubines or second wives as a way of "expanding the family, particularly for the upper classes" (Engel, 1982, p. 9).

> Concubinage also served as a safety valve in the traditional Chinese family. It provided some relief from the very carefully prescribed behaviors for men's roles in the family. The concubine was often chosen by the fellow himself on the basis of personal attraction and romance, in contrast to the mate-selection process in the arranged marriage. . . . As one might expect, it was not uncommon for jealousy to arise among the wives and concubines in a household. (p. 9)

Cross-culturally, the double standard seems evident with regard to who is allowed to have sex with someone other than one's spouse. In her study of 58 societies, Frayser reported that no society gave women the option to have affairs while denying it to men (1985, p. 210).

Hatfield and Rapson (1996) summarized studies of extramarital sexual activity and concluded that in Western countries, two changes have occurred. First, the sexual double standard seems to be eroding, and there is greater similarity in men's and women's experimentation with extramarital sex. Second, in contrast to the past, extramarital relations are occurring earlier, more frequently, and with more partners.

Individuals who ignore the rules prohibiting extramarital intercourse are often severely punished. In 85% of 54 societies studied (Frayser, 1985), forms of punishment include the lover paying a fine to the woman's husband and brother, the lover submitting to a public beating by the husband, the wife submitting to a private beating by the husband, temporary public ostracism, and death. A Kenuzi husband (in Egypt) is allowed to kill his wife if he even suspects her of infidelity.

In most countries, the sexuality (both premarital and extramarital) of women has been controlled by men. "Patriarchy" is a term that originally referred to the supremacy of a father over his family. Patriarchal authority allowed fathers to prohibit premarital sexual behavior of their daughters so as to ensure their marriageability. Anthropologists have observed that even societies that describe women as sexually pure and passive go to great lengths to prevent them from being unchaste. Since most of the world's cultures trace descent through the male line, the purpose of this effort is probably to ensure that paternity of children and their status as heirs are undisputed (Hrdy, 1981, 1993).

Incest

Incest is considered the only nearly universal sexual taboo. Anthropologist Claude Levi-Strauss (1969, 1993) hypothesized that incest prohibition grew out of the need for social alliance. An incestuous couple was seen as one who "automatically detaches itself from the give-and-take pattern of tribal existence" (p. 234). Levi-Strauss saw prohibiting incest not so much as a rule proscribing marriage with one's mother, sister, or daughter, but as a rule that the mother, sister, or daughter be given to others. While virtually all cultures forbid incest, they differ with regard to how incest is defined and socially sanctioned (Davenport, 1987). In some cultures, certain cousins are permitted and even encouraged to have sexual relations, but marriage between them is forbidden. The incest taboo is extended only to primary relatives (parents, offspring, siblings) in some cultures; in others, incest is prohibited among all traceable relatives. The incest taboo may be asymmetrical in that it may apply to one set of cousins (children of same-sex siblings) but not to another set of cousins (children of different-sex siblings). In Chinese culture, all persons with the same surname are subjected to the incest taboo, even though millions of Chinese people with the same surname are not related. The Dahomey of West Africa and the Incas of Peru have viewed sex between siblings as natural and desirable, excluding sex between parents and children (Stephens, 1982).

Social sanctions against those who commit incest range "from ridicule to threats of supernatural punishment to the partners being put to death" (Gray & Wolfe, 1992, p. 645). Frayser (1985) described a variety of sanctions that are applied to those who violate the incest taboo. The Cayapa Indians of Ecuador have been known to suspend violators over a table covered with candles and roast them to death. The ancient Incas also imposed death for violation of the incest taboo.

In some cultures, the sanctions for violating the incest taboo are less severe. Punishment may be as mild as temporary verbal disapproval. For example, the Havasupai Indians of the Grand Canyon merely reprimand offenders verbally. Moderate punishment may involve temporary body damage (such as whipping) or ostracism for a limited period of time.

It has been generally assumed that the incest taboo was universal. However, historical records show that in a number of societies, royalty were encouraged to marry (and therefore, be incestuous with) a family member, especially a sibling. Furthermore, "in some societies there are no obvious incest taboos in the sense of rules (and sanctioned rules especially) against it, only a notion that no one would commit incest anyway" (Brown, 1991, p. 119).

Homosexual Sex

The majority of nonindustrialized societies permit homosexuality. Among the people of East Bay, a village in Melanesia, homosexuality is tolerated only in males. Prior to marriage, young men engage in mutual masturbation and anal intercourse. Many married men are bisexual (Shepherd, 1987).

Batak males (in northern Sumatra) engage in homosexual relations before marriage. At puberty, Batak boys leave their parents' home and sleep in a home with 12 to 15 boys. In this group, each boy is initiated into homosexual practices. After marriage, the majority of Batak men cease homosexual activity (Money & Ehrhardt, 1973).

Homosexuality in industrialized nations is more repressed. In Hungary, homosexuality in women or men is punishable by up to 5 years in prison (Drakulic, 1990). Homosexuals in the former Soviet Union must keep their sexual orientation hidden for fear of government reprisal. However, there is evidence that in many countries of the world (such as French Canada and Hong Kong), people hold more accepting attitudes toward homosexuality (Hatfield & Rapson, 1996).

Female Genital Operations

Female genital operations, sometimes referred to as *female genital mutilation* (FGM), refer to the various practices of cutting or amputating some or all of the female external genitalia—the prepuce or hood of the clitoris, the glans and shaft of the clitoris, the labia minora (small genital lips), and the labia majora (large genital lips). An estimated 85 million to 115 million girls and women have undergone genital cutting (Dugger, 1996). The practice occurs in 28 African countries, as well as in a few Middle Eastern and Asian countries. Typically, the cutting is done by traditional village women, without anesthesia to dull the pain and without sterile cutting instruments. Health complications from genital operations, including infection, hemorrhage, and chronic pelvic inflammatory disease, are not uncommon. In addition, women who undergo this ritual are deprived of experiencing sexual pleasure and are often left with painful scars.

The reasons for the ritual of female genital cutting vary greatly by region and ethnic group. In many cultures that practice female genital operations, the ritual serves as an initiation into womanhood. In other cultures, the practice helps ensure a girl's virginity before marriage and fidelity afterward. Because women in the cultures that practice female

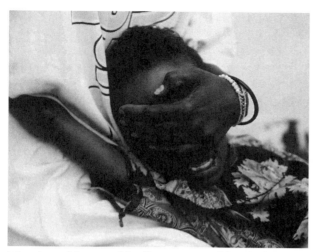
It is estimated that over 80 million women and female children have experienced genital surgeries throughout the world.

genital cutting are economically dependent on men, parents insist on the rite so their daughters are marriageable. Other cultural beliefs include that the "female genitalia are unclean and cutting them away purifies a woman; that the sex drive of an uncircumcised woman is uncontrollable; and that unless the labia of a woman are cut they will grow until they hang down between a woman's knees" (Armstrong, 1991, p. 44).

The practice of female genital operations has become a public issue in the United States. We examine this issue in this chapter's Social Choices section.

Male Genital Operations

The most familiar form of *male genital mutilation* is *circumcision,* which involves the surgical removal of the foreskin, usually during infancy. Circumcision was performed by the Egyptians as early as 4000 B.C. Male circumcision occurs in cultures that share the Judaeo-Christian-Islamic tradition and among the aborigines of Australia and in sub-Saharan Africa.

There are various reasons why some cultures practice male circumcision, including religious, aesthetic, hygienic, and sociological. To Jewish people, circumcision symbolizes Abraham's convenant with God. In some cultures, male circumcision has a sociological function in that it testifies that "the circumcised individual has undergone rituals and ordeals that establish maturity or it is an enhancement of mas-

culinity" (Davenport, 1987, p. 207). In the United States, male circumcision is practiced primarily for traditional as well as for hygienic reasons. Men who were circumcised feel that circumcision for their sons is desirable, and some people feel that a circumcised penis is easier to clean, and therefore, inflammation and infection are less likely to occur. (Circumcision is also discussed in Chapter 9.)

Another form of male genital mutilation that occurs in parts of Australia is *penile supraincision,* which involves making a longitudinal slit through the dorsal of the foreskin. Among Mangaian youths, this practice occurs around age 13 to denote the onset of adolescence. After having received the proper sexual training (on style, timing, and position) by an older woman from the community, the male is supraincised, which certifies that he is ready for sexual intercourse.

A more drastic form of male genital mutilation that occurs in parts of Australia is *penile subincision,* which involves slitting the ventral side of the penis all the way into the urethra. Only subincised men can participate in sacred rituals during which drops of blood are drawn from inside the exposed urethral canal. The blood from this area is viewed as sacred and is associated with mystical powers.

Another form of male genital mutilation occurs among some of the inland Dayak peoples of Borneo. A few Dayak men voluntarily undergo a transverse perforation of the penis through which a wooden pin is inserted. A small knob is attached to each protruding end of the pin. The Dayak people believe that these knobs increase the woman's sexual pleasure during intercourse. This form of genital mutilation is quite painful and provides "an opportunity to display fortitude, hence it signals something about the courage, virility, and stoicism of those who suffer the operation" (Davenport, 1987, p. 208).

THINK ABOUT IT

What sexual beliefs and practices that are viewed as "normal" in the United States might be viewed as strange or abnormal to someone from another culture? What sexual values, beliefs, or norms that characterize other societies would you want to incorporate into U.S. culture? Why?

U.S. POLICIES INVOLVING FEMALE GENITAL OPERATIONS

Although female genital operations (also called female genital mutilation) occur primarily in African and some Middle Eastern and Asian countries, the practice also occurs in the United States among immigrant families who bring their cultural traditions with them. Each year, about 7000 immigrants to the United States (from countries that practice FGM) undergo the procedure either in the United States or during a visit to their homeland (Burstyn, 1995).

Prior to 1996, only a handful of U.S. states had laws banning FGM. In the fall of 1996, Congress passed a federal law banning the practice of genital cutting of females under the age of 18 in the United States. This law also directs federal authorities to inform new immigrants from countries where FGM is practiced that parents who arrange for the genital cutting of their female children in the United States (as well as people who perform the cutting) may face up to 5 years in prison (Dugger, 1996). France, the United Kingdom, Sweden, and the Netherlands have already outlawed the practice; in France, over 30 immigrant families have been prosecuted for violating the ban. Such cases are usually reported to the police by doctors, who detect the practice while examining female patients.

Some U.S. health care providers fear that the ban on FGM will not eliminate the practice, but rather will result in African parents withholding medical care for their daughters in order to avoid detection and prosecution. After African mothers repeatedly requested that their daughters have genital operations in the hospital, physicians at a Seattle hospital proposed offering a largely symbolic form of the ritual, in which they would nick the tip of a girl's clitoris, with her consent, under a local anesthetic. No tissue would be removed. It is not clear whether this procedure would violate the U.S. law against female genital mutilation (Dugger, 1996).

Another policy issue concerning FGM involves giving asylum to refugee women who come to the United States to avoid genital cutting. In 1994, 17-year-old Fauziya Kasinga fled from her home in Togo to escape having her genitals cut off. After escaping to the United States, Kasinga turned herself in to immigration officials, asking for asylum. To win asylum, refugees must show that, because of their race, nationality, religion, politics, or membership in a particular social group, they have either been persecuted or have a "well-founded fear" of persecution. Kasinga's claim for asylum was denied by a judge with the Executive Office for Immigration Review. While awaiting an appeal of the decision, Kasinga was held in prison for more than a year, part of which she spent in a maximum security wing with serious criminals. When asked what she would do if her appeal were denied, Kasinga replied, "I'd prefer to stay in jail rather than go back and face what would be done" (McCarthy, 1996). In the summer of 1996, the Board of Immigration Appeals granted political asylum to Kasinga, recognizing FGM as a form of persecution against women. This ruling set a binding precedent for all U.S. immigration judges. In the current anti-immigrant climate, some citizens fear that this precedent may result in millions of women coming to the United States as refugees.

Finally, some U.S. policies attempt to discourage FGM in the countries that practice this ritual. For example, the federal ban on FGM requires U.S. representatives to the World Bank and other international financial institutions to oppose loans to countries that have not carried out educational programs to prevent it. However, Western governments' efforts to eradicate FGM in Africa or Asia are often perceived by members of these societies as a continuation of the racism, discrimination, and cultural imperialism that these countries have endured historically (Lane & Rubinstein, 1996).

Changing a country's deeply held beliefs and values concerning this practice cannot be achieved by denigration. If Western countries continue to denigrate those who practice female genital cutting, we may be creating "a backlash in which the custom is viewed as intrinsic to the group's threatened identity" (Lane & Rubinstein, 1996, p. 38). More effective approaches to discouraging the practice include the following:

Continued on following page.

1. Respect the beliefs and values of countries that practice female genital cutting. Calling the practice "genital mutilation" and referring to it as a form of "child abuse" and "torture" convey disregard for the beliefs and values of the cultures where it is practiced.

2. Use less inflammatory or derogatory language to describe the practice. Rather than calling it "genital mutilation," we might call it "female circumcision," "female genital cutting," "female genital operations" or "female genital surgeries."

3. Remember that the practice is "arranged and paid for by loving parents who deeply believe that the surgeries are for their daughters' welfare. Parents fear . . . that leaving their daughters uncircumcised will make them unmarriageable. Parents worry about their daughters during the procedures and care for their wounds afterward to help them recover. . . . Parents who do this are not monsters, but are ordinary, decent, caring persons" (p. 38).

4. Lastly, it is important to "recognize the efforts of numerous individuals and groups, in the countries where female genital surgeries are common, who have sought to abolish their practice through education and policy change" and to "endorse and support the efforts of these groups" (p. 39).

From "Judging the Other: Responding to Traditional Female Genital Surgeries, by S. D. Lane and R. A. Rubenstein, 1996, *Hastings Center Report*, 26(3), 31–40. Hastings Center.

Sources: Burstyn, L. (1995, October). Female circumcision comes to America. *Atlantic Monthly*, 28–35.

Dugger, C. W. (1996, October 12). New law bans genital cutting in the United States. *New York Times*, pp. 1, 28.

Lane, S. D., & Rubinstein, R. A. (1996). Judging the other: Responding to traditional female genital surgeries. *Hastings Center Report*, 26(3), 31–40.

McCarthy, S. (1996, July/August). Fleeing mutilation, fighting for asylum. *Ms.*, 12–16.

SEXUALITY IN NONHUMAN PRIMATES

Humans belong to the mammalian group referred to as primates. One suborder of primates is anthropoids, which consists of monkeys in South and Central America (known as New World monkeys), monkeys in Africa and Asia (known as Old World monkeys), larger animals such as gibbons and apes (orangutans, gorillas, and chimpanzees), and humans. While a direct link between lower animals and humans cannot be made, our understanding of human sexuality may be enhanced by examining sexuality among our closest evolutionary relatives.

Frayser (1985) summed up the significance of nonhuman primate sexual behavior:

> . . . the line between nonhuman and human primate sexual behavior is a fine one. Human sexuality is part of the primate sexual continuum, not a separate category. (p. 46)

In making reference to the sexually assertive behavior of a Barbary macaque in estrus, anthropologist Sarah Hrdy (1981) asked, "What earthly relevance does the conduct of this monkey have for understanding her culture-bearing cousin . . . ?" (p. 19). The sexual behavior of animals has been studied with the idea that we can gain insights into human sexual functioning and separate out natural, biological foundations of behaviors from those resulting from social conditioning or influence. Researchers have attempted to determine the impact of polygamous versus monogamous breeding in groups. Debates have focused on the nature of female sexuality. Do female primates experience orgasm? If so, what functions does it serve? Hrdy (1981, 1993) asked, "If we assume that women have been biologically endowed with a lusty primate sexuality, how have cultural developments managed to alter or override this legacy?" (p. 30).

Some of what we know about nonhuman primate sexuality follows.

Social Versus Hormonal Influences

The prolonged dependency period of young primates on their mother results in learning patterns of social interaction necessary to the offspring's survival. If the infant is deprived of social contact with other animals, it will become antisocial, self-destructive, and withdrawn. Male monkeys reared in isolation rarely, if ever, mate. Female monkeys are also less likely to mate. Those who do are more often indifferent and abusive to their offspring (Harlow & Harlow, 1962, pp. 144, 145).

In her study of Old World monkeys, Wolfe (1991) concluded that, for the most part, sexual behavior is learned in a social context with little hormonal influence.

> Socialization in a stable social unit, sexual rehearsal with both same and opposite sex partners by infants and juveniles, and sexual experience while growing to full adulthood have all come to play important roles in the development and maintenance of sexual behavior among humans, Old World monkeys, and apes. (p. 134)

Grooming

Monkeys groom each other (stroke each other's hair, pick off lice). Such grooming may be by the mother to child to build social ties or by adults as foreplay or afterplay to copulation. New and Old World adult monkeys engage in grooming behaviors with each other only when the female is in heat. In addition, just before copulation, male apes and monkeys manually stimulate the female's genitalia. Female apes and monkeys are less likely to stimulate the male genitalia (Ford & Beach, 1972, pp. 53, 54).

Homosexuality

Wolfe (1991) studied female homosexual behavior among free-ranging and captive alloprimates (primates other than humans) and described two females engaging in one or more mounts resembling a heterosexual copulation. While she acknowledged that the label "homosexual" denotes nothing about sexual-object orientation or sexual eroticism, 11 of 180 species evidenced female homosexual behavior. In some cases, female homosexual behavior seemed to be a substitute for heterosexual activities. (No males were available.) In other cases, the homosexual activity seemed to be a result of female preference. However, among female Japanese macaque monkeys, she noted that in no case was female homosexual behavior the exclusive mode of sexual expression if the female was in a group composed of adults and peers of both sexes (p. 133).

Mating Patterns

Just as humans smile at each other alluringly to indicate sexual availability, adult male Japanese macaque monkeys shake tree branches and make loud guttural vocal sounds as a form of self-advertisement. Once in the presence of a specific female, the male monkey may signal further sexual interest by facing the female with his body hair erect and by moving his ears and eyebrows up and down. The facial, anal, and genital areas of these male monkeys also turn bright red during the mating season, which may function to increase their visibility and attractiveness (Gray & Wolfe, 1992). Do nonhuman primates make choices in regard to their partners? Observations of primate mating behavior suggest that primates do not mate randomly, but rather, have preferences regarding a mating partner. Primates do not necessarily engage in sexual behavior for reproductive purposes, but rather, because it is enjoyable in its own right (Frayser, 1985). Both male and female primates have been observed to exhibit strong preferences for mating with a specific primate. Wolfe (1991) observed that some monkeys follow other monkeys around continually, as if they had a romantic crush on their object of desire.

Monogamy

Monogamy is not unheard of among primates; researchers suggest that the percentage of monogamy is between 10 and 18. Wolfe (1991) noted that of 180 species, 10% are monogamous or pair-bonded for life. Hrdy (1981) noted that 18% of primates live in breeding pairs that mutually care for offspring. Monogamy is particularly common among New World primates (Kinzey, 1987). Female Japanese macaque monkeys may have a preference for novel males as mating partners (Wolfe, 1991).

As we close this chapter, we reemphasize the enormous influence culture has on human sexual expression. Earlier, we made reference to the "homosexual" behavior (the term is in quotes because the Sambia have no term for homosexual; they acknowledge only that humans are sexual beings) of Sambia 7-year-olds. When these young boys reach their midteens, they are expected to stop their sexual contacts with males and to "seek out and find exclusive, habitualized, opposite-sex contacts, with their wives" (Herdt, 1991, p. 8). This movement from one sexual target to another is culturally induced. Of this cultural direction and redirection, Herdt (1991) noted:

> What the New Guinea material advises—and that from other cross-cultural and historical periods too—is that sexual function and development are under greater social and cultural regulation, even at the orgasmic level, than we once believed. (p. 11)

KEY TERMS

beliefs 461
circumcision 469
cultural relativism 461
ethnocentrism 461
ethnography 458
ethnology 459
female genital
    mutilation (FGM) 468
female genital
    operations 468
folkways 462
laws 462
male genital
    mutilation 469
mores 462
norms 462
penile subincision 469
penile supraincision 469
values 461

SUMMARY POINTS

The debate continues about the degree to which human sexual expression is biologically or culturally driven. In this chapter, we have emphasized the importance of the latter.

Cross-Cultural Research in Human Sexuality: Ethnography and Ethnology

It is important for ethnographers and ethnologists to understand the language and symbols for sexuality that are used in the culture they are studying. They must also be aware that sexual behavior is often private and informants are usually reporting what they know in their own life or subculture.

What Is "Normal" Sexual Behavior?

Cultures use various criteria to define what is "normal." For example, a specific sexual behavior may be considered normal if it is prevalent, is viewed as morally correct, or is viewed as natural. Most sexual behaviors that occur frequently, are consistent with the values of the prevailing religious and moral values, and result (or can potentially result) in procreation are regarded as normal.

Ethnocentrism Versus Cultural Relativism

Ethnocentrism involves judging other cultures according to the standards of one's own culture and viewing one's own culture as superior. Most people are ethnocentric in that they assume that their cultural norms, beliefs, and values are natural, universal, and correct and that other cultures are strange or wrong. Cultural relativism involves viewing sexual behavior and beliefs of others as different, and as "normal" according to the standards of the culture in which the behaviors and beliefs exist. This perspective on cultural differences involves understanding other cultures according to their own standards. Those who adopt the principle of cultural relativism view the beliefs and practices of another culture according to the values and standards of that culture. A cultural-relativistic view of human sexuality does not, however, imply that all cultural variations in sexuality must be accepted; it merely means that sexual behaviors and beliefs are viewed from the perspective of the cultures that practice the behavior and hold the beliefs.

Cultural Variations in Sexuality

Beliefs, values, and norms are three elements of culture that underlie cultural variations in human sexuality. Cultures exist on a continuum from being sexually permissive (Mangaians) to being sexually repressive (inhabitants of Inis Beag). Cultures also have different beliefs, values, and norms concerning age at first intercourse, nonmarital sex, homosexuality, conceptions of sexuality, and male and female genital operations.

Over 28 countries, most of them in Africa, practice "female genital operations" that involve cutting off the clitoris and small genital lips and stitching together the large genital lips. The practice is arranged by loving parents who deeply believe that the surgery ensures marriageability, and is, therefore, in the best interest of their daughter. Since immigrants from countries that practice female genital operations have immigrated to the United States, U.S. policies have restricted such operations within its borders.

Sexuality in Nonhuman Primates

Nonhuman primates benefit from being reared in a social context with other primates where they learn about mating and caring for offspring. Nonhuman primates reared in isolation are less likely to mate and are abusive to their offspring. Homosexuality and monogamy, while rare, do occur among primates.

REFERENCES

American Council on Education & University of California. (1996). *The American freshman: National norms for Fall, 1996.* Los Angeles: Los Angeles Higher Education Research Institute.

Armstrong, S. (1991). Female circumcision: Fighting a cruel tradition. *New Scientist, 2,* 42–46.

Brown, D. E. (1991). *Human universals.* Philadelphia: Temple University Press.

Cecil, R. (1996). Introduction: An insignificant event? Literary and anthropological perspectives on pregnancy loss. In R. Cecil (Ed.), *The anthropology of pregnancy loss: Comparative studies in miscarriage, stillbirth, and neonatal death* (pp. 1–14). Herndon, VA: Berg.

Davenport, W. H. (1977). Sex in cross-cultural perspective. In F. A. Beach (Ed.), *Human sexuality in four perspectives* (pp. 115–163). Baltimore: Johns Hopkins University Press.

Davenport, W. H. (1987). An anthropological approach. In J. H. Geer & W. T. O'Donohue (Eds.), *Theories of human sexuality* (pp. 197–236). New York: Plenum Press.

Drakulic, S. (1990, July/August). In their own words: Women of eastern Europe. *Ms.,* 36–47.

Dugger, C. W. (1996, October 5). Genital ritual is unyielding in Africa. *New York Times,* pp. 1, 6.

Elliston, D. A. (1995). Erotic anthropology: "Ritualized homosexuality" in Melanesia and beyond. *American Anthropologist, 22,* 848–867.

Engel, J. W. (1982). *Changes in male-female relationships and family life in People's Republic of China* (research series 014). College of Tropical Agriculture and Human Resources, University of Hawaii.

Ford, C. S., & Beach, F. A. (1972). *Patterns of sexual behavior.* New York: Harper Colophon Books. (Originally published in 1951)

Frayser, S. G. (1985). *Varieties of sexual experience.* New Haven, CT: Human Relations Area Files Press.

Freeman, D. (1983). *Margaret Mead and Samoa: The making and unmaking of an anthropological myth.* Cambridge, MA: Harvard University Press.

Gray, J. P., & Wolfe, L. D. (1992). An anthropological look at human sexuality. In W. H. Masters, V. E. Johnson, & R. C. Kolodny (Eds.), *Human sexuality* (4th ed.). LaPorte, IN: HarperCollins.

Harlow, H. F., & Harlow, M. (1962). Social deprivation in monkeys. *Scientific American, 207,* 136–146.

Hatano, Y. (1991). Changes in sexual activities of Japanese youth. *Journal of Sex Education and Therapy, 17,* 1–14.

Hatfield, E., & Rapson, R. L. (1996). *Love and sex: Cross-cultural perspectives.* Boston: Allyn and Bacon.

Herdt, G. (1991). Commentary on status of sex research: Cross-cultural implications of sexual development. *Journal of Psychology and Human Sexuality, 4,* 5–12.

Hrdy, S. (1993). A disputed legacy. In D. N. Suggs & A. W. Miracle (Eds.), *Culture and sexuality* (pp. 19–37). Pacific Grove, CA: Brooks/Cole. (Original work published 1981)

Hrdy, S. B. (1981). *The woman that never evolved.* Cambridge, MA: Harvard University Press.

Kinzey, W. G. (1987). Monogamous primates: A primate model of human mating systems. In W. G. Kinzey (Ed.), *The evolution of human behavior: Primate models* (pp. 105–114). Albany: State University of New York Press.

Levi-Strauss, C. (1993). The incest prohibition. In D. N. Suggs & A. W. Miracle (Eds.), *Culture and sexuality* (pp. 229–236). Pacific Grove, CA: Brooks/Cole. (Original work published 1969)

Malinowski, B. (1927). *Sex and repression in savage society.* New York: Harcourt, Brace.

Malinowski, B. (1929). *Sexual life of savages in north-western Melanesia.* New York: Halcyon House.

Marshall, D. S. (1971). Sexual behavior on Mangaia. In D. S. Marshall & R. C. Suggs (Eds.), *Human sexual behavior: Variations in the ethnographic spectrum* (pp. 103–162). New York: Basic Books.

Mead, M. (1928). *Coming of age in Samoa.* Middlesex: Penguin Books.

Merriam, A. P. (1972). Aspects of sexual behavior among the Bala (Basongye). In D. S. Marshall & R. C. Suggs (Eds.), *Human sexual behavior* (pp. 71–102). Englewood Cliffs, NJ: Prentice Hall.

Messenger, J. C. (1993). Sex and repression in an Irish folk community. In D. N. Suggs & A. W. Miracle (Eds.), *Culture and sexuality* (pp. 240–261). Pacific Grove, CA: Brooks/Cole. (Original work published 1971)

Meston, C. M., Trapnell, P. D., & Gorzalka, B. B. (1996). Ethnic and gender differences in sexuality: Variations in sexual behavior between Asian and non-Asian university students. *Archives of Sexual Behavior, 25,* 33–41.

Michael, R. T., Gagnon, J. H., Laumann, E. O., & Kolata, G. (1994). *Sex in America: A definitive survey.* Boston: Little, Brown.

Money, J., & Ehrhardt, A. A. (1973). *Man and woman, boy and girl.* Baltimore: Johns Hopkins University Press.

Reiss, I. L. (1986). *Journey into sexuality: An exploratory voyage.* Englewood Cliffs, NJ: Prentice Hall.

Shepherd, G. (1987). Rank, gender, and homosexuality: Mombasa as a key to understanding sexual options. In P. Caplan (Ed.), *The social construction of sexuality.* New York: Tavistock.

Sprecher, S., Barbee, A., & Schwartz, P. (1995). Was it good for you, too? Gender differences in first sexual intercourse experiences. *The Journal of Sex Research, 32,* 3–15.

Sprecher, S., & Hatfield, E. (1996). Premarital sexual standards among U.S. college students: Comparison with Russian and Japanese students. *Archives of Sexual Behavior, 25,* 261–288.

Stephens, W. N. (1982). *The family in cross-cultural perspective.* Washington, DC: University Press of America.

Tang, C. S., Lai, F. D., Phil, M., & Chung, T. K. H. (1997). Assessment of sexual functioning for Chinese college students. *Archives of Sexual Behavior, 26,* 79–90.

Wolfe, L. D. (1991). Human evolution and the sexual behavior of female primates. In J. D. Loy & C. B. Peter (Eds.), *Understanding behavior: What primate studies tell us about human behavior* (pp. 122–151). New York: Oxford University Press.

PARAPHILIAS AND SEXUALITY

Chapter 18

Paraphilia: Definition and Overview

Types of Paraphilias

The Origins of Paraphilias: Theoretical Perspectives

Treatment of Paraphilias

Sexual Addiction: A False Concept?

There is no absolute criterion by which to distinguish paraphilic behavior from normal behavior.

Ratnin Dewaraja
Psychologist

Although the Internet has become one of the most valuable information and educational tools of our society, it also has a dark side. Pedophiles, posing as friends, may enter chat rooms with unsuspecting pre-pubescents and arrange to interact with them. Awareness of the presence of pedophiles on the Internet has become a concern for parents who want their children to become computer literate. Ernie Allen, Director of the National Center for Missing and Exploited Children, acknowledged 10 to 12 cases in the preceding year in which children were seduced or lured on-line into situations in which they were victimized (Elmer-Dewitt, 1995). There is also worry that children may access adult-oriented computer bulletin board systems that post images not appropriate for viewing by children (such as photos of bondage, sadomasochism, urination, defecation, and sex acts with animals). In this chapter, we are concerned not only with pedophilia, but also with the wider range of sexual behavior that our society considers unusual or deviant. Such behavior is referred to as paraphilic behavior.

PARAPHILIA:
DEFINITION AND OVERVIEW

A *paraphilia* is an overdependence on a culturally unacceptable or unusual stimulus for sexual arousal and satisfaction. The term "paraphilia" is derived from the words *para,* meaning "deviation," and *philia,* meaning "attracted." Hence, the paraphiliac is attracted to a stimulus that is regarded by the society in which the person lives as deviant. Paraphilic fantasies usually focus on aggression—images of exhibitionism, obscene phone calling, and frotteurism are rehearsals of partner victimization (Levine, Risen, & Althof, 1990). Other characteristics of the paraphiliac are sexual dysfunction (lack of desire, arousal, or orgasm) if the paraphilia stimulus is not present and a seeming inability to develop an intense emotional connection with others (Levine et al., 1990).

The Diagnostic and Statistical Manual of Mental Disorders, Fourth Edition (American Psychiatric Association, 1994, commonly referred to as DSM-IV), defines paraphilias as characterized by arousal in response to sexual objects or situations that are not part of normative arousal activity patterns and that in varying degrees may interfere with the capacity for reciprocal, affectionate sexual activity. The essential features of a paraphilia are recurrent, intense sexually arousing fantasies, sexual urges, or behaviors generally involving the following:

1. Nonhuman objects (fetishism)
2. The suffering or humiliation of oneself or one's partner (not just simulated) (sadism, masochism)
3. Children or other nonconsenting persons (pedophilia, exhibitionism, voyeurism, frotteurism)

All three of these criteria need not necessarily be involved for the label of paraphilia to apply. For example, the pedophile focuses on human subjects (which leaves out the first criterion), and the cross-dresser focuses on clothing, not people (which leaves out the third criterion). What all paraphilias do have in common is that the object being focused on becomes imbued with erotic value, and there is an intense yearning to experience the object. In some cases, the paraphilia is experienced as a compulsion that interferes with work and relationships.

Paraphilia may also involve sexual narcissism, which is primarily an intimacy disorder manifested in sexual behavior. These individuals have considerable difficulty "experiencing a functional, reciprocal, satisfying sexual relationship with their mates. A history of promiscuity and sexual manipulation may be common" (Hurlbert, Apt, Gasar, Wilson, & Murphy, 1994, p. 25). Narcissists are preoccupied with their own sexual needs rather than those of their partners. They also have low self-esteem, which prompts them to seek approval from partners but give none in return.

Hurlbert et al. (1994) compared a sample of men (ages 24–33) with narcissistic personality disorder with a matched sample of men without personality disorders. As compared to the control group, narcissistic men were found to have significantly lower self-esteem, more negative attitudes toward sex, greater egocentric patterns of sexual behavior, more conservative or traditional gender-role orientation, and greater sexual preoccupation.

Some people with a paraphilia are so preoccupied with sex that they feel out of control (Levine et al., 1990). In other cases, the person may feel in control of the paraphiliac impulses most of the time and may lose control only during periods of stress.

In addition to the compulsive quality of paraphilias, it is not unusual for a person to express more than one paraphilia. According to Abel and Rouleau (1990):

> As an initial paraphilia fades, a second paraphilia begins, accelerates in frequency, and may overtake the initial paraphilia as the most common deviant sexual behavior. In this fashion, some sex offenders have as many as 10 categories of paraphilic interest throughout their lifetime. (p. 14)

The relationships of the person with a paraphilia may suffer if the partner becomes aware of the paraphilia. For example, the partner will probably regard pedophilia as unacceptable and may disengage from the person with a paraphilia, who is viewed as "abnormal." Similarly, the relationship may end if the partner is asked to participate in the paraphilia (the partner is asked to be the recipient of the sexual sadist's paraphilia or to dress the partner up in wet diapers [autonepiophilia], for example).

On the other hand, some sexually variant behaviors, referred to by Comfort (1987) as "off-diagonal behaviors," are practiced by couples with the goal of enhancing physical excitement and mutual pleasure. Comfort suggested that these behaviors are a part of mature sexual expression when they are "playful, non-dangerous, not anti-social, and reinforcing to both parties." However, intervention is definitely needed "if a behavior is compulsive, limiting, stereotyped, anti-social or associated with deviant nonsexual behavior" (p. 8).

PERSONAL CHOICES

Should You Disregard Social Disapproval of Paraphilias?

Persons with a paraphilia normally do not seek treatment. As Dewaraja (1987) noted:

> In most instances, the paraphile undertakes treatment at the insistence of society, for example, in exchange for a reduced prison term. When he voluntarily seeks treatment, it is done to escape shame, resulting from social censure. (p. 593)

While some paraphilias are illegal and harmful to oneself (such as asphyxiation) or other people (such as pedophilia or erotophonophilia), other paraphilias may be viewed as not worthy of the guilt, depression, and social disapproval they engender. Examples of such paraphilias include acrotomophilia (amputee partner), autonepiophilia, and formicophilia (ants or other insects crawling on the body).

Individuals with paraphilias that are not harmful to themselves or others might choose to disregard society's negative label of their behavior. Such a choice, in combination with a positive view of themselves, may have productive consequences for them with no negative consequences for society. Comfort (1987) stated that among therapists,

> Most of us now ask, at the practical level, not "is this behaviour normal?" but rather "what does this behaviour signify for this client? Is it reinforcing or handicapping?" and, of course, "is the behaviour socially tolerable?" (p. 1)

THINK ABOUT IT

How might an individual view a paraphilia on the part of his or her partner as desirable or as intolerable?

TYPES OF PARAPHILIAS

In this section, we discuss eight major types of paraphilias identified in the DSM-IV and briefly identify a variety of others. We also discuss legal and illegal paraphilias and consider the question of whether or not rape is a paraphilia.

Table 18.1 identifies and describes eight types of paraphilias. The major emphasis in diagnosis of these paraphilias should be on current, intense urges and fantasies; action on the urges is secondary and need not necessarily be present.

Exhibitionism

Exhibitionism involves an intense, recurrent sexual urge (over a period of at least 6 months), often accompanied by sexually arousing fantasies, to

TABLE 18.1 The Eight Major Paraphilias

Paraphilia	Description
Exhibitionism	Exposing one's genitals to a stranger or having a recurrent urge to do so.
Frotteurism	Touching or rubbing a nonconsenting person in a sexual manner or having a recurrent urge to do so.
Pedophilia	Engaging in sexual behavior with a child or having a recurrent urge to do so.
Voyeurism	Watching a person who is either nude, undressing, or engaging in sexual behavior and is unaware that someone is watching, or having a recurrent urge to do so.
Fetishism	Becoming sexually aroused by actual or fantasized objects (such as leather, lingerie, or shoes).
Transvestic fetishism	Becoming sexually aroused by dressing in the clothes of the other sex.
Sexual sadism	Becoming sexually aroused by actual or fantasized infliction of pain, humiliation, or physical constraint on another.
Sexual masochism	Becoming sexually aroused by actual or fantasized inflicted pain, humiliation, or physical constraint by another.

expose one's genitals to a stranger. The onset of exhibitionist urges usually occurs before age 18, although it can begin later. Few arrests are made in older age groups, which may suggest that the condition becomes less severe after age 40 (APA, 1994).

Money (1986) provided an example of the extent to which the male exhibitionist feels driven to expose himself:

> When the urge does come, it comes so strong that you really want to do it. It just blocks off everything that makes sense . . . everything else that could maybe stop you. . . . You want to do it so bad. . . . I was driving, and the urge just came out from nowhere to do it. . . . I must have passed up about ten or fifteen places where I could have done it, trying not to do it. . . . But it just kept tingling with me. Stop here! Stop there! Stop Here! Go ahead! You can do it! And the feeling that I had inside was one like, if I didn't do it, I'd be missing out on something very, very great. It just kept on going. I ended up driving halfway to Annapolis, trying not to do it, just passing up places. And it got so strong, I just had to do it. I just had to get out and do it. (p. 35)

Exhibitionist individuals expose themselves to people they do not know for several reasons. Sexual excitement is a primary one. Hearing a victim yell and watching his or her horrified face is sexually stimulating for some individuals. Once sexually excited, the exhibitionist individual may masturbate to orgasm.

A male exhibitionist may expose himself to shock women. Exhibiting himself may be a way of directing anger and hostility toward women. Although the woman he exposes himself to has not injured him, other women may have belittled him (or he has perceived it that way); or he has recently been unable to have and maintain an erection, blames his lack of erection on women, and exposes himself as a way of getting back at them.

Some individuals expose themselves as a way of relieving stress. When the stress reaches a peak, individuals exhibit themselves, masturbate, and relieve the stress. Still others expose themselves with a sexually arousing fantasy in which the person observing them will become sexually aroused (APA, 1994).

Some people have referred to exhibitionism, public masturbation, and voyeurism as "victimless crimes"; however, these behaviors can cause harm because victims may be traumatized. Furthermore, in a small minority of offenders, Maletzky (1991) noted that these offenses can predispose the offender toward more aggressive acts, such as pedophilia and frotteurism.

If confronted by exhibitionism, we suggest that a victim remain calm and try not to appear shocked or

Exhibitionism is sometimes regarded as a "victimless" crime.

involve touching or rubbing, often with the genitals, against a nonconsenting person is known as *frotteurism*. *Toucheurism* involves actively using one's hands on the victim. While the person may be distressed over the overwhelming urge to touch or rub against another, he also may act on those fantasies. The person usually chooses a crowded place for the activity. He presses against the sexually desired person while saying, "Excuse me," then moves to another part of the crowd and presses against someone else. This behavior, known as frottage, usually goes unnoticed. But the feelings aroused by pressing against another may be used in a masturbatory fantasy later.

The person with frotteurism may also fantasize about having an exclusive and caring relationship with the person he touches or rubs. However, "he recognizes that to avoid possible prosecution, he must escape detection after touching his victim" (APA, 1994, p. 527). Frotteurism usually begins by adolescence, but most acts occur when the person is 15 to 25 years old, after which there is a decline in frequency.

Pedophilia

Pedophilia is characterized by recurrent, intense, sexual urges and sexually arousing fantasies for at least 6 months' duration, involving sexual activity with a prepubescent child. The pedophilic person has either acted on these urges or is very much distressed by them. To be diagnosed as pedophilic, an individual must be at least 16 years old and must be at least 5 years older than the target child. The target child is generally 13 years old or younger. Although attraction to girls is more commonly reported, individuals with pedophilia may be sexually aroused by both young girls and young boys. Those who are attracted to young boys have a higher recidivism rate (APA, 1994).

Whether or not sex between children and adults is considered acceptable varies across societies and historical time periods. Bullough (1990) observed that "what appears obvious from a historical overview is that adult/child and adult/adolescent sexual behavior has had different meanings at different historical times" (p. 70). For example, during the 18th and 19th centuries in England, a child of 12 could consent to sexual behavior with a middle-aged adult.

alarmed. However, we recommend leaving the situation and immediately making a report to the local law enforcement agency (police, sheriff, or campus security). It may be helpful to law enforcement agencies to obtain reports of "minor" offenses of exhibitionism and voyeurism. One reason is that although sex offenders have a preferred method of offending, if access to that method is unavailable or blocked, they may engage in a less preferred method. Langevin, Paitich, and Russon (1985) reported that all of the voyeurs referred to their sex offender clinic had also committed other sexual offenses. Langevin and Lang (1987) cited two studies of exhibitionist men in which "20% of them had committed one or more violent assaults in the past" (p. 213). Information provided in reports to law enforcement agencies may be helpful in investigating other crimes. It is a myth that "nuisance" offenders have no propensity for violence (Hazelwood, Dietz, & Warren, 1992).

Frotteurism

Recurring, intense, sexual urges (for at least 6 months), accompanied by arousing fantasies that

Even children under 12 "could be seduced with near impunity in privacy" (p. 74).

In addition to the term "pedophilia," a number of other terms have developed to describe adult sexual behavior with children. These include "cross-generational sex," "adult/child sexual interactions," "incest," "man/child association," and "father/daughter sexual abuse" (Bullough, 1990). A wide range of behaviors may also be included in the definition of pedophilia. On one end of the continuum are such activities as undressing the child, looking at the nude body of a child, exposing oneself to the child, masturbating in the presence of the child, and fondling the child. Alternatively, the other end of the continuum includes such behaviors as performing fellatio or cunnilingus on the child; penetrating the child's vagina, mouth, or anus with one's finger, a foreign object, or one's penis; and using various levels of force to do so.

The pedophile is most often an adult male (Fontaine, 1990) who is a relative or family friend of the child. The ratio of heterosexual to homosexual pedophiles is approximately 11:1 (Moser, 1992). Typically, the adult heterosexual man is a family friend visiting the parents of the child. The pedophile may excuse himself as if to go to the bathroom and then sneak into the bedroom of the child for sexual contact, or he may pretend that he is putting the child to bed or saying goodnight when he is actually using the occasion to rub the child's genitals.

Sociologist Edwin Schur (1988) emphasized that traditional male gender role socialization may perpetuate child sexual abuse. Schur suggested that "our culture promotes sexual victimization of children when it encourages males to believe that they have over-powering sexual needs that must be met by whatever means available" (p. 173). Schur said that this belief and the association of sexual conquest with masculinity enable men to think of using children for their own sexual gratification. The implication here is that one way to discourage child sexual abuse is to change our traditional notions of masculinity and male sexuality.

Sometimes an adolescent is the object of the pedophilic person's urges (referred to as *hebephilia*). Sexual behavior between an adult and an adolescent is called ephebosexual behavior. The following illustrates such behavior from the viewpoint of a student.

Our family was having a family gathering with all the relatives for Thanksgiving. It was held in the back yard of my aunt's. I had to go inside the house to get something and while I was inside one of my uncles came in. At that time we were pretty close and so, at first, I didn't think anything of the following events.

My uncle came into the kitchen where I was alone and hugged and kissed me. I kissed him back. Then he kissed me again and because we were close, I didn't think anything about the second kiss. I then moved into the walk-in pantry and my uncle followed me and wanted to hug and kiss me again.

I then realized this was no longer a "friendly kiss." I tried to move from the pantry and he blocked me. I tried not to act scared, even though I was. Trying to dodge him, he moved quickly and knocked a glass jar off the shelf. He told me to get paper towels to clean up the mess. Then my cousin came in the kitchen so I asked her to help with the broken jar and made an excuse to get outside. That was all that happened. To this day, I get chills when I have to be around my uncle, but I'm always careful not to be alone in his presence.

I never told anyone of this event. He is my mother's favorite and closest brother and at the time I decided not to hurt her. (author's files)

Voyeurism

Voyeurism (also called scopophilia) involves recurrent, intense urges to look at unsuspecting people who are naked, undressing, or engaging in sexual behavior. These urges usually involve sexually arousing fantasies. In order to be diagnosed with voyeurism, the person must have had these urges for at least 6 months and either acted on or been distressed by them (APA, 1994). The person who looks at magazines with nude photos or who watches erotic films is not necessarily classified as having voyeurism because the people posing in the magazines and films know that they are being watched. However, a voyeuristic person may look at nude people in magazines or in movies and fantasize that they do not know they are being looked at.

Voyeuristic persons (sometimes referred to as "Peeping Toms") spend a lot of time planning to peep and will risk a great deal to do so. They regard climbing over fences, hiding in bushes, and shivering in the cold as worth the trouble. Peeping is the condition of sexual excitement, which most often results in ejaculation through masturbation either during the peeping or later. The person's targets are usually female strangers. Although some voyeurs are married, they may not derive excitement from watching their wives or any familiar woman undress.

Voyeurism is usually regarded as a male disorder, typically occurring among young men. However, Hurlbert (1992) presented what he believed to be the first reported case study of an adult female voyeurist. The 26-year-old woman he described had a psychological diagnosis of schizoid personality disorder; she was very withdrawn and isolated from social contact. She felt sexual feelings and experienced orgasm only when self-stimulating during voyeuristic activities. She felt humiliated and remorseful over her sexual activities, yet dropped out of treatment, resigned to continue her life as a "loner."

Fetishism

Fetishism involves a pattern, of at least 6 months' duration, of deriving sexual arousal or sexual gratification from actual or fantasized inanimate objects. A diagnosis of fetishism requires that the person has either acted on such urges or has been disturbed by them.

Gebhard (1976) suggested that fetishes are a "graded phenomenon."

> At one end of the range is slight preference; next is strong preference; next is the point where the fetish item is a necessity to sexual activity; and at the terminal end of the range the fetish item substitutes for a living sexual partner. . . . Statistical normality ends and fetishism begins somewhere at the level of strong preference. (pp. 157–158)

Once a fetish begins at the slight preference level, it may progress in its intensity. Figure 18.1 illustrates how a fetish may progress from being a preference, to being a necessity, to being a symbolic substitute for a sexual partner.

Gebhard (1976) suggested that fetishism is an illustration of what philosopher Alfred North Whitehead called "the fallacy of misplaced concreteness": the symbol is given all the power and reality of the actual thing, and the person responds to the symbol just as he or she would to the thing (p. 161). The powerful symbolic component of fetishes may account for the fact that fetishism is virtually non-

existent in preliterate cultures. Rather, "fetishism seems largely confined to literate people taught to be imaginative and to make extensive use of symbolism in verbal and written communication and hence in their thought processes" (Gebhard, 1976, p. 162).

Fetishes may be divided into two types: media and form (Gebhard, 1976). "A media fetish is one wherein the substance rather than the form of the object is the important aspect" (p. 159). For example, a person with a leather fetish responds to leather as an erotic stimulus whether the leather is in the form of a glove, shoe, or coat. "A form fetish is one wherein the form of the object is more important than the material of which it is constituted" (p. 159). For example, a person with a shoe fetish responds to shoes as an erotic stimulus no matter whether the shoes are made of plastic, leather, or cloth. The

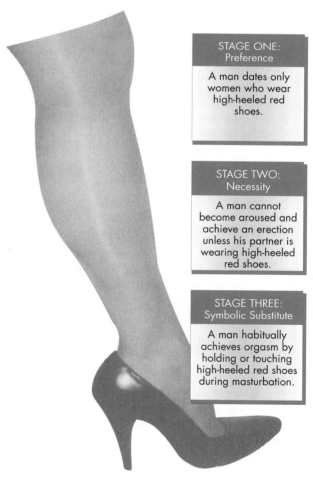

FIGURE 18.1 Stages in the Progression of Fetishism
Source: Based on Gebhard, 1976.

STAGE ONE:
Preference

A man dates only women who wear high-heeled red shoes.

STAGE TWO:
Necessity

A man cannot become aroused and achieve an erection unless his partner is wearing high-heeled red shoes.

STAGE THREE:
Symbolic Substitute

A man habitually achieves orgasm by holding or touching high-heeled red shoes during masturbation.

SALIENCE OF FETISHISM SCALE

The following questions were developed by researchers who were invited to do a study of an organization made up of homosexual and bisexual foot fetishists. This was not a clinical sample, but it involved a large voluntary organization, and the researchers felt that the data they gathered may have wider applicability to other fetishists besides their sample. You may be interested in reviewing the questions to determine the degree to which the fetish was central to the respondent's sex life.

1. Is foot play necessary for your sexual arousal?
2. Is foot fantasy necessary for your sexual arousal?
3. Is foot fantasy usually the main focus of your self-masturbation?
4. What was the frequency of masturbatory fantasies about feet during adolescence?
5. Are feet usually the main focus of your sexual activity with others?
6. How often do you self-masturbate without fantasizing about feet?
7. How often do you self-masturbate while fantasizing about feet?

8. Do you think you could stop fantasizing about feet if you wanted to?
9. Have you ever made a serious attempt to stop your interest in feet?
10. How often do you engage in sexual activity with another without foot play?
11. How often do you engage in sexual activity with another involving foot play?

Scoring and Interpretation   Since the variables used in the scales had different possible ranges, the researchers standardized the scores and made each variable range from 0 to 1. Then they summed the scores for each respondent. The results revealed that while there was a range of salience among the respondents, most clustered at the high end of the scale; 22% had the highest possible score on most of the variables. The salience of fetishism in the men's sex lives was not highly correlated to a measure of self-reported psychological problems. This showed that a man could report that fetishism was very important in his sex life but still have little in the way of psychological problems.

From "If the Shoe Fits . . .: Exploring Male Homosexual Foot Fetishism," by M. S. Weinberg, C. J. Williams, & C. Calban, 1995, *Journal of Sex Research, 32,* 17–27. Copyright © 1995 by the Society for the Scientific Study of Sexuality. Reprinted by permission.

most common form of fetish objects are clothing items, including panties, stockings, lingerie, high-heeled shoes, and boots. Common media fetishes include leather, satin, and latex. Fetishes may also include sounds (a particular song, the clicking of a train on the tracks) and scents (perfume, incense).

Sometimes a parahilia involves both scent and texture, as in *autonepiophilia* (deriving sexual arousal or gratification from wearing wet diapers). One man explained:

> I've had a fetish for wearing wet diapers and latex rubber panties, since being a bedwetter as a boy. . . . Over the years I have been in seven adult diaper clubs and correspond with some 250 to 300 men, who love diapers, too . . . Marriage was unhappy for me. I could not permit myself to enjoy wearing wet diapers at home, except for a short time when I would fake loss of bladder control. (Money, 1988, p. 142)

Transvestic Fetishism

Transvestic fetishism involves recurrent, intense, sexual urges and sexually arousing fantasies, of at least 6 months' duration, involving cross-dressing (a man dressing in a woman's clothes, for example). The person acts on these urges or is distressed by them. The cross-dressing may range from occasional solitary episodes to immersion into a transvestic subculture. The DSM-IV (APA, 1994) classifies the transvestic fetishist's basic sexual preference as heterosexual and describes him as "unremarkably masculine" (p. 531) when not cross-dressed. When wearing female clothes, he typically masturbates (at least initially) "imagining himself to be both the male subject and the female object of his sexual fantasy" (p. 530). However, over time, the sexual arousal motive for cross-dressing may diminish. The cross-dressing may be used as a method of coping with

Cross-dressers are usually heterosexual men who enjoy getting in touch with their feminine side by dressing up as women.

anxiety or depression, or to increase feelings of peace and calm. A subtype of transvestic fetishism involves a permanent desire to dress and live as a woman (gender dysphoria).

While medical and mental health professionals attempt to diagnose transvestic syndromes, transvestites (TVs) and transsexuals (TSs) often resist such categorizations. "Needless to say, members of the TV-TS community do not think of themselves as 'patients,' nor do they particularly like the word 'transvestite,' which seems to imply a compulsive disorder; they prefer 'cross-dresser,' which suggests a choice of lifestyle" (Garber, 1992, p. 4). Calculations from the International Foundation for Gender Education estimate that 6% of the U.S. population are cross-dressers, and 1% are transsexuals.

The TV-TS community has been criticized by gay activist groups as being homophobic, and gay activists challenge statistics suggesting that most transvestites are heterosexuals (Garber, 1992). However, a recent study did find a predominance of heterosexuals among a cross-dressing group. In a survey of Tri-Ess (a national cross-dressing organization) members, the majority of respondents (68%) said they were heterosexual; 10%, bisexual; 2%, homosexual; and 20% were celibate (Bullough & Bullough, 1997).

Four examples of cross-dressing individuals (Bancroft, 1989) emphasize different aspects of the phenomenon:

- The fetishistic transvestite (cross-dressing is sexually arousing, usually involving masturbation)
- The transsexual (cross-dressing is an aspect of expressing one's preferred gender)
- The double-role transvestite (usually a man who spends part of his time in typical heterosexual activities, and part cross-dressing and passing as a woman)
- The homosexual transvestite (sexually attracted to members of the same sex, but cross-dressing is more of a caricature than an impersonation of the other sex)

These categories highlight the three main dimensions of cross-dressing: the fetish aspect, cross-gender identity and role, and sexual orientation and preference (Bancroft, 1989). This range of experiences is represented in the study mentioned earlier of Tri-Ess members. Forty-nine people (from a sample of 372) reported that they had not achieved ejaculation by cross-dressing (Bullough & Bullough, 1997). Nearly one-third (31%) reported that they currently do not experience sexual excitement with cross-dressing.

However, at the other extreme, 21% said they experience sexual excitement at least 75% of the time.

Sexual Sadism

Sexual sadism and sexual masochism are two sides of the same coin in that they both involve associating psychological or physical suffering and humiliation with sexual arousal or pleasure. *Sexual sadism* is characterized by recurrent, intense, sexual urges and sexually arousing fantasies, of at least 6 months' duration, involving acts that hurt or humiliate the sexual partner. In some cases, sadistic people will have acted on these urges; more often, they will not have acted on these urges but, in either case, will be distressed by them.

The term "sadism" refers to the Marquis de Sade (1740–1814), French author, philosopher, and sado-masochist who described literally the experiences of people who enjoyed hurting and dominating their sexual partners. The cries and suffering of the sexual partner are the source of sadistic sexual excitement. Such suffering may be by consenting masochistic partners or by those who are forced to participate. Sadistic acts or fantasies may involve dominance, (forcing the victim to crawl), restraint or bondage (tying the victim to a chair), spanking, whipping, beating, burning, shocking (with electricity), cutting, strangling, mutilating, or killing. However, in some cases, the pain may be only symbolic, as when the sadist "whips" a partner with a feather.

Ernulf and Innula (1995) suggested that sado-masochism is more frequent in the gay culture since "individuals who have accepted one sexual variation

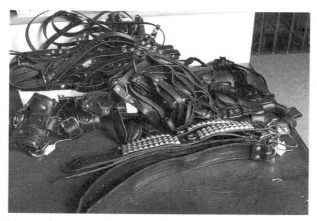

Various devices may be used to tie up a partner (bondage).

in themselves might more easily accept desires for other sexual variations" (p. 647). Alternatively, gay individuals might be more willing to talk about the use of sexual variations than heterosexuals (Ernulf & Innula, 1995).

Sexual Masochism

Sexual masochism is characterized by recurrent, intense, sexual urges and sexually arousing fantasies, of at least 6 months' duration, in which sexual arousal or gratification is obtained through enacting scripts that involve suffering and pain. Such pain may be physical or psychological and may involve being humiliated, beaten, bound, cut, bitten, spanked, choked, pricked, or shocked. While pain may actually be experienced, the diagnosis of the paraphilia may involve only intense, recurrent urges and fantasies for at least 6 months. The person may have these fantasies while masturbating or while having sexual relations.

Gebhard (1976) emphasized that it is not the pain per se that is sexually exciting to the masochistic person, but rather, the enactment of the script that involves pain. In common masochistic scripts, "the masochist must allegedly have done something meriting punishment, there must be threats and suspense before the punishment is meted out. . . . Some masochists dislike the pain while it is being inflicted, but obtain gratification by anticipation of the pain or by thinking about it after it has ceased" (pp. 163–164).

Sadistic and masochistic persons may use each other to act out their sexual scripts. A favorite pattern is bondage and discipline (B and D), where the sadist ties up (bondage) and whips (discipline) the masochist. Often, the sadist will act out a scene by telling the masochist of a series of the latter's wrongdoings and the punishment to follow while the masochist screams for mercy. Both delight in the activity.

Some large cities have "clubs" that specialize in sadomasochism (S and M). The Chateau in the West Hollywood section of Los Angeles is an example. The "staff" consists of 13 women—six dominants (sadists), three submissives (masochists), and four "switch-hitters." (Weinberg, Williams, & Moser [1984] noted that the majority of those who enjoy S and M are equally comfortable in either role.) Equipment includes a wide range of racks, cages, chains, wooden crosses, and whipping posts. The price is a dollar per minute (each treatment is 40 minutes), and more than 1000 customers have been served by being bound, gagged, stretched, and beaten. Similar clubs are located in San Francisco, Miami, and Dallas.

Some partners exhibit mild forms of S and M in their relationship, as illustrated in the following example.

> I like to be tied up and blindfolded. I can't tell what my partner is doing but, on occasion, he has used candles and dripped the hot wax on my body and my breasts. I like it when he orders me around and dominates me. It's not S and M but a step towards it. I, too, tie my boyfriend up and do as I want with him while he is totally submissive. I don't want whips and severe pain, even though we have used handcuffs and ropes; we love each other and know it's fun, and we're not trying to hurt each other. (authors' files)

A less severe form of S and M involves mild spanking in which one partner will playfully spank the buttocks of the partner. The spanking is not regarded as painful by the giver or receiver. Weinberg et al. (1984) noted that the majority of S and M participants are of the mild variety, for whom S and M is "simply a form of sexual excitement which they voluntarily and mutually choose to explore" (p. 388).

In conducting research for his popular counseling book, Alex Comfort (1987) studied what he referred to as "so-called 'bondage' or the playing of 'restraint games.'" He found that it occurred with surprising frequency, not only in fantasy, but also in couples' activities. While he said "the 'bondage' routine is a definite situational fetish for some individuals and a strong preference for others (of both sexes)," a high number of his informants "seemed to be incorporating it into a varied sexual repertoire as one more resource" (p. 13). While this type of "bondage" could be enacted in a sadomasochistic way, he found that couples used it more as a sexual technique, a kind of foreplay, rather than as a compulsive fantasy or activity.

Gebhard (1976) suggested that "sadomasochism is embedded in our culture since our culture operates on the basis of dominance-submission relationships, and aggression is socially valued" (p. 163). The cultural context for sadomasochism is especially salient to gender relationships: "The male is supposed to be dominant and aggressive sexually and the female reluctant or submissive. Violence and sex are commingled to make a profitable package to sell through mass media" (Gebhard, 1976, p. 163). Comfort (1987) noted that not only is sadomasochistic expression reinforced by U.S. society, but the balance between sexual arousal and aggression is made more precarious by the high degree of "non-sexual, free-floating anger and dominance" (p. 5). But this explanation of sadomasochism is incomplete because most men are similarly socialized, but relatively few engage in paraphilic sadistic behavior.

The development of masochistic behavior is easier to explain. Some masochists report having experienced sexual pleasure while being punished as children; for example, the person who was spanked on a parent's knee may have become sexually excited by having his or her genitals rubbed on the parent's knee. These experiences may have become linked in the child's mind.

Some paraphiliac behaviors occur more frequently than others. A team of researchers (Abel et al., 1987) looked at the relative percentages of various paraphiliac behaviors reported by a sample of nonincarcerated men with paraphilias. The most frequently reported paraphiliac behavior was exhibitionism (about 25% of the respondents), followed by frotteurism (18%), nonincestual pedophilia (14%), and voyeurism (10%). The least reported paraphilia in this sample was sexual sadism (about 1%). However, since people are generally unwilling to report such behaviors, most of what we know about people who engage in paraphilic behaviors comes from those who have been caught engaging in illegal acts.

Other Paraphilias

Although we have discussed the major paraphilias presented in DSM-IV, there are many others. Examples of other varieties are presented in Table 18.2.

Legal Versus Illegal Paraphilias

The definitions of paraphilias presented in this chapter, which are based on the DSM-IV (APA, 1994) developed by mental health professionals, do not necessarily meet legal or other nonmedical criteria for what constitutes mental disability. Paraphilias are legal or illegal depending on the degree to which the rights of others are affected. *Formicophilia,*

TABLE 18.2 Other Paraphilias

PARAPHILIA	DESCRIPTION
Apotomnophilia	Becoming sexually aroused by the thought of becoming an amputee.
Acrotomophilia	Deriving sexual arousal or gratification from engaging in sex with an amputee.
Asphyxiophilia	Cutting off one's air supply to enhance orgasm.
Autonepiophilia	Deriving sexual arousal or gratification from wearing wet diapers.
Coprophilia	Using feces for sexual arousal either by watching another defecate or by defecating on someone.
Ephebophilia	Engaging in sexual behavior with an adolescent or having a recurrent urge to do so.
Erotophonophilia	Lust murder, in which the partner is killed as a means of atoning for sex with the individual.
Formicophilia	Becoming sexually aroused by ants, bugs, or other small, crawling creatures.
Gerontophilia	Becoming sexually aroused by elderly individuals.
Klismaphilia	Becoming sexually aroused by receiving an enema.
Narratophilia	Listening to "dirty talk" as a means of becoming sexually aroused. Phone sex companies depend on people with this paraphilia for their income.
Necrophilia	Deriving sexual arousal or gratification from sexual activity with a dead person (or a person acting the role of a corpse).
Nepiophilia	Becoming sexually aroused by babies.
Olfactophilia	Becoming sexually aroused by certain scents.
Partialism	Deriving sexual arousal or gratification from a specific nongenital body part (such as the foot).
Pictophilia	Becoming sexually aroused in reference to sexy photographs.
Raptophilia	Becoming sexually aroused by surprise attack and violent assault.
Somnophilia	Fondling a person who is sleeping so as to become sexually aroused. The person is often a stranger.
Telephone scatalogia	Becoming sexually aroused by calling a stranger on the phone and either talking about sex or making sexual sounds (breathing heavily) (also called telephonicophilia).
Urophilia	Using urine for sexual arousal either by watching someone urinate or by urinating on someone.
Zoophilia	Becoming aroused by sexual contact with animals (commonly known as bestiality).

olfactophilia, and *klismaphilia* do not infringe on the rights of others and are of little concern to the law. Voyeurism, exhibitionism, and pedophilia are examples of paraphilias that interfere with the rights of others and carry legal penalties. Voyeurism and exhibitionism are clinical terms; in the legal system, these criminal acts may be referred to as "secret peeping" and "indecent exposure." They are usually regarded as misdemeanors and are punishable by a fine. (Repeat offenses may involve mandatory outpatient treatment at a mental health facility.) Pedophilic acts are punishable by imprisonment. Legal charges may range from taking indecent liberties with a minor, to sodomy or rape. The majority of apprehended sex offenders are arrested for acts of exhibitionism, pedophilia, and voyeurism (APA, 1994).

Laws regulating sexual behavior vary from state to state. Some states regard exhibitionism as a misdemeanor; others classify it as a felony. The penalty ranges from a fine to a prison term. If the exhibitionist is drunk or has mental retardation, police officers tend to regard his self-exposure differently from those who compulsively expose themselves and are repeatedly picked up for exhibitionism.

Is Rape a Paraphilia?

There is professional disagreement over whether rape should be classified as a paraphilia. Abel and Rouleau (1990) argued that rape is a paraphilia on the basis of clinical interviews with rapists who report having compulsive urges and fantasies to commit rape, feeling guilty afterward, and repeating the behavior. Persons with paraphilias characteristically experience compulsive urges and fantasies and guilt and also repeat the paraphilic behavior. In addition, the age of onset for interest in rape and the age of onset for other paraphilias is similar. Over half of rapists report developing their interest in rape by age 21, the age by which other paraphilias often develop.

The DSM-IV does not list rape as a specific paraphilic disorder. Perhaps psychiatrists do not classify rape as a paraphilia because it is more violent and sexually aggressive than other paraphilias (except some expressions of sadomasochism). In addition, society may be reluctant to accept rape as a paraphilia because paraphilias are associated with less punishment than rape.

THINK ABOUT IT

Have you experienced a preference for a sexual stimulus that you feel borders on a compulsion? To what degree does such a proclivity affect you or your relationships? Are there any potential legal consequences for the movement of this preference into a compulsion?

THE ORIGINS OF PARAPHILIAS: THEORETICAL PERSPECTIVES

Various theoretical perspectives offer explanations for why paraphilias exist or why particular individuals develop paraphilias. Next, we look for clues to the origins of paraphilias within the theoretical frameworks of psychoanalysis, feminism, learning theory, and biological theory. We also explore the origins of paraphilias, using Money's (1986) theoretical construct of "vandalized lovemap" and Freund's (1990) concept of "courtship disorder."

Psychoanalytic Theory

From a psychoanalytic perspective, paraphilias may be viewed as symptoms of unresolved subconscious conflicts. For example, an exhibitionistic man may frighten unsuspecting women by exposing himself to them as a way of rebelling against them. Such rebellion may stem from having a domineering mother or an unresolved oedipal complex (see Chapter 15, "Gender Diversity"), which has left the person unable to engage in heterosexual intercourse. The urge to exhibit himself may be a subconscious symbolic substitute that compensates for the inability to have sexual relations with women.

Kline (1987) reviewed psychoanalytic conceptualization of paraphilias and empirical research designed to test these theories. He concluded that while the evidence was not sufficient to refute Freudian theories, it also did not offer objective support. He lamented that since psychoanalytic theories "have reached a low ebb" (p. 173), it is unlikely that high-quality research will put them to a scientific test.

Feminist Perspective

Paraphilias such as pedophilia and sexual sadism are, from a feminist perspective, expressions of aggression, not sexuality. The pedophile, sadist, and rapist express control and dominance through their paraphilic fantasies and behaviors.

The feminist perspective explains why there are many more men with paraphilia than women with paraphilia: Our culture has perpetuated traditional gender roles that emphasize male dominance, sexual aggression, and control. Some paraphilias may be motivated by expressing hostility and holding the momentary feeling of power over a victim (Bancroft,

1989). An example of the desire to dominate was provided in a description of advertising the sex scenes available on The Amateur Action bulletin board system. Typically, the on-line service received a lukewarm response to straightforward depictions of oral sex. However, when words like *choke* or *choking* were used, the demand from consumers doubled (Elmer-Dewitt, 1995).

Learning Theory

Learning theorists emphasize that paraphilias are learned by means of both classical and operant conditioning. In 1966, Rachman demonstrated how a fetish can be learned through classical conditioning. Using an experimental design, Rachman paired women's boots with erotic slides of nude women. As a result, the participants began to experience erotic arousal to the sight of the boots alone.

Scarf, panty, and red high-heeled shoe fetishes may be a result of classical conditioning. The person may have experienced sexual pleasure when in the presence of these objects, learned to associated these objects with the pleasure, and developed a preference for these objects during sex.

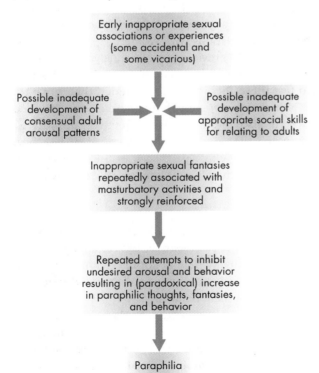

FIGURE 18.2 A Model of the Development of Paraphilia
Source: Durand & Barlow, 1997.

Operant conditioning may also account for the development of some paraphilias. For example, the exhibitionist may be reinforced by the startled response of a woman and seek conditions under which she will exhibit a startled response (exposing his penis). By exposing his penis, he causes her to yell, is reinforced, and wants to repeat the behavior with a new stranger. Orgasm may also be an operant conditioning reinforcer (Weinberg, Williams, & Calhan, 1995).

Similarly, paraphilias may result from negative reinforcement. Negative reinforcement is defined as the strengthening of a behavior associated with the removal of something aversive. A paraphilia may be established because the associated behaviors remove feelings of anxiety, sadness, loneliness, and anger. Hence, when the exhibitionist exhibits to a victim, he feels a temporary reprieve from feelings of anxiety, which are replaced by feelings of excitement.

Levine et al. (1990) noted that some individuals with paraphilias may have "generally poor adaptive functioning" to the stresses of life (p. 101). Figure 18.2 depicts possible conditioning and learning history influences.

Biological Theory

The degree to which biological variables are responsible for the development of paraphilias is controversial. Just as heterosexuality, homosexuality, and bisexuality may be based on biological predispositions, so may paraphilic tendencies. Some people may be biologically "wired" to respond erotically to atypical stimuli. Moser (1992) contended that paraphilias are strong sexual responses to an individualized, specific set of uncommon or inappropriate objects or potential partners and that these "lust" responses are "a basic aspect of sexual identity, set early in life, unchangeable by common sex therapy techniques and are not learned in a classical sense" (p. 66). While he did not define the mechanisms for these presumably innate predilections, other investigators have proposed that there are neurochemical interactions during embryo development that influence cerebral organization (Flor-Henry, 1987).

Paraphilia as a Vandalized Lovemap

John Money (1986, 1988) used the term *lovemap* to describe a mental representation or template that develops within the first few years of life. "It depicts your idealized lover and what, as a pair, you do together in the idealized, romantic, erotic, and sexualized relationship" (p. xvi). In other words, it establishes, or at least influences, the type of sexual partner and activities that will arouse you. Given the standard developmental hormones introduced into the developing fetus at the appropriate time and the traditional heterosexual socialization, people tend to be emotionally and sexually attracted to the other sex. "Normophilic lovemaps" are lovemaps that are consistent with what is culturally defined as appropriate. Lovemaps that involve deviations from what is generally considered as normal and acceptable are known as paraphilias. "On the street they are termed kinky or bizarre sex" (Money, 1988, p. 127). Individuals with a paraphilia are compulsively responsive to and dependent on personally and socially unacceptable stimuli for sexual arousal and orgasm.

The critical years in the development of the lovemap are between ages 5 and 8. "Major erotosexual traumas during this period may disrupt the consolidation of the lovemap that would otherwise be taking place" (Money, 1986, p. 19). Money provided examples of the social experiences that "vandalize" or disrupt traditional sexual-erotic development socialization and showed how these disruptions may contribute to the development of pedophilia.

Pedophiles may have been involved in a relationship with an older man and learned to repeat the age-discrepant sexual experience with a younger boy. "In adolescence and adulthood, they remain sexuoerotically boyish, and are paraphilically attracted only to juveniles of the same age as their own when they became a pedophile's partner" (Money, 1986, p. 21). Often, the experience itself will not be enough to trigger a pedophiliac lovemap. But in combination with a traumatic experience, such as grief over a loved one's death, the man may become particularly vulnerable. Hence, the feeling of having lost a significant other and the enjoyment of sexual pleasure in an age-discrepant context may bond one to that context for reasons related to emotional insecurity and physical pleasure. Freund, Watson, and Dickey (1990) found that pedophilic men were significantly more likely to have been sexually abused as children than individuals who were not charged with a sexual offense against children.

Paraphilia as a Courtship Disorder

Some paraphilias may also be conceptualized as expressions of a common "underlying" disorder (Freund, 1990). The disorder in this case is a distortion of "normal" courtship, which is assumed to consist of a series of four phases in which progressively more intimate expressions of sexual behavior occur. In this theoretical approach, each paraphilia omits most stages of courtship or enacts them only in a superficial way. For example, "the rapist short-circuits all stages and immediately attempts intercourse" (Langevin & Lang, 1987, p. 203). The four courtship phases and examples of paraphilic distortions are presented in Table 18.3.

Another byproduct of the courtship disorder is that the person with a paraphilia may have difficulty loving a person because of his preoccupation with the paraphilic object. The deficient ability to love and the inability to progress through the courtship sequence makes it difficult to have a conventional sexual relationship (Levine et al., 1990).

--- THINK ABOUT IT ---

How can a paraphilia interfere with the development of an intimate love relationship? Which paraphilias would be most difficult for you to accept in a partner?

TABLE 18.3 Courtship Phases and Paraphilic Distortion

COURTSHIP PHASE	PARAPHILIA
Location and first appraisal of a suitable partner	Voyeurism
Pretactile interaction (such as looking, smiling, posturing, and talking to a prospective partner)	Exhibitionism
Tactile interaction	Frotteurism
Genital union	Raptophilia (forced sexual behavior)

Source: Freund, 1990.

TREATMENT OF PARAPHILIAS

The behavioral expression of some of the paraphilias we have discussed (such as exhibitionism, pedophilia, and voyeurism) interferes with the rights of others. When people engaging in such behaviors come to the attention of the law, they are often required to enter a treatment program. In addition, some individuals with paraphilia voluntarily seek treatment before they are caught.

Usually the first step in a sex offender treatment program is a thorough assessment. This involves collecting information regarding the offense of record, as well as a sexual and social history. The therapist usually gathers the law enforcement report, victim statement, presentence investigation, and summaries of previous placements and treatment. Interviews with the client and relevant other people are conducted, and psychological testing may be done. In addition, sexual interest can be assessed through self-report and physiological measurement (Murphy, Haynes, & Worley, 1991). The Multiphasic Sex Inventory obtains reports of deviant behaviors, as well as indications of sexual knowledge and cognitive distortions. Its scales measuring child molestation and rape are the most well-developed, although it does address other paraphilias. The polygraph is sometimes used to corroborate self-reports obtained in clinical interviews. Measurements of penile tumescence (changes in the volume and circumference of the penis) are also used to assess physiological arousal. The penile plethysmograph employs a sensor or transducer that measures and records changes in penis size in response to sexual stimuli (audiotapes or slides).

After a thorough evaluation, treatment begins and is usually focused on decreasing deviant sexual arousal, increasing nondeviant sexual arousal, teaching social skills, changing faulty cognitions, resolving sexual dysfunctions, managing alcohol abuse, or a combination of these tasks.

Decreasing Deviant Sexual Arousal

Effective treatment of a paraphilia involves decreasing the deviant sexual arousal response, or the response to that which society regards as nonsexual stimuli. The therapeutic goal is for the person to no longer require the paraphilic target stimulus as a preferred or necessary condition of sexual arousal. Treatment that focuses on decreasing deviant sexual arousal may involve medications, aversive conditioning, covert sensitization, or masturbatory satiation.

MEDICATIONS The use of medications to assist in paraphilia control is a controversial issue that is discussed in the following Social Choices section.

AVERSIVE CONDITIONING Deviant sexual arousal may also be decreased through *aversive conditioning*. Such conditioning involves pairing an aversive or unpleasant stimulus with the paraphiliac stimulus in order to decrease the deviant sexual arousal and reduce the probability of engaging in the paraphiliac behavior. One example of an aversive stimulus is an unpleasant smell. For the heterosexual male pedophile, this type of aversion therapy is carried out by having the patient look at a series of slides of children and adult women flashed on a wall in the therapist's office. After each picture of a child appears, the therapist administers a noxious odor so that the patient associates this with the visual stimulus of the child. After removing the odor, the therapist changes the slide to that of an adult woman. In this way, the patient associates relief from the noxious stimuli (and, consequently, a more pleasant feeling) with the visual stimulus of the adult woman.

The therapist might also use emetic drugs (which induce vomiting) or electrical shock (Perkins, 1991). Since it is believed that a fetish results from learning to associate a particular object with sexual pleasure, the stimulus object may be reconditioned by associating an unpleasant experience with it. For example, the person might be given emetic drugs to induce vomiting when in the presence of the fetish object. Eleven case studies have reported successful results with this type of therapy, but, the reviewers said, "the results are only suggestive due to the uncontrolled nature of the research" (Kilmann, Sabalis, Gearing, Bukstel, & Scovern, 1982, p. 212).

COVERT SENSITIZATION *Covert sensitization* involves using negative thoughts as a way of developing negative feelings associated with a deviant sexual stimulus. For example, a therapist may induce negative thoughts by saying the following to the patient:

> I want you to imagine going into the bedroom of
> your 7-year-old niece when her parents are in

SHOULD HORMONES OR TRANQUILIZERS BE USED FOR TREATING PARAPHILIC SEX OFFENDERS?

The use of hormones or tranquilizers to quell the sexual lust of the paraphiliac sex offender involves a consideration of the rights of society to be protected from harm versus the rights of an offender to avoid being given medication that may have unwanted side effects.

Depo-Provera (medroxyprogesterone acetate, or MPA) is a synthetic progestinic hormone that lowers the blood level of testosterone and seems to have a direct pharmacologic effect on brain pathways that mediate sexual behavior. In some cases, Depo-Provera removes the paraphiliac preoccupation, "thereby leaving the man more comfortable and able to imagine and act on his sexual interest in his partner without dysfunction" (Levine et al., 1990, p. 99). In other cases, Depo-Provera results in "a complete shutdown of eroticism" (p. 99). While controversial, Depo-Provera has been used to treat exhibitionists, pedophiles, voyeurs, and rapists.

John Money and Richard Bennett (1981) treated 20 adult men with a history of sex-offending behaviors since adolescence with Depo-Provera in doses ranging from 100 milligrams to 600 milligrams per week for periods of 3 months to more than 5 years. Counseling was also an important part of their program and helped to encourage socially appropriate pair-bonded relationships.

Money and Bennett are still evaluating the effectiveness of their treatment program. The specific effects of hormone and counseling therapy have been obscured by patients leaving the program; varying times between hormonal injections; compliance (keeping appointments, staying in therapy); use of alcohol, "street" drugs, and prescription antiepileptic drugs; and, as noted, the establishment of a pair-bondedness with an erotosexual partner. However, "for some patients it proved to be the only form of treatment that induced a long-term remission of symptoms and kept them off a treadmill of imprisonment" (p. 132).

Moser (1992) emphasized that antiandrogen therapy (such as that for pedophiles) is an effective form of treatment in that it will "stop the man from reacting to his lust cues" (p. 68). Moreover, "these men [hormonal treatment of women is rare] report that they still have some capability and interest in conventional sex behavior (consensual acts with an adult partner)" (p. 68).

Psychotropic drugs, especially antidepressants such as fluoxetine (Prozac), are also being used to treat paraphilias (Gijs & Gooren, 1996). These drugs affect the central nervous system instead of hormonal functioning. The success of using serotonin reuptake inhibitors suggests that paraphiliac fantasies may be a type of obsession similar to other obsessive-compulsive and impulse control disorders (Branford & Greenberg, 1996).

Use of hormonal and psychopharmacological interventions should be part of a comprehensive, multidisciplinary treatment program (Gijs & Gooren, 1996). Gijs and Gooren caution that such treatments are indicated only for paraphilias that violate the rights of others or harm the well-being of the person with the paraphilia. They also note the difficulty of obtaining informed consent when assessment and treatment are done in a legal context. Money (1986) pointed out that "some critics claim that paraphilic sex offenders lose their power of informed consent and will sign for any form of treatment in order to escape arrest or imprisonment" (p. xviii). Gijs and Gooren called for attention to the content and process for addressing this concern.

Sources: Bradford, J. M., & Greenberg, D. M. (1996). Pharmacological treatment of deviant sexual behavior. *Annual Review of Sex Research: Volume VII.* Mason City, IA: Society for the Scientific Study of Sexuality.

Gijs, L., & Gooren, L. (1996). Hormonal and psychopharmacological interventions in the treatment of paraphilias: An update. *Journal of Sex Research, 33,* 273–290.

Levine, S. B., Risen, C. B., & Althof, S. (1990). Essay on the diagnosis and nature of paraphilia. *Journal of Sex and Marital Therapy, 16,* 89–102.

Money, J. (1986). *Lovemaps: Clinical concepts of sexual/erotic health and pathology, paraphilia, and gender transposition in childhood, adolescence, and maturity.* New York: Irvington.

Money, J., & Bennett, R. G. (1981). Postadolescent paraphilic sex offenders: Antiandrogenic and counseling therapy follow-up. *International Journal of Mental Health, 10,* 122–133.

Moser, C. (1992). Lust, lack of desire, and paraphilias: Some thoughts and possible connections. *Journal of Sex and Marital Therapy, 18,* 65–69.

another part of the house. As you open the door, you see her asleep in her bed. But as you approach the bed, you begin to feel very nauseous and feel that you are going to throw up. You vomit and feel the particles in your mouth and the stench in your nostrils. You also think that if you act on your urges and are discovered, you will be shamed out of the family.

This scenario is designed to associate negative feelings and thoughts with acting on a sexual urge to touch a child in order to reduce the probability that the patient will engage in this behavior. Covert sensitization may be used to apply negative imagined consequences for offending and positive consequences for imaging alternatives to offending (Perkins, 1991).

MASTURBATORY SATIATION According to Abel, Becker, and Skinner (1985), the most effective intervention to reduce deviant sexual arousal is masturbatory satiation. *Masturbatory satiation* involves instructing paraphiliac individuals to fantasize about their paraphiliac urges during the postorgasmic phase of masturbation.

> The patient is instructed to masturbate to ejaculation as rapidly as possible using nondeviant fantasies, or to masturbate until the usual latency to ejaculation period plus two minutes has passed. Once the patient has ejaculated or the latency period has been exceeded, the patient immediately switches to the use of deviant fantasy, using the most erotic deviant material possible, and continues to masturbate for a total masturbatory time of 1 hour. (p. 118)

Masturbatory satiation has several advantages. First, it is "exceedingly effective" (Abel et al., 1985, p. 119). Second, it provides a powerful pairing of low physiological arousal with the deviant fantasy. Three, it is cost-effective. For every hour of time with the therapist, the patient can have five hours of masturbatory satiation.

Perkins (1991) noted there are limitations, and possibly dangers, of using aversion therapy with those who not only have deviant sexual interests, but also hostility and negative self-images in relating to other people. Although clinicians have been enthusiastic about satiation, empirical support for its efficacy is limited (Over & Koukounas, 1995).

Increasing Nondeviant Sexual Arousal

In treating individuals with paraphilias, it is important not only to decrease deviant sexual arousal, but also to increase nondeviant sexual arousal. Thus, treatment of paraphilias also involves increasing the level of sexual arousal the individual has in reference to culturally appropriate sexual stimuli. For example, the therapist would try to increase the sexual urges of a pedophile to the stimulus of a consenting adult partner. The mechanisms for increasing nondeviant sexual arousal include masturbatory conditioning, exposure, and systematic conditioning.

MASTURBATORY CONDITIONING *Masturbatory conditioning* involves associating the pleasure of orgasm with a nondeviant stimulus. In this way, the previously nonarousing nondeviant stimulus becomes a stimulus for arousal. The therapist instructs the paraphiliac client to fantasize about the paraphiliac urge or behavior while masturbating. Then, as tension mounts and pleasure increases, the client is instructed to switch fantasies from the deviant stimulus (such as a child) to a nondeviant stimulus (such as a consenting adult).

EXPOSURE *Exposure* involves introducing the individual to the nondeviant stimulus for increasingly longer periods of time, during which there is the opportunity to develop positive associations. For example, if the exhibitionist feels uncomfortable in the presence of adult women, the therapist might assign the patient to attend social functions with a male friend and to stand increasingly closer to women at these social functions. Such exposure helps to reduce the fear and anxiety associated with women and facilitates a greater willingness to engage in social interaction with women.

SYSTEMATIC DESENSITIZATION Where the client feels extreme anxiety in the presence of the nondeviant stimulus, systematic desensitization may be employed to reduce such anxiety. In *systematic desensitization,* the client imagines a series of scenes that involve the nondeviant sexual stimulus (such as an adult female), then ranks these scenes according to the level of anxiety or discomfort they produce. Then, while the client is relaxed (the therapist will have taught the person how to relax using a progressive relaxation procedure), the therapist will present the various scenes from lowest to highest anxiety to the client. Being relaxed while fantasizing about the various encounters with women reduces the fear and anxiety associated with women. To ensure generalization, the therapist will ask the person to increase the level of real-life exposure to adult women using the exposure technique described in the previous section.

PERSONAL CHOICES

Can People Control Their Paraphilias?

Therapists disagree about the degree to which persons with paraphilias can control the behavioral expression of their paraphilia. While some feel that those with pedophilia, exhibitionism, and voyeurism are uncontrollably and compulsively driven to express their paraphilia (and will not be able to change these "lust" cues—Moser, 1992), others suggest that they exercise conscious control over their paraphilic behavior.

Pedophilia, exhibitionism, and voyeurism may be conceptualized as requiring a series of choices leading up to the paraphilic behavior. For example, a pedophile who fondles a young boy in the park on a summer afternoon is engaging in a terminal target behavior that was preceded by a number of choices leading to that behavior. These choices may have included taking off from work, looking at child pornography, drinking alcohol, going to the playground, buying candy, sitting on the bench where a young boy was also sitting, talking to the boy, offering the boy some candy, and so on. At any of these choice points, the pedophile may have chosen to engage in a behavior that was incompatible with child molestation. Each of these behaviors, when taken alone, is a relatively easier choice—the person might choose to stay at work, look at alternative magazines, and so forth.

Similarly, the exhibitionist who exposes himself in the library to a stranger may alternatively have chosen to masturbate to ejaculation at home, to avoid alcohol, and to go with a friend to a movie. Finally, the voyeur might choose to schedule time with others when he is particularly vulnerable to "peeping," to avoid walking on another person's property (where peeping often occurs), and to select alternative behaviors, such as going to a movie during prime "peeping time."

In addition to consciously exercising to choose behaviors to control one's paraphilia, it is also possible to control one's level of arousal. Nagayama Hall (1991) studied 169 inpatient adult male sex offenders in terms of their sexual arousal. While listening to erotic tapes, 84% were able to inhibit being sexually aroused as a result of sheer conscious control. The investigator simply asked them to "stop yourself from being sexually aroused" (p. 363), and all but 16% were able to do so.

In addition to making deliberate choices that are incompatible with the expression of paraphiliac behaviors, the person who is concerned about his paraphilia may choose to seek therapy to address such issues as self-esteem, guilt, anxiety, sexual dysfunctions, and lack of social skills. By confronting these issues and ensuring that they do not contribute to unwanted behavior, the paraphiliac is taking deliberate control of his sexual expression.

Teaching Social Skills

Earlier in this chapter, we discussed courtship disorder as an underlying problem in the development of some paraphilias. We also noted that involvement in a relationship can be conceptualized according to a number of phases, such as looking at a potential partner, talking with a new person, and negotiating physical intimacy. Individuals with paraphilias often

> lack skills to establish communication, initiate conversation, maintain the flow of conversation, learn about the interests of others, share intimacies about one's own life with others, empathize with others, and ask for a change in another person's behavior. (Abel et al., 1985, p. 108)

Treatment of paraphilias often involves teaching the person social skills so the person will be better able to initiate and maintain a social relationship that might lead to closer bonding with an adult partner. Social skill training often takes place in a group therapy setting where group members may practice basic communication and interaction skills with each other.

Changing Faulty Cognitions

Some paraphiliac behaviors are justified and maintained on the basis of faulty cognitions. For example, the exhibitionist may think that women are really turned on by the sight of a naked penis and need this experience to get sexually excited. The pedophile may think that children profit from sexual experiences with adults as a form of sex education. The rapist may think that women really enjoy being forced to have sex.

Correcting these cognitive distortions often occurs in the context of group therapy. Group members challenge the irrational beliefs of each other and acknowledge their own irrational beliefs. New beliefs are substituted for irrational beliefs: women are disgusted by exhibitionists, children are harmed by adult sexual exploitation, and women do not enjoy being raped.

Resolving Sexual Dysfunctions

Some paraphilias are continued because of sexual dysfunctions that prevent the paraphiliac individual from engaging in sexual behavior in a pair-bonded relationship. For example, the exhibitionist and voyeur may feel unable to engage in sex with a partner due to erectile dysfunction. They may also suffer early ejaculation or retarded ejaculation and want to avoid exposure of these dysfunctions in a relationship. Unless these sexual dysfunctions are treated, the paraphiliac individual may continue to feel sexually inadequate and perceive no alternative for sexual gratification other than engaging in paraphiliac behavior.

Treating Alcohol Abuse

Some pedophiles, exhibitionists, voyeurs, and rapists report that the use of alcohol lowers their inhibitions and increases the probability that they will engage in paraphilic behavior. Particularly in the case of sex aggression, disulfiram is used to eliminate the use of alcohol. Also known as antabuse, disulfiram taken in pill form remains in the person's system for 3 to 5 days. If alcohol is consumed during this period, severe tachycardia (rapid heart rate), anxiety, nausea, and vomiting will result.

_____ THINK ABOUT IT _____

Assume you were developing a treatment program for a man with pedophilia. Prioritize the various techniques discussed above in developing your treatment plan for this individual.

SEXUAL ADDICTION: A FALSE CONCEPT?

Sexual addiction has been described as a condition in which sexual thoughts or behaviors negatively affect the health, relationships, or work of an individual. The addiction model has been used to characterize the denial, loss of control, and pathological priorization that can occur.

Although a journal about sexual addiction (*Sexual Addiction and Compulsivity*) is published quarterly, and books such as *Contrary to Love: Helping the Sexual Addict* (Carnes, 1990) and *Sex Addiction* (Earle & Earle, 1995) have been written on sexual addiction, the American Psychiatric Association no longer recognizes sexual addiction as a disorder. Wise and Schmidt (1996), reporting on the APA's review of the DSM-III-R use of the concept, noted:

> There is abundant clinical evidence of sexual activity that can be characterized as "excessive." However, the concept of sexual addiction is troublesome in that the term "addiction" has a specific meaning associated with physiological processes of withdrawal. In addition, there is no scientific database to support the concept of excessive sexual behavior as being in the realm of an addiction. Competing concepts of compulsivity or impulsive control disorders are intriguing possibilities but lack database support. The whole issue of excessive sexual behavior is worthy of scientific study, but the interests of research are not served by restricting the focus of these efforts to a process of addiction. (p. 1140)

The American Psychiatric Association does recognize that "excessive sexual behavior" may occur in both women and men and that the clinical description of nymphomania (excessive sexual behavior in women) and satyriasis (excessive sexual behavior in men) may apply. However, how these concepts should be treated is an open question (Wise & Schmidt, 1996, p. 1141).

_____ THINK ABOUT IT _____

How would you distinguish "excessive" sexual behavior from "normal" sexual behavior?

SUMMARY POINTS

Most people have some preference for how, when, and with whom they experience sexual expression. Although a paraphilia involves a preference, it is usually experienced as a drive, and the preference is typically unusual.

Paraphilia: Definition and Overview

Paraphilias are an overdependence on a culturally unacceptable (such as children) or unusual (such as leather) stimulus for sexual arousal and satisfaction. Most individuals who have a paraphilia have an average of three to four different types. Paraphilias may become the major sexual activity in a person's life and may interfere with the person's capacity for reciprocal, affectionate sexual interactions.

Types of Paraphilias

The major paraphilias are exhibitionism, frotteurism, pedophilia, voyeurism, fetishism, transvestic fetishism, sexual sadism, and sexual masochism. Exhibitionists, frotteurs, and voyeurs are usually not violent, but such acts should be reported to law enforcement officials.

The Origins of Paraphilias: Theoretical Perspectives

Theoretical explanations for paraphilias include psychoanalytic (unconscious processes), feminist (control, power, aggression), learning (classical/operant paradigms), biological (innate), and lovemap (biological predisposition plus unusual learning experiences) perspectives. Paraphilias may also be viewed as a courtship disorder whereby the individual has not learned the culturally acceptable social skills for emotional and sexual engagement.

Treatment of Paraphilias

Treatment of paraphilias involves decreasing deviant sexual arousal, increasing nondeviant sexual arousal, developing interpersonal social skills, changing faulty cognitions, resolving sexual dysfunctions, and treating alcohol and drug abuse.

Sexual Addiction: A False Concept?

The American Psychiatric Association's position on sexual addiction is that the concept is conceptually vague, with no empirical support. Specifically, the term "addiction" has a physiological meaning in reference to withdrawal, which has no counterpart in sexuality. The APA recommends abandoning the term.

REFERENCES

Abel, G. G., Becker, J. V., Mittelman, M. S., Cunningham-Rathner, J., Rouleau, J. L., & Murphy, W. D. (1987). Self-reported sex crimes of non-carcerated paraphiliacs. *Journal of Interpersonal Violence, 2,* 3–25.

Abel, G. G., Becker, J. V., & Skinner, L. J. (1985). Behavioral approaches to treatment of the violent sex offender. In L. H. Roth (Ed.), *Clinical treatment of the violent person* (pp. 100–123). Rockville, MD: National Institute of Mental Health.

Abel, G.G., & Rouleau, J. L. (1990). The nature and extent of sexual assault. In W. L. Marshall, D. R. Laws, & H. E. Barbaree (Eds.), *Handbook of sexual assault* (pp. 9–21). New York: Plenum Press.

American Psychiatric Association. (1994). *Diagnostic and statistical manual of mental disorders* (4th ed.). Washington, DC: APA.

Bancroft, J. (1989). *Human sexuality and its problems* (2nd ed.). Edinburgh: Churchill Livingstone.

Bullough, B., & Bullough, V. (1997). Men who cross-dress: A survey. In B. Bullough, V. L. Bullough, & J. Elias (Eds.), *Gender blending* (pp. 174–188). Amherst, NY: Prometheus Books.

Bullough, V. L. (1990). History in adult human sexual behavior with children and adolescents in Western societies. In J. R. Feierman (Ed.), *Pedophilia* (pp. 69–90). New York: Springer-Verlag.

Carnes, P. J. (1990). *Contrary to love: Helping the sexual addict.* Minneapolis, MN: Comprehensive Care.

Comfort, A. (1987). Deviation and variation. In G. D. Wilson (Ed.), *Variant sexuality: Research and theory* (pp. 1-20). Baltimore: Johns Hopkins University Press.

Dewaraja, R. (1987). Formicophilia, an unusual paraphilia, treated with counseling and behavior therapy. *American Journal of Psychotherapy, 41,* 593-597.

Durand, V. M., & Barlow, D. H. (1997). *Abnormal psychology.* Pacific Grove, CA: Brooks/Cole.

Earle, R. H., & Earle, M. R. (1995). *Sex addiction.* New York: Brunner/Mazel.

Elmer-Dewitt, P. (1995, July 3). On a screen near you: Cyberporn. *Time,* pp. 38-45.

Ernulf, K. E., & Innula, S. M. (1995). Sexual bondage: A review and unobtrusive investigation. *Archives of Sexual Behavior, 24,* 631-654.

Flor-Henry, P. (1987). Cerebral aspects of sexual deviation. In G. D. Wilson (Ed.), *Variant sexuality: Research and theory* (pp. 49-83). Baltimore: John Hopkins University Press.

Fontaine, J. L. (1990). *Child sexual abuse.* Cambridge, MA: Polity Press.

Freund, K. (1990). Courtship disorder. In W. L. Marshall, D. R. Laws, & H. E. Barbaree (Eds.), *Handbook of sexual assault* (pp. 195-206). New York: Plenum Press.

Freund, K., Watson, R., & Dickey, R. (1990). Does sexual abuse in childhood cause pedophilia? *Archives of Sexual Behavior, 19,* 557-568.

Garber, M. (1992). *Vested interests: Cross-dressing and cultural anxiety.* New York: HarperPerennial.

Gebhard, P. H. (1976). Fetishism and sadomasochism. In M. S. Weinberg (Ed.), *Sex research: Studies from the Kinsey Institute* (pp. 156-166). New York: Oxford University Press.

Hazelwood, R. R., Dietz, P. E., & Warren, J. (1992, February). The criminal sexual sadist. *FBI Law Enforcement Bulletin,* 12-20.

Hurlbert, D. F. (1992). Voyeurism in an adult female with schizoid personality: A case report. *Journal of Sex Education and Therapy, 18,* 17-21.

Hurlbert, D. F., Apt, C., Gasar, S., Wilson, N. E., & Murphy, Y. (1994). Sexual narcissism: A validation study. *Journal of Sex and Marital Therapy, 20,* 24-34.

Kilmann, P. R., Sabalis, R. F., Gearing, M. L., Bukstel, L. H., & Scovern, A. W. (1982). The treatment of sexual paraphilias: A review of the outcome research. *Journal of Sex Research, 18,* 193-252.

Kline, P. (1987). Sexual deviation: Psychoanalytic research and theory. In G. D. Wilson (Ed.), *Variant sexuality: Research and theory* (pp. 150-175). Baltimore: Johns Hopkins University Press.

Langevin, R., & Lang, R. A. (1987). The courtship disorders. In G. D. Wilson (Ed.), *Variant sexuality: Research and theory* (pp. 202-228). Baltimore: Johns Hopkins University Press.

Langevin, R., Paitich, D. P., & Russon, A. E. (1985). Voyeurism: Does it predict sexual aggression or violence in general? In R. Langevin (Ed.), *Erotic preference, gender identity, and aggression in men* (pp. 77-98). Hillsdale, NY: Erlbaum.

Levine, S. B., Risen, C. B., & Althof, S. E. (1990). Essay on the diagnosis and nature of paraphilia. *Journal of Sex and Marital Therapy, 16,* 89-102.

Maletzky, B. M. (1991). *Treating the sexual offender.* Newbury Park: Sage.

Money, J. (1986). *Lovemaps: Clinical concepts of sexual/erotic health and pathology, paraphilia, and gender transposition in childhood, adolescence, and maturity.* New York: Irvington.

Money, J. (1988). *Gay, straight, and in-between.* New York: Oxford University Press.

Moser, C. (1992). Lust, lack of desire, and paraphilias: Some thoughts and possible connections. *Journal of Sex and Marital Therapy, 18,* 65-69.

Murphy, W. D., Haynes, M. R., & Worley, P. J. (1991). Assessment of adult sexual interest. In C. R. Hollin & K. Howells (Eds.), *Clinical approaches to sex offenders and their victims* (pp. 77-92). New York: Wiley.

Nagayama Hall, G. C. (1991). Sexual arousal as a function of physiological and cognitive variables in a sexual offender population. *Archives of Sexual Behavior, 20,* 359-369.

Over, R., & Koukounas, E. (1995). Habituation of sexual arousal: Product and process. *Annual Review of Sex Research, 6,* 187-223.

Perkins, D. (1991). Clinical work with sex offenders in secure settings. In C. R. Hollin & K. Howells (Eds.), *Clinical approaches to sex offenders and their victims* (pp. 151-177). New York: Wiley.

Rachman, S. (1966). Sexual fetishism: An experimental analogue. *Psychological Record, 16,* 293-296.

Schur, E. M. (1988). *The Americanization of sex.* Philadelphia: Temple University Press.

Weinberg, M., Williams, C., & Moser, C. (1984). The social constraints of sadomasochism. *Social Problems, 31,* 379-389.

Weinberg, M. S., Williams, C. J., & Cahan, C. (1995). "If the shoe fits . . .": Exploring male homosexual foot fetishism. *Journal of Sex Research, 32,* 17-27.

Wise, T. N., & Schmidt, C. W. (1996). Paraphilias. In T. A. Widiger, A. J. Frances, H. A. Pincus, R. Ross, M. B. First, & W. W. Davis (Eds.), *DSM-IV sourcebook.* Washington, DC: American Psychiatric Association.

EPILOGUE

In this text, we have emphasized the importance of making sexual choices, both at the individual and the societal level. Because we are concerned about helping people make informed decisions, this text has focused on negotiating the complexities of sexual decision making and facilitating positive identity foundations. Based on her interviews, Naomi Wolf (1997) spoke of hearing young women casting about for "rules that made sense, for guidance in the chaotic sexual world they inhabit" (p. xvi). It is our premise that decision makers can make better choices for themselves and their communities if they are well-informed about the facts, options, and potential impact of decisions. We recognize that cultural and other contextual factors enhance or limit opportunities, resources, and problem-solving approaches. Nevertheless, we encourage you (students using this book) to assert yourselves in active decision-making processes when it comes to sexuality-related decisions. We urge you to identify values, seek information, adopt theories, evaluate arguments, and obtain consultation to guide you.

When we try to anticipate the types of choices people will confront as they enter the next millennium, we feel that *recognizing complexities* and *increasing tolerance of diversity* will be important. The dichotomous categories we have been using to conceptualize groups of people (such as heterosexual or homosexual; masculine or feminine) are no longer sufficient (Bockting, 1997; Sanders, Reinisch, & McWhirter, 1990). Such binary models "fail to reflect adequately the complex realities of sexual orientation, and human sexuality in general" (Sanders et al., 1977, p. xx). The 1990s have been called the decade of the emergence of the transgenderist role (Bullough, Bullough, & Elias, 1997).

Does acknowledging complexities and increasing tolerance mean that anything goes? No, we are not suggesting that all choices are equally good for individuals or for communities. However, we do see moral thinking, risk reduction, and health promotion to be compatible with showing respect for people who engage in practices or have identities that are divergent from those regarded as typical. Although their rationale ("sexual orientation is not freely chosen") is arguable, we offer the example of U.S. Catholic bishops. On October 1, 1997, the Associated Press (Briggs, 1997) reported that the Administrative Board of the National Conference of Catholic Bishops approved a document urging parents of homosexual children to place love and support for their gay and lesbian children ahead of church doctrine that condemns homosexual activity. The bishops suggested that, in a society full of rejection and discrimination, parents should not reject their gay children.

We think that helping people make more informed sexual behavior choices is one of the most important strategies for preventing negative emotional, health, and social effects. As Pinkerton and Abramson (1997) observed in their article on condoms and the prevention of AIDS, "An ounce of prevention is still worth a pound of cure" (p. 373). Increasing knowledge is an important component of prevention interventions. Comprehensive and empirically validated educational programs should be offered. At the same time, we recognize that "ignorance is not the solution, but knowledge is not enough" (Kirby, 1992, p. 285). A responsible society must also examine the context for sexual decision making, attempt to establish public policies that make needed resources available, and protect community members who are vulnerable to exploitation.

The story of the three baseball umpires, recounted by Sanders et al. (1990), speaks to the nature of scientific inquiry and the potential biases of those who represent it. The first umpire states, "I call 'em the way I *see* 'em." The second umpire answers, "Not me, I call 'em the way they *are!*" The third, more seasoned umpire responds, "They aren't anything until I *call* them!" (pp. xxv–xxvi). We hope you find that the information and ideas expressed in this textbook to be a "fair call" on the state of human sexuality.

References

Bockting, W. O. (1997). Transgender coming out: Implications for the clinical management of gender dysphoria. In B. Bullough, V. L. Bullough, & J. Elias (Eds.), *Gender blending* (pp. 48–52). Amherst, NY: Prometheus Books.

Briggs, D. (1997, October 1). Letter urges Catholics to accept gays. *The News and Observer,* p. A12.

Bullough, B., Bullough, V. L., & Elias, J. (Eds.). (1997). *Gender blending.* Amherst, NY: Prometheus Books.

Kirby, D. (1992). School-based programs to reduce sexual risk-taking behaviors. *Journal of School Health, 62,* 280–287.

Pinkerton, S. D., & Abramson, P. R. (1997). Condoms and the prevention of AIDS. *American Scientist, 85,* 364–373.

Sanders, S. A., Reinisch, J. M., & McWhirter, D. P. (1990). Homosexuality/heterosexuality: An overview. In D. P. McWhirter, S. A. Sanders, & J. M. Reinisch (Eds.), *Homosexuality/heterosexuality: Concepts of sexual orientation* (pp. xix–xxvii). New York: Oxford.

Wolf, N. (1997). *Promiscuities: The secret struggle for womanhood.* New York: Random House.

RESOURCES AND ORGANIZATIONS

ABORTION—PRO-CHOICE

National Abortion Rights Action League
156 15th Street, NW
Suite 700
Washington, DC 20005
202-828-9300

Religious Coalition for Abortion Rights
1025 Vermont Avenue, NW
Suite 1130
Washington, DC 20005
202-628-7700

ABORTION—PRO-LIFE

National Right to Life Committee
419 7th Street, NW
Washington, DC 20004
202-626-8800
http://www.nrk.org/nrlc

Feminists for Life of America
811 East 47th
Kansas City, MO 64110
816-753-2130

CANCER

American Cancer Society and Reach for Recovery
1599 Clifton Road, NE
Atlanta, GA 30329
404-320-3333

Cancer Information Service
1-800-4-CANCER

CHILD ABUSE

Child Help USA Child Abuse Hotline
1-800-422-4453

Clearinghouse on Child Abuse and Neglect
P.O. Box 1182
Washington, DC 20013
703-385-7565

COUPLE ENHANCEMENT

Association for Couples in Marriage Enrichment
P.O. Box 10596
Winston-Salem, NC 27108
1-800-634-8325

American Association for Marriage and Family
  Therapy
1133 15th Street, NW
Suite 300
Washington, DC 20005
202-452-0109

FAMILY PLANNING

Planned Parenthood Federation of America
810 7th Avenue
New York, NY 10019
212-261-4300

INFERTILITY

Infertility and Reproductive Technology
American Fertility Society
1209 Montgomery Highway
Birmingham, AL 35216-2809

Resolve
5 Water Street
Arlington, MA 02174
617-643-2424

MEN'S AWARENESS

American Men's Studies Association
22 East Street
Northampton, MA 01060

NUDISM

American Association for Nude Recreation
1703 N. Main Street
Kissimmee, FL 34744
407-933-2064

RAPE

National Clearinghouse on Marital and Date Rape
2325 Oak Street
Berkeley, CA 94708-1697
510-524-1582

SEX EDUCATION

Sex Information and Education Council of the
  United States
New York University
32 Washington Plaza
New York, NY 10003

Kinsey Institute for Research in Sex, Gender, and
  Reproduction
Morrison Hall 313
Bloomington, IN 47405-2501
812-855-7686

SEX THERAPY

American Association of Sex Educators, Counselors,
  and Therapists
435 N. Michigan Avenue
Suite 1717
Chicago, IL 60611-4067
312-644-0828

Masters and Johnson Institute
24 S. Kings Highway
St. Louis, MO 63108

SEXUAL ABUSE

Child Help, USA
6463 Independence Avenue
Woodland Hills, CA 91367

Voices (Victims of Incest Can Emerge Survivors)
P.O. Box 148309
Chicago, IL 60614
1-800-7-VOICE-8

National Clearinghouse on Marital and Date Rape
2325 Oak Street
Berkeley, CA 94708-1697
510-524-1582

SEXUAL ORIENTATION

BiNet USA
P.O. Box 7327
Langley Park, MD 20787
202-986-7186

Bisexual Resource Center
P.O. Box 639
Cambridge, MA 02140
617-424-9595
BRC@norn.org

National Gay and Lesbian Task Force
1734 14th Street, NW
Washington, DC 20009-4309
202-332-6483

Love Makes a Family, Inc. (Newsletter)
P.O. Box 11694
Portland, OR 97211

National Federation of Parents and Friends of
    Lesbians and Gays
P.O. Box 96519
Washington, DC 20009-6519

The Human Rights Campaign
1101 14th Street, NW
Washington, DC 20005
202-628-4160
hrc@hrc.org
(To receive copies of HRC's Resource Guide to Coming
Out, call 1-800-866-NCOD)

SEXUALLY TRANSMISSIBLE DISEASES

American Social Health Association
(Herpes Resource Center and HPV Support Program)
P.O. Box 13827
Research Triangle Park, NC 27709
919-361-8400

STD/AIDS Information
919-361-8400

People with AIDS Coalition Hotline
1-800-828-3280

National AIDS Hotline
1-800-342-AIDS

National HIV Telephone Consulting Service
1-800-933-3413

1-800-TRIALS-A
For information about AIDS and HIV clinical trials conducted by the National Institutes of Health.
Web site: www.actis.org

1-800-638-8480
The National Library of Medicine provides three on-line AIDS databases: AIDSLINE, AIDSDRUGS, and AIDSTRIALS.

1-800-39-AMFAR
Treatment Information Services of the American Foundation for AIDS Research (AmFAR).

1-800-HIV-0440
Treatment Information Service
Web site: www.hivatis.org

National STD Hotline
1-800-227-8922

National Herpes Hotline
1-919-361-8488

SINGLE PARENTHOOD

Parents Without Partners
8807 Colesville Road
Silver Spring, MD 20910
301-588-9354

Single Mothers by Choice
1642 Gracie Square Station
New York, NY 10028
212-988-0993

TRANSGENDER/TRANSSEXUAL

American Gender Educational Information Service, Inc.
    (AEGIS)
P.O. Box 33724
Decatur, GA 30033-0724
770-939-0244
aegis@mindspring.com

Inner Discovery Network
1745 Pennsylvania Avenue, NW
Suite 108
Washington, DC 20006
http://www.best.com/~cdserv/inform.html

Society for the Second Self, Inc.
P.O. Box 194
Tulare, CA 93275
209-688-9246

The Intersex Society of North America
P.O. Box 31791
San Francisco, CA 94131

WOMEN'S AWARENESS

National Organization for Women
1000 16th Street, NW
Suite 700
Washington, DC 20036
202-331-0066

INDEX

Schmiege, C., 142
Schmitt, D. P., 316
Schnarch, D., 263
Schneider, D., 146
Schnicke, M. K., 285
Scholl, K., 397
Schopenhauer, A., 8
Schover, L. R., 45, 225, 226, 271
Schreiber, N. B., 214
Schreiner-Engel, P., 237
Schroeder, K. A., 413
Schuchmann, D., 373
Schulken, E. D., 280
Schultz, E. E., 304
Schulz, C., 370
Schur, E. M., 300, 482
Schuster, M. A., 117
Schutz, J., 293
Schwartz, I. M., 318
Schwartz, J., 235
Schwartz, P., 91, 387, 412, 414, 415, 463
Schwiesow, D. R., 135
Scott, R. S., 84
Scotti, J. R., 236, 237
Scovern, A. W., 492
Segraves, K. B., 263, 389
Segraves, R. T., 263, 389
Seid, R. P., 412
Seifert, M. H., Jr., 373
Seligmann, J., 122
Sell, R. L., 27, 430
Sellars, T. A., 383
Serber, G., 351
Sexton, D. L., 245
Shahravan, N., 281
Shannon, D., 15
Shapiro, C. H., 166, 169
Shapiro, J. L., 178
Shapiro, J. P., 440
Shaver, F. M., 316, 330
Shaw, J., 264, 267
Sheeder, J., 439
Sheehy, G., 375
Shepherd, G., 468
Sheppard, D. I., 286
Sheridan, P. M., 279
Sherwin, B. B., 44, 45, 406
Shi, Q., 123
Shikai, X., 262
Shoop, J. G., 176
Shue, E., 354
Shuetz-Mueller, D., 262
Siebel, C. A., 279
Sigmon, S. B., 8, 9
Sigmundson, K., 404
Sillen, S., 325
Silver, M. E., 92
Silver, P. S., 83
Silverman, B. G., 120

Silverman, J., 117, 328
Simenauer, J., 363, 364
Simmel, G., 38
Simon, A., 431
Simon, S., 315
Simons, R. L., 142, 326, 333
Simpson, D., 302
Simpson, L. A., 186
Singer, D. B., 58
Singer, I., 70
Siu, B. N., 59, 240
Skeen, D., 30
Skeen, P., 443
Skinner, B. F., 37
Skinner, L. J., 494
Slack, B. S., 236
Slagle, M. A., 232
Sloan, A., 208
Slob, A. K., 244
Smith, D., 217
Smith, K. M., 414
Smith, L., 57
Smith, P. J., 229
Smith, R., 33
Smith, T. W., 388
Smolowe, J., 142
Sobel, A., 216
Sohn, A., 28
Sokol, R. Z., 345
Sonenstein, F. L., 119
Sophie, J., 441
Sorrell, G. T., 295, 329
Spanier, G. B., 388
Spector, I. P., 390
Spiegler, M., 4
Spigner, C., 374
Sprecher, S., 9, 317, 412, 413, 463, 466
Srebnik, D., 351, 352, 415
Staimer, M., 135
Stamey, R., 354
Stark, T., 200
Starr, B., 390
Starr, M., 122
Starrels, M. E., 410
Steiger, T. L., 399
Stein, Z., 149
Steinem, G., 334
Stephens, W. N., 468
Stermac, L., 279
Stern, H., 50
Stern, W., 168
Sternberg, R. J., 328
Sternberg, S., 100
Stevens, G., 134
Stewart, D., 411
Stewart, F., 17
Stifel, E. N., 149
Stinnett, R. D., 281, 333
St. James, M., 333

Stockdale-Woolley, R., 245
Stolov, W. C., 224
Stone, R., 209
Storms, M., 447
Stotland, N. L., 194, 196, 211, 212
Strasburger, V. C., 326
Strassberg, D. S., 30, 263
Strean, H. S., 255
Street, S., 396, 416
Strommen, E. F., 445, 446
Strong, C., 204
Struckman-Johnson, C., 279
Struckman-Johnson, D., 279
Sullivan, A., 437
Summit, R. C., 296
Sumner, G. S., 400
Swaab, D. F., 439
Swan, S., 302
Swartz, P., 342
Swerdloff, R., 146
Swicegood, G., 134
Symons, D., 355, 406
Szasz, G., 30
Szasz, J. T., 350
Szymanski, M., 442

T

Talbert, L. M., 75
Talbert, R. L., 229
Tanfer, K., 158
Tang, C. S., 59, 240, 263, 280, 352, 412, 460, 462, 466
Tannahill, R., 322, 323, 324, 325, 348, 356, 357
Tavris, C., 50, 55, 63, 69, 71, 316, 375, 409
Taylor, R., 28, 90
Teale, P., 439
Tein, J., 296
Teitler, J. O., 121
Tekin, D., 351
Templeman, T. L., 281, 333
Teperi, J., 143
Tepperman, L., 19, 134, 375
Tharinger, D. J., 302
Thomas, A., 325
Thomas, D. J., 227
Thomas, R., 126
Thompson, A. P., 384
Thompson, C., 433
Thornton, A., 374
Thurmond, S., 138
Tiefer, L., 72, 253, 262
Tielman, R., 447
Timmendequas, J., 301
Tissot, S. A., 348
Tjaden, C., 286
Tobin, M., 109
Toman, W., 140

SUBJECT INDEX

A

Abortion, 194–219
  adolescent access to, 376
  adoption as alternative to, 214–218
  attitudes toward, 206–210
  global views and policies on, 202–203, 206, 213
  guidelines for considering, 212
  induced, 194
  medical research and, 204–205
  methods of, 196–199
  physical effects of, 210–211
  prenatal sex selection and, 402
  psychological effects of, 211–212
  reasons for obtaining, 195–196
  reducing the need for, 212–213
  resources on, 501
  spontaneous, 177, 194
  therapeutic, 196
  U.S. legislation on, 199–202
  U.S. statistics on, 194–195
Abortion Attitude Scale, 207–208
Abortion rate, 194
Abortion ratio, 194
Absolutism, 316
Abstinence, 117, 143
  methods of periodic, 151–153
Abuse. See Sexual abuse
Acquaintance rape, 279–280
Acquired immune deficiency syndrome. See AIDS
Acquired sexual dysfunctions, 250
Activating effects, 74
Acyclovir, 111
Addiction, sexual, 262, 496
Adolescents
  abortion decisions and, 376
  physical changes in, 372–373
  pregnancy prevention among, 122
  psychological changes in, 373
  school condom availability programs for, 121–122
  sex offenders as, 290
  sexual behavior of, 373–375
  sexually transmitted diseases in, 102–103, 121
Adoption, 214–218
  barriers to, 214–215
  policies and processes in, 215–216
  psychological reactions to, 216–217
  reasons for choosing, 214, 217–218
Adultery laws, 332
Against Our Will (Brownmiller), 278, 286

Agape, 329
Age. *See also* Sexual life cycle
  extradyadic sexual encounters and, 387
  of first sexual experience, 374–375, 463, 466
  gender role socialization and, 413, 415
  masturbation and, 351–352
Agency adoptions, 215
AIDS (acquired immune deficiency syndrome), 112–115
  homosexuality and, 103, 433
  influence of, on sexual choices, 19
  modes of transmission for, 113–114
  participation in experimental research for, 27
  symptoms of, 114–115
  treatments for, 115
AIDS/HIV Treatment Directory, 115
Akron Center for Reproductive Health v. City of Akron (1983), 200–201
Alan Guttmacher Institute, 144
Alaskan Needle Exchange Study, 31
Alcohol Expectancies Survey, 231
Alcohol use. *See also* Drug use
  during pregnancy, 174, 176
  paraphilias and, 496
  sexual choices and, 8–9
  sexual functioning and, 230
  sexually transmitted diseases and, 103
Ambivalence, 12–13
Amenorrhea, 59
American Association of Sex Educators, Counselors, and Therapists (AASECT), 256, 272
American Cancer Society, 53, 54, 58, 68, 239
American Fertility Society, 167
American Foundation for AIDS Research, 115
American Journal of Pharmacy, 232
American Medical Association (AMA), 199, 202
American Psychiatric Association (APA), 433, 496
American Psychological Association (APA), 211
Amniocentesis, 175, 402
Anabolic steroids, 229–230
Anal intercourse, 361
  condom use with, 120
  HIV transmission and, 103, 361
Anal stage, 36
Anal stimulation, 366
Analysis of research data, 32–34

Anatomy. *See* Sexual anatomy and physiology
Androgen-insensitivity syndrome, 403
Androgenital syndrome, 403
Androgyny, 416, 418–419
Animal sexuality, 471–472
Antihypertensive medications, 229
Anxiety, performance, 252, 415
Aquinas, Saint Thomas, 321
Archives of Sexual Behavior, 25
Areola, 53
Arousal disorders. *See* Sexual arousal disorders
Arthritis, 243–244
Artificial insemination, 137, 167
  of a surrogate mother, 167–168
Asceticism, 316
Assertiveness training, 286
Assessments. *See* Self-assessment questionnaires
Association for Childbirth at Home (ACAH), 183
Attitudes Toward Feminism Scale, 41–42
Augustine, Saint, 321
Autoerotic behavior. *See* Masturbation
Autonepiophilia, 484
Aversive conditioning, 492
Azidothymidine (AZT), 114, 115

B

"Baby blues," 185
Baehr v. Miike (1996), 436
Bancroft's four features of sexual response, 73–74
Bartholin's glands, 50
Basal body temperature (BBT) method, 152
Behaviors. *See* Sexual behaviors
Beliefs. *See also* Sexual values
  as element of culture, 461
Bellotti v. Baird (1979), 200
Biological factors
  and sex characteristics, 396, 397
  in sexual dysfunction, 250–251
Biological theories
  of gender role development, 399–406
  of paraphilias, 490
  of rape, 282
  of sexuality, 35
  of sexual orientation, 438–440
Biosexology, 24
Biphobia, 435, 437
Bipolar disorder, 237–238

Spontaneous abortion, 177, 194
Spurious correlation, 33
Squeeze technique, 265
Standing position, 360
Statutory rape, 278
STDs. *See* Sexually transmitted diseases
Sterilization
    female, 156–158
    male, 158
Stop-start technique, 265
Storge, 329
Straight-walled condoms, 148
Stress inoculation training, 286
Strokes, 235
Structural-functional theory, 39–40
Student Sexual Risks Scale (SSRS), 379–380
Substance use. *See* Alcohol use; Drug use
Suction curettage, 196–197
Superego, 35
Superwoman or supermom, 414
Surrogate mothers, 167–168
Survey research, 27–29
    interviews, 28
    questionnaires, 28–29
    "talking" computers, 29
Swinging, 385
Symbolic interaction theory, 38–39
Syphilis, 111–112
Syringe-exchange programs, 123–124
Systematic desensitization, 285, 494–495
Systems theory, 43, 270–271

T

Tachycardia, 69
"Talking" computers, 29
Tantra, 462
Taoism
    sexual values in, 322–323
    view of orgasm in, 263
Tay-Sachs disease, 171
Teachers
    as influence on gender role development, 410–411
    as influence on sexual values, 326–327
Telephone scatalogia, 488
Television. *See also* Media
    as influence on sexual values, 326
Tertiary syphilis, 112
Testes, 65–66
Testicular cancer, 243
Testicular feminization syndrome (TFS), 403

Testosterone
    decrease in middle-aged men, 383–384
    and development of male sex characteristics, 401
    medications for lowering, 493
Test-tube fertilization, 168
Theories of sexuality
    biological theories, 35
    eclectic view and, 44–45
    integrative model of, 45
    psychological theories, 35–38
    rape theories, 282–284
    sexuality observations and, 43–44
    sexual orientation theories, 438–441
    sociological theories, 38–44
Therapeutic abortions, 196
Therapy. *See also* Sex therapy
    individual vs. conjoint, 255–256
    medical solutions vs., 253
    private vs. group, 267–268
Thornburgh v. American College of Obstetricians and Gynecologists (1986), 201
Three-child families, 141
Time magazine, 299
Timing of communications, 82
Tobacco use, 174, 233
Tonight Show, 15
Touch-and-ask rule, 87–88
Toucheurism, 481
Touching, sexual, 364–365
Tranquilizers, 493
Transabdominal first trimester selective termination, 196
Transgenderists, 405, 499
Transsexuals, 397, 404–405, 485
Transurethral alprostadil, 261
Transvestic fetishism, 484–486
Transvestites, 405–406, 485. *See also* Cross-dressing
Treasury–Postal Service Appropriations Bill (1996), 202
Treatments
    for HIV and AIDS, 115
    for paraphilias, 492–496
    for rape victims, 285–286
    for sex offenders, 286, 289–290
    for sexually abused children, 297, 298
    for sexually transmitted diseases, 108–117
Triangular theory of love, 328–329
Trichomoniasis, 116
True labor, 180
Tumescence, 69
Turner's syndrome, 400
Two-child families, 141

U

UCLA Multidimensional Condom Attitudes Scale, 118–119
Ultrasound, 174–175
Unconditioned stimulus, 37
Unidimensional continuum model of sexual orientation, 427–428
United States
    abortion legislation in, 199–202
    abortion statistics for, 194
    extramarital sex statistics for, 384
    sexual knowledge in, 314–315
    sexual values of adults in, 318–319
    STD statistics for, 101–104
U.S. Commission on Obscenity and Pornography, 335–336
U.S. News & World Report, 186, 333, 439
Urethra, 52
Urethral opening, 52
Uterine cancer, 240–241
Uterine orgasms, 70
Uterus, 57

V

Vacuum aspiration, 196–197
Vacuum devices, 261–262
Vagina, 54
Vaginal condom, 147, 149
Vaginal intercourse, 356–360
Vaginal opening, 52
Vaginal spermicides, 151
Vaginismus, 267
Vaginitis, 116
Vague vs. specific communication, 87
Validity, 34
Values. *See also* Sexual values
    as element of culture, 461
Variable, 25
Vas deferens, 66
Vasectomy, 158
Vasocongestion, 69
Verbal messages, 84
Verifiability, 24
Vestibule, 52
Vibrators, 351
Victims No Longer (Lew), 297
Victorian era, 323–324
Virgins
    sexually transmitted diseases in, 117
    significance of hymen in, 52
Voiding cystourethrogram (VCUG), 294
Voluntary sexual celibacy, 344–345
Voyeurism, 482–483
Vulva, 50
Vulval orgasms, 70

W

Webster v. Reproductive Health Services (1989), 201
WIC (Women and Infant Care) program, 57
Williams v. Zbaraz (1980), 200
Win-win solutions, 93–94
Withdrawal method, 153
Woman-on-top position, 357, 358
Women
  breast examinations for, 53–54
  elderly, 390–391
  gender role socialization of, 412–414
  masturbation and, 349
  menopause in, 382–383
  menstrual cycle in, 58–63
  occupational roles and, 397, 398, 399

Women (*continued*)
  organizational resources for, 501–502
  orgasm in, 69–70
  Pap tests and pelvic exams for, 58
  sexual anatomy and physiology of, 63–68
  sexual fantasies in, 355
  sexual response cycles in, 68–75
  STD susceptibility of, 103
  sterilization methods for, 156–158
  workforce participation of, 17, 19, 397
Women's movement, 19
Workplace
  disclosing one's homosexuality in, 446
  sexual harassment policy in, 304

Workplace (*continued*)
  women's involvement in, 17, 19, 397
World Health Organization, 224
World Wide Web. *See* Internet

Y

Yin-yang concept, 239, 322–323, 347–348
Young adults. *See also* Adolescents; Early adulthood
  sexually transmitted diseases in, 102–103
"Yuzpe method," 154

Z

Zovirax, 111
Zygote intrafallopian transfer (ZIFT), 169–170

CREDITS

This page constitutes an extension of the copyright page. We have made every effort to trace the ownership of all copyrighted material and to secure permission from copyright holders. In the event of any question arising as to the use of any material, we will be pleased to make the necessary corrections in future printings. Thanks are due to the following authors, publishers, and agents for permission to use the material indicated.

TEXT CREDITS

Chapter 1

5 From "The 1997 Body Image Survey Results," by David M. Garner, 1997, *Psychology Today, Jan./Feb. (Vol. 30),* p. 42. Reprinted with permission from *Psychology Today Magazine,* Copyright © 1997 (Sussex Publishers, Inc.); **16** From Sarah Doebbler. Reprinted by permission.

Chapter 2

45 (top) From *Sexuality and Chronic Illness,* by L. R. Schover and S. B. Jensen, 1988, pg. 12. Copyright © 1988 by The Guilford Press. Reprinted by permission; **45** (bottom) From *Sexuality and Chronic Illness: A Comprehensive Approach,* by L. R. Schover and S. B. Jensen, 1988, p. 12. Guilford Press.

Chapter 3

55 From *Healthy For Life,* by Brian K. Williams and Sharon N. Knight, 1994, p. 8.19. Brooks/Cole Publishing Company. Reprinted by permission; **72** From *Healthy For Life,* by Brian K. Williams and Sharon N. Knight, 1994, p. 8.27. Brooks/Cole Publishing Company. Reprinted by permission.

Chapter 4

81 From *An Invitation to Health, 7th ed.,* by Dianne Hales, 1997, p. 216. Brooks/Cole Publishing Company. Reprinted by permission; **91** Adapted from "Sexual Lies Among University Students," by D. Knox, H. Holt, & J. Turner, 1993, *College Student Journal, 27,* 269-272. Copyright © 1993 by College Student Journal. Reprinted by permission.

Chapter 5

101 From "Fact Sheet: Sexually Transmitted Diseases in the United States." 1997, *SIECUS Report, 25*(3), 22-24. Copy-

right © 1997 by the Sex Information and Education Council of the United States. Reprinted by permission; **108** Adapted from "Coping and Depression Among People With AIDS," by J. A. Fleishman and B. Fogel, 1994, *Health Psychology, 13*(2), 156-169. Copyright © American Psychological Association. Adapted by permission of the author; **112** Data from information from the World Health Organization in "The Decade of Death," by C. Gorman, *Time Magazine,* 8/3/92, pp. 32-33; **125** From "Development and Evaluation of a Sexual Decision-Making and Social Skills Program: 'The Choice is Yours—Preventing HIV/STDS'," by J. Noell, D. Ary, & T. Duncan, 1997, *Health Education and Behavior, 24,* 87-101. Copyright © 1997 by Sage Publications, Inc. Reprinted by permission.

Chapter 6

147 From *Healthy For Life,* by Brian K. Williams and Sharon N. Knight, 1994, p. 9.7. Brooks/Cole Publishing Company. Reprinted by permission; **148** From *Healthy For Life,* by Brian K. Williams and Sharon N. Knight, 1994, p. 9.8. Brooks/Cole Publishing Company. Reprinted by permission; **149** (left) From *Healthy For Life,* by Brian K. Williams and Sharon N. Knight, 1994, p. 9.25. Brooks/Cole Publishing Company. Reprinted by permission; **149** (right) From *Healthy For Life,* by Brian K. Williams and Sharon N. Knight, 1994, p. 9.19. Brooks/Cole Publishing Company. Reprinted by permission; **150** From *Healthy For Life,* by Brian K. Williams and Sharon N. Knight, 1994, p. 9.18. Brooks/Cole Publishing Company. Reprinted by permission; **151** (top) From *Healthy For Life,* by Brian K. Williams and Sharon N. Knight, 1994, p. 9.19. Brooks/Cole Publishing Company. Reprinted by permission; **151** (bottom) From *Healthy For Life,* by Brian K. Williams and Sharon N. Knight, 1994, p. 9.16. Brooks/Cole Publishing Company. Reprinted by permission; **152** From *Healthy For Life,* by Brian K. Williams and Sharon N. Knight, 1994, p. 9.15. Brooks/Cole Publishing Company. Reprinted by permission; **154** From "Commentary: Methods Women Can Use That May Prevent Sexually Transmitted Diseases, Including HIV," by M. J. Rosenberg and E. L. Gollup, 1992, *American Journal of Public Health, 82*(11), 1473-1478. Copyright © 1992 by the American Public Health Association. Reprinted by permission; **156** From *Healthy For Life,* by Brian K. Williams and Sharon N. Knight, 1994, p. 9.23. Brooks/Cole Publishing Company. Reprinted by permission; **158** From *Healthy For Life,* by Brian K. Williams and Sharon N. Knight, 1994, p. 9.24. Brooks/Cole Publishing Company. Reprinted by permission.

Chapter 7

184 Adapted from "Conclusion: The Transition to Parenthood: Synthesis and Future Directions, Table 1," by G. Y.

Michaels, W. A. Goldberg, 1988, pp. 352-353. In G. Y. Michaels, W. A. Goldberg (Eds.), *The Transition to Parenthood Current Theory and Research.* Copyright © 1988 by Cambridge University Press. Reprinted by permission of Cambridge University Press.

Chapter 8

195 From *Statistical Abstract of the United States 1995 Update,* Table 113, 1995, and Abortion Surveillance: Preliminary Data—United States, 1994, (1997), *Morbidity and Mortality Weekly Report, 45,* 1123-1127; **197** From *Healthy For Life,* by Brian K. Williams and Sharon N. Knight, 1994, p. 9.27. Brooks/Cole Publishing Company. Reprinted by permission; **198** From *Healthy For Life,* by Brian K. Williams and Sharon N. Knight, 1994, p. 10.26. Brooks/Cole Publishing Company. Reprinted by permission; **199** From *An Invitation to Health, 7th ed.,* by Dianne Hales, 1997, p. 294. Brooks/Cole Publishing Company. Reprinted by permission; **203** Data from *World Abortion Policies, 1994,* 1997. United Nations Department for Economic and Social Information and Policy Analysis [Website]; **205** Data from *World Abortion Policies, 1994,* 1997. United Nations Department for Economic and Social Information and Policy Analysis [Website]; **208** Adapted from *General Social Survey,* 1993. Roper Organization from Website; **213** Adapted from *Birth or Abortion? Private Struggles in a Political World,* by K. Maloy, M. Patterson, 1992, p. 328. Copyright © 1992 by Plenum Publishing Group. Reprinted by permission.

Chapter 9

233 From "Medications That May Contribute to Sexual Disorders," by W. W. Finger, M. Lund, & M. A. Slagle, 1997, *The Journal of Family Practice, 44*(1). Reprinted by permission of Appleton & Lange, Inc; **240** From *An Invitation to Health, 7th ed.,* by Dianne Hales, 1997, p. 399. Brooks/Cole Publishing Company. Reprinted by permission; **241** Courtesy of Wyeth-Ayerst Laboratories. Philadelphia, PA; **243** From *Human Biology,* by Cecie Starr, 1997. Copyright © 1997 by Wadsworth Publishing Company. Reprinted by permission.

Chapter 11

279 Data from Date/Acquaintance Rape Study, by P. Dunn, K. Vail-Smith & S. Knight, 1997, poster presentation, American Public Health Association, Annual Meeting, November 1997. Reprinted by permission; **280** Reprinted by permission of Amanda Tyson; **284** From "Attitudes About Date Rape: Gender Differences Among College Students," by D. R. Holcomb, L. C. Holcomb, K. A. Sondag, N. Williams, 1991, *College Student Journal, 25,* 434-439. Copyright © 1991 by College Student Journal. Reprinted by permission; **298** Reprinted by permission of Trans-

action Publishers. From "The Resolution Model: A Comprehensive Treatment Framework in Sexual Abuse," by N. Orenchuk-Tomiuk, G. Matthey, & C. P. Christensen, 1990, *Child Welfare, 69,* pp. 417-431. Copyright © Transaction Publishers.

Chapter 12

315 Adapted from "Mother and Adolescent Knowledge of Sexual Development: The Effects of Gender, Age, and Sexual Experience," by M. Hockenberry, M. J. Richman, C. Dilorio, T. Rivero, & E. Maibach, 1996, *Adolescence, 31*(121), 35-47. Copyright © 1996 by Libra Publishers, Inc. Adapted by permission; **317** From "A Revision of the Reiss Premarital Sexual Permissiveness Scale," by S. K. Sprecher, K. McKinney, R. Walsh, & C. Anderson, 1988, *Journal of Marriage and the Family, 50,* 821-828. Copyright © 1988 by the National Council on Family Relations, 3989 Central Avenue NE, Suite 550, Minneapolis, MN 55421. Reprinted by permission; **329** Based on "A Triangular Theory of Love," by Robert Sternberg, 1986, *Psychological Review, 93,* 119-135; **331** Adapted from "Sexual Guilt Among College Students," by D. Knox, L. H. Walters, & J. Walters, 1991, *College Student Journal, 25,* pp. 432-433. Copyright © 1991 by College Student Journal. Reprinted by permission; **334** Adapted from *Sex in America,* by R. T. Michael, E. O. Laumann, J. H. Gagnon, & G. Kolata, 1994, p. 157. Little, Brown and Company. Copyright © 1994 by CSG Enterprise, Inc., Edward O. Laumann, Robert T. Michael, and Gina Kolata.

Chapter 13

355 Adapted from "Sex Differences in Sexual Fantasy: An Evolutionary Psychological Approach," by B. J. Ellis and D. Symons, 1990, *The Journal of Sex Research, 27,* 527-555. Copyright © 1990 by The Society for the Scientific Study of Sexuality. Reprinted by permission; **356** From *Healthy For Life,* by Brian K. Williams and Sharon N. Knight, 1994, p. 8.31. Copyright © Brooks/Cole Publishing Company. Reprinted by permission.

Chapter 14

389 From *Health Dynamics: Attitudes and Behaviors,* by W. Boskin, G. Graf, & V. Kreisworth, 1990, p. 209. Brooks/Cole Publishing Company. Reprinted by permission; **390** From *Health Dynamics: Attitudes and Behaviors,* by W. Boskin, G. Graf, & V. Kreisworth, 1990, p. 210. Brooks/Cole Publishing Company. Reprinted by permission; **391** Data from *Sex in America,* by R. T. Michael, J. H. Gagnon, E. O. Laumann, & G. Kolata, 1994, p. 116. Little, Brown and Company. Copyright © 1994 CGS Enterprise, Inc., Edward O. Laumann, Robert T. Michael, & Gina Kolata.

Chapter 15

397 Adapted from *An Invitation to Health, 7th ed.,* by Dianne Hales, 1997, p. 233. Brooks/Cole Publishing Company. Adapted by permission; **414** From *Statistical Abstract of the United States, 1996,* 116th ed. Bureau of the Census, 1996. Table 728.

Chapter 16

427 From *Sexual Behavior in the Human Female,* by A. Kinsey, W. Pomeroy, C. Martin, & P. Gebhard, 1953, p. 470 (fig. 93). W. B. Saunders. Reprinted by permission of The Kinsey Institute for Research in Sex, Gender, and Reproduction, Inc.; **430** Data from *Sex in America,* by R. T. Michael, J. H. Gagnon, E. O. Laumann, & G. Kolata, 1994, pp. 173-178. Little, Brown and Company. Copyright © 1994 CGS Enterprise, Inc., Edward O. Laumann, Robert T. Michael, & Gina Kolata. Reprinted by permission of Little, Brown and Company.

Chapter 17

466 Material prepared specifically for the authors from Robert Bunger, Dept. of Anthropology, East Carolina University, Greenville, N.C. Reprinted by permission; **471** From "Judging the Other: Responding to Traditional Female Genital Surgeries," by S. D. Lane and R. A. Rubenstein, 1996, *Hastings Center Report, 26*(3), 31-40. Hastings Center.

Chapter 18

483 Based on "Fetishism and Sadomasochism," by P. H. Gebhard, 1976. From *Sex Research: Studies from the Kinsey Institute* by Martin S. Weinberg. Copyright © 1976 by Martin S. Weinberg. Used by permission of Oxford University Press, Inc.; **490** From *Abnormal Psychology: An Introduction* by Durand and Barrow, 1997, p. 327. Copyright © 1997 Brooks/Cole Publishing Company; **491** From "Courtship Disorder," by K. Freund, 1990, pp. 195-206. In W. L. Marshall, R. Laws, H. E. Barbaree (Eds.), *Handbook of Sexual Assault.* Copyright © 1990 by Plenum Publishing Group. Reprinted by permission.

PHOTO CREDITS

Chapter 1

4 Oscar Burriel, Science Source/Photo Researchers; **12** ©Robert Kusel/Tony Stone Images; **14** Michael Newman/PhotoEdit; **17** Courtesy of Pharmacia and Upjohn; **20** AP/Wide World Photos.

Chapter 2

25 ©Hulton Getty/Tony Stone Images; **28** Michael Newman/PhotoEdit; **36** David Young-Wolff/PhotoEdit; **38** ©Robert E. Daemmrich/Tony Stone Images; **39** Photo courtesy of Pi Kappa Phi Fraternity.

Chapter 3

56 ©Paul Damien/Tony Stone Images; **68** Reprinted by the permission of the American Cancer Society, Inc.

Chapter 4

82 Jeff Greenberg/PhotoEdit; **83** T. Petillot, Science Source/Photo Researchers; **84** Superstock; **92** ©David Harry Stewart/Tony Stone Images; **94** Superstock.

Chapter 5

109 ©Michael English, M.D./Custom Medical Stock Photo; **110** ©Edward H. Gill/Custom Medical Stock Photo; **111** ©Beckman/Custom Medical Stock Photo.

Chapter 6

140 AP/Wide World Photos; **146** Michael Newman/PhotoEdit; **147** ©Tim Flach/Tony Stone Images.

Chapter 7

173 Michael Newman/PhotoEdit; **180** Michael Newman/PhotoEdit; **181** Crisp, 1997; **187** ©Bruce Ayres/Tony Stone Images.

Chapter 9

224 Spencer Grant/Stock, Boston; **227** ©McIntyre, Science Source/Photo Researchers; **234** AP/Wide World Photos; **239** ©M. Marshall, M.D./Custom Medical Stock Photo.

Chapter 10

252 ©Bruce Ayres/Tony Stone Images; **257** David Young-Wolff/PhotoEdit; **271** Michael Newman/PhotoEdit.

Chapter 11

279 Tom Prettyman/PhotoEdit; **285** Rhoda Sidney/PhotoEdit; **300** AP/Wide World Photos; **301** AP/Wide World Photos; **302** Steven Lunetta/PhotoEdit.

Chapter 12

317 Tony Freeman/PhotoEdit; **319** Tony Freeman/PhotoEdit; **327** Michael Newman/PhotoEdit; **335** AP/Wide World Photos.

Chapter 13

355 Amy C. Etra/PhotoEdit; **365** Michael Newman/
PhotoEdit.

Chapter 14

371 Bill Bachmann/PhotoEdit; **377** Mark Richards/
PhotoEdit; **386** ©Frank Herholdt/Tony Stone Images;
390 Cleo Photography/PhotoEdit.

Chapter 15

398 (left) A. Ramey/PhotoEdit; **398** (right) Michael
Newman/PhotoEdit; **405** (top) ©Chester Higgins, Jr.,
Science Source/Photo Researchers; **405** (bottom)
Danahey, 1997; **416** Tony Freeman/PhotoEdit.

Chapter 16

426 AP/Wide World Photos; **434** ©Ken Fisher/Tony Stone
Images; **448** Authors' files; **449** Deborah Davis/PhotoEdit.

Chapter 17

459 AP/Wide World Photos; **463** ©Brian Yarvin, Science
Source/Photo Researchers; **469** AP/Wide World Photos.

Chapter 18

481 Bonnie Kamin/PhotoEdit; **483** Authors' files; **485**
(left) ©Bill Aron, Science Source/Photo Researchers; **485**
(right) Danahey, 1997; **486** Cindy Charles/PhotoEdit.